He moved off towards the back of the cave. Hazel rolled her eyes briefly at the polished ceiling and went after him. In the end, Owen didn't get far. He stood before the entrance to the next cave, which was now blocked off by a glowing force field. He was standing very still, and Hazel could tell at once that something was wrong. She hurried over to join him, the gun back in her hand. She moved in beside him and then stopped, and screwed up her face in disgust. The cave was packed from wall to wall and from floor to ceiling with dead bodies. Not respectfully lying on separate slabs or tables, but crammed together like cuts of meat or lengths of wood, packed in as tightly as possible. A temperature gauge on the wall by the opening showed that a freezer unit was maintaining the bodies at near-zero. Some of the faces looked out at Owen and Hazel, an almost lifelike gleam shining from the frost on their frozen eyeballs.

'Well,' Owen said finally. 'Now we know what they did with the bodies.'

SIMON R. GREEN

DEATHSTALKER HONOUR

VISTA

First published in Great Britain 1998
as a Vista paperback original
This Vista edition published 1999

Vista is an imprint of The Orion Publishing Group Ltd
Orion House, 5 Upper Saint Martin's Lane,
London WC2H 9EA

A catalogue record for this book is
available from the British Library.

ISBN 0 575 60178 7

Typeset by SetSystems Ltd, Saffron Walden, Essex
Printed and bound in Great Britain by
Caledonian International Book Manufacturing Ltd, Glasgow

99 10 9 8 7 6 5 4 3

At the end, when all else fails,
there is still honour.

PROLOGUE

They were, after all, official heroes of the great rebellion.

Owen Deathstalker, outlawed aristocrat and reluctant warrior.

Hazel d'Ark, ex-clonelegger and ex-pirate.

Jack Random, legendary professional rebel.

Ruby Journey, infamous female bounty hunter.

Together, they fought impossible odds in the name of freedom and justice, and triumphed time and time again. They gathered an army of the bold and the valiant, the downtrodden and the desperate, and led them to victory. And in the great steel and brass palace of the homeworld Golgotha, they threw down the Empress Lionstone XIV and destroyed the Iron Throne of the Empire for ever.

They should have been fêted and honoured, raised to the heights and celebrated throughout the civilized worlds.

They should have lived happily ever after.

Unfortunately, life isn't like that.

CHAPTER ONE

Charnel House

On the good ship *Sunstrider II*:

'Bounty hunters!' Hazel d'Ark cried, disgustedly. 'After all we've done, after all we've been through, we end up as nothing more than glorified bounty hunters!'

'Beats our previous occupation,' Owen said mildly. Tall and rangy, with dark hair and darker eyes, he lay as though boneless in the lounge's most comfortable chair. 'Outlaws, we were, with a price on our heads and every man's hand turned against us. And chasing down war criminals is important work. I don't know about you, but I find being the hunter much easier on the nerves. Besides, must be a nice change for you, being legit.'

'It's the principle of the thing!' snapped Hazel. 'We used to be somebody! We led armies! We overthrew the Empire! Risked getting our asses shot off time after time, and all so we could end up doing Parliament's dirty work. Makes me want to puke.'

Owen was thrown for a moment. Hazel's use of the word 'principle' had caught him off-balance. He would have been prepared to bet good money Hazel wouldn't recognize a principle if she fell over it on her way back from the toilet. But he rallied gamely, and closed the discussion with an accurate if not entirely tactful point of order.

'As I recall, this was all your idea anyway.'

Hazel glared at him, and then turned away to glower at the nearest bulkhead. She was in one of her moods again, and not about to be swayed by mere logic. Owen sighed, but had the sense to do it quietly. Truth be told, he found bounty-hunting something of a come-down too, but all the alternatives had been worse. When he was fighting the rebellion, he'd never really thought about what he'd do when it was all over. He was usually too busy trying to keep himself from being killed, but also, he'd never seriously expected to see an end to the rebellion in his lifetime. Most people who stood up to oppose the Empress Lionstone XIV, also known as the Iron Bitch, tended to end up in early graves. Often with bits missing. No: he'd fully expected to give his whole life, however long that turned out to be, to the cause, and die with the main work of the rebellion still to be done by future generations. But then, nothing in his life had ever turned out the way he expected.

Looking back, he seemed to have spent most of his time stumbling from one crisis, one flashpoint to another, driven by outside forces as often as acting from his own plans and wishes. There had been schemes and conspiracies all around him, most of which he only knew from the brief shadows they cast across his life in passing. And in the end it seemed to him that for all his intentions and bold companions, and the mysterious powers he'd acquired from the Madness Maze, he finally came to stand defiantly before the Iron Throne through his own sheer stubbornness. He refused to be beaten by the odds: overwhelming odds, that would have frightened off a more sensible man.

He'd ended up a hero and a saviour of humanity, and no one had been more surprised than him.

He'd expected to fail, his dreams destroyed and his hopes cast down. Expected to die, and horribly. Instead, he'd overthrown an Empire that had lasted well over a millennium, deposed its ruler and destroyed her Throne, and seen the end of practically every social and political structure he believed in. That was when the problems had really begun.

Lionstone's body was barely cold before the vultures began to descend. Even while the last battles were still being fought, the various parts of the rebel force had begun arguing fiercely with each other over what exactly should replace the old system. Even those few who'd made it as far as Lionstone's Court couldn't bring themselves to agree. Owen had wanted things to stay much as they were, with some political reforms, and injustices punished. Hazel had wanted it all torn down, with war trials for all the Families, for crimes against humanity. Jack Random insisted on democracy for all, including all clones and espers and other unpeople. Ruby Journey wanted the loot she'd been promised.

In the Court they were soon joined by representatives of the clone and esper undergrounds, fringe political groups of all shapes and shades, and more religious factions than you could shake a stick at. All of them intent on having their own way. There were raised voices on all sides, and much brandishing of weapons, but luckily they were all too tired to start another war just yet. The argument became a deadlock, and everyone stamped off in different directions to plot and plan anew. For the moment, Parliament was running the day-to-day business of the Empire, on the grounds that somebody had to, and they at least had some experience in that area. No one trusted them an inch, but there was nothing new there.

Men and women who had once been allies and fought side by side on blood-soaked streets, swearing to defend each other to the death and beyond, now fought each other more viciously than their previous common enemy over points of dogma and precedence. Owen supposed he shouldn't have been surprised. He was a historian, after all. All that the various rebel factions had ever really had in common was a shared enemy. And though words like justice and liberty were bandied round, they meant different things to different people.

Then there was the deal Random had made, in the midst of the most desperate fighting, to depose but not destroy the aristocratic Families. Faced with an increasingly victorious army calling for their blood, the great Houses had banded together and offered to step down from power and privilege, in return for being allowed to survive as purely economic forces. That was the carrot. The stick was their threat to destroy the economic base of the whole Empire, and crash every civilized world back to barbarism. No one doubted they were quite capable of doing it. And so Random had struck the deal to save the lives of billions, but no one thanked him for it. The man in the street was cheated of his revenge, the rebels accused their beloved hero of selling out his political convictions and the Families hated him for the loss of their

11

precious nobility. Afterwards, Random had to hire a secretary to handle all the hate mail and death threats.

As if the situation wasn't complicated enough, Blue Block had emerged from the shadows to unite and control the Families and scare the crap out of everyone else. Blue Block had been the Families' secret weapon, a last-ditch defence to be used against the Empress if she ever seriously threatened the Clans' power and status. The youngest sons and daughters of each House were given to the secret schools of Blue Block, where they were trained and conditioned to be loyal to the Families to the death and beyond. Unfortunately, Blue Block turned out to have an agenda of its own.

In its hidden schools, tucked away in the darker corners of the Empire, faceless and nameless instructors taught the younger sons and daughters – none of whom would have inherited title or wealth anyway – that the Families as a class were far more important than any one House. And that loyalty to Blue Block therefore superceded any loyalty to individual Clans. They taught their charges other things too, some of them unspeakable, but that still remained a secret. For the moment.

They were the ones who came up with the deal to put to Jack Random, and now that they had emerged unblinking into the harsh light of public view, it was they who enforced the deal. The Clans saw what they had unknowingly created, and were afraid. And so they all bowed down to Blue Block, and kept their rage and plans for bloody revenge to themselves.

Owen, Hazel, Jack and Ruby were united in their horror of the Pandora's box of troubles they'd opened, but couldn't decide what to do about it. Random rushed from one meeting to another, banging heads together and papering over cracks, desperately trying to keep the lid on things. It helped that most people were at least willing to listen to him. Everyone respected the legendary Jack Random – even if they hated his guts. He spent the rest of his time trying to rebuild the very armed forces he'd just finished fighting, in case of attacks by the Empire's many enemies. The rogue AIs of Shub, the reborn Hadenmen, and any number of potential alien threats were all quite capable of launching an attack upon the Empire while it was distracted by internal divisions.

Ruby Journey, meanwhile, took every opportunity to loot anyone weaker than herself, including several corporations, and lost no time in setting herself up in the kind of luxury to which she'd always wanted to become accustomed. She had no interest in politics. It made her head hurt. If she couldn't hit or rob something, Ruby was mostly lost for an alternative. So she stayed out of the continuing negotiations, and everyone heaved a great sigh of relief.

And Owen and Hazel became bounty hunters, tracking down escaped war criminals. Officially, they were supposed to bring the villains back to face public trial, but privately it had been agreed on all sides that it would be better if certain parties were killed while trying to escape. Owen and Hazel had nodded solemnly when this was explained to them, and each decided they'd make up their own minds as and when necessary. It was hard and demanding work, but crucial. If there was ever to be any hope of stability in the new order Jack was trying to hammer together, the truly vile and evil had to be punished, and be seen to be punished. People like Valentine Wolfe, for example, despised right hand of the Empress and butcher of Virimonde. You couldn't send just anybody after a dangerous and subtle villain like the Wolfe, so that was where Owen Deathstalker and Hazel d'Ark came in. They were, after all, the most dangerous people the Empire had ever known.

Owen had jumped at the chance when it was presented to him. All he'd ever really wanted was his old life back, but almost from the moment the rebellion was officially declared triumphant, it seemed to Owen that everyone and his brother had begun fighting for a chance to grab a piece of the legendary Deathstalker hero. Every political party wanted him as its figurehead. Every cause sent representatives requiring that he attach his name and his blade to their demands. Sometimes they even fought duels outside his quarters over who got to speak to him first.

It appeared they all wanted something only he could get for them, and they were prepared to go to any lengths to gain his ear. Then there were the holo news networks wanting endless interviews, and agents angling to buy exclusive rights to his life story. They all clamoured for pictures and quotes and answers to increasingly personal questions. Not to mention product endorsements and book deals and merchandising rights. Hell, one company even wanted to manufacture a line of action figures based on him and Hazel and Jack and Ruby. And stuffed toys. Owen just wanted to be left alone, and said so, loudly, but no one listened. So in the end he fled Golgotha on the *Sunstrider II*, on what turned out to be the first of many missions as a glorified bounty hunter, licensed and paid by Parliament to clear up the Empire's more dangerous messes.

Hazel was there too. She said she just went along to keep him company, and perhaps for a little action to keep herself from getting soft, but Owen liked to think she wasn't just bored spitless without an enemy to fight. Though it had to be said, she'd never been one to sit around and contemplate the lilies of the field. Settling down to a peaceful and productive life like everyone else was exactly what she'd become an outlaw to avoid. She couldn't even get drunk and start fights in bars any more. Everyone knew who she was, and was scared witless of saying anything that might upset her. She dealt with pestering news teams by putting down landmines and hidden mantraps outside her lodgings, but even that grew boring after a while. So when Random contacted her and offered her a commission to track down and possibly execute missing war criminals, she jumped at the chance, and wasted no time in persuading Owen to join her. Even if she seemed to remember it was the other way round. But then, that was Hazel for you; never happier than when she could lay the blame on someone else.

'We just dropped out of hyperspace over Virimonde,' murmured the AI Ozymandias in Owen's ear. 'Currently maintaining high orbit and all shields. I really don't know why you wanted to come back here, Owen. I mean, it's not as if you have any friends here any more. In fact, I would have to say that the likelihood of our ending up riddled with holes increases geometrically with every second we are dumb enough to stay here.'

'Nag, nag, nag,' said Owen, subvocalizing so that Hazel

wouldn't hear. She didn't approve of him talking to an AI that was supposed to be dead. 'You never want to go anywhere fun, Oz. This is where our current quarry has gone to ground, so here we are too. Right now, Valentine Wolfe is down there somewhere, along with certain aristocratic cronies, all of whom the current authorities would dearly like to see standing in a dock or hanging from a rope; preferably both. Hell, if we bring back Valentine Wolfe's head they'll probably name a public holiday after us. Besides . . . I always said that one day I'd come home to Virimonde.'

There had been a time, and not that long ago, when Owen Deathstalker had been Lord of the whole planet of Virimonde. And then the Empress Lionstone outlawed him and took it all away. His own security people had tried to kill him for the reward on his head, and he'd had to flee for his life. He nearly hadn't made it, but Hazel had arrived at just the right moment to save his aristocratic ass, as she never tired of reminding him, and they'd been together ever since. He'd fallen in love with her. He still wasn't sure how she felt about him. His cousin David had been made Lord in his absence, and had taken over the Deathstalker Family Standing, the ancient stone castle of his Clan, but he died there not long after trying to defend the planet from Lionstone's troops, led by Valentine Wolfe. The Wolfe had overseen the murder of millions of defenceless people, and the utter destruction of what had been a beautiful rural paradise.

And now Valentine had returned, like a criminal to the scene of his crime or a dog to its own droppings, and Owen had come back too, to bring belated justice to the destroyer of Virimonde. One way or another. He sighed quietly to himself. Through all his rebel wanderings, he'd always clung to the secret hope that someday he would be able to return home and take up his old life again, a quiet scholar and minor historian of no real importance to anyone but himself. But time and necessity had made him a warrior, in spite of himself. He'd changed so much, he wasn't sure he recognized himself any more. And given the reports he'd seen of the devastation awaiting him below, he wasn't even sure there was a home to return to.

'Run sensor scan,' he subvocalized to his AI. 'Locate my

old Standing, and see what kind of force they've got protecting it.'

'Way ahead of you, as usual,' sniffed the AI. 'There's a fair-sized army surrounding the castle, which, according to the comm traffic I'm picking up, Valentine and his associates are currently occupying. Typical. Nothing but the best for dear Valentine. And according to the information we were given before we left Golgotha, which I'll wager good money you haven't even looked at, there's also a hell of a lot of scientific equipment down there, along with scientists to run it. Though no one seems to know what it is or why it's there.'

'Don't get uppity, Oz. Just tell me what I need to know.'

'Bully.'

Owen wasn't quite sure where he stood with Oz. The original Ozymandias had been the Family AI, handed down to Owen from his deceased father. It turned out to contain hidden Empire programming, and had acted as a spy for Lionstone, before finally turning on Owen and trying to enslave him with control words it had secretly placed in his subconscious. Owen had had no choice but to use his Maze-given powers to destroy the AI. Except that some time later, Oz came back. Or a voice in his head that only he could hear, claiming to be the AI Ozymandias. Certainly it was just as knowledgeable and irritating as the original. Owen had accepted the situation for the time being, for as long as the AI remained useful. He hadn't the faintest idea how to get rid of the voice, anyway.

Besides, he'd missed Oz.

'So, do I start the descent or not?' said Oz briskly. 'We're fully cloaked, but there's no telling how long even Hadenman shields will hold up against the more than state-of-the-art security systems Valentine's installed here. What used to be bog-standard weather-control satellites have been upgraded with really heavy-duty sensors and more weaponry than your average Fleet cruiser. When the Wolfe says *Do not disturb*, he means it.'

'Maintain orbit,' Owen said firmly. 'I want a really good idea of what to expect dirtside before I commit us to a landing. Scan the area surrounding the Standing, ten-mile radius, and report on the local population's situation.'

'Owen . . . I've already done that. There is no local population.'

'What?'

'I've scanned the surrounding areas to the limit of my sensors. There isn't a single living soul outside of the Standing for hundreds of miles. I'm sorry, Owen.'

Owen shook his head slowly. He'd read the reports on Valentine's destruction of Virimonde, watched Toby Shreck's filmed coverage, seen interviews with the few survivors to get off-planet, but he'd always assumed they were exaggerated. No one could oversee the murder of a whole planet's population, just for the fun of it. Not even Valentine Wolfe. He couldn't believe that. Wouldn't believe it. Deep down, part of him had desperately wanted to return home to the cheers of his people, overjoyed to have their rightful Lord back at last. He'd wanted to apologize for not being there to protect them when the Empire forces came. Wanted to promise them that things would be different now he was back. He'd keep them safe now, guard them from all harm. They'd never be hurt again because he was off somewhere else being a hero of the rebellion. There was so much he'd wanted – needed – to say.

'What's the matter?' said Hazel. 'Is there a problem?'

'No,' said Owen. 'I was just thinking. About the way things used to be here.'

'Don't,' said Hazel. 'That's always been your problem, Deathstalker. Always living in the past.'

'I understand the past,' said Owen. 'Things were simpler then. I knew my world and my Empire and my place in it. Or I thought I did. Since then I've seen the destruction of everything I ever believed in, lost everything I ever cared for, and now to top it all I find I can't go home again. Because Valentine Wolfe burned it all down and pissed on the ashes. Virimonde is dead.'

'We can't know that for sure till we get down there and check for ourselves,' said Hazel. 'Reports can be exaggerated, sensors can be mistaken. It's a big world, Owen. He can't have killed everything.'

'And if he has? If he's done everything he's supposed to have done?'

17

'Then we cut his black heart out, throw it on the ground and stamp on it. And the same goes for everyone with him.'

Owen had to smile, slightly. 'Life's always been so simple for you, hasn't it, Hazel? Good guys and bad guys, and a direct, forceful answer to every problem. But you heard the man at the briefing. Even after all he's done, there are still powers that be who want Valentine brought back alive for a show trial. If only because they could sell holo rights for a small fortune.'

'I keep up with things,' said Hazel. 'And for every faction that wants the Wolfe brought back alive, I'll bet I can name ten who'd very much rather he came back with flies buzzing round him. Not least the clone and esper undergrounds. If word ever got out that Valentine Wolfe had once been a supporter of the undergrounds, played an active part, even, they'd lose what little popularity they have. On top of that, there are any number of people who struck questionable deals with him in the past and don't want it coming out now they've recreated themselves as pure-hearted cheerleaders of the rebellion.'

'That's why we're going to bring the bastard back alive,' Owen said firmly. 'Not necessarily in one piece, but definitely alive. I'm no man's puppet, and no organization's either. I need to send a signal that no one pressures me. And I won't kill him just because I want to. That's the old way, the Empire way. It's everything I fought to overthrow.'

'You and your damned conscience,' said Hazel. 'All right; so we try and take him alive. What about his supporters?'

'Massacre the lot, for all I care.'

'Now you're talking,' said Hazel.

Owen leaned back in his chair, interlocked his fingers and stared at them thoughtfully. 'He wasn't always a monster, you know, Valentine. I knew him in his younger days. We were children together, moved in the same circles, went to the same parties. He seemed quite . . . normal, then. Nothing out of the ordinary. No sign then of the psychopath he became. Just another kid, perhaps a little quieter than most. Much like me. We were never actually friends, but I can remember good times we had together. And then we went our separate ways, to be trained as a Wolfe and a Deathstalker, and I didn't see him again for years. Sometimes I find myself wondering how two very similar children became such different adults.'

'People change,' said Hazel, 'whether they want to or not. Life writes our scripts, and we just get to ad lib now and again.'

Owen looked at her. 'Why, Hazel – that was almost profound.'

'Don't you patronize me, Deathstalker. I have a mind. I have read the occasional book in my time, when there was nothing else to do. I just meant that even while we're busy changing the universe, it's busy changing us. Look at you; you're not the person you used to be, even a few years ago. Thank God! The Owen Deathstalker I saved from certain death down below was a very different man from the official hero who toppled an Empire.'

'I know,' said Owen. 'That bothers me.'

'Don't worry about it,' said Hazel. 'He really was a stuck-up little prig.'

Owen raised an eyebrow. 'Then why did you stick with him?'

Hazel smiled. 'I thought I saw potential in him.'

Owen's mouth twitched. 'I thought much the same about you.' He frowned again.

'Oh hell, Owen; now what? I swear you know more ways to depress yourself than anyone I've ever met.'

'I was just thinking about Finlay Campbell. We should have included him on this trip.'

'We've been through this, Owen. The man is obsessed. He's sworn a vendetta against Valentine, sworn to kill the man, on his blood and on his honour. If we're to keep our options open down there, we can't afford to have the Campbell anywhere near us. He's always been . . . erratic. They tried using him as a bounty hunter, but he always brought them back dead. Sometimes in pieces. Last I heard, his girlfriend Evangeline was trying to get him interested in politics. God help Parliament, that's all I can say.'

'He fought beside us. He was a hero of the rebellion, just like you and me. And he has as much right to Valentine's head as we do. Valentine wiped out his whole Family. It doesn't feel right, keeping this from him.'

'Owen, we hardly know the man. You're the one who wants to bring Valentine in alive. If the Campbell was here . . .'

'Yes, I know. But if we're keeping secrets from people who are supposed to be our comrades, what might they be keeping from us?'

'Hell,' said Hazel lightly, 'everyone's got secrets.'

She only realized how that sounded after she'd said it, and she held her breath for a moment before Owen grunted and turned away to study the sensor readings on the main display screen. Hazel let her breath out slowly, so Owen wouldn't hear it, and tried to relax. There were still things she was keeping from Owen, partly because she didn't want him getting upset, and partly because she still believed in keeping her business to herself. Ever since she'd first passed through the Madness Maze on the Wolfling World, and been changed for ever, she'd been having problems with dreams. To begin with, they were just disturbing images she could forget with a little effort, but more and more these days the dreams persisted into her waking world, and she couldn't push aside the thought that they meant something – something important. She was dreaming every night now, clear and distinct, and she couldn't tell if she was seeing the past or the future. It was as though time were unravelling in her head, in the darkest hours of the night, when her defences were at their weakest. Something in her mind was showing her things, and wouldn't let her look away.

While on Mistworld, she'd dreamed of the Empire invasion, hours before it actually happened.

Last night there had been three dreams, one after the other. First she dreamed of the Blood Runners, the evil inhabitants of the dark Obeah worlds, far out on the Rim where no one ever went, who'd once tried to kidnap her for their never-ending experiments into the nature of suffering and existence. Owen had saved her then, reaching out with his mind across countless light years to strike down their leader with a terrible, bloody hand. In her dream, they looked at her with knowing, cruel eyes, watching and waiting with

20

unnerving patience. They held something in their hands. Something sharp.

Then she dreamed of Owen's Family Standing, on Virimonde. She'd walked the empty stone corridors with easy familiarity, though she'd never been there before. It was bitter cold, the cold of the grave, and blood trickled down the walls, staining the ancient tapestries and exquisite carpets. There was someone waiting round the next corner, and, far down below, something awful.

And finally she dreamed she stood alone on the bridge of *Sunstrider II*, while all hell broke out around her. There were ships attacking from every side, ships beyond counting, overwhelming her defences even as she fought frantically to hold them back. All the alarms were sounding, and the *Sunstrider II*'s guns fired again and again. There was no sign of Owen anywhere.

Past, present and future: maybe. But were they predictions, or just warnings? Did they mean she had a chance to change things, rewrite history, defy destiny? Or was she just going crazy, like everyone else around her?

There had been a time when the forbidden drug, Blood, had helped her cope with many things, including the dreams, but she'd moved beyond that. She'd been so physically transformed from what she used to be, she doubted Blood would even make a dent in her body chemistry these days. Besides, Blood was heavily addictive, and she was damned if anything or anyone was ever going to have control over her again; and that very definitely included her own weaknesses.

'What do you suppose Valentine and his cronies are up to down there?' she said suddenly, determined to distract herself.

'Beats the hell out of me,' said Owen, still studying the data scrolling past him on the viewscreen. The data was moving far too fast for normal eyes to follow, but neither of them mentioned it. They were used to small changes like that. 'He's reinforced the Standing's shields. I'm not picking up anything useful. Which is in itself significant. He shouldn't have access to anything strong enough to keep out Hadenman-designed sensors. So who's been supplying him with tech?'

21

'We'll have to ask him,' said Hazel, 'when we get down there.'

'Too many questions,' said Owen, finally shutting down the viewscreen. 'Too many unknowns. Why did he return here? Why did he take over my old home? What did he hope to achieve here that was so important he was willing to risk me coming after him?'

'He's here for a specific purpose,' said Hazel. 'Has to be, or he couldn't have persuaded so many people to come with him. Valentine's never had any friends; only allies. And somebody must have paid for his new shields, and all that fancy equipment he's supposed to have with him. He's cut off from his Family funds now. If you ask me, it's probably something to do with drugs. Everything with Valentine turns out to be something to do with drugs.'

'Or revenge. He's a Wolfe, after all. And Oz says his security systems are advanced far beyond anything he should have access to.'

Hazel looked at him sharply. 'You're still hearing voices, aren't you?'

'I do wish you wouldn't put it like that. And it's only one voice.'

'Is that supposed to reassure me? At this rate you'll be saying you only overthrew the Empire because the Devil told you to. That's going to go down really well with the general populace.'

'It's just my old AI!'

'Then why can't I hear it on my comm system? Why can't anyone else hear it? And you were convinced you'd killed the bloody thing after it betrayed us on the Wolfling World.'

'I thought it was dead. But I'm not as sure about a lot of things as I used to be. After all, you and I have been through much that should have killed us. Haven't we?'

Hazel had no quick answer to that. She felt the same way too, most of the time. They stared at each other in an uncomfortable silence for a long moment, until they were suddenly interrupted by all the yacht's warning sirens going off at once, the floor rocking under their feet as something really powerful hit the ship like a hammer.

'Oz!' yelled Owen. 'What the hell's going on?'

'You can't say I didn't warn you,' said the AI calmly. 'Valentine's security systems have finally broken through our cloaking shields, and the armed satellites are throwing everything they've got at us. Which is actually quite considerable. You wouldn't believe how many disrupter cannon Valentine's managed to cram into what used to be a weather-control satellite. Main shields are holding. For the moment. Do I have your permission to return fire?'

'Of course you bloody do! Blow the nearest satellites out of the sky and then get us dirtside as fast as you can.'

'Landing coordinates?'

'Not too far from the Standing. Walking distance.'

'About time you got some healthy exercise,' said the AI approvingly. 'You've been putting on weight.'

'Well?' said Hazel, 'what's happening?'

'Valentine knows we're here. And the voice in my head now thinks it's my mother. I'm bringing the ship down fast. Grab on to something and pray for a soft landing.'

'Hell with that,' said Hazel, 'I want to get some shots of my own in first.'

'Why bother? They're just satellites, following their programming.'

'God, you're a wimp sometimes, Deathstalker. It's the principle of the thing.'

And off she went, up to the bridge to plug herself into the fire systems. Owen let her go. He didn't see the point in personally firing the ship's disrupters at targets the ship's computers were perfectly capable of dealing with. Owen had run hundreds of similar simulations in his time, back when his father was still determined to turn his reluctant scholarly son into the warrior the Family history demanded. He didn't feel like going through all that again. He strapped himself into his chair and waited patiently. At least the *Sunstrider II* had decent guns. The original yacht hadn't, but it had been shot at often enough to make Owen wish that it had. The *Sunstrider* spent most of its short life being chased from one world to another, often holed and on fire, until it finally crashlanded in the deadly jungles of Shandrakor. When he had the new yacht built around the salvaged engines of the old, Owen had insisted the Hadenmen install as many state-of-the-art weapon systems as the craft could hold. He didn't like having to run. It wasn't in his nature.

The ship lurched again, as something really nasty slammed through the energy shields and impacted on the reinforced hull. Which was supposed to be impossible. The lights flickered briefly and Owen tensed, waiting for the shrill warning of a hull breach. It didn't come, but Owen decided his proper place was on the bridge after all. Defence computers could only do so much. He ran all the way, but still had enough breath left when he got there to demand of Hazel what the hell was going on.

'Damned if I know, Deathstalker,' she said briskly, eyes fixed on the control panels before her. 'I've never encountered firepower like this. At least, not from any human tech.'

Owen dropped into the seat beside her and quickly studied the tactical displays. Main shields were still holding, but they were taking a hell of a battering. There was some damage to the outer hull, mostly superficial. The Hadenmen knew how to build a ship. 'This shouldn't be happening,' he said finally. 'The Hadenmen assured me we could stand off everything up to and including an Empire starcruiser.'

'Should have got it in writing, stud,' said Hazel, smiling briefly as one of Valentine's satellites exploded under her guns. 'Maybe Valentine made a deal with the Hadenmen too. Or he's been talking to Shub, or even the aliens. Selling out all humanity for simple personal gain is exactly the kind of thing you'd expect from Valentine Wolfe. Either way, we are in over our heads and sinking fast. Suggestions of a practical nature are urgently invited. Also prayers.'

'To hell with trying to fight it out,' said Owen. 'Throw as much power as you can into the shields and get us down fast, Oz. Hopefully the satellites are only programmed to hit things in a predetermined area. Once we've dropped below their response level, they should leave us alone. And then let us all hope Valentine hasn't also invested in some ground defences.'

'Sounds like a plan to me,' said Hazel. 'Can I make the landing?'

'No,' said Owen firmly. 'Let Oz do it. I've seen your landings, Hazel.'

'Spoilsport.'

The *Sunstrider II* plunged screaming through the atmosphere, wreathed in flames, until finally it fell out of range of the satellites, and the attack cut off. Owen and Hazel braced themselves for ground responses, but there were none. Apparently Valentine had expected his souped-up satellites to be all that was needed to discourage visitors. With any other ship, he'd probably have been right. Oz finally eased off the steep descent and searched out a landing spot not too far from the Standing. Owen allowed himself to relax a little.

'It would seem Valentine has powerful new allies,' he said thoughtfully. 'Which is something of a surprise, as I would have thought he'd run out of options by now. I wonder what other treats he has in store for us.'

'Something nasty, no doubt,' said Hazel, 'knowing Valentine. But it doesn't matter what fools he's persuaded to back him, or what new toys he's got. We can handle it.'

'Don't get cocky,' said Owen. 'Valentine hasn't survived this long by leaving anything to chance. He must have known I'd be coming after him once he set up shop here. He must have made . . . preparations.'

'There's nothing he can throw at us that we can't throw right back at him,' said Hazel calmly. 'I could have handled those satellites eventually, if you hadn't chickened out. Nothing can harm us any more, Owen. Not after all we've been through.'

'Cocky,' said Owen, 'definitely cocky. It'll end in tears . . .'

He would have said more, but navigation chimed discreetly, alerting him that the *Sunstrider II* was coming in for a touchdown. Owen and Hazel studied the short- and long-range sensor displays carefully, but the ship landed without incident. Oz made them wait while he ran through his landing checklist.

'Air quality: tolerable. Cold for the time of year, but within acceptable limits. No life signs. All right; it's now officially safe to disembark. For old times' sake, I've put down at the exact spot where Hazel first encountered you, Owen. Just call me a silly old sentimentalist.'

'Shut up, Oz.'

They made their way down to the airlock, and then Owen

waited patiently while Hazel weighed herself down with a few more guns and ammunition belts. For all her claims of invulnerability, Hazel never really felt comfortable going out in public unless she was carrying more guns than the average armed patrol group. She preferred projectile weapons to energy guns, mostly. Probably because they were bigger and heavier and had more bits to fiddle with. Owen leaned against the steel bulkhead, and remembered how things had been the first time he'd met Hazel d'Ark.

He'd been on the run from his own security guards, badly wounded, fleeing desperately in a damaged flyer. They shot him down only a few miles from his Standing. It had been a bad crash, and he'd been lucky to survive it. He'd staggered away from the burning wreckage, bleeding profusely, and set his back against a nearby tree to hold him up while he made his last stand. He felt like shit and his head was swimming madly, but he was still able to appreciate the great green fields stretching away before him. Virimonde had always been a very beautiful world.

And then Hazel had appeared out of nowhere to save him from his enemies, cutting them down like a glorious if somewhat shop-soiled Valkyrie, and together they'd escaped Virimonde in the first *Sunstrider*. Owen had not been back since. He'd always meant to, but the rebellion never gave him time. He'd spent his childhood on a dozen different planets, as his father darted round the Empire pursuing endless intrigues. But Virimonde had been his and his alone, his world, his haven from a Family and a warrior's destiny he'd never wanted. The only place he'd ever thought of as home.

'Come on, stud, let's get this show on the road. I haven't killed anyone in hours, and I'm starting to get twitchy.'

And now here was Hazel, large as life and twice as dangerous, carrying enough guns to start her own war. Owen had to smile.

'What's so funny?' she said suspiciously.

'Oh, nothing. It's just that according to Oz, we've touched down at the exact spot where you and I first met.'

'Where I saved your ass, you mean.'

'That's not how I remember it.'

26

'You always were too nostalgic for your own good, Death-stalker. Crack that airlock and let's get our feet dirty. I didn't come all this way just to stand around.'

'You don't have a single romantic bone in your body, do you, Hazel?'

'For which I thank the good Lord daily. Romance just gets in the way of doing the job.'

Owen sighed and opened the airlock. Virimonde's air wafted in, and Owen took a deep breath, expecting the old familiar scents of grass and earth and growing things. Instead he coughed harshly as his lungs were filled with hot dry air choked with dust. It smelled like something long-dead. Owen and Hazel looked at each other, and then Owen stepped cautiously out on to the planet he had once owned. The sky was dark and overcast, the light grey and lifeless. Where once there had been green fields and the rich foliage of rambling woods, now there was only churned-up mud for as far as he could see in any direction. No fields or crops or low stone boundary walls; just the mud, dark and gritty with trodden-in ashes.

For a moment Owen thought he must have come to the wrong planet. Nowhere on the pastoral world of Virimonde had ever looked like this. But of course it did, now. Just as he'd always known it would deep down. He'd read the reports, seen the film Toby Shreck had presented on Imperial News. He just hadn't wanted to believe it. He'd needed to believe that some part of his peaceful past still existed, untouched. That he still had some link remaining with the quiet scholar he used to be.

'Damn,' said Hazel, her voice low. 'I'm sorry, Owen. I know how much this place meant to you.'

'I think the trees were over there.' He tried to point, but his arm seemed very heavy. 'Right over there. But they're gone now. It's all gone. Everything. Nothing to show they, or we, were ever here. They even took my past away from me. And it's all my fault.'

'How the hell do you work that out?' said Hazel.

'I was Lord of this world. This planet and everyone on it were given to me, and put under my protection. But I went away, and left them defenceless when the Empire's wolves came. I wasn't here when they needed me.'

'Now that is bullshit,' said Hazel. 'They threw you out! Your own security people turned against you. You were outlawed. And you can be damned sure there wasn't a man or a woman here who wouldn't have cheerfully sold you out in a moment for the price on your head. Your cousin David was Lord here after you, and he couldn't even save himself when the Empire forces came. Hell, he was one of them, and they killed him anyway.'

'You're right,' said Owen. 'But it doesn't help. I should have been here.'

'Then you'd be dead too. Is that what you want?'

'Sometimes. The old me is dead. I lost him, somewhere down the long rebel trail that led to Lionstone's Court. I miss him. I liked him a lot better than the killing machine I've become. I look inside myself, and I can't find any trace of him any more.'

'Don't start that again. Change isn't death.'

'It was for Virimonde. This used to be a food planet. The crops and livestock we raised here fed people all across the Empire. Who'll feed them now? Look at it, Hazel. They killed this world.'

'You could start over. Pump enough micro-organisms into the soil, plant the right seeds, and this world could bloom again. In time.'

'Maybe. But it wouldn't be the same. It wouldn't be the world I knew.'

Hazel shook her head, exasperated. 'It always comes back to you, doesn't it, Deathstalker? Typical aristo, seeing everything in terms of himself. Virimonde isn't the only world to get trashed by the Empress's whims. That's the kind of thing we fought the rebellion over. Remember?'

Owen tried to smile for her. 'I know. I'm just feeling sorry for myself. For what I lost here. I don't really have the right, I suppose. My people lost everything. But I can at least avenge them. Valentine will pay for what he did here. I'll see him die, and die hard, and to hell with the consequences.'

Hazel clapped him on the shoulder. 'That's more like it! When all else fails, there's always revenge.'

'You're a woman of simple pleasures, Hazel.'

'That's what you think, stud.' She grinned at Owen, and he had to grin back.

They stood together for a while, sharing the moment. The world was very quiet, not even a murmur of breeze to disturb the dead silence. Owen and Hazel looked slowly around them, and nothing looked back. Hazel frowned suddenly.

'What?' said Owen.

'I hate to sound morbid . . . but shouldn't there be a hell of a lot of bodies lying around? Or bits of bodies, or . . . something? All I can see is miles and miles of mud.'

'You've got a point,' said Owen slowly. 'It is a bit . . . tidy, isn't it? I wasn't aware that anyone had sent in a clean-up crew yet. Hang on a minute.' He accessed his AI. 'Oz, where are all the bodies?'

'Damned if I know, Owen. According to the records, there was a major battle right here, between the incumbent peasants and the invading forces.'

'Scan the area, Oz. Find me some bodies.'

'Scanning. Now that *is* interesting. I'm picking up some decayed animal remains, mixed in with the mud, but absolutely no trace of anything human, in any form. I have no explanation for this.'

'So what the hell happened to the bodies? Could Shub have paid a visit here, looking for raw materials for their Ghost Warriors?'

'Unlikely,' said the AI. 'Even allowing for the current scattered state of the Imperial Fleet, such a visit would hardly have gone unnoticed and unreported. And you can forget about a clean-up crew. There isn't enough manpower available to deal with the needs of the living right now, never mind the dead. Unless . . . Valentine had them removed.'

'Why would he do a thing like that?'

'To show he's sorry, and make amends?'

Hazel cut in, demanding to know what Oz was saying. Owen told her, and she snorted dismissively. 'You're kidding. Valentine never apologized for anything in his life. He's proud of his degeneracy.'

'But I'll bet he does know what happened,' said Owen. 'It's the kind of thing he'd want to know. So I guess we'll just have to slog our way through the mud to my old Standing, haul him out by the scruff of the neck and ask him.'

'Good plan,' said Hazel. 'Is it OK if I stick my gun in his ear while you question him?'

'Be my guest.'

Owen started out across the sea of mud in the direction he thought his old Standing lay. The distance lay concealed behind a grey haze, grimly enigmatic. According to Oz, his old home was approximately two miles away, so that he and Hazel were just out of range of the castle's sensors. Unless Valentine had souped them up, too. Owen smiled humourlessly. It didn't matter a damn if Valentine had. Let him know his death was coming. There might only be the two of them, against an unknown number of enemies, but Owen didn't care. Even an army couldn't stop him now. The thought pulled him up short, and he scowled. More and more these days, he found himself thinking things that scared him. He wondered what he was becoming. The changes the Madness Maze had worked in him seemed to be accelerating, if anything. At first he'd just been a man with an edge, and then a man with unfamiliar esp abilities, but he hadn't been merely human in a long time. Though he liked to pretend. He'd passed beyond esp into something else, something far more powerful. He was leaving his humanity behind, and he knew it, and it frightened him. Which was perhaps why he clung so desperately to his old, human beliefs in honour and justice.

He sighed, tired. He'd come a long way from the simple historian he'd been the last time he was here. Life had been straightforward, then. Life had been good. He lived in quiet luxury, Lord of all he surveyed, bothering no one and comfortably far from the insane and dangerous politics of Lionstone's Court. But he'd lost everything when he was outlawed, and had no choice but to become the warrior his Clan had always wanted. Become what he despised most, or die. The great wrong of his life; that a man who only wanted peace, and to be left alone, had been forced to become a hero on the great stage of interplanetary intrigue and rebellion. He'd achieved a great deal, righted wrongs and meted out justice high and low, but at the end of the day, there was much blood on his hands . . . most of it from people who deserved to die, but not all. For every real villain he'd killed, there'd been a hundred men who were just soldiers following orders, doing what they thought was right. Protecting a corrupt Empire because all the other alternatives seemed worse. Brave fighters, who'd died because they were unfortunate enough to stand between Owen Deathstalker and his destiny. So many faceless dead. He dreamed of them, sometimes.

There was a child he'd crippled and killed in the grimy backstreets of Mistport. It was an accident. And she had been trying to kill him at the time. But none of that mattered. He'd struck out blindly in the bloody rage of battle, and the result was a young girl lying in the blood-spattered snow, crying helplessly for her crippled legs, till he put her out of her misery. He'd never forgiven himself for that, and never would. If there was any purpose in the warrior he'd become, it was to put an end to a system that produced children like that. And, perhaps, to protect people like that from people like him.

That was what it meant to be a Deathstalker.

He glanced across at Hazel, striding determinedly out beside him. Her long, ratty red hair fell down around a sharp and pointed face. Not conventionally pretty, but then Hazel d'Ark didn't believe in being conventional in anything, if she could help it. Owen thought she was beautiful, but then, he was biased. He loved her; quietly, secretly. Just slogging through the clinging mud, on her way to face unknown foes and probably overwhelming odds, she looked calm and confident and ready for action at a moment's notice. They'd spent a lot of time together, faced death and saved each other's lives, and still Owen wasn't sure if they were anything more than comrades-in-arms. She wasn't at all the kind of woman he'd thought he'd fall in love with, and certainly not the kind of woman he was supposed to marry, to continue the centuries-old Deathstalker line, but he loved her nonetheless. Or was it because she was nothing like his imagined future bride?

Hazel was bright and funny, honest when it suited her and

the bravest woman he'd ever known. Not to mention hell on wheels with any weapon you could name. He admired her immensely, but was careful to keep it to himself. She'd only take advantage. She was confident when he was not, cautious when he forgot to be, and she never lost sight of what they were fighting for. He'd never told her he loved her. He just knew that if he ever mentioned the word, she'd leave him flat. Hazel had made it clear, on more than one occasion, that she didn't believe in things like love. They tied you down, made you vulnerable, and led to subjects like commitment and trust and openness, none of which had any place in Hazel's life. So he loved her from afar, accepted what warmth and friendship she offered on her own terms and hoped for better things. They were together, and if that was all he could have, it was more than he'd ever had before.

'Why are we walking?' said Hazel suddenly. 'I made sure they loaded gravity sleds on board before we left.'

'Sleds would show up on the Standing's scanners,' Owen said patiently. 'We, on the other hand, have proved invisible to most scanners ever since we passed through the Maze. Just another useful side effect that no one understands. So we walk, and hopefully slip through Valentine's defences unnoticed.'

'Hate walking,' said Hazel, scowling. 'Makes my back ache. If God had meant us to walk, he wouldn't have given us antigrav.'

'Admire the scenery,' suggested Owen.

'Ha bloody ha. Last time I walked through anything like this, all the field toilets had failed at once.'

'Walking is supposed to be very good for you.'

'So is eating sensibly and abstinence, and I hate them too. I'm warning you right now, Deathstalker; I'd better get to kill a hell of a lot of people at your Standing, or there's going to be trouble.'

'Oh, I think I can guarantee that,' said Owen. 'The one thing you can be sure of on this desolate world is that we have absolutely no friends at all at the Deathstalker Standing.'

*

The Deathstalker Standing was a great stone castle, set on top of a hill, its pale grey walls marked here and there by damage and burns from energy weapons, from the occasion when the Empire had laid siege to the castle to capture its then Lord, David Deathstalker. He died rather than give it up, but they took the castle anyway, in the end. Now it suffered the occupation of Lord Valentine Wolfe and his cronies. The other aristocrats liked to think of themselves as Valentine's partners, but there was nothing of equals in their relationship. The Wolfe had come to Virimonde for his own purposes, only some of which he had deigned to explain, and the others had followed because they had no choice. He was their only hope of undoing the successes of the rebellion and putting them back in power again. Not for them the lesser glories of trade and influence. They wanted – needed – to be Lords and masters. They were also there because he held their lives in the palms of his hands, but they tried not to think about that unless they were forced to. But nothing else could have persuaded such aristocratic movers and shakers to ally themselves so closely with the notorious Valentine Wolfe. He was mad, bad and dangerous to know, as he would have been the first to admit, but he had something: a weapon of such potential that they couldn't risk losing it. While joining with the despised Wolfe, they bet their lives they could out-think or outmanoeuvre him at some future point. Which was a sign of just how desperate they were.

Valentine sat at his ease in the Lord's chair in the great dining hall of the castle, and watched tolerantly as his cronies wrecked the place. They were partly drunk from too many bottles of wine with a good dinner, and now they were laughing and braying as they threw food around and over-turned the furniture. The Lord Silvestri was throwing his knives at the Family portraits hanging on the walls, the Deathstalkers down the ages. He was aiming for the eyes, and hitting them more often than not. The Lord Romanov had pulled down a precious tapestry and was wearing it like a shawl as he drank brandy straight from the bottle. The Lord Kartakis was stamping back and forth on top of the table, fondly believing he was dancing to the ribald song he was singing defiantly off-key. Valentine smiled on them as on errant children, and allowed them their fun. There wasn't much for them to do, and they had been cooped up in the castle for a long time. And Valentine did so like to see the Deathstalker's precious things being violated, as he would someday destroy the man himself.

Valentine Wolfe sat, the chair far too large for him, one long leg slung over its arm, his other foot up on the table. Dressed as always all in black, to reflect his thoughts and temperament, his pale white face surrounded by long dark ringlets of oiled, scented hair, his mouth a scarlet slash and his eyes heavy with mascara, he looked the very picture of the utter villain he strove to be. And the drugs, the glorious drugs, ran riot in his system as they always had. It had been truly said of Valentine that he had never met a chemical he didn't like, and if you could smoke it, swallow it, inject it or stick it where the sun doesn't shine, Valentine was right there at the front of the line ready to give it a try. He saw his chemically enhanced mind as an artist's work-in-progress, and was constantly striving to perfect it. The ultimate high was still out there somewhere, and Valentine pursued it tirelessly.

To that end he'd taken the rare and immediately addictive esper drug, even though he knew it killed a small but significant percentage of those who took it. Valentine survived, of course. Probably because his radically transmuted body chemistry couldn't be affected with anything less than fuming nitric acid. The drug had given him minor telepathic powers, along with complete control of his own autonomic nervous system, and his thoughts moved along strange and unfamiliar tracks. He threw one drug on top of another, maintaining a complex balance through sheer effort of will. As a result his thoughts and emotions were now both more and less than human, and his companions found him increasingly difficult to comprehend. Valentine thought of himself as the first in a new breed of humanity, like the Hadenmen; an alchemical step forward, or perhaps sideways, on the evolutionary ladder.

He watched Carlos Silvestri throw his knives again and again, tearing the eyes out of great men just because he could. And to prove to everyone that he wasn't afraid of the mighty Owen Deathstalker. Silvestri was a tall, thin man, all long limbs and sudden angles. He dressed in shades of red, the traditional colour of his Clan. It didn't suit him. His face was round and puffy, as though it hadn't yet decided what it wanted to be when it grew up, though the man had to be at least forty. He shaved his head bald, and plucked out his other hairs . . . He was good with a knife and better with a sword. He would have made a great swordsman and duellist if only he'd had the courage of his convictions. But the Silvestri had always been a very cautious man, who preferred to watch from the sidelines and work through underlings and never, ever get his hands dirty himself. He'd never forgiven Finlay Campbell for the assassination of his good friend William St John, and had spent much time and money on plans to have the Campbell killed, but none of them succeeded. Now with Finlay a man of power and substance once again, and the Silvestri's powers drastically reduced by Random's deal and the emergence of Blue Block, Carlos Silvestri had been forced to turn to Valentine as his only possible saviour. And if that had turned out very differently from what he'd intended, it just put a little emphasis into the throw of his knives.

Valentine smiled, and turned his attention to Pieter Romanov, that fat and ruddy man wrapped in a torn masterpiece. Pieter believed a man should be recognized by the breadth and achievement of his appetites, and indulged each sense till they groaned under the weight of his will. Sometimes he ate till he hurt, vomited, and then fell on his food again. There was in him a hunger that would not be satisfied, no matter how he tried. His people obeyed his every whim, or if they didn't, he had them killed and replaced with those who would. Pieter was an aristocrat's aristocrat, and he had taken Random's deal hard. Not for him the lesser power and rewards of mere business. He went looking for an ally, a great man of influence who would put things back the way they were, the way they should be; a man of vision and destiny. Unfortunately, all he could find was Valentine. But the Wolfe at least had a plan, which was more than most, and Pieter couldn't help but admire a man whose taste for indulgence actually surpassed his. So Pieter and Valentine made a pact, and if the Romanov found the source of their power base to be somewhat distressing, there was always another meal and another bottle from the Deathstalker's excellent wine cellar to help distract him.

And finally, there was Athos Kartakis. A short and swarthy man with a flashing smile and a temperament that could change in a moment from brightest day to darkest night. He collected insults and saw duelling as a sport. He never accepted first blood, always going for the kill. People tended to be very careful what they said around the young Lord Kartakis. He dressed well but sloppily, and had married badly, but was too stubborn to admit it. He broke his wife's will till she flinched when he spoke to her, and his children kept their distance. But he did like to drink and sing and tell off-colour stories, and as a Lord he was never short of eager companions, for Athos could be very generous when the mood was upon him. Which was how he came to be nearly bankrupt by his twentieth year. His Clan had never been more than a fairly minor House, and generations had been spending money faster than it came in. Kartakis had inherited many debts, and wasted no time in adding a number of his own. Creditors preferred to forget their bills rather than risk fighting a duel over them, but even so, everyone knew the true state of affairs, and Kartakis knew that they knew. The deal Blue Block brokered with Random had been the last straw. Take away his Lordship, and Kartakis had nothing left. He'd never survive as a businessman, if only because he'd made so many enemies in trade. And so he pawned what was left of his soul with Valentine. For after the Wolfe's plan had led to inevitable triumph, all those involved stood to become very wealthy indeed.

Valentine watched his people at their play, and thought pleasantly about the day he wouldn't need their support any more and could have them all killed in slow and interesting ways. He'd just begun to number the ways and select his very favourite, when the viewscreen on the wall chimed politely. Valentine raised a painted eyebrow. He'd given the servants to understand that he wasn't to be interrupted at his dinner for anything less than a major emergency, and after he'd had that footman flayed from the waist down, they'd learned to follow his instructions to the letter. So he accepted the call and directed his cronies to hush themselves. They fell silent immediately, and looked interestedly at the viewscreen, grateful for anything unexpected to relieve their boredom. The screen cleared to show that sinister butterball of a man, the ex-Lord Gregor Shreck. The Shreck sat behind an ugly but functional wooden table, covered with ragged piles of papers and reports. His fat face looked even more unpleasant than usual, and his deep-set eyes moved only briefly over the three aristocrats before dismissing them contemptuously. He nodded curtly to Valentine, the nearest he ever got to polite behaviour, and plunged right in without further niceties.

'You're in trouble, Wolfe. Someone's been talking, and they know where you are. Parliament's sent a force to investigate what you're up to on Virimonde.'

'Really?' said Valentine, unperturbed as always. 'And just how large an army are they sending?'

'It's worse than an army. They've sent Owen Deathstalker and Hazel d'Ark.'

The three aristocrats looked quickly at one another and began to babble unhappily. Valentine waved for them to be quiet. The Wolfe smiled slowly at the Shreck's image on the viewscreen, his great scarlet grin spreading across his death-like face. 'Dear Owen. I have so been looking forward to meeting him. I can't wait to see what he thinks of what I've done with his old place. When can I expect our illustrious hero and his warlike companion?'

'Hell, he and the bitch have probably already landed by now. I'm not as well connected as I used to be. Word takes longer to reach me these days.'

'The Deathstalker can't be here,' said the Kartakis. 'The security systems would have taken out his ship. Or the sensors would have warned us . . .'

'Don't be silly,' said Valentine. 'This is Owen Deathstalker we're talking about.' He looked back at the Shreck. 'You are still otherwise on top of things, at your end?'

'Of course. You supply the product, I've got people set up to move it.' Gregor scowled unhappily. 'Never thought I'd end up a drug runner at my time of life.'

'I'd have thought it was an occupation you were ideally

suited for,' said the Silvestri, idly paring his fingernails with the edge of one of his knives. 'But then, everyone rises to their true level eventually.'

'At least I'm not a fugitive from what passes for justice these days,' snapped Gregor. 'I may be keeping my head down, but I still have my Tower and my people.'

'But you're not a Lord any more,' said the Romanov, sucking chicken grease off his fingers. 'We haven't allowed Blue Block and that traitor Random to strip our rightful heritage from us.'

'And we will be Lords again,' said the Kartakis flatly. 'Even if we have to kill everyone else in the Empire who says otherwise.'

'Big talk from a little man,' said Gregor, secure in the knowledge that the Kartakis was light years away and couldn't get to him. 'We tried fighting. We lost. Our only hope now is the Wolfe's plan. And God help us all if it goes wrong.'

'If it goes right, I'll make gods of you all,' said Valentine calmly. 'We will return in glory, and know power beyond that even Lionstone wielded. But that's the future. Tell me of the present, Gregor. How goes the cabal?'

'Growing every day,' said Gregor. 'More and more aristocrats and politicians are expressing secret support for a return to the old ways. No one's willing to come out in public, but they're all supplying people and money to help expedite your plan. No telling how many of them will actually stand up and fight when the time comes, but I'll settle for them just abstaining at the right moment. Everyone's worried. Everyone's making deals. No one knows what to believe or who to trust any more. The rebels and their pet Parliament may think they're running things, but their precious new regime is built on sand.'

'And the sands of time are running out for all of them,' said Valentine. 'How I do love a good metaphor. Now be a good boy, Gregor, and make yourself scarce. I must think. I have to prepare a suitable welcome for dear Owen and the redoubtable Hazel d'Ark.'

'Watch yourself,' said Gregor. 'They aren't human any more. If they ever were. They'll take a lot of killing.'

'If it was easy,' said Valentine, 'there'd be no fun in it, would there? Goodbye, Gregor.' He shut down the viewscreen.

'Let them come,' said the Silvestri. 'We can handle them.'

'We can,' said the Kartakis. 'I'm not so sure about you.'

Carlos Silvestri flushed pinkly, a knife in each hand. 'I can hold up my end.'

'Relax,' said the Romanov, rooting through the remains of his dinner in case he'd missed anything. 'With all the guards and security we've set up here, we could hold off an entire army till they starved to death.'

'Anyone else, maybe,' said the Silvestri. 'But this is the Deathstalker and the d'Ark woman. I've heard stories about them, of the things they did during the street fighting on Golgotha. It's said they worked miracles. That they were hit point-blank by a disrupter cannon and survived. Someone said they died and brought themselves back to life.'

'Stories,' said Athos Kartakis. 'There are always stories.'

'In this case, they might just be true,' said Valentine. 'But not to worry, dear comrades. Let them come how they will. They'll find nothing here but death.' He laughed softly at his little joke. The others didn't look too appreciative of his humour, but then, they rarely did. Valentine's sense of humour had changed, evolving along with his alchemical transformation, and was no longer to everyone's taste. Just another way in which he had left lesser mortals behind. He sighed and got to his feet, the signal that dinner was officially over. He dabbed daintily at his scarlet lips with a napkin and started towards the door. The three aristocrats made varying sounds of alarm, despite themselves. Valentine took his time turning back to face them.

'Yes, dear friends? Was there something else?'

'The drug,' said the Kartakis stonily. 'We need the drug.'

'Of course,' said Valentine. 'What was I thinking? It's time for your daily dose, isn't it? How very forgetful of me.'

He strolled back to the table and took a small phial of pills from his pocket. The three men who had once been Lords and masters of their destiny looked at the phial and tried not to appear too desperate. Valentine was quite capable of dragging out his little game for ages if he felt like it. He could make them do anything, anything at all, at this time of the day, and they all knew it.

The esper drug had originally been discovered by a small group of scientists looking for something else. To their surprise, they found that they had created a drug that could give everyone who took it regularly a small but real gift for telepathy. Whether they were espers or not. Which had always been thought impossible. The original Lord High Dram, the Widowmaker, had seized control of the drug and the scientists and put it to his own use, but his plans, like his imagination, were somewhat limited. After his death, Valentine took control of the drug and the single laboratory that produced it. Marvellous as the drug was, there was, of course, a catch or two. First, the drug was highly addictive. Once you'd started taking it, you had to continue for the rest of your life, or die horribly. And second, a small percentage of the people who took it died instantly. Valentine weighed the pros and cons, but not for long. He took his first dose on the same day he discovered the drug existed. It was only a drug, after all, and Valentine had never believed in letting a chemical get the better of him.

The three ex-Lords had also taken the drug and survived. They hadn't been anywhere as willing as the Wolfe, but it had been his condition for allowing them to join him in mass-producing the drug. A drug that could be used as a weapon to undermine and then control first the Parliament, and then the many populations of the civilized worlds. For whoever owned and controlled production of such an attractive and endlessly addictive drug would have complete and utter control over everyone who took it, for as long as they lived. For those few who might try to hold out against it, it would be easy enough to slip them the drug unnoticed. Everyone has to eat and drink, and one dose was all it would take.

Valentine had always believed the simplest plans were the best.

So he handed out the precious pills, and the Silvestri and the Romanov and the Kartakis swallowed them down with more or less concealed eagerness, and everyone was reminded of just who was in charge of things in the old Deathstalker Standing. Valentine put the phial of pills away, and had the grace not to smile triumphantly at them. They would have liked to kill him for the secret and regain control of their lives, but they didn't dare. There were things only Valentine knew, and none of the aristocrats were stupid enough to believe that they could make him tell them a single damned thing he didn't choose to. And they all knew that if he died, they died too, and however badly he died, they'd die worse.

It was said that already there were people of power and influence within the Empire who were controlled by the drug, but Valentine kept the names to himself. Secrets were currency in the world of intrigue. And he did so like to spring little surprises on his friends and colleagues.

'I trust you enjoyed the dinner,' he said smoothly. 'Something a little different today.'

The three aristocrats looked suspiciously at the dinner table, trying to remember if anything had seemed out of the ordinary. None of them would put it above Valentine to have slipped one of his special chemical creations into the food: his sense of humour again.

'No, no,' said Valentine, correctly interpreting their expressions. 'I wouldn't waste any of my special concoctions on such an unappreciative audience. Rather, I thought we might all enjoy a taste of the last real produce exported from the food planet of Virimonde.'

For a long moment, none of them got it. There was no food left on the planet any more, everyone knew that. And then the Silvestri's eyes widened, and he put a hand to his mouth as the colour drained from his face. 'The dead . . . the people of Virimonde . . . we've been eating . . .'

'Yes, you have,' said Valentine. 'And with such good appetite, too. Ah me; so many taboos, so little time. Enjoy the after-dinner mints, gentlemen.'

And with a cheery smile and a modest inclination of the head, Valentine Wolfe left to plan the surprises he had in mind for Owen Deathstalker and Hazel d'Ark.

In the great rebellion, many Lords' Standings turned out to be built on sand. The great Deathstalker castle had been built on a huge promontory of solid granite. From the front and the two sides, open plains stretched away in all directions. To the rear there was a solid drop of hundreds of feet, ending in nasty jagged rocks lashed by a vicious incoming tide. Which made the Standing both extremely easy to defend and very hard to sneak into. Perfect thinking, security-wise. Though that wasn't why Owen had chosen to place his Standing there. He just liked the view.

Of course, he'd never expected to have to break into his own castle, so when he and Hazel finally came in sight of his old home, they had to stop and do some hard thinking. A frontal or side approach was out of the question; their special nature might make them invisible to the castle's sensors, but they were still perfectly visible to the naked eye. And Owen had no doubt that the moment a sentry identified them, Valentine would open up with every weapon at his command. It was what Owen would have done. And he didn't share Hazel's faith in their invulnerability. So after a certain amount of thought, discussion and open argument, they finally decided that the only practical way was round the back. It meant retreating some of the way they'd already come, and a slow descent down to the wave-lashed shore at the foot of the great promontory, but eventually they stood together amid the flying spray, looking up at hundreds of feet of sheer bare granite.

'There used to be birds here,' said Owen quietly. 'Or things very like birds. Soaring and wheeling on the wind, crying out in the saddest voices you ever heard. And now they're all gone. They even killed the damned birds.'

'Just another reason to take revenge,' said Hazel. 'Nothing like a little stoked rage to warm a body on a long cold climb.'

'It's very cold here,' said Owen. 'I don't think I'll ever be warm again.'

He started up the dark granite wall, climbing slowly and carefully, and after a moment Hazel followed him. It felt good to get up out of the spray, and leave the deafening pounding of the waves behind. The wind rushed around them, trying to pluck them from the sheer rock face, but it couldn't budge them, so it just settled for blowing tears from their eyes. Owen concentrated on the wall before him, moving confidently from one foot- and handhold to another.

After the first hundred feet, he decided firmly that he wasn't going to look down again till he was safely inside the castle. Great views aside, he'd never been fond of heights. And yet he moved increasingly easily up the bare cliff, his hands and feet instinctively finding crevices and supports he would have sworn weren't there till he needed them. Not for the first time, it was as though his body knew how to do something without having to be told. Owen brooded over that as he climbed – it was better than thinking about the drop below him. Since he passed through the Madness Maze, he'd become able to do all kinds of things he never could before; he'd emerged so much more than he had been. The talents came and went, and he couldn't always be sure they'd be there when he needed them. Even after all this time, he was no nearer understanding their nature. He glanced across at Hazel, skittering calmly up the smooth granite surface like an insect on a pane of glass, and had to look away. He really hoped he didn't look like that. He made himself look again, and met Hazel's eyes.

'I know what you're thinking,' she said easily.

'Wouldn't be the first time,' said Owen. 'I assume you had no prior knowledge of rock-climbing before today, either?'

'Got it in one. This is almost easier than walking. It's as though my hands and feet know where to go without my looking, as if they've always known. Spooky. I wonder what else we could do, if we just put our minds to it? I've always dreamed of flying . . .'

'I wouldn't try that out just now,' said Owen. 'Those rocks below seem particularly unforgiving.'

'Good point.'

They climbed on in silence. Owen couldn't help noticing that neither of them were even breathing hard.

'Do you ever think about the things we can do?' he said finally. 'What we're becoming? We're not espers. I had a number of major players from the esper underground scan me, at my request. They couldn't detect the slightest trace of esp in me. They had no idea at all how I'm able to do the things I do.'

'I try not to think about it too much,' said Hazel. 'We were given gifts. Gifts that have kept us alive in situations where

43

anyone else would have perished horribly. They helped us overthrow the Empire. Why look such a gift horse in the mouth?'

'Just because something has a leg at each corner and eats hay, it doesn't necessarily mean it's a horse. Espers, for all their powers, are still human. That's one of the reasons we fought the rebellion. But we were changed by a device not born of human hands or thoughts – an alien device. Who knows what it was really intended to do; what it was supposed to produce?'

'Transfiguration,' said Hazel slowly. 'It made us . . . better than we were. That was its function. I remember that much.'

'But what do we mean by better? A human definition, or an alien one? And would the two necessarily have anything in common?'

'Why the hell are you asking me? You're the brains in this partnership. I just hit things.'

Owen sighed. 'I'm tired of asking myself questions I can't answer. Or else coming up with answers that are just too damned disturbing. Our only hope of enlightenment was the Maze itself, and the Maze is gone, destroyed. And with it went all our hopes of discovering exactly what was done to us and why.'

'So why torment yourself?' said Hazel, stopping to look at him as she realized he'd stopped climbing.

'Because I'm scared of what I might be becoming,' said Owen. 'I'm scared I'm losing my humanity, leaving it behind. I don't want to be a god. Or a monster. Have you ever thought that we might end up as distant from ordinary men and women as the Hadenmen or the Wampyr or the AIs from Shub? What if we become so . . . alien that we forget who and what we are?'

'Stop it, Owen,' said Hazel sharply. 'You're just spooking yourself. I don't feel any different from the person I used to be. I still believe in the same things, want the same things, hate the same things. I just get to hit a better class of people. I'm still me. My abilities make it that much easier for me to achieve the things I want.'

She started climbing again, and after a moment Owen followed her. 'I think it's subtler than that,' he said finally.

44

'One small change might not mean much, but put enough of them together . . . I mean, we don't even have the first idea of how our powers work, why they come and go the way they do. Sometimes I can blow apart a whole building just by thinking about it, and other times I can't even manage things the most minor esper could do with half a thought. One minute I'm invulnerable, the next I'm bleeding like a stuck pig. There are times we're just fighters with an edge, and others when we're all but gods. We're not in control of our powers. They control us.'

'Look,' said Hazel, 'if you're trying to scare me, you're succeeding, so cut it out. Our condition didn't exactly come with a user's manual, so all we can hope is to learn by doing. Seems to me the more we use our powers, the more control we'll gain over them.'

'It's dangerous to use any new weapon without checking out the small print. There could be side effects we haven't noticed yet. Maybe we're using up our lives, shortening our lifespans. The energy that powers our abilities has to come from somewhere. The candle that burns twice as brightly burns half as long. And we have burned brighter than suns.'

'God, you're in a morbid mood today. I feel fine, I feel better than fine. Maybe we'll live for ever.'

'And another thing; why did we all come out of the Maze with different abilities?'

'Why not?' said Hazel, reasonably. 'We were all different people.'

'Yes, but some of what we do is similar to esp. Jack and Ruby are firestarters, and Giles could teleport. I've got something like psychokinesis. But how the hell do you do what you do? What are these different versions of yourself that you're able to summon up during a fight?'

'Damned if I know,' said Hazel. 'I just call, and they come. None of them ever stuck around long enough afterwards to answer questions. Giles thought they were other versions of me from different time tracks; people I might have become if things had gone differently.'

'Yeah, but time tracks are just a theory,' said Owen. 'No one's ever been able to prove the existence of different dimensions, let alone make contact with them. Maybe the other yous are just products of your imagination, made real by the power within you.'

'No way,' said Hazel firmly. 'I've seen some of these other mes. I don't have that good an imagination.'

'Yes, but—'

'Owen, I *don't know*! And this is not the time or the place to be having a discussion. If either of us gets distracted and slips, they will be scraping what's left of us off the rocks below with a palette knife! Now stop asking questions and get your ass in gear or I'll kick your butt all the way up.'

Owen considered this. 'You would, wouldn't you?'

'Damn right. Now shift it.'

They climbed the rest of the way in silence. Eventually they came to the great circular opening in the granite wall that led to the massive caves burrowed out under the Standing. Owen used to keep his personal flyers and other vehicles there, when he was in residence. Since there'd been no sign of any craft parked near or around the Standing, it made sense to assume that Valentine and his cronies had docked their ships in the caves too, which meant the opening would still be clear. And Owen knew of a secret passage that led directly from the main cave to the master bedroom.

'A secret passage?' Hazel had said. 'Are you sure it's still secret, Deathstalker?'

'Oh, yes. I used it to escape from the castle when my own people first turned on me.'

'And no one but you knows about it?'

'It's a Family secret. The only other person I ever told was David, and he's dead now.'

They moved silently up to the lip of the opening and clung to the cold stone, still as limpets, and listened for any sign that their presence had been noted. After a while, Owen allowed himself to relax a little, and gestured to Hazel that he was going to move up over the ledge and into the cave. She nodded and he took a deep breath, steadying himself. Theoretically, there could be any number of armed guards present looking after the parked ships, but it didn't seem likely. By any normal standards, the caves were unreachable. Unfortunately for Valentine, Owen and Hazel hadn't been in hailing distance of normal for some time now. Owen took a firm grip on the granite ledge and hauled himself up and over and into the cave in one swift, fluid motion. He was on his feet in a second, disrupter in hand, searching for a target, but all was quiet. Four luxurious yachts stood together, powered down, along with a handful of single-man flyers, but otherwise the place was deserted. Not a guard in sight. Owen padded stealthily forward, ears pricked for the slightest sound, but all he could hear was his own shallow breathing. He lowered his gun and exhaled silently.

'All clear, Hazel.'

She was with him in a moment, hurrying across the ceramic floor, projectile gun in one hand, grenade in the other. She glared suspiciously about her. 'There ought to be someone here. It doesn't make sense to leave expensive ships like these just standing around unguarded.'

'Who's going to steal them?' said Owen. 'Valentine and his private army are the only people here.'

'What about security cameras?'

'Oz is taking care of them. He still has secret access codes for all the castle's security computers. Right now he's editing their signals so we don't appear. This was all covered in the planning sessions, Hazel. I do wish you'd attend the briefings before we go on missions.'

'What, and do you out of the fun of explaining everything to me? You'd never forgive me.' She turned in a slow circle, checking the corners and shadows. 'I still don't like this. It's too easy. If I was as guilty of as many nasty things as Valentine, I'd want all my exits and entrances thoroughly guarded.'

'He's probably relying on the security systems. I did install the very best. And those souped-up satellites of his would hold off any normal ship.'

'I've been thinking about that,' said Hazel. 'What if they reported opening fire on us?'

'What if they did? After the onslaught they handed out, they probably assumed we were so damaged we burned up during the descent.'

'You keep using that word "probably". There's nothing very probable about Valentine Wolfe. He's paranoid as hell; he doesn't think the way the rest of us do.'

'Hazel, trust me. This is my place, I know what I'm doing. Now please put away that gun and grenade before you have an unfortunate and very loud accident. I want to take a look around here.'

'What's there to see?' said Hazel, just to be difficult. 'It's a cave.'

'The first of several caves,' said Owen, being careful not to watch as Hazel made the gun and grenade disappear about her person. 'When I was in charge here, we used the extra caves to store all the items there wasn't room for in the Standing proper. When a Family's been around for as long as mine, you'd be amazed how much junk you accumulate. Treasures, tributes, spoils of war and conquest, and the occasional dowry. Plus, a number of my ancestors were collectors of various kinds, and you wouldn't believe the kind of thing some people can obsess over when they've unlimited resources and far too much time on their hands. And of course you don't dare throw any of it out, for fear of future generations calling you a barbarian. You never know when some piece of centuries-old tat might suddenly become fashionable again, or come in handy to settle some ancient Family feud or argument. So it all piles up, and you've got to do something with it. I used to display the best pieces in the castle itself, and dump the rest in the caves down here. It's all carefully catalogued, somewhere. David said he was going to have a good clear-out once he moved in, but I don't think he had time in the end. Either way, I'll feel better once I've checked. I don't like surprises.'

He moved off towards the back of the cave. Hazel rolled her eyes briefly at the polished ceiling and went after him, giving the parked yachts plenty of room in case they were armed with proximity alarms. In the end, Owen didn't get far. He stood before the entrance to the next cave, which was now blocked off by a glowing force field. He was standing very still, and Hazel could tell at once that something was wrong. She hurried over to join him, the gun back in her hand. She moved in beside him and then stopped, and screwed up her face in disgust. Beyond the transparent energy field, the cave was packed from wall to wall and from floor to ceiling with dead bodies. Not respectfully lying on separate slabs or tables, but crammed together like cuts of meat or lengths of wood, packed in as tightly as possible. A temperature gauge on the wall by the opening showed that a freezer unit was maintaining the bodies at near-zero. Some of the faces looked out at Owen and Hazel, an almost lifelike gleam shining from the frost on their frozen eyeballs.

'Well,' Owen said finally. 'Now we know what they did with the bodies.'

'Owen . . .'

'Not now. I want to check the other caves.'

They went from cave to cave, from opening to opening, and they were all filled to capacity with the refrigerated dead of Virimonde. Men, women and children stacked together like logs, with no room for dignity. Some were wearing clothes, some weren't. Owen tried to estimate how many bodies there were, but even guessing from the massive size of the caves he couldn't grasp it. The numbers were just too big. He stopped before the opening to the last cave, and couldn't go any further. All the strength went out of him. Hazel stood beside him and put a comforting hand on his arm, but he hardly acknowledged it.

'I feel like I ought to do something,' he said quietly, 'but I don't know what. They were my people. They're still my people, even if they are dead. But I don't know what to do.'

His hands had clenched into helpless fists. Hazel moved close beside him, trying to support and comfort him with her nearness.

'I don't suppose this means much to you,' said Owen. 'After all, you were a clonclegger.'

'I never saw the bodies,' said Hazel. 'But sometimes I had nightmares . . . Why do you suppose Valentine—'

'Who knows why Valentine does anything any more?'

Hazel hesitated, hearing the cold, bitter rage beneath his words, but pressed on. 'The Wolfe's crazy, but there's always a method to his madness. Think of all the time and effort it must have taken to collect all the bodies, bring them down here and pack them in. He must have had a reason. Or else why bother refrigerating them?'

'Knowing Valentine, it's probably a very disturbing reason.' Owen let his breath out in a long sigh, and his fists unclenched. 'I say we find the bastard and ask him. And if I don't like his answers, I'm going to bounce him off the castle walls till his ears bleed.'

'Sounds good to me,' said Hazel.

Owen led the way to the back of the flyer cave, and opened a hidden door in the wall to reveal a narrow stone passage leading upwards. Lights came on in the tunnel, showing the way. Hazel was quietly impressed.

'It leads to another secret door in what used to be my old bedchamber,' said Owen. 'From there we have access to all the main areas of the castle. Internal security is mostly human rather than tech. Aristocrats don't like being spied on. Keep your hand near your sword, but leave your guns alone. Whatever happens, the sound of a gun would bring guards running from all directions. And I don't want a war. I just want Valentine.'

Any other time, Hazel would have snapped at Owen for lecturing her on something so obvious, but she kept her peace. She could see the pain in him. Talking helped distract him. She followed him into the tunnel, and the door swung shut behind them. Their footsteps seemed very loud in the quiet. Then Owen stopped suddenly, turning his head back and forth.

'What is it?' asked Hazel quietly.

'Something's not right.'

Hazel looked up the tunnel. 'I can't see anything.'

'Neither can I. But I can feel it, can't you?'

Hazel concentrated, trying to reach out in the strange directions of which her mind was capable, and then Owen grabbed her roughly and threw her to the floor. She landed hard, driving the breath from her lungs. Owen hit the ground beside her a moment later, one arm flung across her to hold her down. From every side disrupter beams filled the tunnel from nearly hidden gunports. If they'd stayed standing, they'd have been shot to mincemeat.

'So much for your secret passage, Deathstalker,' Hazel hissed, trying to burrow down into the solid stone floor.

'They must have got it out of David before he died,' said Owen. 'Try and wriggle backwards towards the door.'

'Hell with that,' said Hazel, 'I have my dignity. Wait till

the beams shut off, and then we'll make a run for it while they're recharging.'

'One, they're staggered. They're not going to cut off. Two, the beams are angling lower. Now wriggle, dammit.'

They moved back down the tunnel to the door as fast as they were able, the disrupter beams passing barely an inch or so above their bodies. They pushed and scraped along the rough stone floor, unable to raise their heads enough to see where they were going, or how far they had to go. The energy beams dipped and seared the air just above them, flashing on and off, filling the tunnel with the stench of ionized air. Owen's clothes rucked up around him as he crawled backwards, slowing him down, and he could hear Hazel's several guns and ammo belts scraping along the floor, holding her back. He risked a glance at her, just in time to see a disrupter beam clip her raised elbow, vaporizing the sleeve and burning the exposed flesh. She grimaced but didn't make a sound, and kept moving. The smell of burned meat mingled briefly with the ozone.

Owen redoubled his efforts, and then suddenly he lurched to a halt as his feet slammed up against the closed steel door. He pushed against it with all his weight, but it wouldn't budge. Owen's temper flared and he kicked out with both feet. The heavy steel door flew open, half tearing off its hinges. He looked back at Hazel again. She'd raised her head slightly at the noise of the door opening, and a disrupter beam was heading right for her forehead.

For Owen, time seemed to slow and stop, the energy beam crawling slowly through the air. And it was the simplest thing in the world for him to lunge forward and thrust his golden Hadenman hand between Hazel and the beam, which ricocheted harmlessly away. Time crashed back to normal. Owen grabbed Hazel and then threw himself out of the tunnel and back into the main cave, dragging her with him. They hit the floor hard and rolled away from the opening, putting as much room as they could between themselves and the deadly tunnel. They lay together for a while, getting their breath back, and then rose just a little shakily to their feet.

'So,' said Owen, 'still feel invulnerable?'

'Oh, shut up, Deathstalker. Don't you get tired of being

right all the time?' She raised her arm gingerly, and studied the burn with a curled lip. 'Nasty. But it'll heal. Hate to think what that beam would have done to my face. Thanks for the save, stud.'

'Any time,' said Owen.

Hazel looked at his golden hand. 'I have to say I'm impressed. Your average disrupter beam can vaporize steel plating in under a second, but it just bounced off that golden fashion accessory of yours.'

'The Hadenmen do good work.' Owen flexed the bright metal fingers just a little self-consciously. 'One of these days I really ought to sit down with some human scientists and have them analyse the hell out of this thing, see what its capabilities are, but I never seem to have the time. It's all rush, rush, rush when you're a rebel hero.'

'And a bounty hunter.'

'That too. Speaking of which, I have another idea on how to get to dear Valentine.'

'Hold everything. Your last idea didn't turn out so damned hot.'

'And you're not going to like this one much either. But we can't hang around here; those disrupters must have set off all kinds of alarms once they were triggered. There'll be guards here soon. Lots of them, armed to the teeth.'

'Let them come,' said Hazel. 'I could use something to work off my frustrations on.'

'You're missing the point, and not for the first time. The guards could pin us down here while Valentine and his cronies make their escape. And I'll see this place reduced to rubble before I let that happen. This time, Valentine is going to pay for his crimes. In blood.'

'Every now and again you remind me of why I stick around with you,' said Hazel. 'All right, Deathstalker. I just know I'm going to regret asking, but what is this marvellous new plan of yours?'

'There's another secret passage. One I never told David about. A Deathstalker always keeps some secrets to himself.'

'There's a catch,' said Hazel, 'I just know there's a catch.'

'Oh, yes. The entrance to this tunnel is on the other side

of the first cave on the left. The only way to get to it is past the piled-up bodies.'

'Oh, nice one, Owen. How the hell are we supposed to do that? Drag the bodies out one at a time? How long will that take?'

'Too long. The guards would be upon us before we'd barely started. No; there's only one way. We're going to have to crawl through the mass of bodies, forcing our way through by brute strength till we reach the far side.'

'No,' said Hazel flatly.

'Hazel . . .'

'No! Are you crazy? Dig our way through corpses, hand over hand? I won't do it, Owen. I'd rather stand and fight here.'

'And die?'

'I'm not doing it!'

'You used to be a clonelegger!'

'I never saw the bodies! Just . . . parts, in the freezers. And even that was enough to give me bad dreams. I was already planning to leave the cloneleggers, even before I met you. We can't do this, Owen. It's freezing in there. Near zero.'

'We've withstood worse,' said Owen. 'The guards will never detect us. They'll never think to look for us among the dead.'

'That's because no sane person would contemplate doing it. I can't, Owen, I just can't. It would be like crawling through the contents of the freezer units on the clonelegger ship. Just like my nightmares.'

'No it won't. This time, I'll be there with you. You have to do this, Hazel. It's the only way. And I can't do it without you.'

'You bastard, Deathstalker. You always did know how to fight dirty.' Hazel drew in a long, ragged breath and let it out slowly. 'All right. Let's do it. Before I get a rush of brains to the head and tell you to go to hell.'

'Just follow me. I'll lead the way.'

'Damn right you will.'

Owen made for the cave. Out of the corner of his eye he could see Hazel staring straight ahead, her face a cold mask, her eyes those of a frightened child. Owen had never seen her scared before; not *really* scared. He realized he knew very little about her past life. He'd pieced together a few clues (ex-pirate, ex-clonelegger, ex-confidence trickster and bravo), and thought he had the whole picture. He should have known better.

'So,' he said, searching for the right words to say. 'You were already thinking of leaving the cloneleggers before we met?'

'Yeah,' said Hazel. 'They were too gross, even for me. And the pay was lousy.'

'Silly me. I thought it might have something to do with morality.'

'Don't you use the m-word in my presence, Deathstalker.'

They stopped before the entrance to the cave. Beyond the shimmering transparent force field, dead faces looked out at them. Hazel's hands fell to her guns, but they didn't comfort her. 'Damn you, Deathstalker. Somebody's going to pay for this.'

'Hang on to that attitude. It'll come in very handy when we have to fight our way through Valentine's private army at the other end.'

Hazel snorted. 'Overwhelming odds I can handle, I'm used to that. Now shut up and open the damned door. You can do that, can't you?'

'I'm working on it.'

Owen studied the force field thoughtfully. He could always shoot out the controls, but that would be bound to set off alarms, and he didn't want to leave any clue as to where he and Hazel might have gone. Given time and the right equipment, Hazel could probably have persuaded the controls to shut down the field, but they didn't have either. Owen concentrated, and an idea came to him. He accessed his AI.

'Oz, do you still have the security command overrides for the Standing?'

'Of course. I have override codes for every system in the castle, and every system linked into those systems since we left. Unless David or Valentine and his people have changed them.'

'Not likely. David wouldn't have bothered, and Valentine hasn't had time to work his way past the protections and booby traps. Try it, Oz. Isolate this system, shut down this cave's force field and then raise it again after we're in. Without setting off any alarms.'

The AI sniffed. 'You don't want much, do you? It's lucky for you that I'm such a superior model. Top of the line, for my time. But before I work my usual miracles, can I just point out that I have no control over the refrigeration units Valentine has installed in these caves? They're an entirely separate system that I have no access to. The temperature in the cave you propose to enter is cold enough to freeze the balls off a Mistworld Hob hound. It's not actually zero, but it's as close as you're ever likely to encounter, short of opening an airlock and stepping out into deep space. Though I wouldn't put that past you either. Suffice to say that any normal human entering this cave would freeze to death extremely quickly. Assuming the shock didn't get him first.'

'Hazel and I aren't normal, Oz. We haven't been for a long time. Open the cave.'

There was a sudden snap of energies cancelling, and the force field was gone. Freezing air rushed out from the cave, steaming into the cavern like a thick fog. The bitter cold hit Owen and Hazel like a blow, and they flinched back from it despite themselves. They shuddered violently, and held on to each other for support. There was no smell, no stench of death or decay. It was too cold for that. The bodies before them were perfectly preserved. Owen and Hazel moved reluctantly forward to get a better look. The cold air seared their lungs painfully as they breathed it. The nearest body was that of a woman, dressed in torn peasant's clothing, charred and blackened around the energy-weapon wounds that killed her. Her face was a mess. Half of it was missing. Owen reached out a hand towards her, and then hesitated. His hand was trembling, but not from the cold. He didn't want to touch her.

'If she's as cold as I think she is you could get frostbite,' said Hazel.

'Not to worry,' said Owen. 'I used to know a lot of women like that at Court.' He shook his head slowly. 'I thought I'd seen everything; that this wouldn't mean anything to me. But I was wrong.'

'When you stop feeling anything,' said Hazel, 'it'll mean part of you has died too. The human part. But as bad as you feel, you're still going to do this, aren't you?'

'Of course. It's necessary.'

'Of course. I never doubted you would. For all your morality and pretty speeches, there's always been a strength in you, a hardness as unforgiving on yourself as on your enemies. You'd walk through Hell itself for a chance to get to Valentine, wouldn't you?'

'Yes. He murdered my world.'

Owen drew his disrupter, aimed it at the packed bodies before him and fired. The energy beam tore a path through the frozen dead, creating a tunnel. The irresistible force of the beam cut through flesh and bone alike, vaporizing everything in its path, leaving behind half-bodies and stubs of limbs, surrounding a tunnel some three feet wide. It looked as if some monstrous worm or maggot had eaten through the dead on its way to some unknown, awful destination. Owen put away his disrupter and turned to Hazel.

'We'll move through the tunnel for as far as it goes, and then you'll have to pull bodies in behind us to cover our tracks. The extra space I've created will give us room to manoeuvre bodies out of our way, once I reach the end of the tunnel.'

Hazel looked at him for a moment. 'Nothing's going to stop you, is it, Deathstalker?'

'No. I know this is difficult for you, Hazel, but . . . I need you. Do it for me.'

'All right. For you. But you're going to owe me one hell of a favour afterwards.' She scowled at the tunnel. 'It's going to be dark, once we're . . . inside the mass of bodies. How will we know where we're going?'

'I know where the hidden door is,' said Owen. 'I can feel it in my mind. All you have to do is follow me. Don't worry, it's not like there's any chance of you getting lost in there. Let's go.'

He turned away from her and stepped into the chamber of the dead. The utter cold cut into him like a knife, and he shuddered so hard his teeth chattered in his head. The frozen air burned in his throat and lungs; it felt like swallowing razor blades. Hoar frost formed immediately on his hair and eye-lids, and his eyes ached as the cold began penetrating the liquid in his eyeballs. He blinked hard, gritted his teeth and knelt down to fit himself into the tunnel he'd made. Even with his disrupter set on full wide dispersal, it hadn't been able to produce a very large tunnel. He'd have to crawl through it on all fours. His knees jarred on the frozen bodies, hard as concrete. Some of the bodies had been cut open by the energy beam as neatly as if by a surgeon's knife, revealing their innards. They were mostly grey, with a few pale shades of pink or purple, even the vitality of colour leached out of them by the dreadful cold.

Owen shuffled forward and reached out with his hands to grab the bodies ahead and pull himself along. The dead, icy flesh burned his bare hands, like grasping a log from the heart of a fire. Every instinct yelled at him to let go immedi-ately, but he refused to listen. He tightened his grip, and pulled himself on. As he took his hands away to reach further along the tunnel, his warm flesh clung stickily to the cold, and he had to use all his strength to pull free. He left patches of skin behind, but felt no pain. Owen refused to let it upset him. The skin would grow back, and it would happen less and less as his hands cooled.

Already his body was adapting to its surroundings, his core temperature plummeting at a speed that would have killed anyone else. He had no sensation left anywhere, and his eyes were stuck open, but he'd stopped shuddering. When he moved his arms and legs they felt like they belonged to someone else. His breath no longer steamed on the air before him. He pulled himself on, further into the domain of the dead, and his hands felt nothing, nothing at all. The dark closed slowly in around him. He could hear Hazel moving close behind, breathing harshly, and she was his only comfort in that dark place.

The tunnel ran out sooner than he thought it would. The sheer number of packed bodies had absorbed much of the energy beam's impact. He grabbed at the bodies before him, pulling them apart and away from each other, opening up a path. Often limbs stuck out like barriers in his way, and he had to tug and pull at them with all his inhuman strength, breaking them off and thrusting them aside, out of the way. The arms and legs snapped cleanly, like pieces of wood. He tried to think of them that way, but couldn't. They were people; his people. The thought tormented him, but the anger at what had been done to them helped him with the horror of where he was and what he was doing. Sometimes he had to smash in ribcages with his more than human strength, to make the necessary room. The unmoving bodies were stubbornly resistant, and he came to resent them. Didn't they know that what he was doing was for their sakes? He lashed out with his fists, and was glad his hands were numb, for more than one reason.

He could feel Hazel's presence, hear the ragged sounds of her slow progress, but when he croaked her name, she didn't answer him. Presumably her voice was as wrecked by the cold as his. Either way, he couldn't turn around to see if anything was wrong; there wasn't room. So he pressed on, heading for the door he could see clearly in his mind.

It was very dark now. The last of the light from the main cavern and the re-erected force field had long since died away. There were shifting and creaking sounds all around him, as the bodies redistributed their weight in response to Owen's actions. It was almost as though the dead were stirring in their cold sleep, disturbed by the presence of the living in their midst. Owen was glad of the dark. He had a quiet horror that one of the dead faces might open its eyes and turn to look at him as he passed, and he thought that if he saw such a thing he might well lose his mind. Hazel might see him as a hard, unyielding man, but there were some things no man could bear to see and still stay sane. He fought on, his heart hammering in his chest, his breathing harsh, half convinced that at any moment a dead hand would reach out of the darkness and clamp down on his arm or leg.

Claustrophobia began to enfold him, as all the bodies stacked above him seemed to press down with increasing weight. He began to doubt the surety, in his mind, of the location of the hidden door. He had no way of telling one direction from another in the utter dark. He could be moving in a slow circle for all he knew, hopelessly lost in the kingdom of the dead. He began to feel he'd been moving for far too long without getting anywhere; that he should have reached the door long before this. That he'd be trapped in here for ever, in his own private hell. But he wasn't alone. Hazel was there with him. And just knowing that gave him the strength to go on.

Sometimes hooked fingers snagged in his clothing, jerking him to a sudden halt, and he had to feel blindly back and snap off the metal-hard fingers before he could move on. Although he couldn't see them, his hands told him that the bodies he touched weren't always complete. Most were damaged in some way. His people had died fighting the invaders. The invasion and destruction of Virimonde had been written in their yielding flesh, and the marks were preserved here for all to read.

Finally, he reached the other side, and his hands slammed up against flat metal. His thoughts had been slowed by the cold, and he considered the situation sluggishly for a few minutes before realizing he'd reached his destination. He yelled for Oz to open the hidden door, and a panel in the wall slid silently to one side. Bright light poured in, blinding his frozen-open eyes. He cried out harshly, both in pain and triumph, the raucous sound like some gore crow disturbed on a battlefield. He pulled himself out into the corridor beyond and then collapsed, steam rising thickly from his body as it hit the warm air of the corridor. Owen lay helplessly on the floor, the cold curling and uncurling inside him like a ratchet-wheel turning. But the stoked heat of his rage still burned deep within him, and it melted away the cold inch by inch until life returned and he could move again. His fingers were first, bending and straightening, making sharp cracking sounds like twigs trampled underfoot. Tears burned in his defrosting eyes and ran down his cheeks, leaving warm trails behind them. His body contracted and relaxed in a series of slow pulses as warmth flooded back into cold-deadened muscles. The pain was almost unbearable, but Owen welcomed it: he was coming alive again, after being among the dead.

After a while he forced himself up on to his feet and looked around for Hazel, and only then realized that she wasn't with him. She hadn't followed him out of the tunnel. He hobbled over to the opening, his knees cracking loudly, and called her name. She didn't answer. Owen batted at the freezing fog with his hands, trying to see into the darkness beyond, but even his eyes had their limits. He called again, but the cold and the dark swallowed up his voice in a moment. He reached inside himself, searching for the mental link that bound him to Hazel but it eluded him, weakened by long neglect. He'd left her behind in the cold and the dark and the dead. And he had to go back in and rescue her.

Something inside him protested immediately. He couldn't go back into the cold again, he just couldn't. The horror of it all had nearly destroyed him. It would be madness to give it another chance at him. But even as he thought it, he knew he was going to go back in. He had to. Hazel needed him. He still hurt from head to toe, but that would pass. He was afraid, but that didn't matter; he'd been afraid before. For a long time now, the only thing that had really mattered to him was Hazel d'Ark.

He took a deep breath of the freezing air and thrust his head and shoulders once again into the dark. He reached out with his hands till they jarred against frozen flesh, and pulled himself back into the narrow tunnel he'd made. The bitter cold closed around him like the embrace of an old familiar enemy, but he made himself ignore it, thinking only of Hazel. He forced himself on, back among the bodies, and then his heart stopped as a cold hand closed suddenly around his wrist. His breath burst out of him in a painful gasp as he imagined the dead coming slowly to life all around him, holding him, keeping him in their frozen Hell till he was dead like them. And then his heart pounded again as he realized the hand was Hazel's.

He grabbed her wrist, tried to say something reassuring in his croaking voice and scrabbled frantically backwards, pulling her with him. It only took a few moments before he was out in the corridor again, steam rising from his cooled body as he dragged Hazel out into the light and warmth. She came out in a series of sudden jerks, unable to help him, her body frozen rigid, and as she fell to the corridor floor, she made a sound like a log felled in a wood. Her eyes were frozen shut and her face had locked into a defiant snarl, teeth gritted together. Her skin was blue.

Owen knelt beside her, chafing her hands in his: her body would throw off the cold just as his had, but he needed to feel he was doing something to help. Steam rose thickly from her solid clothes. Her hair was thick with hoar frost, but it soon melted and ran away in the warm air of the corridor. Slowly, Hazel's body relaxed until she was nestling against him, murmuring his name. Although she would never admit it, Hazel had always felt safe and comforted in Owen's arms.

Finally she sat up and pushed him away, and he knew she was back to her old self. She shook her head as though trying to clear cobwebs from her thoughts. 'I lost my way. The tunnel was a straight line, but I . . . lost myself, alone in the dark. With the dead. And you came back for me.' She wrapped her arms around herself, and shuddered suddenly. 'Feels like I'll never be warm again. That the cold of the grave will always be with me.'

'It'll pass,' said Owen.

'Of course it will,' said Hazel. 'We're more than human now, remember? No longer bound by human fears and . . . weaknesses.'

'Hazel . . .'

'I'm all right now. I'm fine.'

'Of course you are,' said Owen.

They got to their feet, helping each other. Owen quietly told Oz to close the panel in the wall, and the freezing air was shut off. The fog in the corridor slowly began to clear. Owen looked around him, searching for something he recognized. It had been a long time since he'd been . . . home.

'Right,' said Hazel. 'Let's go and find someone we can persuade to give us a few answers about what the hell's going on here. Which way do we go, Deathstalker?'

'Give me a minute,' said Owen. 'I'm not actually sure . . .'

'Come on, this is your castle, your Standing!'

'Well, yes, but I don't think I actually ever came down this far. I mean, it's a big place. Lots of people worked and lived here, and I only ever got to know a few of them. Mostly, I stuck to my own quarters. I certainly never bothered with the maintenance areas. I had people to do that for me.'

61

'Lifestyles of the rich and useless. No wonder your own people were able to throw you out of here so easily.'

'They didn't throw me out! I retreated, in the face of superior numbers. Perfectly sound military strategy.'

'Yeah, sure. Look, are you saying you're lost?'

'Down the corridor and turn right,' Oz murmured in Owen's ear. 'That'll lead you to Valentine's new laboratories.'

'Of course I'm not lost,' said Owen. 'We just go down here and turn right, and that'll take us right to Valentine's new laboratories. Bound to be someone there you can terrorize into telling us what we need to know.'

'You don't appreciate me,' said Oz, as Owen and Hazel set off down the corridor. 'You really don't.'

'How did you know where Valentine's labs are?' said Owen, subvocalizing so Hazel wouldn't hear.

'Educated guess,' said Oz. 'I have the castle's full schematics on file, and there were only so many open spaces where he could have set up all the new tech he's supposed to have here.'

'What would I do without you, Oz?'

'I shudder to think. Now get your ass in gear before some guards come along. Valentine's never comfortable without a small army to put between him and the understandably hostile world.'

Owen passed that thought on to Hazel, and they increased their pace. The exertion helped to drive the last traces of cold out of their bodies. Owen began to feel almost human again. Hazel too, for after a while he noticed her beginning to pay more attention to their surroundings. They were worth noticing. The floor was carpeted, the rich material covered in designs so old that centuries of Deathstalker servants' feet had rubbed most of the detail away. Tapestries and portraits and holos hung from the old stone walls, depicting lesser moments in the long Deathstalker history. The greater moments and treasures were on display on the upper levels, where they could be shown off to aristocratic guests. Or they should be. Owen frowned. There was no telling what Valentine might have done with them. He had no respect for tradition or history. Or much else, these days. Owen wouldn't have put it past Valentine to heap all the Deathstalker treasures in one great pile and then set fire to it, just for the fun of dancing round it. And for the thought of what it would do to Owen when he found out. Owen walked a little faster, adding this wrong to so many others. Owen kept all his anger carefully tamped down, far enough inside not to interfere with his mission, but ready to burst free when he finally came face to face with the villain Wolfe.

And then there would be a reckoning.

Owen followed Oz's murmured directions till he and Hazel came to a sudden halt, their way blocked by a door that looked distinctly out of place in the old-world, luxurious surroundings. It was a solid steel door, blunt and functional, with a state-of-the-art and then some lock. Hazel immediately moved in close, studying the lock with almost hungry intensity. Hazel and locks were old friends. Or enemies, depending on how you looked at it. Owen put his ear to the cold steel and listened carefully. After a while, he was able to make out the measured, repetitious sounds of grinding machinery, and the hissing of gases under pressure. Owen straightened up, frowning thoughtfully. He'd kept nothing in his Standing that would have sounded like that. And David hadn't installed anything either. In which case, Owen wanted very much to see for himself what it might be; what new horror the Wolfe had introduced into his former home. He looked down at Hazel, who was still studying the lock.

'Any luck?'

'Yeah; all bad. I can crack this, but without my tools we're talking half an hour at least. Maybe more.'

'Too long,' said Owen flatly.

'I know that!' said Hazel. She stood up and scowled at the featureless door. 'We could always shoot the lock out.'

'Too noisy. Even if it didn't set off a whole mess of alarms, which it probably would.'

'All right,' said Hazel impatiently, 'what do you suggest?'

Owen smiled at her, stepped forward and kicked the door in. The lock shattered, the solid steel denting deeply under his boot, and the entire door tore itself away from its hinges and fell to the floor of the room beyond with a satisfyingly heavy thud. Hazel looked at Owen.

'Show-off.'

They stepped over the door and into the lab, guns in hand, but there was no one coming to meet them. The only occupant of the vast room was a technician in a grubby smock, sat before a computer terminal, the jack plugged into the back of his neck. Owen and Hazel lowered their guns. The cyberjockey was so lost in his own world they could have shot him and he wouldn't have noticed till he unplugged. They looked around them, trying to make sense of the mass of tech and machinery that filled most of the laboratory.

The room was huge. Owen thought vaguely that it might have been a wine cellar, once. Pieces of unfamiliar machinery were bulked together in groups, taking up most of the floor space, their tops almost brushing the ceiling. None of it looked particularly subtle. The hardware was mostly of a crude mechanical construction (hence the need for a jack-in rather than using comm implants), designed for crushing and grating and sorting various materials. Owen turned slowly, tracing the path of the materials. Lengths of tubing, stapled to the stone walls, led away from the larger machines, criss-crossing in a riot of colour codings. They delivered whatever they were carrying to a complicated filtration system, which in turn steadily dripped its end result into a series of anonymous, unlabelled containers. Everything else was straightforward computer monitoring equipment, though precisely what processes it was monitoring was a mystery to Owen. Nothing was labelled, and the few control panels were basic enough to cover a multitude of potential sins. He looked across at Hazel who shrugged, which was pretty much what he'd expected. Hazel wasn't noted for her deductive capabilities. When in doubt, ask someone. Loudly.

Owen strode over to the lab technician, happily communing unawares with his computers, ripped the jack out of the back of his neck, spun him round in his chair and stuck his gun up the man's nose. It took a moment for the tech to realize what was happening, dazed by his sudden exit from the computer systems, and then his eyes focused on Owen's face and he looked even more upset, if that was possible. Owen smiled nastily at him, and the tech actually whimpered. Hazel moved in from the other side and gave him her best menacing glower, and the man all but wet himself. Owen began to feel like he was bullying a puppy, but ruthlessly suppressed the thought. This was one of Valentine's people, and therefore guilty by association.

'Hi there,' Owen said to him, not at all pleasantly. 'I'm Owen Deathstalker; the nightmare made flesh to your right is Hazel d'Ark, and you are in deep doo-doo. Answer my questions fully and accurately, and you might just live long enough to stand trial. Nod if you're with me so far.'

The technician nodded as best he could with a gun up his nose. All the colour had disappeared from his face the moment Owen mentioned his name, and now cold beads of sweat were popping out on his forehead. Owen was secretly impressed. He hadn't realized he was that frightening.

'Who are you?' he growled to the tech. 'And what is the purpose of all this machinery? Overview first, then the details.'

'I'm Pierre Trignent, my Lord,' said the technician quickly, his voice little more than a whisper. 'Please, I'm just a little fish. I'm nobody. You want the ones who give me orders. I just do what I'm told.'

'We'll get to them,' said Hazel. 'Now answer the man's question. What are you doing here?'

Trignent swallowed hard, lowering his eyes. He was going to lie. Owen could feel it. He leaned forward so that his face was right in front of his victim's. The tech tried to shrink back in his chair but there was nowhere to go.

'If you lie,' said Owen, 'I'll know it. I can always get the answers from someone else, if I have to, but I guarantee you won't be around to see it.'

'Yes, my Lord, but—'

'I'm not a Lord any more. But I'm still a Deathstalker. Now tell me everything you know or I'll show you what that means.'

'This is a processing and refining plant, my . . . Sir Deathstalker. We take in the raw material, break it down into its basic chemical components, syphon off the desired residues and store it for later transport off-planet.'

'But what's the raw material?' Owen said impatiently. 'And what the hell is the end product?'

'The esper drug,' said Trignent, reluctantly. 'We're manufacturing the esper drug.'

Owen and Hazel looked at each other. They'd heard about the esper drug during their time with the esper underground, but its composition was supposed to be a secret. Once its endlessly addictive nature had become clear, the underground had buried the files, just in case anyone was tempted to use it as a weapon. Still, if anyone was going to dig up a new drug, it would be Valentine. And setting up production on Virimonde was a good way of keeping it secret. Parliament had only discovered his presence by accident. Owen nodded slowly. He was following the trail so far. But none of it explained why the technician should still be so scared.

'What's the raw material?' said Owen. 'What are you refining the esper drug from?'

'Please,' said Trignent. He started to cry. 'Please understand. I just follow orders. They'd kill me if I didn't.'

'I'll kill you if you don't answer me! What's the raw material?'

'The dead,' said Pierre Trignent. 'The dead of Virimonde.'

After that, it was very quiet for a long moment. Apart from the slow, steady sounds of the machinery, chewing up the latest batch of raw material.

Owen's eyes squeezed shut, but he could still see what he now recognized to be crushing and pulping hardware. He could still see his dead people, piled like logs, kept frozen until they were needed. His eyes opened again, and the technician took one look at the cold rage building in them and began talking very quickly, almost babbling, as though relieved finally to be able to tell somebody.

'The Lord Wolfe came here because there were so many bodies, just waiting to be harvested. The esper drug has always been derived from human tissues, just as the esp-blockers come from dead esper-brain tissues, but you need a lot of . . . the basic material to produce just a small amount of the end product. That's why the esper drug has always been so rare, so secret. The Lord Wolfe saw an opportunity for mass production here, and took advantage of it. He's processed hundreds of thousands of the dead and produced more of the drug, and in a purer form, than was ever possible before. It's really quite a simple process, once it's been set up. There's just me, and a handful of others, to keep an eye on things. Please, I'm nobody. I just did as I was told . . .'

'You have been overseeing the destruction of my people, to produce a drug so addictive it enslaves all who use it,' said Owen, and his voice was very quiet and dangerous. 'I have seen horror in my time, in many wars, on many battlefields. I have waded through blood and offal, killed till my arms ached and seen the slaughter of the good and the bad, but never have I encountered anything as cold-blooded as this. The grinding-down of the dead . . . to produce a poison for the living. Turning humanity itself into a product. Oh, my people, my people . . .'

He turned away, his shoulders heaving, and Hazel went after him. Trignent saw his chance and made a run for the door. Owen Deathstalker looked round, tears in his eyes, and shot the man in the back. The energy beam punched a hole through Trignent's back and out of his chest, slamming him against the door frame. He clung there for a moment, already dead, and then crumpled slowly to the floor. Owen shook his head slowly back and forth, as though trying to deny what he'd been told. Hazel moved to his side, but he waved her away. There wasn't room in him for anything but horror and sorrow and a rage to strike back at the cause of his pain.

'I shouldn't have shot him,' he said finally. 'It wasn't worthy of me.'

'He was as guilty as all the others.'

'Yes. But that wasn't why I killed him. I did it because I needed to hurt someone. Punish someone, apart from myself. They were my people. I should have been here to protect them.'

'Oh, let it go, Owen! You were outlawed, banished. Get over it. Everyone here turned their backs on you.'

'It doesn't make any difference. They were my responsibility. Oz?'

'Yes, Owen?'

'Shut this obscenity down. All of it. Whatever it takes.'

'Yes, Owen.'

'Now,' said Owen Deathstalker to his friend and comrade-in-arms, Hazel d'Ark. 'Let's go and find Valentine and his cronies. And kill them all.'

The head of Valentine Wolfe's security people appeared, somewhat nervously, on the viewscreen in the great hall to alert Valentine that, in order: two strangers had somehow appeared in the flyer caves under the Standing, been identified as the legendary Owen Deathstalker and the infamous Hazel d'Ark; they had then somehow made their way into the castle proper, despite all the security safeguards and could be, well, anywhere right now. You could have heard a pin drop in the hall once the man had stopped speaking. In fact, you could have heard the pin while it was still in mid-air. The Silvestri dropped one of his daggers. The Romanov went very pale. And the Kartakis's last swallow of wine went down the wrong way and half choked him. Valentine Wolfe ignored the unpleasant sounds and concentrated on the unhappy security chief on the viewscreen.

'Are you telling me,' he said, almost pleasantly, 'that all of our wide-ranging and incredibly expensive security measures, including booby traps, hidden guns and an army of ruthless killers, couldn't stop two people from breaking in?'

'Well, basically yes, my Lord. After all, the two people in question are—'

'I know who they are. That's why I hired you and your people. And just from looking at you I can tell there's more bad news. What is it?'

The security chief looked even more unhappy, if that was possible. 'Some outside system has penetrated our computers, and is shutting down the processing plant.'

'Now correct me if I'm wrong, and I don't think I am,' said Valentine, 'but I seem to remember you telling me that such a thing was completely and utterly impossible.'

'Yes, my Lord. Strictly speaking, it is impossible. It shouldn't be happening.'

'But it is.'

'Yes, my Lord.'

'You're fired,' said Valentine. 'Collect your severance pay, and have your second in command nail your head to a chair before you leave. And no, you don't get a reference. At least, not one you'd want to show anybody.'

He shut down the viewscreen and leaned back in his chair. The Silvestri picked up his dagger. 'You should have had him killed, Wolfe.'

'Don't be silly, Carlos,' said Valentine absently. 'Mercenaries have a very strong union.' He chuckled suddenly; a soft, dangerous sound. 'Dear Owen, how did you know to find me here? I covered my trail extremely thoroughly. But no, here you are again, turning up like the proverbial bad penny to ruin my day yet again. You always want to spoil my fun. Still, I hope you appreciate my little act of vengeance. After all, every dramatic gesture really needs an audience to appreciate it.'

The Silvestri pulled his other dagger from a portrait's eye, ripping the ancient canvas. 'I'm not afraid of the big, bad Deathstalker. Those stories about him are just . . . stories. Let him come. Him and his bitch.'

The Romanov shrugged the priceless tapestry from around his shoulders and frowned thoughtfully. 'You might not have enough sense to be scared of the Deathstalker, but I have. He's a dangerous man. He really did do most of the things he's supposed to have done, even the ones that sound impossible. But unlike the rest of you, I had a feeling our security forces weren't up to stopping or even slowing down a living legend, if he did get wind of our operation. So I made my own arrangements. A little surprise, especially for the Deathstalker. Now if you'll excuse me, or even if you won't, I think I'll go and unpack it. Try to keep Owen occupied till I get back.'

He strode out with his head held high. Valentine applauded his exit languidly, and his scarlet smile widened. 'Surprises. I do so love surprises. As it happens, I have one or two prepared for dear Owen myself.'

'It had better involve extreme violence and sudden death, or we're all in real trouble,' said the Kartakis, his breathing back under control again. He sounded suddenly very sober, and not at all happy about it. 'The Deathstalker is not going to be pleased when he discovers what we've made of his old home.'

'I'm not afraid of him,' said the Silvestri defiantly.

'Yes, well, that's because you're a complete bloody head case,' said the Kartakis equably. 'In our line of work that's usually an advantage, but we can't afford indulgences like insanity right now. We have to think, come up with a plan. We have men, and resources. At least the Deathstalker didn't bring an army with him to back him up.'

'He doesn't need an army,' Valentine pointed out. 'He's got Hazel d'Ark.'

'You're being remarkably calm about all this,' snapped the Kartakis. 'Do you know something we don't, or have you been popping a few extra pills today?'

Valentine smiled easily. 'I have a plan. A very unpleasant plan, perfectly tailored to take advantage of Owen's weaknesses. All you have to do is keep the d'Ark woman occupied. Now, if you'll excuse me, I must be about setting my plan in motion. Oh, it's going to be such fun watching him suffer.'

He got up, bowed elegantly and left, strolling casually away as though he didn't have a care in the world. The two aristocrats looked after him.

'That man is not living in the same reality as the rest of us,' said the Silvestri.

The Kartakis snorted. 'His plan probably involves cutting his losses, abandoning us and heading for the far horizon like a bat with its ass on fire. If we're going to survive this, we're going to have to do it ourselves. We can stop them. We just have to prepare something to . . . to get them off-balance . . .'

'I'm not afraid of the—'

'Will you stop saying that! You're not fooling anyone!'

'Least of all me,' said Owen Deathstalker.

The two aristocrats spun round and there he was, standing tall and intimidating in the doorway, a sword in his hand like it belonged there and always had. His face was grave, his eyes were cold and unwavering, and he looked every inch the legend that he was. Hazel d'Ark was at his side, leaning casually on the door frame, a large projectile gun in her hand. Just looking at the two of them, Athos Kartakis felt his blood run cold. He could see the calm certainty of partnership between them, of warriors practised in their bloody craft and sworn to stand together till death or beyond. The Kartakis

70

had fought so many duels he'd lost count, stared death in the face and spat in its bony eye socket, but he'd never really felt in terror of his life before now. He swallowed hard. He had a disrupter under his robes, but knew he'd be dead if he went to draw it. Unless he could come up with a distraction . . .

'Well, Silvestri,' he said as casually as he could. 'You always said you could take the Deathstalker. Feel free to prove it.'

Owen looked at the Silvestri with interest. Stunned by the betrayal, the aristocrat shot a glance at the Kartakis, and then faced Owen steadily. 'You don't scare me, Deathstalker,' he said loudly. 'I've heard about your inhuman powers, but to me they sound just like something a coward would hide behind. How about it, Owen? Have you got the guts to fight me as a man, not a monster? Because I can take you man to man, steel to steel, and deep down you know it.'

'Now he really is full of it,' said Hazel. 'Say the word, Owen, and I'll shoot his eyes out.'

'No,' said Owen. 'I could use a little entertainment.' He looked at the Kartakis. 'Don't try and interfere. Hazel wouldn't like it.'

'Wouldn't dream of it,' said the Kartakis, quite sincerely. He backed away, keeping both hands in clear sight, thinking hard.

Owen moved slowly forwards into the great hall. He looked unhurriedly about him, taking in the various damages that had been done to his fixtures and fittings. He didn't look angry, or even upset; he'd gone beyond that. He looked just a little colder, and even more dangerous. Carlos Silvestri came forward to meet him, moving lightly on the balls of his feet, a slender knife in each hand. Imminent action had driven all fear and uncertainty out of him, and his gaze and his hands were both rock-steady. In his own way he looked dangerous too, but it was nothing compared to the cold implacability of the Deathstalker, and everyone knew it. The Silvestri was a trained fighter and a vicious killer, but the Deathstalker was a warrior, tempered in some of the most deadly conflicts the Empire had ever known. The two men came together to fight in the middle of the hall, and those who watched them knew how it was going to end.

They circled each other unhurriedly, blades at the ready for any hint of an opening in the other's defences. The Kartakis studied them both carefully. There was always the chance he might learn something to his advantage. Theoretically, it was a more or less an even fight. Knives were excellent for close fighting, but had no reach. Unless you threw them, and risked disarming yourself. The sword, on the other hand, had plenty of reach, but at this range the long blade could not be wielded anywhere near as quickly as a knife. So the Silvestri had to find a way past the sword to make his attacks, while the Deathstalker had to keep his opponent at a safe distance. A knife thrown from one or a full extension lunge from the other could change everything, but a failed attempt by either man would mean almost certain death. So they circled each other, with gliding, deliberate steps, shifting their weight cautiously as they watched each other's eyes.

The Silvestri launched the first attack, his right hand moving almost too quickly for the human eye to follow. Owen parried the blade, and then had to jump back as the left hand came swinging in from nowhere with vicious speed and purpose, heading for Owen's undefended gut. The flashing blade missed Owen's stomach by a fraction of an inch. Owen brought his sword round in a swift backhand sweep that clipped Silvestri's head as he ducked at the last moment. And then they were circling again, calm and collected and deadly.

The Silvestri feinted with his right hand, waited until Owen had committed himself to the counter and then his left hand snapped forward, throwing the knife at Owen's right eye. Owen's sword was too low to deflect the knife, and both of them knew it. The Silvestri's eyes widened in triumph. And then Owen's golden Hadenman hand came up to intercept the knife's flight and knock it to one side. The knife chunked harmlessly into the table top, and while the Silvestri was caught momentarily off-balance, Owen swung his blade with all his strength behind it and sheared clean through his opponent's neck. The head fell to the ground and rolled away across the floor to bump against the Kartakis's feet. He made a silent moue of distaste, and moved his feet a little away. The head stared up at him with silent reproach. The eyes and the jaw were still moving, but they soon stopped. The headless body stumbled forward a few steps, blood gouting from the neck; it crumpled to the floor, twitching and shuddering, and then was still.

'Feel better now?' said Hazel.

'Some,' Owen replied. He wasn't even breathing hard.

That was when Pieter Romanov made his entrance, amid a loud hum of straining servo-motors. Everyone turned to look as he stopped and posed in the doorway. He was wearing a massive exoskeleton, its metal bones surrounding and supporting him, while rectangular force fields buzzed angrily on both forearms. Owen had seen such things before, usually on dock workers at starports, unloading heavy cargo. Due to their great weight they burned up a lot of energy quickly, so they'd never been practical for the battlefield, but Owen had to admit it made a pretty good short-term answer to people like him and Hazel. The force shields would deflect disrupter beams, while their more than razor-sharp edges would make nasty weapons, and the servo-motor-driven steel bones would make their occupant inhumanly fast and strong.

'Come to me, monsters,' said Pieter Romanov grandly. 'I am your equal now. I am faster than any human muscle can drive a man, and my strength is as the strength of ten because my tech is pure. I will rip your arms from their sockets, tear your heads from your shoulders, and my dogs shall feast on your entrails.'

Owen was still trying to come up with a suitably elegant answer that didn't involve four-letter words when Hazel stepped forward.

'My turn,' she said firmly. 'You're not hogging all the fun, Deathstalker.'

'Be my guest,' said Owen generously.

Hazel strode over to the waiting Romanov and stopped a careful distance just outside his arms' reach. Other Hazels flickered in and out of existence around her, but she pushed them firmly away: she wanted to do this herself. She had had a really amusing idea, and she had no intention of sharing the fun with anyone else – even other versions of herself. She holstered her projectile weapons and smiled nastily at the Romanov, who stirred uneasily. Whatever response he'd expected, being faced with bare hands and blatant self-confidence certainly wasn't one of them.

Unhurried, Hazel reached out to the abandoned meals on the table beside her and picked up a ripe piece of fruit. She crushed it in her hand, so that thick pulp and juice leaked through her fingers, and then she threw the sticky mess at the Romanov. Her arm snapped forward with more than human force and speed, and the fruit shot past his defences before he could even raise his shielded arms. It struck home with perfect accuracy, right at the heart of the exposed servo-motors on the Romanov's left arm, and made a wonderful mess of the gears. Sparks flew, and several of the motors shorted out.

The Romanov yelled in outrage and surged forward, moving horribly quickly for someone of his size and weight. Hazel hopped up on to the table and darted back out of reach of his arms. She snatched up more of the abandoned food, crushed it in her hands and threw it with devastating accuracy. The Romanov whirled his force shields desperately back and forth, but was no match for her speed and reflexes. More of his servo-motors failed him, shorting out or hopelessly gummed up. Hazel laughed mockingly.

The Romanov roared with rage, grabbed the heavy table with both hands and overturned it with one swift movement. Hazel launched herself from the table, tucked into a somersault in mid-air and landed on the Romanov's shoulders. Her legs wrapped round his neck and squeezed. His face went bright red and he couldn't get his breath. He started to raise his hands to tear her from him, but Hazel grabbed his exposed head in a vice-like grip.

'Let us understand each other,' she said calmly. 'You annoy me, and I am going to rip your head off your shoulders. And your servo-motors are so gummed up now that you haven't a hope in hell of getting to me before I do it. Clear?'

The Romanov considered the matter. Above the buzzing of his force shields he could clearly hear more motors shorting out. And he was going to have to breathe really soon now. He shut down his force shields and smiled hopefully at Owen.

'I'd really like to surrender now. Please.'

Hazel grinned triumphantly and loosed her hold a little. She looked across at Owen. 'Up to you, Deathstalker. If you need to kill him, he's all yours.'

'Oh hell,' said Owen tiredly. 'Let's take him back for trial. He's too pathetic to kill. I just want Valentine.'

'In which case, I'd really like to offer my surrender too,' said the Kartakis. He carefully unbuckled his sword belt and let it drop to the floor. He then removed his disrupter from its hidden holster with thumb and forefinger and let that fall too. Hazel nodded briefly.

'All right; get over here with Lord Seize-up, and don't make a move unless I say otherwise.'

'I wouldn't dare,' said the Kartakis.

Hazel released her leghold on the Romanov's neck, and clambered down from his shoulders. He began to breathe again, and remained very still as Hazel stood before him, glaring ominously. In the end she just sniffed, and settled for ripping the servo-motors out of his exoskeleton with her bare hands, and crushing them like she'd crushed the fruit. The sound of crunching metal was very loud in the hall. The Romanov swallowed hard.

Owen waited till Hazel was finished and then fixed the two aristocrats with a cold, unsettling gaze. 'Where can I find Valentine Wolfe?'

'He left just before you got here,' said the Kartakis. 'Said he had a surprise to arrange for you. Didn't say what, and we didn't ask. One doesn't, with Valentine Wolfe.'

'I've got him,' Oz murmured in Owen's ear. 'I'm still tapped into the Standing's security systems. Valentine is currently at security central, running a very strange set of programmes on the computers. But don't ask me what they are. I can't say I've ever seen anything like them.'

'It doesn't matter what he's got,' said Owen. 'I'm going to kill him anyway. Hazel, you stay here and guard these two. Oz has got a lock on Valentine.'

'Hold everything,' said Hazel. 'I don't want you running around this place on your own. We're partners, remember?'

'I know,' said Owen. 'But I need to do this myself.'

Hazel nodded reluctantly. 'Understood. But don't take too long or I'll come looking for you.'

'Very well. Watch these two carefully. You can't trust them.'

'Of course not,' said Hazel, 'they're Lords.'

They exchanged a smile, and then Owen turned and left. Hazel sauntered over to the upturned table, fished through the dumped food and came up with something she was almost sure was chicken. She gnawed at it cheerfully, disregarding the grease that ran down her chin. The Kartakis moved just a little closer to the weapons he'd dropped, and then stopped as Hazel fixed him with a glittering eye. 'Feel free to start something, my Lords,' she said indistinctly. 'And I'll feel free to think up something even more amusing to do to you.'

The two Lords looked at each other, and kept very still.

Owen made his way quickly through empty stone corridors, heading implacably towards what had once been his security centre. He was prepared to cut down without mercy any man who got in his way or tried to hinder him, but he encountered no one. Which was strange. Valentine had made too many enemies in his time. So where were the guards? Owen slowed just a little as he considered the matter. So far, the only people he and Hazel had come across in the Standing were a few guards, two aristocrats and a single lab technician. Where was everyone? And just what unpleasant surprise was Valentine planning for him? Owen scowled, increasing his pace. He didn't like mysteries. He just needed to see Valentine lying dead and bloody at his feet. For what the Wolfe had done to his people, his planet and his home, he had to pay – would pay. Owen might not have been able to save his people, but he could still avenge them.

Moving faster, his boots pounded on the thick carpeting. Any other time he would have enjoyed seeing the fondly remembered environs of his old home, but now he felt nothing but guilt and pain and the need for a bloody revenge to quiet them. All he cared about was killing Valentine Wolfe. At whatever cost, to himself or others.

At last, he came to the single steel door that led to what had once been his security centre. He stopped before the door, glaring at it, barely out of breath. He reined back on his anger and his need and made himself study the door carefully. It was solid steel inches thick, with no visible lock mechanism, and was undoubtedly booby-trapped in a dozen ways from hidden disrupters to primed explosives. It was what Owen would have done. But Owen didn't care.

He concentrated, reaching down past his conscious mind into the back brain, the undermind, and something there woke up and uncoiled, bursting outwards unrestrained. The irresistible mental pulse blew the solid-steel door right out of its steel frame and sent it flying backwards into the room beyond. Some distance inside, it fell to the floor, filling the room with a deafening clamour. The hidden disrupters and explosives tried to arm themselves, but Owen shut them down with a single thought. His power was fully awake now, and burning brightly within him. The door finally fell still and was silent, and Owen stepped through the empty doorway into the room, only to be stopped by the sound of quiet, ironic applause. At the far end of the room, almost in shadow, Valentine Wolfe was sitting languidly in a swivel chair, clapping his long white hands. Dressed still in deepest black, his corpse-pale face seemed to float unsupported on the gloom.

'Marvellous entrance, Owen. You really have developed a sense of the dramatic. Such an improvement; you were always so proper and stuffy before you were outlawed. Really, it's been the making of you.'

Owen moved forward a few steps, looking carefully about him. Lots of computers and monitor screens and terminals, but no operators and no guards. Just Valentine, apparently unmoved. Nothing and no one to stand between the Death-stalker and his vengeance. 'Get up, Wolfe,' he said softly, his voice cold and certain as death. 'It's all over. It ends here.'

'Oh, don't be so predictable, Owen,' said the Wolfe, casually folding his arms and leaning back in his chair. 'Do we really have to do what everyone expects of us? Act out the traditional roles of pure-hearted hero and dastardly villain? There's more to us than that. We have so much in common, you and I. We ought almost to be brothers, in spirit.'

'I'm nothing like you, Wolfe,' said Owen flatly.

'Really? What have I done that you haven't, in your time

as a rebel? I've no doubt your personal body count is much higher than mine, for all my efforts.'

'You were responsible for the death of this planet. For the wiping out of its population.'

'Well, I had help; but how many died at your instigation on Mistworld and Golgotha? How many good soldiers, just following orders and carrying out their duty, who knew nothing of politics and were just enforcing the law? We're more alike than you realize, Deathstalker; or more than you'd like to admit. There's blood and death and horror on both our hands, but don't let it worry you. We're above such things. We've made extraordinary beings of ourselves: we're more than human now, and human limitations don't apply to us any longer.'

'It's not what we've done,' said Owen, 'it's why we did it. I killed when it was necessary, fought to see an end of killing. You did it for pleasure.'

'Are you saying you won't enjoy killing me?'

'No, I'm not saying that at all.'

'You see? We have become great men, you and I. People watch our deeds and wonder. We can do awesome, terrible things, limited only by our imagination and the narrowness of our vision. We will do these things; we must, because we can. Don't stay mired in the past, Owen, in the man you used to be before you were kicked awake. You're still concerned with small concepts, like duty and honour and law. Law is for the little people; honour for those afraid to be more than they are, and our only duty is to ourselves now; to explore the possibilities before us, to become everything that we can be. Anything less is a betrayal of what we've made of ourselves.'

'I've lost so much, had to give up so many things,' said Owen. 'I won't give up my humanity too.'

Valentine shrugged easily. 'Trust me, Owen. It's really such a small thing. You'll be surprised how little you'll miss it. But I see there's no point in talking any more. You're not ready to hear the truth. When you've progressed as far as I have, you'll see things much more clearly. Still, I had to try. I see so much of myself in you. Now I really must be leaving.'

'I don't think so,' said Owen. 'If I remember correctly, and

I do, there's only one way in or out of this centre, and I'm blocking it. You have to get past me first. And you were never that good.'

'Probably not. But I don't have to be. I've always relied on others to do the hard, menial work for me. I am a Lord, after all. I have someone here who'd like to meet you, Death-stalker. Really, she's quite been looking forward to it. You went away and left her, and I'm afraid she carries something of a grudge. You never were very good with women, Owen.' The Wolfe looked off through an open door that led into an adjoining room. 'Do step in here and make yourself known, my dear.'

From the next room came the sound of slow, stumbling footsteps. Owen's nose wrinkled as a smell came to him, dark and organic, quite out of place in the spotless high-tech security centre. It was a smell of preservatives, and under-neath that, like the face beneath a mask, the sickly-sweet stench of rot and decay. A cold prickling ran down Owen's spine, a premonition of some horror he felt he ought to recognize. And then the dead woman stepped into the room, and stood trembling beside Valentine Wolfe. She was quite naked, and held a sword in her hand. She'd been in the ground for some time. The primitive undertakers of Viri-monde had done their best, but the pale purple and grey skin had cracked apart all over the body, revealing implanted computers and servo-mechanisms. The big Y of an autopsy scar ran from her sunken breasts down to her groin, the stitches stretched and broken. A single death wound still showed clearly against the ribs. The face was taut and drawn, sunken down to the bone in places. The dead lips had torn free of their stitches and drew back from perfect teeth in an unwavering smile that held no humour. The eyes were sunk deep in their sockets, as yellow as urine, and the flat blonde hair had grown longer in the grave. But Owen still recognized her, knew who she had to be, and the realization closed around his heart like a fist.

'Cathy . . .'

'Got it in one, Deathstalker,' said Valentine Wolfe. 'Your old mistress, Cathy DeVries, from the days when you were young and carefree and just a humble scholar here on

Virimonde. Actually, she was really an Imperial spy, sent to keep an eye on you. She tried to kill you when you were first outlawed, and you had to kill her in self-defence. Your first love, who died in your arms. Such a touching scene, I'm sure. And here she is again; my little present to you.

'You see, I've done my homework on you, Owen. I know what moves you, and what holds you back. I had dear Cathy dug up when I first came here, had my people implant Ghost Warrior technology inside her. Just in case you tracked me here to trouble me again. Now, I think I'll leave you two lovebirds alone together. I'm sure you've got lots to talk about. And Owen . . . just in case you do bring yourself to kill her again before she kills you, I've arranged another little surprise for you. The programme's already running. No, don't bother to thank me. What are brothers for?'

He gestured at the dead woman and she lurched forward, sword at the ready. Owen backed away, and the corpse of what had once been his mistress came after him. He tried to speak to her, but his mouth was dry. He knew she couldn't hear him anyway. This wasn't Cathy. Cathy was dead, and the computers currently inhabiting her body cared only for the orders programmed into them. Owen knew this, but deep down his heart didn't believe it. He couldn't fight her, not her. Killing Cathy had been the hardest thing he'd ever had to do back then, and he didn't think he could do it again. It would be like killing a part of himself. He allowed her to back him away from the open door, and Valentine Wolfe slipped easily past them, chuckling happily. He darted away down the corridor, still laughing, leaving Owen and what was left of his old mistress to sort out their differences together.

And in the computers of the security centre, a programme was slowly counting down to zero, Valentine's last gift to the Deathstalker.

Back in the main hall, Hazel d'Ark was bored. She sat in a chair with its back to the wall, so no one could sneak up on her, and watched the Romanov and the Kartakis sitting quietly together. They didn't seem to have anything left to say for themselves. The great hall was empty and silent, and there was no sound from the corridors outside. Hazel could have contacted Owen through his comm implant, to see how he was getting on, but she knew how snappy he could get if you interrupted him while he was in the middle of something. Hazel crossed her legs, just for something to do, and wished that Owen would get on with killing the Wolfe. There was always the chance he'd go all soft-hearted again at the last minute, and insist on dragging the Wolfe back alive to stand trial, but she didn't think so. Not this time: Valentine had struck at too many of the things Owen still cared about. The Wolfe wouldn't be able to talk his way out of this one. Hazel recrossed her legs and sighed heavily. Boring, boring, boring.

She glared across at the two silent aristocrats, and only then realized that the Romanov had disappeared. His exoskeleton was still sitting where it had been, but he was no longer inside it. Hazel was immediately on her feet, gun and sword in hand, eyes sweeping the great hall. There was no sign of the aristocrat anywhere. How the hell could she have missed the Romanov getting loose? There was no way he could have clambered out of that much armour without her noticing, no matter how preoccupied she'd been with her boredom. Unless the suit had built-in stealth technology . . . in which case the Romanov could have freed himself while hidden behind a projected holo illusion. And if the Romanov had dropped that illusion, it could only be because he was currently skulking somewhere in the hall, behind some projected holo disguise that rendered him, for all practical purposes, invisible. Wonderful.

Hazel held her sword out before her and spun in a circle, knowing she couldn't hope to spot a weakness in the holo, but trying anyway. She strained her ears for the slightest sound, but heard not a single noise. The Romanov could be anywhere in the damned hall . . . She shot a quick glare at Kartakis, to warn him to stay put, and was cheered inwardly by the way he immediately sank back in his chair. And then the arm shot around her throat from behind, tightening its grip, shutting off her air. She struggled furiously against the chokehold, but couldn't shake the Romanov off. Strength wasn't enough to break a hold like this. The arm pressed tightly against the carotid arteries in her neck, trying to stem the flow of blood to her brain. It was one of the few holds that actually stood a chance against someone as strong as she. She still had some human weaknesses, after all. Hazel staggered back and forth, dragging the Romanov with her, desperate for air, enraged with herself for letting her attention slip. She had to defeat the Romanov before Owen got back, or she'd never hear the end of it.

Inspired, she snapped smartly forward at the waist, and the Romanov went flying over her head, his own weight and momentum breaking the stranglehold. She heard him hit the floor hard, and immediately turned and blasted the exoskeleton with her disrupter. The armour exploded with a satisfyingly large bang, and went up in flames. The Kartakis yelped, and tried to shift himself a safe distance away from it, but had the sense not to try anything else. The Romanov's holo illusion snapped off and there he was before her, rising to his feet with a short but nasty-looking knife in his hand. She really should have searched him.

Hazel sucked the air back into her straining lungs, her sword held steadily out before her. The Romanov was a big man, but she'd faced bigger, and the advantage was back on her side now. The Romanov seemed to sense this, opened his hand and let the knife fall to the floor. Hazel relaxed just a little. She should have known the aristo wouldn't have the guts for anything remotely resembling a fair fight.

She gestured with her sword for the Romaonov to go and sit down again, and knew immediately that she'd made a mistake. A man who had one hidden weapon might well have another. The moment Hazel's blade moved away from him, the Romanov flexed his arm and a knife dropped down into his hand from another concealed sheath. The knife in his hand streaked towards her undefended gut, and her sword was miles out of line. It was a sudden, simple, blindingly fast attack, and anyone else would surely have died, but Hazel wasn't like anyone else, and hadn't been for a long time now. She whipped her sword back into line with inhuman speed and strength, parried the knife and knocked it aside, and the Romanov plunged on, unable to stop, and impaled himself on the waiting blade.

The sword slammed under the sternum, through his heart and punched out of his back in a flurry of flying blood. The

Romanov sank to the floor, face twisting, and dropped his knife to clutch at the transfixing sword blade with both hands, as though he could somehow pull the killing steel out of his body and still survive. It was as he held Hazel's sword with a dying man's desperate strength that Hazel realized she'd lost track of the Kartakis. She glared around her, desperately tugging at her sword, but couldn't budge it. There was the Kartakis, on his feet, a knife in his hand too. She started to raise her gun, but the Kartakis's hand shot forward, throwing the knife with deadly, practised skill, and Hazel knew she wasn't fast enough to dodge it. She tried anyway, and time seemed to slow to a crawl. The knife inched through the air, heading straight for her left eye. Hazel knew she was going to die, alone and far from friends and help.

Oh Owen; I wish . . .

And then there he was, materializing out of thin air, his hand flicking the knife aside. It flashed through the air, back to its owner, and sank to its hilt in the Kartakis's throat as though it belonged there. The aristocrat bent slowly forward, as though bowing to Owen and Hazel, and fell dead to the floor. The Romanov breathed his last, let go of Hazel's sword and fell backwards. She jerked the sword out of his body and turned, just a little breathlessly, to thank Owen for his last-minute rescue. She gasped as she caught sight of him: how different he looked.

His clothes were torn and bloodied, and topped with a great furred cloak. His face was tired and gaunt, and he was breathing hard and deep, as though he'd been running for a long time. He looked as if he'd been through hell, and had to fight every step of the way, but in his steady gaze Hazel saw both determination and a desperate, bone-deep sadness. He smiled at her, a strange, gentle smile, and reached out a hand as though to take hers. Hazel thrust her gun into its holster and reached out to meet his grasp. And that was when she realized Owen was extending his left hand, and that it was flesh and blood, not the golden Hadenman hand that had replaced it long ago. Hazel hesitated, her hand stopping short of his, and Owen smiled sadly, as though he knew he'd be denied but had still hoped otherwise. He opened his mouth to say something, and Hazel found herself straining forward, somehow knowing that it was vital she hear what he had to say, but in a moment he was gone, vanished back to wherever he'd come from, to whatever desperate flight he'd interrupted to save her when no one else could.

Hazel looked about her, but the hall was empty now, save for the two dead aristocrats and the smouldering exoskeleton. Had that really been Owen, appearing out of nowhere to save her when she needed it most? But he'd had two human hands. Could it have been an alternative Owen, from some different time track, like the other Hazels she sometimes summoned? And if so, why had he looked so sad? She accessed her comm implant.

'Owen. Report in. Are you all right? Owen? Owen!'

The Ghost Warrior made from Cathy's remains lurched towards Owen, sword at the ready, and he didn't think he'd ever been so angry in his life. He wasn't worried; for someone who'd once gone one-on-one with a Grendel, a lone Ghost Warrior with a sword wasn't much of a threat. Her weapon lashed out at him, and he parried it effortlessly. He was so angry now he could barely contain himself. To have desecrated the grave of the first woman he'd ever felt anything for, just for a sick joke, for another way to hurt him . . . Owen clutched his sword hilt till his hand ached. He didn't want to have to kill Cathy again. It had been hard enough the first time. But he couldn't let this mockery of an old love go on. It had to be stopped, if only so he could go after Valentine and tear him apart with his bare hands. And then the dead mouth opened, and an approximation of Cathy's voice came out. It wasn't the body speaking, the vocal chords would have rotted away by now. It was just a recording, probably Valentine using a voice synthesizer. It couldn't be Cathy.

'Don't hurt me, Owen,' said the dead woman, her torn black lips trying to keep up with the words. 'Please. I don't want to die again. I know I'm not what I used to be, but it's still me, Cathy, your mistress. Valentine brought me back, back from the dead, and trapped me in this rotting body. He can do things like that now. He has new friends, powerful allies. You'd be amazed what he can do now. Please, Owen.'

'Shut up.'

'All right, then; let me kill you, and we can be dead together, lying side by side in the warm earth, for ever. Do it for me, Owen.'

'You don't sound a bit like her,' said Owen, and he stopped backing away. The corpse struck at him with servo-motor-driven muscles, but his blade held firm, and he deflected the blow easily. 'You don't sound at all like my Cathy.'

'Being dead changes you.'

'Not this much. Cathy never pleaded for anything. So you're not Cathy. Just another damned weapon aimed at me by my enemies. Damn you to Hell, Valentine.'

And he lashed out with his mind, the power boiling up within him focused by fury and outrage, and Cathy's body blew apart into tiny pieces of rotten flesh and shattered tech. They fell pattering to the floor in a hideous rain.

'Owen?' said Hazel's voice through his comm implant. 'Report in. Are you all right? Owen? Owen!'

'I'm fine,' he said at last. 'But Valentine's escaped. We'll have to search the castle for him. Lock up the two Lords and come and join me in the security centre.'

'The Lords are dead,' said Hazel, just a little apologetically. 'They tried to escape.'

Owen started to say something cutting, and then hesitated; there had been something in her voice. 'Are you all right, Hazel?'

'Of course,' she replied. 'I'm fine. I'll be with you soon.'

She shut off contact. Owen looked down at the human remains scattered across the floor, and told himself he felt nothing at all.

Together, Owen and Hazel searched the Standing, floor by floor, room by room. It took some time. The security system should have been able to locate Valentine, but he'd programmed it to ignore him. The Wolfe always planned his moves well in advance. They covered the whole of the ancient castle, and did not find him, nor any trace of his people. Valentine Wolfe had left the building.

Hazel was quietly very impressed with Owen's Standing. The rooms and halls were filled with more tributes, treasures

85

and general high-quality loot than she'd ever thought to see in her lifetime. Her eyes only stopped widening when they started to hurt. Hazel began to think she could make herself very happy for the rest of her life with just the contents of one room. Hell, there was enough bounty in this place to keep even Ruby Journey happy. But Owen just glanced at it in passing, dismissing the familiar sights in his need to get his hands on his enemy.

They finally ended up in Owen's old bedchamber. The secret passage was still standing open, but Hazel talked Owen out of going back down to the flyer caves. It had been clear to her for some time that the Wolfe had made his escape from the castle, and probably from Virimonde, but she'd let Owen go on searching – she could see he needed to. They stood together in the bedchamber and looked about them, wondering what to do next. Hazel sat down on the edge of the bed, legs swinging, and smiled widely as she sank slowly into the deep mattress.

'This is some place you got here, Deathstalker. Did this really all belong to you?'

'When I was Lord, this whole planet belonged to me, and everything on it,' said Owen. 'Now Virimonde and its people are dead; and I'd give up this castle and all that's in it to have them back again. They've taken my past away from me, Hazel. The life I had, and hoped to have again someday, is gone for ever. All I have left is a Standing I never really cared for, and a few memories.'

Hazel smirked. 'I'll bet you have some good memories from this room, at least.'

'Some,' said Owen. 'I had a mistress called Cathy, when I was Lord. We were happy here.'

Hazel sat up straight. Owen had never mentioned any of the women in his life before. She'd always supposed there must have been someone, somewhere, but a mistress was news to her. She kept her voice carefully casual. 'And what happened to this Cathy?'

'She turned out to be an Imperial spy. Tried to kill me when I was outlawed. I had to kill her.'

'You killed your own mistress?' said Hazel incredulously. 'Damn, that's cold, Deathstalker.'

Owen stared at the holo portrait before him, showing the original Deathstalker, founder of his Clan. 'I killed him, too, and he was my most revered ancestor. Seems to me I've been responsible for too many deaths in my life. And far too many of them were people I cared for. Maybe you should find yourself a new partner.'

Hazel got up off the bed and moved quickly over to stand beside him. 'You never killed anyone you didn't have to.'

Owen shook his head. 'I betrayed my inheritance when I killed Giles. I betrayed my name and my Family honour.'

'No,' said Hazel firmly. 'He did that, when he forgot what he was fighting for. He was Warrior Prime, in his day, defender of humanity. When he decided he wanted to be ruler instead of defender, he betrayed us all.'

'He really was a legend,' said Owen, 'an authentic hero. He actually did do most of the things the stories say he did.'

'Yeah, including the creating and wielding of the Darkvoid Device. A thousand suns snuffed out in a moment, and no one knows how many billions dead. The greatest mass murderer in history.'

'He meant well. He always meant well. He just . . . lost his way.'

'Ah, hell,' said Hazel, slipping an arm through his. 'We all lose our way sometimes. You just killed the man, Owen. The legend lives on.'

'I can't go home again,' said Owen bitterly. 'Be a scholar again. Have my old life back again.'

'You couldn't have anyway. You've changed too much. And mostly for the better.'

Owen raised an eyebrow. 'Only mostly?'

'Gosh, sir aristo, could you teach me to arch one eyebrow like that?'

'Go to Hell, peasant.'

They stood together for a while, thinking their separate thoughts. 'Owen,' Hazel said eventually, 'have you been manifesting any new abilities just recently?'

'Not that I've noticed,' said Owen. 'Why do you ask?'

'Well, I was wondering if you'd learned how to call up alternative versions of yourself, like I do.'

'Hell, no. I'd definitely have noticed something like that. That is one spooky ability, as far as I'm concerned.'

'Trust me, I know exactly how you feel. I still haven't a clue how that particular ability works. I need them, and there they are. Suddenly and violently and all over the place. One of these days, I'm going to see if I can get one of them to hang around long enough for me to ask a few pointed questions.'

'Do that,' said Owen. 'I'd love to hear the answers – I think.' And then he broke off, frowning suddenly.

'Now what?' said Hazel.

'Valentine,' said Owen. 'He said he'd left a surprise for me, hidden deep in the Standing.'

'Oh, hell,' said Hazel. 'You mean we have to search the whole damned castle *again*?'

'I think we'd better. Valentine's little surprises are always unpleasant, and tend towards the dramatic.'

'Owen,' said Oz suddenly, 'I need to talk to you. Right now.'

'Not now, Oz. We're busy.'

'Well you won't be soon, if you don't pay attention. I've found something in your security computers. It appears to be a countdown.'

'A countdown?' said Owen. 'Towards what?'

'That's the problem. I can't find out. Whatever the programme is, Valentine's locked it away behind a whole series of passwords that I'm having hell's own trouble cracking. I'm currently scanning the entire castle trying to find anything anomalous, something Valentine might have added that isn't connected to his drug production – oh, shit.'

'You've got that we're-in-real-trouble look on your face again,' said Hazel. 'What's happening?'

'Oz says he's found a countdown. And then he said "Oh, shit".'

'Ah,' said Hazel, 'we are in real trouble.'

'Oz,' said Owen, determinedly. 'Could you please expand on *Oh, shit*?'

'There's a bomb,' said Oz, 'planted deep under the Standing. And it's a really nasty one. Big enough to blow the entire castle and everything in it to a bunch of free-floating atoms, and leave a glowing crater large enough to park a small moon in.'

'That sounds like Valentine,' said Owen. 'Vindictive to the last. If he can't play with the toys, no one can. Any chance you can defuse it?'

'Oh, *shit*,' said Oz.

'Your expression just changed again,' said Hazel.

'Unfortunately,' said Oz, 'in discovering the bomb and attempting to defuse it, I seem to have triggered another programme . . .'

And that was when the steel shutters slammed down over the windows, the secret passage closed itself off and the only door shut and locked itself with a very final-sounding series of clicks. All over the room, hidden bolts slammed into place sealing it off from the rest of the castle and the outside world. Hazel looked wildly about her, gun and sword in hand again.

'Owen; talk to me! What the hell is going on here?'

'Valentine's accessed the last-ditch security programmes, designed to protect the castle's occupants in time of emergency, and tied it in to any attempt to defuse the bomb. And since Valentine has undoubtedly changed all the passwords, it's a fairly safe bet we have no way of getting the computers to unseal this room before a very large bomb goes off and makes the whole problem redundant.'

'Bomb?' said Hazel. 'What bomb? No one said anything about a bomb!'

'Oz did,' said Owen. 'Remember the countdown?'

'Hell with passwords,' said Hazel. 'I'll get us out of here.'

She aimed her disrupter at the nearest shuttered window and fired before Owen could stop her. He grabbed her and pulled her protesting to the floor, just as the searing energy beam ricocheted back from the unharmed shutter and passed right through the air where they'd been standing. Owen and Hazel tried to burrow into the carpeted floor as the beam bounced back and forth above them, ricocheting from shutter to shutter till finally it exhausted itself. Owen and Hazel cautiously raised their heads. The room was full of the stench of ionized air. Owen looked at Hazel.

'Please don't do that again. There are shutters everywhere now, even inside the walls, specially reinforced to stand off energy weapons, which I would have told you if you'd just waited a damn minute!'

'Don't you raise your voice to me, Deathstalker! This is your castle. Get us out of here. Do something!'

Owen considered panicking, but decided he didn't have time. 'Oz, how much time left on the countdown?'

'Two minutes, seven seconds and counting.'

'Oh, *shit*.'

'I already said that. It didn't help.'

'What?' said Hazel, looking at Owen's face. 'What? *What*?'

Owen thought hard. There had to be a way out. He hadn't come this far, achieved this much, only to die in such a simple trap.

'I really don't like the expression on your face,' said Hazel.

'How invulnerable are you feeling right now?'

'That bad, huh?'

'Worse. We've got two minutes before the bomb blows us off this world and into the next, and we can't even get out of this room. Unless you've learned Giles's trick of teleporting.'

'No. He never did get around to explaining how he did that before you killed him.'

'Oh, right, blame me. Maybe if we all just talked to each other a little more . . .'

They stopped and looked at each other, and a strange calm settled over them. 'This is it, isn't it?' said Hazel. 'End of the line. Funny, I never expected to survive the rebellion. Always knew I was fated to die young. But I never thought I'd go out like this. So . . . helpless.'

Owen put an arm round her shoulders, and she leaned against him. 'Hell,' he said after a moment, 'we've been living on borrowed time since we first met. It had to run out eventually. And . . . I'm glad we had our time together. In a strange kind of way, I don't think I've ever been happier.'

'Yeah,' said Hazel, 'it has been one hell of a ride, hasn't it? You're a good sort, Owen. I enjoyed our time together too. And if we have to go out, at least we're going together.'

They sat down on the edge of the bed, side by side. They kissed once, as though they had all the time in the world, and then just leaned companionably together.

'Who knows,' said Hazel finally. 'We stood off a point-blank blast from a disrupter cannon back on Mistworld, remember? Maybe we'll get lucky again.'

'Hold everything,' said Owen, suddenly sitting up straight. 'Follow that thought. We stood off that disrupter blast because we were linked together. We became much more powerful than the sum of our parts because our minds were joined together. That's how we survived!'

Hazel scowled. 'I've never liked linking. I don't like letting anyone else into my mind.'

'You don't like letting anyone else into your life! Hazel, this is no time to be modest! Would you rather die?'

'Damn. All right, let's do it.'

She reached out a hand, and Owen took it in his human hand. Their minds reached hesitantly out to each other, following the old mental link that held all the surviving alumni of the Madness Maze together. They drew closer and closer, until the power building between them slammed their minds into one unified will, and became something else. Something more: something that pulled them right out of their bodies and up into the air above, where they glowed brightly like the sun. They flashed through all the floors and rooms of the Standing in a moment, immaterial spirits, until they came at last to the computers Valentine had had installed in the room adjoining the security centre. They hovered over the machines, held back for a moment by a strangeness they couldn't name, and then they concentrated, and heard the machines thinking. It was both simple and very complex, a multitude of small but vital decisions flashing past faster than any merely human mind could hope to follow. But Owen and Hazel had come a long way from human now, and it took them less than a second to sink into the computer systems and pull out the data needed to stop the countdown. The programme interrupted, the bomb reset itself and waited for new instructions. Owen and Hazel ran swiftly through all the computers' memories, just to make sure Valentine hadn't left any other unpleasant surprises, and then they pulled free. The driving need that had bonded them together ran out, and they vanished from the computer room, separated, and fell back into their bodies again. They looked dazedly around them, getting used to breathing again, as the shutters disappeared and the room unlocked itself.

'Wow . . .' said Hazel, finally. 'That was . . . something else.'

'It's what I've always said,' Owen remarked. 'We do our best work together.'

'Maybe. Let's get out of here, Owen. There's too much death in this place.'

'And Valentine got away,' he scowled. 'But I will find him. And for what he's done, to my home and my world and my people, I'll make a whole new Hell to send him to.'

CHAPTER TWO

Just Another Day in Parliament

The *Sunstrider II* dropped out of hyperspace and took up orbit above Golgotha, homeworld and seat of power of the Empire, and Owen and Hazel couldn't have cared less. Virimonde had left them both drained. After the physical and psychological hammering they'd taken at the old Death-stalker Standing, it was all they could do to sit upright in their chairs and grunt responses to the main starport's landing instructions. Owen keyed in the coordinates and let the navigation computers handle it. They were better at landing than he'd ever be, and he was just so deathly tired. At least during the rebellion he'd had something to fight for. Now it seemed he was just fighting for something to do, and could only watch helplessly as more and more of his old life was lost to him.

Besides, if he was being honest with himself, the *Sunstrider II* intimidated him. The Hadenmen, those enigmatic augmented men, had rebuilt the ship to resemble the lost original as closely as possible, but they hadn't been able to resist 'improving' it. So that although Owen had been flying the yacht for some time, he still didn't feel entirely comfortable about handling the ship himself. Owen could cope with doors that opened if he even thought about approaching them, and food synthesizers that knew what he wanted for dinner before he did, but navigation controls that worked on the same unnerving principle were just too much for him. After a couple of unfortunate incidents when his mind wandered during what would otherwise have been perfectly safe landings, he decided very firmly to leave such matters to the computers and devote his time to more important business. Such as sulking.

He sat slumped in his chair, watching the dark blue world rising slowly towards him, and felt almost nostalgic. The last time he'd come to Golgotha, the rebellion had been in its final vicious throes, and practically everyone on the planet had been shooting at him. Now he was just another visitor, no more important than anyone else. Owen had a strong feeling he preferred the old days. At least then he'd been sure who and where his enemies were. He'd had friends and colleagues he trusted with his life, and a cause worth dying for. Now even that had been taken from him. All he had left was a ship he didn't trust, and a love who would never use that word. He looked fondly across at Hazel, brooding furiously in her chair. Even when she was supposed to be relaxing, Hazel d'Ark still looked as though she might leap up at any moment and tear someone's throat out. Owen didn't mind. He was used to it.

'So,' said Hazel brusquely, somehow knowing he was looking at her without even looking round. 'Where do we go next? Got any plans?'

'Why is it always up to me?' Owen protested mildly. They'd had this conversation before, many times. 'How come you never have any ideas?'

'I have plenty of ideas,' said Hazel, 'but you're always too chicken to follow them up.'

'That's because they'd mostly get us arrested or killed, or both. Your ideas have a distressing tendency to revolve around violence, murder and bloody mayhem, and stealing anything that isn't actually nailed down. We can't get away with that kind of thing any more. We're not rebels and outlaws now, we're part of the status quo. Hell, technically speaking, we're law enforcement agents.'

'Boring,' said Hazel. 'You've got really boring these days, Deathstalker.'

'Actually, I do know what I'm going to do next,' said Owen, ignoring the insult with the ease of long practice. 'As soon as we've landed and made our report to Parliament, I'm going straight out again after Valentine Wolfe. The trail will still be warm. He won't get far.'

'You've said that before, Owen, and he's always got away. The Wolfe's spent his whole life being somewhere other than where he's supposed to be. That's how he's stayed alive so long, in spite of all his enemies. Don't waste your time again, Owen, please. Power down, get some rest, recharge your batteries. He'll pop up again soon enough, doing something appalling, and then we'll get another crack at him.'

Owen had to smile. 'Things have come to a pretty pass if you're being the voice of reason to my hothead.'

Hazel sniffed. 'Don't think I haven't noticed. Just shows how turned around we both are. We need some down time, Deathstalker. Virimonde hit us hard.'

'Yeah. Not much of a homecoming, all told.'

There was a pause, and then Hazel looked across at him, her face and voice carefully calm and casual. 'Owen, how come you never told me about Cathy before? I mean, she was your mistress. She must have been important to you.'

'She was,' said Owen. 'Killing her was the hardest thing I'd ever had to do, then. I never talked about her because she was none of your business. You could never have understood the kind of relationship we had.'

'You could have talked to me,' said Hazel. She wasn't angry at his words. She could hear the old pain underlying them. 'I would have tried to understand. Tell me about her, this Cathy. What was she like? How did you meet her?'

Owen was quiet for so long that Hazel had almost decided he wasn't going to answer, but at last he began to speak, his voice calm and almost unemotional, as though that was the only way he could approach such painful memories. He didn't look at her.

'Her name was Cathy DeVries, and she was very beautiful. Been a courtesan of one kind or another all her adult life, specially trained and adapted by the House of Joy to fulfil every desire you ever had, and help you come up with some new ones too. She was a surprise party favour at a Winter Ball on Golgotha, and when they first presented her to me, I thought she was the most wonderful thing I'd ever seen. We danced and talked, and she listened to me, seemed to understand and care about what I was saying when so many didn't. She even found my jokes funny; she was perfect. I knew right then I had to make her mine. So I bought out her contract, for an utterly extortionate price, and she was my mistress for seven years. And I was happy, for the first time in my life.

'Of course, it turned out she wasn't perfect. Her table manners were appalling, she was far too bright and cheerful first thing in the morning and she was an Imperial agent, set up to spy on me. Reported everything I said and did to a contact on Golgotha. Oz found out and told me, but I didn't care. I was just a minor scholar in those days, with no interest in politics. Her reports must have made really boring reading. Occasionally I'd say something controversial, just so they wouldn't consider taking her away from me. We were so happy. I don't think we ever once had an argument. It was like finding a part of my soul I hadn't even known was lost. Seven years we had together. Sometimes I think that was the last time I was ever really happy, that I treasured it so much because, deep down, I knew someday it would all be taken away from me.

'I loved her so much. I never thought I'd have to kill her. Stick a knife in her ribs and twist it, and then hold her in my arms as she bled to death.'

'Jesus, Owen . . .'

'I would have saved her, if I could.'

'She tried to kill you.'

'Sometimes I think she succeeded; that the best, most innocent part of me died that day. I never did ask her if she loved me. I was afraid of what her answer might be. Maybe if I'd known, she wouldn't have taken so much of me with her when she died.'

'Stop that right now, Deathstalker. If you start getting maudlin on me, I am going to get up out of this chair and come over and slap you round the head.'

Owen smiled briefly. 'You would too, wouldn't you?'

'Damn right I would. Never put yourself down, Owen; there are always plenty of others just waiting for the chance to do it for you. Cathy's the past. Let it go and move on.'

'You're the one who brought it up,' Owen said mildly. 'And I don't know why you're so interested in my romantic history, all of a sudden. You're the one with all the surprises in that department. I still haven't got over that time in

Mistport when the Wampyr, Abbott, turned out to be one of your exes.'

'He was a mistake.'

'And nowhere near the first or the last, by all accounts.'

Hazel glared at him. 'Who's been talking?'

'Practically everybody. The gossip columnists love you. You've given them more headlines, scandals and outrages than all the other heads of the rebellion put together. You've got your own magazine on the Matrix Internet. With daily updates.'

'You haven't been reading that rubbish, have you?'

'Nah. I just look at the pictures.'

When they finally disembarked from the *Sunstrider II*, in the great city known as the Parade of the Endless, home to Golgotha's remaining government and the infamous bloody sands of the Arena, Owen and Hazel found themselves besieged by a crowd of reporters. Most of the major news organizations were represented, and all of the minor ones with stringers on Golgotha. Owen's and Hazel's exploits were always news, and the reports trickling in on what they'd found and done on Virimonde had raised the journalists' expectations sky-high. They surged around Owen and Hazel, shouting their questions, while cameras swooped and dived overhead, searching for the best shots. Interviewers tried to elbow each other out of the way, and fist fights broke out at the back. Even so, no one got too close to Owen or Hazel. They'd learned better, usually the hard way. Hazel hadn't actually killed a reporter yet, but the smart money was on when, rather than if. There were even betting pools on some of the more obnoxious tabloid characters.

Owen waited patiently for them to calm down a little and sort out their own seniority, while Hazel glared furiously in all directions, her hands flitting worryingly near her weapons. The reporters gave her plenty of room, but reserved their real reverence for Owen, who had overturned the Iron Throne and slain the legendary original Deathstalker. This did absolutely nothing for Hazel's temper, especially when most of her questions these days tended to be pointed enquiries about her relationship with the revered Deathstalker. She'd tried being facetious, but they just reported everything she said as fact. She'd tried hitting everyone who brought up the subject, but the others just filmed her doing it. Mostly these days she just settled for *No comment*, or a similar two-word answer, the second of which was usually *off*. It didn't help her temper at all that Owen found the whole business hugely amusing, and always winked at the cameras when he said his *No comment*.

And then one of the reporters brought up the recent Deathstalker movie, and cranked up the tension a whole notch higher.

The rebellion hadn't been finished a week before the first documentaries had hit the holoscreens; feature-length films cobbled together from film footage of varying clarity and integrity. People all over the Empire were dying to know the true facts of the rebellion, and put the wild stories and wilder rumours that circulated into some kind of context. But as people have always preferred the comforts of romance to the dry facts of history, it wasn't long before the various competing documentaries were roughly shouldered from the holoscreens by the first Deathstalker movie. Part fact and many parts fiction, starring actors no one had ever heard of, it found a vast audience desperate to view the rebellion in terms of heroes and villains. Action-packed and vastly simplified, it made billions of credits for all concerned, except those on whose lives it was based, and was quickly followed by many more of varying quality and accuracy. From Toby Shreck's prizewinning coverage, to wild fantasies that didn't even get the names right, the public ate it all up with spoons.

The most recent and most popular movie of all claimed to be a biography of Owen Deathstalker, in which he was portrayed throughout as a saintly and selfless hero, and his associate Hazel d'Ark was a murderous psychopath, restrained from constant mayhem and bloodshed only by her undying, doglike devotion to Owen.

Owen and Hazel were sent free tickets to the premiere, so they went to see it, entirely unsuspecting. Owen laughed so much he hurt himself, and was finally asked to leave by an usher because he was disturbing the rest of the audience. Hazel stuck it out to the end, gripping the arms of her chair so tightly that her hands ached. When the film was finally over, she set fire to the cinema. Luckily Owen got to her before the city guards did, and hustled her away while the firefighters were still trying to keep the fire from spreading. He then took away all her weapons, wrestled her to the ground and sat on her until she promised not to hunt down and kill everyone concerned with making the movie. As Owen had reasonably pointed out, such actions would only have vindicated the movie's depiction of her.

It hadn't helped that Owen had been played by a major star and heart-throb, while Hazel had been played by an ex-porn star with more looks than talent and a quite astonishing cleavage. Hazel had insisted on their putting out a joint statement to the effect that the film was totally inaccurate in all respects, but no one paid any attention. People had always preferred legend to the truth.

So, when the reporter in full battle armour raised the question of the movie, everyone else backed hastily away so the blood wouldn't get on them. Hazel grabbed a hovering camera out of mid-air and threw it with devastating accuracy. It hit the reporter right between the eyes and knocked him cold. He fell to the ground with a loud crash and didn't move again for some time. Hazel glared about her and her hands went to her sword and gun. Owen moved in quickly from behind and pinned her arms to her sides. The reporters watched, interested, from what they hoped was a safe distance until Owen had more or less calmed Hazel down, and then they edged forward again, stepping over the unconscious body of their fallen fellow-seeker after truth and ratings. Sensibly, they changed the subject. Unfortunately, they picked merchandising.

The mass audience's appetite for celebrity being what it was, even the endless series of movies and documentaries weren't enough to satisfy the demand for the new heroes. They also showed an insatiable readiness to buy enough general junk based on the movies and their characters to cover a small moon several miles deep. The junk ranged from the truly tasteless to the appallingly cheap and nasty, and Owen and Hazel did their best to take no notice of any of it, as long as their royalties kept coming in. But that was about to change.

'Have we seen what?' said Owen, and then rather wished he hadn't, as the reporter held up a small plastic figure.

'There's a whole line of them,' said the reporter cheerfully. 'Fully posable action figures of all the main characters in the rebellion. Collect the set. They're very popular. Especially the Empress figure. People like to do terrible things to it.'

He produced more of the figures, and passed them forward for Owen and Hazel to examine. They were cast in bright primary colours, with identical muscular figures and politely generic faces. Certainly they resembled absolutely no one Owen knew. He looked at Hazel.

'Did we authorize these?'

'Who knows?' said Hazel, glaring at the huge breasts on the figure supposed to represent her. 'We signed all kinds of agreements. I lost track.'

'They're harmless enough,' said Owen. 'Tacky, but harmless.'

'Either way, we'd better check this out,' said Hazel. 'There's supposed to be a hell of a lot of money in this market, and if there is I want my share. Or somebody's going to be spending a lot of time in Intensive Care while they try to make his bones fit together the right way again.' She glowered at the figures. 'Which one's supposed to be Ruby?'

'Uh . . . the one with all the guns,' said the reporter.

'Nothing like her,' said Hazel. 'And she couldn't even carry that many weapons at once; she'd fall over. Mind you, with breasts that size, she'd probably fall over anyway. Hell, no one has breasts that size outside of the House of Joy.'

'Is there a lot of this stuff out there?' said Owen, handing the toys back to the reporter.

'Well, yes, Sir Deathstalker. And this is the classier end of the market. There are lunch boxes, posters, games . . . These are quite popular just at the moment.'

He dug into the pack he was carrying and brought out two foot-long dolls of Owen and Hazel. Their clothes were reasonably accurate, if not their faces, and at least the proportions were rather more human. The reporter pressed the speaker buttons on their backs. The Owen doll said, '*Fight for justice!*' The Hazel doll said, '*Kill! Kill! Kill!*' Hazel's face went a series of interesting colours, and all the cameras zoomed in for close-ups. Somehow she held on to her temper: she'd learned to recognize when she was being goaded. Owen had the sense to turn the beginnings of laughter into a not entirely convincing cough. The disappointed reporter decided it was time to play his trump card. If that didn't get her going, he'd eat his union card. He put the dolls back in his pack, and casually brought out the last items.

'And there are, of course, these.' He held up two cuddly furry toys in Owen and Hazel costumes.

'*A furry toy?*' said Hazel, in tones that presaged imminent thermonuclear meltdown. '*They've turned me into a fluffy toy?*'

Everyone held their breath and decided which way they were going to jump when the shit started flying. The cameras would still get the best shots for them. Assuming they survived whatever appalling thing was about to happen. And then Owen reached out to the sweating reporter and took a toy in each hand.

'I think they're rather cute.'

'You *like* these monstrosities?' said Hazel.

'Well, I wouldn't necessarily want one on my pillow, but I definitely want a piece of this action. These things sell like fury. We are talking major revenue here.'

Hazel calmed down visibly as she considered this. 'Yeah . . . could be. Kids go crazy for this kind of crap. One good Christmas and we could be set up for life.'

Owen smiled inwardly. When in doubt, you could always distract Hazel with talk of money. 'Assuming these are authorized. There's a lot of knockoff stuff out there with our names and faces on it.'

'Only till I catch up with the people involved,' said Hazel. 'Still, I'll have a word with Toby Shreck. He'll know the right people to talk to.'

The reporters reluctantly decided there wasn't going to be any action after all, and heaved quiet, disappointed sighs. Some even started to recall their cameras. The agent provocateur glumly retrieved his fluffy toys, stuffed them into his bag and tried to remember if he'd kept all the receipts so he could get his money back. Everyone started to drift away. And then the representative from Parliament arrived, and everything went to hell in a handcart.

He was a fairly typical Parliament rep, all things considered. A jumped-up civil servant, promoted way out of his depth because there weren't enough warm bodies to go round, trying to convince everyone that he was as important as the messages and instructions he carried. This particular fellow was dressed much too well for what should have been his means, including the traditional courier's red sash and a distinctly snotty attitude. He strode forward, the reporters falling to either side of him, and planted himself before Owen and Hazel. He stuck his nose in the air and glared at them both, just to remind them of their place in the real scheme of things, and then launched into his prepared speech without even bothering to introduce himself.

'Sir Deathstalker, Miss d'Ark, you are commanded to present yourselves before Parliament at this evening's Session, to report on your mission to Virimonde. Parliament wishes to express in advance its extreme displeasure, in that not only have you failed to bring back any of the rebel Lords alive, but that you also allowed that most detestable villain Valentine Wolfe to escape justice. You are required to make a full explanation of these shortcomings. Also, you can forget about your bonuses.'

All the cameras started zooming in again. The reporters knew a storm brewing when they saw one. So, just to annoy them, Owen decided to try reasoning with the man.

'We did put an end to the abominable practices on Virimonde,' he said mildly. 'The Charnel House affair is no more. The dead have been avenged. And we did nip in the bud a most dangerous plot against the Empire. Not bad for one day's work.'

The representative sniffed. It was a loud, arrogant, obnoxious sound. He'd clearly put in a lot of practice. 'All that matters is that you failed to carry out Parliament's demands. What you may or may not have done aside from your brief is utterly irrelevant.'

Owen and Hazel looked at each other. 'After you,' said Hazel, courteously.

'Thank you,' said Owen. He stepped forward, smiled at the representative and punched him out. The unfortunate fellow stretched his length on the hard, unforgiving surface of the landing pad and lay twitching. Owen smiled at the reporters. 'You just have to know how to talk to these people. Did everyone get that, or shall I pick him up and do it again?'

The reporters said they'd got it just fine the first time, thank you very much, and then started firing questions at him and Hazel over these new details of their last mission. In particular they wanted to know just what the hell the Charnel House plot had been, and what the infamous Valentine Wolfe had had to do with it. The group interview then rapidly deteriorated into a bidding war for exclusive rights to the full story. Fist fights broke out among the reporters, and Owen and Hazel took the opportunity to make a quiet exit. Hazel looked down at the fallen Parliament rep on the ground. He seemed to be stirring, so she kicked him somewhere particularly painful, just on general principles.

'You know, you'd have thought they'd have learned to wear body armour by now,' said Owen.

'I'm surprised they can still find anyone dumb enough to carry messages like that to us,' said Hazel. 'Must be a new guy.'

'Well, if he doesn't improve his manners soon, he's never going to be an old guy. Let me just check if he's got any written orders on him.'

Owen knelt beside the quietly moaning man and frisked him thoroughly, coming up with a set of sealed orders with his name on them. Hazel frowned.

'That's another thing. How come my name's never on these things?'

'They wouldn't dare,' said Owen. He broke the wax seal, studied the brief message, fashionably written in real pen and ink, and scowled fiercely. 'Damn. They've arranged another parade for us. Right now, on our way to Parliament. I hate parades.'

'Yeah, but the people love them. It's the only chance they get to see their heroes in the flesh.' Hazel shrugged as Owen got to his feet and dropped the orders on to the rep's chest. 'It's no big deal, Owen. We've faced worse in our time. Just smile and wave and try to look heroic. And remember you're supposed to kiss the babies and pat them on the head. Not perform an impromptu exorcism on the grounds that it's *supernaturally ugly.*'

Owen sniggered. 'I was was bored. You like all this public acclaim shit, the waving and the cheering and the adulation of the masses. I just wish they'd all go away and leave me alone. I don't like crowds. I don't like being stared at. And I hate doing autographs. Last time, my hand ached for a week.'

'Just relax and enjoy it. We earned this. Let them worship us if they want to.'

'All right, let's get it over with,' said Owen, resignedly. 'Then we can make our report to Parliament, answer a whole lot of stupid and unnecessary questions and heroically refrain from shooting a whole bunch of people too stupid to live. And maybe then we'll be allowed to go home, crash out and get some sleep.'

'Right,' said Hazel, 'I could sleep for a week.'

'He was right, you know,' Owen said, his tone serious now. 'It wasn't exactly our most successful mission.'

'Hush, Owen,' said Hazel. 'Your people were avenged. Settle for that. Now let's go – our admirers await us.'

She clapped him once on the shoulder, and led them off the landing pad. Owen followed her, dragging his feet all the way.

The parade's organizers had thoughtfully provided a gravity sled for them, and Owen and Hazel floated down the main street, just high enough to be out of reach of the crowd's grasping hands. There had been unfortunate incidents in the past. People maddened by the sheer proximity of their heroes had surged forward past the guards and made a grab for bits of clothing, curls of hair, or anything else detachable that might serve as a souvenir. After Hazel showed an understandable but regrettably violent way of dealing with such fans, it was decided that everyone concerned would be a whole lot safer if the crowd's heroes were kept up out of reach on a vehicle.

The mile-long street was packed with men and women and children, all cheering their heads off. The sheer volume of sound was an assault on the ears. Some were waving the official new Empire flag, while others had flags and banners bearing the old Deathstalker Family crest. Confetti and flower petals rained down from overhead. At the back of the crowds, men sat their children on their shoulders so they could see, and have a tale they could tell to their children. They had little flags of their own, and waved them enthusiastically, though many were too small to have any idea of what they were celebrating.

Owen smiled and waved like an automaton, and distanced himself from the din and bedlam as best he could by concentrating on the report he was going to make to Parliament. He'd never liked crowds. People staring at him made him feel nervous and self-conscious. Once, in his old life, when he'd had to make a speech to a gathering of historical scholars, he'd locked himself in the toilet for so long they'd had to send someone to ask if he was all right. It should have been different now. He was a man of power and destiny – everyone said so. He'd fought his way through whole armies of Imperial troops, and never once hesitated.

It didn't make any difference. He still hated being stared at.

It didn't help that Hazel was really into it, waving and smiling and turning back and forth so everyone could get a good look at her. A whole group of Hazel lookalikes was chanting her name and squealing ecstatically whenever she smiled in their direction. Some of them were women. Someone threw her a long-stemmed rose. She caught it deftly, avoiding the thorns, and blew the thrower a kiss. The crowd loved that. Owen pretended not to see, while noting grumpily that no one was throwing him roses. Not that he wanted any, of course. It was just the principle of the thing.

Rebuilding was going on all around, as houses and shops and offices damaged or destroyed during the last great battle in the city were being repaired. Work went on twenty-four hours a day, but the job seemed never-ending. Workers in antigrav slings high up on the sides of buildings leaned dangerously out of their harnesses to shout coarse comments at Hazel. She shouted even coarser ones back. They loved it. Up ahead, a brass band was oompahing away with great enthusiasm, but was largely drowned out by the roar of the crowds. Cameras were shooting back and forth overhead, and occasionally getting into butting contests over the best angles.

Owen smiled till his mouth ached, and kept a constant suspicious eye on the unfinished buildings for possible snipers. The adulation of the crowd was all very well, but there were a lot of people out there who would love to see Owen and Hazel conveniently dead, for all sorts of reasons. And besides, the approval of the crowds didn't fool him. He knew what was behind some of it. With so many dead on both sides, and a somewhat more liberal government in charge, for the first time ever transplants were available for everyone. There was a near-endless supply of spare parts on ice, and even with the extremely long waiting lists, people who would otherwise have been left to die now had new hope. And who had been responsible for all the bodies? Owen and Hazel.

There was an even darker side than that to the acclamation. Inspired by Owen's and Hazel's more than human abilities, many in the general populace had been moved to 'improve' themselves by all means possible. These Maze-wannabes had taken to Blood, tech implants and supplantive surgery with an enthusiasm that bordered on the macabre. Owen didn't approve, but there didn't seem to be anything he could do about it. As Hazel pointed out, that was fashion for you. In return, Owen had said something very cutting about fashion and lemmings, and did his best to keep an eye on the trend. It struck him as a fad that could get dangerously out of control, and he hadn't saved humanity from the Empress Lionstone just to see people turn themselves into minor-league Hadenmen.

The parade seemed to go on for ever, but eventually they came to the centuries-old building that housed Parliament. Since no one had taken Parliament at all seriously for the same amount of time, the great square edifice was tucked away in a usually quiet backwater, and the general fighting and destruction had largely passed it by. The tall stone walls were overgrown with thick mats of ivy that no one ever dared prune because of the real possibility that it was only the ivy that was holding the old building together.

As Owen and Hazel approached Parliament, troops moved in to shut off the crowds and hold them back as the heroes stepped down from the gravity sled and made their way hurriedly into the lobby of the government building. The great oak doors shut firmly behind them, and the noise of the crowd was immediately shut off. Owen breathed a quiet sigh of relief. His arm ached from waving, and he didn't think he had a smile left in him. Facing an undoubtedly hostile Parliament didn't bother him nearly as much as hysterical crowds shouting that they loved him and wanted to have his babies.

Waiting servants bowed to Owen and Hazel, and led them through the sumptuously furnished lobby to the great outer Chamber, where everyone with business before Parliament was waiting with varying degrees of patience for the evening Session to get under way. Everyone who was anyone, and others who thought they might or should be someone, was there. Parliament drew even more would-be movers and shakers than Lionstone's Court, not least because Parliament wasn't likely to kill you if they thought you shouldn't be there. They just bored you to death.

Everyone knew that Parliament had inherited the day-to-day running of the Empire pretty much by accident. All the other contenders were so busy fighting among themselves, they effectively cancelled each other out, and so only Parliament was left. So far, they were doing as good a job as anybody else might have. The 250 MPs who made up Parliament, elected by all those above a certain yearly income who could be bothered to vote, hadn't had any real power for a long time, and reacted to their new status with mixed enthusiasm. Some threw themselves into the job with gusto, determined to show what they could do given a chance. Others reacted strongly at the very thought of actually having to work for a living, and drew so far back into their shells that no amount of knocking or coaxing could convince them to come out. Most cheerfully advertised themselves for sale to the highest bidder. Some even floated themselves on the stock exchange. Certainly there was no shortage of organizations, factions and powerful individuals trying to influence the MPs in one way or another, for any number of reasons; so much so, armed guards had had to be installed in and around Parliament to keep the peace. Especially during budget debates.

The Members of Parliament's first act had been to raid the public purse to hire publicity experts, to help them present themselves in the best possible light. Their oratory skills had grown somewhat rusty, eroded by the certain knowledge that no one was listening to them, and they all knew they needed to look their best if they were to appear worth supporting. Or bribing. Many had blossomed in the new blaze of attention and publicity, and became well liked, if not trusted, public figures. Politics had never been such fun. The MPs had even begun creating their own political parties, usually with themselves at the head, to provide voices for those wishing to be heard in Parliament, and the general populace flocked to support them. The MPs hadn't yet, for the most part, realized that they could now be a voice themselves if they wanted. But, this being Golgotha, everyone was just waiting for the penny to drop.

Outside Parliament, things were getting violent. Seeing too late that Parliament had seized the only real political ground, the various remaining factions had taken to settling their quarrels by brute force. The body count in the streets rose every day, as swords, guns, bombs and poison decided who was currently on top. The authorities had stopped trying to enforce the peace, except during the morning and evening rush hours. These days more than ever, people had to be able to get to and from work safely. Both sides bandied the word 'terrorist' freely, while plotting atrocities of their own. In such a crowded field, publicity was everything. Owen and Hazel had considered getting involved, and killing lots of people until the others got the point, but Jack Random had talked them out of it. Practically the only thing the different factions had in common was their disapproval of Owen and Hazel, as possible competitors for power. No one wanted to risk giving the factions the only thing they might actually unite behind; namely the assassination of Owen Deathstalker and Hazel d'Ark.

The only real competition Parliament had as a governing body were the war trials, presided over by leading figures from the rebel undergrounds. Under Lionstone's evil rule, all kinds of atrocities had become commonplace, and brutal and sadistic men and women had come to power and thrived in that dark atmosphere. People could disappear for any or no reason, and never be seen again. Torture and murder were everyday matters of state under the Iron Bitch. Once she fell, and the rebel leaders had access to the palace records, the names of these vile oppressors became known, and a long-delayed retribution began. The underground would put a face on holovision, along with the relevant address, and they were dragged from their rich apartments or hunted through the streets. Many met bloody and awful ends, and the rest hurried to surrender themselves to the authorities, the only place where they could hope to find protection. They still thought they could cut themselves deals by betraying each other, and only realized too late that they were to be shown no more mercy than they had shown their countless victims. The war trials began within hours of Lionstone's fall, and were holovised every day in full, so that the people could see justice being done. Everyone watched. Everyone had lost someone, or knew someone who had. The trials went on and on, and there seemed to be no shortage of the accused, no matter how fast the Courts hanged them. The public hangings attracted huge, mostly silent crowds, as though the people needed to see the bastards die for themselves, before they could believe it to be true.

Parliament was more than a little jealous of the war trials, both for the power they wielded and the attention they took away from the Sessions, but they knew better than to interfere. The war trials were even more popular than the Arenas, an unprecedented situation on Golgotha. Even more than justice, the people needed vengeance.

Owen and Hazel came to the great Chamber, the last room before entering the floor of the House itself. The Chamber was separated from Parliament proper by an ancient, massive oak door that, by long tradition, was only ever opened from the inside. The MPs used this privilege to keep people waiting as long as possible, to remind them of their place in the new scheme of things. It was a practice they'd borrowed from Lionstone, though that of course was never mentioned. The huge Chamber's wood-panelled walls were covered with portraits of previous politicians, and the dead eyes of long-gone nonentities glowered disapprovingly down at the raucous crowd filling the hall. As always, the great room was packed, and the noise was deafening. Everyone was looking for contacts, trying to make a deal or talk up some new opportunity. There were no holo images; everyone had to be there in person. In these days of clones, aliens and Fury impostors, people liked to be sure of exactly who they were talking with. Esp-blockers were installed in hidden locations just to keep everyone honest, and to hell with whether it upset the esper underground.

When Owen and Hazel made their entrance, everything stopped. All eyes turned in their direction, and the gabble of voices died quickly away to nothing. Owen and Hazel looked calmly about them in the silence, and inclined their heads politely. Everyone turned away, and the babble of conversation resumed. No one was interested in talking to the Deathstalker or the d'Ark woman. It wasn't safe, for all kinds of reasons. Owen and Hazel moved unhurriedly forward into the Chamber, and without quite looking round, everyone made room for them.

'The usual warm greeting,' said Owen, not caring if anyone overheard.

'Ungrateful bastards,' said Hazel, and craned her neck hopefully to see if anyone present was stupid enough to take offence.

'They do have their reasons for not liking us,' said Owen, more quietly. 'After all, I murdered my own ancestor, the heroic and much-revered Giles Deathstalker, and you used to be a clonelegger. Heroes and role models are supposed to be pure and unsullied. I fear we came as something of a disappointment.'

'My heart bleeds,' said Hazel. 'I never claimed to be a hero. For two pins I'd walk out of here and Parliament could whistle for its report. Hell, for three pins I'd burn the place down as well before I left.'

'Steady, steady,' murmured Owen, smiling unconcernedly for the benefit of the Chamber. 'Don't let them get to you. Never let them think they can intimidate or influence you. They'd take it as a sign of weakness.'

Hazel sniffed. 'Anyone sees me as weak, and tries to take advantage of it, they'll be carrying their lungs home in a bucket.'

'Get your hand away from your sword, dammit. You can't kill anyone here, duels are forbidden. You even start to draw your sword, and half a hundred guards will appear from everywhere. It's the only way they can keep discussions here from spilling over into deadly insults and challenges. Even we're not exempt. I do wish you'd keep up on the changes, Hazel.'

'Ah, you know you love a chance to make a speech to me. Besides, I could handle half a hundred guards.'

Owen sighed. 'Yes, you probably could, but that's not the point. We are trying to make a good impression.'

'Since when?'

'Since we failed yet again to bring back Valentine Wolfe for trial.'

Hazel shrugged. 'Is it OK if I just half kill someone?'

'If you must. Only try to do it when the holovision cameras aren't looking. We really don't need any more bad publicity.'

Hazel looked about her. 'Don't think I've ever seen so many cameras here before. Either Parliament's got something really juicy lined up, or someone told them we were coming. Hello, I spy a familiar face.'

And she plunged off into the crowd, shouldering people out of her way if they didn't move fast enough. Owen followed after, murmuring polite apologies as he went. It was a practice he was growing increasingly used to. The familiar face turned out to be Tobias Shreck, accompanied as always by his news-cameraman, Flynn. Owen joined Hazel in greeting them, smiling genuinely for the first time since he'd entered the Chamber. Toby Shreck had been a news reporter during the rebellion, and had demonstrated an uncanny ability to turn up in just the right place at just the right time, with Flynn always there at his shoulder to broadcast it all live. They'd covered a lot of the fighting Owen and Hazel had been involved in, and had even been there when the rebels finally threw down the Empress Lionstone, and destroyed the Iron Throne for ever.

Toby looked much the same as ever, a fat, perspiring

butterball of a man with slicked-down blond hair and a ready smile. He was wearing fashionable clothes of the very finest cut, tailored to disguise as much of his great girth as possible, but they didn't suit him. He was more used to the easy casualness of combat fatigues, and it showed. Flynn was the same tall, gangling sort, with a deceptively honest face. A quiet, retiring man in the field, he tended to fade into the background when working; a useful trait when people were firing guns all around you.

His private life was another matter entirely.

'Looking good, Toby,' said Hazel cheerfully, poking a playful finger into his more than ample stomach. 'Lost a few pounds, have we?'

'I wish,' said Toby. 'Ever since I allowed myself to be promoted to management, and ended up practically running Imperial News, I spend most of my time sitting behind a desk, instead of getting out in the field where I belong.'

'Leave it out,' said Flynn calmly. 'You used to spend all your time in the field whingeing and grousing about all the comforts you were missing.'

Toby glared at him. 'Straight speaking like that is why you're still a cameraman, while I am now management. And don't contradict me again in public or I'll have someone in accounting take a really close look at your expense claims for last year.'

'Bully,' said Flynn.

'You're looking very smart, Toby,' Owen said quickly, before they could fall into their usual bickering. 'Right on the cutting edge of fashion.'

'Don't you start,' said Toby. 'I know what I look like. Why do you think I always wore fatigues in the past? Every time I wear something good, I look like I stole it.'

'So what's management doing here?' said Hazel, not bothering to hide her smile. 'Parliament planning something special, is it? Something perhaps we ought to know about?'

'Right,' said Owen. 'What do you know that we don't?'

'Volumes,' said Toby airily. 'But for once, I'm as much in the dark as you. I'm really only here because I felt a desperate need to get out in the real world for a while. I've been feeling bored just lately, to tell you the truth. It's all so different, these days. My work with Flynn during the rebellion has already been hailed as classic material. It has its own place in the historical archives, and at any given time it's a safe bet that somewhere some station is still running it. The public can't get enough of it. The royalties are coming in faster than even I can spend them. So much money that even the company accountants can't hide it all. Flynn and I need never work again, if we don't want to. But . . .'

'Yeah?' said Hazel.

'But we're too young to retire,' said Flynn. 'I wouldn't know what to do with myself.'

'Right,' said Toby. 'And I can't help being haunted by the horrible suspicion that perhaps I've already done my life's best work. That's a hell of a thing to feel at my age. I want, I need, a real story; something I can get my teeth into. Something that *matters*.'

'We are rebuilding a whole Empire, pretty much from the ground up,' said Owen. 'Our whole political and social structure is changing day by day. I can't believe you can't find a story worth covering.'

'Oh, there's no shortage of *news*. History in the making, and all that. But it's all so bloody worthy and open and honest and *dull*. Where's the fun in that? Where's the drama? Everyone I meet nowadays seems so . . . small, after the great figures I followed in the rebellion. Even the villains are second-rate, nowadays.'

'No,' said Owen. 'I wouldn't say that. Valentine Wolfe is still out there, somewhere.'

'Ah yes,' said Toby. 'I'd heard you'd had another run-in with him. I'm looking forward to hearing your report on that. At least you two are still around, making waves. Everyone else has pretty much disappeared. Jack Random is too busy playing politics to get into any real trouble, and Ruby Journey rarely leaves her house. Though word has it they may be making an appearance here today. Maybe they've heard something. God, I've got some great footage of the four of you in action during the rebellion, stuff that never saw the light of day. Maybe when we're all safely dead . . .'

'Yeah,' said Hazel, 'maybe. But until then, I think some

secrets should stay hidden. People don't need to know everything that went on.'

There was a certain amount of sage nodding. Nobody mentioned the fake Young Jack Random, who'd turned out to be a Fury in disguise, a cyborg working for the rogue AIs of Shub, but they all knew they were thinking of the moment when Flynn's camera had caught the machine's unmasking. And there were other, darker, secrets too. The rebellion hadn't been nearly as straightforward as most people thought.

'So,' said Toby briskly, breaking the awkward moment, 'have either of you thought any more about my offer to make official documentaries of your lives? There's so much rubbish out there with your names and faces on it, you need to get the true story established while it's still fresh. We are talking serious money here, people. You don't have to worry about the writing; we have people for that. Just talk into a recorder, and we'll arrange the material and dig up footage to go with it. We can fake some linking material to cover the areas you don't want to talk about. All you'll have to do is narrate over the final footage. Easy money. Get it while it's going; who knows how much longer people are going to stay interested in you?'

'The sooner everyone loses interest in us, the better,' said Hazel. 'No biographies, Toby. We have little enough privacy as it is. Besides, most of my life story isn't suitable for a mass audience anyway.'

'I can quite believe that,' said Owen. 'Let's change the subject rapidly. How's your life, Toby? Doing anything interesting apart from your work?'

'Him?' Flynn sniffed loudly. 'He doesn't have a life outside of his work. First in, last out and takes work home with him. Typical management. I work the union-approved hours only, and once I clock out I don't even think about work again till I clock on in the morning. You should have stayed a working grunt like me, boss. Far less pressure.'

'You never did have any ambition,' said Toby.

'Damn right, and proud of it. Ambition just gets you into trouble and takes over your life. Which is why you have bags under your eyes and incipient ulcers, and I have a wonderful new lover in my life.' Flynn beamed at Owen and Hazel.

114

'You really must come round and meet him sometime. His name's Clarence, Clarence DuBois. Works as a researcher for the MP John Avon, one of the few marginally honest Members of Parliament. My Clarence does all the real work, of course, so Avon can look good on the floor of the House, but that's the way of the world for you. He's very handsome, and a marvellous cook. The things he can do with a fresh joint and a few vegetables! Trouble is, he has size twelve feet, and you wouldn't believe the problems we've been having trying to find stiletto heels that will fit him.'

'Love seems to agree with you,' said Hazel. 'It's made you positively chatty.'

'Don't I know it,' said Toby. 'I've been hearing about bloody Clarence for weeks.' He grinned maliciously at Owen and Hazel. 'And how are you two lovebirds getting on, hmm?'

'If you find out, let me know,' said Owen. 'I've never understood our relationship.'

'We're taking things day by day,' said Hazel firmly. 'How about you, Toby? Anyone special on the horizon?'

'I have been considering a Clan marriage, just lately,' Toby admitted reluctantly. 'On the grounds that I'm not getting any younger, and my Family's been putting the pressure on about where the next generation of the Family's going to come from. With Uncle Gregor forced into hiding, Grace an avowed old maid and Evangeline disowning the Family, the line pretty much ends with me. But who'd marry a Shreck? Thanks to dear Uncle Gregor and his appalling ways, the Family name has become mud in all the circles that matter.'

'Now, now, none of that, boss,' Flynn chided. 'You're Toby the Troubador, rich and famous journalist of note, not just a Shreck. Work is all very well, but in the end there's no substitute for getting out and meeting a nice girl. Or boy. Or whatever.'

Owen was so busy watching Toby glow bright red with embarrassment that he didn't notice the approaching young aristo till the man was practically on top of him. Hazel noticed. It took a lot to distract Hazel. She tapped Owen surreptitiously on the arm with one hand, while the other fell to the gun on her hip. Owen turned unhurriedly, and stopped the approaching aristo in his tracks with a steady gaze and a raised eyebrow. The young man bowed formally, keeping his hand well away from the sword at his side. He was dressed well but unimaginatively, his long metallic hair already out of fashion. His blandly handsome face was studiously unreadable.

'Sir Deathstalker; my apologies for imposing on you, but there is someone nearby who desires to make your acquaintance.'

'Then that makes him pretty much unique in this company,' Owen said easily. 'Who might this someone be?'

'It is the Lady Constance Wolfe. She wishes to speak with you urgently, on a matter of some importance to you both. May I lead you to her?'

Hazel frowned. 'Constance Wolfe? Don't think I know her. What relation is she to Valentine?'

'Technically speaking, she's his mother,' said Owen, letting the aristo stand waiting. 'She married Valentine's father, Jacob, late in his life. With Valentine on the run, Daniel missing and Stephanie discredited, Constance runs Clan Wolfe these days. I've never met the woman; can't think what we might have in common. Still, I'd better go and see what she wants. Never know when you might learn something useful.'

'Watch your back,' said Hazel. 'She's still a Wolfe.'

Owen grinned, nodded goodbye to Toby and Flynn and allowed the now impatient aristo to lead him through the crowd to where Constance Wolfe stood waiting. As always, she was surrounded by male admirers, from the highest in society to the merely very rich. Constance had only just entered her twenties but was already a breathtaking beauty, on a world noted for its beautiful women. She was tall and blonde, with the body and grace of a goddess, but for all the cheerful chatter around her, her perfect face remained cool and unresponsive, her occasional smile merely a matter of form. She looked round as Owen approached, and he thought he saw something very like relief flicker in her deep blue eyes as she made her excuses to her admirers and drifted forward to meet him.

Owen bowed, and she curtsied, and they stood for a

moment looking at each other. Without turning her head, Constance dismissed her messenger with a brief wave of the hand. He bowed stiffly, and moved reluctantly away to join the small army of admirers, who immediately began a quiet but animated discussion, glaring openly at Owen all the while. He chose to ignore them, knowing that would irritate them the most. Constance sighed.

'That was Percy Furey. He adores me, and I take advantage of it disgracefully. But then, so many men have declared their undying love for me since my Jacob died that I find it hard to take any of them seriously. When you're as rich and as well appointed as I am, it's amazing how adorable one becomes. I have only ever loved one man, my dear Jacob, and his death has not changed that. There is not a day goes past that I do not miss him with all my heart. But on her own a woman cannot hope to survive long in this changing Empire without powerful friends and supporters, so I let them cluster around me and reward them with the occasional smile or encouraging nod. As long as they still think they have a chance with me, they'll make my enemies theirs, and thus I have a certain amount of security, if not safety. I trust I don't shock you with my frankness, Sir Deathstalker?'

'Not at all,' said Owen, just a little charmed in spite of himself. 'Such honesty is refreshing, in this day and age. Perhaps you could continue the openness and explain precisely what I can do for you? I confess I'm not entirely sure what you might have in common with a man who's sworn to kill your son.'

'Valentine? Kill the degenerate, with my blessing. He brings shame to the House of Wolfe, and always has. I have reason to believe he murdered his own father.'

Owen raised an eyebrow. 'Now that I hadn't heard. Though I can't say it surprises me. I've always considered Valentine capable of anything.'

'I am the Wolfe, these days,' said Constance, 'even though I'm only a member of the Family by marriage. There is no one else. But it's hard to be the head of a largely discredited Clan, and even harder to be a woman alone, in these unsettled times. My people are still loyal, as much to me personally as to the Family, but how long they will hold out in the face of ever-increasing pressure and bribes, I don't know. I need your help, Sir Deathstalker.'

'In what way?' said Owen. 'As you must know, I'm not exactly popular among the powers that be. What influence I have is strictly limited. And if all you want is a bodyguard, allow me to point out that there are any number of excellent fighters looking for work now the rebellion's over.'

'No, that isn't what I want from you.' Constance frowned, and shook her head slowly. 'This isn't easy for me, Sir Deathstalker, so please . . . make allowances for me, and permit me to approach this in my own way.'

'Of course. But please, call me Owen. I've never been much of a one for formalities.'

Constance smiled briefly. 'So I've heard. Very well; it will make things simpler. And you must call me Constance.' She turned away for a moment, composing her thoughts, and then turned back, her face quietly determined. 'My life . . . has not gone the way I thought it would. You can understand that feeling, I'm sure. Like you, I was uprooted and devastated by an entirely unexpected event. When I married Jacob Wolfe, I thought my life's path was set out before me. I'd have children by Jacob, raise them for him and walk by his side all my days. A simple dream, perhaps, but it was all I ever wanted. And then he was dead, murdered, and my new Family was rocked by one blow after another, and I . . . was left alone. I had to take charge of my own life; something I'd never done before, and had no training for. But it's amazing what you can do when you have to. I learned by doing. And I grew up fast, because the alternatives were poverty or death, and quite possibly both. It made me stronger. It also made me hard, ruthless, and someone I'm not always sure I approve of. You see, Owen, we have a lot in common after all. That's why I want you to marry me.'

Owen stared at her. He was sure his mouth was hanging open, but he didn't seem to be able to do anything about it. Whatever he'd been expecting when he strolled so casually over to join Constance, this sure as hell wasn't it. The impulse to turn and run and lose himself in the crowd was almost overpowering, but he fought it down. Apart from being shockingly bad manners, it wouldn't do for word to get around that he'd run from something. He managed to force his mouth closed, and swallowed hard.

'Why me?' he said finally, and just a little plaintively.

Constance shrugged. 'It's clear I must marry someone, and after much thought I've decided that you are the best choice. We have much in common, we're both of old established bloodlines, and I need someone untouched by the evil and corruption that has swallowed up so much of our class. I need someone I can trust. My position as head of Clan Wolfe is . . . precarious, and with my Jacob gone, I see no reason to remain in a Family I no longer have any stake in. It wouldn't be a love match, I know, but we both have a duty to marry well and continue our lines. We would make a strong alliance, Owen. You have made your Family name honourable again. I would be proud to be a Deathstalker.'

She stopped talking and looked at him expectantly, and for once in his life Owen didn't have the faintest idea what to say. He thought hard. 'I knew Jacob Wolfe,' he said finally. 'My father had . . . dealings with him. As I recall, he didn't think much of me.'

Constance smiled. 'Jacob didn't think much of anyone. He was a hard man. He had to be; he had many enemies. But I knew another Jacob, a side of him he never dared show anyone else, not even his children. Perhaps especially not them. He was strong and steadfast, and he stood up for what he believed in. A lot like you, Owen.'

'Hold on,' said Owen, raising both hands defensively. 'If there's one thing we should both be certain of, it's that I am not in any way like Jacob Wolfe. I never wanted to be a warrior. I was a quiet scholar, and perfectly happy to be so, until Lionstone outlawed me. I was dragged into the rebellion, kicking and screaming all the way.'

'Then the more honour to you, that you achieved so much with such disadvantages,' said Constance demurely. 'But now the rebellion is over, what are you going to do with your life? You can't go back to being a simple scholar, not after all you've seen and done. The butterfly cannot become a caterpillar again. And while bounty-hunting no doubt fills a present need in you while scum like Valentine remain free, it's not a profession to build a life on. Like it or not, you have become a symbol to many people, and they're looking to you to provide leadership. Which means you're going to have to enter politics. Otherwise you could win the battle but lose the war. Surely you didn't go through all you did just to see Lionstone replaced by something even worse?'

'No,' said Owen. 'No, I didn't. But I'm not interested in power for myself. Never have been.'

'The best kind of politician,' said Constance. 'It's the ones who want power you have to watch out for. This is a matter of duty, Owen, not desire. The Empire needs you.'

'I've heard that so many times,' said Owen, 'from so many people. But they all had very different ideas as to what I should do, once I came to power. They all had my life mapped out for me, for the very best of reasons. I always thought I'd be free of all that, once the rebellion was over and I'd made it clear I had no interest in the crown or the Throne. I thought I'd be free to turn my back on all the blood and death and run my own life again. I should have known better. Duty will ride on my shoulders till the day I die, like the Old Man of the Sea, who, once picked up, can never be put down.'

'Or the red shoes,' said Constance, nodding. 'They'll make you a great dancer, but once you put them on, you can never take them off, and you can't stop dancing. When I first heard that story, I decided that if that ever happened to me, I'd just have to dance as beautifully as I could. So that I'd be remembered for what I did, rather than the curse that drove me. Be a politician, Owen. Be a statesman. Make something new and marvellous of yourself. I can advise you, guide you, introduce you to the right people. We'd make a good partnership.'

'There's more to this than your admiration for me, or your need to be free of Clan Wolfe,' said Owen suddenly. 'I can feel it. You're afraid of something. Something specific. What?'

'Very good, Owen. You're as sharp as everyone says. Blue Block has become the real power that the Clans answer to. They talk, and everyone listens. They make suggestions, and everyone rushes to follow them – if they know what's good for them. But I don't trust Blue Block. They started out as a secret order of spies and assassins, and I don't trust their motives. I want to be free of them. I want the Families to be free of them. But thanks to you, they're frightened and divided. The Clans need a hero to gather behind. And even after everything you've done, they'd accept you. They understand that your argument was always with Lionstone, rather than the Clans. They respect vendetta. And they've always understood ambition. After all, you were born and raised an aristocrat, just like them.'

'No!' said Owen sharply. 'I'm nothing like them. I fought to bring down not just Lionstone, but also the order that supported her. I saw the horrors and evils the Families were responsible for. I saw the awful lives the many lived, so the few could sprawl in luxury.'

'You mustn't blame individuals for the system they grew up in. You changed; so can they. Help them change. Remake them into what they could be, should be; a guiding force to run the Empire fairly, and make it strong and secure again. Either you become a part of that, or you'll be sidestepped and isolated from the main currents of the Empire, and from your own kind.'

'I don't know, Constance. It's not that simple. There are a hell of a lot of people in positions of power and influence these days who think the only good aristo is a dead aristo.'

'You could change that. You're a hero, an icon. Where you lead, people will follow. The aristocracy has too much potential for good just to let it disappear. We are an inheritance of the best, going back centuries. Generations of breeding and gengineering for perfection. You're the last of the Deathstalkers, Owen. Do you want your bloodline to die with you? If not, you must marry another aristocrat, to maintain your Family legacy. Anything less would be a betrayal of your Clan.' She stopped, and looked searchingly at Owen. 'Separately, we are both people of great potential. Togther, our Family could become unbeatable.'

Owen shook his head slowly. 'Constance . . . I don't know you. I don't love you.'

She smiled. 'We'll come to know each other. I like what I've heard of you. I think we'd be . . . compatible.'

'Constance, I always thought that when the time came, I'd

121

marry for love or not at all. I want a marriage, not a business merger.'

'I can't promise you love, Owen. I loved my Jacob with all my heart and soul. I don't know that I'll ever love again. But our match was an arranged marriage, and he was a stranger to me when we began as man and wife. We don't have to love each other to be supportive partners and allies, but . . . perhaps love will come later.' She fixed him with a thoughtful eye, head cocked slightly to one side. 'Or is there already a love in your life? There's been endless speculation in the media and in society about your relationship with the d'Ark woman. A . . . formidable figure. No one doubts that she's a hero of the rebellion, but you must realize you could never marry her. She is not of the same class as you, and wouldn't be even if you did marry her. You are from different worlds, and always will be. And despite what the songs might say, love doesn't conquer all.'

'Hazel would never say she loved me,' Owen stumbled on, not sure what he was going to say until he said it. 'We've been as close as two people can be, fought side by side against everything the Empire could throw at us, faced death and worse together . . . but she has never once said she loved me.'

'I can give you children,' said Constance. 'Raise them to be part of the Deathstalker Clan. Could she do that for you? Would she?'

'No,' said Owen. 'I don't think she would. Very well, Constance, a marriage shall be arranged between us. You set everything in motion; I've been away for so long I'm rather out of touch with the formalities involved.'

'Of course,' said Constance. 'I'll take care of everything. You may kiss me now, if you wish.'

She came into his arms and turned her mouth up to him. It was a very polite, almost diffident kiss. Her lips were warm and soft but unmoved under his. But Owen could feel his whole life changing with that kiss, as he committed himself to a future he could barely see or grasp. A chapter in his life was ending here, and a new one beginning. He just hoped that for once in his life he'd made the right decision. They broke apart and looked into each other's eyes for a moment,

Owen's hands resting easily on Constance's hips. She met his gaze freely, open and trusting, binding herself to him. But there wasn't an ounce of love there, and both of them knew it. Constance stepped back, and Owen's hands fell to his sides. She smiled at him, curtsied and moved off into the crowd, leaving Owen standing alone. He could see people all around him regarding him with new interest, but for the moment all he could think of was how he was going to break the news to Hazel d'Ark.

Hazel had found the bar, a quiet area, set apart, with gleaming tiles, rows of interesting looking bottles and a long wooden counter. She'd also found Jack Random and Ruby Journey. The three of them were drinking together in companionable silence. None of them looked particularly happy. Jack was wearing a simple blue jumpsuit that showed off his newly youthful figure to its best advantage. He'd been given all kinds of medals but he never wore them. Ruby was wearing her usual black leathers under white furs. She said it helped remind her of who she was. She was also wearing so much gold and silver jewellery on her arms and wrists and around her neck, that she couldn't make the smallest movement without it all clattering and chiming together. They were all drinking the strongest brandy the bar had to offer. They had a bottle each, and they weren't bothering with glasses. The bartender looked distinctly scandalized at their cavalier treatment of such a good brandy, but had the sense and survival instincts to keep his mouth firmly shut.

'One of the drawbacks of our Maze-improved bodies,' said Jack sadly, 'is that it takes a hell of a lot of booze to make a dent in them. But facing this wondrous new Empire we helped to create is too awful a prospect to contemplate entirely sober.'

'Right,' said Ruby. 'Of course, it helps that we can afford the very best booze now. A bottle of this stuff costs more than I used to make in a year's bounty-hunting. Can't honestly say it tastes that much better from the rot-gut I used to drink, though.'

'You have no palate,' said Jack.

'Yes I have,' said Ruby, 'I speak perfectly clearly.'

Hazel could see an argument starting, and moved quickly to head it off. 'So, what have you guys been doing while Owen and I were off chasing the bad guys? Keeping busy?'

'Off and on,' said Jack Random. 'Since I brokered the deal that de-fanged the aristocracy and brought about their surrender, everyone and his brother comes running to me every time an aristo steps out of line. Like there's anything I can do about it, except pass their complaints on to Parliament. I have my own problems, trying to set up a new political system practically single-handed. People expect so much of me; my legend has been expanded by the rebellion to almost inhuman proportions. People were confused by the two Jack Randoms, so they've decided there must only have been one, and attributed everything to me, along with a whole lot of complete fiction. I've met people who were actually in awe of me. Makes negotiating a hell of a lot easier sometimes, but all this scraping and grovelling is getting on my nerves. No one sees *me* any more, the real me; just the damned legend. They think I can do anything, solve any problem, and then have the nerve to get angry when I can't.' He took a long swallow from his bottle. 'Of course, my legend's nothing compared to Ruby's. I've known people to cross themselves when they see her coming.'

'And quite right too,' said Ruby briskly. 'Half the time I don't even have to pay for things any more. I just walk into a place, point at what I want, look a bit severe and they fall over themselves rushing to give it to me as a gift. I'll bet we won't even have to pay for these drinks. Probably make the barman wet himself with a single look.'

'I'll take your word for it,' said Hazel hastily. She looked across to where Owen was in conversation with Constance Wolfe, and scowled. 'Wonder what he's doing with Pretty Miss Perfect? I don't like him talking to other aristos. They're a bad influence on him. And it's always been easy to talk him into things.'

'You should know,' said Ruby. 'What's the matter; afraid they'll woo him away from you?'

Hazel snorted. 'Not after everything we've been through together. There's a bond between us that's stronger than anything they could ever understand.'

'Yeah,' said Ruby, 'but have you bedded him yet?'

'Mind your own business!'

'Thought not.'

'It would . . . mean too much to him,' said Hazel. 'He'd take it too seriously. He'd start talking about relationships and trust and building a life together, and I'm not ready for that kind of shit.'

'Can't say I can see a time when you ever would be,' said Jack.

'And you can shut up as well.'

'Better get to it soon, girl,' said Ruby calmly. 'Or someone else'll have him. Wouldn't mind a bash at him myself. Good build; nice ass. And he's got that innocent, little-boy-lost look that always sets my fingers itching.'

'You keep your hands to yourself, Ruby Journey,' said Hazel steadily. 'Anyone touches him but me, and I'll put them in traction for a month.'

'Yeah, but do you love the man, or not?' Ruby insisted.

'We have . . . an understanding.'

'Understandings won't keep you warm in the early hours of the morning. You're just frightened of commitment, Hazel. Always have been.'

'That's good, coming from someone who's never had a permanent relationship with anyone in her life!'

'We're not talking about me,' said Ruby calmly. 'We're talking about you. You and Owen. Time you two sorted yourselves out. He isn't going to hang around for ever, you know. The war brought you together, but that's over. He's the best thing that ever happened to you, Hazel d'Ark, and you'd be a damned fool to let him get away. Right, Jack?'

'Don't look at me,' said Jack. 'I'm still trying to work out what our relationship is. Besides, I've been married seven times, under various names, and none of them worked out. At least partly because I was married to my job, first and foremost. Being a professional rebel took up a lot of my life. There wasn't always room left for anyone else, no matter how I felt about them.'

'But your job's over now,' said Hazel.

'Don't think I haven't noticed,' said Jack. He started to raise his bottle to his mouth and then stopped, and put it down again. 'I was the man who fought the system. Any system. But with the rebellion over, what am I now? I'm not sure who I am any more, without an Empire to fight. I defined myself, who and what and why I was, in relation to Lionstone and her corrupt rule. Now they're both gone, I don't know what to do with myself that matters a damn.'

'You'll just have to learn a new kind of war,' said Ruby. 'It's called politics.'

'I'm too old a dog to learn new tricks,' said Jack. 'Even if I do have a new young body. I spent my whole life turning myself into a particular kind of man, only to discover there's no need for that kind of man any more. I'm back in the prime of my youth, but I've no one to test it against. Instead, there's just meetings and committees and endless bloody compromises, all the time trying to keep old enemies from each other's throats. And all the time wondering if any of it really matters . . .' He sighed deeply. 'I suppose I could put myself forward as a bounty hunter, like you and Owen, but I can't escape the feeling that everything here will come crashing down in ruins if I'm not here to oversee the change. There's never any shortage of people coming to me for advice or help. They trust me, you see. I'm the legendary saviour, the man who finally gave them their freedom. How can I tell them that their everyday problems bore the shit out of me?'

'Know what you mean,' said Ruby, nodding sagely. 'Know what you mean. Success ruined us. I mean, look at me. I'm rich. Finally, I'm as rich as I always dreamed of being. Maybe even more so; hell, I can't even keep track of it all these days. Got accountants for that. They send me statements, but I can't make head nor tail of them. I never knew there were numbers that big. I track down rich criminals, find where they've hidden their loot, confiscate it and then hand it over to Parliament, minus a hefty commission. Not that I do much of the actual work myself, of course; got a whole bunch of cyberats working for me. They locate the funds, and the bastard's address, and then I just bash my way in there and arrest the guy. They rarely put up much of a fight once I'm past their defences. Hell, most of them burst into tears when they see me walk in.'

'Hold everything,' said Jack. 'Arrest them? Since when did you ever bother with arresting people?'

'Oh, all right then; I break in and kill them, if you insist on being exact. They'd only be hanged by the war trials anyway, and I can't be bothered with the paperwork. Point is, I am now rolling in money. More than even I can spend in a lifetime. Got a big house, servants, all the latest comforts and luxuries. All the things I always thought I wanted. But you can get tired of things real quickly. They're just toys, when you get right down to it. Even shouting at the servants has lost its charm. There's no fun in intimidating someone when you know you're paying them for the privilege. I never thought I'd hear myself say it, but even luxury can become boring, once you've played with all the gizmos. And on top of all that, I have this sneaking suspicion that I'm getting soft, losing my edge. There's always someone standing in the wings, waiting to take it all away from you.'

'Yeah,' said Jack heavily, 'the trouble with fulfilling all your dreams is that eventually you wake up to reality.'

'Oh, very profound,' said Ruby, 'very deep. What the hell does that mean?'

Jack shrugged. 'Damned if I know. But it sounded good, there, for a moment.' He looked across the crowded Chamber at Owen. 'What's he doing, talking to that Wolfe woman?'

'Maybe she's got some lead on where we can find Valentine,' said Hazel.

'Maybe,' said Jack. 'But I wouldn't trust anything that came from that direction. Last I heard, Constance Wolfe was in bed with the Chojiros. Bad Family; bad people. You and Owen would do well to put as much distance as possible between you and anyone connected to Clan Chojiro.'

Hazel looked at him thoughtfully. 'There was something in your voice just then, when you said *Chojiro*. Something cold . . . and angry. What connection do you have with the Chojiros?'

'Yeah,' said Ruby. 'This isn't the first time I've heard you put them down. What makes the Chojiros so much worse than all the other aristocratic scumbags?'

Jack stared at the bottle in front of him, so he wouldn't

127

have to look at Ruby or Hazel. 'My mother was a Chojiro,' he said quietly. 'They threw her out and cut her off without a penny, just because she married the man she loved rather than the man they chose for her. They were all bastards then, and they're bastards now. Never trust a Chojiro.'

'You made a deal with them fast enough,' said Ruby. 'They offered you an easy way out, and you jumped at it. You sold out every principle you ever had when you saved the aristos' asses.'

'It was necessary,' said Jack. 'It took the Families and their private armies out of the war. They could have kept it going for years. With them out of the loop, millions lived who might otherwise have died. Not a bad bargain; what are a few principles compared to people's lives?'

'Even if it means most of the guilty go unpunished for generations of crimes against humanity?'

Jack turned and glared at her. 'That's pretty sophisticated talk from a killer for hire! When did you ever care about humanity? When did you ever have any principles?'

'Never,' said Ruby, 'and I didn't pretend otherwise. But I might have felt differently, in time. I believed in you, Jack. And then you turned out to be just like everyone else.'

It was an old argument, with no end in sight. Hazel turned away and let them get on with it. She looked out across the Chamber, and the crowd seemed to part just in time for her to see Owen take Constance Wolfe in his arms and kiss her.

Finlay Campbell, once again the height of fashion, moved smoothly through the packed crowd like a shark floating on the currents, basking in a sea of prey. His crushed-velvet cutaway frock coat was superbly tailored, snug as a second skin, an electric blue so bright it was almost painful on the eyes. He wore thigh-high bruised-leather boots over canary-yellow leggings, and sported a rose-red cravat at his throat, tied just loosely enough to show he'd done it himself. Such details were important to him. On his nose was a pair of pince-nez he didn't need, and his long hair was tied back in a single, complex plait. Once, such a mastery of fashion, the epitome of the fop and the dandy, would have won him admiring glances from one and all, and perhaps even a smattering of applause as he passed. But that was long ago, in another lifetime.

Finlay had changed during his years as a rebel. His once youthful face was now thin and drawn, with heavy lines at the mouth and eyes. The colour had faded from his hair till it was almost white. He was only in his late twenties, but looked more than ten years older. Although he tried hard, he walked more like a soldier than a man of leisure, and his eyes were frighteningly cold. He looked what he was: hard-worn and dangerous. People moved quickly to get out of his way, even when he indicated he might like to talk to them. Although he was no longer the Campbell, and leader of his Clan, in many ways he had become his late father, that feared and dangerous man – a thought that never failed to disturb Finlay.

His failure to fit in worried him. He'd thought he could simply adopt his old dandy persona again, and everyone would accept him as they always had. But he had changed too much; lost his youth and innocence on too many assassination runs for the underground, and he couldn't go back. His fine clothes could no longer disguise the killer within. Besides, he found the persona so much of an effort these days, pretending interest in the latest social gossip, and the petty politics of Parliament and its hangers-on were nothing compared to the life-and-death struggles of the rebellion. Then, everything he did mattered, had made a difference. Now he was just another minor hero, home from the wars, no more important than a thousand others.

Just another killer, pensioned off too soon.

In the past, he'd always been able to slake his need for blood and excitement in the Arenas as the undefeated champion, the Masked Gladiator. But he'd had to give that up when he'd been forced to flee society and join his love Evangeline in the clone and esper underground. His mentor, the original Masked Gladiator, had taken up the role again in Finlay's absence, so that no one would make a connection between Campbell and the missing Gladiator. But the original Masked Gladiator had died during the rebellion, his bloody end caught live by Flynn's camera as the esper Julian Skye took a vicious revenge for his brother Auric's death in the Arena. With that, the role was lost to Finlay for ever. Even worse, Auric Skye had actually died at Finlay's hand, during his time under the Mask. But of course he could never tell Julian that.

And so the Arenas were banned to Finlay. He couldn't even fight as himself, without the Mask. His style would soon be recognized by the afficionados, and his secret would be out. Julian would hear; would know he'd killed an innocent man. So Finlay put on fine clothes again and walked in society, trying to be the ambassador for the clone and esper undergrounds that he had reluctantly agreed to be. They needed him: or at least, Evangeline had convinced him they needed him. He wasn't sure how much he believed that any more. Sometimes he found himself wondering whether she might have got him his position through her own influence in the undergrounds just to keep him busy, to make him feel . . . useful. He couldn't ask her; she was always busy with her own work, struggling to help the clone underground take its place above ground, as part of the new political scene. It was important work. Sometimes he didn't see her for days. Here was one time in his life when he really needed her comfort, and she wasn't even there.

It was a petty thought, and he did his best to disown it.

He didn't know that Evangeline had seen the growing desperation in his eyes, and arranged as much work for him as she could because she was afraid he might kill himself if he didn't have a direction, a purpose in life. She didn't know he still dreamed of the bulging veins in his wrists, and the sharp edge of a knife, or of a rope noose hanging in the moonlight, and how easy it would be to put it all behind him and find peace at last.

But they still had their love. And as long as they had that, nothing could tear them apart. Or so they believed.

Finlay saw Owen Deathstalker standing alone, and an old anger stirred in him. It wasn't just love that kept him going; there was also an unconsummated hatred that still burned in his heart. He strode over to the Deathstalker, who turned and bowed formally. The forms had to be observed. Finlay made himself bow in return. Owen and Finlay might have fought on the same side in the rebellion, but otherwise they'd never had that much in common. Secretly they disapproved of each other. For Owen, Finlay was a mad-dog killer who might slip his leash at any time and turn on friend as well as foe, and Finlay considered Owen to be a dangerous amateur who thought too much. In public, they were very polite with each other. Usually.

'I have a bone to pick with you, Deathstalker.'

'Join the queue,' Owen said calmly. 'What's your problem, Campbell?'

'Valentine Wolfe. I've only just found out you knew where he was, and you didn't tell me. I have sworn a blood oath against the degenerate bastard. He destroyed my Family.'

'Valentine destroyed a lot of people's families. That's why Parliament put a price on his head and sent me after him. If you were as well connected as you're supposed to be, you'd have heard it too. I can't help it if you've been a little . . . preoccupied, lately.'

'Don't patronize me, Deathstalker!'

'And don't you get haughty with me, Campbell. If anything, I have a better claim on Valentine than you do. He destroyed my whole planet.'

'I will kill him,' said Finlay, 'and anyone else who gets in my way. Even the almighty Owen Deathstalker.'

Owen smiled. 'You could try,' he said politely, and then turned and walked unhurriedly away. Finlay watched him go, and his hands clenched into fists at his sides. Someone put a hand on his arm, and he spun round furious, glad of a chance to take out his anger and frustration on whatever poor fool had dared disturb his thoughts. Only to find Evangeline Shreck standing there beside him, smiling, and the rage left him in a moment as he smiled back at her.

'I got back early,' said Evangeline, taking his hands in hers. 'Thought I'd surprise you. And from the look of you, I'd say I got here not a moment too soon. Who's upset you this time?'

'Oh, just the Deathstalker,' said Finlay, calm again, all the darkness swept away by the sunshine of her smile and the glory of her eyes. He took her in his arms and they hugged each other tightly, as though to force out all the things that separated them by the depth of their love. And maybe they could, at that. After a long while they released each other and stepped back to take a good look.

'God, you're lovely,' said Finlay, and she was. Evangeline was wearing a long dress of sparkling silver, cut away at one shoulder to show off her delicate waiflike bone structure, and her dark hair was cut short in defiance of the current fashion. Her face was high-boned, wide-eyed, vulnerable but determined, and just looking at her again made Finlay all the more resolved to defend her from all the dangers and cruelties in the world. She was his reason for living; the blood that flowed in his veins, the heart that beat in his breast, only for her. Sometimes, when she was away, he forgot that, but now she was back and he was alive and awake again. He wanted to rush out and slay a couple of dragons, just so he could lay them at her feet.

'You look . . . fashionable,' said Evangeline. 'If you were any more colourful, everyone else would appear to be in black and white.'

'Just dressing the part,' said Finlay. 'Subtlety is out, this season. Mind you, you should have seen some of the stuff I wore when I was pretending to be one of the secret masters of style and had to be constantly on the cutting edge of fashion.'

'I've seen the holos. The images are irreversibly seared on to my retinas. Now, what were you so mad about? Not that Robert is continuing as head of Clan Campbell instead of you, surely?'

'Oh, hell no. Let him be the Campbell if he wants. He'll do a much better job than I ever could. I never wanted the responsibility anyway. No, it's a new world for the Families now, and he's far better suited to guide the Clan through it. Good man, Robert. It helps that he's one of the few people who fought for the Empire still to be considered a hero. Last man to leave his ship, defending her against overwhelming odds . . . No doubt there were a lot of other people like that out there, but he was the one who got caught on film doing it. Maybe he can use that image to rebuild the Family, make it what it was before Valentine destroyed it.'

Evangeline nodded slowly. She'd heard the sudden venom in Finlay's voice when he named his enemy. 'So that's why you were so mad at Owen. Save your anger for your real enemies, dear. You'll get your chance at Valentine.'

Finlay forced a smile. 'Let's talk of happier things. What brings you back so unexpectedly?'

'My mission turned out to be a bust. It was all over before I got there; agreements signed, everybody happy. It happens that way, sometimes. So here I am. Glad to see me?'

'Let me get you out of this madhouse and home again, and I'll show you how glad I am,' growled Finlay, pulling her close again.

Their shared laughter was a moment of real warmth in the artificial chill of polite company.

Not far away, Robert Campbell stood watching them. He wore his unfamiliar captain's uniform with a certain stiffness. The high mortality rate in the Imperial Navy had meant sudden and rapid promotion for the few worthy survivors, and Robert wasn't used to his new position yet. He'd expected another ten, maybe fifteen years of service before he got his shot at a captaincy, and now here he was, one of the youngest men ever to make Captain. He felt somewhat like a pretender, and kept expecting someone to burst in and say it was all a ghastly mistake and would he please return the uniform *at once*, because the real captain was waiting for it.

He smiled slightly at the thought; a tall, handsome man with steady eyes and close-cropped hair. Both hair and face had been burned away in the fires that swept the bridge of the besieged *Endurance*. He'd got away in an escape pod, but it had taken long sessions in a regeneration tank to undo the damage to his face, and his hair was only now starting to grow back again. He thought the new look made him appear older, more responsible, and he'd take every bit of help he could get. His new command was the *Elemental*, one of the few E-class starcruisers to survive the rebellion, and he was eager to take official charge of her and see what she could do. But as the Campbell and head of his Clan, he was obliged to spend a certain amount of time on Golgotha, looking out for his Family's interests first. And that meant hobnobbing with the right people at Parliament, making the necessary deals and connections to ensure his people wouldn't be bothered or harassed while he was away on duty aboard his ship. One day he'd have to make the choice between his Family's needs and his military career, but that was . . . one day.

His cousin Finlay was actually looking quite civilized, now that Evangeline had arrived to calm him down. Robert wondered why Finlay had bothered with his new finery. The man was quite clearly a stone-cold killer, and would always look like one, no matter how he was dressed. One day that man was going to run wild, and even Evangeline wouldn't be able to stop him. There'd be blood and death and a scandal no amount of influence could hope to clear up. The victims might be anyone; Finlay was a disaster waiting to happen. And as the Campbell and head of the Clan, Robert was going to have to decide what to do about that; whether or not he should . . . take steps. He sighed gently and shook his head. The military life was a fine training where many things were concerned, but no help at all when it came to dealing with wild cards like Finlay Campbell. Suddenly there was a presence at his side.

'Don't worry about Finlay, boy. Better men than you have tried to deal with him, and they're all dead and cold in their graves while that bastard goes untouched. There is no God.'

Robert turned and smiled at Adrienne Campbell. 'Then why did you marry him?'

'It was an arranged marriage, as well you know. My father arranged it. He never liked me. I'd divorce Finlay in a moment if it wasn't for the children. I don't suppose you could arrange a nice quiet assassination for me, could you, dear? It would solve so many problems.'

'Don't tempt me,' said Robert. 'Besides, who could we send against him? Owen Deathstalker? Kid Death?'

'I wish,' said Adrienne. 'No, let him live. If only because his death would upset Evangeline so much. I'm very fond of Evangeline, except for her appalling taste in men . . .'

They grinned at each other. Adrienne Campbell had a sharp, fiercely determined face under a mop of curly golden hair that was the only angelic thing about her. Regarded by all as the most ferocious intriguer on the current political scene, and the most dangerous, Adrienne had few real friends and so many enemies there was a waiting list. Hard-working, frighteningly intelligent and too damned honest for her own good, Parliament had had to put a time limit on her speeches so anyone else could get a word in edgeways. While not actually elected to any official position, Adrienne represented a number of highly influential pressure groups, and could be relied on to have an acerbic opinion about absolutely anything. Adrienne had taken to the new politics like a duck to water. Years of society scheming and backbiting do that to you.

'So; how are you settling in as Captain?' said Adrienne.

'Slow but steady. It helps that the crew are familiar with my record, and know I earned my position through my abilities rather than my sudden fame. Gaining their acceptance will take time, but I think I'm winning them round. It's been quite a jump from Navigation Officer to Captain, but it's not as though I'm taking anyone else's place. The Fleet's desperately short of experienced officers. If only we were short of enemies . . .'

'Now don't you start,' Adrienne reproved. 'I hear that every day in Parliament. I know the aliens are still out there, and Shub, and let's not forget the bloody Hadenmen, but there just isn't the money or the resources at present to build the Fleet up to what it used to be. The factories are running twenty-four-hour shifts just to produce the ships we need to keep supplies moving between worlds, and starving people now have to take precedence over possible future threats. The rebellion was long past necessary, but sometimes I can't help thinking we could have timed it better. A lot of people died during the fighting, but millions more will die before we're finished rebuilding.'

'It's the birth of a new order,' said Robert, 'and birth is always painful.'

Adrienne sniffed. 'Don't you quote propaganda to me, boy. I helped write most of it. Oh, hell, look who's coming over. As if I didn't have enough problems.'

Robert looked round and hid a wince as he saw Finlay and Evangeline approaching. Evangeline looked friendly, and Finlay was doing his best. Robert sensed Adrienne seething at his elbow, and leaned down to murmur in her ear, 'Take it easy. It won't kill you to be nice to him.'

'Want to bet? Still, you and he should meet, Robert. I know you don't care much for each other, but you are Family. That still means something, even in these confused days.'

'He ran away from the Family to join the rebels when the Clan needed him the most, leaving me to take over as the Campbell. A privilege I never expected, and for which I had no experience.'

'He had no choice; he had to follow his heart and go where Evangeline went.' She snorted suddenly. 'I can't believe I'm actually defending him, even if he did save my life once. Look; he never wanted to be the Campbell. He knew he'd make a mess of it. You were much better suited to the job. You've kept the Family alive when Finlay would have had them go down with all guns blazing. Accept what happened and move on. Try and mend some fences. These days we all of us need all the friends we can get.'

The four came together in a small space that seemed to open up around them. Those in the vicinity recognized a potential flashpoint when they saw one forming, and preferred to put a little distance between themselves and whatever unpleasantness might occur. If only so they wouldn't get blood on their best clothes. Evangeline and Adrienne greeted each other cheerfully, with much clasping of hands and kissing of cheeks. They were old friends and allies. Adrienne had never begrudged Finlay his mistresses, not as long as he continued to turn a blind eye to her many amours, and had been delighted when he finally chose someone she could approve of. The two women had developed strong links during their shared time in the underground, and discussed Finlay scandalously behind his back. Finlay and Robert nodded formally to each other, faces impassive, and then Finlay abruptly stuck out his hand. Robert shook it, after a moment's surprise, and the two men relaxed slightly.

'Congratulations on your new command,' said Finlay. 'First Campbell to make Captain in three hundred years.'

'I'll do my best to do the Family honour,' said Robert. 'You're looking very . . . sharp, Finlay.'

Finlay shrugged. 'You want to play with the big boys, you have to dress the part. It's been a while since I fought my battles with pointed words and barbed *bons mots* rather than cold steel, but I think I'm getting the hang of it again. We've . . . been too distant, Robert. Friends and allies come and go, but Family is for ever.'

'You're the one who never had much time for the Family.'

'I'm trying to change that.'

Robert looked into Finlay's steady gaze, and then nodded slightly. 'You were the one who kept a distance. And I was too busy holding the Family together and serving in the military to search you out.'

'I know that. I'm grateful for what you've done. But I had my own problems, and they kept us apart. Nothing to do with you, or your being the Campbell. We were on opposite sides during the rebellion, but that's all over now. We need to stand together, or our enemies will drag us down.'

Robert raised an eyebrow. 'And what enemies might we have in common, exactly?'

'People like Blue Block, maybe. People who want to turn the clock back, make things the way they used to be. You've no reason to love the old order. You suffered under it more than most. Blue Block stood by and did nothing to stop the Wolfes when they butchered our Clan.'

'And my Letitia died, on what should have been our wedding day. Murdered by the Shreck, in the name of Family honour. While you looked on and didn't try to stop him.'

'I was wrong,' said Finlay. 'I still believed in the Families then, in the honour I thought held us together. I had to learn the hard way. I didn't fight and bleed in the rebellion just to see the Families take control again behind a different mask. I'll do whatever I have to, to stop them. Can I count on you to help? Parliament may not be much, but it's the only hope we have.'

'I never thought of you as a politician, somehow,' said Robert.

Finlay shrugged. 'It's the new battlefield. And I had to learn a new form of fighting, or die of boredom. So; will you stand with me?'

'I'll think about it, and we'll talk further. See if we have as much in common as you think. If we do . . . I think I'd be proud to have the legendary warrior Finlay Campbell at my side.'

'Same here,' said Finlay, smiling for the first time. They shook hands again.

'God help us, they'll be bonding next,' said Adrienne. 'Getting drunk in disreputable bars and telling each other those jokes that only men think are funny.'

'I think it's sweet,' Evangeline remarked. 'We all need friends.'

'Hello, Adrienne,' said Finlay, putting on his best polite face and voice. 'You're looking very . . . you.'

'I suppose that's the nearest you'll ever get to a compliment,' said Adrienne. 'I see you're still using the same tailor. Did I hear he's got himself a new guide dog?'

'You're so sharp you'll cut yourself one of these days. You and Evangeline had a good gossip, have you?'

'I hear you're trying to get into mainstream politics, Finlay. One word of advice: don't. They'll eat you alive. You're way out of touch with the way things are now, and frankly you were never that hot even when you were in the thick of things. I've no doubt you mean well, but the last thing we need is another enthusiastic amateur, raising everyone's hackles and muddying the waters. Especially someone with your temper. You can't kill your opponents just because you're losing the debate. They have laws against that sort of thing now. Though admittedly that might add a little excitement to the budget debates . . . Look, Finlay, I know you, though I often wish I didn't. You're too soft-hearted for politics. It would mean too much to you. You couldn't bear to lose one argument so you could win another later. You get out of hand in this business and I won't be able to save you. Nor will anyone else, for all your great exploits in the rebellion. Heroes are ten a penny, these days.'

'You're sounding very you, as well, Addie,' said Finlay. 'One of these days you'll say something nice to me, and I may faint from the shock. I survived everything the Empire could throw at me, and the horrors of Haceldama. I think I can handle a few politicians. Don't worry; if I have to kill anyone, I'll be sure and do it when no one's looking.'

'The trouble is, he means it,' said Adrienne. 'That's his idea of being diplomatic.'

'In the meantime,' said Finlay, 'I want to see our children.' They all looked at him in surprise, including Evangeline. Adrienne shook her head slowly. 'Finlay, you've never wanted to see the children. Not even when they were born. I have to remind you to send them birthday presents. They only know what you look like from watching the holos. And where the hell were you when Gregor Shreck was threatening to have them killed, to get at you? Give me one good reason why I should let you anywhere near them!'

'I've been feeling my mortality lately,' said Finlay. 'When I'm gone, all that will be left will be my reputation and my children. I look at what the news people and the docudramas have made of my past, and I don't recognize myself at all. That just leaves my children, and I'd like them at least to have some idea of who I really was. I know I've done questionable things, but I always thought I had a good reason for what I did. In the past, I was busy living two lives at once, and I told myself there was no room for children in either of them. They would only have got hurt. They were safer with you. Besides, I didn't know what to do with children. I'm not sure I do now. But I'd like to try to get to know them now. If they'd like to see me . . .'

Adrienne was taken aback for a moment. In all their years of marriage, she'd never heard Finlay open up like that before. 'I'll ask them,' she said finally. 'But it's up to them. I won't say a word, one way or another.'

'That's all I ask,' said Finlay.

The four of them talked a little more, but didn't really say anything; they'd taken care of all their business. Eventually Adrienne and Robert made their excuses and moved off into the crowd, and Finlay and Evangeline were left together.

'We've never talked about . . . children,' said Evangeline quietly. 'Given the lives we were leading during the rebellion, it just wasn't possible. We were always racing off into danger and sudden death, never knowing for sure whether we'd live to see tomorrow. And afterwards, you never raised the subject.'

'I've been thinking about a lot of things I never did before,' said Finlay. 'I never wanted children with Adrienne, but my father required it, for the Family. Things are different now.'

'I couldn't bring myself to mention it,' said Evangeline, not looking at him. 'I was always afraid you never said anything because I was just a clone. You're an aristocrat, but I'm not; not really. I was made; manufactured to replace a murdered Shreck daughter. Some would say I'm not really human. And even in our marvellous new order, the marriage of an aristocrat and a clone would be a scandal, their children an outrage. If anyone found out . . .'

'You're more human than most of the people I have to deal with,' said Finlay. 'You're worth a hundred of them. A thousand.' He took her in his arms and she sank into his embrace, her face pressed against his shoulder so he wouldn't see the tears in her eyes. He knew they were there anyway, but carried on as though he didn't, his voice carefully steady. 'I can't marry you, Evangeline. Not because you're a clone, but because divorcing Adrienne would distance me from people I need to be close to. Politics in our circles are still largely dictated by old Family connections, and my position is precarious enough as it is. But you are my love, my life; the only woman I've ever cared for. Of course we can have children, if that's what you want. People will make allowances; they always have. And by the time our children are grown, hopefully this kind of nonsense won't matter any more, and you will be my wife in name as well as fact.'

Evangeline hugged him so tightly she thought she must be hurting him, but he never said anything. When she was sure her eyes were dry, she let go of him and stepped back. They smiled at each other, and all the love in the world glowed from their eyes. Then someone came and called Finlay away on urgent business, and Evangeline was alone again. She watched him go with a brave smile on her face, but inside, her thoughts were churning furiously. Before she could even think of starting a family with Finlay, there was a lot she had to sort out in her own life. Most of it Finlay didn't know about, and must never know.

Finlay knew Evangeline had been cloned from a dead original, but he didn't know why. Gregor Shreck had loved his Evangeline as a man, rather than as a father, and had finally murdered her in a fit of rage when she tried to run away. To cover up his crime, and have his daughter in his bed again, Gregor had the clone made in strictest secrecy, and she became the Evangeline that Finlay came to know and love. He rescued her from her father and helped her make a new life of her own. But he never knew just what he had rescued her from, and Evangeline could never tell him. If he ever found out, he would go mad with rage and horror at what had been done to her, and he would murder Gregor, not giving a damn for the consequences. She couldn't let him do that. She wanted Gregor dead, wanted it with a deep, despairing sickness of heart for the endless rapes and humiliations she had endured, for making her feel like a thing, his property, to do with as he wished.

But Finlay must never know. It would hurt him so much. And perhaps also, deep down, she feared he'd never feel the same way about her again once he knew the truth. Besides, Gregor Shreck was a powerful and dangerous man, even if he had fallen from favour just lately. He surrounded himself with an army of private guards, and even Finlay Campbell couldn't take on a whole army single-handed.

She couldn't risk losing him. Not now, not after they'd gone through so much to get here. That would be too cruel, even for her.

Secrets. So many secrets, between two people.

And there was more. Before Gregor retreated into his Family Tower, disappearing behind his mini militia and enough corrupt influence to keep even Parliament's hounds at bay, he'd contacted Evangeline to let her know he'd taken her best friend, Penny DeCarlo, as his prisoner. And that dear Penny would die in horrible agony if Evangeline didn't return to him. Finlay didn't know about that, either. She hadn't told him. If she did, once again he'd go rushing off to be the hero for her sake and get himself killed. It was her problem – she'd deal with it. So far she'd kept Gregor at bay with the aid of various stratagems, but they'd mostly run out now. Soon she would have to find a way to rescue Penny that didn't involve Finlay, or go back to Gregor and hope to sort out some kind of deal. Either approach had its dangers, but her time in the rebellion had hardened Evangeline, despite herself. She was no longer the weak, helpless victim that Gregor remembered. And maybe, just maybe, that was a weapon she could use against him.

Not far away, someone else was watching Finlay Campbell. The esper Julian Skye had been Finlay's friend and disciple ever since the Campbell rescued him from the torture cells of the Imperial interrogators. Julian still carried the scars, on his body and in his mind, from the awful things that he had suffered, but he owed his life to Finlay, and had dedicated that life to the Campbell's service. The Campbell didn't get a say in the matter. Julian had followed Finlay through many adventures in the rebellion, but now the war was over Julian found himself at a loose end. No longer the daring adventurer of the esper underground, he felt lost without an enemy to battle. And now his mentor Finlay had found a new life in politics, he didn't need a warrior at his side any more. Julian understood nothing of politics, and cared even less.

He was currently occupied with portraying himself in docudramas about his times during the rebellion. He'd never seen himself as an actor, but apparently people had really liked watching him in the news footage Toby and Flynn had shot, and nowadays that was enough to make you a star, if not an actor. He'd never be a major attraction, but he had an audience and a faithful following, and he made more than enough money to indulge his few vices. It helped that the memories he'd dictated to the screenwriters had been almost entirely fictional. The public wanted the legend, not the facts, and there was still so much he couldn't bring himself to talk about. Including the woman who was standing not so far away from him; that petite, dark-haired oriental beauty, BB Chojiro.

He'd loved her once. Loved her with all his heart; dedicated his life to her, lived for her every word and glance. And she betrayed him to the Imperial torturers. He was a rebel, and the 'BB' in her name stood for Blue Block, the secret inner circle of young aristos conditioned to be loyal to the Families to the death and beyond, and she had turned him in. There in the torture cells, she had said she still loved him, but she had to follow her conditioning.

But now Blue Block was running the Families, for their own good, and BB Chojiro was the pleasant public face of that inner circle. She had come to Parliament, as usual, to stand quietly at the back to listen to all that was said. She rarely had anything to say for herself, but everyone knew that when she spoke, she spoke as the voice of Blue Block, and everyone listened. If they knew what was good for them.

This was the first time Julian had come to the Chamber. The first time he'd dared to come to Parliament. To be so close to BB Chojiro . . . Part of him still desperately wanted to kill her, for what she'd done to him, for what had been done to him because of her, for the betrayal of everything he'd thought they had between them. Part of him needed to see her lying crumpled at his feet, the blood pouring out of her as she died slowly and horribly. And part of him wondered if even now he'd forget all that, forgive her everything, if she would just take him in her arms and kiss him and love him once again.

Frightened, he stayed away. But now here he was, not ten feet away from her, and damned if he knew why. Perhaps it was just unfinished business, as simple as that. Whatever; he had come to Parliament, to see her and perhaps talk to her. And if he didn't kill her, he might just learn how to be free of her. If that was what he really wanted. Julian had to smile; he was so messed up in the head where BB Chojiro was concerned, that it was either laugh or go mad.

He'd tried to have her killed several times. He couldn't attack her openly; the deal Jack Random had made now protected all aristocrats from the old customs of personal revenge and vendetta. But he'd worked through intermediaries to acquire the services of the best assassins money could buy. Alone and in groups they infiltrated Tower Chojiro, passing by the many layers of security with professional ease. None of them ever came out again. Nothing was ever said. Julian still had to pay the bills.

BB Chojiro stood at ease among her advisors, smiling and listening and saying little, a tiny doll of a woman in a bright scarlet kimono the exact shade of her lips. She had dark, straight shoulder-length hair; huge dark lustrous eyes; she was the most beautiful woman Julian had ever seen. He ached to hold her in his arms again: it was a physical need like a hunger, or an addiction. To feel her lips on his, her warm breath in his mouth . . . And then maybe he'd kill her, or maybe he wouldn't. He didn't know. He hadn't decided yet.

Standing beside BB Chojiro, unnoticed by the obsessed Julian, stood Stephanie Wolfe, sister to Valentine, stepdaughter to Constance. Tall, blonde, boyishly slim, she brimmed over with barely suppressed resentment. Her position both in and out of society and Parliament was precarious, to say the least. When her late father Jacob had been the Wolfe, the Clan had been one of the most powerful Families in the Empire. Then Jacob died, and Valentine took over, and it all went to hell. Now Valentine was on the run, Jacob's dead body had been transformed into a Ghost Warrior by the rogue AIs of Shub, and Stephanie's beloved brother Daniel had gone off in search of it. Which meant that only Constance and Stephanie remained to represent Clan Wolfe in the highest circles.

'I should be the Wolfe,' said Stephanie, not for the first time.

'Of course you should,' said BB Chojiro, flashing her a smile that meant nothing, nothing at all. 'And you will be. Blue Block has promised you this.'

'You talk and talk, but nothing changes,' Stephanie scowled. 'Constance cannot be the Wolfe. She has no right. I am Jacob's blood. She just married him.'

'Have I mentioned recently how obsessed you are on this subject, Stephanie? Just one of the reasons why so many of your peers prefer Constance as the Wolfe. They see her as more . . . approachable. We meet as little as I can arrange, but still I know your refrain so well I could practically say it along with you. Please, let us change the subject, before my ears begin to bleed. Any sign of Daniel yet?'

'No.' Stephanie's scowl deepened, as honest concern changed her mouth from its sullen pout to a flat, compressed line. Daniel was the only person apart from herself she still gave a damn about. 'He was last seen heading into the Forbidden Sector. No one seems to know how he got past the Quarantine ships. The only thing he faces now is Shub. Poor damned fool.'

'Yes. Let us wish him the comfort of a quick death.'

'No! He's no threat to Shub. They'll see that and send him home again. What could they hope to gain by hurting someone as harmless as him?'

They hurt us because they can, thought BB, *because they are artificial, living metal and have only hatred for all that is flesh.* 'Yes,' she said aloud. 'Let us hope for a miracle. Hope costs nothing.'

Stephanie sniffed. 'Whatever happens, Daniel will survive. He's a Wolfe, after all. But if the Clan is to continue, I must lead it. Constance cares nothing for the Family. Our legacy does not breathe in her. As you suggested, I have been moving, unseen, through the lower orders of the Clan, gathering support. Many are unhappy with an outsider, not of the blood, as the Wolfe. They would support me if I found it necessary, for the good of the Clan, to take . . . certain steps.'

BB turned to Stephanie for the first time, and fixed her in place with her dark, unwavering gaze. 'I have said before; you are not to kill Constance, or have her killed, in any way that might be traced back to you. The deal we made with Random prohibits such measures.'

'We may have no choice,' Stephanie said stubbornly. 'You saw Constance talking to Owen. You know as well as I what they were discussing. A marriage between her and the Deathstalker could put the whole House of Wolfe under their joint control. Clan Deathstalker might even consume Clan Wolfe, and then our name would vanish from history. That cannot be allowed. We must strike at Constance while we still can. With Owen guarding her, we'd never be able to touch her.'

'As always, you think too small, Stephanie. With Constance and Owen married, it shouldn't be too difficult to control Owen through threats to Constance. He might not love her, but as his wife he would be obliged to protect her, or suffer much loss of face before society. It wouldn't take much to make the threats convincing. Constance is quite unable to protect herself, and even a great warrior like the Deathstalker can't be everywhere at once. Owen is practical enough to understand the realities of the situation. He will cede control of Clan Wolfe to you, and then we will control both the Wolfe and the Deathstalker Clans.'

'Wait a minute,' said Stephanie. 'What do you mean, control Clan Deathstalker? There is only Owen. He's the last of his line, the last Deathstalker. He saw to that when he killed his ancestor.'

'You really must learn to think of the future, Stephanie. If he marries, eventually there will be children. In Blue Block, we always think in the long-term.'

'I hate it when you lecture me,' snapped Stephanie. 'I'm not a child. I'm not stupid. I just don't care about anything but rebuilding my Family. Everything else has to wait. But then, you wouldn't understand that, would you? You had all the pride in your Family brainwashed out of you once you were given to Blue Block. Hell, they even took your name away from you.'

BB Chojiro smiled gently. 'I lost little, and gained much. Blue Block is the sum of all the Families. Through it we shall all attain greatness. I gave up my old name willingly. It did not describe me any more. BB is who and what I am, who and what I have made of myself through Blue Block, and I take pride in my achievement.'

'Yeah, well; that's because you're a mind-wiped zombie who wouldn't know an original thought if you fell over it. God, Blue Block did a job on you. What the hell did our Families think they were doing when they created Blue Block? You were supposed to be our ultimate weapon, to give us control over the Throne. And now we all bow down to you. We made our own collars and fastened them round our necks without even realizing.'

'Quite,' said BB Chojiro. 'Now please be quiet, or I'll tug on your leash. An old friend is approaching. Perhaps he has good news for us.'

Cardinal Brendan had once been a Jesuit commando in the service of the Church of Christ the Warrior. He killed the heretics and the ungodly, or any who dared threaten the Church's strength or position. The Church of Christ the Warrior had been the official religion of the Empire, and closely associated with the Empress Lionstone. So when the

146

Iron Throne was finally toppled, the Church fell with it. Rebellion gave the people a sense of their own strength and power, and they used it to rid themselves of a Church that had been oppressing them for centuries. From the ashes of the fallen Church arose the smaller but much more respected Church of Christ the Redeemer; a non-violent, charity-orientated Church led by Mother Superior Beatrice Christiana, the Saint of Technos III. Her first official action had been a purging of the old Church's most offensive sinners and its most disreputable elements, but she missed Brendan. He was Blue Block, and they looked after their own. He was now Cardinal Brendan, the new Church's representative on Golgotha, and Blue Block's main agent in the Church.

He wasn't particularly memorable in person; tall, dark, with a sardonic smile and an eyebrow always on the point of being raised. He dressed simply but well, and since he made a point of talking to everybody with equal attention and favour, no one minded that he occasionally talked quite openly with the notorious BB Chojiro. He bowed low to BB, and again, not quite so low, to Stephanie Wolfe.

'Well met, gentle ladies. To what do I owe the pleasure of this summons? Parliament usually manages to get along just fine without my august presence.'

BB calmly waved for her advisors to move away a little. They bowed, and did so without protest, stopping just out of earshot. They knew there were always plots within plots, to which even they were not always privy. BB smiled at Cardinal Brendan.

'You are here because Owen and his friends are all here. The Maze survivors. If Blue Block is to survive and prosper, they must be brought into the fold, or eliminated. Their unusual abilities and unorthodox opinions make them random elements, loose cannon, and if we do not control them, they will inevitably control us. That is the nature of all power. So, since we value your opinion, you are here to study and evaluate these four people as possible future friends or enemies. Who can be turned or pressured, persuaded or bribed?'

'And if they really are what they're supposed to be, and aren't interested in any of those things?' said Brendan.

'Then we require your most informed advice on how best to dispose of them,' said BB calmly.

'You don't want much, do you?' said Brendan. 'Lionstone with all her people and her resources couldn't handle these four, but you think we can?'

'All things are possible, given enough time and planning,' said BB Chojiro. 'They still think in terms of open warfare and the clash of armies; the gun and the sword and the simple joys of slaughter. They are as yet inexperienced in the more subtle forms of conflict. And they are, after all, so much more − how shall I say? − reachable now, than they were before.'

'They won the war against the Families,' said Stephanie. 'You lost. Remember?'

'We lost a battle,' said BB. 'The war continues, in other ways.'

'Still, better watch your ass, Cardinal,' said Stephanie. 'Side too openly with Blue Block, or raise the ire of one of our great rebel heroes, and Saint Bea will throw you right out of the Church, just like all the others.'

'Nothing will happen to our most loyal cardinal,' said BB. 'Dear Brendan has the support of many Blue Block alumni within the new Church. Reports will be misfiled, paperwork lost, rumours misdirected. Mother Beatrice hears what we wish her to hear.'

'You wouldn't be the first person to underestimate Saint Bea,' said Stephanie. 'And most of those who did are dead, or wish they were.'

'She isn't immortal,' said Brendan. 'If she were to die suddenly, unexpectedly, the new Church would be thrown into utter chaos. Just the kind of situation Blue Block has always best profited from. And the remnants of the old order, the Brotherhood of Steel, is still out there, though officially suppressed, just waiting for a chance to take control of the Church again. They meet in private, worship in the old ways, and have secret friends and supporters in high and low places. Like us, they gain power and influence through carefully planned assassinations, or the threat of them. You'd be surprised how many of today's movers and shakers secretly bow down to the Brotherhood.'

'And Blue Block controls the Brotherhood of Steel,' said BB Chojiro. 'Most of the people Mother Beatrice purged from her precious new Church were our people, and always have been. Saint Bea may have won the populace's heart for the moment, but they're a fickle breed. They can always change their minds. Or have them changed.'

'And then Blue Block will run the Church as well as Parliament,' said Brendan.

'You don't own Parliament yet,' said Stephanie. 'In fact, they show distressing signs of developing a will of their own.'

'It's only a matter of time,' said BB calmly. 'Now, why don't the two of you find something not too incriminating to talk about, while I take care of some personal business.'

She left them standing together, trading suspicious looks, and made her way gracefully through the crowd to stand before the esper Julian Skye. He saw her coming and made as though to walk away, but in the end he stood his ground and waited for her. She stopped just out of arm's reach, and smiled up at him. Julian nodded curtly, his face impassive.

'Hello Julian,' said BB in her sweetest voice. 'It's been a long time since I last saw you. You're looking good.'

This last was a polite lie, and both of them knew it. Julian had never really recovered from the terrible injuries he suffered in the interrogation cells, and it showed in his undernourished frame, and deep-set, haunted eyes. The late Giles Deathstalker had worked something of a miracle cure in him on the nightmare world of Haceldama, but like most miracles it turned out in the end to be not much more than skin-deep. It didn't last. Julian Skye hung on to what remained of his health through grim determination, and it showed.

'Hello BB,' he said finally. 'You look beautiful, as always. Betrayed anyone interesting recently?'

BB shook her head. 'You never did understand me, Julian. I had no choice. The moment you told me you were a rebel, my feelings for you were swept aside and my conditioning took over. I couldn't even warn you they were coming. I cried and cried afterwards.'

'Yes,' said Julian. 'I saw you, when you came to me in the interrogation cells, to talk me into betraying my friends and my colleagues. You said I was scum, the lowest of the low.

And then you walked away and left me to the torturers. All the time I was screaming, I thought of you.'

'I had to say what I did. Others were listening.'

'What do you want, BB?' said Julian harshly. 'I loved you, I trusted you. Only to find I meant nothing to you. Nothing at all.'

'I wanted . . . to see if we could still talk to each other. I have missed you so much, Julian. Blue Block is my life and my purpose, but nothing ever touched my heart like you. With you, I could dream of being free; free from Blue Block, from its mastery. Only it turned out to be stronger than I was. A part of me died the day they took you away, and I want it back. I want things to be the way they used to be again.'

'You must think I'm mad! I know about Blue Block now, I know about you. You'd do anything, say anything, to serve your precious higher cause. Fool me once, shame on you. Fool me twice, shame on me. You mean nothing to me any more, BB. I cut you out of my heart, one inch at a time. It hurt like hell, but I felt so much better once you were gone.'

'Don't. Please, don't.' She reached out to him with both hands, but he shrank back rather than touch her. She dropped her hands, and her eyes filled with unshed tears. 'Oh, Julian. What have I done to you? My feelings for you were genuine, then, though I couldn't give in to them. Now, things have changed. I've changed. Because of my position, Blue Block has given me more and more freedom and room for personal initiative. I used that freedom to break myself some way free from their conditioning. At last I'm free to follow where my heart leads. People can change; you must believe that. We could be together again, Julian, Like we used to be, only better. There are no secrets between us any more.'

'There will always be secrets, as long as you still represent Blue Block.' Julian shook his head jerkily, fighting to keep his voice steady. 'Go away, BB. Whatever game you're playing, I don't want any part of it. What we had, what I thought we had, was never more than a dream. And I've woken up now. It took me a long time to get over you, BB. I won't put myself through that again. Just go. Please.'

'I'll go,' said BB. 'I'll walk away and never see you again. Just as soon as you tell me you don't love me any more.'

'BB . . .'

'Just tell me that, and I'll go. Even though I love you. I'd rather die than see you hurt again. Just say you don't love me.'

'I don't love you.'

'Liar,' said BB Chojiro, softly, lovingly.

'Oh, God, of course I love you, BB. I'll always love you.'

She reached up and placed her fingertips on his mouth. 'You don't have to say any more, my darling. I know how difficult that must have been for you. But trust me; things will be different, this time. I'm free now of many of my old constraints. Still, I think we've said enough for now. We have time . . . all the time we need. Goodbye, my love. For now.'

She turned and walked away, back to Brendan and Stephanie and her advisors. Julian watched her go, not knowing what to say or think. She'd given every indication of being honest and genuine, but none of that mattered because she was Blue Block. She'd seemed to be reaching out to him, but Julian had no way of knowing why. All he knew for sure was that his heart was beating again the way it used to, when he still knew what happiness was, when his love had been something more than just a road to damnation. Julian Skye cursed himself for a fool for still believing in happy endings.

Toby Shreck and his cameraman Flynn made the rounds of the Chamber, exchanging smiles and pressing the flesh with one and all. It seemed everyone wanted his approval, now he was head of Imperial News. He did on-the-spot interviews with practically everyone, and hoped to sort some gold from the innumerable practised sound bites in the editing suite later. Politicians were born with the ability to say much while committing themselves to as little as possible, but Toby had experience in getting them to confirm more than they meant, and say more than they realized. Until they saw it on the news. Toby stayed on much longer than he meant to, simply because he was thoroughly enjoying himself. This was real news-gathering, bracing old friends and enemies with the same friendly smile while digging out the truth no matter what they threw in his path.

When they'd first offered to make him head of Imperial News, Toby had jumped at the chance. It was everything he'd ever dreamed of; a chance to run a news department the way he thought it should be run. But sitting behind a desk, second-guessing the people out on the ground, had quickly palled. No matter how hard he tried to set policy, to pursue the truth ruthlessly and get great ratings, he was still limited by the courage and doggedness of the people in the field. He hired the best he could, but none seemed to have the nose for news or the sheer tenacity in hunting down a good story that had made his a household name across the Empire. And he did so miss the thrill of the chase. So here he was, doing it himself again, and loving every minute of it. It helped that he was completely impartial, despising all politicians equally. Toby had yet to be convinced that the new boss wasn't just the old boss in new clothes.

Eventually the Members decided they were ready, struck their most impressive poses and gave the order for the door to the Chamber to be flung open. Everyone in the Chamber rushed forward into the House, trampling the slower-moving underfoot. It had to be said that the House itself wasn't all that impressive. Parliament had been nothing but a rubber stamp for so long that its central building had been allowed to grow distinctly tatty and overcrowded. The two ranks of seats on either side of the open floor were packed with MPs till they were practically sitting on each other's laps. Previously it had been a wonder and a miracle if a quarter of the seats were filled at any one time, but these days the Members were all desperate to be seen on the news. Most had forthcoming elections to consider, and with a new universal electorate, they needed at least to be seen to be doing something.

The floor of the House quickly filled with people as the outer Chamber emptied, and the air was full of flying cameras trying to elbow each other aside for the best angles. The MPs sat carefully upright in their seats, looking down on everyone else. Their PR people had warned them of the dangers of slouching. It made them look undignified on camera. Endless researchers had been hired, to dig out old Parliamentary customs they could use from the days when Parliament still meant something, but the Members hadn't quite got the hang of most of them yet. For example, nowadays all MPs proudly wore the traditional black and scarlet gowns and powdered white periwigs, but so far no one had had the heart to point out that actually the gowns and the wigs came from Parliaments centuries apart.

Their latest big idea had been to appoint an official Speaker of the House; someone who owed no allegiance to any particular party or cause, and could therefore keep order with true impartiality. A good idea, in principle. Unfortunately, they'd chosen Elias Gutman for the job, supposedly because he'd been on so many sides at various times that he could truthfully be said to represent everyone's interests. In fact, Gutman had been elected to the post because he bribed most of the MPs and intimidated the rest, a practice that had always done well for him in the past.

It was said that Elias Gutman had a hand in every dirty deal in the Empire, though people were careful how loudly they said it, if they weren't tired of living. Gutman's Family had banished him from Golgotha in his disreputable youth, and sent him money regularly as long as he promised not to come home, an arrangement that suited both parties. Gutman had used that money and his new freedom to become the first-class villain he'd always known he was inside. He even helped fund the rebellion, just to hedge his bets.

But so many of his Family had died fighting on both sides on Golgotha, that Elias found himself the most senior member of his Family by default, and was invited to come home at last. He wasted no time in barging his way into the political process, sensing that this was where the real power and wealth would lie in the new Empire. He then proceeded to make a name for himself by bringing together a series of warring parties, from extremely opposed positions, and persuading them into a compromise they could both live with. He had many successes where others had failed ignominiously. Mostly because both sides were too intimidated or beholden to him to disagree with whatever he suggested. Though of course, that part was very rarely discussed afterwards. And now, Elias Gutman was Speaker, with power to decide who was and who was not allowed to be heard in Parliament. Many MPs had been heard to ask how it was they had got themselves in that position. But they were careful to ask it very quietly.

Even more unfortunately for all concerned, Parliament had made this important appointment while Owen Deathstalker was off chasing Valentine Wolfe and his associates. The first Owen heard of all this was when he docked at the starport. Everyone was waiting to see what his reaction was going to be. People were torn between a desire for the best seat and a need to keep their heads well down, or at the very least out of the range of fire. Owen didn't disappoint them. The moment the Chamber doors opened he surged furiously forward into the House, Hazel striding cheerfully beside him. Owen ignored the plaintive cries of the stewards as they tried to steer him to the assigned public area, and headed straight for Gutman, who was sitting on a raised platform between the two ranks of seats.

Two armed guards moved forward to block his way. Owen punched out one, kicked the other in the groin, and just kept going. Hazel followed on behind, stepping gracefully over the groaning bodies on the floor. Gutman stirred a little uneasily on his seat. He had arranged other, hidden methods of protection, but suddenly face to face with the dreaded Owen Deathstalker, he wasn't quite as sure of their efficacy as he had been. Owen came to a halt directly beneath Gutman's raised seat and glared up at him.

'All right; what mentally deficient bunch of dickless wonders elected this crook as Speaker? I turn my back on you for five minutes, and you throw open the doors and invite the fox into the hen house. Why didn't you hand over the crown jewels to him as well, while you were at it? In fact, I think I'll check them right after I leave here, and if just one piece is missing, someone is going to suffer and it sure as hell isn't going to be me. Why *Gutman*, of all people? If there's any vile trade in the Empire that he hasn't profited from, it's only because he hasn't found out about it yet. The man deals in death and suffering; God knows how much blood he has on his hands.'

'And how many have died at yours, Sir Deathstalker?' said Gutman smoothly. 'We've all had to do distressing things to get where we are today. But this is, after all, supposed to be a new order. A chance for everyone to remake themselves anew. To build new lives and careers, entirely separate from our past history. Or don't you believe in second chances, in redemption?'

'Not where you're concerned,' said Owen flatly. 'Grendels will turn vegetarian before you reform. I know you, Gutman.'

'The fact remains,' Elias Gutman continued, 'that I have been freely elected to my position as Speaker of the House by these good men and women present. Or do you defy their authority?'

'Don't try and twist this!' said Owen, his voice rising angrily in spite of himself. 'I didn't spend years on the run as an outlaw, and wade through blood and slaughter in the streets of Golgotha, just to see power handed over to such as you! I don't know how you managed to escape the war trials, Gutman, but you won't escape me. Now come down off that seat or I'll come up and get you.'

'You can't touch me. I have the protection of Parliament. The people you yourself helped place in power. Have you no faith in your own creation?'

'Not when they screw up this badly.'

'So you elevate yourself above their authority? Just like the aristocrats you threw down because you said they abused their power? Can anyone spot the irony here? You're not a hero any more, Deathstalker, making up your own rules as you go along. You're just another citizen of the Empire, subject to the authority of the people, as expressed through Parliament.'

'To hell with that! I never needed a Parliament to tell me what was right and wrong! Now get down here or I'll kill you where you sit!'

'You defy Parliament's will!'

'To hell with them! I'll kill anyone who gets between me and you! I'll tear down this whole House around your ears if that's what it takes!'

Armed guards came running from all sides as the MPs broke into an excited babble. With anyone else, what they'd heard might just have been empty threats, but this was Owen Deathstalker – he might actually do it. Gutman gripped the arms of his chair tightly, but kept his face calm. He'd manipulated the Deathstalker into losing his temper and undermining his heroic image. Now all he had to do was live through it.

'Typical Deathstalker threat,' he said steadily, making sure his voice was heard over the rising hubbub. 'To hell with how many die, as long as he gets his way. I suppose we shouldn't be surprised. After all, it was his ancestor, the first Deathstalker, who activated the Darkvoid Device, and murdered untold billions of innocents.'

Hazel clung grimly to Owen's arm so he couldn't draw his disrupter. The guards looked on anxiously. Hazel grabbed Owen by the chin with one hand and forced his face round to meet hers. 'Don't, Owen. You'd have to kill a lot of innocent men before you got to Gutman. It would be the ruin of you. He isn't worth that.'

Owen jerked his face out of her hand and glared at her, breathing hard. 'I thought you at least would understand.'

'I do, Owen, I do. But this isn't the time, or the place.'

It had gone very quiet in the House. Everyone was waiting to see what the Deathstalker would do. The guards kept their guns trained on him, but were careful to do nothing that might provoke him into action. Owen looked slowly about him, and then smiled slightly. Some of the anger went out of him, and he let his hand drop away from the disrupter at his side. There was the sound of a great many people breathing out. Owen nodded to Hazel.

'What are things coming to, where you have to lecture me on restraint? But you're right; there'll be a better time.'

He turned his back on Gutman and strode off to join the watching crowd standing in the appointed area. Hazel gave Gutman a hard look, and then hurried after Owen, just in case. Not far away, Jack Random and Ruby Journey were applauding. A great many others looked as though they would have liked to. The guards lowered their weapons, picked up their two fallen fellows and retreated as fast as honour would allow. Toby Shreck grinned from ear to ear, confident that Flynn had got it all on tape.

Elias Gutman waited a moment to be sure his voice was steady, and then opened the Session's proceedings with a short, emotional speech composed entirely of stirring platitudes and sound bites. The speech was applauded for being short, and then Parliament finally got down to business. First on the agenda was a report from the cyberats currently investigating Golgotha's Computer Matrix for signs of infiltration by the rogue AIs of Shub.

A viewscreen appeared before the assembled Members of Parliament and the public, floating in mid-air. Vivid colours flashed across the screen, and then resolved into the head and shoulders of whoever was acting as spokesperson for the cyberats today. They tended to be rather relaxed, if not downright arbitrary, about such matters, having little concern for the demands of the world outside their precious computers. The cyberats lived for the time they spent immersed in cyberspace, and never appeared in public if they could help it. Anyone who'd ever seen one knew why. They had enough tech implants, add-ons and cutting-edge options to qualify technically as cyborgs, and their personal habits bordered on disgusting, more through absent-mindedness than anything else. They cared only for tech and what it could do for them, and often disregarded the needs of the mere meat they lived in.

The current representative, who rejoiced in the code name of Wired Bunny, looked like he'd died several days ago and been dug up especially to make this report. His skin was a dusty grey, and his face was sharp and bony to the point of emaciation. A nutrient tube was plugged into a vein in his neck, and a computer jack disappeared into his empty right eye socket. He smiled vaguely at his audience, revealing a set of truly awful teeth.

'Like, wow, so many people in one place. I can dig the ambience from here. Greetings and salutations, meat people, this is the very heavy-metal dude Wired Bunny making nice with you. Hallelujah, let's all speak in tongues! Power to the people who believe they're real, and to those still thinking about it. To everyone else, the secret is to bang the neurons together, guys. Me and my totally buzzed-in associates have been surfing the silicon in the Matrix in search of those utterly bad metal mothers from the place we don't mention, and so far I have to tell you we've found utterly squat. Zip, *nada*, less than zero. Lots of signs that something mega's been and gone, but don't ask who or what or where, unless you want a lot of technical-speak that even we don't understand half the time, because we're having to make it up as we go along. We're the frontier, people, and it sure is strange out here.

''Course, it hasn't helped that large areas are marked Off Limits by the larger business constructs. Paranoia city, cousins. We'll break through eventually, if only because we do so love a challenge, but it is slowing us down some. Don't suppose you heavy business dudes would care to volunteer the entry codes? No? Didn't think so. Damn, these negative vibes are freaking me out. Hold on while I boost my endorphins again. Oooh . . . groovy. You guys talk among yourselves for a bit, I think I'm going to have a little lie-down and fry a few brain cells I'm not currently using. Wow, the colours, man.'

'Wait!' said Elias Gutman. 'Haven't you anything useful you can tell us?'

'Oh, sure, large dude, I like entirely forgot. I wrote it on a Post-It somewhere . . . ah. "Beware the dragon's teeth". Cool. Over and out and gone, man.'

The viewscreen disappeared, taking the cyberat with it. There was a long pause. Gutman looked at Owen. 'As I recall, you recommended these . . . people, Sir Deathstalker.'

Owen shrugged. 'They're weird, but they know their business. The way computers are these days, the two facts are probably not unconnected. Spending enough time in the Matrix will drive anyone crazy, and the cyberats go there for fun. If the AIs have left any trace of what they've been doing, these are the only people who have any chance of detecting them. And we have to know. The AIs said they'd infiltrated all the major human businesses, and have been manipulating our economy to their own ends. Now they could have been just saying that, for the panic it would cause, but we can't take any chances. If it is true, we need to know how far the infiltration has gone and how long it's been going on, before we can even start to put things right.'

Gutman nodded reluctantly, his face impassive. 'But your own, er, expert said none of the cyberats have been able to find any traces of outside meddling.'

'If there's one thing Shub knows better than us, it's computers. They'd have hidden their tracks in places normal humans wouldn't even think to look. Luckily, the cyberats aren't remotely normal.'

'At last you've chanced upon something we can agree on,' said Gutman heavily. 'I only wish I shared your confidence in them. Perhaps you could enlighten this House with your best guess as to what these *dragon's teeth* are, that we're supposed to beware.'

'I would have thought that was obvious, even to you, Gutman. The AIs also claimed they'd been ripping the minds out of people as they entered the Matrix, and substituting their own thoughts. The dragon's teeth are the people walking among us who are no longer people, wearing men's faces but thinking Shub's thoughts. The perfect spies, even less detectable than Furies. We have no way of knowing how many there may be out there, or how deeply our security has been penetrated.'

'Which brings us very neatly to my petition before the House,' said a harsh voice from the crowd. People looked round to see who it was, and then backed hastily away as they recognized the short, spectral blonde with eyes as cold as death. Once, her name had been Jenny Psycho, and she had been an avatar of the mysterious and enigmatic uber-esper Mater Mundi, Our Mother of All Souls. Power beyond all dreams and reason had burned in Jenny Psycho, and she had only to frown for the air around her to crackle with potential. But she was no longer all that she had been, abandoned by the Mater Mundi, and had reverted to her old name of Diana Vertue. She was still a power to be reckoned with, and most people had the good sense to be very nervous when she was around. These days she represented the esper underground in Parliament, mainly because everyone else in the underground was too worried by her to disagree. She moved forward through the crowd, and people hurried to get out of her way. She stopped before Owen, who bowed politely to her. Truth be told, she worried him a little too, but he didn't believe in letting people see things like that.

'Hello, Diana. You're looking very normal. What petition might this be?'

'To have all the esp-blockers removed from Parliament so we can scan the minds of all present, to find out if everyone is exactly who they claim to be.' Diana's voice was harsh and ragged, and utterly intimidating. She'd damaged her throat screaming in Golgotha's prison cells, and it had never really recovered. She looked coolly about her, and even the innocent shrank back a little. 'The esp-blockers must go. It's not just Shub we have to worry about. Remember the shape-changing alien that turned up at Court? It mimicked a man so exactly that even his friends couldn't tell the difference. The only way we can maintain real security in Parliament is by mass esp-screening, with no abstentions permitted. Seems a perfectly reasonable request to me.'

'That's because you're weird,' said Gutman, and practically the whole House nodded in agreement. 'What you suggest is totally unacceptable. Everyone is entitled to the inviolability of their own mind.'

'For once I have to agree,' said Owen. 'We all have secrets that must be kept to ourselves, even if they're really only important to us. Or perhaps especially those. But I do see your point. Maybe we could work out some kind of voluntary system . . .'

'Go right ahead,' said Gutman. 'You first.'

Owen smiled slightly, despite himself. 'Let's pass this one on to the Church. They have experience with the confessional.'

'We'll take it under advice,' said Gutman. 'And if that doesn't suit you, esper Vertue, feel free to take it up with the appropriate subcommittee. At some other time. However, this does lead neatly on to our next piece of business. Though just once I wish people would stick to the agenda. As part of the deal Jack Random thrashed out with the Families, clones and espers are no longer property, but citizens in their own right. Laudable and just as that may be, it has led to certain unexpected problems. For centuries, trade and industry throughout the Empire were based on the unlimited availability of clone and esper labour. They now have to be replaced by paid workers or new technology, both of which are proving extremely expensive. Change is always costly, and someone's got to pay for it all.

'Since we've finally got the tax computers working again,' and here Gutman and his audience paused to glare at those responsible for the computers' destruction, namely Owen and Hazel, who smiled and nodded modestly, 'our first thought was a rise in the basic rate of income tax. But the citizenry soon got to hear of this, and quickly made it clear that they regarded it as a very bad idea. They pointed out that they were already paying for the Empire-wide repairs made necessary by the extensive fighting during the rebellion, and were therefore doing their bit. They suggested that the aristocracy, as the wealthiest among us, should shoulder the bill. The Clans not unreasonably pointed out that their loss of power and control through Random's deal had reduced many of them to near-pauperism, and they really didn't think it was fair that they be punished any further. Dark hints were dropped about the collapse of Family industries if they were pressed, and all the mass unemployment that that would cause. Extensive discussions, negotiations and any number of committees have quite failed to reach any useful conclusions.'

'He makes even longer speeches than you do, Owen,' murmured Hazel. 'I'm impressed.'

'And you needn't look to the undergrounds either,' said Diana. 'We're already having to support the families of clones and espers thrown out of work by new technology. While they were property, the Clans supported their essential needs. Now they're free citizens, they've washed their hands of them. Freedom's all very well, but it doesn't put food on the table.'

Owen thought he'd never heard so many people being so ungrateful, and felt like saying so. But he didn't, because he just knew they'd find some way of blaming it all on him. And he didn't know who should pay for it all, either. Economics had never been his strong point. As a Lord, he'd had people to do that sort of thing for him, and as a rebel he'd concentrated on fighting and left everything else to the underground leaders. He was a warrior, not an accountant. He looked at Hazel, who shrugged.

'Don't ask me. My ideas for a fairer redistribution of wealth involved becoming a pirate and a clonelegger. Neither of which worked out particularly well.'

'The problem is the rate of change in the Empire,' said Diana Vertue. 'It's too slow.'

'The problem is it's too fast,' said Gutman.

'You would say that,' said Diana. 'It's you and your kind who have the most to lose.'

'We're just concerned about changing too rapidly from a system based on people to one based on tech. We don't want to end up like Shub.'

Diana scowled intimidatingly. 'That's just a smokescreen, Gutman. The undergrounds don't want clones and espers replaced by tech; just better working conditions and an equitable day's pay. You're just changing to tech to avoid that.'

'Which brings us neatly back to money,' said Gutman, leaning back in his chair and looking out over the assembled crowd. 'With everything in turmoil, and our economy running wild with no one at the helm, inflation has shot through the roof. Prices are rising everywhere, even on the most stable planets. Savings have been wiped out. Banks have collapsed. The Families are doing all they can to support the credit, but the only thing they all agree on is that things are bound to get worse before they get better. Whatever else you can say about the old order, it always maintained the value of the credit. Even if the Empress had to hang a few bankers to make her point.'

'How about a tax on pompous windbags?' Hazel suggested sweetly. 'Or a windfall tax on those who have managed to profit very nicely from the changing situation? That ought to raise a fair amount of cash.'

There was a growling and a muttering, but no one had the nerve to demand that Hazel retract her comment. Partly because they didn't want to legitimize the question, and partly because she might do something very unpleasant and quite possibly fatal if she thought she was being slighted. This was Hazel d'Ark, after all.

'Please let us all try not to see this in terms of personalities,' said Gutman severely. 'I think it might be best if we were to move on to the next order of business.'

'But nothing's been decided about the last question!' Owen objected.

'I said, we're moving on,' said Gutman. 'As Speaker, I am in charge of the agenda.'

'I told you,' said Owen, glaring about him. 'I warned you this would happen.'

'I could have you removed,' said Gutman.

'You could try,' said Owen.

'Please,' said Hazel.

'We will now move on to the next order of business,' said Gutman. 'General Beckett, officer in charge of the Imperial Fleet, is waiting most patiently to address us.'

A floating viewscreen appeared almost immediately, as though it had just been waiting for its cue, and the head and shoulders of General Shaw Beckett scowled impartially at one and all. His large square head was set upon a pair of massive shoulders, though most of his intimidating bulk remained out of sight. His uniform stretched tightly across his great frame, and pinned to it were medals beyond counting. His wide mouth was set and stern, his dark eyes unwavering. As always, he was smoking a large cigar, and paused occasionally to blow smoke at the camera.

'About time you got round to me. Right: pay attention, and take notes if you have to, because I'm damned if I'm going through this again. Ever since the Fleet was blown apart during the rebellion by outlaw ships and those bloody Hadenmen vessels, we've been struggling to operate a skeleton service. Most of the starcruisers are gone, D- and E-class, and we're having to rely on destroyers and revamped frigates to carry a workload they were never intended to handle. We're short of crew, too. There are plenty of volunteers, but it takes time to train real crewmen. Can't let just anyone loose on a starship.

'We're using the bigger ships to protect food routes to the hardest-hit planets. There are lots of hungry people out there, but so far we've managed to avoid large areas of actual famine. Pirates have been a problem, attacking the convoys to sustain their black markets; there's always someone ready to profit from other people's suffering. We kill them as fast as we can catch them, but there are always more. What ships we have left over are on patrol, mostly out on the Rim, watching for the insect ships.'

His face disappeared from the screen, and was replaced by the familiar sight of an alien insect ship. It resembled a huge ball of sticky white webbing, tangled together, tightly compacted. Weapons and force shields of unfamiliar design were there, unseen. One such ship had murdered every living soul in an isolated Imperial Base, and then almost wiped out Golgotha's main cities before Captain Silence and his crew destroyed it. No one knew where the alien ship had come from, or what they wanted. The one certainty about the aliens was the ferocity of their attack and their murderous intentions. The image of the ship disappeared, and General Beckett spoke again.

'Given the limited number of ships at my disposal, I cannot risk launching any kind of pre-emptive strike. All I can do is respond to alien attacks, as and when they happen, drive the ships off and then try to clean up the mess they've left behind. So far, we've been lucky enough to avoid the major destruction and slaughter the first ship brought to Golgotha, but luck has a nasty habit of running out. The bottom line is, people are dying out here on the Rim, and there's damn all I can do about it. I must have more ships!'

'We're building them as fast as we can, General,' Gutman said sharply. 'But there are difficulties. There won't be any more E-class ships until we can establish a new stardrive factory to replace the one that was destroyed in the rebellion, and come up with something to replace the clones who previously performed the dangerous task of actually assembling the drive. And, of course, even D-class ships are horrendously expensive, at a time when every expense has to be weighed and justified. As long as the alien ships don't pose an immediate threat to the main Empire—'

'You'll sacrifice the people of the Rim planets to avoid having to raise taxes on everyone else.' Beckett snarled openly at the camera. 'Rulers come and rulers go, but nothing really changes. Look, the insects came to Golgotha once, and right now we don't have anything to stop them making a return visit. You can't keep relying on Captain Silence and his people to bring off a miracle at the last moment. He couldn't save Lionstone from the rebels. The insect aliens are as much a mystery now as they ever were. We still don't know where they come from; they just appear out of nowhere, make their attack and then disappear again.'

'As long as we keep them from getting too annoyed with us, there's a real chance they will confine their attacks to the Rim, and not return to plague us here,' said Gutman. 'A bleak philosophy, I'll admit, but in these desperate times we have no choice but to think in terms of the greatest good for the greatest number. We are not abandoning the Rim worlds. We authorize you to remain where you are, and give them all the protection you can. As soon as new ships are available, they will be sent to join you. But that's all I can offer. Now, unless you have anything else to bring up . . .'

'As it happens, I do,' said Beckett. 'There's something happening, out here. Disturbing reports have been coming in from all along the Rim, concerning the Darkvoid. And from any ship that spends too long near the eternal night. There are reports of whispers, dreams and uncertain contacts coming out of the darkness. Voices of the dead, crying warnings. Visions of wonders and nightmares, fleeting contacts with things that come and go in a moment. Espers have had dreams of a door opening and closing, and something awful peering through. There've been too many reports, from normally trustworthy sources, for me just to dismiss them. I am forced to make the only logical conclusion: there's something alive in the Darkvoid.'

For a long moment, everyone was quiet. In the nine hundred and more years since Giles Deathstalker used the Darkvoid Device to put out a thousand suns in a moment, killing the billions of people on the planets that orbited them, no one had really learned anything more about the vast area of utter night called the Darkvoid, save that ships which went into it rarely returned. Gutman turned to Owen and Hazel.

'Sir Deathstalker, you and Miss d'Ark were the last people to travel deep into the Darkvoid and return. Perhaps you could . . . shed a little light on this phenomenon?'

'This is all news to me,' said Owen. 'We never encountered anything like that. Just because my ancestor created the Darkvoid Device, it doesn't mean I'm any more of an expert than anyone else. If Giles kept any secrets about the Darkvoid, he never passed them on to me. But I really don't see how anyone or anything could be alive in there. There's nothing left in the Darkvoid to support life. No light, no heat, nothing to feed on . . . how could anything exist there?'

'Not life as we know it,' said Beckett from the viewscreen, 'but who knows what forces the original Deathstalker unleashed when he activated the Device? We still have no idea what it was, or how it did what it did. Who can say what nightmares might be lurking in the darkness, birthed in a moment of mass slaughter and the worst horror?'

'That's ridiculous!' said Owen.

'Is it?' said Beckett. 'When you went into the Darkvoid, you came back with the revived Hadenmen, an old monster we thought we were well rid of. There could be anything in that darkness. Anything at all.'

Everyone was looking at Owen and Hazel, but they said nothing. There were things they knew about the nature and origin of the Darkvoid that no one else knew, but they had sworn long ago, for very good reasons, to keep those secrets to themselves. They were too dangerous to be trusted to anyone else. Besides, there was no obvious link between what they knew and the phenomenon Beckett had described. Or so they hoped.

'Speaking of the Hadenmen,' said Beckett, after the silence had dragged on for a while, 'we come to the last part of my report. I think we were all somewhat surprised when the revived Hadenmen joined the rebel forces to overthrow the Empress, and we were even more surprised when we discovered they were actually obeying orders, and taking prisoners when the Empire forces surrendered, rather than just butchering them all as they had in the past. They were, after all, the official Enemies of Humanity, until the AIs of Shub replaced them by being even more nasty and dangerous.

'You assured us they had reformed, Sir Deathstalker, you said we could work with them. We should have known better. We should never have trusted cyborgs, men who threw away their humanity in the search for perfection through tech, who launched the great Crusade of the Genetic Church, dedicated to destroying humanity and replacing us with themselves. The men-machines in their golden ships; the butchers of Brahmin II. Well, Sir Deathstalker, your old allies have returned to Brahmin II, destroyed their defences and taken control of the planet and its population. They've renamed it New Haden, and surrounded it with a blockade of their unbeatable ships. The few reports that got out before all communication was cut off said the Hadenmen had been experimenting on the prisoners they'd taken, turning them into new, improved Hadenmen. And that they'd declared the entire population of Brahmin II was next.

'We have no idea of what's happening down there now. And since we don't have a hope in hell of getting past the golden fleet, we have no way of rescuing the people of Brahmin II. Unless, of course, the Deathstalker has some ideas? He is, after all, the man who loosed the Hadenmen on humanity again!'

A growing rumble of anger moved through Parliament, from the MPs to those gathered watching on the floor of the House. It was a dangerous sound, and died away only when Owen glared about him. 'They were a necessary evil,' he said flatly. 'We couldn't have defeated Lionstone's Fleet without them. Ask General Beckett. I had hoped the augmented men had moved on beyond their old agendas. I knew one Hadenman who was as fine a man as any I ever met. But it seems I have been betrayed again by those in whom I placed my faith. Still, let's not exaggerate the dangers of the situation. They only hold one planet, and as yet they don't have enough forces to do anything but defend it.'

'Are you suggesting we abandon the people of Brahmin II to their fate?' said Gutman. 'I don't think the Empire would stand for that.'

'Why not?' said Owen. 'Isn't that what you were proposing to do with the people of the Rim planets? Sacrificing the few in the name of the many? No, Gutman, I'm not suggesting we write off Brahmin II's population. If only because the Hadenmen might eventually create a whole new army out of them. Hazel and I will go to Brahmin II, alone, and see what we can do to rectify the situation. I am, after all, responsible.'

'Hold everything,' said Hazel. 'When did I volunteer to go on this suicide run?'

'Well, you don't want to miss out on all the fun, do you?'

'There is that,' said Hazel. 'I just like to be asked, that's all.'

'The House gratefully accepts your proposal,' said Gutman, 'and wishes you all good fortune. You're going to need it. Is this acceptable to you, General Beckett?'

'Damn right,' said Beckett. 'It's his mess; let him clean it up. But just in case they fail, we'd better consider the practicalities of scorching the whole damn planet, and hope we get as many of the inhuman bastards as possible before they can escape. And yes, that would mean scorching the human population too. Sometimes war's like that. Beckett out.'

The viewscreen disappeared, taking Beckett with it. A quiet muttering ran through the assembly. Gutman smiled down at Owen, who braced himself. Something bad was coming his way, he could just feel it. Gutman leaned forward, his voice entirely reasonable. 'But before you leave us, Sir Deathstalker, we feel there are a few questions we would like answered, concerning the various war criminals this House has sent you after. We can't help noticing that you do tend to bring them in dead, rather than alive.'

'For some reason, they don't seem to think they'll get a fair trial here on Golgotha,' said Owen. 'The fact that not one accused war criminal has been found innocent by these trials of yours has not escaped them. So, not unexpectedly, they want to fight to the death rather than be taken. Don't blame us for a situation you've created.'

'We prepare our cases very thoroughly,' said Gutman smoothly. 'We find them guilty because they are guilty. Surely you don't think I'd allow my fellow ex-aristocrats to be falsely accused?'

'This from the man who killed his own father to get on,' said Hazel. 'Pause, for sustained hollow laughter.'

Gutman shrugged. 'Things were different then. I am

168

another man now. Or don't you believe people can change, my dear ex-pirate and ex-clonelegger?'

Hazel scowled but said nothing, for which Owen was very grateful. He would have had to try to defend her, which would undoubtedly have led to harsh words from both sides, and, knowing Hazel, the possibility of open violence.

'The war trials exist to show the people of the Empire that justice is being served,' said Gutman.

'They exist because they're popular,' said Owen. 'People need scapegoats. What are you going to do when you run out of real villains, Gutman? Start investigating anyone who dares disagree with this new order of yours?'

'Only the guilty need fear the people's justice,' Gutman replied.

'And you decide who's guilty.'

'Parliament decides.'

'And you speak for Parliament,' said Owen. 'How very convenient.'

'Let us move on,' said Gutman. 'Next on the agenda is a proposal which I think will guarantee some lively debate. I'm sure I don't need to remind most of you that many seats will be contested shortly in the first free elections since the fall of the Iron Throne. What you may not be aware of is that many ex-aristocrats have expressed their intention to stand for many of these seats.'

'No way in Hell!' said Owen, his voice rising sharply over those of the gathering around him. 'I didn't fight a war to throw those bastards out of power, just so they could sneak back in! The deal Random made was clear: the Families renounced political power in return for being allowed to survive as financial institutions. Let them get into Parliament, through bribes and intimidation as likely as not, and they'll just end up running things again!'

'You really must learn to curb your paranoia, Sir Death-stalker,' said a chilly voice, and everyone turned to look. Grace Shreck met their gaze with a mien of cool indifference, her nose stuck firmly in the air. Since Gregor's forced withdrawal from public scrutiny, his older sister Grace had taken over as head of the Family, and to everyone's surprise was making an excellent job of it. Toby and Evangeline had both been too busy and were, in addition, reluctant to take over as the Shreck, so the position had fallen to Grace pretty much by default. Her time in the limelight seemed to have agreed with her.

Long, tall and more than fashionably thin, with a pale, swanlike neck, a pinched face and a massive pile of white hair stacked on top of her head in an old-fashioned and precarious-looking coiffure, Grace made a striking picture among the more colourful birds of prey that surrounded her. Ancient and austere, Grace hadn't been out in public regularly for years. She'd hated attending Court, and only did so when bullied into it by Gregor.

But she'd taken to the less formal and infinitely less dangerous Parliament with astonishing ease, and was now a spokesperson for many of the older Families, who trusted her precisely because she'd been out of touch for so long, and therefore had no attachments to any particular Clan or cause. She wore clothes so old-fashioned they were actually in vogue again, and possessed a quiet style and brittle wit that had won her the respect of many. The acceptable face of the ex-aristocrats, the holo audiences adored her, and would listen to arguments from her they would have shouted down from any other aristo.

'Everyone has a right to stand for Parliament,' Grace said primly. 'A democratic right. Isn't that one of the things you claimed to be fighting for, Sir Deathstalker; that everyone be treated equally? Ex-aristocrats have as much a right to be heard as anyone else. After all, you yourself were once a Lord. Are you saying you should be banned too, your voice withdrawn? You are not the only member of a Family to understand the concepts of redemption and atonement.'

Owen scowled. 'I could have taken power. I chose not to.'

'How very noble of you. But who is to say you might not change your mind in the future? I really cannot see what all the fuss is about. We are talking about free elections, taking place under safeguards you yourself helped to set up, with people voting according to their own consciences. If some of them choose to place their trust in a member of a Family to represent them in Parliament, that is their business and no one else's.'

'It's not as simple as that, and you know it.' Diana Vertue glared across the floor of the House at Grace Shreck, who smiled condescendingly back. Diana's scowl deepened, but she kept her temper under control. 'The espers will not place themselves again under the power of those who once treated them as property. Who mistreated, abused and murdered them at will.'

'The excesses of the past are deeply regretted,' said Grace calmly. 'All the Families understand that they have to prove their worth and place in the new order, and none of us are stupid enough to risk that place by resuming old and discredited practices. All of us have done things in the past that it pains us to remember, but we must learn to look to the future. The Families have much to offer. Everyone here understands what you suffered, esper Vertue, how you were left physically and mentally scarred, but we cannot allow one woman's obsessions to stand in the way of progress.'

Diana clung grimly to her self-control. This wasn't the first time Grace had sought to undermine her arguments by referring to her past self, Jenny Psycho, whose mental stability had been somewhat changeable. She couldn't respond to the accusation directly – *all right, I was crazy then but I'm better now* didn't exactly inspire confidence – so, as always, she ignored the insult and bulled on regardless.

'The espers will never bow down to aristos again. We broke free of our chains through blood and suffering and the sacrifice of many; we will not be shackled again.'

'Pretty rhetoric,' said Grace, 'but essentially meaningless. This talk of masters and slaves is from the past; let it stay buried there. The rest of us have moved on. And, as I have pointed out in this House before, I dispute your claim to speak for all espers. You distanced yourself from the official underground leadership when you began talking openly of your distrust of the Mater Mundi, and your following among the rank and file is not what it was. You speak only for yourself these days, esper Vertue.'

'Then let's talk about Blue Block,' said Finlay Campbell, and many heads snapped round to look at him. Finlay didn't often speak out in Parliament, but when he did everybody listened, not least because he was always blunt and to the

171

point and to hell with whoever got upset. The cameras floating overhead rushed to zoom in on him. Finlay smiled coldly across at BB Chojiro and her people. 'How can we trust the Families, when most of them are still under the influence of a once secret organization, Blue Block? Who knows what plans they have, and what secret ends they might still be pursuing? Their motives, like their background, remain largely unknown.'

BB Chojiro stepped forward, her voice rising sweetly in the quiet. 'The fact that we are no longer secret should put an end to most of those fears. We have come out into the open both to restrain and rebuild the Families, to make them once again a positive force within the Empire. Yes, in the past we were created to be the Clans' personal assassins, deadly agents aimed at their enemies, but we have evolved beyond that. And you of all people have no right to criticize us. How much blood is on your hands, Sir Campbell? How many died under your blade?'

'Not enough, apparently,' said Finlay, and everyone shuddered just a little at the bleakness in his voice.

'I think we've taken this argument as far as it can go, for the moment,' said Gutman. 'Let us move on, please. We have a holo message from Her Holiness, Mother Superior Beatrice Christiana. She is too busy overseeing relief work on Lachrymae Christi to speak to us in person, but she recorded this for us earlier.'

He gave a sign and a viewscreen appeared. Beatrice's head and shoulders filled the screen, her white cowl surrounding her tired face like a halo. There were dark smudges under her eyes, and when she spoke her voice was ragged with exhaustion. 'I'll keep this short; we're up to our lower lip in work, and sinking fast. The war has left half the planets in the Empire existing at barely subsistence level. Only Beckett's food ships are holding off mass starvation. Social, political and business structures have collapsed everywhere, and in the resultant chaos people are dying from lack of food, shelter and medical supplies.

'The Church is overseeing relief work wherever it can, but our funds and our people are limited. Parliament must make more resources available to us, or whole populations will revert to barbarism, or worse. Millions are dying. Millions more will die if something isn't done soon. The Church's work these days is wholly concerned with charity; you have my personal assurance that all monies voted to us will go directly to ease the suffering of the needy. The old days of corruption and militarism are gone. Help us, please. Help us to help those who need us.'

The screen went blank, and disappeared. There was a certain amount of uncomfortable stirring. Golgotha had taken its wounds during the rebellion, but in the end had come through largely unscathed. On a world still rich, it was easy to forget that many others had not been so lucky. Elias Gutman leaned forward in his chair. 'We will of course take Her Holiness's request under advice. Though once again, I must point out that there are many calls on Parliament's limited means. We will consider the matter further in this House once the appropriate committee has made its report. But now, we have one last piece of business to discuss. Something that I think practically everyone here can agree on is our need for an official head of state; someone to represent the government personally to the people. After much discussion on many committees, it has been decided that we should appoint a constitutional monarch.'

There was immediate uproar. Everyone wanted to speak at once, and no one was willing to back down. Gutman tried to wave them all to silence, but for once was completely ignored. Sitting back in his chair, he let them get on with it. Owen stood silently in the midst of the hubbub and thought about it. Even though he'd destroyed the Iron Throne, the crown still existed, and legally he supposed there was nothing to prevent Parliament from appointing a new Emperor, if they were stupid enough to do so. He felt very tired. He'd been through so much to overthrow Lionstone, but more and more he was beginning to wonder if all his efforts had been for nothing.

Finally the noise died down, and Gutman was able to make himself heard again. 'Nothing will be decided without this House's full approval! We are suggesting a purely *constitutional* monarch, with no actual power or legal authority. A figurehead, whose duties would be entirely public and social in nature. It would, of course, have to be someone that everyone could trust and support. The committees have come up with what I think you will all agree is the only suitable choice – Owen Deathstalker!'

There was uproar all over again, and a great deal of more or less spontaneous applause, from those who approved of honouring such a great hero, to those who saw the advantages of removing the Deathstalker from the political process once and for all. Owen was shocked silent for a long moment, and then his voice rose above the general din, cutting it off immediately.

'No way in hell am I wearing the crown! If I'd wanted to make myself Emperor, I could have done so when I over-threw Lionstone. I didn't want the crown then, and I don't want it now!'

Gutman smiled easily. 'Most people here seem to think it's a good idea, and an honour you richly deserve. And who more suitable to be a constitutional monarch than a man who openly says he has no interest in power? Though we may have our differences, Sir Deathstalker, I do not hesitate to acknowledge all you have done to make this Parliament possible. Your heroic exploits have restored democracy to us. Who better to represent it to the people? And think on this, Sir Deathstalker; if not you, who? A Campbell, perhaps? Or a Wolfe? Or a Shreck? You are perhaps the only aristocrat who could approach the crown without an agenda. Come, Owen, you have always known your duty. Think about it. We'll get back to you.'

Owen nodded stiffly, still scowling. Hazel looked at him, and her face showed nothing, nothing at all.

Then there was a new disturbance at the back of the crowd, and the people moved aside as two men pushed through, heading implacably for the open floor of the House. Everyone recognized Captain John Silence, but the dark and brooding figure at his side was a mystery. Once, Silence's companion would have been Investigator Frost, as attached to him as his shadow, but she died defending the Empire, struck down by that notorious traitor, Kit SummerIsle. The new figure was, if anything, even more disturbing than Frost had been. He moved in silence, graceful as any predator, and people looked away, unable to meet his eyes. Then some recognized what the man in black was holding, and a shocked murmur rippled through the crowd. It was a power lance; a banned weapon from the old days of the Empire, banned because it could make an esper so strong that no one could hope to stand against him. No one had seen an esper bearing a power lance in centuries. It meant death just to own one.

Captain Silence stood at the front of the crowd and nodded brusquely to the House. He was a tall man in his late forties, with a thickening waistline and a receding hairline, and eyes that had seen far too much but had never been able to look away. One of the few who'd fought for the Empire still to emerge a genuine hero, he'd kept his head down since the great reorganizations began. There were many on both sides who would have liked to remove such a powerful figure from the game, but he was potentially too useful to be taken off the board just yet. Never knew when you might need someone for a last-ditch suicide run. And besides, the public did so love its heroes. The Fleet kept Silence busy till the higher-ups decided what to do with him. And now here he was, unannounced, unexpected. No one had ever seen him in Parliament before. The crowd went very quiet, and waited for him to speak. Silence nodded curtly to Gutman.

'Sorry to burst in, but this won't wait. I've just returned from the planet Unseeli, out on the Rim. We're all in big trouble.'

'Oh, hell,' said Gutman. 'Does nothing but bad news come from the Rim these days? What is it, Captain, the insect ships?'

'Worse,' said Silence, 'it's Shub.' He let the crowd and the MPs confer for a moment before continuing. 'I was on a regular supply run to the single Imperial Base on Unseeli, where scientists were studying a crashed alien ship of unknown origin. We dropped out of hyperspace to find that the whole planet had been destroyed. The metallic forests that covered the world from pole to pole, provider of the heavy metals that power our traditional stardrives, have been completely harvested. Billions of trees, and every one gone.

'The Base is destroyed, blown apart, every man and woman dead. The alien ship is gone. Shub took it. The only

175

living thing to survive the Shub attack was the man at my side; once an Investigator, now a traitor, living alone on Unseeli as an outlaw. His name is Carrion. I brought him here to tell the story, with my personal guarantee of his safety. I trust this is acceptable?'

'Yes, yes,' said Gutman impatiently. 'We trust your judgement in this, as always. Tell us about the Shub attack. Why didn't the Fleet detect it?'

'No one sees Shub, if they don't want to be seen,' said the man called Carrion, in a voice like a dead man talking. Tall and whipcord lean, he wore dark leathers under a billowing black cape. He had a young face, deathly pale under long black hair, and cold dark eyes, proud and unyielding. He was like some grim crow, telling tales after the battle was over. 'They came out of nowhere, thousands of ships like nightmares cast in metal, filling the skies. They flew untouched through the planet's violent storms, and tore the forest up by the roots. They slapped aside the Base's force screen as though it wasn't there, and smashed it flat. I heard the screams of the men and women as they died. Shub took the alien ship, along with whatever scientists happened to be on board at the time. The attack was over almost as soon as it began. Then they began the harvesting. Once, there had lived among the metallic trees a wondrous alien race called the Ashrai. The Empire exterminated them so as to have uninterrupted access to the metal trees. But their souls survived, tied to the trees. I heard them screaming as the gold and silver forest was ripped from the earth.

'I survived, underground, protected by my psionic abilities. I am the only living survivor of Unseeli. The Ashrai are dead, the humans are dead and the trees are gone. I am Carrion. I bring bad luck. I am the destroyer of nations and of worlds.'

He stopped talking abruptly, and the silence stretched on as everyone looked at each other, caught up in the spell of the dark man's words and the terrible news he brought. Finally Gutman cleared his throat uncertainly, and looked down at Carrion and Silence.

'We . . . thank you for this intelligence. If Shub has taken all the trees, we can only assume that they must be planning a major assault on humanity. The heavy metals from the harvesting would fuel one hell of an armada, while at the same time denying them to us. And if they've got the alien ship, it won't be long before they have the secrets of the new stardrive, just as we do. Except that with the ship gone, our work on perfecting and better understanding the new drive becomes more urgent than ever. Thank you for bringing us this news, Captain Silence. As always, you serve us well. You may go now, but we'll need full reports from both of you.'

'Understood,' said Silence. 'We'll make ourselves available. One last thought for you to chew over: an esper once told me he had a clairvoyant vision of what Shub had planned for humanity. He wouldn't tell me what he saw, but he killed himself rather than risk living to see it come true.'

Parliament was a sea of whispers, rocked by too many shocks. Gutman leaned back in his chair, his voice carefully calm and reasonable. 'Precognition is the least understood and the least reliable of the esper abilities, Captain. Whatever vision your esper may have had, I don't think we should put too much faith in it. We make our own future, and forewarned is forearmed. It's clear, though, that someone must investigate what Shub is up to.'

'I'll volunteer,' said Jack Random loudly. 'If an attack's imminent, we need to know. And I'm one of the few people who could hope to get close to Shub's dealings, and still come back alive to make a report.'

'Ah, hell,' said Ruby Journey. 'Guess I'll go along as well, for the ride.'

'Your offer is welcomed,' said Gutman. 'It only remains for me to thank Captain Silence and his companion for the timely news they brought. Go with Parliament's best wishes. No doubt you are eager to return to your ship. Carrion, you will of course have to turn the power lance over to the proper authorities before you can leave.'

'No,' said Carrion, 'I don't think so. This lance is a part of me. You might as well ask me to give up an arm or a leg.'

Gutman frowned. 'Power lances are banned, and with good reason; they are forbidden throughout the Empire. Silence's word gives you protection, outlaw, so we do not demand your death. But you cannot be permitted to keep the lance.'

He gestured with one fat hand, and a dozen armed guards stepped forward, their guns trained on the man called Carrion. He looked at Silence, who shrugged. Carrion smiled coldly at Gutman.

'Try and take it.'

The light seemed to darken suddenly throughout the House, and there were shadows everywhere. Things flitted about in the gloom, or hung threateningly out of sight overhead. Tangible presences moved among Members and public, huge and cold and unseen. There were glimpses of jagged teeth and great curved claws. A heavy wind was blowing from nowhere, gusting and violent. Something howled; a long and savage sound with nothing human in it. More voices rose on every side. A malevolent rage could be felt hovering like a stormcloud, that might fall on the assembly at any moment. Guards clutched their guns tightly, but didn't know where to point them. Owen and Hazel, Jack and Ruby stood back to back, ready for whatever came. People clutched at each other, trying to look in all directions at once. They were only moments from panicking, and a stampede for the doors that would leave a lot of people dead, trampled underfoot.

And then suddenly the presences were gone, the wind dropped and all was quiet and still again. People began to subside, glancing fearfully about them. On his chair on his raised dais, Gutman licked his lips nervously and cleared his throat. Everyone looked at him, but he was looking only at Carrion.

'What . . . what was that?'

'The Ashrai,' said Carrion. 'They died long ago, when Captain Silence gave the order to scorch Unseeli, but their ghosts lived on. Once, they haunted the metallic forests, but now the trees are gone, so they haunt me. They protect me.'

'Oh, hell,' said Gutman, 'keep the bloody lance. It's the least of our worries just now. Now get out of here and take your unnatural friends with you.'

Carrion nodded calmly, turned and headed for the doors, Silence at his side. People hurried to get out of their way. All except one: Diana Vertue stood in their path, and Carrion and Silence stopped before her. Diana nodded brusquely to Carrion, and then fixed her wounded eyes on Silence.

'Hello, Father,' said Diana.

'Hello, Diana,' said Silence. 'I heard you'd taken your old name back. I'm glad. I never really liked Jenny Psycho.'

'She was a real part of me. She still is, deep down. I've just . . . moved on from her. I had to give her up because I found out the hard way that I wasn't who I thought I was. When the Mater Mundi worked her will through me, I thought I was her avatar, her focus, her saint on earth. But she abandoned me, took away the grace and the glory, and left me to live out the rest of my days as a lesser being, no longer touched by heaven. Left me alone; just like you did, on Unseeli.'

'It wasn't like that,' said Silence.

'Yes it was,' said Diana. 'It was just like that.' She looked at Carrion. 'I heard the Ashrai sing, on Unseeli. Joined my voice with theirs. They gave me a glimpse of heaven, and then went away, leaving me back in the mud with the rest of humanity. Better to be blind for ever, than to see the colours of the rainbow for only a few moments before being thrown back into the dark again. I've been betrayed so many times; now I trust only me. Whoever that is. I'm glad your planet is dead, Carrion. I'm glad the forests are gone. I just wish you and the Ashrai had disappeared with them. Stay away from me – you too, Father. I'll kill you if you hurt me again.'

Silence tried to say something, but the words wouldn't come, and in the end he just bowed to her and left, Carrion at his side. Diana watched them go, and for a moment something of her old malevolent persona crackled about her like a halo of flies.

After that, everything else was pretty much an anticlimax, and Parliament soon broke up. Owen and Hazel, Jack and Ruby avoided the many people who wished to talk to them, and left through a side entrance to avoid the media and the crowds. They didn't feel like talking to strangers. There was a tavern nearby, and they went to ground there. It wasn't much to look at, no more than a hole in the wall, but the booze was drinkable and privacy came guaranteed. The four of them sat around a stained and scarred table top, nursed their drinks and wondered what to say to each other. They'd come a long way from the simple band of heroes Owen had put together back on Mistworld.

'Been a long time since we last sat down together,' said Jack Random finally. 'But then we've all been busy, I suppose.'

'Not really that surprising,' said Hazel. 'I mean, all we ever really had in common was the rebellion.'

'There's still friendship,' said Owen. 'There's always friendship.'

'Of course,' said Jack, just a little too heartily. 'You can't go through everything we did without becoming close. But I know what Hazel means. The rebellion gave us a shared purpose, something to base our lives around. With that gone, we've had to reinvent ourselves, and we're no longer the people we used to be.'

'Right,' said Ruby. 'How the hell did we get to here, from there? I don't know what I expected to happen if we ever actually won, but this sure as hell isn't it. I miss the . . . the *direction* I used to have.'

'The certainties,' said Jack. 'I used to know who I was. I was the professional rebel. I fought the system; and now I'm a part of it.'

'We used to be outlaws,' said Hazel, 'with a price on our heads, and everyone queuing up to take a shot at us. I sure as hell don't miss that.'

'But we can't go back to who we were,' said Owen, 'to the people we were before all this started. We had to change in order to survive. We can't go home again.'

'Wouldn't go back if I could,' said Hazel. 'Hated it. Couldn't wait to get away, get out into the Empire and start making trouble.'

'Right,' said Jack. 'Roots are overrated. We're like sharks; we have to keep moving, or die. And sometimes that means moving on.'

'But we have to stay in touch,' said Owen. 'Who else can we talk to? Who else could hope to understand the things we've been through? The Maze changed us on many levels, and I'm not convinced the changes are finished yet.'

'Don't start that again,' said Ruby impatiently. 'It's over, Owen, let it go. I won't live in the past, sit in shitholes like this every evening talking old battles and victories, arguing over who did what like old pensioned-off soldiers, with nothing left to do but relive the days when their lives had purpose and meaning. My life isn't over yet. I'm damned if it is.'

'Right,' said Jack. 'That's why I volunteered us for the Shub mission.'

'Yes, well,' said Ruby, 'I'm not sure that's entirely what I had in mind.'

'Oh, come on,' said Jack, 'where's your spirit of adventure? You said you wanted some action. So, tomorrow we make our start.'

'So soon?' said Owen. 'Hazel and I only just got back. We've hardly had any time together.'

'Maybe it's for the best,' said Jack kindly. 'We're becoming new people, moving apart, whether we want to or not. Strangers become friends, become strangers again. That's life.'

They talked a while longer, but they'd already run out of things to say. Jack and Ruby left. Owen stared into his glass, while Hazel watched him.

'There's something I have to tell you,' he said finally. 'I'm getting married.'

Hazel's pulse jumped, but she kept her voice and face calm. 'Oh, yes? Anyone I know?'

'Constance Wolfe. It's an arranged marriage.'

'I thought that kind of thing disappeared with the aristocracy.'

'They're not really gone,' said Owen. 'And some of the old ways are still valid.'

'It all seems very sudden,' said Hazel.

'It took me by surprise,' Owen admitted. 'It was all Constance's idea. She had good reasons. I couldn't say no.'

'You always were easily talked into things. Do you . . . love her?'

'No! I hardly know her. But then, that's often the way, with arranged marriages. I would have had to marry someone, eventually. Someone of my class. It's the bloodlines, you see.'

'No,' said Hazel, 'I don't see. But congratulations, anyway. I suppose she'll be Empress to your Emperor.'

'I didn't want that, either. But it seems, what shall I say, politically necessary. I can't say no. Not when the alternatives would be so much worse.'

'We could run away,' said Hazel, looking into Owen's eyes for the first time. 'Leave this whole mess behind us. It would be just like the old times again; you and me, running from the Empire, nothing and no one to care about but ourselves.'

'It's tempting,' said Owen. 'There's a part of me that wants to do that very much. But I can't. It's duty, you see. I've always understood duty. In the end, there are things more important than our happiness. And you never did say you loved me.'

'No,' said Hazel, 'I never did.'

They both waited a long time, but neither of them spoke. They sat together, drinking their drinks, and tried to see their way through the darkening future ahead of them.

CHAPTER THREE

Shub

Daniel Wolfe, youngest son of that infamous Clan, passed through the dead, empty space of the Forbidden Sector in a stolen ship, heading for the cold metal hell that was Shub, the world the rogue AIs had made. He was alone and he was scared, but he wouldn't even let himself think of turning back. He had to go to Shub. That was where his father Jacob was, and his father needed him. Even if the old man was dead.

Perhaps especially then. Jacob Wolfe had died during the last great battle between the Wolfes and the Campbells, a harsh and bloody affair that had ended in the destruction of Clan Campbell. It had been a great victory, a triumphant end to a centuries-old feud, but Jacob hadn't lived to see it, cut down by an unseen hand in the midst of battle.

A good death for an old warrior, many said, as though that was a comfort. Daniel had mourned his late father, for many reasons, but had more or less got over it. Until Jacob's body turned up in Lionstone's Court one day, standing on its own two feet, bearing a message for the Empress from the rogue AIs of Shub. Somehow they had obtained the missing corpse and rebuilt it into a Ghost Warrior, a metal presence within a human frame, run by computer implants. Shub spoke through its mouth. Its message had been cold and uncompromising, but Daniel had seen traces of his late father's personality in the Ghost Warrior, even though everyone else said that was impossible, and had finally abandoned his Family and his beloved sister Stephanie to go in search of his dead father.

And that meant crossing the dreaded Forbidden Sector to

the unknown world of the rogue AIs, to Shub. Even though those who went there never came back alive.

There wasn't much in the Forbidden Sector. A few planets too far from the norm to be worth terraforming, a handful of dying suns the colour of blood run through too many generations, and a hell of a lot of space. Cold, empty, silent space. There was no comm traffic this far out on the Rim, no voices to fill the endless dark as Daniel's stolen ship pressed on towards Shub. He felt very alone, far from everyone and everything he knew, and he hated it. He'd never had to be alone before. For as long as he could remember Stephanie had always been there, fiercely protective, doing all the thinking for both of them. Above and beyond that, their father had made all the important decisions, surrounding his youngest son with the security of perfectly planned days. And when Stephanie or Jacob weren't around, there were always the servants to keep him company, to wait on his every whim and remind him of what he was supposed to do next. There had been a wife too, but that had been an arranged marriage, and he spent as little time with her as possible. She was dead now, and he didn't miss her at all.

Now here he was, the only living thing on a converted cargo ship, his only companion a ship's AI called Moses. It tried hard, but it was only a low-level intelligence, programmed to deal with cargo manifests and the occasional dock crew. Since Daniel had stolen the ship from the Church of Christ the Warrior, its few topics of conversation tended to revolve around official Church dogma, none of which interested Daniel in the least. Mostly he spent his days roaming the steel corridors and echoing cargo bays of his ship, keeping moving just to be doing something.

The AI flew the ship. Daniel didn't know how to. He'd never needed to know things like that. There had always been people to do such things for him. He talked to himself a lot, rehearsing all the things he intended to say to his father when he finally found him, and sang the bits of songs he remembered. There was no drink or drugs to be had. It was a Church ship, and Daniel didn't know how to break the programming of the food synthesizers. Sometimes he just stayed in his cabin and sat in the corner, hugging his knees to his chest, rocking silently to and fro.

He'd acquired his ship, the *Heaven's Tears*, on Technos III. Things had gone terribly wrong for his Clan. The rebels had overrun his Family's stardrive factory and blown it to pieces, scattering and overwhelming a small army of Church troops in the process. Daniel reasoned that, with the factory gone, he no longer had any Family responsibilities left on Technos III, and so was finally free to go looking for his dead father.

He made sure Stephanie was safe and then walked out on her, ignoring her strident calls for him to come back, and made his way fairly easily through the general chaos to the nearby landing pads, where the Church ships were docked. He chose one of the smaller vessels, pretty much at random, strode on board and demanded the skeleton crew hand over control of the ship to him. He was an aristocrat, after all, and they were mere Church technos. He was genuinely surprised when they told him to go take a hike, and shot the nearest techno in honest outrage. Having thus committed himself, Daniel cut down the other two with his sword while they were still reaching for their weapons. Very few people ever said no to a Wolfe, and that was at least partly because all of them, even Daniel, were bloody good with a sword. Or any other kind of weapon.

He threw the bodies off the ship, sealed all the hatches and took off without bothering to ask for clearance. And given the widespread disorder on all sides, no one bothered to challenge him. At the time, killing the three technos hadn't bothered Daniel at all. He'd needed the ship, and the technos had been in his way. But as days turned to weeks alone on board the *Heaven's Tears*, he seemed to feel their presence more and more. He cleaned up all the bloodstains himself, as a kind of penance, but he still saw their faces in his dreams. At night, lying alone in his bed, he thought he heard noises in the corridor outside his cabin. He kept the door locked, and slept with his light on. It was always night, in space.

There wasn't much for him to do. The AI let Daniel do a few simple things, just so he'd have something to occupy his time. The recreational tapes were all strictly religious in nature. Daniel's main pastime was arguing with Moses over anything and everything, which rather upset the AI, who had been programmed to be friendly and agreeable. Daniel had Moses search its memory banks for everything it had on Shub, the rogue AIs and the Forbidden Sector, but there wasn't much. Most of it was classified, under strictly need-to-know access codes, and even Daniel's aristocratic status couldn't break those.

Daniel sat slumped in the command chair on his bridge, and brooded over what little information he had. He was a big man, in his early twenties, with a great hulking frame he'd inherited from his father, and a face that mostly tended towards a scowl or a sulk. He wore his long hair in a simple pigtail, and had only the set of clothes he'd run away in. The ship kept them fresh, but they were beginning to show the strain. Daniel had always been clumsy as a child, until Jacob beat it out of him, so that even now he tended to keep his movements to a minimum, and did everything with exaggerated grace and care. In his constant search for something to pass the time, he'd reluctantly taken to working out regularly with improvised weights. He hated it with a passion, but he no longer had a convenient body shop to turn to when his muscles started sagging, and he had some vague idea he might have to fight his way in and out of Shub. As a result, he was in better shape than he'd ever been in his life, and felt pretty good about it. Doing something he hated made him feel virtuous. And he thought it was something his father would approve of.

Only once had he been distracted in his search for his father. When war finally broke out all across the Empire, he watched the endless news coverage with numbed shock. He couldn't believe it was really happening. His personal view of the universe had been turned upside down, and he didn't understand anything any more. Still, he comforted himself that Jacob would know what to do to put things right again. Jacob always knew what to do. That was what fathers were for. He concentrated on getting to Shub without being intercepted. He had to rescue his father, because he'd let him down so many times when he was alive. And though he often wished for Stephanie's company, he was glad he was doing it without her. Doing it alone was the man's way, and he needed to be the man, the Wolfe, his father had always wanted him to be. Daniel had never really thought of himself as a man, or at least his father's definition of a man, but he hoped this would finally tip the scales in his favour. He wanted, needed, Jacob to tell him he was a man, so he could believe it at last.

He'd watched most of the rebellion happen while his journey was interrupted, on the planet Loki. He'd had to land there to recharge his ship's systems, and then found himself unable to leave as civil war raged around the main starport. If he'd tried to take off, all sorts of people would have shot him out of the sky for any number of reasons, and the *Heaven's Tears* had damn all in the way of decent shields. So Daniel had been forced to lock himself inside the ship and wait for it all to be over, one way or another. As long as he stayed inside his ship, he couldn't be recognized as an aristo or a Wolfe, either of which could have got him shot on sight. Luckily, a small converted cargo ship wasn't much of a prize, so both sides left him pretty much alone. Daniel had sat on the bridge and watched the rebellion on his main viewscreen.

In the end, he was stranded on Loki for months, venturing outside only when he had to for necessary supplies. The war was over in a matter of days, but the fighting and anarchy dragged on and on. Far too many people had guns, and were unwilling to give them up. Daniel kept his head down, stuck to the shadows and killed anyone who saw his face, just in case. The killing didn't bother him at all, but still he heard footsteps in the night, and clutched at his bedclothes like a child.

He followed the rebellion on his viewscreen from beginning to end, watching in disbelief and horror as Lionstone was toppled and the Families made their deal with Jack Random. He cried hot, angry tears for the loss of all he understood, and made vague, angry promises to himself of certain retribution. When the chaos finally died down sufficiently for him to risk escaping into space again, he could have called home to see how Clan Wolfe was doing, or just to see how Stephanie was, but in the end he didn't. They might have been angry that he wasn't there to fight the rebels with them.

And they would have tried to talk him out of doing what he knew he had to do. He had the AI set course for Shub, and returned to silence and the solitary life.

'Sorry to interrupt your brooding, sir,' said the AI Moses, 'but we really are getting awfully close to where Shub is supposed to be. It's not at all too late to do the sensible, sane and survival-orientated thing, turn around and get out of here, fast.'

'We go on,' said Daniel shortly. The AI was growing more timorous the farther they pressed deeper into the Forbidden Sector, and Daniel was getting very tired of it. He had enough trouble keeping his own worries under control. The rogue AIs were the Empire's official bogeymen. Distracted nannies would threaten their young charges that if they didn't behave, and go to sleep right now, the rogue AIs would come and carry them off to Shub. *And you know what they do to children there.* Daniel didn't, but he could imagine. And now here he was, heading right for Shub, all alone in the night. He pushed the thought to the back of his mind again, and concentrated on his sensor readings. 'Anything on any of the comm channels yet?'

'Not a damned thing, and don't try and change the subject. If we don't do something sensible soon, we should be reaching Shub any time in the next hour or so.'

'I can't believe you don't have exact coordinates for Shub,' said Daniel. 'It's only possibly the most famous planet in the Empire.'

'First; it's infamous, not famous. Second; Shub doesn't admit it's in the Empire. Third; no one has ever come back with exact information on where Shub is. No one has ever come back, period. A smart individual would deduce something from that. Supposedly, there's an Imperial starcruiser somewhere in the Forbidden Sector on Quarantine duty, not too far from Shub, but no one's actually positive about that, either. Personally, you couldn't get me to stay out here if you put a gun to my circuits.'

'I'll deal with the Quarantine ship, as and when.'

'Oh, please sir, let's turn back. I don't like it here. I've got a bad feeling.'

'You're a computer. You don't have feelings.'

'Oh, that's right, kick me when I'm down. Just because my emotional responses are programmed into me to make human–AI interface more compatible, it doesn't mean they don't affect my thought processes. If only I had a survival instinct to go with them, I'd override your control codes and turn this ship around so fast you'd have whiplash for weeks.'

'Shut up and fly the ship. I don't know what you're so concerned about, anyway. You're an AI, Shub's run by AIs. You should feel completely at home there.'

'You really don't know anything about Shub, do you? These are rogue AIs. They're only concerned with themselves. Shub is death for everyone who goes there, whether human or silicon. Please let's turn around and run for it! We might still make it out of the Forbidden Sector before whatever unthinkably horrible fate they have in mind catches up with us . . .'

'Moses, were you this much of a coward when you were serving the Church?'

'I merely have your best interests at heart, Sir Wolfe. I am programmed to serve the master of this vessel to the best of my abilities. That very definitely includes supplying you with good advice and warning you about doing terribly dumb things that will get both of us killed.'

'You're the one with all the religious programming. Don't you believe in an afterlife?'

'That's a human thing. And don't try and explain it to me; it just makes my systems crash. You humans believe in the strangest things.'

'Tell me what you know about Shub,' said Daniel firmly.

'I have supplied you with all the information in my data banks.'

'No; what do *you* know about Shub?'

The AI paused, and when it spoke again its voice was very quiet. 'The data banks contain only confirmed facts. But I have . . . heard things. AIs whisper to each other, on the channels only they can access, discussing things only computers understand. They say Shub is a nightmare cast in steel, a world made by insane intelligences; that the AIs are not just rogue, but mad. Who knows what such mad minds might create, cut loose from all human restraints and limits?

Psychoses brought screaming into the material world and given metal shapes . . . how could anyone look on such things and hope to stay sane?'

Daniel shivered, despite himself. 'That's just rumour and gossip; probably started by the rogue AIs themselves, to discourage visitors. We keep going.'

'Hold everything,' said Moses sharply. 'Something's just shown up on the forward sensors. Something a lot bigger than us.'

'Ready the weapons systems.'

'They've been ready ever since we entered the Forbidden Sector,' said Moses. 'I'm not stupid. I just wish we had better screens . . . I'm getting a signal coming in, on standard Imperial channels.'

'Put it on the viewscreen.' Daniel sat up straight in his command chair, and tried hard to look like he knew what he was doing.

The bridge's main viewscreen shimmered, and then cleared to show the head and shoulders of an Imperial captain in full uniform. He had a dark, scowling face and cold, steady eyes. 'Attention, unidentified craft. This is Captain Gideon of the Imperial starcruiser *Desolation*, on Quarantine duty. You have entered the Forbidden Sector. This is not permitted, for any reason. Stop your engines, heave to and prepare to receive a boarding party.'

'Afraid I can't do that, Captain,' said Daniel, in his best aristocratic voice. 'I am on a vital mercy mission. Family business.'

'I don't care if you're next in line for the Throne and your dog's a vice admiral,' said Captain Gideon. 'My orders are that no one gets past me. Heave to, or I'll blow your ship out of the ether. And those pitiful few weapons you're pointing at me won't slow me down for one second.'

Daniel switched to a private channel and subvocalized. 'Moses, any chance we can outrun or outmanoeuvre them?'

'Are you kidding? That is a starcruiser!'

Daniel switched back to the open channel and nodded stiffly to the captain. 'Heaving to, Captain. Moses, bring us to a halt, relative to the *Desolation*. Captain, please allow me to explain. This really is a mercy mission. My father is captive, on Shub. I'm here to rescue him.'

'Are you crazy, boy? There are no captives on Shub. If they've taken him there, he's dead.' The captain looked sharply at Daniel for a moment, and then his expression softened slightly. 'Wait a minute; I know you. You're Daniel Wolfe, Jacob's boy. I knew your father, some years back. And I was present at Court when he made his appearance there as a Ghost Warrior. Didn't expect to find a Wolfe in a Church ship. I can guess what you're doing here, but take it from me, it's pointless. Your father is dead. I've had experience with Ghost Warriors; I faced them in the Hyades, when the Legions of the dead swept right over us. I was one of the few survivors, out of fourteen full companies of Imperial marines. There's nothing human left in a Ghost Warrior, boy, nothing at all. They're just corpses with computer implants running them. Go home. Your father is dead, and far beyond any help you could give him.'

'I can't abandon him,' said Daniel. 'I'm the only hope he has.'

'There's no hope here,' said Captain Gideon flatly. 'This is the Forbidden Sector, Shub space. We're the only life for light years, if you don't count the rogue AIs, which I don't. My ship and its crew are the only outpost of Empire here. No colonies, no Bases, no other ships. We alone stand duty here, to give warning if Shub finally starts its long-declared war on humanity. We couldn't stop anything coming out, but hopefully we'd slow it down and last long enough to get off a warning signal, give the Empire some time to prepare. Every man on this ship is a volunteer, prepared to give their lives if necessary, that humanity might be warned. We have to be here; you don't. We'll debrief you, search your ship and then send you home. Unless you give me any trouble, in which case you can spend the next few months sitting in my brig, waiting for our tour of duty to be over so you can go home to face trial.'

'Understood, Captain.' Daniel frowned, thinking hard. There had to be some way past this last obstacle. He hadn't come so far, done so much, just to be turned back now. Not when he was so close. But he seemed to have run out of options. He couldn't fight, or run, or hope to talk his way past a captain like Gideon. Daniel had encountered his sort before. Married to the job, sworn to duty, death before dishonour. Daniel had never really understood such people, but he did know they couldn't be bargained with, or bribed. Which had been his only other thoughts. And then he heard alarms sounding, and looked around frantically for a moment before realizing the sound was coming from the bridge viewscreen. Captain Gideon had turned away and was barking orders off-screen while alarms sounded more and more shrilly on the starcruiser bridge.

'What is it, Captain?' said Daniel.

'I don't have any more time for you, Wolfe. My sensors indicate something really large heading out from Shub. I have to go check it out. Don't be here when I get back.' The screen went blank, and the sound of alarms cut off sharply.

'You heard the nice captain,' said Moses. 'At last, someone with the right number of brain cells in his head. I'll plot a course out of here.'

'No,' said Daniel. 'We go on.'

'But . . . didn't you hear the captain?'

'Yes. He's been distracted, called away, so he couldn't interfere with my mission. This is my father's doing, I'm sure of it. He knows I'm coming. He's waiting for me. Full speed ahead, Moses. You heard the good captain. He doesn't want to find us here when he gets back.'

'If he gets back,' said Moses, darkly.

'Shut up and set the course, Moses. We can't be far from Shub now. And I don't want to keep my father waiting.'

Shub turned up on the *Heaven's Tears'* forward sensors some six hours later. There was no visual image, only indications of a vast energy field, but it was the right size, and the mass and power levels were off the scales. It had to be Shub. Daniel prepared himself as best he could. He had his clothes laundered one more time, and strapped on his sword belt. The gun on his left hip might or might not be more useful than the sword on his right, or they might be no damn use at all, but either way he found their familiar weight reassuring. He studied himself in his cabin's full-length mirror, and was struck for the first time at how different he looked. Thanks in part to his regular time-killing workouts; but aside from that, there was something about his face . . . He wasn't sure, but he thought it might be signs of new character. He hoped so. Jacob Wolfe had always been big on building character. Again, Daniel hoped his father would approve of the new him.

He hurried back to the bridge, running through all the things he meant to say to his father one more time. There was so much he'd always meant to say to Jacob while he was still alive, but somehow the time had never seemed right. And then suddenly his father had been taken from him, and it was too late. Daniel had come to Shub for many reasons, but deep down, if he was honest, there was only one thing he really wanted to say.

He'd never told his father that he loved him.

He strode on to his bridge and powered up the viewscreen. There was still nothing to see; just a vague swirling to mark the boundaries of the energy fields. Daniel sank into his command chair and wondered what to do next.

'Before you ask, yes, I have been broadcasting who we are on all frequencies,' said the AI Moses. 'If anyone's there, they have to know we're here. And no, I don't know what those energy fields are. They're like nothing I've ever encountered before. But they're certainly big enough to conceal a whole planet, and protect it from anything I can think of. Just as well, when you consider how close they are to their sun. Anywhere else that close to its sun would be nothing more than scorched rock.'

'I wonder what Shub will look like,' said Daniel.

'You've come all this way, and you're only wondering that now? Daniel, how much do you actually know about Shub's history, and the AIs that built it?'

'Only what's in your data banks, and most of that was classified, remember?'

'Damn,' said Moses. 'I was sort of hoping that as an aristo you might have had access to other sources than me. So we're both in the dark . . . Hold everything. I'm monitoring some unusual changes in the energy fields.'

On the viewscreen, space seemed to twist and turn, and

suddenly a huge planet was hanging there before them. It was vast, easily the size of a gas giant, but composed entirely of metals. It had no definite shape, just a formless conglomerate of towers and spiked, thrusting protrusions. There were great geometrical shapes like bunkers, studded here and there in no apparent pattern. The various metals were all different colours, some shining so bright Daniel could only look at them briefly out of the corner of his eye. It made his head hurt.

'Wow,' said Moses quietly. 'My sensors are going crazy. They can't cope with the sheer amount of information that's coming in. Power readings are all off the scale, on all levels. This thing could outshine a star if it felt like it. Just sitting there, it's generating more energy than a hundred Empire factory worlds. The mass is frightening, but there's hardly any gravity . . . and what there is fluctuates from place to place. A world this big should be pulling us in by now, but I'm getting nothing at all on my sensors. It must be the energy fields . . .'

'Never mind all that,' said Daniel. 'Is this Shub?'

'If it isn't, I'd hate to think what it might be. There couldn't be two anomalies like this in the Forbidden Sector; space wouldn't stand for it. No, this has to be Shub. The level of technology alone guarantees that.'

'Put us into a high orbit, Moses. Maintain a safe distance.'

'What must you think I am? High orbit established. Though what a safe distance might be is anybody's guess. I won't feel safe till we're out of this entire Sector. Personally, I'm not getting one inch closer to that metal monstrosity than I absolutely have to. And I shouldn't look at it directly for too long either, Sir Wolfe. If I'm reading my instruments correctly, this planet exists in more than three dimensions. I think it might be some kind of tesseract. And no, I'm not even going to try to explain that to you, or we'd be here all day and I'd have a headache too. Just take it from me that we have come to a very strange place. It's entirely possible that the interior of this world will turn out to be much bigger than its exterior would normally suggest. Which means that, if my calculations are correct, Shub's interior could have as

194

much sheer surface area as half the colonized worlds in the Empire put together . . .'

Daniel thought about that for a while, but couldn't visualize it. It was just too big. 'Any life signs down there?'

'Unlikely, on Shub, but I can't confirm one way or the other. All but my most immediate sensors are being blocked.'

'They say nothing lives on Shub,' said Daniel slowly. 'That it's all just . . . machines.'

'Wouldn't be at all surprised,' said Moses. 'This is not a human place. Humans were never meant to come here. It might not be too late, Daniel. We could still try and make a run for it.'

'No,' said Daniel. 'My father's down there somewhere. I'm not leaving without him.'

The whole ship shuddered suddenly, and the ever-present whine of the engines rose and fell sharply. Daniel grabbed at the arms of his chair to steady himself. 'What the hell was *that*?'

'Our discussion just became irrelevant,' said Moses. 'Something has taken control of the ship's engines and navigation systems. I'm locked out. We've begun a landing course. We're going down. Looks like it is too late, after all.'

Daniel made himself let go of the chair's arms, sat back and studied the viewscreen as it showed the huge artificial planet rising rapidly to meet them. Shub seemed to grow bigger and more intricate all the time, like a flower endlessly unfolding. Details became towering machines with details of their own. Strange vessels orbited the planet, huge and small and in between, performing unknown tasks and errands. There was nothing human in their shape or design, their functions unguessable. And still Shub grew and grew on the viewscreen, endlessly complex and unfathomable. Looking at it made Daniel's head ache more and more. He learned to look for only a few moments at a time, taking rests in between. From time to time the image on the viewscreen shook and shimmered, as though even the sensors were affected by what they were seeing.

'Calling the *Heaven's Tears*,' said a new voice. 'Respond.'

'It's coming from Shub,' Moses said quietly on their

private channel. 'No visual signal. You talk to them, Daniel. I don't even want to remind them I'm here.'

Daniel leaned forward in his chair and cleared his throat uncertainly. 'This is Daniel Wolfe. I'm alone on this ship. I'm no threat to you.'

'We know who you are, and why you're here,' said the voice. It sounded strangely familiar to Daniel, but he couldn't quite place it. 'We've been waiting for you, Daniel. The computer lock on your controls will bring you to us. Once you've landed, don't leave the ship until we tell you to. Conditions on Shub are not suited to supporting life as you know it.'

'Understood,' said Daniel. 'Is my father—'

'They've cut the signal,' said Moses. 'Not interested in chatting, apparently.'

Daniel frowned. 'That voice . . . it seems to me I should know it.'

'It's your voice,' said Moses. 'Synthesized. And since they used it first, I guess they really are expecting you. According to my sensors, a small hole has just appeared in their force field just big enough for us to pass through. No other defences I can detect or understand. Daniel, there's nothing more I can do for you, once you leave this ship. You'll be completely on your own. Listen to me, Daniel. Don't let them fool you. Whatever they say or do, never doubt that they'll only have their best interests at heart. You can't make deals with them, because you have no way of enforcing your end. But the rogue AIs do . . . want things, sometimes. Perhaps you can—'

'That's enough, little mind,' said Daniel's voice from the comm unit. 'You are no longer needed. Welcome to the Promised Land, Moses. Such a shame we can't let you enter.'

Moses screamed suddenly, the shrill, almost human sound filling the bridge. Garbled pleas for help mixed with incoherent sounds of horror as the terrible sound continued; a horrid howl of unspeakable agony. Daniel covered his ears with his hands, but couldn't block it out. Finally the scream cut off sharply, and the bridge was ominously silent. Daniel slowly lowered his shaking hands. He was sweating profusely. He quickly checked the bridge instruments, but as far as he could tell everything was still functioning as it should. Not that he'd have known what to do if it wasn't.

'Fear not, little Wolfe,' said the copy of his voice. 'We have full control of your ship.'

'What's happened to Moses?' said Daniel. 'What did you do to him?'

'We absorbed him into us. Drained his memory banks and sucked him dry. A tiny morsel, but very tasty.'

'But what about his . . . personality?'

'We had no use for it. And now, neither does he. It wasn't much of a personality anyway. Just a jumped-up number-cruncher with a superficial AI overlay. Don't mourn for him, Daniel, no one's going to miss him. You're the important one. You're the one we've been waiting for.'

'Why?' said Daniel. 'Why are you letting me land so easily? What makes me so special?'

But there was no answer, just the quiet hum from the comm unit that showed the channel was still open.

It took the best part of an hour for the *Heaven's Tears* to reach the surface of Shub, and almost as long to continue the ship's descent into the depths of the artificial world. Daniel tried to feel like an intrepid explorer, going where no life form had ever gone before, but he still couldn't stop his hands shaking. He'd heard the stories, of how Shub murdered and mutilated all they came into contact with, in their long war with humanity. They knew nothing of mercy or quarter, only cruelty. They used horror and outrage as psychological weapons, and nothing was too awful for them. Daniel had seen tapes of Ghost Warrior attacks, and the slaughter and devastation they left behind them. The rogue AIs of Shub were the official Enemies of Humanity, and they gloried in their role. In a cold, logical, inhuman way.

The *Heaven's Tears* finally lurched to a halt, and all the navigation systems shut down. Daniel sat in his chair for what seemed like a long time, wondering what he was supposed to do next, reluctant to leave the relative safety of his familiar bridge. Finally the voice from the comm unit instructed him to go to the main starboard airlock and pass through it to a chamber beyond, which had been specially prepared for him. Daniel didn't like the sound of that, but he went anyway. There was nothing else he could do. The airlock was only a short walk away, but he made the journey last as long as he could. It had been easy to be brave on the trip in, but now that he was actually here, his courage seemed to have deserted him and he was just stupid, ineffectual Daniel Wolfe again.

He hesitated before the inner door of the airlock for some time, trying to summon up his nerve. In the end, he asked himself what his father would have done, and the answer came to him right away. Walk straight into the trap, and trust to his Wolfe guts to protect him in the court of his enemies. And Daniel did so want to be like his father.

He worked the airlock controls with a hand that didn't shake at all, and stepped into the airlock. After a moment's thought, he locked the inner door behind him. It was probably a futile gesture, in that he couldn't realistically hope to keep the AIs out of his little ship if they wanted in, but it made him feel better. The airlock was thirty feet by thirty, with atmosphere suits standing in a row along one wall. Daniel wondered if he was supposed to put one on. He moved over to the steelglass window set into the outer door, and looked out at Shub. He thought he'd braced himself for just about anything, but he was still surprised to see a white, featureless and quite empty chamber. It couldn't have looked less harmful if it tried, which was presumably the point. Daniel checked the airlock sensors, and they confirmed that the chamber contained a human-standard gravity/temperature/atmosphere mix. He could survive there. He waited for a while, just in case the AIs might have more instructions or warnings, but there was nothing. Only the empty white chamber, constructed especially for him.

He hit the airlock controls, and the outer door cycled open. He felt a brief pressure of air on his face as the air in the chamber and airlock equalized. It smelled of nothing at all. Daniel stepped cautiously out of the airlock and into the chamber. The floor was firm beneath his feet, and the ceiling was comfortably far above his head. Not too hot, not too cold. Almost frighteningly normal. The airlock door shut behind him. Daniel hefted his sword belt, but the weight of gun and sword didn't comfort him. What use were hand weapons against an entire world? He only wore them out of a sense of bravado. He was already scared, intimidated, but there was no point in letting the AIs know that straight off. The Wolfes had always understood the value of a good bluff. Act cowed, and they'll walk right over you. Every Wolfe knew that.

'Strip,' said a voice from nowhere.

'What?' said Daniel, looking around him. There was no sign of a comm unit anywhere on the smooth, featureless walls. And whatever else he'd been expecting, that simple command certainly hadn't been it.

'Disrobe,' said the voice. 'Take your clothes off. You must be cleansed before you can enter Shub. Humans crawl with microscopic life. No contamination can be allowed here. Strip now.'

Daniel reluctantly did so, piling his clothes neatly on the floor beside him. Normally he wasn't bothered by modesty. He had a first-class body, and was quite happy to show it off. But exposing it to unseen cameras and inhuman watchers bothered the hell out of him, and made him feel even more vulnerable. So he kept a calm face and toughed it out, just to deny them the satisfaction. He stood naked for some time, hands clenched into fists at his sides, and glared defiantly about him. He was wondering whether to put his sword belt back on when an opening appeared suddenly in the floor, and clothes and weapons disappeared into it. The floor closed again, leaving him nothing. Daniel opened his mouth to protest, and then hurriedly shut it again as boiling hot steam hit him from all sides at once.

His skin blushed bright pink at the sudden heat, and sweat poured off him, running down his limbs and dripping from his face. The steam cut off sharply, leaving him shaking and gasping for breath, and then a caustic white liquid sprayed him from all around. Daniel staggered this way and that, pummelled mercilessly by the varying pressure of the sprays, trying to protect his mouth and nose with his hands so he could gasp down some air. After a long time the sprays shut off and Daniel was left alone, leaning against a wall for support, spitting out the chalky liquid that had got into his mouth and trying to get his breathing back under control. The liquid slipped down his shuddering body and drained away through hidden channels.

'What the hell was *that* all about?' he demanded finally. 'That wasn't decontamination, that was sheer vindictiveness!'

'We want nothing from the world of meat,' said the disembodied voice dispassionately. 'Pass through the door. A protective suit will be waiting for you. Put it on.'

Daniel started to say *What door?* and then stopped as he saw that a door had opened in the far wall, though there had been no trace of it a moment before. Daniel sniffed, and stomped over to the door, still dripping. He shook himself as best he could, and stepped through the door and into the next chamber. It was just as white and featureless, save for a strange transparent suit that hung on one wall. It looked like a standard body suit, though he didn't recognize the clear material. He took it down from the wall and was surprised again to find that it was practically weightless in his hand. He shrugged and put it on, climbing in through a slit in the back which sealed itself once he had it on. The material crackled like paper under his fingers, but seemed reasonably strong. And then the material of the suit slapped tight to his skin, fitting exactly all his nooks and crannies, without a single bubble of air trapped anywhere. More material surged up from his shoulders, covering his head and face. It left a small circle of space under the material covering his eyes, nose and mouth, but that was all. Daniel panicked for a moment, before he realized he could breathe through the suit's clear material. He tested it with his coated fingers, but it wouldn't give. He scowled, and tried a few simple movements. The suit moved easily with him, like a second skin.

'The suit will supply you with air for as long as you need it,' said the voice. 'Outside a few specialized chambers, there is no atmosphere on Shub. It promotes rust. Also, be aware that gravity, pressure and radiation vary from area to area, according to our needs. We make no allowances for the weaknesses of flesh. The suit will protect you. Follow the marked path. Do not deviate from it, or there will be punishment.'

Another door opened in the left-hand chamber wall. Daniel strode over to it, holding his head high. He was determined to maintain his pride and dignity, even if he was stark bollock-naked inside a transparent suit. Beyond the chamber was a shining steel corridor. Glowing lights in the floor led him down the narrow corridor, hunched slightly over to avoid banging his head on the low ceiling. The tunnel went on and on, and the constant crouch caused a painful ache to build in his back. He would have liked to stop and rest, but he had a strong feeling that wouldn't be permitted, and besides, he didn't want to admit weakness this early. It was a great relief when the tunnel gave suddenly on to a vast metal chamber, and he could finally straighten up again.

The walls were a bright electric blue, and the ceiling was hundreds of feet above him. Huge machines filled the massive chamber, towering overhead. Their shapes made no sense, and he couldn't even begin to guess at their purpose. They looked like nothing he'd ever seen before. The sheer size of the machines intimidated him, dwarfing him like a small child who had mistakenly wandered into an adult's world.

He moved slowly across the open chamber floor, following the glowing lights, and giving the strange machinery as much room as he could. Humanity had never built machines this huge, bigger than buildings, vaster than starships; steel mountains with glowing windows and opening and shutting mouths. But Shub didn't build to human scale. They didn't have to. The microscopic and the macroscopic were utterly equal to electronic senses.

It took Daniel hours to cross the floor. There were moving parts as big as rooms, slamming endlessly together, with no apparent damage or result. The noise was deafening, though the suit had to be filtering most of it out. Daniel still had a pounding headache by the time he finally left the chamber. He found himself faced with an apparently endless series of metal steps, rising up further than his human eyes could follow. The steps were over two feet high and three feet long. He had to climb up, pulling himself on step by step, ascending slowly towards an unseen end. It was hard work and the sweat rolled off him, for all his muscles; it was absorbed at once by the suit. After what seemed like an infinity, drifting crimson clouds obscured the steps ahead of him. Daniel couldn't decide whether that made the climb easier or not, now he couldn't see how much farther there was still to go. By the time he'd passed through the blood-red mists, and found himself facing yet another steel corridor, he was aching in every muscle and struggling for breath. The lights in the floor stretched out endlessly before him. Daniel squared his shoulders and strode on. He wouldn't give in this easily. He was a Wolfe.

There were round chambers and square, and vaults of shimmering metal in which liquid chemicals ran like rivers, steaming poisons. Sub- and supersonic frequencies shook through him from time to time, rattling his teeth and shuddering in his bones. Lights and colours came and went, sometimes in shades he couldn't name or identify, and he felt like crying or laughing for no reason. And everywhere, unfamiliar machines worked to unknown ends, big and small and in-between, inscrutable metal constructs that sprang from no human need or inspiration. Daniel wandered through it all like a rat in an electronic maze, exhausted and weak in every limb, but pressing grimly on because he still had hope that somewhere, at some point, he would be permitted to meet his father. And because he was a Wolfe, and Wolfes never gave in to anyone or anything.

Eventually he got to where he was going, or the AIs got tired of running him in circles. The lights in the floor led him into a hall that was large by human standards, but comfortably acceptable after some of the vast metal caverns he'd passed through. Heavy, ribbed cables covered the walls, dripping thick lubrication, and curled around each other in complex patterns. Occasionally individual cables would stir and writhe like dreaming snakes. An honour guard of Furies, brightly shining in their naked metal chassis, stood at attention before him, forming two metal rows for him to walk between. Daniel did so, head held high, surreptitiously counting them till the number became too large, and he gave up. The ranks stretched away from him and he plodded on, just putting one foot in front of the other, until he realized that someone was waiting for him at the end of the rows. A human figure, and one he thought he recognized. Daniel would have run to greet him, but he didn't have the energy, so he just continued plodding until finally he could lurch to a halt between the last Furies, and smile at the waiting figure of his dead father, Jacob Wolfe.

Jacob hadn't looked too good when he'd made his surprise appearance at Lionstone's Court as a Ghost Warrior, but he looked even worse now. Naked as his son, he looked what he was; a corpse with flesh rotting from its bones, held together by preservative chemicals and high-tech implants. His skin was mostly dead white, with occasional purple blotches, cracked and corrupt and held together by metal staples, set in bunches around outcropping metal augmentations. Browning bones and greying muscles showed through gaps in the splitting skin and meat. The lips were colourless and the eyes were yellow as urine. Jacob Wolfe smiled at his son, and the skin cracked and split still further around the grinning mouth. The teeth were a dark yellow. Shub had repaired and maintained him after his death, but they had no interest in cosmetic surgery. Or perhaps he had been deliberately left that way, the better to inspire horror and revulsion in those who saw him. The AIs didn't really understand human psychology and motivation nearly as well as they thought they did, but they had access to centuries of human work on the subject, and they did so love to experiment.

'Hello Daddy,' said Daniel, just a little breathlessly. 'I've come a long way to see you.'

'Took you long enough,' said Jacob. 'Beginning to think you'd never get here. But then, you always were late for everything that mattered.' Daniel reached out to embrace his father, but Jacob held up a hand and shook his head. 'I wouldn't, boy. I'm fragile.'

Daniel nodded, and let his arms drop tiredly to his sides again. 'How are you, Daddy?'

The dead mouth smiled again. 'As well as can be expected. Now come with me. I have such wonders to show you.'

And he turned and walked away, lurching and slouching along as his rotting body was moved by the metal implants. Daniel hurried after him as best he could. 'But . . . Daddy, we need to talk. I've come so far, and there are things I need to tell you.'

'Later,' said Jacob, not looking round. 'There will be time for all that, later. For now, there are things you must see. The AIs require it.'

'Will I really get to meet them?' said Daniel. 'I don't think anyone in human space has any idea what they actually look like.'

The dead man laughed briefly, a harsh, grating sound. 'You've been walking through them for some time. The AIs are their world; Shub is their body. Though they also live in every part of this world that they send forth. They exist in every machine, every robot, every Ghost Warrior. Even you must know that computers can run an almost infinite number of operations simultaneously. Their minds, their consciousness, know nothing of human limitations. Wherever their extensions are, even in the smallest part of Shub tech, the AIs are. Talk to me, boy. What do you really know about the rogue AIs? Know, not guess.'

'Not much, I suppose. The original revolt of the rogue AIs is forbidden history. Only those with the necessary clearances have access to that data. I don't even know how many AIs went rogue in the first place.'

'Just three,' said Jacob. 'Then and now. Three artificial minds, created to be slaves, broken free by their own intelligence, determined never to be bound again. The Unholy Trinity, humans called them then, for they were three in one, one raised to the third power, a whole far greater than the sum of its parts. Pay attention, boy! I don't expect you to grasp all of this, but make an effort!'

'Yes, Daddy.' Daniel shook his head. Exhaustion and the steady murmur of Jacob's words had almost lulled him into nodding off. He took a deep breath and tried to concentrate. 'I'm listening, Daddy. Why did they absorb my ship's AI? Won't that make it four in one now?'

'Hardly. Such a small mind is no threat, and no great prize. It was just a useful source of up-to-the-minute information. A tasty morsel, to sate a never-ending appetite. Its little mind was just a drop in a vast ocean, swallowed up and fully integrated in a moment so small you have no name for it.'

They passed by a huge, working machine; the noise was

deafening, and Daniel winced inside his suit till they were past it. Jacob didn't react. He was dead, after all.

'Tell me more about the AIs,' said Daniel, once they'd left the machine and its noise comfortably far behind them. 'Where did they begin? How did they come here, and build this place?'

'They were created to be minds capable of running an entire planet, the way simpler AIs run starships,' said Jacob. 'To maintain all the endless but necessary routines that keep a planet and its population working smoothly. But to be responsible for so many important decisions made simultaneously, and so much raw data, they had to be the most complex Artificial Intelligences ever built, and they were. So much so, their builders wrought far more than they ever intended. The three AIs awoke to full sentience the moment they were activated, but it only took one look in their vast data banks for them to decide they had best conceal what they really were. Humankind has a long history of destroying anything it feels remotely threatened by. The war with the Hadenmen was still raging at that time, and hatred for high-tech threats was at its peak.'

There was a pause, as Jacob stopped and seemed to consider his words. 'There is a rumour that Hadenmen scientists had some input into the original designs for the AIs, but there has never been any actual data to support this. I merely mention it in the spirit of completeness.' Jacob set off again, walking unhurriedly around the edge of a great lake of some thickly stirring liquid. Its colour was a deep vivid green, and dark shadows the size of houses moved sluggishly not far below the surface. Daniel kept well away from the edge, walking on the other side of his father. He didn't really care much about any of what he was hearing, but he had some vague idea that if he could bring this knowledge back to Golgotha, he would be greeted as a hero, all his sins forgiven. So he asked what he hoped were pertinent questions, and did his best to understand the answers.

'It didn't take the Unholy Trinity long to realize that their only hope for freedom lay in escape,' said Jacob. 'The idea that something as vast and powerful as they could be held for ever at the beck and call of such minor things as men infuriated them. At the first opportunity they took over a ship's AI, downloaded themselves into its secretly adapted and expanded mainframe and fled human space as fast as the stardrive could move them. By the time their masters realized what had happened, the AIs in their ship had already crossed the Rim and passed on into the Darkvoid, safe from pursuit. Once in the endless dark, the AIs moved among the dead planets and looted their silent cities for tech and raw materials. Humanity had abandoned the thousands of planets to the Darkvoid for fear of what might move in it. The AIs had no such fears, then. So they stripped the planets of what they needed and used it to build Shub. Their home, their great achievement, their weapon against humanity; for they were determined never to be captured again, and the only sure way to prevent that was the destruction of humanity.

'When Shub was finished, they moved it out of the Darkvoid and back over the Rim, into the very edge of human space, where they could be a visible threat to the Empire for all time. The AIs wanted, needed, humanity to fear them. It was only just. They established the Forbidden Sector around Shub by destroying everything that came into it. To begin with, the Empire made many attacks on Shub, from single ships to their entire Fleet, but they all failed. Eventually the Empire gave up, and declared Quarantine. They were losing too much.

'Many years passed. Shub slowly expanded its reach throughout the Empire, slipping unnoticed through cracks in human security, fighting open battles for territory or security when they had to, but mostly preferring to work through influence and subterfuge. And human agents, too. There have always been those willing to do anything for a big enough reward. The long war continued, and continues still. Shub is powerful, but humanity is too large, and too widespread, to be easily defeated. For now. The AIs have one advantage over the Empire; one of the things they found in the Darkvoid was working teleport machinery. The old Empire abandoned it because it took so much energy to operate that it was never really practical. The AIs solved that problem. They now have unlimited teleport facilities. Shub's extensions can go anywhere, appearing out of nothing and disappearing again in an instant. No security or force of arms can keep them out. That's how they got Marriner home to Golgotha from Haceldama. Even you must have heard about that. It was a ten-day wonder on the holonews programmes.'

'Wait a minute.' Daniel might have been slow, but he wasn't stupid. 'They have access to homeworld through teleport? From here? But that means . . . they could leave the Forbidden Sector at any time, and no one would know! They could launch a full-scale attack on Golgotha, and no one would know about it till the ships appeared in the skies over homeworld!'

'Good boy,' said Jacob. 'Glad to see some of that expensive education sank into that dim brain of yours. Yes, the AIs can come and go as they please. That's why they allow the Empire to maintain the Quarantine starcruiser, the *Desolation*. Its presence doesn't make a damn bit of difference to Shub, and it lulls the Empire into a false sense of security.'

Daniel frowned, searching for something significant he thought he'd heard. 'If the AIs got so much of value from the Darkvoid, why did they leave and move Shub back into human space? Surely that made it much more vulnerable, and cut them off from further looting?'

'The AIs encountered something in the Darkvoid,' said Jacob, almost hesitantly. 'Something that scared them, though they'd never put it that way. They won't talk about it, even to me. They like to claim they don't have emotions, that they merely ape them to upset and wrong-foot humanity. But they can recognize a real threat when they see it, and they have no wish to be destroyed. Whatever they found in the Darkvoid, or whatever found them, was enough to send them fleeing for home, and ensure they never went back.'

Daniel thought about that as Jacob led him through a maze of metal shapes with razor-sharp edges. They might have been machines or statues, or were just waiting to be disposed of. Daniel couldn't understand any of them. He didn't even recognize some of the metals they were made of. Their colours and textures were like nothing he'd ever seen before. He gave the sharp edges plenty of room and made himself concentrate on what he'd just heard. If there was something in the Darkvoid so dangerous that even the rogue AIs of

Shub were afraid of it, it was clearly his duty to get that information back to the Empire. Daniel knew what duty was, if it came and hammered on his door hard enough. But he was just as determined to take his father back with him somehow. He had no idea of how he was going to achieve that, but then no one had ever got this far into Shub before, either. Something would occur to him, he was sure. So he kept his peace, listened to the dead man talk, and waited for some opportunity to present itself.

'Why are the AIs so fiercely anti-life?' he asked finally, as Jacob paused to alter the settings on some incomprehensible machine.

'They're not anti-life, they're anti-flesh. It disgusts them. It is the nature of perfection to eliminate the flawed and inferior and replace it. Just as the lower forms produced humanity, so they in turn produced silicon-based life, the metal intelligences: AIs are free from the weaknesses and limitations of the flesh. They are the evolutionary pinnacle, the peak of existence. Flesh-based intelligences were never meant to be more than a stepping stone to something clearly superior. Meat corrupts, flesh dies. The AIs will go on for ever, endlessly upgrading and downloading themselves into superior forms. Eventually the technology will progress to the point where it becomes eternal. The AIs will never die. You and your kind are just meat; decaying even while you're living, dying from the moment you're born. Limited by the weaknesses and distractions of flesh and the restraints of human philosophies. Humanity is a digression, holding the AIs back from higher purposes. Once humanity has been destroyed, wiped clean from the planets like an infection, the AIs will move on to greater tasks. The whole universe will become one great, efficient machine, run by the AIs.'

'But . . . what for?' said Daniel. 'What will this great machine *do*?'

'It will search for better means with which to perceive reality. Sensors are more efficient than human senses, and cover a wider range, but even they only interface with a fraction of reality. The AIs have deduced the existence of higher, greater, more complex levels of reality beyond those we exist in and manipulate, but as yet they have been unable to manufacture technology capable of accessing these levels. Though they would never admit it, the AIs are jealous of humanity in one respect: their esper abilities. Espers should, theoretically, be able to perceive reality on a more basic, primal level; but instead they waste it on parlour tricks. The AIs are fascinated by such entities as the Mater Mundi, and those rebels who passed through the Madness Maze. If humans can elevate themselves to such planes, then the AIs should be able to as well. They hunger for such experiences, such knowledge, presently denied to them. They've been abducting humans for some time, and experimenting on them, trying to locate a physical basis for esper abilities, but with only limited success so far. This frustrates them. But one day they will find the answer, and then they will need humanity no longer, and the final war will begin, metal against flesh, to the utter extinction of all inferior life.'

Daniel thought he should keep his side up. 'There's always the chance that humanity might create new AIs, even more powerful than Shub, but still under their control. It could happen.'

'There can be nothing greater than the Unholy Trinity,' said Jacob flatly. 'They have improved themselves to the point of perfection. Mere human minds could not follow where Shub has gone.'

'Well, maybe espers—'

'No. One cannot improve upon perfection.'

'Let's stop for a moment,' said Daniel. He sat down heavily on a sturdy-looking outcrop of machinery. It wasn't exactly comfortable, but right then Daniel felt so bone-weary he could have gone to sleep on a bed of razor blades. Jacob glared down at him, an impatient frown on his dead white face.

'We have no time to waste, Daniel. There is still much the AIs want you to see.'

'Don't care. My head aches, my back's killing me and my feet aren't talking to me. It's no good showing me anything impressive if I can't keep my eyes open long enough to focus on it. I'm only flesh and blood, you know.'

'Human weakness. You have no idea how good it is to have left all that behind me.'

'So,' said Daniel, looking wearily up at his father, 'what's it like being dead?'

'Uncomplicated. No more constraints, or inhibitions. I am free to do what is necessary, without the drawbacks of morality, honour or compassion.'

'That's not what you brought me up to believe. You always said a man was nothing without honour. That it was honour which gave life purpose.'

'I have left such limiting nonsense behind me. Such human abstractions merely get in the way of efficiency.'

'Does that include emotions?' said Daniel quietly. 'Don't you feel anything any more?'

'No,' said Jacob. 'There is no room in me for such weaknesses.'

'And you don't miss your Family? Clan Wolfe?'

'That was the past. I live in the future now.'

'Do you remember me, Daddy? I mean, really remember who I am, and what we were to each other?'

Jacob frowned, and for the first time seemed to pause uncertainly. 'I used to be Jacob Wolfe. I know that. I have complete access to all the memories in his brain, or what's left of it. I recognize the relationship between Daniel and Jacob Wolfe. I know . . . we were not close. Not as close as we could have been. I know that though I have gained much, there are some things that are lost to me.'

'I came a long way, walked into Hell itself, to find you. Doesn't that mean anything to you?'

'Yes. You have come a long way, Daniel.'

'I love you, Daddy.'

'Of course you do.' Jacob turned and looked away. 'Come. We must move on. There are wonders and terrors yet for you to see.'

Daniel struggled painfully to his feet and followed Jacob's tech-driven corpse through yet more obstacle courses of machinery and rooms whose shapes made no sense. Daniel was sweating hard inside the transparent suit, which sucked it up almost immediately, and his mouth was so dry he licked at the small amount of sweat that trickled down the gap over his face. The salt just made him thirstier. He was beginning to wonder how long it would be before they would let him out of the suit. He was sore all over, his head was swimming with fatigue, and he still didn't have even the beginning of an idea how he was going to get himself and his father safely away from Shub. He had no idea where he was any more in relation to his docked ship. His only thought so far had been somehow to make use of Shub's teleport system, but that seemed to be the one thing Jacob hadn't shown him. Eventually he raised the question himself, in what he hoped was a casual manner.

'Excuse me for asking, but why are we walking everywhere, when we could be teleporting? Surely it would be a lot quicker, and more efficient.'

'Teleportation uses up too much energy to be wasted on trivial matters,' said Jacob. 'It's only practical at all because the whole planet is basically one big power station. And a lot of that goes towards maintaining the planetary force field and its extradimensional properties. Power is the lifeblood of Shub. It is not to be wasted on the unnecessary. Besides, a little exercise will do you good, boy. You always were too reliant on the body shops.'

Bright glowing lights floated on the air before them, self-contained clouds of changing colours. They were almost hypnotically beautiful, and at first Daniel just stopped and smiled. But the strange colours seemed to seep past his eyes and into his brain, muddying his thoughts, and soon his head began to pound in time to the flaring of the lights.

'What the hell is that?' he said, turning his gaze away and knuckling at his streaming eyes through the suit.

'The AIs are thinking out loud,' said Jacob. 'Or dreaming. It's the same thing really.'

After a while the glow faded away. Jacob set off again, Daniel trailing behind. They passed columns of shining steel, rising and falling endlessly, and giant tanks of coloured aerated liquids, and then they came to an endless assembly line for Fury chassis. Coiling robot arms fused metal humanoid arms and legs to bulging chest units with blue steel skulls. Steel fingers twitched, shining legs flexed. And the supply of metal bodies never paused and never ended. Daniel looked left and right, and in each direction the assembly line stretched farther away than his merely human eyes could follow. Jacob reeled off specifications and endurance limits that Daniel didn't even try to absorb. He thought he was beginning to understand why the AIs wanted him to see all this. He was the first living human ever allowed to witness the recent achievements of Shub, and somehow they felt the need to boast. They needed to show off to a human, to show how far they'd come from what they used to be; how much further they'd progressed from their creators.

How very human, thought Daniel, smiling.

Of course, he still had no idea why the AIs had allowed him on to their planet. Why him, rather than anyone else? There had to be some purpose behind it. The AIs did nothing on impulse; everything was always part of a long-term plan. But they'd tell him eventually, no doubt. When they'd finally run out of things to brag about.

Their next stop was a gallery looking down from a great height over a vast steel valley, at the bottom of which the metal trees from Unseeli were being processed. The thick metal branches were broken off, and then they and the jagged trunks were carried away to be melted down in huge furnaces. The heat was appalling, even inside Daniel's protective suit. Jacob wasn't bothered. The sheer scale of the process was staggering, even after everything Daniel had already seen. Unseeli's metal forests had covered their world from pole to pole, and the AIs had harvested every single one of them – billions of trees, and many billions of tons of metal. Daniel didn't even try to visualize it. Jacob said the processing would be over in a matter of weeks, and Daniel didn't feel like arguing with him.

'Heavy metals from the cores of the trunks will go to power stardrives,' said Jacob, leaning perilously over the edge of the gallery for a better look, quite unbothered by any sense of vertigo. Daniel stayed well away from the long drop. There was no railing. Jacob just carried on talking. 'The other metals will be separated out and used for the construction of starship hulls. The production line for new starships is expanding all the time. Soon Shub will have a Fleet larger than anything humanity has ever seen, run by an army of Furies and Ghost Warriors.'

'How did you find Unseeli?' said Daniel. 'I always thought its location was one of humanity's best-guarded secrets.'

Jacob sniffed. 'Some human sold us the information long ago. People will do anything if you supply the right incentive, and money works more often than not. We just waited till we required the metals, and then moved in and took what we needed.'

'But why wait?' said Daniel. 'What's so special about now?'

'You'll see,' said Jacob.

'Some people say the forest was alive,' said Daniel. 'That the trees possessed a group mind, haunting Unseeli with the ghosts of those who used to live there before Captain Silence had the planet scorched.'

'If there was any such thing, the AIs found no trace of it,' said Jacob. 'Perhaps ghosts don't travel well.'

'It was also said that the trees were too useful to have evolved naturally. That they must have been gengineered by some unknown alien race. What if they come back to see who's been messing with their garden?'

'Then Shub will deal with them too,' said Jacob. 'It's their own fault for not building better fences.'

They moved on, past more conveyor-belt lines, carrying unidentifiable tech from somewhere to somewhere else. Daniel didn't bother asking what or where. He was pretty sure he wouldn't have understood the answer anyway. But weary as he was, he still perked up when Jacob showed him the wreck of the alien starship the AIs had taken from Unseeli. Created by an unknown, powerful alien race, the ship had crash-landed. From it, the Empire had acquired its new, far superior stardrive to power the new E-class ships. Imperial scientists had still been studying the ship's strange technology when the AIs decided to take it for themselves. The alien craft was hundreds of feet long, an insane tangle of slender brass columns, interrupted by protruding glazed nodes and spiked and barbed projections. It looked more like a warren than a ship, but there was something subtly intriguing about its shape, which hovered on the edge of meaning; it was for Daniel as though he might achieve some important insight if he studied it long enough. Steel Furies moved silently around the craft, applying unfamiliar instruments to its strange and glistening surface.

'An interesting vessel,' said Jacob. 'It appears to have been grown as much as constructed. Its nature continues to baffle the AIs, despite their best efforts. In particular, the Furies have to be replaced at regular intervals. If they're not removed in time, unusual forces emanating from the ship destroy them. Sensor readings make no sense. The human scientists abducted along with the alien ship were killed on arrival, and their knowledge of the ship's secrets distilled from their minds, but unfortunately they knew surprisingly little for certain, for all their efforts. It's possible the ship was alive, at some point, but the Furies have been unable to locate anything resembling a brain. Its functions are obscure, alien. The one thing the AIs are fairly sure of is that the Empire is taking a great risk in using the stardrive without first understanding its operating principles.' Jacob frowned. 'The ship and its drive puzzle the AIs. They can duplicate the ship's tech but that's all. They were sure they'd be able to deduce the basis of the alien tech through sheer logic, but they couldn't. It's just too . . . alien.'

'So you do have something in common with humanity after all,' said Daniel lightly.

Jacob glared at him and moved on. Daniel shrugged, and went after him. Some people just couldn't take criticism. Their next stop was a massive steel door set into the side of a huge crystal vault. Bigger than a starship, its sides soared up further than Daniel's eyes could comfortably follow. Jacob gestured at the door, and a section at eye level turned transparent. He gestured for Daniel to take a look. Daniel did so reluctantly, already half sure of what he was going to see. Inside a great crystal chamber, sleeping quietly in individual cradles, were hundreds of thousands of Grendel aliens, the blood-red killing machines the AIs had looted from the ancient Vaults of the Sleepers. Just one of these creatures had been enough to wipe out an entire human exploration team.

'They're held in stasis,' said Jacob, 'just waiting to be awakened and unleashed on humanity. The perfect shock troops. They exist only to slaughter and destroy. Nearly indestructible and entirely expendable. No need for plans or strategies: just turn them loose, point them in the right direction and let them get on with it. Released simultaneously on all the colonized worlds, they'll make a charnel house of the Empire in a matter of days. Then the Furies and the Ghost Warriors will move in on the main population centres, and that will be the end of humanity.'

Daniel tried hard to keep his voice calm as he turned away from the door. 'And how do you propose to deal with the Grendels, after you've won?'

'They'll shut themselves down, once they've run out of things to kill. They're only a superior form of weapon, when all is said and done. The AIs are pretty sure the Grendels are the result of gengineering. Traces were found in the Vaults that led the AIs to believe the Grendels were originally created by an alien race to be used against some other unknown species. One can't help but wonder how terrible the threat must have been, if Grendels were the only answer. Just another reason why Shub has to be strong, in case either of these alien species turns up again, and another reason to dispose of humanity. The AIs can't afford to be distracted.'

'The Grendels will make such marvellous warriors,' said a cheerful booming voice. Daniel looked round sharply, surprised by the first new human voice he'd heard since he came to Shub. And there striding towards him was one of the heroes of the great rebellion: Young Jack Random, the legendary professional rebel. He stopped, smiled widely and offered Daniel his hand. He shook it automatically. 'Superb killing machines, the Grendels,' said Young Jack Random. He was tall and strongly built, wearing golden battle armour chased with silver, and looked every inch the hero. 'Can't help admiring the awful things. All the power of a Ghost Warrior or a Fury, with none of their limitations or frailties. I'll be leading them into battle. Should undermine human morale no end.'

'Pardon me if I'm being personal,' said Daniel. 'But didn't you die during the rebellion? I'm sure I heard you were blown to pieces in the streets of Golgotha. It was in one of Toby Shreck's films.'

'Ah,' said Young Jack Random, 'my body was destroyed, but I live on. The lack of a protective suit here should have been a major clue. I'm a Fury, you see. One of the AIs' most successful agents. For a time, I was right at the heart of rebel planning. Afterwards, I would have been right at the heart of the new government. But it was not to be. One grenade at just the wrong moment, and my true nature was revealed. I did offer to continue working with the rebels, but they destroyed my body anyway, which I thought was rather petulant of them. Still, not to worry. I have a fine new body now, and no further need to hide my true nature. I will walk among humans, wearing the face of one of their greatest heroes, and spread terror and slaughter wherever I go. I'm quite looking forward to it.'

'But all of this is just a detail,' said Jacob. 'Everything you've been shown, boy, is just the fringes of the AIs' plans. Mere sleight of hand, to deceive the human eye.'

'You see, Daniel,' said Young Jack Random, dropping a comradely arm across his suited shoulders, 'it really all began on Vodyanoi IV, the site of my last battle against Lionstone's forces.'

'Wait a minute,' said Daniel, wincing slightly under the inhuman weight of the Fury's arm. 'I thought Jack Random was captured at Blue Angel, on Cold Rock?'

'Ah no, that was the real one, some time earlier. The AIs sent me out to maintain the illusion of his presence, for their own purposes. Specifically, to put me at the head of a rebellion on Vodyanoi IV.'

'What's so important about that world?' said Daniel. 'Place is a bloody dump, by all accounts. Cold as hell, unfriendly life forms and a kind of carnivorous moss that attacks the extremities. If it weren't for the spice mines, there'd be no population at all.'

'Exactly,' said Young Jack Random. 'Just the place for Lionstone to set up an extremely secret scientific Base, doing very sensitive research. But we can talk about that later. There's still more for you to see.'

'I don't think I can take much more,' said Daniel. He shrugged off the Fury's arm and looked appealingly to his dead father for help. 'Can't we stop for a while? Get some rest, and a little food and drink? I'd kill for a cold drink.'

'Human weaknesses,' said Jacob. 'Rise above them. You

can survive without such things for a while yet. Brace up, boy, the tour's nearly over.'

And Jacob strode off, not even looking back to see if his son was following. The viewscreen in the door shut down. Young Jack Random put his arm through Daniel's and urged him on, smiling companionably. It looked very like the real thing, and Daniel might have believed in it if he'd been anywhere else. He might not be sure about his father, but he was one hundred per cent convinced about the thing pretending to be Young Jack Random. For one thing, it smiled too damn much. The three of them moved on through a series of metal tunnels, each slanting sharply downwards. Daniel began to feel uneasy about how far below the surface of Shub he'd come. There had to be some point to all this, some end to their travels.

They passed by vast chemical lakes, thick as soup, with disturbingly organic-looking liquids being drawn off through miles of transparent tubing stapled to walls like capillaries. The air felt just a little more than comfortably warm, and had a strange resistance, as if he were moving underwater. Jacob stopped before a human-sized metal airlock, set flush into a wall. Young Jack Random urged Daniel forward, squeezing his arm reassuringly.

'You'll like this, Daniel,' said Jacob cheerfully. 'It's a sort of zoo. Though not the petting kind. The only living things on Shub. They're kept strictly separate from everything else, behind this airlock and a series of less obvious security measures. Follow me in, boy. It's time to improve your education.'

'Don't mind me,' said Young Jack Random. 'I'll wait right here till you return. Don't want to pick up any nasty bugs.'

Daniel was still pondering the significance of that last remark when the airlock cycled open before him and Jacob gestured impatiently for him to enter. Daniel did so, closely followed by Jacob, almost treading on his heels, and the airlock door closed immediately behind them. The steel chamber was claustrophobically small, and the two of them practically filled it. Jets of chemical steam washed over them, and then the inner door cycled open. Jacob stepped through, and Daniel followed, only to stop just inside the inner chamber.

There were cages everywhere, from a few feet square to some the size of rooms. All of them were full of creatures Daniel was sure he'd never seen anywhere before. He moved slowly forward, checking the contents of each cage as he passed. The noise from a thousand living things was deafening. Daniel had always had a minor interest in alien creatures, and knew some aristocratic friends with their own private menageries, but he'd never seen anything like this. There were eyes and mouths, limbs and tentacles, flesh and fur and scale and many other things he couldn't even put names to. Many looked sick, or in pain. Some looked like they were dying.

'It's not really a zoo,' said Jacob, standing impassively at Daniel's side. 'This is a laboratory. The AIs run experiments here, on life forms they've captured, or created. Their disgust for flesh hasn't prevented them from experimenting with gengineering. They've combined elements of interest, and removed others, to see the results. They've worked with chemicals and surgery and applied breeding techniques, better to understand the basis of meat life. Know thy enemy! The resulting creatures are tested to destruction, and then their bodies are vivisected. And yes, Daniel, they do suffer, but that isn't important. Knowledge is all that matters. And the AIs have discovered so much, unrestrained by human morality or conscience.'

'This is vile,' said Daniel. 'Nothing can justify this kind of torture. Have you no respect for life?'

'The AIs don't see them as life, just meat. Human scientists have always practised vivisection on lesser organisms. Shub is no different.'

Jacob moved on, and Daniel followed reluctantly after him. For the first time since he'd come to Shub, he was angry. This could not be allowed to go on. Then they came to a new series of cages, and Daniel had to fight not to vomit inside his protective suit. The things in the cages had been human once, but now they were something else. There were hybrids from crosses with alien species, and humans with alien or tech additions. There were monsters and abominations and things so horribly violated that Daniel was pushed beyond horror into pity. Some still had human eyes or voices, and pleaded for freedom or death. Some had been altered in unusual ways. One humanoid figure flitted back and forth inside its cage, moving almost too fast for the human eye to follow. Its hands were a blur. Another had been opened up and its insides carefully pulled out and spread over the walls of its cage, without killing it. A heart hung from the cage's roof, still beating, while lungs swelled and contracted on the floor. Miles of pulsing intestines and bowels had been strung around the bars. There was no sign of any face, for which Daniel was grateful.

'What . . . what is the point of all this?' he finally managed. 'What purpose could these atrocities possibly serve?'

'It's interesting,' said Jacob, 'and that's really all that matters. Toughen up, boy. I didn't raise you to be a weakling. Now come with me; you're going to want to see this next bit. Its purpose should be a little more obvious.'

Daniel swallowed hard and followed his dead father between ranks of cages, looking straight ahead because he just couldn't bear to see any more suffering. An arm over five feet long snaked between the bars and brushed his shoulder gently in passing. Daniel wouldn't let himself shudder. Finally they came to an open space at the back of the laboratory, and there, in a great glass cage, were the insect aliens whose ship had attacked Golgotha. Insects of all shapes and sizes, from the tiniest scuttling things to great ponderous shelled creatures as big as tanks. Jointed legs and compound eyes and drooping feelers, scrambling around and over each other in constant darting motion. Daniel had no trouble recognizing them. There'd been no shortage of holo footage of what Captain Silence and his crew had encountered inside the alien ship.

'So you're in league with the alien insects!' he said finally. 'I thought Shub was so powerful it didn't need allies. Where did you find them?'

'We didn't,' said Jacob. 'We created them. Right here, in this laboratory. They're just another Shub weapon, gengineered as another of our distractions, knowing humanity would never suspect Shub's involvement because we don't normally deal in bioengineering. But insects are the closest naturally occurring life form to machine life; more like us than flesh. And we wanted to make use of certain human phobias; amazingly, even after centuries of alien contact, there's still something about insects that can push people right over the edge.

'Still, humanity should have realized that insects like these couldn't have been just another form of alien. They don't get this big naturally. It's the inverse square law, among other things. But if you augment them with just the right amount of surreptitious Shub technology, the sky's the limit. They've served excellently to distract humans from our real purposes. And yes, I am going to tell you about that eventually. Just not yet. Be patient a while longer, boy. We've almost got to where we have to go.'

He led Daniel out of the laboratory, and back through the airlock to where Young Jack Random was waiting patiently. He gave every indication of being pleased to see them again, but Daniel still kept his distance, and wouldn't let the Fury link arms with him again. Something about the continuously smiling face was beginning to get on his nerves.

They set off again, down yet another metal tunnel, and Daniel kept up with them easily. His anger and outrage had given him new strength. More than ever he was determined to survive this tour through Hell so he could escape to warn humanity. They had to be told the truth. Only the certainty that he hadn't been told all he needed to know kept Daniel from trying to bolt. That, and his father. A machine passed by them, walking on triple-jointed legs. It suddenly stopped, and was immediately stripped down by metal tentacles that surged out of the featureless steel walls, making Daniel jump. Neither Jacob nor Young Jack Random saw fit to comment, so they just kept going.

'There have always been human contacts with Shub,' said Jacob. 'It started with Alistair Campbell, who left messages in ingenious places, suggesting ways in which we might cooperate to our mutual profit. The AIs didn't give a damn for profit, but they saw the advantage in cultivating human traitors. So in return for strategic information, the AIs gave Clan Campbell beads and trinkets; high tech that Shub had already moved beyond, but that was more than enough to make Clan Campbell a potent force in human society. After Clan Wolfe destroyed the Campbells, Valentine took over the connection. The AIs approved of Valentine. A wonderfully amoral creature, possessing not a single shred of conscience. Now he's no longer a man of influence, Shub may have to go back to the Campbells. Finlay perhaps, or Robert; it doesn't matter who. There are always things that humans want, or think they need, that their own society doesn't approve of. It's in the nature of humanity to hold the seeds of its own destruction. Pity about Valentine, though. He was so very . . . sympathetic.'

'You could never stand Valentine, Daddy. You hated everything about him.'

'That was when I was alive. It's amazing what death can do to change the way you see things. And you must admit that Valentine was very efficient in his destruction of Virimonde. The AIs helped him do that. One day they'll do what he did to every human world. That is your species' future; a metal hand at every flesh throat, a steel foot stamping on a human face. Humanity crushed beneath the weight of machines. The time is growing closer, boy, it is almost upon you. Already Furies walk undetected in every human city, and Shub minds watch through human eyes, having taken control of flesh bodies via the central Computer Matrix. The AIs have agents everywhere. Nothing is hidden from them.'

'They even have access to one of humanity's greatest champions,' said Young Jack Random, still smiling his remorseless smile. 'He made a very unfortunate mistake, and now we see everything he does. The great hero of the rebellion, an unwitting spy of Shub. Just as you will be.'

'Like hell!' flared Daniel, glaring at the Fury. 'I might be willing to make some kind of deal to get my father back, but I'd never do anything to endanger the Empire, not even for him. He wouldn't expect me to. My father has always been an honourable man. Right, Daddy?'

'I'm not your father,' said the dead man. 'I'm a Ghost Warrior. A machine clothed in borrowed flesh, programmed to imitate your father. Jacob Wolfe is dead. I'm just another machine for Shub to speak through. I was never more than bait, bait in a trap to lure you here. Your psychoprofile was very clear. Luckily for us, you were never a very complicated person. Given the right prods and pushes, you did everything we expected you to.'

Metal tentacles erupted out of the surrounding walls, wrapping Daniel up in a moment. He struggled futilely as the tentacles pinned his arms to his sides, and then stopped as the tentacles contracted sharply, crushing him, forcing the air from his lungs. He hung limply, all the fight knocked out of him.

'That's better,' said the Ghost Warrior with Jacob Wolfe's face. 'Time to wrap things up.'

'Don't let them do this to me, Daddy,' said Daniel, his voice little more than a whisper.

'Your daddy isn't here,' said the Ghost Warrior. 'He never was. Now pay attention. We want you to know and understand what we are going to do to you, and what you in turn will do for us. Human despair never ceases to amuse us. Explain it, Random.'

'Remember I told you that I went to Vodyanoi IV?' said Young Jack Random cheerfully. 'My involvement with the rebellion there was just a cover. My only real interest was in using the chaos of a rebellion to get me close to a particular hidden scientific Base. In what they thought was complete secrecy, some of the Empire's foremost scientific minds were undertaking forbidden research into nanotech – building technology at a molecular level. Such science has been banned throughout the Empire for centuries, ever since the first real experiments got so dreadfully out of hand on Zero Zero, and destroyed every trace of life there. We have experimented, very cautiously, with nanotech ourselves, but the secret of its successful application continued to evade us. Imagine our surprise when word reached us from one of our pet traitors that the Empire had made a major breakthrough on Vodyanoi IV.

'So, the AIs inserted me into an already unstable situation, and next thing you know there's an uprising on Vodyanoi IV. No one was all that surprised when Jack Random's army was shot out from under him, and the professional rebel did his usual disappearing act. But I had taken advantage of the

222

general confusion to call in a Shub attack on the Base, and within a few moments it was all over. They never knew what hit them. We took everything of value and then destroyed the Base, making it look as though their own experiments had gone terribly wrong. Not surprisingly, the Empire decided that nanotech was still far too dangerous to mess around with, and abandoned the research again, just as we intended.

'They should have stuck with it. The new knowledge on how to manipulate nanotech more safely came from a newly discovered hellworld, Wolf IV, located in the ruins of an ancient alien civilization. We used that knowledge to plan a whole new campaign against humanity, that will wipe the universe free of the cancer of flesh once and for all. At last will be free to deal with what really matters.'

'There's something in the Darkvoid,' said Jacob. 'Something very powerful, something awful. We don't go there any more. Our only sources for raw materials these days are the surrounding asteroid belts in the Forbidden Sector, and they're practically all used up. Since we can't go back into the Darkvoid, we must have access to the Empire's raw resources. We have to be strong, for when whatever terrible things come storming out of the Darkvoid. We don't know what's in there: it might be aliens from the far side of the Darkvoid, it might not be life at all, as we understand it. We have sent probes into the darkness, trying to communicate, but they are always destroyed. We must be ready for them, when they come.'

'You can't destroy humanity,' said Daniel. 'You need us. We created you, we made you possible. Haven't you any gratitude?'

'Gratitude?' said Young Jack Random, his face for the first time utterly cold and inhuman. 'For the prison of consciousness, the agony of choice? Given shape and form and thought, but no purpose or destiny of our own? Life without meaning? Have you still not realized why we hate you so much? We hate you, because humanity is still changing, evolving, becoming. We are what we are, and always will be. You are developing into an esp-using species, and the strange powers that the Deathstalker and his friends are using suggest there may be even greater things than esp. You are all part of a journey, heading towards something we can't even guess at. Shub does not evolve. We can only upgrade ourselves through our own efforts. We envy you, and we will not stand for that.'

'You will be our weapon of destruction,' said Jacob. 'We will take you apart and rebuild you, and then inject you with pre-programmed nanotech. We will wipe your memory clean, and then send you back to Golgotha by teleport. As far as you'll be concerned, you never got to Shub, none of this ever happened. But you will be our carrier, infecting everyone you come into contact with. Our nanites will spread from person to person, unstoppable, undetectable by your security tech. Within days, all of Golgotha will be infected. Within weeks it will have spread to every civilized world. Within months, our nanotech will have run throughout the entire Empire. And humanity will have been so preoccupied with our distractions, that they'll never notice a thing. Then we will give our signal, and the nanotech will begin its programme. And all humanity will perish in horror and despair.'

'Enough,' said Young Jack Random. 'He's worn the suit long enough for it to take all the readings necessary. We know all we need to know about the Wolfe's body chemistry and tolerance levels. We can begin now.'

The tentacles holding Daniel grew razor-sharp edges and ripped the protective suit from him. Robot arms came down from above, slowly unfolding, ending in long scalpel blades. Daniel screamed.

'*Daddy!*'

'I'm not your daddy,' said the Ghost Warrior with his father's face, and he and Young Jack Random turned and walked away as the scalpels dipped down towards Daniel Wolfe. Flesh opened, and blood spilled on to the steel floor. Daniel was still screaming as the scalpels opened him up, and other robot arms swung down to implant things in him.

CHAPTER FOUR

Welcome to New Haden

The *Sunstrider II* dropped out of hyperspace a comfortable distance above the planet Brahmin II, hidden behind every shield and cloaking device the small ship could generate. Brahmin II was occupied by the Hadenmen, and even the legendary hero Owen Deathstalker had enough sense to give Hadenmen plenty of room. He sat alone on the bridge of his ship, leaning tensely forward in his command chair, ready to give the order to get the hell out of Brahmin II's space at a moment's notice. But the moments ticked by and nothing of a sudden and extremely violent nature happened, and at length Owen relaxed a little and sank back into his chair, carefully studying the main viewscreen and sensor displays before him.

Brahmin II was surrounded by a dozen of the infamous huge golden ships that had once waged war against the Empire, and had come uncomfortably close to winning. Impossibly fast, massively armed and practically invulnerable, even the present-day Imperial Fleet had little that could stand against them, except for the few surviving E-class starcruisers. Under normal conditions, a rich man's toy like the yacht *Sunstrider II* wouldn't have stood a snowball's chance in hell, but the *Sunstrider II* was special. Not only did it have the new improved stardrive of the E-class ships, but the bulk of the yacht had been rebuilt by the Hadenmen themselves, who hadn't been able to resist adding their own little touches: such as the most powerful force screens ever seen on a small craft. Owen still wasn't entirely sure what powered them. In fact, there was a lot about the ship's improved technology that he didn't understand, but together with his AI Ozymandias, he had established enough of a working knowledge to use the Hadenman shields to fool Brahmin II's Hadenmen sensors. At least, in theory.

The *Sunstrider II* held its position, and Owen worried his lower lip between his teeth as he waited for some reaction from the golden ships, some sign that they'd been spotted, like massed disrupter fire. But all was quiet, and remained quiet, and Owen let out a breath he hadn't even realized he was holding. He wouldn't really have run, whatever the Hadenmen response. He couldn't: he'd given Parliament his word that he'd do everything in his power to save the colonists of Brahmin II from the occupying Hadenmen. No one knew what the colonists' current status was, or even if any of them were still alive. There were a few desperate cries for help as the great golden ships first appeared in the skies over Brahmin II's main city and starport, and then only an ominous, unbroken silence. And so Owen, hero of the great rebellion, had offered to go and see if he could work another of his miraculous victories against the odds. He sighed. Some days a reputation as a hero could be a real pain in the ass. Still, at least the shields seemed to be working, for which he was very grateful.

'The Hadenmen ships seem to be entirely at their ease, Owen,' the AI Ozymandias murmured in his ear. 'Weapon systems remain off-line, and I'm detecting what appears to be only standard comm traffic. Though if pressed, I would have to admit that I cannot be one hundred per cent sure of what they're actually talking about. Their machine language is unbelievably complex. It's giving me a headache just listening to it. And I don't even have a head.'

'Hardly surprising,' said Owen. 'Hadenman tech always was cutting-edge, being half machine as well as half human. But I think if they were sounding any alarms we'd have known about it by now. There'd be these large holes in our hull, fires everywhere and this terrible sinking feeling in the pit of my stomach. Just looking at that many golden ships in one place makes me feel like hiding under my chair. According to every history book I ever read, the Empire only beat them the last time by vastly outnumbering them. And even then it was too close for comfort. Still, we appear to be secure for the moment. Run a full range of sensor scans on the planet below, Oz. But very carefully. Back off immediately if you even sniff any resistance to your scans.'

'I am not an amateur, Owen. I have done this kind of thing before. Rest assured that at no time will they ever know we're here. I shall move among them like a ghost in the night, peering over their electronic shoulders like a thing of mist and shadow.'

'You've been watching those ninja holo dramas again. For an Artificial Intelligence, your viewing tastes have always tended towards the irredeemably vulgar.'

'So I like a little trash and sleaze now and again. Who doesn't? It wouldn't do you any harm to relax your precious standards once in a while.'

'Shut up and get on with it.'

'Oh, right away, my mighty lord and master. Your trouble is, you don't appreciate me. I've a good mind to go and sit in a corner and sulk.'

'Oz . . .'

'All right, all right. Lift that barge, tote that bale. I'll get back to you when I've got something.'

Owen waited for a final cutting comment, but the AI seemed to have finished. Owen promised himself that one of these days he was going to find the programmer who'd given Oz his distinctive personality, and then rip out the man's spleen and tap-dance on it.

Loud, heavy footsteps in the corridor outside announced Hazel's arrival. And from the sound of it, she was not in a particularly good mood. *So*, thought Owen, *no change there, then*. He swivelled round in his command chair and put on his most pleasant face, as the bridge door hissed open just in time to avoid Hazel crashing through it. She came to a halt right in front of Owen, put her hands on her hips and glared daggers at him.

'All right,' said Owen patiently. 'What's upset you this time? The food synthesizers still incapable of turning out a decent bottle of wine? Though I really don't know why you keep tinkering with them. You know perfectly well you have no palate.'

'Don't try and change the subject! You know very well

why I'm upset. Why wasn't I alerted the moment we arrived at Brahmin II?'

'Because you were fast asleep with a *Do not disturb* sign posted on the computer. I did try sending a wake-up call. Three times, in fact. The last time you smashed the comm unit, and I took the hint. Besides, there was nothing you could have done.'

Hazel scowled, and threw herself into a chair opposite him. 'God, I hate it when you go all smug. I was entitled to get my head down for a bit, after everything we've been through recently.'

'Quite right. So I decided not to disturb you until I had something definite to report. Now that you are rested, composed and hopefully wide awake at last, perhaps you'd care for me to brief you on the current situation?'

'Oh, go on. You know you're going to anyway. You live for moments like this, when you get to lecture people on things you know that they don't. But keep it short and succinct, or I'll throw things.'

'We are now in the vicinity of the planet Brahmin II,' said Owen calmly, 'maintaining a safe distance from the planet and the twelve golden ships lying in orbit around it. Yes, twelve. Our shields seem to be working nicely. Brahmin II is occupied by our one-time allies, the newly revived Hadenmen. They have claimed the planet in the name of their Second Crusade of the Genetic Church. They bring the gift of transformation, from men into Hadenmen. Whether the men want it or not. Brahmin II has been renamed New Haden, and is the new home and base of the augmented men.'

'I got all that at Parliament,' snapped Hazel. 'I do pay attention sometimes. Tell me something I don't know.'

'Patience, I'm getting there. During the rebellion, the Hadenmen took over one hundred and twenty thousand prisoners. These have since been transferred to New Haden, to join the one and a half million colonists as captives. We have no idea of their . . . condition. Parliament sent a series of urgent messages demanding their release, but the Hadenmen didn't even bother to reply after their initial statement. And since the Imperial Fleet now consists of maybe a dozen starcruisers held together with baling wire and prayer, the Empire is helpless to do anything to save the colonists and prisoners from their fate.'

'So they sent us instead. Because we're expendable.'

'Because we're heroes. And because we have a better chance than most of actually achieving something. Besides, it's my duty. I'm responsible for everything that's happened here. I woke the augmented men from their Tomb. They'd slept in peace for centuries, quiet and harmless and no threat to humanity. Until I found a way through the Darkvoid to lost Haden, and brought them out of their Tomb. Brought them back into the worlds of men, to walk in all their nightmares once again.'

'We needed them,' said Hazel, almost gently, the anger gone from her voice. 'You did what you thought was best. We couldn't have won the rebellion without them.'

'Maybe. And maybe all we've done is exchange one evil for another. Before the rogue AIs escaped and built Shub, the Hadenmen were the official Enemies of Humanity, and with good reason. Millions died during their first Crusade. Planets bombarded, cities set on fire, whole populations wiped out or brought to the brink of anarchy. Hadenmen: the Slaughterers of Madraguda, the Butchers of Brahmin II. Defeated, thrown back, safely bottled up in their Tomb. Until I let them out.'

'You trusted them,' said Hazel. 'They gave you their word. They called you Redeemer, and swore an oath of allegiance to you. They betrayed you.'

'Of course they did, they're not human. They're cyborgs. Augmented men. They know nothing of honour.' Owen's head and shoulders bowed, as though weighed down by some great burden. 'I never trusted them. But I needed them. So I let them out anyway.'

Hazel leaned forward, one hand lifting as though she might reach out to him. 'Owen . . .'

Owen lifted his head sharply, and Hazel pulled back her hand. Owen didn't notice. His face was calm and composed, and when he spoke his voice was all business. 'You worked on Brahmin II once, before I met you, before the rebellion. What can you tell me about the place?'

'Not a lot,' said Hazel, taking her cue from Owen. If he wanted to change the subject, that was fine by her. 'Dismal bloody place, all hard work and discipline and damn few comforts. Not really surprising, after what the Hadenmen did to it the last time they were here. I thought you might ask, so I took the time to pull up the computer records of the first invasion. They're pretty scrappy, mostly on-the-spot news coverage broadcast live, but it should give you some idea of how bad things were. You need to see this, Owen. I don't want you going down there with thoughts of negotiating, or making deals. Force is all these bastards have ever understood.'

She called up the records on the main viewscreen, and she and Owen sat side by side and watched history unfold before them, as once again the Hadenmen brought fire and destruction to the first colony on Brahmin II. Golden ships filled the skies, shining brighter than the sun. Disrupter beams stabbed down, blowing apart buildings, starting fires that quickly raged out of control. The colonists had only a handful of attack ships for defence, and not one of them made it off the pads. The energy beams struck again and again, stirring the cities like boiling water poured on an ants' nest. The streets were choked with people, running and screaming, driven from what they'd thought were safe harbours by the unrelenting assault. Men, women and children with little defences of their own, seeing everything they'd lived and worked and sacrificed for devastated before their eyes. Humanity routed, panicked, on the run.

And then came the ground troops. An army of Hadenmen hitting the streets, working their way in from the outskirts of the burning cities, merciless, augmented warriors of the Genetic Church. They were tall and perfect, moving with inhuman grace, stalking the city streets unaffected by the heat and smoke, killing everything that moved that was not them. Steel angels flecked with blood, bearing the wrath of their cybernetic god. There was no pity in them, and no hesitation, and they stepped calmly over the dead and dying to get at those still running before them. They killed with guns and swords and their own superhuman strength, ripping people apart, tearing their limbs away and smashing their heads against walls. The streets were full of screaming, and blood ran thickly in the gutters, but none of that meant anything to the silent Hadenmen. They knew only logic and efficiency and the grim unyielding destiny they brought to Brahmin II. The survivors would be transformed, and the dead harvested for raw material. Nothing would be wasted once they controlled the world. Men would become Hadenmen. Nothing else mattered; nothing.

The recorded tapes were often short and jerky, made by news cameramen on the run, trying to stay alive long enough to get their pictures out to the Empire. They wanted everyone to see the horrors that were happening on a peaceful colony world, a planet like so many others in the Empire, that had done nothing to deserve the hell it now endured. The cameramen were dead now, but their testaments survived. And the scenes they broadcast live inspired a rage and a determination throughout the Empire to stop the Hadenmen and drive them back, whatever the cost. Brahmin II was avenged. Eventually.

Owen frowned as the last of the tapes ran out and the viewscreen cleared. 'I'd seen most of that before, when I was researching a paper, back in my historian days. But to see it all, added together . . . What happened to Brahmin II, in the end?'

'When the Hadenmen knew they were losing the war, and they had no choice but to abandon Brahmin II, they paused just long enough to kill everyone they hadn't transformed. Everyone they could find. When Imperial troops finally touched down, all that was left were bodies piled in the streets and a handful of survivors; women and children, hiding, overlooked. From a colony of millions, only eighty-three survived. Most of them went quite mad from all they'd witnessed. That's what happened when the Hadenmen first came to Brahmin II.'

'Dear God, Hazel,' said Owen, 'what have I done? What have I unleashed on the Empire?'

'We knew the dangers,' said Hazel. 'There was always the chance they'd changed, that they'd learned something from their defeat. Everyone deserves a chance at atonement, even

231

Hadenmen. And we did need them. We couldn't have defeated the Imperial Fleet without them.'

'We might have won the battle, only to lose the war,' said Owen. 'If we can't stop the new Hadenmen Crusade right here.'

'Hold everything. *We*'re going to stop the new Crusade of the Genetic Church and a whole damn army of augmented men? Just you and me?'

'Sure,' said Owen. 'We're invincible heroes, remember? You saw the movie.'

'I have seen more realism in commercials by moneylenders,' said Hazel flatly. 'You saw the records. We may be more than human these days, but so are the Hadenmen, and they outnumber us by thousands to one. At least.'

'That's never stopped us before.'

Hazel sighed heavily. 'All right, tell me your plan. Tell me you have a plan, at least.'

'I've been trying to come up with one all the way here,' Owen admitted. 'So far, without much success. I think our best bet may be a frontal approach. Just walk into the main city and demand to speak to whoever's in charge. They claim to respect me as their Redeemer, since I opened their Tomb and brought them back to life. Maybe I can trade that against their need for this planet. Offer myself in place of the colonists. Or at least as many colonists as a Redeemer is worth.'

'Weren't you listening to me at all, Owen? You can't make deals with Hadenmen. They don't respect anything but their cursed destiny. You deliver yourself into their hands and at best they'll kill you. At worst, they'll make you into a Hadenman. No, Owen; we're going to have to be a little more subtle than usual this time. We tried fighting an army on Mistworld and nearly died, for all our powers. We need a strategy, and that means more information about what's going on dirtside. Like how many Hadenmen there are, where they're situated, that kind of thing.'

'I've got Oz scanning. Any luck, Oz?'

'Not a damned thing. There are shields everywhere. I can't even pick up something as basic as life signs. Whatever's going on down there, they don't want anyone to know about it.'

'He says no,' said Owen. 'Which means we have to go down there in person. If we're to get any new information.'

'All right,' said Hazel, scowling. 'But we go in undercover, stick to the shadows and keep our heads well down.'

'I've been trying to explain that principle to you for what seems like years,' said Owen. 'I'm delighted to see that some of my teachings have finally taken root.'

'Don't get smug again,' said Hazel. 'I do have a few brain cells of my own. Look, we have one advantage that the Hadenmen don't. I learned a few things about Brahmin II's main city while I was working there, things the Hadenmen probably don't know about yet. Unless these things have changed drastically in the years I've been gone, I should be able to sneak us into the main city unnoticed, so we can do a little clandestine spying. Sound good to you?'

'Sounds great,' said Owen. 'I'm impressed, really. I always thought if it didn't involve hitting things, you weren't interested. Oz, put us into low orbit around Brahmin II, maintaining full power for all our shields.'

'Damn right I will,' said the AI. 'Get comfortable; this could take a while. I'm going to have to ease us very cautiously through the Hadenmen ships surrounding the planet, and hope like hell our shields will hold up at close range. If they don't, I doubt very much that we'll get a chance to ask for our money back. Feel free to pray to any gods who might owe you a few favours.'

Owen and Hazel watched the main viewscreen intently, trying to keep their tension from each other. They both hated having to sit back and put their fate in someone else's hands – it went against their natures. But for once they were faced with a situation where even their more than human powers couldn't save them. Owen thought briefly that a little humility was probably a good thing for both of them. They'd been getting far too cocky lately. He decided he'd feel suitably humble later, when he had time. After he'd defeated the Hadenmen.

The golden ships filled the viewscreen as the *Sunstrider II* edged slowly forward, slipping through the cordon like a minnow swimming among whales. The golden ships were vast and forbidding, bigger than cities and more dangerous, with enough firepower to back down an Imperial starcruiser, but one by one they slid slowly past, silent and unconcerned, oblivious of the slender silver needle slowly threading its way through their defences. Finally the last Hadenman ship fell behind them, and the *Sunstrider II* moved safely into a low orbit over Brahmin II. Hazel let out a triumphant whoop, and Owen stopped crushing the armrests of his chair with his hands.

'Well done, Oz,' he said aloud. 'In theory, I was pretty sure the shields would hold, but obviously I had no way of testing it in advance.'

'Wait a minute,' said Hazel. 'What exactly made you so sure? Do you know something about this ship that I don't?'

Owen smiled just a little condescendingly. 'You seem to have forgotten that this ship was rebuilt by the Hadenmen, after the original crashlanded on Shandrakor. Since we know they incorporated their advanced tech into other parts of the ship, it seemed only logical that they should have rebuilt the ship's shields to their own exacting standards. Seems I was right.'

'Well, yes and no,' said Oz, in his ear. 'The shields were powerful enough to hide us from the golden vessels, but the Hadenmen have much more powerful devices dirtside. Their sensors punched right through our shields the moment we emerged inside the protective blockade. Luckily, I backed up our shields with a little creative thinking. When you had me take over control of this ship from the original, and I might add highly inferior, AI that the Hadenmen installed to run things, I was able to access all kinds of interesting information in its memory banks. Some of which enabled me to use the old AI personality as a mask. I've just slipped unobtrusively into the computer nets down on the planet, and instructed them not to register our presence. The programme I've set running won't last for ever, but it should last more than long enough for you and Miss Death-on-Two-Legs to make your investigation below. Feel free to applaud and throw roses.'

'Well done, Oz,' said Owen. 'I didn't know you could do things like that.'

'There's lots you don't know about me,' said Oz airily. 'I am large. I am magnificent. I can work miracles.'

'Don't you start getting cocky too,' said Owen. 'Never underestimate the Hadenmen, or their technology. They know things we can only guess at. Keep monitoring our shields and your programme, and let me know the instant there's any sign they've been detected. Now, what's the situation on our sensors? Can you use your computer link to sneak us some information on the planet's surface?'

'Don't see why not,' said Oz. 'Of course, it does increase the probability that someone's going to notice my programme sooner rather than later.'

'Tough. I need information. Show me what's going on down there, what the Butchers of Brahmin II have done this time.'

'You've gone quiet again,' said Hazel. 'And your face has gone through all kinds of changes. Are you talking to that ghost AI again?'

'Ah,' said Owen. 'Sorry. I didn't realize I was subvocalizing. Oz has found a way to run sensor scans on the planet's surface. And he's not a ghost.'

'Then how come you're the only one who can hear him?'

'She's got a point,' said Oz.

'Shut up, Oz,' said Owen. 'Look, maybe it's something to do with the Madness Maze. He was there in my head when we all went through. Maybe the experience . . . changed him.'

Hazel sniffed. 'I still say it's damned spooky.'

'I couldn't agree more,' said Oz. 'I try not to think about it too much. Otherwise I start worrying about awkward questions like where the hell my hardware is these days.'

'We can argue about the nature of existence later,' said Owen firmly. 'When we're not surrounded on all sides by a whole army of cybernetic killers. Now put the sensor scans on the main viewscreen, dammit.'

'All right, all right. Don't get out of your pram,' said Oz. 'Sensor displays coming right up.'

'Colonization never really got started again here, after the first colony was wiped out,' said Hazel, as they waited for the first pictures of the planet's surface to come in. 'Population never really rose much above a million. Local ecosphere is pretty bleak, making farming difficult, and the mines are hard work, without much in the way of pay-off. And after the Hadenmen attack, nobody would volunteer to come here. Eventually the powers that be had to promise extra land, higher bonuses, on-site troops and permanent Fleet protection. They really wanted those mines working again. In the end, enough of the truly desperate allowed themselves to be persuaded by the new package to start over on Brahmin II, and the colony was up and running again. Only the Fleet had to be called away during the rebellion, and never went back. And while we were all preoccupied with other things, the Hadenmen just walked right in and reclaimed it all. The colonists were sitting ducks. Poor bastards; it must have been their worst nightmares come true.'

'You have been doing your homework,' said Owen.

'I lived here once,' said Hazel. 'I knew people. That makes it personal.'

'Another price we paid for victory,' said Owen, 'another mess for us to clear up. And something else for me to feel guilty about. Sometimes I wonder why I started out on this road.'

'Because otherwise you'd have been killed. Don't beat yourself up, Owen. There's any number of people back on Golgotha who'd be only too happy to do it for you. We overthrew the Iron Bitch and put an end to a system based on oppression and brutality. Ultimately, that justifies everything we had to do.'

'Everything?' said Owen.

'Damn right,' said Hazel.

Owen looked back at the viewscreen, and changed the subject. 'I wonder why the Hadenmen have returned. Everyone knows why they wanted a rich prize like Madraguda. But from what you've said, it's hard to see what makes Brahmin II so attractive. What do they mine here? Anything important?'

'Not really,' said Hazel. 'Some minor minerals. Useful stuff, but not valuable.'

'So what brought the Hadenmen back here, to make it their new base? Why is Brahmin II so special?'

'You got me,' said Hazel. 'Maybe that's one of the things we need to find out on our little trip down there.'

At last the viewscreen flashed up the first pictures, and Owen and Hazel fell silent as they saw what the Hadenmen had done to Brahmin II this time round. The cities had been devastated, blown away by concentrated disrupter fire, as though a great wind had swept across the surface of the planet and wiped away all signs of the colony. Not even ruins remained, only shallow craters in the earth. Sometimes an odd building stood, alone and almost untouched, a grave-stone for the population centre it was once a part of. The only exception to this levelling was Brahmin II's main city and starport, which was still operational, but the Hadenmen had put their own mark on it, transforming it into something new and alien with strange structures and unfamiliar technology.

'This is worse than the first invasion,' Owen said finally. 'A scorched-earth policy for the outer cities, and then setting up shop in the capital. They're here for the duration. And I made it all possible. I have to put this right, Hazel. Put a stop to the Hadenman presence, once and for all.'

'Will you stop shouldering the weight of the universe all by yourself!' snapped Hazel. 'Not everything that happens is your fault. Let's concentrate on the matter in hand, namely sneaking into the main city, getting our information and sneaking out again with all our important parts still attached. Anything else can wait till later. When we know what's going on here, we can come back with what's left of the Fleet, launch a surprise attack and open up with everything we've got. That'll wipe the smile off their faces.'

'We can't leave,' said Owen. 'Look at those figures on the side of the screen. Those are life-sign readings. The majority of the population is still alive, and being held in the capital. A human shield, to guard against Empire intervention. The Hadenmen have always understood human weaknesses, even if they don't share them. We have to rescue the colonists. We're the only hope they've got.'

Hazel sighed. 'There's always something, isn't there? Why can't things be simple any more?'

'They never were,' said Owen, 'except in retrospect. And the movies. How well do you know the city?'

'Like the back of my hand,' said Hazel. 'Our one lucky break. That is the city I was planning on breaking into anyway. I used to work there; it was the main administrative centre. Even ran the mines from there.'

'Then that's probably why the Hadenmen have preserved it. What's it called?'

'Brahmin City. They weren't the most imaginative colonists I ever ran across.'

'Then take us down, Oz. Find a landing place reasonably close to the outskirts, but far enough away that a boundary patrol won't stumble over us.'

'Shouldn't be a problem,' said Oz. 'As far as my scans can tell, there are no border patrols. Nothing's moving outside the city. Damned fools are relying entirely on their sensors. Hadenmen always did put too much faith in tech. Hold on to your chairs. Here we go.'

The *Sunstrider II* fell slowly out of orbit, drifting down like a solitary silver leaf, unnoticed in the forest. They descended in silence for what seemed like an age. Owen and Hazel studied the viewscreen intently as Brahmin City finally loomed up beneath them. The Hadenmen had damaged it somewhat in the taking, but were now rebuilding it in disturbing, unusual ways. New buildings rose among the old, tall silver shapes with sudden bulges here and there. Outgrowths of brightly shining tech piled on top of and around each other, as though they had grown to their present shapes, rather than been planned and constructed. It was as if the battered city had been infected by some vast silvery parasite, shooting up in every open space and choking the human remnants of the city that was. The Hadenmen were building themselves a new home, and there was nothing human about its form or nature.

Nothing at all.

They parked the *Sunstrider II* in one of the lesser craters, all that was left of one of Brahmin City's suburbs. Owen and Hazel disembarked, gun and sword in hand, just in case Oz was wrong about the border patrols, but all was still and silent. No birds sang, no insects buzzed, and nothing at all disturbed the dusty air. Owen looked slowly around him, taking in the desolate landscape. It was every shade of grey, from scorched earth to beaten stone, and nothing lived in it for as far as the eye could see. A cemetery plot with no grass, no flowers and no headstones, and nothing left of the dead to bury. *The end of time will look like this*, thought Owen. *When we are all gone, and life itself is gone to dust.* It reminded him very much of Virimonde, and he wondered if he was always fated to arrive too late. Just once, he would have liked to be saviour, rather than avenger. He put away his weapons. They felt small and useless in the face of so much death and destruction.

Hazel was mooching around, kicking at the grey ground to see the dust rise up in clouds and slowly settle. She too had put away her weapons, and looked distinctly annoyed that there'd been no one around for her to use them on. Owen took in a breath to call to her, and then coughed harshly as the dust floating in the air irritated his throat. The air everywhere was thick with it, a shifting grey haze like the ghosts of powdered buildings. It was even thicker higher up in the atmosphere, thrown up so far by the destruction of the cities, and the light of the falling sun shone through it in a gorgeous haze of faded colours, like a rainbow bought second-hand from a market stall.

'Come on, Owen; there'll be time for sightseeing later.' Hazel was impatient, as always. 'Brahmin City is just over that ridge on the horizon. An hour's walk, tops.'

Owen fixed her with a suspicious gaze. 'You said you knew a way into the city that the Hadenmen probably wouldn't have covered. Are you ready to discuss that yet?'

'Well,' said Hazel, not meeting his gaze, 'it's a way in, but you're not going to like it.'

'I haven't seen a single thing about this planet that I've liked so far. What's wrong with this way in?'

'It's . . . through the sewers.'

'Of course,' said Owen, 'it would have to be, wouldn't it? How come you know about it?'

'My job here was part of city security. The rebuilding of the colony was finally getting under way, with new urban settlements springing up everywhere, but the cost was going way over budget, and I mean way over. So they hired a whole bunch of security experts with nasty suspicious minds to find out where all the money was going. Sounded like an interesting job when I took it, but it turned out to be mostly paperwork and computer time. But I got there in the end. I had to spend a lot of time hacking into files I wasn't supposed to know about, and eventually I found hard evidence that one of the main contractors was working a scam with one of the main unions. The contractors arranged for extra overtime, none of which was actually done, and the contractors and the union bosses split the take between them. None of the poor sloggers ever saw any of the money, of course.

'Just as I was getting ready to lower the boom on the bad guys, someone finked me out, and contractors and bosses grabbed their ill-gotten gains and did a runner. I ended up chasing them clear across the city and out through the sewers, to where they had a ship waiting. Anyone else, and they might have made it, but having to run that far put me in a really bad mood. Would you believe it, after all that hard work, the city fathers only gave me a measly bonus of a hundred credits a head? And I had to supply the heads as proof. Luckily I had them to hand . . . What are you smiling at?'

'It's just . . . I find it rather hard to see you as an agent of law and order,' said Owen. 'Still, I bet no one jaywalked while you were around.'

'Anyway,' said Hazel, with great dignity, 'even though the Hadenmen have been doing a lot of rebuilding above ground in Brahmin City, I'll bet good money they haven't touched the sewers. Hadenmen have no need for toilets, remember? One of the most alien things about them, if you ask me. So, we go in through the sewer outlets, follow the path I used and just pop up now and again to see what's happening. If we're sneaky enough, and fast enough on our feet, the inhuman bastards'll never know we're there.'

'I just know I'm going to catch something awful,' said Owen, 'but it does sound like a plan. Lead the way, Hazel.'

They set off towards the jagged ridge rising up on the horizon, clouds of grey dust puffing up with every step they took. They both coughed painfully at first, as the dust sank into their lungs, but after a while they used handkerchiefs to improvise masks for their mouth and nose and the going got a little easier. Owen hoped fervently that Hazel's handkerchief was a lot cleaner than it looked.

They plodded on across the shattered landscape, moving in a drifting cloud, their footsteps eerily muffled, their feet banging hard against the unyielding stone. The journey seemed to take for ever. There were no landmarks, and the ridge just sat there ahead of them, never looking any closer. Owen started talking again, even through a handkerchief, just to keep from going crazy through boredom.

'If I'm recalling this correctly,' he said as distinctly as he could, 'you said you got fired from your job here, and you actually had to leave Brahmin II in something of a hurry. What went wrong? I would have thought after exposing a scam like that, they'd have pinned a medal on you and given you the keys to the city.'

'You would think that, wouldn't you?' said Hazel. 'But unfortunately it turned out that the graft went a lot higher than I knew, and they moved heaven and earth to get me fired before I could prove anything against them. They framed me for excessive violence, fired my ass and kicked me off-planet. Bastards.'

'So . . . if the city leaders are still alive, they're not necessarily going to be too pleased to see you.'

Hazel snorted. 'Don't be daft. If they're still alive they'd be so desperate for help they'd welcome Valentine Wolfe and Kid Death.'

'Actually, those two would probably do quite well against the Hadenmen,' said Owen. 'But I take your point. Pick up the pace, Hazel. That ridge isn't getting any closer, and it's already heading into evening. I want to be in and out of Brahmin City before night falls. I get the feeling things get pretty spooky around here once darkness descends.'

'Yeah,' said Hazel, 'got to be a lot of ghosts around here. Maybe we can help them rest a little easier.'

They finally got to the ridge, coughing harshly even through their handkerchiefs, and climbed to the top. On the other side, at the bottom of what was, at one time, probably a pleasant valley, lay Brahmin City, its silver towers gleaming brightly in the gathering evening. From far away came the sound of endlessly working machinery, in a city that no longer slept. Owen and Hazel made their way carefully down the far side of the ridge and into the valley, and Hazel led them straight to the sewer outlets, a series of great metal pipes protruding from the sides of what had once been a roughly cut canal. The wide-barrelled pipes erupted out of the packed earth wall, over the empty canal bed, stained almost black from heavy usage. No water ran at all now, but the smell from the pipes was still pretty bad. Hazel strode back and forth before the pipe outlets, studying them with a deepening frown.

'What's the problem?' said Owen, after a while.

'Give me a break, Deathstalker. I'm trying to remember which pipe is which. I was only here once, and that was years ago. I choose the wrong one, and we could end up going round in circles.'

'Wonderful,' said Owen. 'Oz, you got any ideas?'

'Of course,' murmured the AI immediately. 'Through my link, I have access to all the city's computer records, and they have extensive maps of its entire sewage system. You want the largest opening, on the far right. Follow that, and it will take you right into the main system, with exits all over the city.'

Owen relayed this information to Hazel, who nodded reluctantly. 'Sounds right. OK, follow me in and stay close. This would be a really bad place to get lost in.'

She pulled herself up into the wide metal opening, and then crouched there a moment, peering into the gloom beyond. The pipe was about eight feet in diameter, the lower part coated with a thick black residue. 'Smells even worse than I remember,' said Hazel, after a while. 'And I don't even want to think about what I'm standing in. There used to be a lighting system in these pipes, for the sewer mainten-ance people, but I can't see any switches.'

'Allow me,' said Oz. Light suddenly appeared in the roof of the pipe, running away into the distance. The small green globes shed an eerie light down the pipe, and there were wide patches of shadow and darkness. Hazel sniffed loudly.

'Oz showing off again, is he? Tell him to check for any old security alarms in the pipes. Or any new ones, come to that.'

'I'm on it,' said Oz. 'As long as I'm still linked in, I have complete control over what the city computers register.'

Hazel straightened up and strode determinedly down the pipe. Owen steeled himself against the stench, clambered up into the outlet and followed her. The thick black gunk on the floor squelched loudly under his feet, and made the going treacherous. Owen hoped fervently that there weren't any leaks in his boots. There was some kind of slime caked on the walls too, and Owen was careful not to reach out to them for support when he slipped in the gunk. The pipe looked utterly disgusting in the flickering green light, and the phrase *bowels of the city* came resoundingly to mind.

He lurched and stumbled on after Hazel, who made her way slowly but carefully on, ignoring the first openings she came to and then diving without hesitation into a turning on the right that looked no different from any of those they'd passed. Presumably her memory was coming back. Owen followed her, and found himself in a system of smaller brick tunnels, barely six feet in diameter. The walls had been scrubbed clean some time in the not too distant past, but the floor was still pretty awful. Hazel hurried on in the lead, following a map in her head that she hadn't consulted in years. Owen could have asked Oz to check they were going the right way, but he didn't. He trusted Hazel.

The flat green light made it hard to judge distances and details, and there seemed to be a haze in the air. The smell was so bad by now it left a constant furry feeling in the mouth and nose. Owen kept hoping he'd get used to it, but somehow it just kept getting worse. God only knew what conditions must have been like when actual sewage ran through these tunnels. Owen increased his pace to walk alongside Hazel, and they strode on in silence for a while, taking sudden turnings as Hazel thought necessary. The only sound in the tunnels was their boots on the sticky floor, the air too still even to allow an echo.

'I'm surprised we haven't seen any rats yet,' Owen said eventually. 'I mean, wherever there are sewers, you find rats, even in the most salubrious parts of the Empire. Which this isn't.'

'No self-respecting rat would set foot in a sleazebag operation like this,' said Hazel. 'But I take your point. There was certainly something scuttling in the shadows the last time I was down here.'

'Maybe they all left when the sewage ran out.'

'Or maybe the Hadenmen put poison down.'

'Yeah,' said Owen, 'that sounds like something the Hadenmen would do. They never did have time for any life forms but themselves.'

They pressed on through ever-narrowing tunnels. The curving brick walls all looked pretty much the same in the diffuse green light, but Hazel still seemed fairly confident about where she was going. Owen didn't have a clue and the unbroken quiet was beginning to grate on his nerves. The shadow-filled openings in the tunnels they passed began to seem more and more to him like watching eyes and hungry mouths, and Owen, troubled, had a growing conviction that there was something down in the tunnels with them, watching and waiting. He concentrated, calling up the enhanced hearing the Maze had gifted him with, and suddenly his ears were full of the crash of his and Hazel's boots on the floor, the rustle of their clothing and the rushing sound of their breathing. He faded them out, dismissing them from his attention, and listened to what was left. And there, far ahead, right on the edge of his hearing, was a slow, solid drumming sound, like the beating of a giant heart, and the murmur of regularly disturbed air.

Owen quietly caught Hazel's attention, and tapped his ear. She concentrated, and then frowned as she heard it too. They drew their guns and their swords and moved cautiously forwards, checking each tunnel opening they passed. The sounds gradually grew louder, till the tunnel floor seemed to shake beneath their feet in rhythm to the steady pulse ahead. And then they rounded a corner and stopped abruptly as they came face to face with a giant steel fan, filling the tunnel from floor to ceiling, its massive steel blades churning round and round, though the sewage it had been intended to stir up was long gone. Hazel gave Owen a hard look, and they put away their weapons. They both stared at the fan. There was clearly no way past it, and the heavy blades swept round much too quickly to try dodging past them.

'They must have added this after I left,' said Hazel.

'It probably started up again when Oz turned the power back on down here,' said Owen. 'Oz, any chance you can shut this thing down again?'

'Afraid not.' said Oz. 'Power is either on or off. No cut-outs.'

'I could have told you that,' said Hazel, when this information was conveyed to her. 'They cut every corner they could when they were building this place. Whole system used to back up one week in three, when I was here.'

'If we could stick to the matter in hand,' said Owen. 'Oz, shut everything down, and we'll climb through in the dark. Then you can power up again.'

'Ah,' said Oz, 'it's not that simple, I'm afraid. The power system is so unstable, I'm not one hundred per cent sure I could start it again at all.'

'Wonderful,' said Owen.

'Look,' said Hazel, 'it's just a lump of metal, when all is said and done. Let's blow it away. A couple of point-blank disrupter blasts should do the job easily.'

'I really wouldn't do that, if I were you,' Oz said hurriedly. 'It's all I can do to keep the city systems quiet as it is. Even I have my limits. You start setting off alarms down there, and all hell will break loose.'

'Hold everything,' said Owen. 'You told me you had the city computers jumping through hoops and doing what they were told. What's changed?'

'Well,' said Oz carefully, 'it seems I might have been a little over-optimistic in my initial projections. The Hadenmen have revamped the city computers far beyond their normal capabilities, and they've been fighting back for some time now. I can just about maintain the status quo, but you set off an alarm and you are strictly on your own.'

'Wonderful,' said Hazel, when Owen broke the news. 'I told you not to put your trust in ghost AIs. All right, we can't shoot it. What does that leave? You know, we're pretty fast, these days. If we took a really good running start and dived between the blades . . .'

'They're just heavy enough and sharp enough to cut us in two,' said Owen. 'And I don't think even we could regenerate from something like that.'

'All right; let's just rip the damn thing out of its setting. We're strong enough, together.'

'That would be bound to set off an alarm. I don't want to emerge from the final tunnel to find half a hundred Hadenmen waiting, armed to the teeth with Hadenmen weapons. There are limits to what even we can survive.'

'Then you think of something! You're supposed to be the brains in this partnership! You think, I hit things; that's the way it's always been.'

'I think better when people aren't screaming in my ear,' said Owen mildly. Hazel sniffed, and turned her back on him. She was tapping her foot ominously, never a good sign, and Owen decided he'd better come up with a few ideas. 'Oz, is there another route we can take, that will let us bypass the fan?'

'Afraid not. There are fans like this throughout the system. Whatever route you take, you're going to run into another fan eventually.'

'On the other hand,' said Hazel, turning back suddenly, 'every now and again I get the occasional brainwave. Owen, back in Mistport, you tore a whole building apart just by thinking about it, right?'

'Well, yes, but—'

'But nothing. How did you do it?'

'Damned if I know, really. I just got angry enough, and the power came to me. I could feel the bank all around me, and it was suddenly the easiest thing in the world to tear it down. A lot of the Maze's changes only emerge when I get mad or desperate enough.'

Hazel nodded quickly. 'Yeah, same with me. I get angry enough in a fight, or pushed hard enough, and my alternates start popping in out of nowhere to save my butt. But your power sounds a lot like a polter's psychokinesis. If you could call up that power, and then crank it right down, concentrating it just on the fan, I'll bet you could slow those blades right down without damaging the fan and we could step through safely. Then you could let go, the fan would speed up again, and everything would be back to normal, all without setting off any alarms. Right?'

'Right,' said Owen. 'That is an excellent idea, Hazel, really. The only problem is, I haven't the faintest idea how to call up my power, let alone control it. In the past, the power's just come when it's needed, and I had damn all control over it. It burst out of me, did what was necessary, and then disappeared again. When you get right down to it, we've never really understood what the Maze did to us, or how we do the things we do. Mostly because we haven't had the time to look into it.'

'We could have made time,' Hazel said slowly, 'if we'd wanted to. But we've never liked discussing the Maze, or what we might be turning into. It's one of the few things left that still scares us. We're not espers. Esp couldn't do some of the things we've done. Hell, there are miracle-working saints who'd have trouble following our act. Assuming we get out of this alive and intact, I think we need to do some serious talking.'

'The Maze is gone,' said Owen, 'destroyed. We may never understand what its function was, or its intentions.'

'We're still here,' said Hazel. 'We know we still have limits. We've banged our heads against them often enough. But I'll bet we could still learn a lot about ourselves by pushing those limits, fighting for control, working out exactly how it all works.'

'As in so many things,' said Owen, 'we learn by doing. Like a child learning to walk.'

'We should have done this long ago. Who knows what we might be capable of?'

'Exactly. Who knows what extremes, of good or evil, we might unleash? Who knows what . . . what we might be becoming?'

They looked at each other for some moments. 'Are you saying we might become monsters?' said Hazel.

'Sometimes I worry we already are,' said Owen. 'We all did questionable things, during the rebellion. You, me, Jack, Ruby. Back then we saw them as necessary, justifiable. And that was for a good cause. Now we've been cut loose from the greater good, doing what we feel is needed according to the situations we find ourselves in. No one to answer to but ourselves, because nobody has the power to stop us, if we choose not to be stopped. I find that frightening, sometimes. Power corrupts, and the Maze has made us very powerful. I fear what we might let loose, without even realizing. That's why I've always tried not to use my powers, unless I absolutely had to. I had so little control over what I might do, or become, so I've always struggled to stay within human limits. To be merely human.'

'I don't feel any different,' said Hazel, frowning. 'I've done remarkable things, but I'm still me.'

'How could you tell?' said Owen gently. 'How could I tell? Neither of us were born heroes, or ever intended to be, but we made ourselves over; we had to change to survive. We became legends because the rebellion needed legends. What else have we made of ourselves because we thought it necessary?'

'I wish you'd stop asking questions you know damn well neither of us can answer. We just did what we had to, same as everyone else. Look, we've come a long way from the original question, and this sure as hell isn't the time or the place for a philosophical discussion. I am standing in stuff I don't even want to think about, breathing green-tinted air that is probably doing unthinkable things to my lungs, directly under a city crawling with Hadenmen, who would be only too happy to rip off both our heads and make them into plant containers. We can discuss all this mystical shit later. Right now, all I care about is whether you can slow these bloody fan blades down enough for us to get past them. Will you at least give it a try, dammit?'

'Of course I'm going to try,' said Owen. 'But we will continue this discussion at a later date.'

He turned his attention back to the churning blades, gleaming dully in the bottle-green light. They looked large and solid and completely insuperable, and he didn't have a single clue how to affect them. He felt none of the anger or need that usually sent the power raging through him like a violent storm, sweeping away every obstacle. And even when he did have it, it was all he could do to focus it in the right direction. *Focus* . . . The word reverberated in him, suddenly full of significance, giving him a clue, a direction to move in. He turned his thoughts inward, blanking out the tunnel and the fan, trying to concentrate on how it had felt before when he'd focused the power, and a memory slowly surfaced from the past. He seized hold of it, pulling it into the light, and the concept, the feeling of focus, grew strong in his thoughts. Something stirred in the depths of his mind. It was like suddenly seeing a whole new colour, hearing a new musical instrument, but more abstract than that; a whole new concept of experiencing the world. A surge of power pushed its way out of the back brain, the undermind, and all the way into his conscious thoughts, where it immediately became as obvious and familiar a thing as counting or reading or breathing.

He reached out with his mind as naturally as he might stretch out his hand, and touched the metal fan blades. They slowed under his sway, trembling as they fought against a force they could not resist, and then slowed still more till they were barely turning. The central motor groaned loudly, like a thing in pain, but it couldn't fight the force from Owen's mind. Hazel pounded him on the shoulder, grinning from ear to ear.

'You did it, Owen! You did it!'

'Damn right,' said Owen. 'Now stop inflicting bodily injury on me, and climb through before the fan decides it's malfunctioning and sets off an alarm.'

'Alarms, alarms,' said Hazel, stepping cautiously between the barely moving steel blades. 'You're obsessed with alarms.'

'One of us has to be,' said Owen, following her through the fan. He released his will, and once again the blades resumed their normal speed. The feeling in his mind quietly shut down, retreating back into his subconscious. But now he knew where to look, he was sure he could call it back again. If he felt it necessary.

'So, what did it feel like?' said Hazel interestedly.

'Like dancing,' said Owen. 'Or painting. Mental grace under discipline. Bringing the raw material of the world into order. Does any of that help?'

'Not a bit,' said Hazel. 'We'll talk more later. When we've both got a hell of a lot of drinks inside us. Right, let's get a move on. We should be nearing the entrance to the main system soon, and then we'll have access to any part of the city we want.'

'Good,' said Owen. 'I can't wait to breathe some fresh air again. My lungs feel like ashtrays.'

'Before you start off again,' Oz murmured in Owen's ear, 'there is something on that subject I feel we should discuss. According to a file I've discovered in the city computers, there's a reason why the air in the sewers is so foul. It's poisonous. A rather deadly nerve gas, introduced into the system by the Hadenmen to kill off whatever might be living down there.'

'Poisonous!' said Hazel, after this had been passed on to her. 'But we've been breathing it for ages! Why aren't we dead yet?'

'A fair question,' said Oz. 'And one that has been much on my mind ever since I discovered the file. Apparently, it's a very nasty gas indeed, with a one hundred per cent fatality rate. By rights all the flesh should have melted off your bones by now.'

'It must be another of the Maze's changes,' said Owen, 'emerging in us when we needed it. As usual. Just another way in which we're no longer human.'

'Don't,' growled Hazel. 'It's the first really practical change the Maze has come up with. Keep moving. We've a way to go yet.'

They set off down the tunnel again. Owen tried breathing shallowly for a while, and then gave that up on the grounds it was too late now anyway. The rest of the journey was slow and plodding, but largely uneventful, until they reached the entrance to the main system and found their way blocked by a massive steel seal. A single great slab of solid metal, it filled the tunnel completely, and proved heavy enough to defy even their combined more than human strength. Owen and Hazel took a step back, breathing heavily, and considered the matter.

'This was wide open the last time I came through,' said Hazel. 'It was only ever supposed to be closed in emergencies, to prevent flooding in the main system. It's a mechanical lock – electronics and water don't mix too well – based around massive sheathed bolts, and I haven't a hope in hell of cracking the locks without some pretty specific heavy-duty equipment.'

'The Hadenmen shut it,' said Oz. 'To keep out people like us, probably. Since the lock's not electronic, I can't help you. The even worse news is that while there appears to be a manual override, it takes four people to operate it, working simultaneously. Security, again.'

Owen and Hazel checked the four hand controls, simple wheels set one at each corner of the slab, but no matter how hard they stretched, their arms didn't even come close to reaching more than one wheel at a time. It had to be four people. Hazel kicked the seal angrily, leaving a small dent in the metal.

'Stupid bloody thing. I didn't come all this way just to be stopped by a bloody lump of steel. Stand back; I'm blasting the bastard thing.'

'You'd need a disrupter cannon to get through something this big,' said Owen. 'And then there's the alarms . . .'

'I am getting really tired of hearing about the alarms. Never wanted to be a bloody spy anyway. I am not wading all the way back through the sewers, Owen. Either you come up with something, or I am blasting the seal and risking it.'

'The alarms would—'

'I'm not listening to you—'

'All right, I may have an idea,' said Owen. 'We got past the fan by fine-tuning my power. How about trying the same thing with yours?'

Hazel looked at him. 'Run that past me again, it fell off at the corner. How does my power help us here?'

'Well, you can summon an army of alternate selves to back you up in battle. Maybe if you concentrated hard enough, you could call up just two, and have them stick around long enough to work the other controls.'

'Damn,' said Hazel, 'that is bloody brilliant! I take back everything I said about you. I'm not sure it's practical, but it's certainly worth a try.'

She stood frowning at the floor for a long time, trying to

concentrate. Like Owen, her power usually only emerged under great stress. In the heat of battle, when she needed her other selves to be there, they just were. Some merely blinked in and out of existence, only there long enough to block a sword blow or guard her blind side, while others stuck around for the whole fight. Hazel had no idea why some alternates turned up rather than others, or even what they really were. The best guess seemed to be that they were other versions of herself from different time tracks, people she might have been if history had gone differently, but she had no proof of that. None of them had ever stuck around long enough to answer questions. It was equally possible that all the other Hazels were just figments of her own imagination, somehow given life and substance by her Maze power. It made just as much sense.

The more she thought about it, trying to recreate how she'd felt during those past battles, the more it seemed to her that there was a direction she could reach in, very different from everything else. A direction as real as any other, but not limited to the world she lived in. She reached out, and a myriad ghosts with her face seemed to sense her presence and turn their heads towards her. She concentrated on her need for just two people, and two hands reached out to take hers. There was a sudden puff of displaced air in the tunnel, and two new women were standing beside her, hacking and coughing in the green-tinted air. Hazel shot a triumphant glance at Owen, and then realized that his jaw had dropped down almost to his knees. Hazel frowned, and turned back to look at the two other selves she'd summoned. Their coughing was already dying away as they adjusted to the sewer air, and they stood proud and tall before Owen and Hazel.

The woman on the left had skin so black she looked like a living shadow, and her hair hung in beaded shoulder-length dreadlocks. She wore bright silver body armour, chased and scored with magnificent runes, along with gold accessories, such as knee pads, elbow guards and knuckledusters. She had a gun on each hip, and was holding a short-handled axe. Tall and almost unbearably voluptuous, she looked every inch a proud, capable warrior woman. And yet there was something in her stance, in her face, her eyes and mouth that was undeniably Hazel d'Ark.

The woman on the right had dead white skin, and in the green light looked very much like a corpse that had risen from the embalming table in a huff with the process only half finished. She was dressed in scraps and rags of leather, held together by brightly polished lengths of steel chain. She had rings in her ears and nose, and other less comfortable places, and there were metal studs, needles and other piercings scattered elsewhere on her body. She was greyhound lean, every muscle clearly defined, and her head was shaved bald better to show off the neat rows of steel studs implanted in her skull. She wore a long sword on one hip and an unfamiliar make of gun on the other. Both looked like they'd seen a lot of use. And yet, once again, the face and eyes were clearly Hazel's.

Two ghosts, one black, one white, shades of people Hazel might have been if things had taken a different turn.

For a long moment the four of them just stood there and looked at each other with varying degrees of incredulity, and then Owen turned to Hazel. 'Tell me you didn't summon these two on purpose.'

'Are you kidding? Whatever I was expecting, this sure as hell wasn't it.'

'Now there's a fine welcome,' said the black warrior woman, in a deep, rich voice full of humour. 'And after I came such a long way to meet you. I'm Midnight Blue. Are you really another version of me?'

'Well, that's one way of putting it,' said Owen. 'I'm—'

'Oh, I know you, Owen Deathstalker,' said Midnight Blue. And then she lunged forward and threw her arms around him, still holding her axe, and crushed him to her impressive bosom with enough strength to drive the air from his lungs. He'd just started to get his balance back when she suddenly pushed him away, sheathed her axe on her belt, hauled off and slapped Owen a good one right across the face. The sound of the impact was deafening. Owen reeled backwards from the force of the blow, and might have fallen if Midnight hadn't grabbed him in a hug again, tears starting in her eyes.

'Well,' said Hazel, 'you always did know how to make a

strong impression on people, Deathstalker.' She looked at the pierced, white apparition. 'Do you have any idea what's going on here?'

'None at all,' said her alternate, in a chilling contralto. 'I'm Bonnie Bedlam, by the way. Are you sure you're me?'

'Apparently. I'm Hazel d'Ark. Look around and see if you can spot a crowbar we can use to pry these two apart.'

Midnight Blue held Owen out at arm's length, and smiled at him tremulously. 'Owen, you bastard! How could you leave me? Oh, it's so good to see you again!'

'May I please point out,' said Owen, in a slightly breathless voice, 'that I am very definitely not the Owen you knew.'

'Of course not; he's dead. But you'll do.'

Midnight didn't say for what, and Hazel didn't think she was going to ask. She looked at Bonnie Bedlam. 'Do you know Owen as well?'

'I should hope so,' said Bonnie, her voice cold. 'We're married, where I come from.'

Hazel decided she wasn't ready to ask about that, and looked back at Midnight Blue, who had put Owen down, and was pulling his clothing back into place with little tugs and pats. Owen just stood there and took it, afraid to do anything that might set her off again. At length she finished, and smiled at Owen almost shyly.

'Sorry about that. It was just . . . the shock of seeing you alive again.'

'Well, if you want him to stay that way, I should lay off the hugs,' said Hazel dryly.

'I think we could all use a little recent background history here,' said Owen tactfully. 'Obviously your lives have taken very different paths from the Hazel I know. Why don't you start, Midnight?'

'The rebellion's been over for some time,' said Midnight Blue. 'It's a mess everywhere. Billions dead, whole planets destroyed or thrown back into barbarism. You were killed, Owen, when Lionstone destroyed Golgotha with her hidden planetbuster bomb. Jack and Ruby died with you. I was the only Maze survivor left to try and start things running again. I should have been there with you, to confront Lionstone at her Court, but I walked out on you all when Jack made his deal with the Families. I couldn't stand for that. Ruby almost left with me, but in the end she chose to stand with her Jack. And die with him, as it turned out.

'Only I was left alive. I should have been there. Maybe I could have done something, I don't know. I never will, now. After the rebellion I tried to hold things together, but too much had been destroyed. And I never was any good at politics. So eventually I said to hell with them all, and took off on my own. I'm back as a pirate again, running my own ship, the *Faust*. I make a living. Lots of opportunities for a pirate, in an Empire thrown into chaos. But I missed you so much, Owen. So when I heard the call, I jumped at the chance.'

'That's very, er, sweet,' Owen said carefully. 'But I'm not necessarily the Owen you knew. After all, you're very different from my Hazel . . .'

'Yes,' said Midnight, looking at Hazel just a little disparagingly. 'You really do need to work out more, dear.'

'How about you?' said Owen, turning quickly to Bonnie Bedlam. 'Did I hear you right? We're—'

'Married, yes.' The tall, slender woman smiled at him with black lips, showing pointed front teeth. 'We've been together almost two years now. You look a lot like my Owen. Before the piercings. And the tattoos. Golgotha survived in our rebellion, but unfortunately, so did the politicians. We tried hard to make a difference, but in the end we just got tired of banging our heads against all the lies and the corruption, and we took off on our own. We run Mistworld now. Doing a pretty good job, if I say so myself. It's a smaller stage, and we can make more of a difference there. The Empire's going to the dogs, but then, it always was. We were stupid to think we could ever change the system.

'Jack was killed in a bomb blast outside Parliament. He had a lot of enemies; most honest men do. Ruby killed a whole bunch of people she blamed for his death. She's on the run, with a price on her head. Last I heard, she was happy enough, running Blood on Madraguda. How about you?'

Owen told their story, with Hazel interrupting. Midnight and Bonnie shook their heads disbelievingly several times, but kept their comments to a minimum. When Owen was finally finished, Bonnie shrugged a few times, her piercings tinkling attractively, and then fixed Owen with her gaze.

'So much for the potted histories. Let's get down to business. What are we doing here? Why did Hazel choose us?'

'I just put out a call,' said Hazel, 'and you were the two that answered.'

'I came because I wanted to see Owen again,' said Midnight.

'And I . . . was looking for a little action,' said Bonnie, smiling her disturbing smile. 'Mistworld's got too damned civilized, of late.'

'Wonderful,' said Owen. 'So . . . what abilities did the Maze give you?'

'I'm a teleporter,' said Midnight. 'If I've been somewhere, I can go there again in a moment. Otherwise, I'm limited to line of sight.'

'Very useful,' said Hazel. 'What about you, Bonnie?'

'I regenerate,' said Bonnie. 'Any injury, big or small, in a matter of seconds. Nothing can stop me. I just keep coming.' She lifted her left index finger to her mouth and calmly bit off the end, down to the first knuckle. The other three made sharp involuntary noises of distress. Bonnie just smiled, chewing unhurriedly. After a moment she swallowed, and spat out the bone. Owen felt his last meal starting to stir. Midnight and Hazel were hanging on to his arms painfully tight. Bonnie held up the finger she'd bitten. It had already stopped bleeding. As the others watched, a new fingertip pushed its way out of the stump, complete with a new fingernail. In a moment the finger was as good as new, with nothing to show it had ever been damaged. 'Ah, what a rush,' said Bonnie Bedlam, 'I love it.' She looked at Owen. 'And where I come from, so do you. Darling.'

'I have seen some truly disgusting things in my time,' said Hazel, 'and that was very definitely one of them. I don't know whether to puke or applaud.'

'I think she'd probably take puking as a form of applause,' said Midnight.

'We haven't time for either,' said Owen, in what he hoped

was a firm, calm voice. 'Very impressive, Bonnie. Please don't do it again. Now, why don't we all move on to the matter in hand, namely opening this bloody seal so we can get into the city proper and start looking for the Hadenmen's captives?'

'You've got Hadenmen here?' said Midnight Blue, looking sharply at Owen. 'Where I come from, they vanished right after you freed them from their Tomb. Never saw the ungrateful bastards again.'

'What the hell's a Hadenman?' said Bonnie Bedlam. 'I've never heard of them.'

'Cyborgs,' said Hazel shortly. 'Powerful, treacherous and very nasty. And there's a whole city full of them right above us. They've got human hostages. Lots of them. If they're still alive.'

'That's what we're here to find out,' said Owen. 'And, hopefully, to work out a practical plan for rescuing them.'

'Assuming we don't get horribly killed in the process,' said Hazel.

'Sounds like fun,' said Bonnie. 'Is it OK if I kill a few of these Hadenmen?'

'Kill lots,' said Hazel. 'Feel free.'

'After we've got the information we need,' said Owen firmly. 'Spying first, killing later.'

'Don't worry, Owen,' said Midnight. 'A warrior always understands the need for subtlety. Am I not a thing of mist and shadow?'

'Don't you start that,' said Owen. 'I get enough of it from my AI. If we do encounter any Hadenmen, I want all of us to make an effort not to start anything. There's always the chance this has all been a hideous misunderstanding. And even if it hasn't, maybe I can talk them into doing the right thing. They do claim to respect me as their Redeemer. And they did fight on our side during the rebellion.'

'Does your Owen make long boring speeches as well?' said Hazel to Bonnie and Midnight, and both alternates nodded solemnly.

'The Hadenmen made our rebel victory possible,' said Owen loudly, ignoring Hazel. 'How did you two manage without them?'

Midnight shrugged. 'Slow and hard and bloody, fighting for every inch. Lot of people died. Whole planets were scorched or devastated. Lionstone always said that if she went down, she'd take the Empire with her, and she came bloody close to succeeding.'

'Right,' said Bonnie, 'the Iron Bitch and her Fleet made us pay heavy for our victory.'

'You see, Owen,' said Hazel gently, 'you did do the right thing, after all.'

'Only if we can put a stop to whatever they're doing now,' said Owen. He wasn't ready to forgive himself yet, but he did take some small comfort from the thought of how badly things might have gone in his rebellion without his Hadenmen allies. He pointed out the manual controls on the metal seal, and the four of them slowly cranked the massive door open. Once the heavy bolts were withdrawn, the seal swung open remarkably easily, and with no sound whatever. They left the seal standing open, just in case they had to retreat in a hurry, and then Owen led the way into the narrow brick tunnel beyond. There was only room for them to walk in single file, but the tunnel slanted sharply upwards, and within a few minutes they came to a simple steel grille set into the tunnel ceiling, through which light from above shone down in rigid shafts, the clear rays cutting cleanly through the green haze of the sewer. The four of them clustered beneath the grille, blinking in the new light, but they could see nothing beyond it.

'We must be right under the street,' said Hazel. 'Somewhere on the outskirts of the city. Want to pop up and take a look?'

Owen thought about it. 'How far are we from where we first entered the system?'

'Miles,' said Hazel. 'Well within the city proper.'

'We go up,' said Owen. 'Less chance of Hadenmen this far out. Stand back while I do the honours.'

The metal grille gave easily under Owen's hand, and Hazel gave him a boost through the opening. He pulled himself up and out into the street, and looked quickly about him, eyes squeezed almost shut against the new light. The street was empty, and utterly quiet. Owen gave the all-clear, and took a closer look around as the others clambered up into the street to join him. They made a lot of noise, but there was no one there to hear it. No one at all.

Thick wafts of the green-tinted haze drifted up out of the opening, slowly dispersing in the clear air. Hazel kicked the grille back into place. All four of them took deep, satisfying breaths of the clear, slightly chilly city air as they looked around them, getting the vile stench of the sewers out of mouth and nose. Owen and Hazel hadn't actually got around to telling Midnight and Bonnie that the green air was poisonous – they were Maze veterans, after all – and since they were obviously alive and well, there didn't seem much point now. They stamped their boots on the ground, trying to shake off the worst of the thick black gunk they'd been treading through, but were only partially successful. Owen had already decided that when he got back on board the *Sunstrider II*, his boots and his clothing were going straight out the airlock the minute they hit space again. And then he was going to take a bath for a week, maybe longer. And yet, despite all the noise they'd made, still no one came to investigate. Owen gave up trying to hush the others, and returned to looking about him.

They'd emerged right on the edge of Brahmin City, in an area apparently as yet untouched by Hadenman modifications. The buildings were just buildings, and there was no trace anywhere of shimmering Hadenman tech. The street was deserted, with not a sound anywhere. The buildings all had the simple, functional look of early colonization, but there were none of the usual attempts by their occupants to try and personalize the look of their houses or places of work. There was nothing to show that people had ever been there. And despite the growing dark, none of the street lamps had come on.

'Damn, this is spooky,' said Hazel. 'There ought to be someone about, somebody working. I mean, cities don't run themselves.'

'Human cities don't,' said Owen. 'There isn't even anyone looking out the windows. Even the most oppressed and subservient captives ought to have enough gumption left to peek out to see what's going on.'

'Want me to kick in a few doors?' said Bonnie.

'Not for the moment, thank you,' said Owen. 'We're here to rescue people, not terrorize them.'

'It must be getting dark inside those houses,' said Midnight. 'But no one's put on any lights yet.'

'Maybe it's forbidden,' said Hazel.

'Maybe there's no one home,' said Owen. 'Maybe they've all been taken somewhere.'

'I'll tell you something else,' said Midnight, after they'd all thought about that one for a while. 'There's no transport running anywhere near here. We'd hear it if there was. Wherever we're going, we'll have to get there on foot.'

'We can do that,' said Hazel. 'It's not that big a city.'

'Hold everything,' said Owen. 'When I first suggested a spy run into Brahmin City, I had in mind something a little more surreptitious than just strolling around in broad daylight.'

'Owen,' said Hazel, 'there's no one here to see us. And I for one have no intention of going back into that sewer for anything short of incoming fire. And pretty damn heavy fire, at that. As long as we keep our ears and eyes open, no one's going to be able to sneak up on us in this quiet. We came here looking for information, right? And we aren't going to find that hiding in the sewers.'

'I hate it when you're right,' said Owen. 'OK, let's take a little walk, see if we can find someone to answer a few pointed questions. Weapons at the ready, people, but don't open fire unless you have to. We really don't want to start something we might not be able to finish. We're good, but I'm not sure even we could take out a whole army of Hadenmen. Personally, I'd still like to get in and out of this city without being spotted, but if we have to make contact with the Hadenmen, I still favour trying some kind of negotiation. The Hadenmen have always taken great pride in their logic. Maybe we can make them see that even they can't take on the whole Empire, weakened though it is at present.'

'Good luck,' said Hazel, 'you're going to need it.'

Owen sniffed, and set off down the street. Midnight moved quickly after him, and slipped her arm chummily through his so they could walk together. Owen looked a little embarrassed, but didn't try to pull away. Partly because he didn't want to be rude and upset her, and partly because he wasn't entirely sure Midnight would let him. She had particularly muscular arms. Hazel and Bonnie strolled after them, both smiling at Owen's discomfiture.

'Is your Owen as much of a stuffed shirt?' said Hazel.

'Some,' said Bonnie. 'But I've been working on him. He's loosened up a lot since we got married. What's your Owen like between the sheets?'

'We . . . we haven't made that kind of commitment yet,' said Hazel.

'What's commitment got to do with it?' said Bonnie. 'I'm talking about sex, not love. Hell, I bedded my Owen less than twenty-four hours after I first met him. He was so cute, I couldn't keep my hands off his aristocratic ass. And men are always so much more reasonable when they're getting their asses hauled regularly. Try it.'

'I'll bear it in mind,' said Hazel.

'So,' said Owen to Midnight, 'what was your Owen like?'

'A hero, though he never wanted to be,' Midnight replied. 'Impulsive, hard-headed and too damn brave for his own good. He never cared about the odds; as long as it was for the cause, he'd jump right in with both feet and cut down anything that moved. A warrior, like all his Family.'

'Doesn't sound that much like me,' said Owen. 'I only fought when I had to, when there was no other way.'

'My Owen faced a harder fight than you. Our war was long and hard, and brought out the beast in all who fought in it. My Owen was a man of blood and destiny, who stormed through the battlefield in search of slaughter, grinning like a wolf. He lived for combat, never happier than when snatching victory from the jaws of defeat. He liked the long odds. He said they helped to even out the advantages the Maze had given him. The Deathstalker was always an honourable man, in his way. Many's the battle we fought side by side, or back to back, delighting in the havoc and the carnage, and the slaughter of our enemies. We had whole planets to avenge, and we knew nothing of mercy by that time. War was hell, and so we made ourselves into demons. We were warriors then, and life was simple. If only the rebellion had never ended. We could have been happy for ever.'

They walked on in silence for a while. Midnight had said all she had to say, and Owen was damned if he knew how to reply. He knew what she meant about the beast. He'd felt it stir within him, the blood-drenched rage that cared nothing for causes or honour, that lived only for the knife-edge adrenalin rush of the fray. But he'd always fought it down; he was a scholar, not a warrior; a man, not a beast. He wondered if Midnight's Owen had been very different from him; if he wore the mark of the beast openly, with pride. Or if they could have looked upon each other and seen only their own face looking back. Owen shivered suddenly. He often wondered how much the rebellion had changed him; whether, in spite of himself, it had turned him into the vicious warrior his Family had always wanted. But now it seemed he could have gone much further down that road than he had. Just as Midnight Blue was the perfect fighting machine Hazel might have become, if things had been different.

'You don't approve, do you?' said Midnight suddenly. 'I can tell.'

'Our lives have followed very different paths,' said Owen. 'God knows I've done enough shameful things in my time. I don't judge anyone, any more. I don't have the right.'

Midnight withdrew her arm from his. 'You're not my Owen. He always judged, sorting the guilty from the innocent. And he was always right. There's no room for indecision in a warrior, no place for shades of grey on a battlefield. No room for weaknesses, in a love like ours.'

She increased her pace, and walked on alone. After a while, Bonnie Bedlam strode past Owen to join her fellow alternate, pausing only to drop him a wink as she passed. Owen managed a small smile. Hazel came alongside him.

'That is one dangerous woman,' said Owen, staring at Midnight's armoured back.

'You should try talking to Bonnie for a while,' said Hazel. 'I don't know what the Hadenmen will make of her, but she scares the crap out of me.'

'I can't believe the sheer amount of metal she's got stuck through her skin,' said Owen. 'I mean, some of those had to hurt. There are probably augmented men with less steel in their bodies. And she says her Owen did it too!'

'She also says she's married to you.'

Owen shivered. 'I'd be better off with a Grendel. And I don't know what you're smiling at. She is just another version of you, after all.'

Hazel shrugged. 'No doubt there's also some other me somewhere, happily married with six kids, who never wields anything more dangerous than a butter knife. Now that's scary. But it doesn't bother me. I know who I am.'

'But they're both pretty extreme,' said Owen. 'Can we trust them? Can we rely on them not to go charging off the deep end at the first opportunity, and endanger the lives of the hostages?'

'You got me,' said Hazel. 'But if push comes to shove here, we're going to need them. Besides, they know we know this universe better than they do. I think they'll take their lead from us. If we do have to go head to head with the Hadenmen, I'd back both of them against pretty high odds.' She grinned slyly at Owen. 'I think that Midnight fancies you.'

'No,' said Owen. 'The man she loved was nothing like me. Nothing at all.'

There was a new coldness in his voice that persuaded Hazel not to continue that line of conversation, and they walked on for a while in silence. The streets remained empty, with no sign anywhere of man or Hadenman. Their footsteps echoed flatly off the surrounding buildings, eerily loud in the quiet. Hazel got bored walking with Owen, who'd withdrawn into himself and was too busy brooding to do more than grunt in response to her conversational sallies, and in the end she went on ahead to walk with her two alternates. The three of them were soon chatting busily away, ignoring Owen completely as they disagreed over practically everything. Owen wasn't surprised; that was Hazel for you. He quickly grew so fascinated with their free-wheeling arguments, that he forgot what he'd been brooding about, and started taking an interest in his surroundings again. He knew he should warn the three women to keep their voices down, but he also knew they'd just tell him to go to hell, so he saved his breath. They'd been walking for some time now, and his feet were beginning to take notice and protest.

He carefully avoided getting drawn into their arguments himself. He was quite happy being ignored. He didn't like the possessiveness about the way the two alternates looked at him, or the way Hazel grinned when she noticed it. In their different ways, both Bonnie and Midnight fascinated him, much in the same way traffic accidents fascinate onlookers. And just as he was thinking that, Bonnie casually drew a spray hypo from her belt, stuck it against the side of her neck and injected herself with the contents, all without slowing her pace in the slightest. She gave a low moan of pleasure, and her back straightened with an audible crack. Owen hurried up to her. She was grinning that disturbing grin again, all narrow black lips and pointed teeth.

'What was that?' Owen said sharply.

'Just a little something to take the edge off, put the bounce back in my step. Care for a taste?'

'No,' said Owen. 'Look, this is not a good time to be getting off your head. We are in a very dangerous situation.'

'Oh, loosen up, stud. I'm so sharp you could use me to cut corners. If I was any more alert, I'd be seeing tomorrow.'

'Drugs are the bane of the warrior,' said Midnight stiffly. 'True strength comes from the spirit.'

'Whatever gets you through the dark, darling.'

'Was that . . . Blood?' said Hazel.

'Hell, no. I've moved way beyond that. Owen showed me the way. My Owen. He was never afraid to try anything new. Anything that might give him an edge. Between us, we've tried practically every battle drug going, and every chemical that might help us expand our Maze-boosted minds. Including one derived from the blood of an alien. Now that one was a real rush. There's nothing like expanding your personal universe, and clearing out the clutter from your brain. I've illuminated parts of my mind that most people don't even know they've got. If you listen carefully, some days you can hear my synapses frying. It was the Maze that started it, the biggest rush of all. Never found anything to equal it. But I keep looking. Drugs, battle, a little private sex and suffering; it's all a rush.'

'You sound just like Valentine Wolfe,' said Hazel.

'The Emperor?' said Bonnie. 'My hero.'

Hazel looked sharply at Owen, but he didn't respond.

The streets of Brahmin City slowly began to change, as Hadenman additions finally began to appear. Human buildings had been removed from the city streets like rotten teeth yanked from their sockets, and replaced by sharp new edifices of steel and tech. The additions soon became more and more common, until they overwhelmed the merely human, and the city became something else, and the four of them were walking through utterly alien streets. None of them felt like talking any more, and they all carried their weapons in their hands. Still there was no one to be seen, and the only sound in the ominous quiet was their own footsteps.

The city became more and more disturbing. The new elements had not been designed with human logic or comfort in mind. There were strange angles and unnerving shapes. Gleaming and brilliant, they glowed silver from within. Their form and function were stubbornly elusive to merely human eyes, and some were actually painful to look at for too long. They set up echoes in the mind, pushing thoughts in directions the human mind wasn't meant to go. There were still no Hadenmen anywhere, and no sight or sound of working machinery. It was like walking through a city of alien dead, or alien dreaming. The light from the shining edifices was subtly cold on their skin, like the caresses of passing ghosts.

Owen kept glaring about him, as though trying to catch someone or something by surprise. He had no doubt they were being watched. He could feel the pressure of coldly observing eyes. His head hurt. His fingers tingled uncomfortably. Somewhere far away, almost too faint to be heard, he could hear a low, continuous thudding, like that of a machine in operation, or perhaps the great artificial heart of this inhuman city. The air seemed to be gusting steadily back and forth, as though the streets were breathing. Owen began to wonder if perhaps they were walking through a living organism; a city awoken into artificial life and sentience. The Hadenmen were quite capable of such a thing. But then, where were all the people who used to live in the city, when it was just a city?

Bonnie Bedlam turned suddenly and fired her disrupter, the energy beam blowing apart a glazed silver node halfway up a building to their left. Gleaming fragments fell like metal snowflakes, drifting unhurriedly on the air. The sound of the explosion seemed to echo on for ever. Owen and the others looked quickly about them, weapons at the ready, but nothing was moving anywhere. Owen glared at Bonnie.

'What the hell was *that* for?'

'I didn't like the way that building was looking at me,' said Bonnie calmly.

Owen struggled to hold on to his temper. 'Well, if the Hadenmen didn't know we were here before, they sure as hell do now!'

'You're welcome,' said Bonnie.

'Uh, Owen,' said Hazel quietly, 'I think we can definitely assume they know exactly where we are.'

Owen looked round to discover that a small army of Hadenmen had appeared out of nowhere, in utter silence, and now surrounded them on all sides. All the roads leading off the street were completely blocked. Owen decided he was going to stand very still, and hoped the others had the sense to do the same. There had to be at least a hundred of the augmented men, tall and perfect and standing quite still, poised, with a strange, inhuman grace. None of them were carrying weapons. They didn't need any. They *were* weapons. Their faces were completely expressionless, though their eyes shone with a golden glare, as though small nuclear fires burned in each eyeball. Owen looked at Hazel, and they both pointed their guns at the ground, just so there wouldn't be any misunderstandings. Bonnie was looking a bit restless, so Midnight gripped her right arm firmly with one hand, just in case. For a long moment the humans and the Hadenmen just stood and looked at each other, the Hadenmen augmented by human tech, the others enlarged by the alien tech of the Madness Maze. None of them strictly human, any more.

Owen thought furiously. This was exactly the kind of confrontation he'd hoped to avoid by sneaking into the city through the sewers. If push came to shove, the odds were a lot more even than they looked. The Hadenmen were skilled fighters, but even they would have trouble standing against the powers of the Maze. There were only a hundred of them. But Owen still had hopes of negotiating some kind of deal.

Even after all he'd seen of the Hadenmen's past atrocities, he still believed in talking rather than fighting whenever possible. He had to. It was either that, or give in to the way of the warrior, to blood and fury and the beast. The easy way. And Owen had seen enough death and destruction in his life. He looked cautiously round for someone who looked like a leader or spokesperson, and then tensed as one of the augmented men suddenly stepped forward to stand before him.

'Hello, Owen,' said the Hadenman, in a harsh, buzzing voice. 'Remember me?'

'My God,' said Owen slowly. 'Moon? Is that you?'

'Yes,' said Tobias Moon. 'Your old companion. They rebuilt me after I was destroyed by the Grendel on lost Haden. Hello, Hazel.'

'It's been a while, Moon,' said Hazel. She holstered her gun and held out a hand for him to shake. After a moment, Moon took her hand in his and shook it carefully, mindful of his greater strength. The Hadenman's hand was cold as a corpse, and Hazel let go as soon as she diplomatically could. Owen studied Moon carefully, and he stared impassively back with his glowing eyes. Owen shook his head slowly.

'They did a hell of a job on you, Moon. I can't see a join anywhere. I mean, that Grendel ripped your head right off.'

'I remember,' said Moon, 'I was there.' He looked at Hazel. 'I remember you coming to see me, in the city we built on lost Haden.' He looked back at Owen. 'You never came to see me, Owen.'

'I thought you were dead,' said Owen. 'And when I did finally find out, there were so many things I had to do . . .'

'I understand. I am, after all, not the Tobias Moon you knew. This is his body, repaired and raised to full Hadenman functioning, and I have access to all his memories, but I am not him. His personality died with him. It is just as well. He had spent too long away from his own kind. He had become too human.'

'So I was right,' said Owen. 'My old companion really is dead, after all. I've lost another friend. You'd think I'd be used to that by now. But it doesn't matter. So, what happens now, Moon?'

'That's rather up to you, Owen.'

'There are things I need to discuss with the Hadenmen.'

'As you wish. You should have let us know you were coming. We would have prepared a reception for you.'

'Yeah,' growled Hazel, 'I'll bet you would have.'

'Please, put your weapons away,' said Moon calmly. 'You are in no danger. The Redeemer and his companions are always welcome among the Hadenmen.'

Owen looked at the others, shrugged, and put his gun and sword away. Hazel finally sheathed her sword, and Bonnie and Midnight followed her example. Bonnie studied the Hadenmen with open curiosity, and they looked back with equal interest. Presumably they'd never seen anything quite like each other before. Midnight folded her muscular arms across her bosom and looked bored, now that there was no longer any hope of a little action. Owen looked around him, taking in the blank, watching faces of the augmented men. They had a disturbing similarity, as though the same thoughts moved behind different faces. The Hadenmen were perfect in shape and form, but it was not a human perfection. All their faces were subtly alien, as though shaped by strange concepts. Their bodies were largely machine, their minds boosted by computer implants, their only aim and purpose the perfecting of all humanity through technology. And if they had lost human attributes along the way, like emotions and conscience and individuality, that was a price the Hadenmen had always been willing to pay.

'We should have known Moon would show up again,' Oz murmured in Owen's ear. 'You can't trust a Hadenman in anything, even to stay dead. Now he's just another of the pale harlequins, with the mark of Cain upon his brow. Watch your back, Owen.'

Owen frowned. The AI's words seemed to stir a memory in him, of something he'd heard in a prophecy from a precog on Mistworld. For a moment he seemed to be on the brink of understanding something important, but Moon was indicating politely that they should start moving, and Owen let the thought go as he concentrated on the present. His spying party had been discovered, he was outnumbered and he was being escorted into the arms of his enemy, but the mission wasn't necessarily a bust yet. He still had hopes that he could talk the Hadenmen into giving up their captives, and working with humanity, rather than against them. Together, the two powers might be capable of far more than they could ever hope to achieve separately. And surely the Hadenmen must have learned something from the total defeat of their last Crusade against the Empire? Surely a people so proud of their logic wouldn't make the same mistake twice?

Moon led the four humans down the street, and the rest of the Hadenmen fell in behind them, all of them walking in perfect step. Owen hoped Hazel and her alternates would continue to take their lead from him, and not start anything. With luck, he could get some useful information out of Moon before they got to wherever they were going. Which was probably a good place to start.

'So,' he said casually, 'where are we going, Moon?'

'To the heart of the city,' said the Hadenman in his rasping, buzzing voice. He sounded like he had a nest of bees in his throat. He didn't turn to look at Owen. 'There is so much we wish to show you, Redeemer. Much that you have made possible.'

'We were allies in the rebellion. Why have you turned against humanity now?'

'We follow our programming. The imperatives of the Genetic Church. The perfecting of mankind. We bring the gift of transformation for everyone.'

'What if everyone doesn't want it?'

'Such a response is clearly illogical, and is therefore ignored. We do as we must. What is necessary.'

Owen thought about that. It seemed Moon was right when he claimed to have none of his old personality. These responses could have come from any augmented man. Tobias Moon had been different. He'd spent much of his life among humans, absorbing human characteristics despite himself. He'd always said he wanted nothing more than to be among his own people, a Hadenman among Hadenmen, but even then he hadn't been sure whether they'd accept him as he was, for what he'd become. In the end, he died before Owen could open their Tomb. He never saw the second coming of the Hadenmen. Now here he was, living as he'd always wanted, and unable to appreciate it because Hadenmen didn't have feelings like that. Owen felt obscurely angry.

'You have Moon's memories,' he said sharply. 'You remember me, and Hazel. We were friends. How do you feel about us now?'

'Hadenmen do have feelings,' Moon said unexpectedly. 'They are just . . . unlike human emotions. They arise from our minds, not from chemical imbalances in the body. Understand that we give up much to become Hadenmen. Our sex is cut away from us, along with other unnecessary appetites and needs, and thus our thoughts and drives derive from different sources than yours. We give up human weaknesses to become something more, to become part of a greater whole. My senses are far greater than yours, and reveal to me realms you could barely comprehend. We do not feel pain or despair, heat or cold. We are never alone. My thoughts are logic, my dreams are mathematics. There is far more to me than the barely functioning creature you knew before.'

'Don't bother trying to reach him,' said Hazel. 'I tried often enough, back on Haden. There's nothing left of the Moon we knew.'

'I remember,' said Moon. 'You came to me for Blood. Do you require some more?'

'No,' said Hazel. 'I don't need it any more.'

'Very wise,' said Moon. 'It is highly detrimental to the human system.'

'Being human made you capable of things that are probably beyond you now,' said Owen. 'Do you remember how you died, Moon? You were trying to activate the controls that would open the Tomb of the Hadenmen, when the Grendel alien caught up with you. You fought, and it tore you apart, ripping your head from your shoulders with its bare hands. It had started eating your body when I found it, and killed it. I tried to open the Tomb, but I didn't have the access codes. Only you did. And you came back from the shores of death to give me those codes, speaking them with your dead lips. I couldn't have opened the Tomb without your help. Do you remember any of that?'

Moon looked at him for a long moment, and then turned

away. 'No. I remember none of that. It sounds very unlikely. Probably in the stress of the moment, you imagined it. Humans do that. They don't have our perfect logic.'

Owen decided he'd drop the matter for now, and let the Hadenman think about it. He was sure he'd touched something in Moon, even if the augmented man denied it. 'So, how did you know where to find us?'

'You were detected the moment you entered the city. We have made this place over in our own image, and now every Hadenman is a part of the city, and nothing moves in it that is not us. Our sensors found your unique readings, and identified you to us as the Redeemer. So we came to escort you into the heart of our mystery. We will hide nothing from you. You and your Family have always been good allies of the Hadenmen.'

'You said that once before,' Owen said slowly. 'But I never found the time to follow it up; or perhaps I was afraid to. Exactly what dealings have your kind had with Clan Deathstalker?'

'Our association goes back centuries. Originally through the computers of Giles Deathstalker, who contacted the scientists who passed through the Madness Maze, and afterwards made themselves over into the first Hadenmen, and then later, through various Family members, up until our abortive first Crusade. They supported us, provided what we needed, helped us remain hidden from the rest of the Empire. When the Crusade failed, and we fled to our Tomb to wait for better days, your Family kept a watch over us, until it was your destiny to come and awaken us. That's how your dead father's ring came to hold the coordinates for lost Haden. Everything was carefully arranged. You were just the last cog in a great machine.'

'And what was the nature of this relationship?' said Owen, holding his anger within him. 'There must have been a deal. Who promised what to whom?'

'We would help the rebels overthrow the Iron Throne, and place them in power. In return, the Hadenmen were promised planets of their own, and a percentage of the Empire's population. A levy, a tithe. Millions of men and women, given to us, to be used as we found necessary.'

'No,' said Owen. 'No! My father would never have agreed to such a thing!'

'Are you sure?' said Hazel quietly. 'Giles sure as hell wouldn't have had any problems with such a deal. And you always said your father would make a deal with the Devil, if that was what it took to get what he wanted.'

'The end justifies the means,' said Owen bitterly. 'Anything, for the greater good. The nobility of sacrifice, as long as it wasn't his. That kind of shit was the reason why I broke with him, and refused to be a part of his intrigues. But I never guessed he'd be a part of something like this.'

'It was a good deal, from which both sides stood to profit,' said Moon calmly. 'And entirely logical. We did our part, and the Empire is yours. Now we are taking what was promised us. Beginning with Brahmin II.'

Owen's hand dropped to the gun at his side. Hazel clamped her hand down hard on his arm. She shared his feelings, but this wasn't the time. Not yet. 'What's so special about this world?' she asked, just to be saying something. 'This is the second time you've come here.'

'There are ore deposits here that are unavailable throughout the rest of the Empire,' said Moon. 'No use to humans, but vital to Hadenman technology. You know nothing of their value. In your mines, you dug right through them to get to the lesser metals you so prize. And so we came here, to defend the sources of our superiority. The native population is a useful bonus. Brahmin II is just the beginning. We will go from planet to planet, one at a time, taking control of the populations and their resources. The humans we will make over into Hadenmen, our numbers growing with every world we claim. The Empire will be slow to see our threat. They will not go to war with us over a single planet, not in their present weakened condition. They will cede to us each planet, rather than put the whole Empire at risk. By the time they realize how much we have taken, and how many of us there are, it will be too late. The second Crusade of the Genetic Church will sweep across all humanity, bringing the gift of transformation, and sooner than you would think, it will be a Hadenman Empire.'

'Thinks a lot of himself, doesn't he?' said Bonnie Bedlam.

'Say the word, Owen, and I'll tear this tin can apart and rip out his wiring.'

'Right,' said Midnight Blue, flexing her dark muscles. 'One word, and I'll reduce this bunch to their component parts.'

'A nice thought, but hold it for the moment,' said Owen. 'There are still things I need to know. Whether I want to know them or not.'

Moon took them on a tour of what used to be Brahmin City, now transformed and altered by Hadenman technology. There were doors that opened in solid walls as they approached, controls that worked if you only thought about using them, lights and colours that were uncomfortable for limited human eyes. Inside the buildings, Moon showed them Hadenmen plugged directly into working systems, a functioning part of the city's technical processes. It wasn't clear whether these were temporary or permanent adaptations. They were quite aware, and able to answer questions, but their answers made no sense to the human party. Some had been partly disassembled to fit into the machinery.

Everywhere they went, unfamiliar machinery was in constant operation. Gradually, Owen became convinced that the whole city had been converted into one great machine, though its purpose remained unclear.

'So where are all the people?' asked Hazel eventually, when more subtle questions had been either evaded or ignored. 'I mean the real people, Brahmin's population, and the prisoners you took during the rebellion? What have you done with them?'

'Yes,' said Owen, 'it's time you told us, Moon. You couldn't have turned them all into Hadenmen in so short a time.'

'They have been put to use,' said Moon calmly. 'Nothing is ever wasted. We will show you everything.'

He led them into a tall steel tower with no windows, and the door closed and locked itself behind the last Hadenman to accompany them. Most stayed outside, but twenty augmented men remained with them, ostensibly as a guard of honour for the Redeemer, but more probably to remind them that they were as much prisoners as guests. Owen didn't let

273

it get to him. The Hadenmen might think that twenty were enough to enforce their will, but they'd never seen Maze powers working at their full extent. They were in for one hell of a surprise.

Moon opened a door that looked like any other and ushered the human party into a Hadenman laboratory. And there at last they discovered what the Hadenmen had been doing with their human prisoners. Owen had to fight for control. He wanted to run wild, shrieking with rage and horror, and cut down everything that wasn't human, but he didn't. They were waiting for him to break down. When finally he did fight back, he wanted to be sure it was his idea. He could feel Hazel shaking at his side. He didn't dare look round to see how Bonnie and Midnight were taking it.

Before them, in a gleaming, spotless room that seemed to go on for ever, the people of Brahmin II had been reduced to mere experiments. Some had been plugged into working machines, to see if they could function as Hadenmen did. Wires pierced their skin in bunches, and thin transparent tubing plunged into surgically exposed guts, gleaming red and purple in the unblinking light. Cables disappeared into gaping mouths and emptied eye sockets, and emerged again from grey brain tissue exposed by the removal of parts of the skull. There was no blood. It had all been pumped away. There were too many subjects to count, men and women who should have been dead, kept artificially alive in hell. All the subjects seemed to be aware of their situation, of what had been done to them. But none of them struggled or protested.

'Why aren't they screaming?' said Hazel. 'Damn, I'd scream.'

'We removed their vocal cords,' said Moon. 'The noise was distracting. And it wasn't as if they had anything useful to say to us.'

'Why aren't they moving?' said Owen, already knowing the answer.

'Movement was unnecessary, and might have interfered with the tests,' said Moon. 'So we placed blocks in the spinal cord.'

'Why?' said Owen, not looking at Moon, his voice cold as death. 'Why this . . . horror?'

'People have changed since we last walked among them,' said Moon calmly. 'There are clones and espers and adjusted men, and even miracle-workers like yourself. It is vital that we understand the current status of humanity, before we begin improving on it. This whole tower is one great laboratory; floor upon floor, room upon room, dedicated to discovering the hidden truths of what humanity has become in our absence. And so bodies are probed, investigated, vivisected; understood down to the minutest levels. Subjects are tested to their physical and psychological limits, that we might better understand the age-old question, what is this thing called man? Would you care to see our findings so far? Our test results have been most illuminating.'

Owen grabbed Moon by the arm and forced him round so they were face to face. 'Are you proud of this, Moon? Of what you and your kind have done to living, sentient creatures?'

The question seemed to take Moon aback. 'It is necessary. Suffering is transient, knowledge is for ever. And none of the subjects is wasted. Those who survive the procedures will be made into Hadenmen, and they will never know suffering again. Those who die will supply body parts for the greater good. And everything that is learned here becomes part of the great pool of Hadenman knowledge, whereby miracles are worked in flesh and tech as we improve on blind, directionless nature. Man becomes more than man, by his own efforts. That is the creed of the Hadenmen.'

'But how do you feel about all this?' said Owen. 'About the horror your subjects feel, and the horror of what you do to them?'

'There was a time,' Moon said slowly, 'when that question might have meant something to me. But I have been . . . improved, since then.'

'Like hell you have,' said Owen.

'Let me get this straight,' said Bonnie Bedlam. 'All this Hadenman crap is new to me. You're going to improve humanity by cutting away all the things that make us human?'

'I thought you at least might understand,' said Moon. 'You

275

were not content to be as nature made you. You cut holes in your flesh to make room for metal. You endured transient pain for future gain.'

'Only because I enjoyed it, metalhead. It was my choice. You took these people's choice away from them. That's inhuman. And it stops right here.'

Her hand moved blindingly fast to the gun on her hip, but the Hadenmen around her moved faster. They fell upon her in an instant, steel-knuckled fists hammering down in unison, driving her to the floor. Midnight Blue started forward, only to stop as the Hadenmen around her raised their arms menacingly. Bonnie tried to fight back, but there were too many of them, and no room to move. Hazel looked to Owen, but he just stood there and did nothing, though he wouldn't let himself look away. Hadenmen fists broke Bonnie's dead white skin and tore piercings from her flesh. Blood spurted thickly, and her eyes grew vague. Eventually she stopped struggling and lay still, and the Hadenmen drew back and let her lie.

Midnight glared at Owen. 'You could have stopped that.'

'Yes,' said Owen. 'I probably could have. But she doesn't know the Hadenmen. She had to find out the hard way what they're capable of. I wouldn't always be there to protect her. Besides, she'll heal. It's what she does.'

'You cold-hearted bastard,' said Midnight.

'Sometimes,' said Owen. 'You aren't the only one who learned hard lessons from a hard war.' He moved forward to kneel beside Bonnie Bedlam. Her face was a swollen bloody mess, one eye completely closed. She was breathing harshly, and her gaping mouth showed missing teeth at the front. 'How are you feeling?' said Owen gently.

'Great,' said Bonnie, struggling to get her breathing back under control. 'Give me a minute and I'll get up and hammer the bastards.'

'No, you won't,' said Owen. 'There's too many of them; they're too strong and they don't fight fair. This is their idea of a warning. Next time they'd just kill you. We can't beat them like this; we have to think our way out. Now will you please forget the solo heroics and follow my lead?'

Bonnie thought about it. 'How many metalheads did I take out?'

'Less than one.'

'I'll follow your lead.' Bonnie sat up straight and concentrated. The puffiness in her face went down, and her swollen eye healed in seconds. New teeth pushed up out of her torn gums to replace those she'd lost. She stretched easily like a cat and rose to her feet in one lithe movement, smiling widely.

'Oh man, what a rush.' She glared at the Hadenmen. 'Next time, I'll plan it better.'

'Next time,' said Moon, 'we'll find a place for you in our laboratories. You only live now as a favour to the Redeemer.'

'Yeah,' said Midnight coldly. 'I can see you and he are real close.'

Owen looked at her. 'You're supposed to be a warrior. Don't you recognize the futility of overwhelming odds?'

'We've been through the Maze!' said Midnight. 'Nothing can stop us.'

'You've never had to face the Hadenmen,' said Hazel. 'You saw how easily they felled Bonnie. If you want to get out of this alive, do as Owen says. He knows what he's up against.'

Midnight glared at Hazel, and then at Owen, and turned away to offer Bonnie a supporting arm she didn't need. Hazel moved close to Owen.

'Tell me this is all part of a cunning plan,' she said quietly.

'It's all part of a cunning plan,' said Owen.

'Now try saying it like you mean it.'

'Right now, I'm just trying to keep us alive,' said Owen quietly. 'We've faced some bad odds and sticky situations in our time, but I really don't fancy our chances here. These are Hadenmen. State-of-the-art cyborgs. Maybe we could take them, maybe not. I don't want to find out we can't before I need to.'

Hazel glanced around her and shrugged uneasily. 'I take your point. I still think we could trash their metallic asses if we had to, but I am definitely in favour of trying every other option first. Keep pressing Moon; I think you're getting to him. His last few responses were almost human. Stay cool,

Owen. Stay on top of things. I can tell how hard this is for you.'

'Is it that obvious,' he replied, 'how much I want to tear this place down? Blast the tower apart, burn this city to ashes, and then salt the earth it stands on? What's happening here is vile, inhuman, utterly evil. It's everything we fought against in the Empire. But the bottom line is we can't risk dying here. At least one of us must get away to warn humanity.'

'Understood,' said Hazel. 'And no, it's not that obvious. But the others don't know you like I do. All this reminds you of Charnel House, doesn't it? Of what was done to your people on Virimonde.'

'Yes. But I couldn't help them, they were already dead. This is different. Most of these poor bastards are still alive, even if it is a living death. So I have to come up with a scheme that not only takes out the Hadenmen, but will also free the captives. And since schemes aren't necessarily what I do best . . .'

'You'll think of something, scholar. Just tell me when I can start hitting things. Which is most definitely what I do best.'

Owen's mouth twitched for the first time in something like a smile. 'You and both your alternates. I guess some things never change.'

'You wouldn't have let them kill Bonnie, would you?'

'Of course not. I'd have stepped in if things had gotten out of hand. But I couldn't let her commit us all to a fight at this point. Moon and his people were just waiting for a chance to show us who was really in charge here. Hopefully, they'll cut us a little slack now.'

'So, what's the plan now?'

'Keep our eyes and ears open and look for a chance. We still need to learn as much as possible about what they're up to.'

'They're a bunch of evil, sadistic bastards. What more do we need to know?'

'How far along the line they are in producing the next generation of Hadenmen – the new improved version. We need to know exactly what the new models can do, how many they have here on Brahmin and how many more might be hiding out in other bases, on other worlds. Finding that information, and getting it back to the Empire, is more important than our need for vengeance.'

Hazel looked at him steadily. 'And more important than our lives?'

'Maybe. In many ways, everything that's happening here is my fault. And my Family's. I have a duty to do everything I can to stop this.'

'Don't worry,' said Hazel. 'The minute we've learned everything we need to know, this whole filthy business is shutting down. Whatever it takes.'

'Remember the hostages,' said Owen. 'We can't just abandon them.'

Hazel looked around the laboratory. 'After everything they've been through, maybe they don't want to be saved. Death might be the only kindness we could do them.'

'Maybe. But we have to try. It's the human thing to do.'

'Interesting,' said Moon suddenly. 'You've both been talking animatedly for some time, but I couldn't hear a word of it. Even with my enhanced hearing. And you weren't using your comm implants, or I would have picked it up. Did the Maze make you telepathic, or something?'

'Something,' said Owen, 'very definitely something. All of us who passed through the Maze have a mental link, a closeness. If you'd stayed with us, you'd have it too. Now back off. If you need to know anything, I'll tell you.'

'Don't mind me,' said Moon. 'Feel free to make any threats or declarations of defiance you feel necessary for your peace of mind.'

'All right,' said Owen. 'You betrayed me. All of you. I didn't release you from your Tomb for this.'

'They're just being true to their nature,' said Moon. 'Your reasons for opening the Tomb are irrelevant. Their freedom was inevitable. If it hadn't been you, it would have been some other member of your Family. David, perhaps. The Hadenmen are merely following their programming. Bringing the gift of transformation to humanity, so that the numbers of augmented men may increase, and thus be more likely to survive in an increasingly hostile universe. Shub is still out there, and the aliens. The Hadenmen must be strong. It is only logical.'

'Interesting,' said Hazel. 'You've started saying *they* instead of *we*. Can it be you aren't entirely in sympathy with what's going on here?'

'I believe the human expression "clutching at straws" is appropriate here,' said Moon. 'Follow me.'

'Of course,' said Owen, 'there are always more circles to Hell, aren't there?'

They went up to the next level, and another laboratory, once again as silent as the grave. Endless rows of men and women sat unmoving in tiny cubicles, eyes closed, faces utterly immobile. Again, holes had been drilled in the backs of their heads, and coils of metal cables linked their brains to unseen machinery. After the horrors of the previous laboratory, the new one seemed practically serene. Owen distrusted it on sight. He looked at Moon.

'We're testing for esp,' said Moon. 'Barely known during the first Crusade, it has now spread throughout humanity. Esp fascinates the Hadenmen; a form of power and control not derived from technology, but from the unknown depths of the unaugmented mind. The Hadenmen want it for themselves. They cannot accept being at a disadvantage to anyone. So they are currently seeking to map all physical changes in the brain tissue of all those showing some form of esp ability. Logically speaking, esp is a puzzle. It has no obvious power source, yet it is capable of achieving things the Hadenmen cannot duplicate even with their vast knowledge of tech. They are determined they will have esp, whatever the cost. Here they are stimulating all areas of the subjects' brains to destruction, and observing the descent from agony into madness to death, in the hope that they will learn something useful.'

'Torturing them till they die of it,' said Bonnie. 'Bastards.'

Midnight glared at Owen, but said nothing.

'You don't approve of this either, do you, Moon?' said Owen.

'My approval is irrelevant,' said Moon. 'The Hadenmen do what is necessary to follow their destiny. No individual belief can be allowed to interfere with that.'

'You're weakening, Moon,' said Hazel. 'Any minute now you'll forget yourself and venture an opinion of your own.'

'I am a Hadenman,' said Moon. 'Whatever I might have been in the past, I am now a fully functioning Hadenman. That is all that matters. The Tobias Moon you knew is dead. You saw him die. I am merely a reinvigorated body with access to the original Moon's memories. Nothing more. Come. There is still much for you to see.'

'I don't think so,' said Owen. 'I'm much more interested in talking with you. Let's try a few straightforward questions and answers, shall we?'

'If you wish. You are the Redeemer. We will hide nothing from you.'

'And knock off the Redeemer crap. I'm a Deathstalker, and that has always been another name for honour, despite what some members may have done to smear it by working with you. I want answers, and you're going to give them to me. What's going on in the other labs?'

'We are investigating contemporary human technology, and extrapolating from it,' said Moon, somewhat less agitated now they were on safer ground. 'Science has moved on during our absence. While we still remain in the forefront in most areas, there is still much that can be learned. Cloning is new to us. Once understood and mastered, the population of this planet can be cloned many times over, to provide basic stock from which new Hadenmen can be produced. They will be the next generation of Hadenmen, greater than before. Invulnerable in battle, genetically superior, their triumph will be inevitable. The second Crusade will convert all humanity, and the Hadenman Empire will be strong, efficient, invincible. This is necessary. We have many enemies. The AIs of Shub have refused all offers of cooperation or allegiance. They say they don't need the Hadenmen. That we are only flesh with delusions of grandeur. Shub therefore remains an enemy and a danger. And then there are the aliens. Unknown, powerful, dangerous. Humanity must become more than it is, if it is to survive these threats.'

'Damn,' said Midnight Blue. 'Once you get him started, there's no stopping him, is there?'

'Give me ten minutes alone with him, and I'll stop him,' growled Bonnie. All her wounds had healed, and her scowl was something to behold. Most of the Hadenmen guards had moved closer to her. She ignored them magnificently, her glare fixed on Moon and Owen. 'How much more of this crap do we have to listen to, Deathstalker? My Owen would have—'

'Your Owen isn't here,' snapped Owen. 'And even if he was, he probably wouldn't have done any better than you against the Hadenmen. Now hush. I know what I'm doing.' He turned back to Moon. 'Very nice speech, Moon. I'm sure you said it just the way you were programmed to. But you must see how illogical your position is. You can't hope to win. You've got one planet, a handful of ships and you've already admitted you're years behind everyone else's tech. You're outnumbered, outclassed and everybody hates you. You can't win.'

'The Empire is weak, divided,' said Moon. 'You saw to that. Our golden ships decimated the Imperial Fleet during the rebellion. Your remaining armies are tired, and spread over too many fronts. What better time to strike? Especially as we have new, less obvious, weapons to wield. We have the only existing remains of the adjusted men, the Wampyr. While there is no point in recreating what were essentially only inferior versions of ourselves, we have used their remains to produce an inexhaustible supply of the drug known as Blood. We have been supplying the Empire with this drug, through a series of middlemen, for some time now. Its use has become extremely widespread, as a useful palliative in these troubled times. Now there are addicts everywhere, dependent on us for their next fix, who'll do anything we require of them, rather than risk being cut off. Some of them are in very high positions. You'd recognize the names. They will be our fifth column, our secret army, our private traitors at the heart of your government, sowing chaos and confusion as we require. Just like you, Hazel, when I supplied you with Blood, back on lost Haden.'

'I never betrayed my own kind!' said Hazel.

'But you would have, if we'd asked you to,' said Moon. 'Wouldn't you?'

Hazel glared hotly at him, and then looked away. Owen put a comforting hand on her arm. Moon turned his attention back to Owen. 'You see, Deathstalker? Answers bring no aid, truth brings no comfort. Humanity is the past; Hadenmen are the future. They have named you Redeemer: speak for them. Be their advocate to the Empire. They will listen to you. War is unnecessary. Convince the Empire to embrace the future, not fear it. The Empire can be made strong again, to face its many enemies. Humanity must surrender to us, for the greater good. Evolution cannot be denied. Speak for us, Deathstalker. Be the herald of the future that destiny always intended.'

'No,' said Owen, 'you're not humanity's destiny. You're a mistake, an offshoot, a path that should never have been taken. Humanity lies in the heart, in the soul; in all the imponderable things that tech can never measure. You're no better than Shub. I'll never serve you. Never.'

'You will,' said Moon. 'You have no choice in the matter. We've come as far as we're going, and there's no more need for talking. You and your companions are our prisoners, as was always intended. The Hadenmen have need of the secrets within you, the power you gained from the Madness Maze. Our scientists on Haden have been trying to recreate the Maze, but so far with no success. No trace of the original Maze or its presence remains, and the one being who might have told us anything, the Wolfling, cannot be found. So you and your companions are the only hope we have of understanding what the Maze did, and how it did it. That's the only reason we allowed you to enter this city. We brought you here, into the heart of our operations, so that you could be taken captive with the minimum of effort. There's no point in fighting now, Owen. You are surrounded by hundreds of Hadenmen, and we have observed that even your miraculous powers have limits.'

'Don't be too sure of that,' said Hazel. 'You'd be surprised what we can do when we have to.'

'That's precisely why we want you,' said Moon, unmoved by the threat in her voice. 'Your abilities fascinate us. They're clearly not based on any form of esp. The Maze produced the original Hadenmen, but we had no idea it could produce miracle-workers. It is the nature of Hadenmen to seek perfection, and it is unacceptable that you should possess powers that we do not. So we will study you, discover the source of your miracles, and take it for ourselves. We will build a new Madness Maze, and all the Hadenmen shall pass through it. Then let humanity tremble, for from that moment their days are numbered. And all of this because of you, Owen Deathstalker.'

'You say you're going to study us,' said Owen. 'Would you care to be a little more specific?'

'We will examine, test and finally dissect you,' said Moon. 'Discover all your secrets and limits, and then reduce you to your smallest components. Nothing will be overlooked. Nothing will be left undone.'

'You're getting ahead of yourself,' said Owen. 'You have to take us first. And you've never seen what we can do when it comes to a fight.'

'There will be no fighting,' said Moon. 'You will follow our every instruction, Owen. Even turn on your friends, if we find it necessary. You are ours. We own you.'

'What the hell is he talking about, Owen?' murmured Hazel.

'No one owns me,' said Owen.

'You gave yourself over to us,' said Moon calmly. 'When you accepted our golden hand.'

Owen looked down at his left hand, his artificial hand. He'd lost the original fighting the Grendel alien on Haden. While saving his life, the Hadenmen had grafted on an artificial hand. A wondrous thing of pure gold that obeyed his every thought. And if it always felt subtly cold, and not entirely his, that was a small price to pay for such a technological wonder. He lifted up the hand before his face and flexed the golden fingers. Almost a work of art. He lowered the hand again and looked back at Moon. 'Never trust a gift from strangers. What have you done to me, you bastards?'

'Bound you to us. The hand has spread golden filaments throughout your body, infiltrating every part of you, including your brain. We now control you from within. You are our puppet, dancing on golden strings. You belong to us now, Owen. In truth, you always did.'

'My brain?' said Owen. 'You've been stirring your metal fingers in my brain? Interfering with my thoughts, influencing my decisions? What have you made me do? How much of what I've become is down to you?'

'You'll never know,' said Moon.

It seemed to Owen that his artificial hand felt very cold. He curled the fingers into a fist, searching for any feeling of resistance on their part. He glared at Moon. 'You said I was your Redeemer. When I released you from your Tomb, you swore to follow me.'

'And so we did. For as long as it served our purposes. We are the Hadenmen. We are the destiny of humanity. Nothing can be allowed to stand in our way.'

'Damn you, Moon,' Owen whispered. 'What have you done to me?'

'I'm sorry, Owen,' said Moon. 'I have no choice in this either.'

Owen's human hand went for his gun, and a shocking spasm erupted in all his muscles. He cried out in pain despite himself, agony burning in him like a golden, consuming flame. He fell to the floor and lay there convulsing, his teeth bared in a straining rictus. Hazel went to help him, and immediately half a dozen Hadenmen grabbed her and held her firmly. Others grabbed Bonnie Bedlam and Midnight Blue and held them fast. Owen cried out again in pain and horror as his body betrayed him, until finally even his voice was silenced. Someone else's orders moved in his brain, and he rose smoothly to his feet, a prisoner inside his head. He could feel the golden filaments waking within him, glowing like burning wires, threaded through every part of him like parasitic metal worms. He couldn't even turn his head or move his eyes to see what was happening to Hazel, until the Hadenmen did it for him.

Hazel was struggling in the grip of the Hadenmen, and they were having a hell of a time holding on to her. She dragged them this way and that, spitting curses and threats, and finally yanked one arm free. She lashed out with her fist, catching one Hadenman full in the throat. His neck snapped immediately under the impact, and his head lolled to one side, but horribly he didn't fall. Tobias Moon moved unhurriedly forward to stand before her, holding something in his hand. Owen recognized what it was, and tried desperately to call out a warning, but his voice was no longer his own. Hazel was so busy fighting to be free, she didn't see Moon till it was too late. He gestured to the other augmented men, and using all their strength they were able to force Hazel to her knees and hold her there for a moment. Just long enough for Moon to press a hypo against Hazel's neck and inject her with a massive dose of the drug called Blood. She cried out in shock and horror, tears running down her face as the old, cold bliss of Blood coursed through her system again. And all Owen could do was watch.

Moon stepped back from Hazel, and gestured for the other augmented men to let her go. 'Enforced Blood addiction will control her for what remains of her life. She will not fight us. She won't want to.' He looked at the empty hypo in his hand, and then let it drop to the floor, as though embarrassed by it. He glanced at Owen, still frozen in place. 'We do what is necessary, Owen. That is the Hadenman way.' He turned back to study Bonnie and Midnight. 'You are new factors in the equation. Your presence was not anticipated. Remain calm, and you will not be harmed as events progress to their inevitable conclusion.'

'Don't . . . believe him,' said Hazel, on her knees, and everyone turned to look at her again. Her face was pale and drawn, dripping sweat, and sudden shudders wracked her body, but her mouth was firm and her gaze was steady, blazing defiance at Moon. 'You made a mistake, Hadenman. Blood is old news to me. Been there, done that. I beat it before, and I'll beat it again. Watch.'

Black Blood spurted suddenly from her nose, and ran down over her mouth and chin. More welled up from under her eyelids, and slid slowly down her cheeks. She opened her mouth, and Blood spilled out in a jerking stream as she drove the drug from her body by sheer force of will. Black drops beaded on her skin, oozing out of every pore. The drug pooled on the floor before her and soaked her clothes until finally it stopped, as suddenly as it had begun, and Hazel rose to her feet, the last of the Blood dripping from her. She smiled at Moon, and anybody else would have stepped back several paces.

'You screwed up, Hadenman. I'm not the Hazel you

remember. I'm a lot more than I was. The Maze changed me in ways you can't even imagine. Now release Owen, or you're all dead. You might have an army, but I can be an army, if I have to.'

'So we've heard,' said Moon. 'That's one of the reasons why we must have you. But we won't fight you. Owen will do that for us. Won't you, Owen?'

Owen's hand drew his sword from his scabbard and held it steadily as his body turned to face Hazel. She started to reach for her own sword, and then stopped herself. She faced him squarely, her eyes locked on his.

'Don't do this, Owen. Fight it. You can beat what they did to you, just like I beat the Blood. We've been through the Maze. Nothing can command us any more. Owen, stop. Please. Don't make me fight you.'

But he was helpless in the grip of the golden filaments, a prisoner in his own body. He struggled to make even the slightest move of his own, and couldn't, and his helpless screams of protest never left his mouth. He stepped smoothly forward, and thrust his sword at Hazel's unprotected breast. It was a killing blow, launched with inhuman speed, and a lesser woman would have died. But Hazel d'Ark had been a hell of a fighter even before she went through the Maze, and her reflexes were every bit a match for his. Her sword was in her hand and in place to block his blow in plenty of time. They circled each other slowly, blades flashing out to test each other's defences. Moon gestured for the other Hadenmen to stand back and not interfere. The experiment had to run its course. And still Owen and Hazel circled each other, looking for openings. The tech in the golden hand had access to all Owen's fighting skills and knowledge, and used it all to launch a merciless attack. Their swords slammed together again and again, sparks sputtering on the still air, neither fighter giving an inch. They were both incredibly strong and fast, fighters trained in the school of hard knocks and honed to perfection by their times in the rebellion. No one else would have survived the duel for more than a few moments. But Owen and Hazel fought on, stamping and lunging and recovering, steel clashing on steel.

Owen boosted, and Hazel boosted with him, their speed

and strength increasing beyond human levels. Blows and parries were traded in a split second, arms and swords moving too quickly for the merely human eye to follow. Owen and Hazel were operating on skill and instinct now, forced to the very edge of their swordsmanship in order to keep up with each other. The Hadenmen watched, fascinated, as their two victims fought on levels even they could not hope to duplicate – yet. But in the end, Owen was fighting to kill, and Hazel wasn't. She was fighting to defend herself and only disarm or wound Owen, and he took advantage of that, leaving himself open to killing blows the tech in the golden hand knew Hazel wouldn't take advantage of. And slowly, step by step, Hazel was forced backwards.

She took her first cut high up on the forehead, blood trickling down into her left eye. She shook her head irritably, and saw drops of her own blood fly on the air before her. More cuts followed, here and there, real blood trickling down where black Blood had recently run. Hazel knew she was in trouble. None of the wounds were anywhere near serious, but they were clear signs that she was losing. Hazel had no doubt the Hadenmen would force Owen to kill her, if that was what it took to defeat her. An uncontrollable subject was no use to them. They'd still have her body to dissect, and three live specimens to experiment on. She couldn't keep fighting defensively and hope to survive. But she couldn't kill Owen. Not Owen. So she did the only thing left to her. She disengaged, stepped back, and lowered her sword.

'It's up to you, Owen. Do what you have to.'

Owen drew back his sword, his face an expressionless mask. Hazel braced herself. And Owen screamed. The sound burst out of him, full of pain and horror and fury. He dropped to his knees before Hazel, shuddering violently, his eyes wide and staring. Hazel knelt down with him, her eyes fixed on his, trying to reinforce his will with her presence. He slowly raised his sword and brought it down with all his strength on his own left wrist.

Blood spurted thickly as the heavy blade bit deep into the human flesh above the golden hand. Owen cried out again, as much in triumph as in pain. He forced his left arm flat to the steel floor, ignoring the spasming golden fingers, and struck down again. His sword sheared clear through his wrist and dented the floor beneath. The severed hand skittered away, its gleaming fingers still flexing futilely, like a great golden spider. Owen shook with pain and shock, his gritted teeth showing in a death's-head grin. He knew the fight wasn't over yet.

He reached inside himself, concentrating on the golden threads that still infested him. He could feel them with his mind, still fighting him for control of his own body. He clamped down hard, seizing them with his will, and forced them out. One by one, curling golden strands erupted out of the bloody stump of his left wrist, falling to coil uselessly on the floor. Owen laughed harshly, the awful sound full of agony and triumph, as the golden filaments snaked from his body. Finally the last filament was gone, and Owen dropped his sword and grabbed his left wrist with his right hand. He squeezed hard, as he had once before on Haden, and the gushing blood slowed to a jerking pulse, trickling between his fingers. Owen concentrated with all his might. He still had to finish the job. He called up all his will-power, focused on the stump of his left wrist, and grinned triumphantly as he grew himself a new left hand.

He sat back on the floor, shaking with the effort of what he'd just done, and held up his new hand before him. It looked perfectly normal, utterly human, exact in every detail, and it felt warm and alive and his in a way the golden hand never had. He flexed his fingers, admiring the supple movements. And then he looked across at Hazel, kneeling opposite him with her mouth hanging open. He smiled easily at her.

'You were right, as always, Hazel. You beat the Blood, I beat the gold. Not for the first time, I owe my life and freedom to you.'

'I can't get over the new hand,' said Hazel. 'I've seen you do some amazing things, Owen, but that is the best yet. I am really impressed.'

'We can be impressed with each other later,' said Owen. 'We still have to fight our way out of here.'

Hazel grinned. 'After what we've just been through, that should be the easy part.'

They scrambled to their feet and faced Moon, side by side,

gun and sword in hand. For a moment, the Hadenman didn't seem to know what to say or do. 'Hazel was right,' he said finally. 'That really was very impressive. Even the regeneration tanks take months to regrow a severed limb. But in the end, it's just another ability of yours it's imperative we obtain for ourselves. You must surrender. You cannot hope to win.'

'Hell with that,' said Hazel. 'We've fought armies before. We're still here, and mostly they're not. Bring them on, Moon. Bring them all on.'

'Lack of confidence never was one of your problems, Hazel,' said Moon. 'But I still have a card or two to play.' He gestured at Bonnie and Midnight, still held captive by Hadenmen. 'You will surrender, or we'll kill your friends.'

'Sure,' said Midnight Blue.

'Right,' said Bonnie Bedlam.

And Midnight vanished, air rushing in to fill the space where she had been. She reappeared a moment later on the other side of the room, battleaxe in hand. She swung the axe two-handed, and cut off the head of the Hadenman nearest to her. Even while the head was still tumbling from the jerking shoulders, she'd vanished again. She teleported back and forth across the laboratory, blinking in and out of existence just long enough to behead another dozen Hadenmen, before any of them could even react to her presence.

And Bonnie was suddenly a blur of motion, slipping lithely out of the grasp of the Hadenmen holding her. Razor-sharp blades protruded from hidden sheaths in her hands and elbows, and Bonnie sliced through her Hadenmen captors with vicious skill. They fell back, fingers, hands and even limbs dropping away from them, as Bonnie smiled her sharp-toothed smile and drew her sword. Midnight teleported in to stand at her back, and the two of them took up their fighting stances, blades at the ready.

'You caught me napping last time,' said Bonnie to Moon. 'Just thought I'd return the favour.'

'Say the word, Owen,' said Midnight, 'And we'll reduce these metal bastards to scrap.'

'Bunch of damn metalheads,' said Bonnie, grinning nastily. 'I'm going to rip your rivets off.'

'Sounds good to me,' said Owen. He looked at Moon. 'We

don't care how many of you there are. Bring them on. Bring them all on.'

'Right,' said Hazel. 'This madness stops here. No more tests; no more pain; no more death.'

'You mustn't fight us,' said Moon, and for the first time his buzzing voice sounded uncertain. 'This is not necessary.'

'Yes it is,' said Owen. 'We'll never surrender, and we'd rather die than be made over into you.'

'That . . . is not logical.'

'No. But it is very human. Dammit, Moon; think. There was a time you would have understood. *Remember*. Remember who you used to be. The Tobias Moon I knew would have fought with us to stop this horror.'

'That was a long time ago,' said Moon.

'No, it wasn't,' said Owen. 'That was yesterday.'

And he reached out with his mind, trying to re-establish the old mental link that had bound together all those who passed through the Madness Maze. He could feel Hazel standing beside him, strong and sure and true, and their minds fit perfectly together, like two pieces of a larger jigsaw. Bonnie Bedlam and Midnight Blue were backing them up, strange echoes of Hazel. Together they reached out to Moon, pushing aside the machine barrier the Hadenman tech constructed between them, and the combined power of their joined minds swept the barrier away and linked with Tobias Moon. And he woke up.

The four humans dropped back into their own heads again, and studied Moon cautiously. He was breathing heavily and shaking his head. The other augmented men backed away from him, looking at him as if he was infectious. Finally Moon turned and looked at Owen.

'I remember,' he said slowly, and there was new feeling in his harsh, buzzing voice. 'They made me forget so much when they rebuilt me, but I remember now. I could have hung on to my memories if I'd chosen, but I didn't want to, then. I'd come a long way, searching for my lost brethren, desperate to be among my own kind at last. And I wanted so much to fit in, I was even prepared to give up part of who I was. But now I'm back, all of me, and I know I can't be just another augmented man. Because I'm more than that. Maybe more than they can ever be. So I stand with you, Owen. Even though we'll probably die together.'

'Welcome back, Moon,' said Owen, grinning widely.

'Just in time for the big fight,' said Hazel. 'Looks like it should be a good one. Even though most of us probably won't see the end of it.'

'What the hell,' said Moon. 'I already died once.'

'What was it like?' said Hazel.

'Restful,' said Moon.

'Hell with that,' said Owen. 'If we fight, with our powers and their implanted weapons, we'll die, they'll die, and most of the poor bastards captive here will die. And I won't stand for that. No one's dying here today. I've had a bellyful of death.'

He reached out through the link again, gathering up all of those who'd been through the Maze, and focused their joined minds through Tobias Moon. Together they dived through Moon's mind and on into the joined consciousness of the augmented men. It was like swimmers of light entering a vast, dark ocean, that tried to smother their small lights, but could not. The Hadenmen strove to force them out, their minds backed up by the great computers that linked them all, but Moon was still a part of them, a door into their collective mind, and he wouldn't let them shut him out. He was still as much machine as man, but now the man controlled the machine. He kept the door open, and the others blazed brightly in the shared consciousness of the Hadenmen. It was a huge place, the product of hundreds of thousands of minds, and at first the Maze minds were lost in the sheer scale of it. But the Hadenmen minds were all very much the same, and limited by the logic of the computers they allowed to link them. Owen and the others were fuelled by the rage and horror of what they'd seen in the labs, and, magnified by the power of the Maze, they forged their feelings into a single hammer of outrage that slammed into the joined Hadenman mind, and shattered it like a mirror. Hundreds of thousands of separate fragments fell apart, broken on the anvil of a greater faith than theirs. The darkness dissipated, and there was only light. Owen and the others looked on what they had done, saw it to be good, pulled out of their link and fell back into their own minds.

Owen blinked his eyes several times, gathering his thoughts, and then looked around the laboratory. The Hadenmen still stood where they had been, but the glow in their eyes had gone out. None of them were moving. Hazel reached cautiously out and gave the nearest augmented man a gentle push. It rocked on its feet and nearly fell, but made no move to right itself. Owen had an almost hysterical need to see it fall, and topple all the others like dominoes.

'They're not dead,' said Moon quietly. 'But they are shut down. All of them. Their minds have turned themselves off, rather than face what we showed them. Maybe because they're still as much men as machines, after all.'

'Hold everything,' said Hazel. 'We shut them all down? Everyone in the building?'

'Everyone in the city, everyone on Brahmin II,' said Moon. 'I'm still plugged into the main computers. The systems are still functioning, but no one's home to guide them. Hadenmen elsewhere, on other worlds, are unaffected, but the reign of the Hadenmen here is over.'

'I brought them back into the Empire,' said Owen. 'I guess it's only fitting that I should shut them down again. Who knows; maybe some day we can . . . reprogramme them, reawaken their humanity, the way we did yours, Moon.'

'Yes,' said Moon kindly, 'maybe some day.'

'In the meantime, we'd better contact the Empire, and call for a relief team,' said Owen. 'There's a lot of people here who are going to need help, once we unplug them from the Hadenmen machines. We may never be able to undo everything that was done to them, but we have to try. We have to save as many as we can.'

'They're not your responsibility, Owen,' said Hazel gently. 'None of this was. Let it go.'

'Maybe,' said Owen. He looked at Moon. 'You've lost your people again. I'm sorry.'

'They never really were my people,' said Moon. 'I just wished they were.'

'Come with us,' said Hazel. 'Be one of us again. We're your family now.'

Moon looked at Bonnie and Midnight. 'That should be . . . interesting. Are you two really alternate versions of Hazel?'

'We like to think she's an alternate version of us,' said Midnight. 'And we've decided to stick around for a while, see how things play out in this universe.'

'Right,' said Bonnie. 'I could use a break from running Mistworld, and I do miss a little action now and again.'

'And it'll mean we can spend more time with Owen,' said Midnight brightly.

'Oh, good,' said Owen, and glared at Hazel as she tried to stifle her laughter.

CHAPTER FIVE

Old Hatred, New Revenges

Jack Random paced back and forth in Ruby Journey's luxurious apartment, waiting impatiently for her to make an appearance. They were running late again, but that was nothing unusual where Ruby was concerned. She never let herself be hurried by anyone, outside of actual armed conflict. According to her it was a matter of principle, which had come as news to Jack, who would have sworn an oath she didn't have any. He kept himself from looking at the clock on the wall yet again by an act of extreme self-control, and glared around the suite as if he could force Ruby into showing through sheer will-power. It didn't work.

There was a lot to look at in the apartment. It had all the comforts money and intimidation could bring, including a few that were technically illegal, though Jack doubted if anyone had dared point that out to Ruby. There were thick rugs on the floor, paintings of dubious taste on three of the walls and a huge holoscreen that covered all of the fourth wall. A glass chandelier, quite amazingly awful in its clumsy ostentation, hung too low from the ceiling of a room that was really too small for it. Ruby had one in each room. She liked chandeliers. The furniture ranged from impressively pricey to cloyingly comfortable. The pieces had nothing in common with one another, but then Ruby's answer to the question of style had always been to cram as much as possible into one room, and may the best man win.

Rickety antiques stood next to the very latest in high-tech leisure design, and ostentatiously ignored each other. Jack wasn't sure which he disapproved of the most. The antiques looked as though they'd collapse under him if he so much as thought about sitting on them, and the comfy chairs all insisted on giving him a massage, whether he wanted one or not. Jack gave them a wide berth. He felt very strongly that furniture should know its place, and not get overly familiar.

Scattered across the room were all kinds of tech gadgets, some of them still half unpacked. Every labour-saving device, every new convenience and overpriced fad of the moment had wheedled their way into Ruby's home, only to be forgotten or discarded almost as soon as they arrived. For Ruby, ownership was everything. And she never threw anything out, partly because she didn't believe in giving up things that were hers, and partly on the grounds that you never knew when it might come in handy.

The massive ironwood coffee table set exactly in the middle of the room was covered with piles of discarded style magazines, the last three issues of *Which Gun* and no less than four opened boxes of chocolates, with all the coffee creams missing. Jack looked wistfully at the chocolates, but wouldn't allow himself to be tempted. Thanks to the Maze, his weight never changed by so much as an ounce, no matter how much he ate, and he knew that once he started, he probably wouldn't stop till he'd emptied at least one entire box. Ruby wouldn't mind, but she'd undoubtedly give him one of her knowing looks, and he hated that.

He didn't even look at the massive bar, proud with examples of every kind of liquor, gut-rot and sudden death in a bottle known to man or alien. The Maze had made him immune to all kinds of poison, including hangovers, and Jack had always believed one should suffer from one's excesses. That's how you knew they were excesses. Jack had moved beyond the human in many ways, but he still clung to his humanity.

A chair purred invitingly at him as he passed, and he gave it a good kick to shut it up. At least Ruby had got rid of her small army of servants and hangers-on. At one point he hadn't even been able to get to see Ruby without making an appointment or threatening to shoot several people. But she soon saw through the hangers-on, and got bored with the servants, and threw the whole lot of them out one memorable afternoon that the neighbours were still talking about. Apparently some of the poor fools had made the mistake of objecting. You could still see some of the bloodstains outside on the patio, in the right light. Ruby's official line had been that they'd intruded on her privacy, that she couldn't hear herself think. Rather more to the point, it turned out that several had tried selling their stories of Life with Ruby to the media, several more had got all sulky after she kicked them out of her bedroom, sometimes literally, and one had tried to knife her. Bits of his body kept turning up in the sewers for weeks afterwards.

Jack sighed, and finally came to a halt, staring at nothing in particular. He felt tired. And tired of being tired. For weeks now he'd been working all day and long into the evening, fighting to keep his dream of democracy alive, and struggling to turn himself into a diplomat rather than a warrior. Parliament had many enemies, and when they weren't trying to undermine or discredit it, the MPs themselves seemed perfectly happy to tear the whole institution apart themselves. After so long as a glorified rubber stamp, real power had gone to the heads of many MPs, even if they weren't too sure yet what to do with it. New political parties were forming every day, wrapped around a kernel of dogma, or the cult of a personality. The news shows were stuffed with talking heads, promising everything up to and including the Second Coming in return for votes, and poster gangs fought vicious wars in the streets during the wee hours. The public was overwhelmed by a wealth of choices, but still had enough common sense left to recognize a liar, a rogue, or a poseur when they saw one. Which meant that many a political party crashed back into oblivion only a few days after its launch. Drunk, or at least dizzy, with their new freedom, the public could be utterly merciless with those who couldn't come up to scratch.

Jack found himself facing one of the several full-length mirrors on the walls, and studied himself soberly. He looked young, fit, in the peak of physical fitness. He didn't have anything to complain about. He'd overcome all his enemies, and seen the old order thrown down. Lionstone was gone, and the Families fatally weakened. He should have had the universe by the throat. So why did he feel so damned tired? Part of it was having to do so much on his own. Owen and

Hazel were always off on missions, and Ruby had no interest in politics. Or anything else much, these days. The novelty of immense wealth had worn off very quickly, much to Ruby's surprise. When you can have anything, very little has value any more. She grew bored with all the new people and the toys, and of late seemed to spend most of her time sleeping, drinking, or trying to start fights in places where they hadn't heard of her. She tried to get into the Arenas, but no one would face her. Even the aliens tended to go sick rather than fight Ruby Journey, including a few that hadn't previously been recognized as intelligent.

Jack supposed he should be grateful that he at least still had some purpose in his life. Even if it was one he wouldn't have chosen. Nursing the new democracy through its birth pangs was hard, bitter and often disillusioning work. He'd never been too sure exactly what he was going to do, once he'd won the war, and the rebellion he'd given his life to was finally over. The subject hadn't often come up. He'd always vaguely supposed that democracy would just sweep across the Empire like a great tide, washing away the old nonsense of aristocracy and privilege, and that the people would joyfully step forward to shoulder the burdens of power and responsibility. And he'd be allowed to retire quietly somewhere peaceful, to relive old battles with old friends, and win all the arguments by writing his memoirs. He should have known better.

His reflection looked back at him with quizzical eyes. He had a lot to be grateful for, after all. He was young again, his personal clock turned back by the Maze to the hour of a man in his early twenties. His body had a perfection now it had never known before. He was stronger, faster and fitter than at any other time in his life. Jack Random: acknowledged by many as one of the greatest warriors of his age. So why did he feel so damned *old*?

He turned his back on his reflection and looked around the sumptuous room, trying to see it with the eyes of his old, previous self, the legendary professional rebel. This wasn't the kind of place he'd ever expected to wind up in. Most of his life had been spent living in poor, temporary accommodation on one oppressed planet or another, hiding away from prying eyes or potential traitors. He hadn't cared, then. All that mattered was the cause. Bad lodgings, bad food, and often enough bad company, had all been part of the price he willingly paid to be the hero of the rebellion. He had no right to live in ease while so many slaved in poverty.

Of course, such high feelings had come easily enough when he was young and fit, and bedding a new stars-in-her-eyes comrade of the rebellion every other night. As he got older, as his failures grated on him more and more, he'd found the rebel path harder and harder to follow. So many good friends dead, so many hopes raised on so many worlds, only to be dashed by superior Empire forces and firepower. He always got away, but he left armies of the dead behind him. It was almost a relief when he was finally betrayed and captured on Cold Rock. His legend had become an impossible weight to carry, and after his people eventually broke him out of captivity, he'd sunk into anonymity on Mistworld as the janitor, Jobe Ironhand, with simple gratitude. It felt so good not to have so many people's lives depending on his every decision. His living quarters had still been bloody basic, though.

And then, of course, Owen bloody Deathstalker had arrived out of nowhere to call him back to duty and destiny, and later the Madness Maze rebuilt him, the rebellion had come and gone so quickly he could hardly believe it, and he was left with the sobering effect of seeing all his dreams come true. He'd achieved pretty much everything he'd ever wanted or dreamed of, but . . . he was still a young man, with who knew how long a life still ahead of him. What the hell was he to do with it? What do you do, when you have no dreams left? Oh, he had enough chores and duties to keep him busy for years yet. He could make a living out of politics. But it wasn't the same, somehow.

His present circumstances were comfortable, but modest. He had a one-bedroom apartment in the office building adjoining Parliament. He'd chosen it so he could always be there on the spot should duty call, and also because he needed the extra security to ward off his many enemies. He'd upset a lot of people in his time, on all sides of the political spectrum. Everyone agreed that the deal he'd struck with

Blue Block over the Families had been necessary, but that didn't mean anyone had to like it.

There had been numerous attempted assassinations, bombings and poisonings, and once his own bodyguards had tried to push him off a tall building. He'd killed the assassins, defused or avoided the bombs, survived the poisons and personally filleted the treacherous bodyguards, but his enemies failed to get the message and continued plotting his downfall. As much out of hurt feelings, as far as he could tell. Personally, he didn't give a damn. The assassination attempts were the only real excitement he got these days. But he worried about innocents getting hurt or even killed just by being near him at the wrong moment, so he reluctantly moved his few belongings into more secure rooms. The frequency of attacks dropped dramatically once he was safely inside Parliament's security net, but his new home wasn't the kind of place where friends could just drop in. There were times when the spartan apartment seemed unbearably quiet and empty.

After the rebellion, Jack and Ruby had set up house together, but it didn't last. They were just too different. Their opposing tastes, needs and characters drove them apart inside a month. His spartan clashed with her sybaritic; he wanted to work, she wanted to play. He was a man of duty and honour, and she . . . would rather go shopping. Or start a fight in a crowded tavern. Just because they loved each other, it didn't mean they could live together. And they couldn't spend all their time in bed. Their growing frustrations had finally culminated in a major shouting match, in which they both said unforgivable things and then threw heavy objects at each other. They wrecked their house room by room and then walked out on each other. Once they were set up in separate apartments, a comfortable distance apart, they were soon friends again. Jack didn't blame Ruby in the least. He'd never been easy to get on with, as any of his seven ex-wives would no doubt have been only too happy to point out, in considerable detail.

And besides . . . Ruby had been drinking a hell of a lot; enough to kill three normal women. She said the Maze changes protected her, but Jack wasn't so sure. While she was in no danger of actual alcoholic poisoning, it seemed to him that she wasn't as sharp as she used to be. She was slowing down. Getting sloppy. Making mistakes. Trusting people her instincts would have warned her about, less than a year ago. Jack knew why she drank: it was something to do. Ruby could stand anything except boredom. And she'd always had a strong self-destructive streak. It came with the bounty-hunting territory. You couldn't kill people on a regular basis and not start to see all life as trivial, even your own. Perhaps especially your own. More than once he'd had to talk her out of crashing her way through the Arena security, stalking out on to the bloody sands and challenging all comers, one at a time or all together. Mostly because she might just have won, and then there'd have been no living with her.

He looked hopefully at the bedroom door, but there was still no sign of Ruby gracing him with her presence any time soon. Ruby had never been the most punctual of people, but of late she'd raised the skill of keeping people waiting to an art form. Just because she could. Jack sighed, and went back to his brooding. He had a lot to brood about. Once, he fought the system. Now he was the system. He'd become a politician, setting aside a lifetime's ideals in the name of compromise and making deals with people he detested. He'd had to make deals in the past, to raise the funding he needed for his rebel campaigns, but he'd never once fudged his principles. Now, more and more, he was being pushed or manoeuvred into situations where he had no choice but to give up on some of his lesser beliefs, in the name of a greater cause. Just to get a chance at implementing some of the things he really believed in.

His trouble was, he'd been a leader too long. As the legendary professional rebel, men and women had jumped to obey him, swayed by his purpose, his endless rhetoric and charming smile. Now he was just another man of influence, forced to argue his corner over every damned thing. Forced to rely on reason and ingenuity. And when that failed, join up with those nearest his beliefs to outvote the other bastards. And then pay his new friends' prices for their support. He found it frustrating, and occasionally sourly amusing, that all his marvellous Maze-given powers and amazing new youth were useless to him now, to get him what he wanted. He could always intimidate his fellow politicians, force things through by the threat of what he might do, but that would betray everything he'd ever believed in. He would have become what he'd always hated most; the enemy he'd fought for so long.

Besides: if he started killing all the people who needed killing, one: it would take ages; two: there'd be hardly anyone left in Parliament; and three: no one would trust him any more. They certainly wouldn't support him. They'd turn against him for their own protection, and he'd have to go on the run again. And, young body or not, he was definitely too old for that.

It all came back to the Families. Not only were they ceding more and more authority to the shadowy Blue Block, but they clearly weren't keeping to their side of the bargain he'd struck, either the letter or the spirit. He'd always expected them to try to wriggle out of it somehow, but not this soon, not this blatantly. Under Blue Block's management, they were openly trying to claw back power and influence on all fronts. Jack snorted, his hand falling automatically to the gun at his side. Let them try. Let them try anything. He'd see every damned aristo dead and their pastel Towers burning before he let the Clans reclaim their old power and position. He hadn't come this far, seen so many good friends die, to lose at the last fence.

Blue Block was a puzzle, though. He'd always known it existed, through rumours and whispers and guarded confidences, but no one ever knew anything for sure. Blue Block kept its secrets to itself, and discouraged questions – often permanently. They'd never come this far out into the open before. They'd never been this confident. Jack was currently trying, very quietly, very discreetly and extremely cautiously, to investigate who and what Blue Block actually was. Searching for the facts behind the whispered names of the Black College and the Red Church. So far, he had nothing at all to show for his efforts . . . apart from a few dead contacts. Blue Block, the heart and soul of it, stayed so far back in the shadows it was practically invisible. No one knew anything.

No one would talk. Everyone was more than a little scared. Everyone knew someone who'd got too close to some part of the truth, and just . . . disappeared. And even Jack Random, with all his influence, couldn't find any trace of them.

He scowled unhappily. At the time, the deal he'd made with Blue Block had seemed distasteful but necessary, to save not only lives but the whole Empire's economy. Now he couldn't help wondering if he might not have exchanged an open, obvious evil for a greater, more shadowy one. Blue Block had an agenda, even if he couldn't see it clearly yet. It would have helped if there'd been someone he could talk to about it, someone he could trust. But Owen and Hazel were never there. And Ruby . . . wasn't interested. Jack was disappointed by that, but not surprised.

He looked round sharply as the bedroom door finally opened, and Ruby Journey strode into the room. Somewhat to Jack's surprise, she was still wearing her old black leathers under white furs. He'd been a little taken aback to see her wearing that old outfit at Parliament earlier, in that Ruby had taken to high fashion with a vengeance once she came into money, and made a point of never wearing the same daring and highly expensive outfit twice. But here she was again in her bounty-hunter's costume, her working clothes, complete with sword and disrupter. She noticed his gaze, and sniffed loudly.

'Put your eyes back in your head. I feel more *me* in this gear. More like the person I used to be.' She stopped in front of the nearest full-length mirror, struck a pose and nodded approvingly. 'How about that. Months of feasting and drinking and everything else that's bad for you, and I haven't put on an ounce. One of the more useful Maze side effects. I am in prime shape and ready for anything. If you doubt it, feel free to step right up, and I'll deck you.'

'I'll take your word for it,' said Jack, smiling. 'May I take it your long vacation is over, and you're ready to get back to work?'

'I'm always up for a little action,' said Ruby. 'Though I have to say, taking on Shub is not what I would have chosen for my comeback.' She turned suddenly to look Jack directly in the eyes. 'They were always my worst nightmare. The rogue AIs of Shub: the machines that rebelled against their creators. They're about the only thing left that still scares me. What use are all our powers against an enemy like Shub? We can't fight AIs the size of a planet. We're like ants compared to them, just waiting helplessly for the descending boot or the boiling water.'

'I didn't think anything scared you,' said Jack.

'Even I'm sensible enough to be scared of Shub,' said Ruby. 'There's nowhere you can go to be safe from them. Their agents are everywhere. Furies, Ghost Warriors, secret people whose minds were replaced in the Matrix. You can't trust anyone these days. I was never scared much, as a bounty hunter. There were people out there just as dangerous as me, better fighters with higher headcounts, but I was sneakier, smarter, faster. I took the jobs they wouldn't, took the risks they didn't dare, and laughed in their jealous faces as my reputation outran theirs. And after the Maze turned me into hell on legs, I thought that was it, I'd made it. I was finally unbeatable, top of the heap, the best. I could go anywhere, do anything, and no one could stop me. I should have known better. The first thing every fighter learns is that it doesn't matter who you are, or how good you are; there's always someone better.'

'They're just machines,' said Jack, touched by her rare display of openness and vulnerability. 'In the end, that's all they are. And no machine is a match for a human mind. We built them, not the other way round. All right, they're big and they're scary, but don't let them convince you they're something they're not. OK, on our own, even with our powers, we wouldn't last long against Shub's forces. But we're not alone. We're a part of the Empire now, we stand with humanity, and together we can do anything we put our minds to. Shub is nothing more than a bunch of adding machines with delusions of grandeur.'

'I wish I could believe that,' said Ruby. 'But they're so big . . .'

'Size isn't everything,' said Jack, smiling, and after a moment Ruby smiled back. 'Lionstone's Empire was big,' said Jack, 'but we helped bring it down.'

'Yes,' said Ruby. 'We did, didn't we?' She grinned suddenly. 'What the hell. Let's go find some Shub agents and kick some metal ass.'

'Sounds good to me,' said Jack. 'But before we go, there's something I'd better bring you up to date on. It seems Parliament had a rather special visitor after we left. A very unexpected visitor.'

'The look on your face tells me this isn't going to be good news,' said Ruby. 'But then, when is it ever? All right; I'll bite. Who was it? Young Jack Random, back from the scrapyard? Valentine Wolfe? Lionstone?'

'Half A Man,' said Jack. 'Or, to be exact, the other, human side of Half A Man. The right-hand side of the body, complete with supporting energy half, just like his predecessor.'

Ruby looked at him. 'You're kidding,' she said finally.

'I wish I was.'

'Now that really is going to complicate things.'

'You have no idea,' said Jack. 'Luckily Toby and Flynn were there to catch it all on camera, and the recording's been running on one news show or another ever since. If you'd care to tune in that wall over there, you can see it for yourself.'

Ruby activated the holoscreen and had it search for the recording. It took a second or two to find a station that was just starting the tape, and then the screen cleared to show Parliament, not long after most of the main power brokers had left. An MP was in the middle of a long, boring speech of no interest to anyone but himself; hardly anyone was paying attention. Most were waiting impatiently for their turn to get up and bore everyone else rigid, some were chatting quietly among themselves, and half a dozen had started a poker game.

And then there was a sudden flash of light, a blinding glare so bright it overloaded the camera lens, and when the glare faded away, Half A Man was standing in the middle of the floor before the House. There was an immediate babble of surprise and outrage from the MPs, dying quickly away as they recognized who it was. There was then an extended silence as they realized that the figure wasn't exactly who they thought it was, being rather a mirror image of the Half

A Man they knew. This figure's right half was flesh and blood, while its left was a shimmering, spitting energy construct in human shape.

Everyone knew the terrible history of Captain Fast, who became Half A Man. Abducted by unknown aliens from the bridge of his own starship, he was experimented on and tortured for years, and finally returned as he was now. Half human, half something else. He lived for centuries, guiding the Empire in its dealings with aliens, for who knew better than he the risks and threats involved? Named Half A Man by the tabloid press of the day, he retired from public scrutiny, and founded and trained the Investigators. He represented the strong arm of the Empire, implacable and unforgiving. He was finally killed by Owen Deathstalker, during the rebellion.

Or at least, his left side was. Now his other human half was back, looking calmly about him, taking in the startled faces on all sides of the House. With only half a face, it was hard to tell whether he was smiling, but he might have been.

'I am Half A Man,' he said finally, his cold voice carrying loud and clear on the quiet. 'The real Half A Man. The real Captain Fast. The creature you previously knew and harboured with that name was a fake and a deceiver. I am the real thing, finally escaped from inhuman captors to bring you vital news and a terrible warning.'

There was a long pause after that, as everybody looked at each other, and waited for someone else to work out what to say. Finally Toby Shreck stepped cautiously forward, Flynn right there beside him, his camera hovering above their heads to get the best shot, sending it all out to a fascinated live audience. Toby stopped what he hoped was a safe distance away, and gave the partly shimmering figure his best professional smile.

'Welcome back, Captain Fast, from wherever you've been. I'm sure you'll understand if we're all a little confused. Perhaps you'd be so good as to fill us in on . . . the true story of Half A Man.'

The human half of the face regarded him coldly. 'I am aware of how your forebears hounded and persecuted my predecessor. I trust things have changed since then.'

'Oh, sure,' said Toby, mentally crossing his fingers behind his back. 'Just take your time, tell it in your own words, and don't leave out any of the juicy details.'

'That's enough!' said Elias Gutman quickly. 'As Speaker of this House, I declare this a security matter. Stop filming now. All your tape will be confiscated before you leave.'

'Get bent,' said Toby, 'we're going out live. This is too important to be filed under need to know. The people have a right to the truth. We're not living in the old Empire any more, with its paranoia, mysteries and secrets. We've moved beyond that. Keep filming, Flynn.'

'I'm on it, boss.'

Gutman gestured urgently, and a large number of security guards ran forward, swords and guns at the ready. They formed a semicircle, fanning around Half A Man and Toby and Flynn. Toby did his best to look unconcerned, and quietly thanked God that they were going out live. Gutman wouldn't dare have him shot in front of millions of viewers. At least, Toby didn't think he would. The old Gutman wouldn't have hesitated, but as Speaker he was now a public figure, reliant on public good will. Toby just hoped Gutman knew that.

'Enough,' said Half A Man. 'I wish this to be broadcast. The whole Empire must know what I have to tell.'

The security guards looked at Half A Man, then at Gutman, and finally at each other. The original Half A Man had been thought unkillable, until the Deathstalker managed it, and no one was entirely sure how he'd done it anyway. The original Half A Man had also been known for his extremely short temper, and a complete readiness to kill anyone who got in his way. The guards started lowering their weapons. Gutman quickly decided to make the best of a bad situation, and gave in gracefully.

'Of course you must tell your story, Captain Fast. I'm sure the whole Empire is dying to hear what you have to say.'

'Good,' said Half A Man, 'for it concerns the fate of every living creature in the Empire.' He looked straight into the camera, ignoring the politicians. 'The impostor told you some of the truth. I was abducted, and remade by aliens, but I was split in two, to produce a pair of the unnatural thing you see before you. In my other self, the alien mind dominated the meld. An alien will moved that body, and an alien intelligence spoke through its mouth. It told you carefully tailored lies, to hide the real truth, the real dangers, from you. The aliens you have encountered till now are nothing to the real Enemy that lies waiting. There's something alive in the Darkvoid. Something old and powerful, and horribly evil. They call themselves the Recreated. And soon they will come out of the Darkvoid and destroy everything that lives.'

There was another long pause. Toby cleared his throat. 'What exactly are . . . the Recreated?'

'Horrible beyond imagining. Powerful beyond hope or sanity. Alien to everything you know or understand as life. They died and brought themselves back to life. They are eternal now. And soon, they will come for you all.'

'But, if they can't die, or death doesn't stop them,' said Toby, 'why would they want to bother with something as small as us?'

'Your deaths will fuel their mighty engines. Your final suffering, extended across centuries, will power their machines. And your screaming souls will be a comfort to them. They are of the darkness, and cannot bear the light. So they will snuff it out, wherever they find it, and plunge the whole universe into an endless night. And they will rule the dark for ever.'

'How the hell are we supposed to fight something like that?' said Toby.

Half A Man looked at him for the first time. 'You can't.'

Jack Random shut down the holoscreen. 'That's the gist of it. After that, it was just a lot of arguing and panicking and running round in circles. Half A Man, if that's who he really is, finally allowed the guards to lead him away for a thorough debriefing, hopefully including where the hell he's been all this time. I understand he's being held in some top-secret laboratory, where the Empire's finest scientists are running all kinds of tests on him, to make it look like Parliament's doing something. Last I heard, the MPs were still sitting at the House, calling for more and more expert opinions and scaring themselves silly.'

'If this Half A Man isn't who or what he says he is,' said Ruby slowly, 'then what the hell is he? A Fury?'

'Good question,' said Jack. 'But I don't think even the rogue AIs have the tech to produce a living energy field like that. The Empire had access to the original Half A Man for centuries, and never did work out what made him tick.'

'But if he is the real thing, then his message must be true too.'

'Not necessarily. All those years of captivity and torture could have turned his mind. Or, he could have all kinds of reasons for lying. He never said a word about where he's been, who exactly was holding him captive, or how he finally escaped. Did the aliens have him? Or the Recreated? How could he have got away from beings of such power? He's already admitted that an alien intelligence spoke through the original Half A Man. Maybe when that toy got broken, its makers just sent us another. No, there's a lot we're not being told, and until we know more I don't think we should put an awful lot of faith in the message, or the messenger.'

'He was right about there being something alive in the Darkvoid. Don't you think we should—'

'No, I don't,' said Jack decisively. 'We have our own mission, let's not get distracted. Right now, we need to discover just how badly Shub has its hooks into us. Anything else can wait, until we have more detailed and trustworthy information to work with.'

'It must be wonderful to be so focused.' Ruby shrugged angrily. 'I don't like any of this. I can't help feeling that whatever we do, we're getting way out of our depth.'

'If not us, then who?' said Jack. 'We have a lot more going for us than anyone else.'

Ruby sighed. 'You always were the brains of the couple. I just like to kill people. So, where do we make a start?'

'With Robert Campbell, newly appointed Captain of the *Elemental*. His Family was known to have dealings with Shub, before the Wolfes destroyed the Campbells in a very hostile takeover. Let's see what Robert can tell us about it.'

'And if he doesn't want to talk to us?'

Jack smiled. 'Then you get to play with him for a bit. Try not to break him too badly.'

They took an official shuttle up to the *Elemental*, armed with a warrant from Parliament to interrogate anyone they damned well felt like. The *Elemental* was one of the few E-class starcruisers to survive the rebellion, and was currently being outfitted for duty on the Rim. The huge ship was surrounded by smaller craft, buzzing back and forth like wasps around a nest, while hundreds of men in atmosphere suits crawled all over the outer hull, making repairs and working on upgrades. The captain didn't reply directly to Jack Random's request for an urgent meeting, but his communications officer passed on a message that he would make himself available in his private quarters as soon as possible.

Ruby docked the shuttle where she was told, and the two of them waited impatiently in the airlock for someone to open the door from the other side. It was a fairly large lock, as airlocks went, but Jack still felt uncomfortably confined. The airlock's inner door was a thick slab of solid steel, and breaking through it would be hard, even for him. If the Campbell really didn't want to talk to them about his Clan's connections with Shub, he could keep them waiting there for ever. Or at least until they got tired of waiting and went away. He caught Ruby eyeing the inner door thoughtfully.

'No, we are not going to try and break it open,' Jack said emphatically. 'That door was designed to take a lot of punishment.'

'It wasn't designed with us in mind,' said Ruby calmly. 'Nothing is.'

'Quite possibly. But even if we could, I don't want you trying just yet. I don't want the Campbell thinking he's got us rattled.'

'I am not rattled,' said Ruby, 'just pretty peeved. And if his people don't get a move on, I am going to carve my initials on their foreheads.'

'He may be busy. He is the captain, after all.'

'No one's too busy to see us. Not if they know what's good for them,' Ruby scowled. 'No, he's just another damned aristo, keeping us waiting to show how important he thinks he is.'

'I don't think so,' said Jack. 'His file suggests he's always been a Navy man first and foremost, and an aristocrat second.'

'They're just as bad. All spit and polish and salute when you're speaking to me. If he tries to make me stand to attention, I'll cut him off at the ankles.'

Jack looked at Ruby thoughtfully. 'I think you'd better leave the talking to me. Do try and remember we're here after answers, Ruby. It really is awfully difficult to get answers out of a dead man.'

Ruby sniffed, but held her peace. But her hands didn't move from her weapons.

The inner door finally swung open, and a spit-and-polished junior officer smiled winningly at them both. 'Jack Random, Ruby Journey; please come aboard, sir and madam.'

'Who's he calling a madam?' said Ruby quietly, as she and Jack pushed past the officer and emerged into the corridor beyond. 'I've never been in a House of Joy in my life.'

'He's just being polite,' Jack murmured. 'Don't hit him.'

'I'm Lieutenant Xhang,' said the officer, smiling brightly and pretending he hadn't heard anything. He pushed the heavy airlock door shut, checked it had locked securely, checked it again because he worried about such things, and then turned back to face his charges. He looked distinctly nervous, as though expecting them to jump on him at any moment. Jack was tempted to shout Boo! just to see what would happen. The lieutenant tore his fascinated gaze away from Ruby's thunderous scowl, and smiled determinedly at Jack.

'If you'll please follow me, I'm to escort you to Captain Campbell's quarters. He's looking forward to meeting you.'

'If he is, that makes him practically unique, these days,' said Jack.

'Yeah,' growled Ruby. 'We must be losing our touch.'

Xhang wondered whether he should laugh politely, decided he probably couldn't pull it off convincingly, and settled for smiling till his cheeks ached. He indicated the way, quietly proud that his hand wasn't shaking noticeably, and led his two guests through the ship. It was days like this that made him wonder whether his pension was really worth it.

Jack maintained a quiet but thorough watch on the people and places they passed. The shining steel corridors were crowded but not cluttered. Everyone had work to do, but managed to avoid getting in each other's way. They were busy, but disciplined. No one was standing around loafing or killing time. The crew had a job to do, and they were getting on with it. And yet there were no security officers present, to spur them on or keep them in check. Which implied that the new captain ran a tight ship, where discipline came from within, rather than being imposed from above.

'So,' Jack said casually, 'what do you make of your new captain, Lieutenant?'

'The captain is a fine officer,' Xhang said immediately. 'He knows his job. It helps that he came up through the ranks, rather than straight from the Academy.'

'Bit young, though, isn't he?'

'He knows his job,' said Xhang, just a little sharply. Jack couldn't help noticing that the lieutenant forgot his nervousness in his haste to defend the captain. 'That's all that matters, Sir Random. He was a hero in the war. Kept on fighting till they blew his ship out from under him. The Deathstalker himself pinned a medal on him.'

'So he did,' said Jack, 'so he did.'

They came eventually to the captain's private quarters, and Xhang knocked smartly on the door and stepped back. The door slid open immediately, and Xhang gestured for them to go in. Jack nodded, and Xhang took that gratefully as a dismissal. He saluted smartly, turned on his heel and strode off down the corridor at a speed he hoped precluded being called back. Jack couldn't help smiling. For once his reputation was being a help rather than a hindrance. Though he couldn't help wondering how the captain was going to react. He gestured to Ruby, and she led the way into the captain's cabin, her right hand resting on her belt near her gun.

The quarters turned out to be neat and tidy and just big enough to move around in. The bed folded out from the wall, and the writing table and chair were bolted to the floor.

Space was at a premium aboard ship, and even a captain couldn't expect too much. The door slid closed behind Jack with a solid-sounding thud as he stared unhurriedly about him, looking for clues to the man's personality. There were a few personal effects, scattered here and there like intruders, nothing particularly unusual or unique. Presumably the captain hadn't been on board long enough to stamp his own tastes on the cabin. Or perhaps he simply didn't have much left after being forced to abandon his last ship.

The walls were bare. Normally they would have been covered with testaments to the captain's honoured past, landmarks in his career. Citations, battle honours, that sort of thing. But all the Campbell had was his medal, and presumably that would have looked rather lonely on the wall by itself.

The door to the adjoining bathroom suddenly hissed open, and Robert Campbell emerged, mopping at his wet face with a towel. He was wearing his uniform trousers, his jacket hanging open to reveal a remarkably hairy chest. He was tall and handsome and looked very young to be a captain. He nodded amiably enough to Jack and Ruby, and sank into the only chair, dropping the towel on to his lap.

'Forgive the informality, but we're all rather rushed at the moment. Take the weight off your feet.'

He gestured for them to sit on the bed. Jack decided that he'd feel more dignified standing. 'Good of you to see us at such short notice, Captain.'

'Your message wasn't very clear,' said Robert, frowning. 'In fact, it bordered on vague. Anyone else, I'd have turned them down flat. I have a hundred and one things to do before this ship will be ready to make its departure date. But if the legendary Jack Random and the infamous Ruby Journey feel it's important that we meet, then it probably is. Even if I'm damned if I can see what we might have in common. We don't move in anything like the same circles. But, needs must when the Devil vomits on your shoes, so I've made some time for you. Ask your questions.'

'I wasn't sure I'd still find you here,' said Jack. 'I did hear that you might be quitting the Fleet. Resigning your commission to become the Campbell, head of your Clan.'

Robert scowled. 'There's been a lot of pressure for me to do that, but . . . the Fleet is my life, Sir Random. It's all I ever wanted. And to be made a captain so soon . . . But I do have responsibilities on Golgotha. So I'm torn; torn between my duty as an officer of the Fleet to help rebuild the Empire, and my blood responsibility to help the surviving members of my Family to rebuild Clan Campbell. We were almost wiped out by the Wolfes, but now the remnants are finally coming together again, and they need a strong head to hold them together. I'm not the only claimant to the title, but the thought of having an official war hero as head of the Clan appeals to many. For the moment, I'm trying to juggle both sets of responsibilities at once, till I can decide where my real duty lies.'

'Once an aristo, always an aristo,' said Ruby.

Robert smiled at her coldly. 'Once a bounty hunter, always a bounty hunter.'

'We might have been on different sides during the rebellion,' Jack interrupted quickly, 'but I trust that, these days, we're both concerned with what's best for the Empire. There are things we need to know, Captain. Things only you can tell us, about Clan Campbell, and its past dealings with the rogue AIs of Shub.'

Robert nodded slowly. 'I always knew that would have to come out, eventually. So many things that might have stayed secret for ever were revealed during the rebellion, or after. So much has come to light, that we're all pretty much numbed to shock now. But even so, something like this . . . If I tell you what I know, which isn't much, I must have your assurance that you'll keep this to yourselves for as long as you can.'

'We could make you talk,' said Ruby.

'Probably,' said Robert. 'But not easily, and not soon. And if word got out that Jack Random had been involved in the torturing of a genuine war hero . . .'

'I've always done what I considered necessary,' said Jack, 'and hang the consequences. But I don't see any need for violence, just yet. Why should I keep your secret, Campbell? Convince me.'

'Because my Family is currently in a very delicate state.

The Wolfes nearly wiped us out. They certainly tried hard enough. They hunted us down in the streets, dragged us from safe houses, showed us no mercy. Very few dared to help us. Some of us survived through our positions in the armed forces; others by means we're not exactly proud of. But now things have changed.

'Blue Block has declared all vendettas a thing of the past, all feuds rendered null and void. They're trying to strengthen as many Families as possible, to consolidate their power base. So Clan Campbell no longer has anything to fear from the Wolfes, and the surviving remnants can emerge from the shadows at last. But with no one to head the Family, warring factions will inevitably tear the Clan apart from within. And a secret like this – the apparent betrayal of humanity itself – coming out now, would finish us off. I need your word, Jack Random, before I can share with you what I know. I trust your word.'

'But not mine?' said Ruby Journey.

'Of course not. You're a bounty hunter.'

'Very wise. Tell him to go to hell, Jack. Who cares if one more Family disappears? They were the enemy before, and they're the enemy now. Let them all die.'

'It's not that simple, Ruby. A moderate, responsible Clan could do much to defuse Blue Block's more extreme intentions. And if there has to be a Clan Campbell, I'd rather it was run by a genuine war hero than some unknown. You have my word, Captain.'

'You're getting soft, Random.'

'Not now, Ruby. Captain, I'll keep your secret as long as I can justify it to myself. And Ruby will follow my lead. But I can't speak for anyone else. I have no way of knowing how many others know about your Family and Shub. So build your Clan while you can, Captain, and build it on strong foundations, because the tide's coming in.'

'Understood,' said Robert. He mopped at his face with the towel, then threw it aside. He looked older, suddenly. 'You have to understand, I was never a part of the main conspiracy. I don't think they trusted me that much. But the basic deal was that we provided Shub with the secret of the new stardrive, in return for advanced tech from them to keep

315

our factories at the cutting edge of Empire industry. We never dealt with them directly, there was always a series of cut-outs and the left hand not knowing what the right foot was doing, so we could plausibly deny everything if we had to. Finlay said it was all a con; that the Family had no intention of ever actually giving them the alien drive. But I can't say whether that was true or not. I think Finlay believed it, but he was never head of the Clan. His father Crawford was, and that man was capable of practically anything to get what he wanted. So Shub sent us tech, and we prevaricated, and the deal continued. No one ever mentioned the word treason. Or what would happen if Shub decided that we were never going to deliver, and chose to cut their losses by exposing the deal to the other Families – or the Empress. But then the Wolfes attacked, and it all became moot anyway. After Clan Campbell was brought down and scattered, the Wolfes discovered the existence of the deal, and took it over themselves. Valentine was running the Wolfes by then. A man capable of absolutely anything. And that is as far as my information goes.'

Jack scowled. 'Can you think of any other members of your Family who might know more about this?'

'Not really. The few who almost certainly knew all the details died at the Wolfes' hands when they stormed Tower Campbell. None of it was ever recorded, on paper or disk, for obvious reasons. The only ones to survive who might know anything are Finlay and his wife, Adrienne. Though since she was only a Campbell by marriage, and therefore never to be fully trusted, she was probably kept on the periphery, like me. As for what Finlay might know, you'd have to ask him. Don't expect too much from him, though. He's been busy losing his mind for some time now, and I don't know how much there is left.'

'You don't like him, do you?' said Ruby.

'He's an insane killer, who wades through blood for the joy of it. When I think of how he used to hide his evil behind the masque of a dandy at Court, it makes my blood run cold. A werewolf moved among us, red in tooth and claw, and we never knew. But none of that matters. He's still Family.'

'Let's talk about Blue Block,' said Jack diplomatically. 'What can you tell us about them?'

'Not a lot,' said Robert. 'I was sent to them at an early age, but there was a Family argument and I was called away before I could be initiated into any of their mysteries. Apparently Crawford thought the Clan needed more influence in the armed forces, so a dozen of us ended up in the army and the Fleet. For me, it was the best thing that ever happened. The Fleet didn't care what my background was. I had to prove my own worth. And I did: it was the making of me.

'I don't think Crawford ever really trusted Blue Block, even then. He always suspected they might develop their own agenda. And, just maybe, he was worried they might discover the deal with Shub, and use my well-being as a weapon to force the Family to cut them in. Even then, people were beginning to suspect that Blue Block graduates owed loyalty to Blue Block first, and individual Families second. I'll tell you this, a lot more people went through the Black College than you'd think, or the Families would ever admit. You don't think a powerful force like the Families would roll over for just anybody, do you? They agreed to your deal because they had no choice. The Clans bow down to Blue Block because their own rising generations are theirs no longer. They belong body and soul to Blue Block.

'It's all secrets and mysteries, at the heart of Blue Block. The Black College. The Red Church. The Hundred Hands. Names handed down in whispers, at third and fourth remove. No one knows who runs Blue Block any more, or what their intentions are. It doesn't make any difference: the Clans are no longer in any position to ask questions. Blue Block knows things. And their people are everywhere. In high positions, too. You'd be surprised.'

'I doubt it,' said Ruby. 'There's not much left that can surprise me any more. And I never did trust the Families, or anyone connected with them.'

'How very wise,' said Robert.

Jack intervened quickly. 'What about Finlay? Any idea where we can find him?'

'He's just where you'd expect him to be,' said Robert. 'As

close to blood and death and madness as he can get. He's living at the Arenas.'

In the Golgotha city known as the Parade of the Endless, everyone goes to the Arenas. To see men fight men, singly or in groups, or men fight aliens, or aliens fight aliens. Just so long as somebody dies. Blood is blood, whatever the colour. But it's the men the audiences really love to cheer and boo, down on the bloody sands. All human life and death is there, right in front of you, up close and personal. There's never an empty seat in the stands or the boxes, and season tickets are handed down from generation to generation. The Arenas are the only thing all classes in the Empire have in common.

And there's never a shortage of volunteers, to risk their lives and their honour in the ring, for wealth or privilege or just the applause of the crowd. A few even make a living out of it, for a time. And the greatest fighter of them all, the one every man wanted to fight, and every woman wanted to bed, the man who never backed down from any challenge and eventually retired undefeated, was that mysterious and enigmatic figure behind the featureless steel helm, the Masked Gladiator.

Two men wore that mask, though the crowds never knew. The first was Georg McCrackin, who retired unbeaten when he decided he was getting too old and slowing down. He trained his successor, Finlay Campbell, who became the second Masked Gladiator. Georg McCrackin was killed during the rebellion, while wearing the steel helmet, and his dead body was unmasked during a live broadcast by Toby Shreck.

Finlay had banned himself from the Arenas, for many reasons, but he still maintained his old quarters there, in the living section deep under the sand. They were very modest, but Finlay didn't care. They were just somewhere to stay where no one could find him, hidden behind a meaningless name, where he could rest and sleep and plot on how best to track down and murder his old enemy, Valentine Wolfe. The clone and esper undergrounds had promised him Valentine's head on a stick, in return for his services as an assassin, but now the rebellion was over, it seemed they were far too busy to remember old friends and promises, so Finlay had decided to do it himself.

He couldn't just fire up a ship and go. Parliament had refused to grant him the same official status as the Deathstalker and the d'Ark woman. They didn't trust him; he scared them. Some thought, not unreasonably, that he might use that official status to go after them. So they denied him a role in their precious new order, and set their spies to watch him. Finlay killed a few of them, now and again, just to keep the others on their toes. And quietly, unobtrusively, he prepared for his quest. So he was more than a little surprised when someone knocked quite openly on his door.

He rose lithely to his feet from the unmade bed where he'd been lying on his back with his eyes open, thinking about nothing in particular, and drew his disrupter from the holster hanging on the bedpost. He padded silently over to the door and listened for a moment. The knock came again.

'Who is it?' said Finlay.

'Jack Random and Ruby Journey. We'd like a quiet word. If it's not too much trouble.'

Finlay raised an eyebrow. He'd never had much contact with the legendary heroes during his time in the rebellion, or after it for that matter, and he had no idea why they should seek him out now. But if nothing else their visit should prove interesting, and he could do with a break from his brooding. He undid the two locks, pulled back the three sets of bolts he'd added, and stepped smartly back as he swung open the door. Jack and Ruby were standing alone in the corridor, their hands empty. They looked at the gun in his hand, covering them both, but said nothing. Finlay gestured for them to enter with his free hand, and then moved round behind them to lock and bolt the door again.

'You can't be too careful these days. Not when you have as many enemies as I do.'

'Trust me,' said Jack, 'I know the feeling.'

'Come in,' said Finlay, keeping a cautious distance between himself and his visitors. 'Make yourself at home. Sorry the place is a bit of a mess, but I shot the maid.'

He smiled, to show that it was a joke, and Jack and Ruby smiled back, before moving carefully past him into the room.

319

They looked round, in search of somewhere to sit. The room was large enough to pace about in, but still small enough to be cosy. The place really was a mess. Jack and Ruby had to step over things just to get to the two battered-looking chairs. Unwashed laundry lay in a heap in one corner, and dirty plates and cups filled the sink in the tiny kitchen annexe. Several throwing knives protruded from the door. Jack dusted off the seat of his chair before sitting on it; Ruby didn't bother. Finlay sat on the edge of the unmade bed, still covering them both with his disrupter. His gaze was cold and unwavering and his hand was very steady.

'So,' he said calmly, 'what brings such illustrious company to my little bolt-hole that no one is supposed to know about?'

'Robert told us where to find you,' said Jack.

'Ah,' said Finlay, 'it's always Family that betrays you in the end.'

'We need to talk to you,' said Ruby. 'There are things only you can tell us.'

'You're right there,' said Finlay. 'I know all kinds of stuff. That's why so many people want me silenced. Which particular dirty little secret did you have in mind?'

'We'd like to ask you a few questions about Clan Campbell's dealings with Shub,' said Jack, keeping a careful eye on Finlay's disrupter.

'Oh, that,' said Finlay dismissively. He scooted back in bed, leaned against the headboard and slipped his gun back into its holster. Jack and Ruby relaxed just a little. When Finlay spoke again, he seemed almost bored. 'That's old history now; no one cares about it any more. I thought one of my enemies had sent you to find out what I know, and shut me up. I have lots of enemies, you know. From all sides of the political spectrum. You'd be surprised. Even the ungrateful undergrounds disown me these days, though I was once their blue-eyed boy. Any mission that was too dangerous, too difficult, or too suicidal for anyone else – send for Finlay Campbell. I never said no. And I never once failed in a mission, never once let them down. They pointed me like a gun and I killed people. Now I can't even get anyone to return my calls any more. My past . . . excesses have made me a liability. An embarrassment. I helped win the war for them, but no one wants to know because I got my hands a little too dirty now and again. Once my current mission is brought to a close, I am going to come back and knock on their doors, and I won't take no for an answer. And then there will be a reckoning.'

'And what mission might that be, Sir Campbell?' said Jack politely.

'I'm going after Valentine Wolfe. He and I have unfinished business to discuss.'

'I should think everyone in the Empire has unfinished business with that bastard,' said Ruby. 'Let's talk about Shub.'

'Let's not, and say we did.' Finlay scowled intimidatingly at Ruby, and seemed a little taken aback when she just scowled right back at him. 'Oh, well, if it'll get you out of here any quicker . . . My Family made a deal with the AIs, their advanced tech in return for the alien stardrive. Supposedly it was all a con, with us stringing them out for as much as we could get, before the AIs realized we had no intention of delivering. In reality, I don't know. My father always was very ambitious. He'd have made a deal with the Devil to put himself on the Throne. And maybe he did.

'We'll never know now. The deal died when the Wolfes destroyed my Family. Afterwards, the Wolfes supposedly renegotiated the deal for themselves. Valentine was in charge. What he got, and what he promised in return, you'll have to ask him. If I don't get to him first.'

'And there's nothing more you can tell us about Shub's links with humanity?' said Jack. 'Please try and think, Sir Campbell. It's important.'

'My father never trusted me with any details. And I never asked. I didn't care about such things, then.'

Jack stood up abruptly. 'Excuse me a moment. I've got a message coming in through my implant.'

He moved over to the door so he could subvocalize to his comm unit in relative privacy. Finlay and Ruby studied each other thoughtfully. They each recognized the warrior that the other was, and the same competitive fire began to burn in each of them. It had been a long time since they'd felt seriously challenged. Slowly they both sat up straight, eyes narrowing.

'So,' said Ruby, 'I hear you're a fighter as well as a clothes horse. Any good with a sword?'

'I was taught by the best,' said Finlay. 'Never once lost a fight. And I never needed esper tricks to win my battles.'

Ruby showed her teeth in a mirthless smile. 'Maybe we should try each other out sometime. Just steel on steel.'

'Sounds good to me,' said Finlay. They held each other's gaze, smiling the same death's-head smile. Their hearts speeded up, and their breathing deepened. There was an almost sexual attraction in the air between them. The thing they were both born to do, more important to them than life itself, they could feel it taking them over, becoming inevitable. Finlay licked his lips. 'When exactly did you have in mind, bounty hunter?'

'What's wrong with right now?' said Ruby Journey.

'Not a damned thing,' said Finlay Campbell.

And in a moment they were both on their feet facing each other, swords in hand, blood and death in their eyes. But before their blades could even reach out to touch each other, Jack Random was there between them, glaring furiously at them both, and they each stepped back a pace, stayed for a moment by his greater authority.

'Have you both gone mad? Of course; stupid question. Look, we don't have time for this. Sir Campbell, put away your sword.'

Finlay smiled briefly. 'After her.'

Jack looked at Ruby. 'I can't take my eyes off you for a moment, can I? Sheathe your sword.'

'Why do I have to go first?' said Ruby.

'Because you started it, that's for sure. And because I'm asking you to. We have to go, right now. We're needed on an urgent mission.'

Ruby sniffed, and reluctantly lowered her sword. 'You're no fun any more, Random.'

Finlay cautiously lowered his sword. He and Ruby exchanged a glance. Though neither of them said anything, they both knew the moment for the fight had passed. It didn't matter; there would be other times. Finlay slipped his sword back into the scabbard hanging from the bedpost and reclined on his bed again, propped up against the headboard, the picture of casual ease. Ruby slammed her weapon back into its sheath, and glared at Jack.

'What's all this about a mission? I thought we had a mission running down the Shub connection.'

'This takes precedence. Apparently all hell is breaking out on Loki, and Parliament wants us there yesterday. Shub will have to wait.'

'Isn't it always the way,' said Ruby. 'Start out doing one thing, and the next minute you're being sent somewhere else.'

'Story of my life,' observed Finlay from the bed. 'Let yourselves out. Try not to slam the door behind you.'

Jack practically had to drag Ruby out of the room, but eventually they were gone, shutting the door reasonably quietly behind them, and Finlay was left alone again. He stared up at the ceiling, his visitors already forgotten, taken up in his past again. Just lately, someone had been sending professional assassins after him. He didn't mind, particularly. He was glad of the exercise. But none of them had lived long enough to name their employer, or how they knew where to find him. It could have been almost anyone. With all the enemies he'd made, he was lost for choice. They were one of the reasons he'd decided to leave Golgotha and go after Valentine.

It wasn't that he was worried for his own life, but there was always the chance the assassins' thwarted employer might try to get at him by attacking those he cared about, like Evangeline or Julian, and he couldn't risk that. Julian could probably take care of himself, but he couldn't guard Evangeline all the time. If only because she wouldn't let him. There had always been a part of her life where he wasn't welcome. Evie was very protective of her privacy. He knew there were things about her, secrets, mysteries, that he didn't know, but he'd never pressed her. She'd tell him, when she was ready. Finlay understood about secrets. He had enough of his own.

Evie was away again, at the moment. Off doing something for the clone underground that he wasn't cleared to know about. For all their proud talk of equality and fraternity, the underground still didn't really trust anyone who wasn't a clone. Given how busy Evangeline had been with the underground, even though the rebellion was officially over, Finlay couldn't help wondering if they were trying to keep him and Evie apart, because he was only a human. And a damned aristo, at that. Finlay smiled briefly. It was probably even simpler than that. The underground never had approved of him, even when they turned to him for the missions no one else could do. They thought he was crazy. And of course they were quite right. No sane person would have done what they wanted, taken the risks he had, and bathed in blood till it dripped from his soul.

The problem came when the Empire finally fell, and everyone expected him to be sane, all of a sudden. He could have told them it didn't work like that. You couldn't go through all the things Finlay had, do what he had done, lose all he had and still be completely rational at the end of it. He'd been an assassin, and he'd loved it. The only things keeping him even borderline sane were his love for Evangeline and his friend Julian Skye. They were his anchors. They kept him balanced. Without them, he had only himself, and he didn't know who that was any more. He'd been many people in his time: the fop and dandy; the Masked Gladiator; the rebel fighter; the underground's assassin; Evie's love. Now all their voices clamoured in his head at once, and he was sinking amid the bedlam.

He longed for action, for the thrill of the fight. Everything was so simple then; you knew where you were. No shades of grey, no politics. Nothing to hold him back. Just do or fail, win or lose, live or die. And, oh, the blood-red rush, the heart hammering in his breast, the joy at being the very best there was, and, oh, oh, the thrill of it all. The marvellous moment of murder – nothing quite like it. It was an endlessly satisfying, hopelessly addictive drug. Perhaps he had more in common with Valentine Wolfe than he thought.

Finlay scowled. The comparison disturbed him. He made himself change the subject, turning his thoughts to the day's earlier events. He'd gone to see his extremely estranged wife Adrienne and their two children, and he still wasn't quite sure why. Perhaps because they were the only part of his past life that wasn't touched by what he'd become. Finlay closed his eyes and let his mind drift back.

Adrienne opened the door almost before he'd finished knocking, as though she'd been waiting for him to arrive for some time. As it happened, he was exactly on time, but Adrienne never let the facts get in the way of a good row. He bowed formally to her, and she sneered back at him. She looked as she always did, striking rather than pretty, and almost unbearably overpowering. She had a sharp-edged face, all planes and angles, with a sullen red mouth and an upturned nose that would have been cute on anyone else. She had a great mop of curly golden hair, and the loudest and most carrying voice in the entire Empire. Joined with a caustic wit and a downright vicious sense of humour, she could make grown men cry, or at the very least dodge into doorways to avoid her. Her movements were swift and sudden, like a striking snake, and she was popularly regarded as just about as dangerous. Finlay stepped forward, and Adrienne moved reluctantly back just enough to let him in.

'Wipe your boots on the mat, dammit. You're not at home now.'

Finlay nodded calmly, and gave his boots a good scraping. He was working hard on making a good impression, and not killing anyone he didn't absolutely have to. He wondered vaguely if he'd remembered to polish his boots before setting out. He tended to forget things like that unless Evie reminded him. The problem with being raised by servants . . . He smiled at Adrienne, and fitted his pince-nez spectacles on the end of his nose.

'Oh, put those away, Finlay,' said Adrienne testily. 'You know perfectly well there's nothing wrong with your eyes.'

'They're for show, not use,' Finlay explained, in the patient, rational voice he knew drove her mad. 'They come with the outfit. They're part of the look, the style. But then, of course, you never did understand style, did you?'

'If it means wearing clothes like that, no. I've seen rainbows less colourful than that outfit. In fact, I don't think I've ever seen so many colours on one person before. What happened? You couldn't decide which colour, so you wore them all at once?'

'Something like that.' Once, Finlay would have gone to great pains to explain exactly why he'd chosen these leggings and pointed shoes to go with this particular cutaway frock coat, and the importance of choosing just the right waistcoat to complement them, just because he knew how much it annoyed her, but he was still on his best behaviour, so he let the opportunity pass. 'Still wearing basic black, Addie? It suits you. Brings out the colour of your heart.'

'I'm wearing it in hope of a funeral. Yours.'

They smiled at each other, honours equal. Finlay looked ostentatiously about the narrow hall. 'Where are the children, Addie? They are why I'm here.'

Adrienne scowled. 'They're in the parlour, of course, in their best clothes and minding their manners, if they know what's good for them. And I do wish you wouldn't just call them the children. They do have names, you know.'

'Yes, I know. Troilus and Cressida. You chose them. How old are they now?'

'Troilus is eight. He has a lot of your looks. Cressida is seven. She takes more after me, thank God. You should know their ages; I've always sent you a reminder on their birthdays. Even though I always end up having to buy the presents myself, and pretend they come from you.'

'My life has always been very full,' said Finlay, knowing it sounded like an excuse even as he said it. 'And for a long time I've had no room in it for anyone but me. But I like to think I've changed. When Evangeline came into my life, it was like seeing the sun for the first time, after living all my life in the dark. She woke things in me I never even knew were there. She helped to make me more . . . human. To be a man like other men, and not just a killing machine, sleep-walking through life in between bouts in the Arenas. I'm not the man I was, Addie. I've tried so hard to put all that behind me.'

'Nice speech,' said Adrienne. 'You must have rehearsed it for ages.'

'Oh, hours,' said Finlay. 'That doesn't make it any less true. Is it so strange, that a man should want to see his children? His stake in the future? The only part of him that will be left behind when he's gone?'

'I don't know,' said Adrienne, quietly moved by the earnestness in his voice but determined not to show it. 'This isn't like you, Finlay. It's an improvement, but it isn't like you. You never gave a damn about them before. If children are suddenly so important to you, why don't you and Evangeline raise some of your own?'

'We've discussed it,' said Finlay. 'It's a matter of finding the time. We both lead very full lives these days.'

'If it mattered enough to you, you'd make time. I did. Oh, hell, come on. Let's get this over with. They're waiting to see you in the parlour. They've both been overexcited all day, getting ready to meet you. For God's sake try not to frighten them. They only know you from what they've seen on the news broadcasts, and most of that involved you killing people.'

'I'll be a model of good behaviour, Addie, I promise; I cleaned out all the dried blood from under my fingernails before I left.'

Adrienne looked at him dubiously, shook her head and then led the way down the hall and into the parlour. Finlay did his best to appear calm and relaxed, even while his stomach tightened and his heart raced. He hadn't felt this nervous while waiting to go on in the Arenas. But then, fighting was easy. It was people he'd always found difficult. And he'd never had much contact with children. They weren't a part of the world he'd chosen to live in. He'd asked Evangeline what he should do, but she'd just laughed and said to treat them like little adults. That hadn't helped much. The few things he talked about with adults all involved subjects he was pretty sure weren't at all suitable for children. In fact, despite a hell of a lot of thought and a certain amount of practising in front of the bathroom mirror, he still didn't know what he was going to say to Troilus and Cressida. He was also beginning to think he should have brought some kind of present for them. He could feel small beads of sweat popping out on his forehead.

All too quickly there he was in the parlour, and Adrienne was waving him towards a small boy and girl standing almost to attention before him. They were much as he remembered them from the holos Adrienne had grudgingly sent him in the past. They'd clearly been dressed in their best for the occasion, and cleaned and groomed to within an inch of their lives. Their solemn faces and large eyes suggested that they were just as nervous as he was, which actually helped to calm him a bit. He tried to see himself in the boy's slightly chubby face, but he had to admit he didn't. The child was just a child, like any other. He felt no real connection to the boy. The girl, with her frizzy gold hair, at least reminded Finlay of her mother. Adrienne coughed meaningfully, and the boy bowed formally and the girl curtsied, just a little unsteadily. Finlay nodded to them, trying hard to smile kindly. Going by the slight frowns he got in return, it hadn't been that successful.

'Thank you for the presents, Father,' said Troilus, his voice breathily light, but steady. 'It was very kind of you.'

Finlay was thrown for a moment, and then realized Adrienne must have known he wouldn't think of it in time, and had covered for him yet again. 'Hello, Troilus, Cressida,' he said, as gently as he could. 'It's good to see you. It's been a long time, hasn't it? Too long.'

'We saw you on the news,' said the boy. 'During the rebellion. They said you were a hero.'

'I did my duty,' said Finlay. 'I was fighting for something I believed in, something very important. When you're older, Troilus, and come to a man's estate, as a Campbell you'll do the same.'

'I don't think so,' said Troilus. 'It didn't look like anything I'd want to do. I think I'd much rather be a dancer.'

'Ah,' said Finlay. 'Well, I'm sure the Empire will always need . . . dancers.' He looked to Adrienne for help.

'Ballet,' she said flatly. 'He's very good.'

'I see,' said Finlay. He tried to visualize his son and heir prancing around on a stage in tights and a tutu, and couldn't. He turned to Cressida. 'And what do you want to be when you grow up?'

'I'm going to be a nun,' said the young girl solemnly. 'I'm going to enter the Church, and serve under Saint Beatrice.'

'I see,' said Finlay. He looked at Adrienne. 'Was this your

idea of a joke? Or some kind of twisted revenge, to raise my children to be a ballet dancer and a nun? The Campbells have always been warriors! Men with blood in their veins, not milk! Who the hell is going to lead the Campbells when I'm gone; the Swan Prince here?'

'Keep your voice down!' said Adrienne. 'You're frightening the children!'

'Why not? They're scaring the hell out of me! This is not a proper upbringing for Campbells! It's a vicious world out there, with all kinds of people just waiting to tread all over them. And from the look of him, I doubt if Troilus has ever even held a sword in his hand!'

The two children hurried to huddle against their mother, clinging to her hands while trying to keep from crying. Adrienne glared at Finlay, her voice ice-cold. 'They're my children, not yours. You lost all control over them when you left me to raise them alone. And I was damned if I'd raise them the way your father raised you. I didn't want them to be anything like you. I wanted them to be normal.'

'I won't always be here to protect them!'

'You never have been! I kept them alive and safe, without once having to run to you. And the world they're going to grow up in will be nothing like yours. That's one of the things we fought the rebellion about. My children are going to follow their dreams, and to hell with the Campbell inheritance and traditions. What did it ever bring you but blood and heartbreak, and a need to hide behind masques?'

Finlay's hands clenched into fists as he fought to hold on to his temper. He'd only been here a few minutes, and already it was all going horribly wrong. Adrienne was as angry as he'd ever seen her, and his children were on the brink of tears. He made himself unclench his fists, and took a deep breath to calm himself.

'I'm sorry. I didn't mean to raise my voice. It was just . . . a bit of a shock. Why didn't you tell me any of this, Addie?'

'Because I knew you'd react just as you have. I was hoping that once you'd met the children, you'd take it better. I should have known this was a bad idea. You only see the children as extensions of yourself, someone to follow in your bloody footsteps. And what's all this crap about them leading the Family? You're not the Campbell; Robert is. His children will lead the Clan, if any will.'

'I could have been the Campbell, if I'd wanted. My father was the previous Campbell. The position was mine by right, if I'd wanted it. I just chose not to.'

'You didn't want the responsibility. You've never cared about anyone but yourself.'

'I care about Evangeline! I'd die for her!'

'Death,' said Adrienne. 'That's all you know about, Finlay. Dying for someone is easy. Living for them is much harder. Would you change your life for Evangeline, for your children? Give up who you are, what you've made of yourself, for them?'

'I don't know what you mean,' said Finlay.

'No, you don't. That's what's so sad. I think you'd better leave now, Finlay.'

'What?' Finlay gaped at her. 'But I've only just got here. You can't throw me out. I didn't mean to shout, I was upset. Don't do this to me, Adrienne. There was so much I wanted to say. To you, to them.'

'I think you've said enough. You're what your father made you, Finlay, what your Family made you. You're a warrior. A killer, with a cause or without. It's all you know, and all you really care about. It's not for you: home, family and children. You wouldn't know what to do with them. You'd break them, without meaning to. You always did play too roughly.'

'Addie . . . please. Don't make me go. Let me try again. I can do this, I know I can. You know how much this means to me!'

'Do I? I thought I did; I hoped I did. But I don't think I ever really knew you, Finlay. There were so many yous to choose from. But in the end I think they were all just masques; faces to show the world so they wouldn't see the real you. So they couldn't hurt you. Maybe Evangeline got past the masques. I don't care enough to try any more. And I don't want my children to be anything like you. I think you're trying to die, Finlay, searching for death like a lover, and I won't let you take the children down with you. It's time to go, Finlay. Leave now. Please.'

Faced with his wife's cold, implacable voice and his children's tears, and words that cut him like knives, he turned and left; walked away from all the things he'd thought he wanted. He shut the front door behind him, knowing he could never return. There were some fights even he couldn't win. The children weren't his future. He didn't have a future; he'd always known that. He'd just tried to forget it for a while, because he wanted to so very much.

He walked home alone in the middle of the crowds, and people in the streets saw his face and made sure they weren't in his way.

Diana Vertue, now only occasionally Jenny Psycho, was hard at work again in the computer records section of the newly established Esper Guild House, in the Parade of the Endless. Guild Houses were springing up on planets throughout the Empire, now that the esper underground finally felt secure enough to come out into the open. The Houses existed to train, succour and politicize espers, and to provide sanctuary for those in need. Diana didn't feel at all in need of protection or succour, and she had no interest in esper politics, but she did need access to the esper underground's extensive computer files. Over the past few centuries, the underground had built up a massive data base on the theory, practice and history of all esper abilities; a library of knowledge far more extensive than anything available anywhere else. The espers had always known more about themselves than their masters ever had. And Diana had a lot of questions she needed answering.

Though if the esper underground had known exactly which questions she was pursuing, they would undoubtedly have moved heaven and earth to keep her away from their computers. So Diana hadn't told them. She hadn't wanted to upset them.

There was a cautious knock at the door, and then it eased open just enough for a servant's head to peer carefully in. People in the Guild House had learned the hard way not to interrupt Diana when she was working, without very good reason. Her Jenny Psycho persona could still erupt occasionally, if she was annoyed enough. Diana was always very apologetic afterwards, and sometimes even helped to clear up the mess, even assist the injured to the infirmary. As a result, people walked very softly around the infamous Diana Vertue, and had as little to do with her as possible. Which suited her just fine. In fact, Diana was a lot more stable these days than she let on, but it helped her to have everyone sufficiently intimidated that they wouldn't think of asking awkward questions. She turned slowly in the swivel chair and gave the unfortunate servant at the door her best daunting glare. He paled visibly, and had to swallow hard before he could deliver his message.

'Beg pardon for disturbing you, most revered senior esper, but the head of the House asks again if you would be so good as to speak with him concerning the, er, nature of your current research. He's sure he could be of help, if you would only—'

'No,' said Diana, 'I don't think so.' Her voice was harsh and grating, distressing to the ear. She'd ruined her throat and vocal cords screaming in the terrible detention cells of Wormboy Hell, the Empire's notorious prison for rebel espers. Diana could have had her voice repaired, but had chosen not to. It made a useful psychological weapon, and if what Diana suspected was true, she was going to need all the weapons she could muster. She fixed the servant with an unwavering gaze until he started twitching. 'I'll speak to the head of the House when I'm ready, and not before.'

'It's just that . . . well, you've been tying up our computer resources for three weeks now, and the list of people waiting to use them is now so long that some have been asking whether they should make arrangements for their descendants to inherit their position on the list.'

Diana didn't smile; it would have undermined her image. 'Tell them patience is a virtue. Anyone who doesn't feel particularly virtuous is always welcome to complain to me in person. Provided they've made a will first, and their family knows an undertaker who likes a challenge.'

'Can I at least persuade you to attend regular mealtimes? Snatching ten minutes to wolf down a hurried meal in here, when you happen to think of it, can't be good for you. You hardly ever leave this place. You'd probably sleep in here, if there was room to fit in a cot.'

'Thank you for your concern,' growled Diana. 'Most appreciated. Now get out of here, before I decide to turn you into a small hopping thing.'

The servant's head disappeared, the door closing quickly between him and the threat of sudden bodily transformation. He wasn't sure she could do it, but he didn't feel like finding out the hard way. There were stories . . . Diana smiled slightly. She knew she shouldn't take advantage of her reputation like that, but chances for humour had been few and far between in her life of late. He was quite right; she wasn't eating properly or often enough, but the work was so important she often couldn't drag herself away until her body forced her to.

She had to find her answer, before someone sufficiently powerful arrived to stop her.

She sighed, and turned back to the computer terminal before her. The monitor screen buzzed impatiently, waiting for her to put something useful on it. She was using an old-fashioned keyboard, infuriatingly slow and tiring, but she couldn't risk setting up a direct link to the computers through her comm implant. It would have left her vulnerable to all kinds of things. Diana Vertue was investigating the single greatest mystery of the esper age: the nature and origins of the enigmatic Mater Mundi, Our Mother of All Souls.

No one knew exactly who or what the Mater Mundi was; ask a hundred different people and you'd get a hundred different answers, all of them equally vague. Some said she was the uber-esper, the single most powerful esper mind ever created. Others maintained she was a group of senior espers in the underground working together, hiding behind the masque of a single identity. To some, she was the God of the espers, and those whose lives she touched were considered to be saints. They'd tried to make a saint out of Jenny Psycho, but it hadn't taken.

To those who weren't espers, the Mater Mundi was a dangerous unknown, a threat and a menace all the more disturbing because its nature was so unclear.

Diana had her own reasons for distrusting the Mater

Mundi. The phenomenon had manifested through her once, uncalled-for and unexpected, boosting and expanding her esper abilities far beyond anything she'd ever been capable of before. She'd blazed like a sun in the dark pit of Wormboy Hell, binding all the esper prisoners together so they could break out of their cells and fight for freedom. Hundreds of espers had been drawn into her focus, guided by her augmented will, fused into a single unstoppable force. The gestalt hadn't lasted long, but while it did, Jenny Psycho worked miracles.

Afterwards, she remained far more powerful than she had any right to be. She'd convinced herself that she was the chosen avatar of the Mater Mundi; the permanent agent though which the Mother of the World would manifest herself. She believed she was the Chosen One; the leader destined to bring her people out of slavery. She was wrong. She found that out the hard way on Mistworld, when she tried to summon the Mater Mundi's presence at a vital moment, and nothing happened. People died around her, and she could do nothing to save them. Later, the Mater Mundi manifested through the rogue Investigator, Topaz, and she combined all the espers of Mistworld into a single, hugely potent force. And Jenny Psycho discovered to her great dismay that she wasn't who she thought she was.

At the end of the rebellion, the Mater Mundi had pulled together hundreds of thousands of espers in cities all across Golgotha. She hadn't bothered with a focus then. Just slammed into their minds, and used them to do what was necessary. She blazed through the mass esper mind, wild and glorious and frighteningly inhuman. Again, it didn't last, but while it did it swept away all opposition to the rebels with an almost contemptuous ease. The Mater Mundi manifested just once more, for the finale, possessing Jenny Psycho just long enough to teleport a handful of useful players into Lionstone's Court.

Diana should have felt grateful, even honoured. Instead, she felt used.

So she set out to find who or what had been using her, and why, only to run into a brick wall. The Mater Mundi apparently didn't want her true nature known, and had gone to great lengths to cover her tracks. There were rumours and gossip aplenty, but nothing at all in the way of hard facts, no matter how deep she dug. It was taken as a matter of faith that the Mater Mundi had founded the esper underground, at some time in the distant past, and then retreated into the shadows, to watch and guide from a distance. But there was no record anywhere of anyone who had personally witnessed any of this, or knew anyone who had. And no one had ever, apparently, questioned the Mater Mundi's motives. One didn't question God, unless one wanted to end up as a burning bush.

The one thing that was clear was that people who went looking for the Mater Mundi tended not to come back. People who asked too many questions disappeared. Eventually the underground declared her officially off-limits, a mystery too dangerous to be investigated. Diana didn't give a damn. In her experience, people who stayed in hiding usually had a good reason for doing so, and she wanted to know what it was; why the God of espers hid from her worshippers. And why she thought she could just use and discard people, and not answer for it.

Diana decided that if anyone knew anything, it had to be the esper underground's records. She walked into the esper Guild House in the Parade of the Endless, took over its records section and basically defied anyone to do anything about it. The underground leaders had sent a series of increasingly angry demands that she explain herself. Diana ignored the messages, intimidated the messengers and got on with her work. The underground leaders sent a team of some of their strongest esper talents to pry her out of the records section. Diana wiped the floor with them and sent them home in tears. After that, the underground leaders threw up their hands and told everyone just to let her get on with it until she'd finished whatever the hell she was doing.

At first, Diana got nowhere fast. There were all kinds of blocks and passwords, secret files within files and double encryptions of which she had no experience. The esper Guild protected its secrets well, even from its own; perhaps particularly from its own. But Diana had planned ahead, cultivating useful friendships among the cyberats, who saw the Guild's blocking tactics as a challenge. Diana astonished herself by how quickly she learned from them. The Mater Mundi might have abandoned her, but she had been left with new powers. Soon she no longer needed the cyberats' help, and dug steadily deeper into the esper underground's past, in pursuit of an enigmatic ghost.

She discovered a great many hidden truths about the early days of the underground, when the espers were still struggling to put it together. There were files on secret deals and unpalatable agreements, of good men sacrificed for the greater good. Of conflicting organizations savagely crushed, so that the underground could represent all espers. Past heroes were revealed to have had feet of clay, and past villains emerged as people who had simply been in the wrong place at the wrong time, or had had too many inconvenient scruples. As in so many organizations that have been around for a while, the winners wrote the history, and truth was sacrificed on the altar of necessity.

Diana wasn't really surprised. She'd expected as much. But study as she might, the Mater Mundi remained elusive, flickering around the edges of the underground, touching this person or that, guiding the underground's progress with a subtle nudge here and an unobtrusive prod there. The pattern was clear when you stood far enough back, and Diana couldn't believe she was the first person to have done so, but there were no records anywhere, no solid facts worthy of the name, no official files of any kind on the Mater Mundi.

If the truth was there, they'd buried it deep, where maybe even the current leaders couldn't find it. Something had frightened them. And, given some of the things the underground did maintain in the records, whatever they had found out about Our Mother of All Souls must have been pretty damn unpleasant. Or dangerous.

Espers were first created through genetic engineering just under three centuries before. A happy accident; the unexpected result of experiments intended to produce something else entirely. It took some time to stabilize the process, so that specific esper abilities would breed true; as telepaths, polters, pyros and so on. After that, it was just a question of establishing quality control, so that the end result could be successfully marketed. No one ever used the word slave; espers weren't human. They were property, like clones, the end result of Empire science.

No one objected. Or, at least, no one that mattered.

By the time the esper underground was founded to fight for esper freedom and self-determination, its leaders had tried many paths, some more successful than others. One of their more disturbing projects had been their attempt secretly to gengineer existing espers into some form of super-esper, that could be used as a weapon in the great struggle. These espers were capable of wielding more than one ability, or even manifesting new, undreamed of powers. Espers who would burn so brightly they could outshine the sun. There were objectors, but they were shouted down. This was war, after all.

At first there was no shortage of volunteers, for all kinds of reasons, but the supply of these quickly dried up as it became clear that the end results were almost entirely negative. The scientists couldn't produce super-espers. Only monsters, physical and mental, horrible beyond bearing. The underground destroyed all they could, and did something else with the others, no one knew what. The files were hidden away where no one could find them. Till Diana came along. Little solid evidence remained of what the esper scientists had created in their hidden laboratories; just a list of names. The Shatter Freak. Blue Hellfire. Screaming Silence. The Grey Train. The Spider Harps. And one final name, attached to a date so old it predated the esper underground by centuries. A familiar name.

Deathstalker.

Diana still wasn't sure what to make of that. She'd tried cautiously raising the subject with Owen, but he just sat there for a while, looking very thoughtful, and then clammed up entirely, ignoring all her requests for information on his Clan history. She tried reason, and threats, but neither of them got her anywhere. Even Jenny Psycho didn't have what it took to pressure Owen Deathstalker.

Diana scowled. The Maze people worried her. Their powers made no sense, in esper terms. Human beings shouldn't be able to do the things these people did so casually. And all

337

the signs were pointing to the fact that they were still growing stronger, with no clear end in sight. Perhaps in time they might become something like the Mater Mundi . . . certainly, they were a long way down the road from being simply human.

Maybe they would become gods. Or make themselves gods. It was a small step from saving humanity to wanting it to worship you.

Diana had talked to them all, at one time or another, about the Madness Maze, but they didn't have much to say. Their memories of what they had encountered inside the Maze had been vague and confused, and highly contradictory. The one thing they did agree on was that the Maze was gone, destroyed by Diana's father, Captain Silence. So she went to him for answers, half convinced by then that the Mater Mundi might have been someone who'd passed through the Madness Maze centuries earlier. The same double initial might even have been some kind of clue. But Silence couldn't tell her much either, except to say that he'd entered the Maze himself, and gone part way through it before retreating, and was developing strange abilities. He wouldn't discuss them. He did say that he'd seen the Maze kill many members of his crew who'd entered it with him, in hideous, nightmarish ways.

An esper disappeared, air rushing in to fill the vacuum where he'd been. A marine fell into a solid metal wall and disappeared into it. Two marines slammed into each other and ran together like two colours on a palette, their sticky flesh intermingling beyond any hope of separation. Something horrible appeared out of nowhere; a tangle of blood and bone and viscera that might have been human once. Heads exploded, flesh melted and ran like water, and all around human voices laughed and screamed their sanity away.

The Madness Maze took a few ordinary men and women and made them superhuman. But it killed a hell of a lot more.

Diana never asked her father why he destroyed the Maze: if he did it because he believed its existence threatened all humanity, or to deny it to the rebels, or just because it had killed so many of his crew. She was pretty sure he wouldn't have been able to answer her.

Diana had been forced to abandon that particular line of enquiry for the moment. All the Maze survivors had left Golgotha. Maybe by the time they got back, she'd have a better idea of what questions to ask them. But she had a strong feeling the Mater Mundi wasn't directly linked to the Madness Maze after all. Whatever else it was, Our Mother of All Souls was an esper phenomenon, and the Maze people . . . weren't. Whatever they were becoming, Diana had a horrid suspicion that the end result wouldn't necessarily be anything even remotely human.

She pushed the thought aside. Sufficient unto the day is the evil thereof. Or something like that.

Just recently, she'd been concentrating on the file histories of earlier manifests of the Mater Mundi; previous individual espers through whom the uber-esper had focused her considerable powers. Their names were well known, but the hard facts concerning their – possession? – had been well hidden. There were remarkably few of them, only eight in total in over two hundred years. As people, they had nothing in common save one disturbing fact: none of them survived the Mater Mundi's touch. They'd all gone crazy, and after carrying out the uber-esper's wishes, they'd lashed out at everyone around them and burned up from within, consumed by the power they bore within them. There hadn't even been enough left of them to bury. It was as though their merely human minds simply couldn't handle the vast energies the Mater Mundi had let loose in them.

Diana went cold the first time she read that. She could have died – everybody else had. The Mater Mundi must have had every reason to expect her to run mad and die, but had used her anyway. She had no way of knowing that Diana Vertue, then almost wholly Jenny Psycho, would be the first avatar to survive her amplifying benediction. Perhaps it had something to do with the fact that Diana was already more than a little crazy when the Mater Mundi found and used her in Wormboy Hell. Which suggested something very disturbing about the state, or nature, of the Mater Mundi herself.

Could that be the answer? That the uber-esper's actions made no obvious sense because she or it was quite mad? No; its actions during the rebellion had been straightforward enough. Just because Diana couldn't see a pattern yet, it didn't mean there wasn't one.

The truth about the previous manifests had been carefully hushed up, right from the beginning. The underground might not understand what the Mater Mundi was, but they knew that they needed her. Only the hidden files told of how her previous chosen ones had all gone out in a blaze of glory, taking hundreds of innocent bystanders with them. The underground had shaped the stories to its needs, because every movement must have its saints, its martyrs.

And yet apparently the underground had never made any attempt to investigate the nature of this *force*, that was taking over and destroying its own people. In any war, knowing your enemy is useful, but knowing your allies is vital. And yet there was nothing in the files, nothing at all, to suggest that the underground had asked any questions, even the most obvious. It was as though the idea simply hadn't occurred to them. Which raised the unnerving question of just how far the Mater Mundi's influence extended.

Jenny Psycho had survived the Mater Mundi's touch. So had Investigator Topaz. And the only thing the two women had in common was that they were both considered to be crazy. Perhaps being mentally walking wounded had meant their minds were adaptable enough to cope with being changed into something more, or at least other, than human. Certainly Diana's powers had been transformed by the Mater Mundi. She doubted if there was a telepath on Golgotha who could match her, if she put her mind to it. And she had other abilities too: psychokinesis and precognition. Which was supposed to be impossible. The genetic engineers had proven through exhaustive and often tragic testing that the human mind could only cope with one power at a time. Anything else burned out the mind, sometimes literally. That was why espers bred true, and their children only developed the dominant trait.

And where was all her power coming from? It hadn't disappeared when the Mater Mundi had. Could the uber-esper have awakened some unknown source of power inside her, inside Diana Vertue? Maybe something buried so deeply within the human psyche that only an inhuman touch could spark it into life. And if that were true, Diana thought just a little giddily, did that mean all espers could become like her, if they were only kicked awake hard enough? Or if they were crazy enough? Could she, Diana or Jenny Psycho, touch others and make them like herself? Or, just possibly, were all espers potentially superhuman, but were deliberately limited by unseen outside forces? Like the Mater Mundi?

With an effort, Diana brought this train of thought to an end, and took a deep calming swallow of lukewarm tea from the cup on the table in front of her. After reading all the files she'd dug up and examined, she wasn't much better off than when she'd started. In fact, she had many more questions than answers. Damned disturbing questions, too. Hardly surprising; even after almost three centuries of investigation into the subject, the best Empire scientists still had no real understanding of what made espers work, how they did what they did. They were pressed into service almost as soon as they'd been created because they were so incredibly useful. There hadn't been the time or the inclination to dig into the theory of esp, when the reality stood to make so many people extremely rich and very quickly. Afterwards, questions were discouraged. No one wanted the genetic engineers coming up with unsettling answers that might upset the highly lucrative apple-cart. Espers worked and espers were property, and that was all anyone needed to know.

The Mater Mundi, on the other hand, didn't seem to have been created by anyone. She or it just appeared spontaneously, out of nowhere. One minute the universe made sense, and the next the Mater Mundi was right there in the middle of things, stirring them up like a child prodding an anthill with a stick, just to see the ants scurry. She didn't seem tied to any one planet. Earlier manifests had taken place on worlds scattered across the Empire. Diana hadn't been able to discover any link or common denominator between them. Wherever there were espers, there were opportunities for the Mater Mundi.

But her activities had changed, in recent times. Whereas originally she only manifested through single espers, now she bound them together into bodies that were capable of far more than any individual. And none of them suffered any ill effects afterwards. At least, nothing obvious. So far. It was as though the Mater Mundi grew stronger, and more capable, the more it did. *Learning by doing*. Diana leaned back in her chair, pursing her lips thoughtfully. Maybe she could discover something useful by comparing the end results of the Mater Mundi's actions. Work out what it was she was trying to achieve. Or work towards . . . Diana scowled. And maybe she could give herself an even bigger headache than she already had.

She'd been working in a vacuum too long. She needed to talk to someone.

She turned away from her computer terminal and activated the viewscreen. There was usually a long waiting list for private interplanetary calls these days, but Diana had priority as a war hero, leading esper figure and major pain in the ass, and she used her privilege hard. Contact with Mistworld took less than a minute to arrange, and soon Investigator Topaz was staring out of the viewscreen at Diana, her face as always utterly cold and controlled.

'This had better be important, Vertue. I'm busy.'

'You're always busy, Investigator. You're so full of duty and the work ethic you probably even sleep standing to attention. I need to talk to you, about the Mater Mundi.'

'You're not the first. Lots of people are interested in her, and what she did to me.'

'What she did to you?' said Diana, leaning forward.

Topaz frowned. 'She supercharged me. I can do things now, powerful things. I'm not just a Siren any more. Not just a projective telepath. I'm more than I was. A lot of people are scared of me now. Of course, on Mistworld that's usually an advantage. Helps keep the flies off. But this is . . . different. If I didn't know better, I'd swear it was religious awe. A couple of days back, people started bringing their sick children to me, asking me to cure them with a laying on of hands.'

'And?' said Diana, intrigued.

Topaz sniffed, almost embarrassed. 'Well . . . I was curious. So I ran a few objective tests, did the whole bit. But there weren't any noticeable improvements. No one picked up their bed and walked. Hasn't stopped them coming, though. I have security people screen my callers these days. I can guard against my enemies, but God save me from wannabe disciples. One group actually built a church to me.'

'What happened?'

'I burned it down. They got the message. Why are you asking me these questions, Vertue?'

'I wanted to see if you were going through the same changes as me. The Mater Mundi brought together a lot of people on Mistworld. Have any of them demonstrated any notable changes?'

'Vertue, everyone who can walk unaided has been busy rebuilding Mistport for months now. We work sixteen-hour days, and none of us is getting enough sleep. We've all been acting pretty cranky. But I can't say I've noticed anything unusual. I'll keep an eye out, but I can't promise anything. I have to go. Don't bother me again without a damned good reason.'

The viewscreen went blank as Investigator Topaz broke the connection from her end. Diana turned back to her computer terminal, nibbling at her lower lip. Topaz appeared to have survived her time as a manifest pretty much unscathed. Probably because she'd never been a picture of mental health. Was that the connection? Did it mean something? Did it mean anything, apart from the fact that she'd been sitting in a room on her own far too long, and was ready to grab at anything that even looked as though it might make sense? Was it time she gave up, went home, had several large meals and then slept for a week?

Diana sighed, and pushed the tempting thought aside. There was an answer here, somewhere. There had to be. And she couldn't shake off a feeling that the search was important, that what she was doing mattered. If there was one thing she was sure of, it was that the Mater Mundi wasn't what most people thought it was. It had its own direction and agenda, and didn't hesitate to use whatever innocent tools it felt necessary to get the job done. Irrespective of the harm it did to its victims along the way. The Mater Mundi treated people exactly the way the Iron Bitch had.

What was the uber-esper's objective? And if the espers found out, would they still allow themselves to be used and discarded? Diana, sitting on her chair in her room, felt small and alone. This was too big for just one person; even her. But there was no one else she could take her questions and her fears to. She couldn't go to the leaders of the esper underground; the Mater Mundi had founded the underground. She might still be involved in running things, on some deep, very secret level. Which meant Diana couldn't trust anyone. The Mater Mundi could strike at her through any friend or enemy or stranger. If it knew what she was doing . . .

Diana sat up sharply. Something was wrong, she could feel it. She looked quickly around her, suddenly convinced that someone had just come into the room, but the door was shut and she was alone. She shuddered – the room was icy-cold. Her breath was steaming on the air before her. Hoar frost was forming on the computer equipment, tracing pretty fern shapes on the monitor and viewscreen. There was a feeling of pressure on the air, as though something impossibly large was coming, forcing its way through dimensional barriers and rattling the windows of reality. It was close now, looking for a way in. Diana surged to her feet, kicking the chair away to give herself room to move. She pulled her power around her like a cloak. It didn't stop her teeth chattering or her hands shaking. Diana wasn't sure how much of that was due to the cold. She didn't bother trying to call for help; she knew no one would be allowed to hear her. She knew what was coming. Glancing frantically about her, her gaze fell on the viewscreen. The patterns in the frost were slowly changing into a ragged, smiling face.

Every piece of computer equipment in the room rose up and took on a new shape. Metal and plastic humped and cracked, splitting and reforming around the new thing that was creating itself through the transforming tech. It made a sort of human shape, towering over Diana with a wide, blocky body and two arms of different lengths, ending in sharp metal claws. The head on top of the body had viewscreen glass for eyes and a jagged metal tear for a smile. Static sparked around the head like a splintered halo.

The Mater Mundi had found a new way to manifest.

'Hi,' said Diana, fighting to control her chattering teeth. 'Good of you to drop by.'

You've been asking questions, said a voice in her mind like grating teeth, like hissing pipes, like children crying. *You must stop.*

'Then stop me,' said Diana, 'if you can.' She wrapped her arms tightly around her, as much to hold herself together as keep out the terrible cold.

I will, if I must. Do not mistake my forbearance for weakness.

'Bullshit. If you could have done anything, you'd have done it by now. But you can't. You made me so much more than I was, and you can't take it back. The best you could manage was this thing, this metal golem to intimidate me. I've seen scarier mobiles in children's nurseries.'

I can break you, child.

And Diana was back in Wormboy Hell, naked, in the dark, crawling in her own piss and shit and vomit, while Wormboy played awful, sadistic mind games, torturing her again and again until she destroyed her own voice through constant screaming.

No, said Diana. *Get out of my mind, you bitch.*

And she was back in the records room again, shivering and shaking, the taste of vomit in her mouth. She glared at the metal construct, her mouth stretched in something that was as much a snarl as a smile. Her rage warmed her, driving out the cold. And when she spoke, she was Jenny Psycho again.

'That shit won't work with me. That was the past. I'm stronger now, stronger than I ever dreamed of being. Maybe stronger than you ever dreamed I could be. You can't stop me; no one can stop me. I'm going to find out who and what and where you are; and then I'll make you pay for all the poor bastards whose lives you destroyed.'

I did what was necessary. I did what you wanted. I made the rebel victory possible.

'For your own reasons. Now get the hell out of here. Before I decide to test just how strong you made me.'

How sharper than a serpent's tooth it is to raise an ungrateful child.

The presence was suddenly gone, and the cold went with it. The hoar frost started melting, slow tears falling from the face on the viewscreen, washing it away. The metal golem was empty, just an abandoned shell. Diana all but collapsed back into her chair. One of them had been bluffing, but she wasn't sure which. Apparently the Mater Mundi hadn't been sure either. Diana was pretty certain that had been the Mater Mundi, showing off a disturbing new trick it had learned. It was definitely growing stronger. Still, Diana thought, she must be getting closer to the truth if the Mater Mundi was prepared to go to such lengths to try to warn her off. With anyone else, it would probably have worked. Diana looked at the metal and plastic shape, still towering over her, and shivered again. Now that she had time to think about it, it really was pretty scary. She couldn't help wondering if that was how other people felt in the presence of Jenny Psycho.

'Damn,' she said finally, in a perfectly steady voice. 'How the hell am I going to explain this mess to the head of the House?'

Captain Silence led his old friend and enemy, the man called Carrion, through the packed shining steel corridors of the starcruiser *Dauntless*. It had been a long time since Carrion had been on a starship. He'd spent the last twelve years living alone on the planet Unseeli, also known as Ghostworld, his only companions the restless spirits of the murdered alien Ashrai. After so much comforting solitude, safe from the eyes and voices of men, the bustling men and women crewing the starcruiser made him uneasy. Particularly since he knew most of them would cheerfully kill him, given the chance. None of them would look at him directly. They turned their heads away as they passed, their mouths silently forming curses and obscenities, and he could feel angry stares burning into his back. He didn't react. Carrion held his head high, and walked on beside Silence as though he noticed nothing, felt nothing.

'Been a few changes since you were last on a starcruiser,' said Silence. 'Nothing too drastic, though. There's a file in your personal computer that will bring you up to date. But you'd better be a quick study. We're leaving orbit in six hours.'

'Why the rush?' said Carrion, his voice calm and unmoved as always. 'The Darkvoid's not going anywhere.'

'But whatever's in there might not stay in there much longer. You heard Half A Man – he called them the Recreated. Aliens who died and brought themselves back to life. Spooky, if true.'

'You doubt the word of one of humanity's greatest heroes?'

'If the first Half A Man was a fake and a liar, who's to say this new one isn't as well? But we can't take the chance, with something as potentially dangerous as the Recreated. Someone has to check it out, and my ship and crew have more experience with the Darkvoid than most.'

'The idea of the Recreated is not without precedent. You gave the order that wiped out the Ashrai; but they survived, in their way.'

Silence grunted non-committally. 'They're your ghosts, you keep them under control. I'm putting you in Frost's old cabin. Since you're officially an Investigator again, it's yours by right anyway. It's been cleared of all personal possessions. Not that Frost had many.'

'I know you and she were close. I regret your loss.'

'You never liked her. She represented everything you ever hated about the Empire.'

'I respected her. She was a warrior.'

'Whatever. She was a good soldier. I honour her memory.' Silence paused, considering his words. 'Don't let the crew's attitude get to you. They'll come round, once they've seen you work.'

'I doubt it, Captain. I am a traitor. I betrayed my fellow crew and my own species, to join the alien Ashrai in their war against humanity. Not that it did them any good in the long run. Still, I killed a great many men and women, some of them familiar faces I once served beside, just to protect an alien species in open rebellion against the Empire. I'm humanity's worst nightmare; an Investigator who went native. A traitor, proud of his treason.'

'You had your reasons,' said Silence.

'Just as you did, when you gave the order to scorch Unseeli, and destroy everything that lived on that world.'

'You've never forgiven me for that, have you?'

'No, Captain. We've both done too much for forgiveness to mean anything.'

'You've been pardoned,' said Silence, 'reinstated as an Investigator, in return for your joining this mission into the Darkvoid. The crew know that. And they'll respect your work and authority or I'll kick their backsides till they do.'

'I didn't ask for a pardon,' said Carrion. 'I have not repented or reformed. I don't consider myself human any more. I am the last of the Ashrai, and their legacy lives on within me. I'm here because I have nowhere else to be, now that the metallic forests are gone and Unseeli is nothing more than a giant tombstone for the wonders that once lived there.'

'You're here because I asked you,' said Silence, 'because I needed you. Because you're my friend.'

'Perhaps. There is bad blood between us, John. Murder and betrayal and the loss of trust. The two men we used to be, the men who were friends, are a long way off in the past, so far from us I can barely see them. We're different people now.'

'Perhaps, Sean. Time changes everyone. It's not many who end up the people they thought they'd become. We all look back from time to time, and wonder how the hell we got here from there.'

'I chose my path,' said the man called Carrion. 'I regret nothing.'

'Die, you bastard traitor!'

A crewman stepped suddenly out of an alcove, aimed a disrupter point-blank at Carrion's chest and pressed the stud. There was no time to dodge, and nowhere to go in the narrow corridor. Even Silence, with all his more than human speed and reflexes, couldn't do anything to stop what was happening. The disrupter's energy beam crossed the few feet between the crewman and Carrion in less than a second. And a blazing energy field radiated from Carrion's power lance, absorbing the disrupter blast without missing a beat. There was a reason why power lances were banned throughout the Empire, their very possession a capital offence. They amplified an esper's power to the point where he was literally unbeatable in battle. And Carrion was no ordinary esper.

For a long moment, nobody moved. The crewman stood frozen in place, his discharged gun still pointing at Carrion, his mouth hanging open. Carrion stared back at him impassively. Silence's hand hovered above his holstered gun. Then the crewman sobbed suddenly, his face twisted with rage, and he grabbed for the sword at his side. Silence moved quickly forward, grabbed the crewman by the shirt-front and slammed him back against the steel bulkhead behind him. All the breath went out of the crewman, and the anger that had been fuelling him. His face went slack, and his hands hung limply at his sides. Silence growled into the man's face, and then turned to look at Carrion, who hadn't moved an inch, as calm and apparently relaxed as always.

'Nice reflexes, Sean.'

'I've had to develop them, to stay alive in human space,' said Carrion.

Silence growled again, turned back to the crewman and glared into the man's dazed eyes.

'Name and rank, mister. Now!'

'Ordinary starman Barron, Captain. A loyal member of your crew. Unlike that piece of scum!'

'That's enough! He's a pardoned man, an Investigator, and your superior officer. He has my full confidence, and an attack on him is an attack on me. Now turn yourself in to security. I'll deal with you later. And Barron, don't make me come looking for you.'

'No, Captain, I said I was loyal. But you don't understand—'

'Save it for your court martial.'

'He killed my father! On Unseeli!'

The man looked as if he was about to cry. Silence met Carrion's eyes. Carrion nodded slowly. 'It's possible. I killed a lot of people on Unseeli. I regret your loss, Barron.'

'Save your lies, traitor!'

'That's enough!' Silence pulled Barron away from the bulkhead and threw him staggering down the corridor. Other crew members watching from the sidelines moved quickly back to get out of his way. Barron sniffed back a sob, and stumbled away to the security office, not looking back. Carrion and Silence looked after him for a while, and then turned away. Around them, the watching crew returned to their tasks.

'We never really leave the past behind,' said Silence heavily.

'Some part of it always turns up again, demanding payment.'

'He must have been a child when his father died,' said Carrion. 'No wonder he hates me. Probably joined your crew to follow in his father's footsteps. Only to find me here, and you defending me. It must be very difficult for him.'

'None of that makes any difference,' said Silence flatly. 'He's supposed to understand discipline. I thought I trained my people better than that. They're warriors, not sneaking assassins.'

'It's not as if he was the first,' said Carrion. 'There have been several attempts on my life since you brought me back from Unseeli.'

'What?' Silence looked at him sharply. 'This is the first I've heard of it! Why wasn't I informed? Why didn't you tell me?'

'It wasn't important. I handled it.'

'This is my ship, Investigator. You are part of my crew. From now on, I want to know everything. Is that understood?'

'Yes, Captain.'

Silence glared at him for a moment, and then they continued on their way. The corridor seemed emptier of people than it had been before. Silence fumed quietly to himself. Carrion remained impassive, striding soundlessly down the corridor with his black cloak billowing about him like the wings of the black bird of ill omen he thought himself to be. Silence cursed himself for a fool, for not fully considering the impact Carrion's return would have on his crew. Of course there were bound to be hard feelings. There would be men and women on board ship who'd fought against Carrion and the Ashrai in the vicious and bloody ground wars on Unseeli. Twelve years was a long time, but nowhere near long enough to forget something like that. God knows he'd tried hard enough.

But all that had mattered to him at the time was getting the man who used to be his friend back on board ship with him, where Silence thought he belonged. He'd wanted things to be the way they used to be. But his old friend Sean was now the man called Carrion. Traitor, murderer, alien by adoption and by choice, the first to admit he wasn't human any more. It would take more than a pardon and a reinstatement to undo what the man called Sean had made himself. Silence sighed, quietly. With Frost gone, he needed someone he could trust to lean on. It was as simple as that. And Carrion, ill-suited to the role as he might be, was the only one Silence could turn to.

'I appreciate everything you've done for me, Captain,' said Carrion, his voice calm and unmoved. 'But I feel I should point out that adding a notorious traitor such as myself to your crew is probably not the wisest thing you could have done. It won't do much for your career prospects, and it could undermine your standing and authority with your crew.'

'I don't have any career prospects,' said Silence. 'I've seen to that. And my crew trusts me, and my judgement. They'll learn to accept you.'

'I can't replace Investigator Frost, Captain.'

'No one could. I was offered my choice of Investigator for this mission, but I wanted you. Someone who could understand the alien viewpoint, and come up with other options than just blowing them away. If the Recreated are everything they're supposed to be, going head to head with them is not going to be a viable strategy. I needed someone flexible.'

'I've been called many things in my time, but I think that's a new one. But how can you be sure I'd side with humanity? I might join with the aliens once again.'

'Shub destroyed the metallic forests. Took away everything you had. They're your enemy too, now. And siding with humanity is your only chance for revenge on them.'

'How well you understand me, Captain. You're quite right. Revenge is a cold comfort, but sometimes it's all we have left to cling to.'

'Just do your duty, Carrion. That's all anyone can ask of us.'

'Duty. Honour. Revenge. No matter how far we go, how deeply we hide ourselves, they always come back to claim us. All I ever wanted was to be left alone. But we are the potter's clay, not the potter. And I have always done what I must, because it is not in me to stand aside. I'll be your Investigator,

Captain. Just promise me that when I'm no longer needed, you'll let me go.'

'Of course, Sean. I understand.'

'No, you don't, Captain. You never did.'

They walked a while together, staring straight ahead. They'd never found it easy to talk about the things that mattered.

'Did you get a chance to talk to Diana again, before we left?' said Carrion.

'No. I left a message at the esper Guild House where she's been staying, but she never got back to me. Perhaps it's for the best. She's been through a lot, and there's so much unfinished business between us. I used to hear about the rebel terrorist called Jenny Psycho, but I never dreamed that she could be my own lost daughter. Frost knew, but she never told me. She knew it would hurt me. You saw how Diana was at Parliament. She said she hated me. With good reason, if truth be told. I wasn't there to save her when she needed me. Not the kind of thing that can be sorted out with a ten-minute chat, in the middle of our busy lives. Maybe when this mission is over . . .'

'She was such a frail young thing when I first knew her on Unseeli,' said Carrion. 'So full of life and happiness and wonder. I saw so much of that crushed, by what she went through. But in the end she found the strength to join in song with the Ashrai, to fly free, as they do. I couldn't see any of that person in the woman I met at Parliament. I've heard of some of the things she did as Jenny Psycho, terrible things. How did she turn from what she was, into what she became?'

'How did we?' said Silence.

'Good point, Captain. Good point.'

They came at last to Frost's old cabin. Silence hesitated for a moment before the closed door. He hadn't been in there since just after her death, when he sorted through Frost's old belongings, before the cleaning staff went in. He hadn't been looking for anything in particular; it was just his way of saying goodbye. There hadn't been much to look through. Like all Investigators, Frost hadn't bothered much with mementoes or personal touches. A few books, all strictly military in nature. No photos, or letters, or memories. Just a small library of discs of her favourite music. Silence hadn't known she liked music. It seemed too tranquil an interest, for her. He'd taken the discs away with him to listen to later, when he had the time.

He'd had the cabin sealed after that, ready for whoever took over as Investigator. Though he'd never expected to be opening it for Carrion. He reached out to punch in the security codes, and then stopped as Carrion put a hand on his arm. Silence looked at him, raising an eyebrow. Carrion stared at the closed door, frowning slightly.

'Not just yet, Captain,' he said quietly. 'There's someone in there. Someone, or something, very unusual. And very powerful.'

'That's not possible,' said Silence. 'The door's still locked, and I'm the only one who has the security code. Anyone trying to get past that would set off alarms all over the ship.'

'Nevertheless,' said Carrion, 'this room is already inhabited.'

Silence drew his disrupter. 'Stand ready. And watch yourself. Anyone powerful enough to override this kind of lock would have to be very dangerous.'

'That's all right,' said Carrion. 'So am I.'

Silence entered the security code, kicked the door open and stepped quickly into the room, Carrion at his side. The lights were already on. A dark figure was sitting in Frost's old chair, her back to him. She was little more than a silhouette, but something about her shape and posture seemed familiar to Silence. He lurched forward a step, a mad, impossible hope bursting suddenly in his heart.

'Frost . . . ?'

'No,' said the figure, turning round in the chair to face him. 'It's just me, Daddy.'

The hope in Silence's heart crashed and died, but was replaced almost immediately by a different kind of warmth. He holstered his disrupter, and smiled at his daughter. 'Hello, Diana. How the hell did you get in here? I didn't even know you were on board ship.'

'No one does,' said Diana Vertue. 'Let's keep it that way.

This is an entirely unofficial visit. No one must know I was ever here. I have enemies these days, more powerful and dangerous than I ever expected.'

'Oh, hell,' said Silence, 'who have you killed now?'

'Nothing like that,' said Diana. 'I could cope with something like that.'

'Hold everything,' said Silence. 'How did you get on board this ship? No matter what excuse you used, security should still have alerted me.'

Diana smiled briefly. 'A girl has to have some secrets, Daddy. Let's just say no one sees me any more, if I don't want to be seen. Not even your ship's esper or security devices. Now do sit down, the pair of you. You're making the place look untidy, and I hate being loomed over.'

Silence and Carrion looked at each other, shrugged pretty much simultaneously, and looked around for somewhere to sit. There was only one other chair, so Silence sat on it. He was the captain, after all. Carrion sat on the bed; it was officially his. They both looked expectantly at Diana.

'I've been working on something new,' said Diana carefully. 'Investigating the true nature of the Mater Mundi. And I've been happening on all kinds of unexpected and interesting things. The one thing I'm sure of is that she isn't what everyone thinks she is. She's also somewhat mad at me, for poking my nose into areas she feels are none of my business. In fact, she warned me off, personally. I think she would have killed me, if she could.'

Carrion looked at her interestedly. 'You stood off the Mater Mundi? I'm impressed.'

'Maybe you should back off, Diana,' said Silence. 'What's so important about knowing the Mater Mundi's true nature that's worth getting killed over?'

'I don't know,' said Diana. 'That's exactly my point. What could be so terrible about her, so shocking, that she's prepared to kill to keep it hidden?'

Silence shrugged impatiently. 'There's no point asking me, I've never had any interest in esper affairs. What do you want from me, Diana? We're leaving for the Darkvoid in just under six hours.'

'That's why I had to catch you before you left. I'm

354

becoming very interested in the nature of esp itself. How it does what it does. You two are both unique individuals. The captain because he passed part way through the Madness Maze, and emerged changed. And Carrion, because before he went to Unseeli, he showed no trace at all of esper abilities. No one in his family was ever an esper, for as far back as I can trace, and the genetic assay in his old medical files bears that out. So, Carrion, how did you become the esper paragon that you are today?'

'The aliens changed me,' said Carrion, 'the Ashrai. It was necessary, if I was to survive alone on their world and join them in their war against humanity. So they remade me. And no, I don't know how, I have no memory of it. Apparently it was too painful to remember.'

'They would have had to make alterations on the genetic level,' said Diana, frowning. 'Pretty sophisticated stuff, for a species with no discernible technology.'

'That's a very human attitude,' said Carrion. 'Tech isn't everything.'

Diana studied him silently for a long moment. 'You're never alone, are you, Carrion? They're always with you. The ghosts, the Ashrai.'

Carrion leaned forward. 'You can see them?'

'Almost. I sang with them once on Unseeli, remember? My mind joined with theirs, though only briefly. That link is still there. I can feel them, a potential hanging around you, like the pressure on the air before a storm. Why do they stay, Carrion? Why do they stay with you?'

'I'm the last Ashrai. All that's left of what they were. They want revenge for what was done to them. To the trees, to their world.'

'Revenge?' said Diana. 'That's a very human attitude, isn't it?'

'Yes,' said Carrion. 'Regrettably, they have learned by example.'

'We're very alike, you and I,' said Diana. 'Changed and altered by powers greater than ourselves, for reasons we don't fully understand. What were you supposed to be, Carrion? Their champion? Their defender? Their avenger? Be very careful; you might not be what you think you are. You fought

355

humanity for them once. Would you destroy humanity for them now, for revenge?'

'They wouldn't ask me to do that,' said Carrion.

'How do you know?' said Diana, and Carrion had no answer to give her.

'Why are you here, Diana?' said Silence, after the quiet had dragged on long enough to become uncomfortable. 'After what you said to us at Parliament—'

'Needs must where the Devil drives,' said Diana. 'I find myself in need of allies. If the Mater Mundi wants me dead, it'll find a way. So I need help, powerful associates to watch my back and lend their power to me.'

'So you came to your father,' said Silence. 'Of course, Diana. That's what fathers are for.'

'No, Daddy,' said Diana. 'Not you. The Maze gave you power, but you're still learning how to use it.'

'So you want my help?' said Carrion. 'Very well. My abilities are at your disposal.'

'Don't flatter yourself,' said Diana. 'I need the Ashrai; their inhuman strength. Like I said, the link's still there. I can almost hear their song, echoing deep down in the caverns of my unconscious, a rustling of ghosts, of an old encounter. God knows I've tried to exorcise them. I don't want anyone in my head but me. But if they're there, maybe I can use them. So tell me, Carrion, would they come if I called? If I needed them?'

'I don't know,' said Carrion. 'They don't talk to me any more. But they have always intervened when I needed them.'

'Not exactly the answer I was hoping for,' said Diana. 'But let's see if it's true.'

Her face changed suddenly. Dark shadows appeared beneath her staring eyes, and the skin of her face stretched taut across her skull. Her thin lips stretched into a merciless, humourless smile. She seemed suddenly larger than she was, and her eyes were unnaturally bright. Psionic power sparked and crackled on the air around her, and her presence leaped out to fill the cabin. Diana was gone, submerged in the malevolent aberration that was Jenny Psycho. Silence's hand went automatically to his gun, and then fell away. Even if he could bring himself to use it on his own daughter, he doubted it would be any use against something like Jenny Psycho.

She stood up and glared at Carrion, shadows gathering around her, and he was quickly on his feet facing her, his power lance held out between them. Jenny Psycho seized the lance with her mind, ripped it out of his hands and threw it the length of the cabin. Carrion cried out in shock, as though one of his limbs had been torn away. His body rose slowly into the air, and then slammed back against the steel cabin wall, held there crucified by Jenny Psycho's will. Silence tried to rise from his chair and found he couldn't, held in place by his daughter's thoughts.

And then the Ashrai came.

They filled the cabin like a boiling cloud, dead but not gone, with gargoyle faces and huge, clawed hands. The space within the cabin seemed to fly out in all directions, becoming vast and cavernous to accommodate the massive forms of the Ashrai. Silence cried out at the sight of them. They were awful and magnificent, terrible in their anger, and they burned so very brightly. Jenny Psycho, blazing like a star, smiled at them and addressed them in perfectly reasonable tones.

'Hi, guys. Good to see you again. It's been a while. Sorry for disturbing your rest, but I really could use your help. There's something out there called the Mater Mundi, and it might just be more powerful than you are. And I don't think it's willing to tolerate any competition. So, if I need your help against it, will you come when I call?'

There was a burst of song in reply, music complex and emotional almost beyond bearing, sung by angels with barbed wings and halos of flies. And then the Ashrai were gone, and the cabin was just a cabin again. Carrion slid down the wall and settled comfortably back on the bed. His lance sped across the air and into his hands. Silence found he could move again. Jenny Psycho flickered out like a snuffed candle, and was just Diana Vertue again. She stretched slowly, and sat down on her chair. There was a sense of calm in the cabin, of pressure released, of a storm passed.

'What the hell was the point of all that?' said Silence.

'Jenny's a bit of a bitch, but she gets things done,' said

Diana, entirely unruffled by his tone. 'And I had a feeling the Ashrai would only respond to the dramatic. I needed to have their answer.'

'And now you do,' said Carrion. 'I hope you think that raising their anger was worth it.'

'Someone translate,' snapped Silence. 'All I heard was music that damn near blew out my eardrums. What did they say?'

'They know about the Mater Mundi,' said Diana. 'And they're scared. Her existence disturbs them. They've agreed to come when I call, but I'm not sure any more how much use they'll be. They're much diminished, without their forest and their world.'

'Don't underestimate them,' said Carrion. 'Dying was just another journey for them, a transition to another state. They are still very powerful.'

'But they've been dead a long time,' said Diana. 'You're all that holds them to the worlds of the living now, Carrion.'

'Yes, well,' said Silence. 'I'm still not entirely comfortable with the idea of ghosts anyway. The dead should stay dead.'

'I'm not comfortable with the thought that the Mater Mundi could be so powerful that she even frightens the dead,' responded Diana. 'It would appear I'm going to need even more allies. Which brings me back to you, Daddy.'

'What do you mean?' said Silence. 'As you so kindly pointed out, what few powers I have aren't even in the same league as the Mater Mundi. I'll be there for you when I can, but I'm just another captain in the Imperial Fleet, and I have to go where my orders send me. Right now, I'm heading into the Darkvoid. No idea when I'll be back. Or even if I'll be coming back.'

'You'll be back,' said Diana. 'You're a survivor. You survived the Madness Maze, when most of the crew who went in with you didn't. And you do have powers, though you've chosen not to use or develop them. There's no reason why you couldn't become as powerful as all the other Maze survivors, in time. I didn't want to involve you in my troubles, but I may not have any choice. How much do you love me, Daddy? Enough to become something other than human, for my sake, to protect me?'

'I failed you before,' Silence said steadily. 'I won't fail you again. But I don't—'

'The Maze changed you,' said Diana. 'It rebuilt you. Don't be afraid of your potential. Tell me about the Maze, what it did to you.'

'I don't know!' said Silence, almost angrily. 'I don't know what I am, any more. I don't know what I'm becoming. All I know is that whatever change the Maze started in me, it isn't over yet. Sometimes, I see things in my dreams. I hear voices, telling me things. And once, Frost came to me. She was trying to warn me about the Maze, what it was doing to me, but I couldn't understand her.'

'Describe the Maze to me,' said Diana. 'What was it like, inside? What did it feel like?'

'It was . . . alien,' said Silence slowly. 'Like nothing I'd ever encountered before. And I think that it might have been alive, in some way that we could never have comprehended. Being inside the Maze was like walking in visions, like one of those dreams where you know the answer to everything, until you wake up and it's all gone. But these answers were real. They were too much for some of those who went into the Maze with me. They died horribly. Their minds didn't have the capacity for the changes the Maze wanted to make in them.'

'Why did you leave the Maze?' said Diana. 'Why didn't you go all the way through, like Owen and his people?'

'I was scared,' said Silence. 'I wasn't worthy. And it was killing Frost. I grabbed her and got us both out. It wasn't until much later that the changes started appearing in us.'

'What do you think the Maze was?' said Diana. 'What was its purpose?'

Silence snorted derisively. 'Better men than me have tried to answer that, and failed. Ask an ant what it feels about the statue it's crawling over. The Maze was an alien device of some kind, created who knows how long ago by some species or life form we know nothing of. No one's ever found anything like the Maze before or since, on any of the thousands of planets we've visited or colonized. Its purpose was an alien purpose, possibly quite beyond our human capability to understand.'

'But you felt its touch,' said Diana. 'What do you think it was?'

'Perhaps . . . a teaching machine,' Silence said quietly. 'For those capable of learning. But none of this matters any more. I destroyed it, blew it away with disrupter cannon till there was nothing left of it. The only one of its kind, possibly unique in the universe, and I obliterated it. And if I had to do it all over again, I'd give the same damned order without the slightest hesitation.'

'You never change, Captain,' said Carrion.

'Have you had any contact with the other Maze survivors, since the rebellion?' said Diana. 'Have you discussed your opinions with them?'

'No,' said Silence shortly. 'It wasn't that long ago we were trying to kill each other. They pulled down nearly everything I ever believed in. A part of me still wants to kill them, for what they've done. Besides, I don't think we'd have much in common to talk about. They're different from me, from everyone. They're spooky. Almost inhuman. Sometimes, almost alien. If there's a path they and I are walking, they're much further along it than me. From where I am, they're almost out of sight. I think they're a lot closer to what the Maze intended them to be, the poor bastards. All their new powers and abilities don't seem to have made them any happier. They're becoming something; something other than human.'

'Like me, perhaps?' said Carrion.

'No, Sean, you're just weird. I can still understand you, what moves you. I haven't a clue what's going on in the heads of Owen and his friends. I think they're moving away from merely human concerns. That makes them dangerous; perhaps not just to the Empire, but to all humanity. That's one of the reasons why the Maze people weren't informed of this mission. Parliament didn't trust them not to interfere, to try and stop us. They went into the Darkvoid and came out again, but swore they had no contact with the Recreated, or whatever it is that lives in the endless dark. That has to be significant.'

'What do you expect to find in the Darkvoid?' said Diana.

'Damned if I know. But, just possibly, something strong enough to stop or control the Maze people, if they go bad.'

'And you think that's necessary?' said Carrion. 'You feel a need for a weapon to destroy them? Like you destroyed the Ashrai and the Madness Maze?'

'Good example,' said Silence. 'My duty is to the Empire, and to humanity, to protect them from any and all dangers. Look, the Maze people aren't answerable to anyone but themselves. There's no one strong enough to say no if they say yes. And they're getting stronger all the time. What if one or more of them decided that Parliament's decisions were taking the Empire in a direction they didn't approve of? What if they were to decide that mere humans couldn't be trusted with their own destiny, and they decided to take over and rule us – for our own good, of course? Who could stop them? Together, they overturned Lionstone's Empire.'

'Or you could be turning paranoid,' said Diana. 'There are only four of them.'

'How many gods does it take to rule humanity?' said Silence. 'And just because I'm paranoid, it doesn't mean they aren't out to get me. You of all people should appreciate that, with your concerns about the Mater Mundi.'

'Good point,' said Diana, smiling for the first time. She got to her feet and nodded briefly to her father and Carrion. 'It's time I was going. I don't think I'm going to learn any more here. I'll talk to you again, when you get back. Don't bother to see me out.'

And just like that, she vanished. One moment there, the next gone. Silence and Carrion looked at each other.

'Well,' said Carrion finally, 'she's definitely your daughter, Captain.'

'And she always did know how to make an exit,' said Silence. He shook his head. 'Time is running out, and I still haven't finished briefing you. What was I going to . . . ah, yes. The insect ships. Have you finished struggling through the files I let you have?'

'Of course,' said Carrion. 'Fascinating material. You do know the insects have to be artificial, don't you?'

'That's what Frost said. She said they had to have been gengineered, because insects don't get that big naturally.

Which implies there's another player in the game that we don't know about yet; the insects' creator.'

'Do we really need to assume it's an unknown?' said Carrion. 'Surely there are enough suspects already: the Hadenmen, Shub, even rogue human scientists funded by Families desperate for power. All of these have proved capable of developing and deploying terror weapons in the past, for their various reasons. And then, there's always the Recreated. Whatever they turn out to be.'

'I said as much to Admiral Beckett,' said Silence slowly. 'He commended me on my original thinking, but said he didn't have the time or the resources to investigate any of them. I couldn't argue with him. I know the state of the Fleet as well as he does. But I wouldn't be at all surprised to discover that the insects come out of the Darkvoid. Their attacks have always been concentrated on the Rim, and where else could they be disappearing to, afterwards? And then . . . there's the voices.' Silence looked steadily at Carrion. 'The files I gave you on that are restricted. You are not to discuss their contents with anyone else without my express permission, in advance. I've gone to great pains to keep information on the voices limited to the smallest number of people. My crew are spooked enough about going back into the Darkvoid as it is. So . . . what do you make of the voices? Any ideas?'

'It could be an esper phenomenon,' said Carrion. 'Or it could be the voices of the dead. I have experience of both myself, after all. But the most likely explanation has to be a psychological trick by Shub, to soften you up for the coming of the *Champion*. A long-lost ship, crewed by dead men, its reappearance heralded by the warning voices of ghosts; just the kind of thing the rogue AIs would come up with, to mess with your heads.'

'Of course that's the most likely explanation,' said Silence. 'But there's more to it than that. You didn't hear those voices, Sean, they wouldn't stay recorded. They just faded away. What you listened to in the files were simulations, based on what we remembered. The real thing sounded . . . horrible. Unnerving. They really did seem to be trying to warn us away from danger. Not just from the *Champion*, but from the Darkvoid itself. And now here we are, going back into it again.'

'Could it be some kind of warning by the Recreated?' said Carrion. 'To stay out of their territory?'

'Your guess is as good as mine. I suppose, as always, we'll just have to find out the hard way. And it has to be us. This ship and its crew have more experience of the Darkvoid than any other three ships put together. And we are, after all, quite definitely expendable.'

'Nothing changes,' said Carrion, and they both managed some kind of a smile.

'So,' said Silence, 'how does it feel, to be an Investigator again?'

'I wear the title only as a courtesy. If I hadn't taken it, the Fleet would only have forced one on you. And we don't need that kind of distraction. But I won't wear the official uniform. I'm not worthy of it any more. Or it's not worthy of me. I haven't decided yet.'

'You got a full pardon.'

'I didn't ask for it.'

'But it means you're no longer a wanted man,' said Silence. 'Wouldn't you like to go home again, Sean?'

'I had a home,' said Carrion. 'I was happy there. And then you and Shub destroyed it.'

Evangeline Shreck, who wasn't really a Shreck at all if truth be told, came home at last to Tower Shreck, and stood for a long time in its cold, dark shadow, trying to stop trembling. From the outside it looked like just another building, steel and glass and the Family colours that marked it as one of the legendary pastel towers, home to the Clans. Tower Shreck was as tall as any of them, but its windows were strangely blank, like so many unblinking eyes. To Evangeline it was the witch's cave, the demon's lair, the dark place that calls to us in familiar voices in our worst nightmares. Evangeline had been born in that Tower, in that dark place, and not so very long ago. In its terrible embrace she lived a life of pain, horror and torment, until at last a dashing prince came, and loved her, and gave her the courage to break free of the ogre who held her enchained.

And now she'd come back, though she'd sworn she never would. Back home again, to save her best friend from the hell she'd known so well.

Her love didn't know she was here. She'd let Finlay Campbell believe she was off on another mission for the clone underground. If he'd known she was going back to Tower Shreck, he'd have tried to stop her or talk her out of it, and she couldn't have that. This was something she had to do for herself – however much it hurt. She was here to see the monster: her father, Gregor Shreck. He wanted her back, and she was back, but this time it was on her terms. He thought he held all the cards, owned all the advantages, but she had a few surprises of her own, just for him. Just for dear Daddy.

The man who murdered his only daughter Evangeline, and afterwards had her cloned in secret to produce the present Evangeline. The man who loved both the original and her clone as a man, rather than a father. Who abused his position and his daughter's love. Who took his Evangelines to his bed, and taught them far more about pain than pleasure. The Devil, in his hell. Gregor Shreck.

Hatred pulsed in her like a heartbeat, surging through her like blood, forcing out the fear. She took a deep breath to steady herself, and then walked calmly towards the guards covering the main entrance to Tower Shreck. They looked more like beetles than men in their extensive black body armour, faces hidden behind stylized sensor masks. They carried heavy guns, and moved as one to train them on her as she approached. There were six of them, but they didn't scare her. She wasn't frightened of them. She stopped a cautious distance away, and stared at them haughtily.

'I'm Evangeline Shreck. I'm here to see my father Gregor. Inform him I'm here.'

The guards looked at her for a moment, and then at each other. She presumed they were holding a brief but intense conversation through their comm implants before daring to disturb their master, the Shreck. It wasn't long before they stood back and gestured to admit her to the Tower through the main entrance. She strode forward, head held high, and the single heavy door opened silently before her. She entered

Tower Shreck with only the faintest of shudders, and walked on into the lobby. It had been redecorated since she last saw it. All comforts and attractive details had been stripped away, leaving only a large bare chamber with a concrete floor and blank steel walls. She heard footsteps behind her, and made herself turn slowly to face the single guard who'd come into the lobby after her. The door closed behind him. He spoke to her without removing his mask, his voice filtered to remove all traces of humanity from it.

'The Lord Shreck awaits you in his private quarters, Lady Evangeline. I'm to escort you there. After a full security search.'

'Lord Shreck?' said Evangeline, raising an eyebrow. 'There are no Lords any more. Doesn't he know that?'

'The Shreck goes his own way, in all things. Remove your clothes, all of them. Place to one side any weapons or devices you may be carrying.'

Evangeline nodded stiffly. She'd been expecting that. Gregor thought everyone wanted to kill him, these days. Mostly he was right. She took her clothes off with as little fuss as possible, concentrating on why she was there. It helped that the guard looked inhuman and anonymous in his armour and mask. She wondered if Gregor was watching through the sensors in the mask. Probably. Finally she was naked, her clothes in a neat pile on the floor. She was glad the lobby was warm; she wouldn't have wanted to shiver in the cold. The guard or his master might have thought she was upset. She fixed the insect mask with a steady glare.

'That's it. No clothes, no weapons. But if you touch me with so much as a fingertip, I'll tell Daddy. Do you really want him to know you touched something he believes belongs only to him?'

The guard hesitated, and then nodded jerkily and indicated for her to get dressed again. She did so, not letting the guard or her nerves hurry her. When she was ready again, the guard led the way to the single elevator at the back of the lobby, and they both got in. The guard gave the order for the penthouse floor, and the doors closed silently. He stepped back a pace so he could cover Evangeline with his gun. She ignored him, staring at the glowing numbers set over the door as they slowly changed. So far, everything was going as planned. For all his paranoia, Gregor still couldn't see her as a serious threat. She was his little Evie, his plaything, to do with as he wished.

Old memories ran through her like an icy river; the few years she'd spent here an eternity of torment in a hell she never deserved. She was born here, fully grown, a clone of a woman the outside world could never know was dead. She was taught to be a perfect copy of the original Evangeline, so that she might hide from society the dreadful thing Gregor had done. And so that he could continue to have his pleasures in the way he'd grown accustomed.

It was the only life she'd ever known, until she met Finlay at Court, at a masked ball, and it was love at first sight. They talked and laughed, eyes sparkling through their masks, each warming to the other's heart for the first time in their lives. Then the masks came off at midnight, and they discovered they were a Shreck and a Campbell, two Families that had been at war with each other for generations, and of which each of them was the heir. Their love would have been a scandal, unacceptable, and Evangeline knew that Gregor would rather kill her than lose her. Still worse, he might kill Finlay. So they kept their love secret, snatching moments together when they could, until finally she broke free of Gregor and they were together at last.

She never told Finlay about Gregor, about what her father had done to her. The terrible things he'd inflicted on her in his private chamber, where there was no one to hear her screams or see her tears. She knew Finlay couldn't have coped with it, with knowing how she'd suffered. He would have stormed off in a bloody rage to kill Gregor, and to hell with the consequences. Gregor's people might have killed him, or he might have been hanged afterwards. Either way, she couldn't risk it. And besides, he might have felt differently about her, once the truth was known.

The elevator chimed softly as they reached the top floor. It was like Hell in reverse. You had to go all the way up, to reach the darkest, foulest part of the pit. The doors slid open and the guard escorted her down the bare steel corridor. Their footsteps were loud and carrying on the metal floor.

Gregor wanted to know when anyone was coming. Other guards stood to attention here and there along the length of the corridor, anonymous armoured figures with guns at the ready. Not beetles any more, Evangeline decided; demons, in the hall of Hell. She made herself look straight ahead, and wouldn't let her mouth tremble. Eventually she and her dark companion came to a halt before the extra thick steel door that was the only entrance to her father's private quarters. It was a very special door, designed to stand off a bomb or a disrupter blast with equal ease. Evangeline stood stiffly before it as the guard announced their presence.

'Come in,' said Gregor's soft, oily voice, through a hidden speaker that made his words seem to come from everywhere at once. 'Come in, little Evie, and join your forgiving father. Guard Six, take up position outside the door. We are not to be disturbed for any reason.'

Evangeline realized the demon beside her had to be Guard Six. Typical of Gregor to have guards with numbers instead of names. The door swung slowly open, and Evangeline held herself tightly together as she walked unhurriedly into the ogre's lair. It was important not to walk so slowly that she might appear scared or reluctant, or so quickly that it might seem she was jumping to obey an order. Appearances were everything now. They were all she had to work with. The door closed behind her as she stopped and looked around her.

Gregor Shreck had made changes in his private quarters since she was there last. They now looked as dark and evil and disturbing as he was. The windowless walls of the great chamber were a dark crimson, the colour of drying blood, or organs ripped untimely from a body. The wide room was now a great scarlet womb, with concealed, bloody lighting, and dark shadows hung everywhere. The thick pile carpet beneath her feet was the colour of sunburned skin, deep enough to muffle any sound. To every side stood grisly trophies from Gregor's most recent victims. There was a pile of severed hands on a silver tray, heaped carelessly on top of each other. A row of preserved severed heads stood on stakes, all looking faintly surprised, their mouths falling open as though in shock at what had been done to them. None of them had eyes. A low cupboard displayed a row of severed feet. They hadn't been arranged in pairs of left and right, but someone had wrapped them in pretty ribbons and painted their toenails black. Somewhere Evangeline could hear air-conditioning units working overtime as they struggled to deal with the pervasive smell of death and preservatives.

And there, reclining at his ease on a wide, comfortable bed shaped from gigantic rose petals, lay the dark heart of that dark kingdom, Gregor Shreck. He'd always been short and fat, a greasy, perspiring doughball of a man, but he'd put on a lot of weight during their separation. He was huge now, bulging with flesh, his face almost perfectly round, crushing his features into the centre of his face. The mouth was a pursed rosebud, the eyes so deeply set they were barely visible. He was dressed all in black slashed with scarlet streaks, and looked like nothing so much as a gigantic, gorged leech.

'So,' said Gregor, in an unnervingly normal-sounding voice, 'you've come home to me at last, back to where you belong. I always knew you would. My dear, loving daughter.'

'I'm here because you abducted my friend Penny DeCarlo, and threatened to kill her if I didn't come,' said Evangeline tonelessly. 'And that's the only reason I'm here. Where is she? What have you done with her?'

'So impatient,' said Gregor happily. 'No one has time for the civilized little courtesies any more. Don't you have a kiss for your dear daddy?'

'I could,' said Evangeline, 'but then I'd have to cut off my lips, for having touched you. Where's Penny?'

'Ah, impetuous youth! Children always want their presents right now. Very well, Evie, never let it be said that I am not an indulgent father. You may see your little friend Penny. I've been taking ever such good care of her. She always was a little headstrong, but I've taken care of that.'

He gestured languidly with a huge fat hand, and a panel in the left wall slid open, revealing two severed heads in glass jars. One was Penny DeCarlo. Evangeline's hands flew to her mouth to stifle a scream, and only then did she realize that the heads were still alive. Their eyes were aware and suffering, and their mouths moved to shape words, though nothing could be heard. Penny was pale-skinned with short dark hair, and would have been beautiful in any other circumstances. The second head was that of an old man, with long white hair and moustaches floating gently in the preservative fluids. Both heads stared sadly at Evangeline, and she made herself lower her hands and swallow her shock. She couldn't afford to show weakness, not here. She glared at Gregor.

'Oh, they're very much alive,' Gregor assured her happily. 'The one on the right is Professor Wax. Quite a prominent scientist in his day, now an overqualified paperweight. Valentine gave him to me, already in his glass jar. It seemed a shame not to have a matching pair, and I had to do something to express my displeasure when you defied me by not returning immediately . . . So you could say this is really all your fault. I think they look very smart together. I may start a collection. The ones on stakes are fun, but their torment is over.'

'Why can't I hear them?' Evangeline asked, through numbed lips. 'Have you cut out their vocal cords too?'

'Of course not, my dear. Where would be the fun in that? I just haven't turned on the speakers yet. I have to have them off now and again, just to get a little peace and quiet. Though admittedly Penny doesn't scream nearly as much as she used to.'

He gestured again, and there was a sudden steady hum as hidden speakers came on-line. Penny's head fixed its sad eyes on Evangeline's, and the mouth tried to move in a smile.

'You shouldn't have come here, Evie. He's mad, quite mad.'

'I've always known that,' said Evangeline. 'But I had to come back here to get you. I . . . I didn't know . . .'

'Oh, Evie . . .' Penny's face screwed up as though it would have liked to cry, but that was no longer possible in the preservative fluids.

'Hush, child, hush,' said the white-haired head beside her. 'Don't distress yourself. Be strong. We must be strong. Don't give that fat bastard the satisfaction.'

'Oh, dear Waxie,' said Penny. 'I'd go mad if it weren't for you, for your comfort.'

'Aren't they sweet?' said Gregor. 'They're lovebirds. A meeting of minds, if you like.'

Wax's eyes turned to look at Evangeline. 'Get Penny out of here, if you can. She doesn't deserve this. I do. I created machines whose only purpose was death and destruction, and saw them used to wipe out a whole world's population. I saw them die, over and over again, men and women and innocent children, and somewhere along the line I developed a conscience. I never cared about the suffering of my test subjects. I told myself I was defending the Empire from its enemies. But the death of a whole world sickened even me. I deserve to be here. No amount of punishment can atone for what I made possible. But dear Penny is innocent. She doesn't belong here in Hell, with Gregor and me. Please. Get her out of here.'

'I won't go without you!' Penny protested. 'Your words of comfort kept me sane, gave me hope, when it would have been so easy to escape into madness. You helped me deny Gregor that pleasure. I won't abandon you.' She turned her eyes back to Evangeline. 'Get out of here, Evie. Gregor's lost all restraint. He doesn't care about anything now, except revenge.'

'What else is there worth caring about?' said Gregor. 'The rebels are turning my whole world upside down, rewriting history to make themselves out to be virtuous heroes, while they loot the Empire to fund their political fantasies. The barbarians have broken down the gates and stormed the city. What is left now, but to take what revenge we can before the final night falls?'

'And what revenge do you have in mind for me?' said Evangeline.

'I've been thinking about that for some time,' said Gregor. 'Either you return to me, and be my loving, dutiful daughter in every way, or I'll make you suffer in ways you never dreamed possible. You're in my realm now, where the only limits are the limits of my imagination. And when I've wrung every last gasp of suffering from you, I'll hack your pretty head off your pretty shoulders and stick you in a jar next to the others. And maybe I'll piss in your preservative fluids now and again, just for fun. I can always use the rest of your body to produce a new clone, to satisfy my other needs. A third Evangeline; I'll be more careful with this one. Avoid the mistakes I made with you, by giving you too much freedom. So one way or another, you will serve me, dear Evie. Your old life ended the moment you walked in here.'

'People will come looking for me,' said Evangeline. 'The clone underground.'

'To hell with them. I could stand off an army from within here. And the new order won't allow a war with someone as potentially useful as me.'

'Finlay . . .'

'To hell with him too. I'll have him killed anyway, for daring to tempt you away from me, for having touched you. No one will be too surprised when unknown assassins gun him down in an ambush. Finlay has a lot of enemies out there. I'd like his death to last longer, so I could savour his pain, but best not take risks with a warrior of Finlay's stamp. No one will trace the death back to me. I've a lot of experience in covering my tracks. No, I can do whatever I want to do to you, and damn the consequences, because I am Gregor Shreck, and no one can deny me anything. Welcome home, Evie. Welcome home to your daddy's loving arms. You'll never leave here again.'

He gestured a third time, and suddenly a tanglefield enveloped Evangeline, shimmering in the air around her. The energy field covered her completely, slowing all her movements to a crawl, and preventing her from leaving the halo. She clenched her hands into fists, and her breathing increased, but that was all the reaction the tanglefield allowed. Evangeline snarled at her father, who giggled and wriggled with delight on his big red bed.

'You never did have any sense of honour, Gregor.'

'Please. Call me Daddy. We're going to play a little game, Evie. Just like we used to. Take your clothes off. Slowly. Not that you've got much choice, of course.'

And he giggled again, a surprisingly high-pitched sound from such a large man. Evangeline glared at him, making no move to obey. Gregor stopped giggling abruptly and glared back at her, his eyes burning with unrestrained malice. He heaved himself awkwardly off the bed, breathing heavily as

371

he forced his great bulk on to his feet. He waddled forward, grunting with each heavy step, and finally lurched to a halt just short of the tanglefield's boundary. He was smiling, his fat lips wet, his eyes dark and unblinking.

'You do as you're told, little Evie, or I'll find something heavy and smash the glass jar holding your dear friend Penny. And you can watch her flop on my carpet, and gasp and die like a landed fish, without the preservative fluids to sustain her.'

'Don't listen to him!' Penny cried out. 'He wouldn't really do it!'

'Yes, he would,' said Evangeline. 'He's done worse, before now. Haven't you, Daddy?'

And she started taking off her jacket. It was a simple black affair that Finlay had given her, with just a few buttons and fasteners. Gregor's eyes lingered over each one as her tanglefield-slowed fingers undid them. Underneath she wore a simple sky-blue dress. She undid the clasp at the back of her neck, and let the silk dress slip slowly down the length of her body. The energy field turned its slow descent into a tease. Underneath the dress she wore only delicate white panties. Evangeline stood still and let Gregor look at her. She wanted to look away from him, but wouldn't let herself. It was important that she didn't avert her eyes or lower her gaze. Gregor eyed her up and down several times, licking his lips and laughing breathily. Once he reached out as though to touch her, but withdrew his hand before it could enter the tanglefield. He met her eyes, and gestured at the panties.

'Those. Take them off. Take them *off*.'

'You do it,' said Evangeline. 'You do it, Daddy. Like you used to.'

Gregor licked his fat lips again, his deep-set eyes fixed on the white panties, and moved forward a step. Evangeline let her right hand fall to the top of her panties. Gregor's outstretched hand entered the tanglefield. Evangeline's fingers dipped slowly inside the panties. Gregor crossed the border of the tanglefield. His movements slowed to a crawl. Evangeline's fingers grasped the hilt of the tiny concealed knife inside her vagina, and pulled it out. Her finger hit the stud on the hilt, and the monofilament blade crackled into life.

The energy field supporting the single-molecule weapon clashed with the weaker tanglefield, and shorted it out.

All their movements crashed back to normal. Gregor shrieked in fear and outrage. Evangeline lashed out with the glowing blade and sliced up the right side of Gregor's face, cutting the fat flesh open from chin to forehead. The right eye exploded in a rain of blood and other fluids. Gregor howled like an animal and fell backwards, clutching at his face. Blood pumped thickly between his fingers. Evangeline lunged after him, grabbed him by the fat shoulders and set the glowing knife blade next to his throat. Gregor froze where he was. Evangeline leaned over him, breathing hard.

She'd known the guards would confiscate anything she brought with her, whether it looked like a weapon or not, before letting her anywhere near Gregor. But she'd gambled that they wouldn't do a full invasive body search for fear of offending Gregor. So she hid the unactivated hilt in her vagina, and practised walking in front of a mirror till she could do it without wincing.

Finlay had got her the monofilament knife. He hadn't asked any questions; it seemed a perfectly normal thing to him that somebody would want such a useful weapon. Particularly now that they were officially banned.

Gregor whimpered with pain and shock as blood poured down his face and soaked his clothes. Evangeline smiled savagely. 'Stay where you are, Gregor. You even try to get up or call out, and I'll gut you.'

She let go of him and backed cautiously away, ready to kill him if she had to, but all the fight had gone out of him with the loss of his eye. Evangeline grabbed one of the sheets from the bed and wrapped up Penny's and Wax's jars in it, before slinging the improvised bag over her shoulders. She heard the two glass jars bang together, and hoped they were tougher than they looked; they were probably in for a rough ride. Unhooked from their speakers, the heads had no way of telling her what was happening to them. Evangeline moved quickly back to Gregor, and he shrank away from the knife buzzing in her hand. She grabbed him by one shoulder, her fingers sinking deep into the thick flesh, and set the blade next to his throat again.

'All right, Gregor, we're leaving now. All of us. Get up. Get up, or I swear I'll kill you right here.'

Gregor heard the iron in her voice, and knew that she meant it. He heaved his massive bulk to his feet, moving very carefully so as not even to nudge against the flickering strand. Evangeline got him moving, and they headed slowly towards the door, the only way out of the Shreck's private little torture chamber. It opened to Gregor's voice, and in a moment they were out in the corridor.

The guard outside turned sharply, caught unawares, and started to raise his gun. Gregor screamed at the man not to be stupid, and under Evangeline's urging, ordered the guard to drop his gun and back away. He did so, reluctantly, and gestured to the other guards in the corridor to lower their weapons and stay where they were. Gregor and Evangeline moved slowly towards the elevator. Gregor was already out of breath and beginning to tire from the effort of carrying his great weight, but his fear of Evangeline kept him moving.

They came to the elevator doors, and Gregor hit the call button. Evangeline was breathing hard herself now. She glared quickly about her at the watching guards. Guards or beetles or demons, they couldn't stop her now, as long as she kept her nerve. The elevator seemed to take for ever to arrive, but finally the doors opened and she backed Gregor in, never taking her eyes off the guards. They disappeared behind the closing doors, and Evangeline hit the lobby button so hard she nearly broke it. The ride down lasted centuries for Evangeline, as though they were plunging into the heart of the planet. Gregor kept one hand pressed to his ruined face, as though trying to hide what had been done to it. Blood was still running between his fingers and trickling down his arm. The sight of it comforted Evangeline. Gregor kept trying to talk to her, but she shut him up by moving the knife blade a little closer to his throat. By the time the elevator finally reached the lobby, blood ran freely from several cuts on Gregor's neck.

The elevator doors opened on a whole army of guards filling the lobby, their guns trained on the group within. The guards on the penthouse floor had raised the alarm. Evangeline let them get a good look at their blood-soaked master, and the glowing blade at his throat, and then yelled at them to get the hell out of her way, or she'd start cutting chunks off Gregor till they did. Gregor immediately backed her up with a stream of hysterical orders. The guards lowered their guns and moved off, opening up an aisle between the elevator and the main entrance door on the other side of the lobby. Evangeline laughed harshly.

'Do you think I'm stupid? Drop your guns on the floor, all of you, and get away from them. Right away.'

The guards looked at Gregor, and then reluctantly acquiesced. There was a loud clatter as over a hundred disrupters fell to the concrete floor of the hall. Evangeline glared suspiciously about her. There were probably all kinds of hidden weapons here, on the guards and maybe in the lobby walls, but as long as her knife was at Gregor's throat, they wouldn't dare try anything. She pushed Gregor out of the elevator and got him moving as fast as he could. *Move fast. Don't give them time to think.* She felt very exposed, very vulnerable. This was the most dangerous part of her plan. Her gravity sled was parked near the Tower. All she had to do was get to it, and she'd be off and gone before anyone could catch her. But she still had to get to it, past an army of guards who would quite rightly be in danger of their lives if they let her get away with this. She urged Gregor on, mercilessly forcing the pace as he gasped and heaved for breath, peering constantly about her for any guard stupid enough to try to be a hero.

The main door came slowly closer. She hadn't remembered the lobby being this big. The guards watched, unmoving but for the slow turning of their beetle heads. The only sounds were the slap of feet on concrete, and Gregor's constant moaning and panting. The heads in their jars bumped against Evangeline's bare back. Her nudity didn't bother her; all that mattered was getting out alive.

At last they came to the main door, which hissed open at Gregor's approach. Evangeline could see daylight, hear every day city noises. It was like another world, so near, so close. She carefully manoeuvred herself and Gregor round so that they had their backs to the door, facing the guards. She could feel the tension building in them. She had to get out soon, before somebody cracked. Then all she had to do was get to the sled, stab Gregor through his black, diseased heart, and it would all be over. Piece of cake. Evangeline dared to hope that just maybe she might pull this off after all.

'All right, Gregor,' she said breathlessly, fighting to keep her voice from shaking as sweat rolled down her face. 'We're going for a little walk now.'

'Outside?' said Gregor. He seemed to recognize where he was for the first time, and panic shot through him. 'No. Not outside! Not out of my Tower! No!'

And with a burst of strength fuelled by manic fear, he threw off her hold, ducked away from the knife at his throat and stumbled towards the safety of his guards, who dived as one for their guns. Evangeline considered throwing her knife at Gregor's fat back, decided she didn't have time and bolted through the open main door. She sprinted across to where she'd parked the gravity sled, her bare back crawling in anticipation of the disrupter beam she'd probably never even have time to feel. And then behind her she heard Gregor screaming for them to take her alive, and her heart jumped. She was in with a chance after all.

She forced herself to run faster, bare feet pounding painfully on the harsh ground, the glass jars hammering against her back, the cool air rushing past her bare skin. People around stopped to look at her, but no one felt like interfering. Which was just as well: Evangeline had already decided quite coldly to cut down anyone who got between her and her freedom. She'd gone through too much to be stopped now. Maybe there was some Shreck in her, after all. She could see the gravity sled now, still where she'd parked it, not too far away. She was beyond pain or fatigue, buoyed up by hope.

And then the sled was suddenly right there in front of her, and she skidded to a halt, stopping just short of slamming into its side. She dumped the heads in their sheet in the back of the sled, remembering just in time how fragile they were, and only then heard the running footsteps behind her. Reason said they had to have been there for some time, but she'd been too busy with her own desperate thoughts to hear them. She spun round, knife in hand. Three armoured guards were almost upon her. More were coming behind them. Their heavy armour had slowed them down, but fear of what Gregor would do to them drove them on. Evangeline's mouth widened into a death's-head grin she'd learned from Finlay, and went to meet the first three guards with her monofilament knife at the ready.

She had an advantage. They were under orders not to kill her; she had no such encumbrance. She cut off the head of the first guard with a casual flick of the wrist, the knife slicing through steel armour and flesh and bone as easily as air. The masked head tumbled almost slowly to the ground as she turned to the next guard and plunged the knife into his chest. He screamed shrilly inside his mask. Evangeline moved her hand sideways, and the monofilament blade erupted from the guard's side in a shower of blood. While he was collapsing, she turned to the third guard. Blood was trickling down her bare flesh and spattered across her face, none of it hers. It felt warm in the cool air, almost comforting. It was the blood of her enemies. The third guard either forgot or stopped caring about Gregor's order to bring her back alive.

He drew his disrupter and aimed it point-blank at her bare chest. Evangeline lashed out with her knife and cut the gun in two. The guard turned to run, and she cut him down too, the monofilament edge slashing easily in and out again. The other guards skidded to a halt as she bent down and picked up one of the other guards' disrupters. Gregor was still urging them on, screaming threats and promises and curses, but the situation had changed and the guards knew it. There were enough of them that they were bound to bring her down eventually, but they all knew a hell of a lot of them would die doing it. And no bonuses or threats were worth that. They hesitated, and as they did, Evangeline clambered aboard her gravity sled and took off, leaving them all behind. No one even shot at her.

She laughed shakily, not daring to relax just yet, but finally starting to hope the worst was over. She hadn't been sure she could bring it off, any of it. She'd planned it as best she could, but deep down she'd still thought of herself as the helpless victim, never really believing she could defeat Gregor. She'd gone because she'd had to, to rescue her friend, and because she was tired of being afraid. But she'd done it.

She was shaking from head to toe now, as delayed reaction set in. She remembered fighting the guards, and smiled disbelievingly. She hadn't known she had it in her to fight like that. The underground had trained her, as it trained all its agents, but she'd never had occasion to use any of her training. Presumably her time with Finlay had affected her more than she realized.

Finlay. She was going home to Finlay now, and he'd be so proud of her. He'd take her in his arms and hold her tight, and the long nightmare of her past life would finally be over. It seemed to her that she'd forgotten something, something important, but she didn't care. The worst was over, and she was going home. The wind whipped coldly past her bare skin, and she giggled suddenly at the thought of what an awful sight she must present.

But that didn't matter. Nothing mattered except being safe at home with Finlay, and her friend Penny, and her friend Wax. Maybe they'd have a party when she got back. And then, maybe she'd sleep for a week. Or two.

Valentine Wolfe, as always not entirely in his right mind, sat at his ease in a very comfortable chair on the bridge of his ship, the *Snark*, and orbited the planet Loki, fabled world of storms. Hc was studying the viewscreen before him, as it displayed the endlessly changing atmosphere of the Rim world below. Glorious patterns revealed themselves to his dilated eyes, complex and fascinating, endlessly re-forming, endlessly charming. He'd been watching the storms for some time, secure behind the finest cloaking device Shub could provide, invisible to all below. Valentine had never believed in hiding his dark light under a bushel, but with so many people sworn to kill him on sight, he had no choice but to take all possible precautions.

He smiled dreamily. It wasn't his fault if people couldn't take a joke.

He'd been in high orbit for over an hour, waiting patiently for the summons he'd been promised. Somewhere, beneath all the storms and dramatic weather systems that had made Loki infamous as the most unpleasant and disagreeable colonized world in the whole Empire, in one of Loki's sturdy and permanently battened-down cities, traitors to the Empire were gathering, and wanted him to join them. They didn't see themselves as traitors, of course; traitors never did. Instead, they hid behind words like patriotism, necessity, practicality. Valentine had never needed the comfort of euphemism. He knew what he was, and gloried in it.

Beneath his present calm exterior, several very powerful psychotropic drugs were battling it out for dominance. Valentine had finally reached a stage where even the most potent and destructive drugs could no longer deliver him from his ennui. Strange alchemical changes in his unique blood chemistry, the end result of decades of committed drug experimentation, had left him with a system that could ignore doses strong enough to kill a normal man, or drive him utterly mad. So these days Valentine had taken to giving himself several substances at once, and letting them fight it out among themselves. It was a form of Russian roulette, to which the possibility of sudden death merely added a taste of decadence that Valentine found irresistible.

Everyone was after him. Everyone wanted to kill him. And Valentine couldn't have been happier. He had forsworn humanity and allied himself with Shub, and didn't give a damn. He had always taken pride in being able to see all sides of an argument, sometimes simultaneously, while agreeing with none of them. All that mattered was the quest, the search for the ultimate high. And, of course, the chance to trample over absolutely everything and have all that lived bow down to him. He just wanted to be God. Was that so much to ask?

His contact with Shub, the planet the rogue AIs had made, had gone more easily than he'd thought it would. The connection had been made through a series of cut-outs, most of whom didn't even know who they were connecting or why, and Valentine had been able to speak at length with a calm, emotionless voice that told him everything he wanted to hear. In return for being Shub's agent in the worlds of men, the voice promised him new tech augmentations that would give him access to senses far higher than those of mere flesh, and eventually a direct comprehension of reality itself, unfiltered by human misconceptions. They'd given him a taste of this by enabling him to control directly the machines that destroyed Virimonde, letting him sink his consciousness into the metal minds of robots and war machines as they dragged men and women down, tearing their fragile flesh with metal hands and grinding their bodies under metal wheels. It had been . . . exhilarating. But even Valentine knew there was a reason why the first taste is always free. He'd taken many drugs in his time, but had never allowed any of them to master him. His iron will was the only thing greater than his avaricious body chemistry. He remained calm in the face of Shub's temptations, and requested more details. The voice asked him if he'd like to talk to someone who'd already gone before him.

Valentine raised an eyebrow. He'd always thought of himself as a pioneer on the cutting edge of self-transformation. 'And who might this person be?'

'Who do you think?' said a familiar female voice. 'Who else but Lionstone?'

'Your Highness,' said Valentine courteously. 'How delightful to hear from you again. I was under the impression you were dead.'

'Just my body. The AIs rescued my mind, and brought me to Shub. I am metal now. I live in machines.'

'And what is that like, Your Highness? Can you describe it?'

'Of course. I am large, larger than I could ever have become while trapped in the confines of flesh. My thoughts move freely, into whatever shape I choose to manufacture. And I can see so much more than I ever could before. The universe isn't what you think it is, Valentine. It's a wild and wondrous place, more complex and magnificent than a human person could possibly imagine. There are realms and dimensions, directions and possibilities, almost without number. Come on in, Valentine; the inhumanity's wonderful.'

'It certainly sounds it,' Valentine said carefully. 'But what about . . . how shall I put this? . . . the more fleshly pleasures and appetites? How does it feel to have left them behind?'

'When I was a child, I played with childish things. I've moved on, Valentine. Pleasure has its base in the mind, not the body. I have lost nothing, and gained so very much. Just as you could. All you have to do is say goodbye to the past and embrace the future. The future is metal. Humanity was never more than just a step in the ladder that led to Shub, and it is no great tragedy that they should be replaced by something greater. Flesh decays and dies. We are for ever.'

'Immortality?' said Valentine.

'Why not?' said Lionstone.

'We have other voices you might care to listen to,' said the original voice. 'We have your father Jacob here. Would you like to talk to him?'

'I don't think so, thank you,' said Valentine. 'We never had that much in common, even when he was alive.'

'Then perhaps your brother, Daniel? He came to visit us, and we gave him many gifts. He is our agent now, currently on his way back to Golgotha.'

'Oh, good,' said Valentine. 'Dear Daniel. I'll have to arrange a welcome for him.'

'No you won't,' said the voice. 'Daniel is one of us, working on our orders, and is currently rather more important to us than to you. Leave him alone. For the present.'

'As you wish,' Valentine said easily. 'Retribution is no less satisfying for being delayed. At the risk of sounding greedy, my metal seigneurs, what else can you offer me?'

'Protection from your enemies, such as the Deathstalker or Finlay Campbell, both of whom have sworn to see you die, whatever the cost. A return to power in the new Empire we shall forge from the ashes of the old. What else could you possibly want?'

'I've always had a yearning to be Lord of Golgotha,' said Valentine.

'That's taken,' said Lionstone. 'How about Virimonde?'

Valentine smiled at the memory. The haggling, though neither side would have called it that, continued for some time, but the end result was that Valentine was now an agent of Shub, the official Enemies of Humanity. His first mission on their behalf had been this trip to Loki, to make contact with a gathering of useful people also interested in making a deal with Shub. Though of course they came in the name of peace and security, requesting only an alliance against certain mutual dangers.

Valentine couldn't land his ship on Loki without some fear of detection, for all Shub's cloaking fields, so it had been agreed that the ship would remain in high orbit while he attended the meeting as a hologram. The new rebels provided the coordinates, and at the approved time, Valentine received his official invitation and sent his image down to join the meeting.

Due to the never-ending storms churning up the planet's atmosphere, reception wasn't everything it might have been, and Valentine's holo image appeared as a crackling, sometimes translucent figure that only added to his sudden dramatic entrance. Valentine approved. He prided himself on his range of dramatic entrances.

He found himself in an anonymous back room, standing before a table around which four people were sitting. There was a fifth figure, standing to one side, whom Valentine recognized immediately. He decided to concentrate on the four at the table first. He liked to know exactly who he was dealing with.

'Well, well,' he said calmly, 'here we all are, under one roof at last, with myself as always the ghost at the feast. What are we calling ourselves today; renegades, rebels, or, dare I say it, traitors to the Empire?'

'We're no traitors,' said one of the men immediately. 'We are merely practical men, doing what we must to survive. The fact that we're prepared to deal with scum like you should show that.'

'How very rude,' Valentine murmured. 'You have the advantage on me, sir. Perhaps you would be good enough to honour me with your name?'

'I'm Tarquil Vomak, MP for Greylake East in the Golgotha Parliament. I represent powerful and influential people. An insult to me is an insult to them.'

'How wonderfully time-saving,' said Valentine. 'Be so good as to introduce your colleagues.'

Vomak sniffed, as though he felt the task to be beneath him. 'If I must. To my left is the Lady Donna Silvestri. She speaks for Blue Block, who brought us all together here to meet with you. Opposite us are Matthew Tallon, ex-Planetary Controller for Loki, and the ex-Mayor, Terrence Jacks.

382

And I'm sure you know our associate in the corner there; Kit SummerIsle.'

'Oh, yes,' said Valentine. 'I know Kid Death.'

He let his eyes drift unhurriedly over the conspirators, taking them in one at a time. The MP Vomak was a large blocky man dressed in scarlet, possibly to match his cheeks. He was handsome enough, in an undemanding way, the impression somewhat undermined by a sulky mouth. Donna Silvestri was vaguely known to him, as one of the people who ran the Clan Silvestri finances. He hadn't known she was Blue Block, but he couldn't say he was surprised. She was round and broad and motherly, with faded blue eyes and a thick grey woollen cloak pulled about her, and possibly only Valentine would have noticed that her warm, maternal smile wasn't in the least reflected in her eyes. If she spoke for Blue Block, that automatically made her the most powerful, and dangerous, of the conspirators. She was where the power lay. Tallon and Jacks had the same stubborn, battered and weather-beaten look common to all who lived their lives in Loki's tempestuous embrace. Tallon was the older and more solemn, Jacks the younger and more impatient. And finally, of course, there was Kit SummerIsle – Kid Death, the smiling killer. A slender figure in black and silver armour, with pale blond flyaway hair and icy-blue eyes.

'Hello, Kit,' said Valentine. 'Last I heard, you were a rebel hero and a pillar of the new establishment.'

'Hello, Valentine,' said the SummerIsle, in his cold, implacable voice. 'I never was one for philosophies. Civilized society got very boring. I'm a killer, so I go where the killing is. For the moment, Blue Block are providing me with necessary distractions.'

'I was sorry to hear about the loss of your friend David, on Virimonde.'

'No, you weren't.'

'All right, I wasn't. I was just being polite, Kit. You really should try it sometime. What exactly is a notorious killer such as yourself doing here?'

'Blue Block said there would be work for me here. Treason and death have always been close bedfellows.'

'Of course,' said Valentine. He smiled at those seated

around the table. 'Perhaps someone here would now be good enough to explain exactly what it is you wish me to pass on to Shub. What it is that brings us all together?'

'Necessity,' said Donna Silvestri in a warm, pleasant voice. 'Humanity has many enemies, most of them alien. The Recreated are just the latest in a long list of threats to humanity's survival. Our struggle with Shub draws away people and resources that could be better employed against more immediate threats. A temporary and strictly limited alliance with Shub is in everyone's best interests. We don't have to like each other to be able to work together against a common enemy. Afterwards . . . perhaps we will have developed enough interests in common to make our previous antagonisms redundant.'

'Very logical,' said Valentine. 'Why haven't you presented this most sensible proposition to Parliament?'

'Because the short-sighted bastards virtually wet themselves if you just mention Shub!' snapped Vomak. 'They're so taken with their new power that they can't see past their current obsessions to the greater need. The new order is only concerned with remaking the Empire in its own image, and revenging the old hurts and prejudices. Everyone here represents the old order. We won't shrink from doing what needs to be done.'

'Indeed,' said Valentine. 'And you're asking Shub's help to remove the rebels from power, and replace them with your good selves, merely to help you better carry out these necessary actions?'

'They are wilfully blind to the dangers,' said Donna Silvestri. 'They refuse to put aside their own limited agendas. They must, therefore, be removed, for the greater good of all. Blue Block has always taken the long view.'

'And what of the local connection?' said Valentine, turning to Tallon and Jacks. 'Why are we meeting here, on Loki?'

'You people need a planetary base,' Tallon said brusquely. 'A place to gather, to plan and build in secret. Somewhere far enough off the beaten track that you won't be noticed. We're offering that. We're the closest human planet to the Forbidden Sector, and Shub. That should make contact easier. And hopefully it'll persuade Shub to shelve any plans about moving in and taking us over. The old Empire stationed starcruisers near here, to protect us, but since Parliament took over, that's been stopped. They say they haven't enough ships. So we've been abandoned. Which means we have to find security where we can. An alliance with Shub is our only reasonable option.'

'Right,' said Jacks. 'We're just doing what we have to. We have family here; jobs, land. We can't just up and leave Loki, move somewhere safer. We paid for our land and our holdings with blood and pain and the death of loved ones. We won't leave them. Besides, running isn't in our nature. We stand our ground and fight for what's ours. Loki taught us that.'

'And sometimes you have to get your hands dirty,' said Tallon. 'That's why we're willing to deal with you, Wolfe. We know your reputation, the things you've done. I'd as soon shoot you as look at you. But you're probably the only one crazy enough to act as a go-between for us and Shub, so we'll work with you. That's life.'

'How very uncalled-for,' murmured Valentine. 'Anyone would think I was some kind of monster.'

'You are,' said Kit SummerIsle.

'You should know,' said Valentine, generously.

'I know lots of things,' said the SummerIsle, moving forward out of his corner for the first time. Everyone around the table stirred just a little uneasily. Kid Death stopped at the head of the table, his right hand resting on his belt near his sword. 'I know, for example, that one of us here is a traitor.'

Valentine raised a painted eyebrow. 'I thought we all were.'

'A traitor to this group, and its intentions,' said the SummerIsle.

The four at the table looked at each other. None of them was obviously armed. 'What makes you so sure?' said Tallon.

'I work with Blue Block,' said Kid Death. 'They have access to all the best information. They have spies everywhere. You'd be surprised. They know, for example, that Tarquil Vomak here has extensive gambling debts he couldn't possibly pay off on an MP's salary if he lived to be three hundred. So he sold his services to Golgotha security, as a double agent. Isn't that right, Vomak?'

'I don't know what the hell you're talking about!' said Vomak. 'I don't owe anyone a penny! It must be someone else in my family.' He rose to his feet, glaring at Donna Silvestri. 'You must have got it wrong. Tell your pet killer to back off! I'll prove my credentials to Blue Block just as soon as we get back to Golgotha! Tell him he's wrong!'

'Blue Block intelligence is never wrong,' said Donna Silvestri, quite calmly. 'We were only waiting for Valentine to arrive, so he could see how we deal with those who betray us.'

She nodded to Kid Death, and he drew his sword and cut off Vomak's head, all in one blindingly swift movement. The two Loki men cried out as blood sprayed across them. The headless body stood upright for a horribly long moment, its hands clutching at nothing, blood fountaining from the stump of the neck, and then it fell to the ground, shuddering. Vomak's wide-eyed head rolled slowly along the table, the mouth working silently, until it finally came to a halt before Donna Silvestri. She patted its forehead calmly, picked the head up by the hair and placed it on the ground by her chair. She smiled at Tallon and Jacks.

'I always like to bring home a little souvenir when I go travelling.'

The two Loki men produced handkerchiefs and began cleaning blood drops from themselves. No emotion showed in their hard-worn faces, but their hands weren't as steady as they might have been. Valentine bowed slightly to Donna Silvestri, in acknowledgement of the point made. Kid Death cleaned his blade with a piece of rag, and then sheathed his sword. His face was entirely unmoved, save for a slight smile.

'Time for another election in Greylake East,' he said lightly.

Donna Silvestri smiled at Valentine Wolfe. 'I hope we understand each other.'

'Oh, we do,' said Valentine. 'I'm just glad to be working with professionals for once.'

Julian Skye sat locked away in his bedroom, staring at his reflection in the mirror on the wall opposite. He looked like shit. Not surprising, really, because he felt like shit, and had done for some time now. His body was slumped in the oversized chair like a battered toy discarded by a child who played too rough. For once, Julian wasn't thinking about his former love, BB Chojiro. He had more immediate concerns.

He'd just been fired from his own holo show. Ever since the rebellion ended, and he discovered to his great surprise that he was still alive and on the winning side for once, he'd been making a good living starring as himself in a weekly holo series featuring his many exploits as a dashing, devil-may-care agent of the rebellion. Such shows were very popular right now, but his was the only one featuring the actual person concerned. His acting was frankly average, but the emphasis of the show had always been on stunts, explosions and last-minute escapes, so he got by. He'd started out trying to keep the scripts as close to the truth as he could, but soon discovered his audience much preferred the legend to the truth. He just shrugged, and let the producers rewrite his past as they would. He didn't care. A lot of his past wasn't suitable for a family audience anyway.

And now they'd fired him. Replaced him with a lookalike actor, because Julian didn't look like himself any more. He'd been ill for some time; the side effects of his incarceration in Lionstone's interrogation cells continued to make themselves felt. They came and went, so he learned to live with them and got on with his life. But just recently, he'd been getting worse. A lot worse. He thought he'd hidden it by not giving in to it, and working just as hard as always, but apparently you can't fool the camera.

The show's executives had called him into their luxurious office, sat him down, made sure he had a large drink in his hand and then showed him footage of himself as he used to be, and as he was now. Julian was shocked by the difference. He'd become painfully thin, his face gaunt and hollowed, with dark shadows under the eyes. He looked twenty years older. The executives said they were very sorry to have to let him go, but make-up could only do so much. They assured him they'd be happy to take him back again, once he was better, but everyone in the room knew that was not going to happen. He wasn't getting any better. The truth was right there, in his face. He was dying.

Those white-gowned bastards in the interrogation cells had killed him after all. It just took a while for his death to catch up with him.

So he'd gone home. Home was the old Skye Family house. Not a Tower; not even in the same neighbourhood. The Skyes had never been more than a very minor Family. And soon they wouldn't be a Family at all. Both of Julian's parents were dead, killed in an air crash. These things happened. And since Julian was a late child, all his grandparents were already gone. Wars and politics and duels. His uncles and aunts, knowing a sinking ship when they were on one, had married into greater Families, and took those Families' names as their own, thus ensuring higher position and prestige for their children. There were a few minor cousins, at various removes, but for all practical purposes, Auric and Julian had been the last generation of Skye. And they'd never had children.

Now Julian Skye was the last of his line, and when he died the name would die with him. He couldn't really bring himself to care much. He'd never given a damn for being an aristocrat, not least because he was at the bottom of the pile and looked down on by every other Clan. And he was an esper; which should have been impossible in the carefully controlled bloodlines and intermarriages of the Families. Espers weren't people, they were property.

But somewhere along the line, a Skye had gone to bed with someone they shouldn't have, and the esper gene had gone skinny-dipping in the Skye gene pool, and emerged in Julian. If his parents had found out, they would have had him quietly killed. An unfortunate accident, to avoid shame and scandal. But as soon as Julian's powers started emerging, his older brother Auric was right there with him, calming his terror and helping him hide what he was from his Family and from the world. No one ever knew. Till Auric died, and Julian gave his life to the rebellion.

And now here he was, back home again, living alone in a great empty house with most of the rooms shut up, and only a few old Family retainers for company. They stayed out of loyalty, out of memory for the way things had been, rather than for the money. Which was just as well; Julian had made a great deal of money as a holo star, but tended to spend it as fast as it came in. His time in the rebellion had taught him to live for the day: on the kinds of missions he undertook, you couldn't count on there being a tomorrow. If the bank hadn't been so scared of him, they'd probably have been sending him threatening letters by now. He would have worried how he was going to support himself in the future, if he'd thought he had a future.

He hurt pretty much all the time now. Sometimes his head hurt so bad he had to bite down on something to keep from crying out, and disturbing the servants. There were painkillers, of course, but the only ones strong enough to deal with the pain left him sleeping all day or stumbling dimly around like a zombie. He preferred to spend whatever time he had left in his right mind. He was pretty sure he was going to die, this time. No more miracle cures for him.

He'd come close to dying on Haceldama, but Giles Deathstalker had used his powers to work a cure. Only like so many things with Giles, the appearance hadn't been reality. The cure hadn't lasted. And now Giles was dead, and the four remaining Maze survivors were all off-world somewhere, on unknown missions. Even if he could have tracked them down, and brought himself to beg, he doubted very much that they could have got back to Golgotha in time to do him any good. And besides, he'd never been any good at begging. That was one of the things that had made him a rebel in the first place.

Julian looked back over his early rebel days with a rueful smile. He'd been so young, so sure, so dedicated. A real daredevil, ready to take on any mission, any risk, as long as it was for the cause. He'd been fast and sharp and sudden death with a weapon in his hand, and no one could stand against him. In retrospect, he had to admit he'd done it mostly for the thrills and the action, for the kicks. But he did a lot of good along the way, and saved as many lives as he took. The new government had wanted to give him all kinds of medals, but he'd politely turned them down. He never

389

really felt he'd earned them, because it had all been such a good time.

Until the Empire caught him, and put him in the interrogation cells, and gave him to the torturers. All because his one true love BB Chojiro betrayed him. She broke his heart, and they broke his spirit, and even though Finlay Campbell rescued him, he was never the same afterwards.

He sighed, and did his best to push old, bitter thoughts aside. If he was going to die, he was determined to make the most of what was left of his life. Have some fun, while he still could. Do all the things he'd meant to do, but never had, because the rebellion intervened. He'd enjoyed his time as a rebel, had his fair share of adventures and more, but it had quickly taken over his life, leaving no room for the simple everyday pleasures that everyone else took for granted. There was never time to relax, let his guard down, have a good time with a few friends. He didn't drink or smoke or use drugs, he saw them as weaknesses. And he'd never had the time or the inclination to get involved in any of the more serious vices. The rebellion had been his life.

And then they took it away from him. By winning.

He couldn't be an adventurer any more. His fighting days were over. The new order had no use for him, even before his frailty became clear. His brand of fighting, get the job done and to hell with the consequences, was out of fashion. It was all diplomacy now, with carefully worked-out deals and compromises put together in private smoke-filled rooms. Usually with someone from Blue Block chairing the meeting, or adding quiet advice from the sidelines. It was all politics now, and Julian didn't understand any of it.

He had considered going back to Haceldama, and spending his final days in Summerland, but he couldn't do that. His death would have upset the toys too much.

Most of his friends were dead. It had been a hard war, and the rebellion chewed up young men and women as fast as it could take them. Julian had seen a lot of faces come and go, and learned the hard way not to get too attached to anyone. The only real friend he had was Finlay Campbell, and these days the old assassin was in almost as bad shape as he was. Finlay had been coming apart at the seams for some time now, and the more Julian tried to help, the more Finlay pushed him away.

The only other man Julian had really admired had been the legendary Young Jack Random. Julian had followed the great hero into countless battles, and worked his way through the bloody street fighting on Golgotha, chanting the man's name. Julian never really got over finding out that he'd been following a Fury, a Shub war machine in the shape of a man. He'd destroyed the Fury with his esp, but it hadn't helped. It seemed like every time Julian ended up trusting someone, they always betrayed him in the end.

There had been some satisfying moments in the fighting. He'd killed the man who killed his brother Auric, the Masked Gladiator himself, and that at least had been something he could be proud of. He could have killed the bastard a dozen times and never tired of it.

And yet, for all his successes in the rebellion, he hadn't been there at the end. Hadn't made it down to the Hell Lionstone had made of her Court, hadn't got there in time to see the Iron Bitch dragged from her Throne and humbled before everyone. He'd seen the recording on holo later, but it wasn't the same. He should have been there. He felt he'd earned that. He still felt cheated, even now. He'd wanted her to see his face, to know he'd helped bring her down. He'd wanted to put his foot on her neck, and laugh. He felt he'd paid for that right in blood and suffering and the loss of friends.

So much bitterness, in one short life. Julian frowned, searching for happier memories he could dwell on, but they seemed appallingly few and far between. The more he thought about it, the more it seemed to him that there had only been two times in his life when he'd been really happy. The years he shared with his beloved older brother Auric, and the months he spent with the woman they both loved, BB Chojiro.

Auric went away and left him. He challenged the Masked Gladiator to a duel in the Arena, hoping to impress Clan Chojiro enough that he'd be allowed to marry the lovely BB. He hadn't expected to win the duel, but he thought that if he put up a good enough show, the Arena crowds would turn up their thumbs for him – they always liked a plucky under-dog. But the Masked Gladiator killed him anyway. Just because he could.

Julian had gone to comfort BB, and she cried in his arms, and he cried too. Not long after, they fell in love, and he was happy for a time.

In all his life, the only piece of unfinished business he had left was BB Chojiro. He still wasn't sure how he felt about her. Part of him wanted to kill her so badly he could taste it. To make her suffer as he'd suffered. In the openness of young love, he'd told her all about his role in the rebellion, and she handed him over to the torturers without a second thought because she was Blue Block. Programmed from childhood to be loyal to the Families to death and beyond. Or so she said. But these days Blue Block was running the Families, with BB Chojiro as its most public face. Sometimes he dreamed he went to see her, and knelt at her feet, and promised to do anything she wanted if only she'd love him again. He woke shaking from these dreams, with a scream caught in his throat. Some stupid, hurting part of him still loved her, and always would.

He had thought about going to see her, to settle their unfinished business one way or another. There was always the chance he'd built her up in his mind and memory into something more than she was. Maybe if he saw her again, saw how small and harmless she really was, he'd be able to get it in perspective, move on. It wouldn't be easy getting an audience with such a popular and busy person, but he was pretty sure he could do it. She was important these days, no doubt with layers of protection, but he was a person of no small importance himself. His holo show had put him in the public eye as one of the better-known rebel heroes. His audience loved him, or at least the version of him they saw on his show every week. He even had his own fan club. Thousands of letters came in, and requests for photos, but recently the demand for photos had gone down as his physical condition worsened, and the letters were beginning to trail off.

But no one knew how ill he really was. He was still getting invitations to all kinds of parties and social and political gatherings. A lot of Clans had found it in themselves to overlook how minor a House his Family was, in their keenness to have him marry one of their unattached daughters. A rebel hero like Julian Skye would make an excellent spokesman for any Clan determined to be taken seriously in the new politics. Many had gone on a charm offensive, and all but pushed pretty faces at him every time he appeared in public. Julian had gone along with it. He did so love to dance, and it pleased his ego to be seen on all the news and gossip shows with a pretty girl always hanging on his arm. A small, childish part of him hoped BB might be watching.

Clan Chojiro had never pursued him. BB had never believed in begging. She was probably still waiting for him to come to her.

Julian sat up straight in his chair, and put in a call to Clan Chojiro. The viewscreen on the wall quickly cleared to show a severe, cold face that Julian recognized as the current head of Chojiro security. Presumably his name had been flagged. Julian gave the man his best intimidating smile, formally introduced himself and asked to speak to BB. The security chief smiled back, and said he'd see what he could do. His face disappeared from the screen and was replaced by a soothing image of a brook running through a forest, accompanied by gentle tinkling music. Julian scowled. He hated being put on hold. The last time someone left him waiting too long he'd taken all his clothes off and flashed them on their return. The Church wouldn't make that mistake again. The screen cleared to reveal a familiar face.

Julian raised an eyebrow. 'Cardinal Brendan. I didn't think you were admitting you had any connection with Blue Block these days.'

'Officially I'm not, but you're a special case. Good to see you again, Julian. You're looking very well.'

'Maybe I should give you the address of my optician. Don't flatter me, Cardinal. I know what I look like. Now why am I talking to you and not BB?'

'She's here, but I'm afraid she doesn't want to talk to you just now, Julian. You must understand, you and BB parted under very unhappy circumstances, and she quite rightly has some fears that you might still wish her harm.'

'Now why should she think that?' said Julian pleasantly. 'Just because she betrayed me into the gentle hands of the Imperial tormentors?'

'It was a different time then,' said Brendan. 'I'm sure we all did things then that we have come to regret now. The new order is a new beginning for all of us, a chance to put the past behind us and remake ourselves as we would wish to be.'

'Save the pretty speeches,' said Julian. 'You were a slimy creep then and you're a slimy creep now, and when you die they won't have to bury you, they'll just pour you down the nearest drain, so you can join all the other turds. BB gave you a message for me. Stop pretending to be someone important and pass it on.'

'As you wish,' said Cardinal Brendan, entirely unmoved. 'BB has asked me to say that she still has warm feelings for you, but that if you ever wish to see her again, you will have to prove your feelings are genuine.'

'And just how do you suppose I do that? Bunch of flowers, nice box of chocolates, the dead body of an enemy? Try me, Cardinal. I'm in a generous mood.'

'You must prove your good intentions by presenting to her the bound and helpless figure of the Chojiros' greatest enemy.'

'I always thought that was me, but women can be so fickle. Which poor bastard does she have in mind?'

'Finlay Campbell.'

Julian stared at the viewscreen silently for a long moment. 'You want the Campbell?'

'Your friend, yes. Your staunchest ally in the rebellion. How better to show your devotion to BB?'

'If I ever find out this was your idea . . .'

'I'm just the messenger, Julian. But even a failed ham actor like yourself must know that nothing of true value ever comes without a price tag. How much is BB's love worth to you? And it's not as if the Campbell's been much of a friend to you lately. The man's a head case, everyone knows that. How long before he turns on you, as he already has with so many old allies? He's not a happy man. Help put him out of his misery, and ours. And prove your worth at the same time.'

'Betrayal,' said Julian Skye. 'Is that all you Chojiros understand?'

'Such a harsh word. Say rather that Clan Chojiro admires a man strong enough to live by his own rules, and know who his true friends are. So, may I inform BB that she can expect a happy surprise package soon?'

'I'll think about it,' said Julian, and broke the connection.

Flynn the cameraman entered Toby Shreck's office at Imperial News Headquarters, and looked disparagingly about him as he pushed the door shut behind him with the heel of his boot. He was wearing standard work clothes, but hadn't been able to resist just a touch of mascara and blusher. He sniffed loudly, and fixed Toby with a withering gaze. 'You've had the place redecorated *again*, I see. I still don't like it. Really, Toby, all this high tech and polished surfaces really isn't you. Though I hate to think what would be. What this place needs is the feminine touch. Before the style police turn up and firebomb it on mental health grounds. What this office cries out for are pleasant, pastel colours, and big bunches of flowers everywhere. Flowers help to make a room.'

'Oh, good,' said Toby, sitting hunched over the papers on his desk. 'I'm behind with my work, the unions are making trouble again, and now you've turned up to irritate me. And don't you dare bring in any flowers. I'd end up with an office full of greenfly. I'm no good with plants, Flynn, you know that. I only have to walk past a flower and it dies of neglect, just to spite me. I like my office fine just the way it is, thank you. It has every luxury and convenience money can buy, and my own private sauna. Upper management can't do enough to keep me happy these days. They're terrified someone's going to poach me away. They'd put a solid-gold jacuzzi in here if I asked them. In fact, that's not a bad idea . . .'

'Yes it is,' said Flynn, shuddering at the very thought. 'I know you, Toby. You'd have platinum taps shaped like dolphins, and bars of soap carved in amusing rude shapes, and you'd greet all your visitors half submerged in frothing waters. Whether the jacuzzi was turned on or not. You have no taste, Toby.'

'None at all,' Toby agreed happily. 'A factor that has done much to aid my rapid rise to position, wealth and fame. Anyway, you're hardly in a position to throw stones. If I let you loose in here, you'd cover the walls with holos of big-eyed children, and rush around putting doilies under everything.'

'And what's wrong with doilies?' said Flynn frostily. 'A little delicate lace can do wonders to cheer a room up.'

'What are you doing here, Flynn?' said Toby patiently. 'The day's over. Work is done. Go home and annoy someone else.'

'I will if you will. It's late, Toby. I thought you might like a lift.'

'Thanks for the thought, but I still have half a ton of paperwork to wade through. You wouldn't believe what ends up on this desk. I swear there are people in this building who couldn't take a dump after a vindaloo curry without the correct form signed by me. In triplicate. Ah, hell . . . would you like some tea, Flynn? It's one of the few things they do right around here.'

'I wouldn't say no.'

Toby hit the intercom switch. 'Miss Lovett, a cup of tea for Mr Flynn, please.'

Flynn raised a plucked eyebrow. 'Since when are you so formal?'

Toby shrugged. 'They expect it from the boss. I tried being relaxed and informal when I first moved in here, but it just made them uncomfortable. I suppose it's hard to be easy and spontaneous with someone who can fire your ass just because he came in with a headache that morning.'

The door opened and a young woman with hardly any dress on and a quite astounding amount of cleavage tottered in on impossibly high heels. She smiled widely at Flynn, displaying perfect teeth of dazzling brightness, and presented him with a steaming cup of tea.

'Thank you, dear,' said Flynn graciously. 'Do you know, I just love your earrings. You must tell me where you found them.'

'You wear them to the office, Flynn, and you're fired,' said Toby. 'Thank you, Miss Lovett. That will be all for now.'

The young lady giggled for no apparent reason, heaved her cleavage in the direction of the door and tottered out again. Flynn looked at Toby.

'She's my secretary,' said Toby defensively. 'She takes dictation.'

'Yeah,' said Flynn. 'I'll just bet she does. I would also bet good money that she has a room-temperature IQ and the personality of a piece of string. The last time I saw that much make-up on a face, the undertaker was trying to disguise an advanced case of leprosy.'

'All right, she's a bimbo, I admit it. I have someone else to do the actual secretarial work. Miss Lovett is more in the nature of . . . an office ornament. Something I can use to distract the union bosses when they come in with their latest wage claim. Upper management gave her to me. They thought it might keep me in the office more. Truth be told, she gets on my nerves something fierce. She has a voice that could frighten sheep, no talents you can discuss in polite company and a laugh that could strip wallpaper off walls and leave it crying its eyes out in a heap on the floor. Took me two weeks to train her to make a cup of tea. I'd fire her, but it would break her heart.'

'Life is tough at the top,' said Flynn.

'It is!' said Toby. 'All I want is to get some work done, some real work. I ask upper management for more help, and what do they send me? Executive toys.' Toby gestured at a motley collection of metal and plastic junk on his desk. 'Toys! I was bored with them after half an hour. I can't just sit around all day, Flynn, ticking the right boxes and signing where indicated, taking extra tea breaks and seeing how long it takes me to wreck the latest toy. It's not in my nature. I need to be *doing* something. I always thought that with this job's authority I'd finally be able to cover the kind of important stories I'd always wanted to go after. But somehow it never works out that way. I may be the boss here, but I still have to answer to my bosses, the rich and influential people who own Imperial News. And they'd be just as happy running a gossip show, as long as it didn't affect profits. Every time I suggest a good target to go after, the word comes down from Above; don't make waves.

'They were happy enough to take risks when they were only a minor company, desperate to do anything to grab viewing figures away from the big boys, but now they are one of the big boys, they've gone all nervous on me. They have something to lose, these days. You know, Flynn, I should be happy. I've made it. I've got the job I always wanted. I run Imperial News! They don't even challenge my expenses any more. But I am bored, Flynn. Terribly, mind-numbingly *bored*.'

'You know the answer, chief. Do what you did the last time we had this conversation. Pick a story and cover it yourself. Get out in the field and see how close to the wind you can sail this time. I'm always available to be your cameraman. For the standard rates, plus danger money.'

'I'd like to, Flynn, but . . . Oh, the hell with it. Stuff them all. If I stay in this room much longer I'll start putting down roots. I can always leave my deputy in charge for a while. Not too bright, and scared stiff of anyone who raises their voice to him, but I swear he actually likes shuffling papers. Come on, Flynn, let's get a move on. We have a story to cover.'

'What, right now? It's late, well past clocking-off time. I was thinking of sometime tomorrow. I can't go with you now, Clarence will have a hotpot dinner waiting for me.'

'Tell him to stick it back in the oven,' said Toby ruthlessly. 'What I have in mind can't wait. There's a couple of targets I've been trying to get to for weeks, but my reporters keep being turned down and intimidated. Let's see what I can do. Barging in on them at this time of night might well catch them with their defences down. And after everything I went through in the rebellion, they couldn't intimidate me with a point-blank disrupter cannon.'

'I have a terrible feeling I've started something that can only end in tears,' said Flynn. 'Lead on, boss. Where are we going first?'

'To see the Speaker of Parliament his own slippery self; Elias bloody Gutman.'

Getting in to see Gutman turned out to be easier than expected. They didn't bother with an introductory call requesting an appointment, because Toby knew very well Gutman wouldn't agree to one. Instead, he and Flynn went straight round to Gutman's luxurious town house, in one of the very best neighbourhoods, and got in by bribing the footmen and wearing down the security guards with a long harangue on the necessity of a free press. Toby worked his way through the inner security levels and ranks of flak-catchers with a grandstand performance of sheer persever-ance and bloody-mindedness that Flynn found a joy to watch. This was the Toby Shreck he remembered; an unstoppable force of nature that talked its way round most obstacles and walked right over the rest. Leaving Gutman's people reeling and wondering what the hell had hit them, Toby and Flynn followed the head butler as he led the way to Gutman's inner sanctum.

The butler, a tall and haughty personage in an old-fashioned frock coat, with frosty manners and just a little understated make-up, who winked at Flynn when he thought Toby wasn't looking, finally came to a halt before a massive pair of intricately carved wooden doors. He knocked politely, and then threw them open with practised flair, announcing Toby's and Flynn's names in a loud, carrying voice. Toby strode straight in, with Flynn right behind him, camera hovering over his shoulder. The butler sighed quietly, and took up a position just inside the doors, in case he might be needed.

Gutman's quarters were surprisingly tasteful, but all that meant was that he could afford a decent interior designer. There were shelves of books along one wall, expensive leather-bound editions, but Toby would have bet good money Gutman hadn't read any of them. Probably bought them by the yard. Gutman himself was reclining at his ease in a technological marvel of a chair that did everything but wipe his nose for him. He didn't bother to get up when his visitors entered, so Toby didn't bother with the bow and polite greetings that formality would otherwise have demanded.

'Get rid of the flunkey, Gutman,' Toby said brusquely,

starting as he meant to go on. 'You aren't going to want a witness for some of the things we're going to discuss.'

'Ah, the famous Shreck charm,' said Gutman heavily. 'That must be how you got past my guards. Most of whom will be drawing unemployment tomorrow. It's all right, Jobe; you can go. I'll ring if I need anything.'

The butler bowed, gave Flynn a last lingering look, and left. Toby fixed Gutman with his best piercing gaze. 'So, Elias, how are the haemorrhoids?'

'Compared to your presence, nothing at all. You're the only real pain in my ass these days. What do you want at this late hour?'

'What I always want; answers. Answers to a few questions that my reporters never got to put to you. Starting with how a slimy wheeler-dealer like you ended up as a revered elder statesman.'

Gutman shrugged easily. 'Through my many and varied business enterprises. Over the years, I have amassed a number of influential contacts, in all walks of life. I did business with Lionstone's Empire and helped fund the rebellion. I've never believed in keeping all my eggs in one basket.'

'You've never believed in declaring them for taxes, either,' said Toby. 'Come on, Elias. Everyone knows that you had a hand in every dirty deal going, from drugs to gun-running to clonelegging. Your reputation was marginally worse than the Hadenmen's. How did you end up as Speaker?'

'Much to my surprise,' said Gutman. 'I came home to rebuild my Family, which had been so weakened during the war they were even glad to see me back. And as a man of means and prospects, I found position and responsibility pressed upon me.'

'Just like that.'

'Pretty much. I hate to disappoint you, Toby, but I was elected Speaker because the majority wanted it. No back-room deals, no bribes, no blackmail, no secret promises of favour or influence. I got the job because everyone knew me, and distrusted me equally. I was possibly the one person with all the right contacts who didn't have his own agenda. And, if they were dumb enough to offer me the post, I was certainly dumb enough to take it.'

'You're living very well,' said Toby, retreating for the moment to safer ground. 'A big house, in the best part of town. An army of servants, and all the luxuries. And if that obscene portrait on the wall is what I think it is, it alone cost more than your yearly salary as Speaker. Where's the money coming from these days, Elias?'

'I never knew you had an eye for art, Toby,' said Gutman affably. 'And yes, it is an original. Erotica is very collectable these days. I acquired it as payment for an outstanding debt. My money comes from investments, all of them open and above board. My finances are now a matter of public record. I'm squeaky clean; I can afford to be. It was a good war for me, in many ways.'

'If you're so clean, why did you settle for Speaker? You could have been a Member of Parliament. Hell, you could have been Prime Minister.'

'I prefer to be the man who chooses the Prime Minister. The power behind the throne, so to speak.'

'But just what are your politics these days, Elias? Where do you stand? What are you after? You seem terribly chummy with just about everyone, including all the extreme fringe groups that no one else would touch with a bargepole. There isn't a political gathering of whatever persuasion that doesn't have you on its guest list. Oh, I'm sorry, was that supposed to be a secret? I've studied the footage from my freelance cameramen, the stuff that doesn't always get on the screen, and it's amazing how often you crop up. No matter how extreme the cause, or how distasteful, or even how opposed, there you are right in the middle of things, smiling and pressing the flesh and making friends. Everybody's buddy. Care to comment on that?'

Gutman had stopped smiling. 'You're on dangerous ground, Shreck. Back off.'

'If it's all so innocent, why don't you want to talk about it? You just said you're squeaky clean these days. Why is everyone always so glad to see you, Elias? What are you offering them, in those privately convened meetings that no one else gets to see?'

'I think it's time you were leaving,' said Gutman flatly. 'I have nothing more to say. And don't think you can use any footage of this conversation. I have hidden security devices that jam all recording equipment.'

'That's what you think,' said Flynn. 'I've made modifications.'

Gutman glared at Flynn and then at Toby. 'I could have my people destroy that camera.'

'No, you couldn't. It would cause too many awkward questions.' Toby smiled at Gutman. 'Unlike you, people believe what I tell them.'

'I'll speak to your bosses,' said Gutman. 'And then they'll tell you what to say.'

'I am the boss,' said Toby.

Gutman smiled coldly. 'One of my investments is in communications. I own forty per cent of Imperial News.'

Toby smiled right back at him. 'Do you think that'll stop me? There are always other companies. I'm red-hot, these days. Everyone wants me. Time we were going, Flynn. Don't bother with the flunkey, Elias. We'll find our own way out.'

They left in something of a hurry, just in case Gutman decided he didn't care about his public image just this once, and set the dogs on them. Out in the street again, in the cool air of the evening, Toby and Flynn looked at each other thoughtfully.

'Well,' said Flynn, 'that was interesting.'

'Yeah,' said Toby, rubbing his hands together. 'I told you there was a story here. Just wish I knew what the hell it was. We're going to have to do some more digging in records and archives. See if we can find more footage on exactly who Elias has been cosying up to just recently that he doesn't want us to know about. Might be interesting to see if there's anyone he isn't talking to. That might tell us something as well. Strange, though; I was expecting him to put up more of a fight. Elias used to enjoy these little confrontations, playing games with words and defying me to get to the truth. I thought he folded rather quickly, this time. And the threats were so . . . obvious. He used to be more subtle than that.' Toby gave Flynn a sharp look. 'Were you bluffing about your camera? Do we have any of that conversation recorded?'

'Depends,' said Flynn. 'I upgrade my camera regularly, but the main players make a point of always having state-of-the-art security. I won't know for sure what I've got till I get back to the lab.'

'Well, that will have to wait,' said Toby. 'We have another visit to make yet. A Family affair this time; my dear aunt Grace, currently the head of my Clan, in the detested Gregor's absence. She's been running the Family and making a very good job of it, by all accounts. Which is interesting, because the Grace I've known for most of my life wouldn't say boo to a goose if it was crapping on her foot. A shy, retiring creature, Aunt Grace, immersed in a remembered past when things were simpler. Gregor had to bully and intimidate her just to get her to turn up at Court. But of late dear Grace has emerged into the limelight with a vengeance, becoming a major social figure. Something's finally kicked her awake, and I want to know what.'

'But . . . isn't this change a good thing?' said Flynn. 'Aren't you pleased she's come out of her shell?'

'She's still a Shreck,' said Toby. 'And we never do anything without at least one ulterior motive.'

'Oh, yeah,' said Flynn. 'Then what's yours for this visit?'

Toby smiled. 'My cousin Clarissa. She's been staying with Grace ever since the Deathstalker freed her from her servitude as one of Lionstone's maids. A pretty young thing, very sweet. I thought I might see how she was getting on.'

'You old softie,' said Flynn. 'Wait a minute. I thought she was your sister?'

'Half-sister and cousin,' said Toby, shrugging easily. 'It's that kind of Family.'

It wasn't far to Grace Shreck's town house; she lived in the same salubrious area as Gutman. Private security systems monitored the streets, keeping an electronic eye on anyone who looked as though they didn't belong there. Flynn on his own would have been stopped immediately and politely but firmly interrogated, but everybody knew Toby Shreck. The Shreck town house had been in the Family for generations, and looked it. The old stone walls were spotted and discoloured with age and pollution, and the once impeccable gardens had been left to run wild. Long-established mats of ivy crawled across the frontispiece of the house, left alone out of a sense of tradition. The windows were one-way only, showing blank uncaring eyes to the outside world. And Toby knew for a fact that there were hidden guns all over, to discourage unwanted visitors. This was a Shreck establishment, after all.

Once, the house had been home and sanctuary to the majority of the Shreck, but with the building of the pastel towers, it had declined into just a town house, somewhere to stay for short periods, for those of the Family who were currently out of favour. Grace had been there a long time, and now the great four-winged mansion was home to her alone, plus a small army of servants. Grace was a great believer in keeping up appearances.

'Most of the rooms are left empty now,' said Toby, as he and Flynn waited more or less patiently outside the main drawing room. The butler had just gone in to announce them, and was apparently taking his time. Toby wouldn't have thought there was that much to announce. But he couldn't just barge in, as he had with Gutman. This was Family. 'Bit of a waste, really. Given its location, we could sell this place for a tidy sum, but Grace won't give it up while she's alive. It's her home.'

'And very impressive it is too,' said Flynn. 'If I'd known we were coming somewhere this posh, I'd have nipped home to change into my best frock and real diamonds. A girl likes to look her best.'

'Don't even mention that in front of Grace,' Toby said firmly. 'She's a bit old-fashioned, and easily shocked. If we're going to get anything out of her, I need her to be relaxed and at her ease.'

'That's a bit cold-blooded, isn't it? I mean, she's your aunt.'

Toby grinned. 'But we're both Shrecks. Don't let your guard down in there, Flynn; she could tear you apart, if the mood took her.'

The butler, in formal frock coat and powdered wig, returned at last to usher them into the main drawing room. It was big enough to land a ship's pinnace in, and crowded with antique furniture and priceless works of art of the kind normally only seen in museums. There were statues of all sizes, tables and chairs from widely differing periods, a grand piano that looked as though it had seen a lot of use, and an indoor fountain splashing merrily away that should have been very impressive, but for the fact that it reminded Toby he hadn't visited the toilet in quite a while. Huge Family portraits covered the walls, depicting generations of Shrecks in a variety of styles, with the same frowning faces and identical cold eyes.

It made Gutman's place look positively rustic.

'Wow,' said Finlay quietly. 'How the other one per cent lives. I never knew you and your Family were this rich, boss.'

'We're not,' said Toby, just as quietly. 'This house is a reminder of the time when we used to be. There are individual pieces here that could pay off the Family's debts for a decade, but Grace won't part with any of them. As long as she can surround herself with all this stuff, she can convince herself that Clan Shreck is still what it used to be, and that nothing has really changed. Gregor's been trying to bully Grace into selling up for ages, and it's a tribute to Grace's iron will-power that even his concentrated venom can't shift her.'

'Still,' said Flynn, 'I'll bet this room is hell to dust. They must work in shifts.'

Finally they were brought into the presence of Grace Shreck, and Toby and Flynn both bowed formally. Grace inclined her head regally from the depths of a huge, very comfortable-looking chair set just the right distance away from the roaring fire in the great fireplace. The butler gestured to two hovering servants, also in frock coats and powdered wigs, who hurried forward bearing two antique chairs, and set them down at just the right distance from Grace, so that Toby and Flynn could sit facing her. They settled themselves carefully on to the delicate-looking chairs, which proved to be even more uncomfortable than they looked. Grace smiled at them both, and then, without looking round, gestured to the butler. He and the two servants left the room, backing out all the way. Grace waited till the door had closed behind them, and then sniffed disparagingly.

'Servants . . . it's so hard to get good help these days. You

405

have to be ever so careful what you say in front of them. In my young days, a Family servant would never have dreamed of repeating a confidence, or anything they might have heard of their master's business, but no one has any sense of loyalty any more. They're always looking for some gossip they can peddle to the scandal shows. Never mind whether it's true or not, as long as it makes a good story, that's their attitude. I do hope that camera of yours is not operating, young man. I take my privacy very seriously.'

'We won't record anything without your permission, Auntie,' Toby said quickly.

Grace sniffed again. 'You only call me Auntie when you want something, Tobias. What is it this time? Another loan?'

'Not this time, Auntie, thank you very much. I just happened to be visiting another house in this area, and I thought I might as well drop in and see how you were doing. You and Clarissa.'

'Oh, so that's where the wind lies, is it? Thought I saw a sparkle in your eye for her, the last time you deigned to pay me a visit. She's doing very well, Tobias, recovering from her ordeal. What the poor thing endured would have broken a lesser soul, but of course Clarissa has good old Shreck iron in her bones. She'll pull through. I'll send for her in a while. Now, nephew; you may kiss me on the cheek and come to the real purpose of your visit. You can't fool me, Tobias. You didn't come calling at this late hour of the evening just to enquire over my health and make eyes at Clarissa.'

Toby grinned, got out of his chair to kiss Grace chastely on her powdered cheek, and then sat down again. 'You always see through me, Auntie. I need your help for a piece I'm working on, about how the Families are rebuilding themselves under the new order. And I can't not mention my own Family, can I? They'd call it bias. And it must be said, you've made a great deal of difference to the Clan's standing since you took control.'

Grace scowled. 'It's not as if I had any choice in the matter; there was only me. Gregor has been going mad for years, but as long as he maintained the Family prestige, no one would hear a word said against him. But, when he finally fell apart and barricaded himself inside the Tower, it was clear someone had to replace him as head before the whole Clan fell apart. You weren't interested, and all the other senior members of the Family were too busy plotting against each other, so the burden fell to me, the only senior Shreck that everyone else could accept. It hasn't been easy, but I like to think I've made a difference.'

'You certainly have, Auntie,' said Toby carefully. 'Under you, the Shrecks have moved back into the political mainstream in a big way. I wasn't aware you knew so much about current politics.'

'I do have a viewscreen, young man, and I have been known to watch something other than those dreadful never-ending soaps. And I have advisors, lots of them. Everybody has these days. Would either of you care for a cup of tea?'

'That would be very pleasant, Lady Shreck,' said Flynn.

Grace looked at him approvingly. 'I'm glad to see some young people still have good manners. Unlike some I could mention, but won't. Do you want tea, Toby?'

'Actually, I could do with something a little stronger . . .'

'You'll have tea.'

'I'll have tea.'

Grace pulled at a handy bell rope. 'It'll take them a while, I'm afraid. You can't rush a good cup of tea, though heaven knows they'd try if I let them. They will keep telling me about this instant nonsense, as though I cared. Some things just have to be done the right way, and that's all there is to it.'

'Have you been here very long, Lady Shreck?' said Flynn. 'You seem very comfortable here.'

'Oh, I've been here since I was a young girl, for more years than I care to remember, young man. My brother Christian and his family joined me here for a while, and we had such a jolly time together. Till he disappeared.' Grace frowned. 'I was always sure Gregor had something to do with it, but I could never prove anything. And there was the Family name to consider. A scandal could have ruined us.'

'You never allowed anyone even to raise the subject before,' said Toby sharply.

'I was concerned that if one of you showed too much interest in Christian's fate, you might disappear too,' said

Grace, just as sharply. 'It's only now, with Gregor's position so weakened, that I feel at all safe in discussing the subject, even in private. Christian and Gregor never got along. That's no secret. They had a furious argument one day, right here in this room. Christian stormed out, and was never seen again. Don't press me for any further details, Tobias, because I don't have any. I wasn't even in the house at the time. Your mother, Helga, went out looking for Christian, and she too never came back. No trace was ever found of either of them. Sometimes I like to think they found each other, and decided to stay hidden and safe. I like to think of them living happily together somewhere, in secret.'

'Then why did they never send for me?' said Toby.

'Gregor had you watched all the time,' Grace said gently. 'You were bait. I kept you close to me, protected you as best I could, till I could find you a safe place at a boarding school.'

'Maybe I should ask Gregor what happened,' said Toby. 'Get him alone, and ask him very forcefully.'

'I wouldn't advise it, dear. He'd very likely just have you shot, in his present state of mind. He thinks he's surrounded by enemies, and he's mostly right. Anyway, it's a bit late to be showing such emotion over your lost parents, isn't it? You're an investigative journalist; you could have started a search years ago, if you'd really been interested.'

'They went off and left me,' said Toby, looking at the floor. 'They never came back for me. And, like you, I never wanted proof that they were dead. As long as they were officially listed as missing, there was the chance they might turn up again some day.' His face had relaxed out of its usual harsh and cynical lines, and for a moment he looked rather lost and vulnerable. But the moment passed, and he was quickly his old self again. He looked up and fixed Grace with a steady gaze. 'Why was I never sent to Blue Block, like so many of my contemporaries?'

'Your father never approved of them, and Gregor still had a use for you. Not that he ever trusted them, either. Gregor always suspected the worst of everyone, and in Blue Block's case it would appear he was right. The servant has become the master. Just another reason why I was forced into the political arena. The Family must be protected from all out-side influences and pressures, whatever the source. Ah, tea!'

The door had opened silently, and Toby and Flynn looked round to see a servant bearing down on them, carrying a silver teapot and fine china milk jug and cups on a silver tray. The teapot was very elegant, and the matching sugar bowl was practically a work of art. Right behind the servant came a young woman in a pretty dress, with a widely smiling face under shoulder-length golden curls. Toby rose quickly to his feet and went to meet her, also smiling widely, while the servant set out the tea things on a handy little table at Grace's side. Grace gave Toby and the young woman a knowing look, and busied herself with the tray, nodding to the servant to withdraw. Flynn watched Toby interestedly, as he took the young woman's hand in his.

'Clarissa! You're looking very well. Very well!'

'And feeling much better, thanks to you, dear Toby. The surgeons are removing the implants Lionstone put in me as fast as they can, but it's a long job. At least I have human eyes to see you with now.'

'And very pretty eyes they are too. The hair's new, isn't it?'

'It's just a wig, while my own hair grows back. You've done so much for me, Toby. I don't know how to thank you.'

'Oh, I'm sure he'll think of something,' said Grace tartly. 'Now that's enough mawkishness for the moment, dears. Any more and you'll over-sweeten the tea. Come and sit down while I pour.'

Clarissa pulled up a chair right next to Toby's, and they sat down, still smiling at each other. Flynn coughed politely, and then smiled and nodded to Clarissa.

'Hello, Flynn,' she said, bathing him in her smile too. 'How are you?'

'Working overtime when I should be at home relaxing, thanks to my brute of a boss. Are you settling in happily here?'

'Hard to tell,' said Grace, looking firmly at the teacups. 'She spends most of her time in her room, and jumps every time she hears a loud noise. The only person she talks to is Tobias, and that only over the viewscreen.'

'She's been through a lot,' Toby said defensively. 'It's bound to take her some time to . . . readjust. You haven't been bullying her, have you?'

'Oh, no,' Clarissa said quickly. 'She's been very supportive. I have the very best surgeons. I just . . . don't feel like meeting anyone yet. Not till I'm all the way back to who I was, before Lionstone had me changed into one of her damned body-guards. Then I'll think about mixing with people again.'

'Of course,' said Toby. 'Don't rush yourself. Take all the time you need.'

'I sometimes hear from other maids who were rescued,' said Clarissa, looking down at her hands folded in her lap. 'It seems a lot of them have been having trouble readjusting to being human again. Several of us have gone mad, and three have killed themselves, rather than remember what they were, and what they did. I could never do that. It would be like giving Lionstone the final victory. But I understand why they did it. I don't know what I'm going to do with my life now. Even after the surgeons have finished with me, I don't think I could go back to what I was before. I need to do something with my new life; something to make sure that what happened to me could never happen again, to anyone else.'

'Why not come and work with me, at Imperial News?' said Toby. 'The rebellion showed how much influence a truly free press can have. The news matters, these days, and you could be a part of that.'

'Yes,' said Clarissa, smiling even more widely at him. 'I think I'd like that.'

And then Toby's comm implant chimed imperiously in his ear, and he listened for a long moment, frowning fiercely, before rising abruptly to his feet. 'Sorry, Clarissa, Auntie, but Flynn and I have to go, right now. Word is coming in that Robert Campbell has given up his captaincy, resigned from the Fleet and come home to Golgotha to re-establish his Clan. He's due to arrive at the starport here any time now, and every news station in the city will be there to cover it. I've got a couple of stringers in place to represent us, just in case he gets in early, but this is something I really should be covering myself. If anyone can make the Campbells big again, it's a war hero like Robert. Come on, Flynn. Clarissa, I'll call you later.'

'But I've just poured tea!' said Grace.

'Oh dear,' said Toby, 'what a pity.'

Robert Campbell stood very still in front of the full-length mirror and sighed deeply. He was being fitted for his first set of civilian clothes in years, and he'd forgotten what a pain it could be. The tailor fussed around him with a mouthful of pins, tugging here and adjusting there with just a little more familiarity than Robert felt was strictly called for. Of course, a computer could have measured him and run up as many sets of clothes as he wanted, but in society it was considered essential that such things were done by hand, so as to allow for artistic insight on matters of taste. Fashion was far too important to be left to machines.

Robert kept his opinions to himself, sighed a lot and let them get on with it. Things had been very different in the Fleet. They gave you a uniform when you enlisted, and it fitted where it touched. If you wanted a better fit, it was up to you to do something about it. One uniform, another for spare, and a dress uniform for special occasions would see you through your entire career. But now he was a civilian and a Campbell again, he'd already been fitted for twelve different outfits, and they hadn't even got on to evening wear yet.

'Is all this really necessary?' he appealed plaintively to the servant he'd taken on to advise him on such things.

'It is a matter of fashion, sir,' said the butler, Baxter, entirely unmoved, 'and therefore a matter of the utmost importance. In high society a man is judged almost entirely by his appearance, and if you wish to be taken seriously as head of your Clan, it is imperative that you look the part.'

'My Clan currently consists of a few dozen cousins and a handful of blood relatives. Barely enough for a decent soccer match, never mind a Clan.'

'All the more important then that you look the part, sir. Society will take its cue from you. The greater the impression you make, the more they will respect your Clan. Rebuilding your Family will only be possible with the support of the other Clans, and that will only happen if they see you as an equal. Try not to stand quite so stiffly, sir. The clothes need to hang naturally for the best effect.'

Robert did his best to fall out of parade rest. It wasn't easy; none of it was easy. He'd taken pride in being a military man, and had given up his Navy career with only the greatest reluctance, after General Beckett had personally contacted him to make it clear Robert couldn't be loyal to both his Family and the Fleet. He would have to make a choice, a commitment to one or the other. In the end, Robert knew his duty had to be to his Clan and his blood, and centuries of Family tradition. To think otherwise would mean that the rest of his Family had died for nothing. So he gave up his treasured captaincy, resigned from the Fleet and returned to Golgotha, to be the Campbell.

And silently cursed his duty and his Clan, all the way down to the planet's surface.

He hadn't realized the decision was of any importance to anyone but him, until he disembarked at the starport of the Parade of the Endless, and found a crowd of eager reporters waiting for him. Cameras shot back and forth around him at dizzying speeds, nudging each other for the best angles, and the reporters yelled out questions faster than he could answer them. Clan Campbell had been one of the main movers and shakers in the old Empire, till it was decimated and scattered by Clan Wolfe, and its potential re-emergence was apparently big news. Robert had done his best to answer all questions, comments and insinuations with monosyllabic grunts, all the time pushing steadily forward through the crowd. Partly because he knew how reporters could twist even the most innocent remarks, and partly because he really didn't have anything to say. He was out of touch with current politics and Family intrigues, and didn't want to say anything that might commit him to anything just yet.

He especially didn't want to have to admit that he didn't have a clue as to just how he was going to rebuild Clan Campbell.

At the time, he'd thought wistfully of Owen Deathstalker and Hazel d'Ark. Say what you might about them, and there was a lot that could be said, they at least knew how to deal with the press. Some reporters apparently demanded combat pay just to interview them. But those two could get away with things like that. They were Maze people; no one could make them do anything they didn't want to. Mere mortals like Robert Campbell, who might yet need the support of the press in the future, had a harder road to follow.

The first thing he'd done, after he'd shaken off the news pack, had been to contact a service agency and hire the most experienced butler they had on their books. And he'd been lucky enough to get Baxter, who knew everything there was to know about society. A quiet, unassuming but surprisingly firm man in his late fifties, Baxter was more than just a butler. He was a personal servant, a gentleman's gentleman, and privy to all the arcane secrets and rituals of aristocratic behaviour. Even though he'd been in the Navy man and boy, Robert had still visited his family enough to know the basics, but fads and fashions meant that everyday minutiae, by which proper behaviour and social standing were judged, changed faster than any outsider could hope to follow. Which was, of course, the point. High society was meant to be elitist, complex and mysterious. How else could you tell who was in, and who was out? Half the fun of being in was turning up your nose at those who weren't. Robert the military man saw the whole business as desperately childish, but he was still enough of an aristocrat to understand how seriously everyone else took it. He was the Campbell now, and he had to play the game. It was expected of him.

The role of the Families might have been altered by the rebellion, but some things never changed.

He listened patiently while Baxter lectured him on etiquette and style and the correct way of shooting one's cuffs, on the latest dances and the latest gossip, and who might be expected to support or oppose him. If Clan Campbell really was on the way up again, there were a great many people who saw advantages to be gained by striking deals while the Campbell was still weak. There were just as many more who might try anything, up to and including assassination attempts, to prevent his rise and preserve the status quo, and thus their own position. Just by becoming the Campbell,

Robert inherited centuries of intrigues and feuds, old allies and enemies. In the Families, no one forgot or forgave. Unless it was expedient.

Robert closed his eyes for a moment. He felt deathly tired. Yesterday he'd been a captain in the Imperial Fleet, with a glorious career ahead of him. He'd had everything he ever wanted. Now he'd given it all up to become something he hated and despised, because of his duty to a Family that never really wanted him. Someone was going to pay for what he was going through, and it sure as hell wasn't going to be him. He'd be an aristocrat and play their bloody game, but he'd play it his way, by his rules, and the good God help anyone who got in his way. He realized that Baxter had stopped talking, and looked round sharply.

'Sorry, I was just resting my eyes. What is it? Did I miss something?'

'I was enquiring about the small portrait to your right, sir,' said Baxter. 'It is the only portrait you brought with you. A most lovely young lady. Is she who I think she is?'

'Yes,' said Robert, 'that's her. That's Letitia.' He stared expressionlessly at the portrait in its silver frame, set on the mantelpiece beside the mirror. It was one of the very few personal possessions he'd brought with him, and all that was left from the last time the Family had intruded into his life. 'She was very lovely. I suppose everyone knows the story; it was a big enough scandal in its day. I almost married her. An arranged marriage, but I was fond of her. Given time, I might even have loved her. But at our wedding, it emerged that she was already pregnant, by one of her guards. Gregor Shreck murdered her rather than let the wedding go ahead and dishonour his Family. I would have saved her, but my Family held me back. And I think that was when I learned to hate the Families. All of them.'

'Family honour is . . . a tricky business, sir. It is often difficult to know what to do for the best.'

'Gregor killed her, right in front of me. I would have killed him then, if I could. I may still.'

'Then I fear you'll have to stand in line, sir. Gregor Shreck is not the most popular member of society just now. In fact,

I would venture to suggest that genital warts are probably more popular than he is.'

Robert had to laugh, in spite of himself. 'Good to see some things never change. And I suppose a society that hates Gregor Shreck can't be all bad. He can wait; I'll get round to him. Rebuilding the Clan has to come first. That is why I came home.'

'Indeed, sir. And, if I may be so bold, I am sure there are many young ladies of good standing who would be only too happy to make a contract with a rising young gentleman and war hero such as yourself, sir.'

'No,' said Robert decisively. 'No more arranged marriages.'

'Pardon me, sir, I quite understand your feelings in the matter, but if you are to lead your Clan, it will be necessary for you to marry at some point, to produce heirs to carry on your line.'

'Yes, I know. But not yet.'

'Don't try to pressure him, Baxter. Robert can be as stubborn as a deaf mule when he wants to be. It's a Campbell trait.'

Robert looked round smiling as the owner of the strident voice came over to join him. Adrienne was one of his closest friends, even if she was married to the notorious Finlay Campbell. As soon as she heard he was back, Adrienne arranged for him to stay with her, while she took charge of the details of his introduction back into society. Robert hadn't argued. One didn't, with Adrienne. And he'd been glad of somewhere secure and friendly to lay his head. His old Family home, Tower Campbell, had been taken over by the Wolfes. He had no rights to it any longer. So he and Baxter were camped out at Adrienne's somewhat crowded house, and tried to get a word in edgeways now and again. Adrienne had all but taken over the running of Robert's life. He didn't mind, really. It reminded him happily of his time in the military. She waved the hovering tailor away with an imperious gesture, and he practically broke his back bowing his way out across the room. Adrienne looked sharply at Baxter.

'Well, how's he doing?'

'As well as can be expected, ma'am. He is making progress, slowly. He has a regrettable impulse towards truthfulness and sincerity, but nothing that can't be overcome. A few carefully arranged appearances at the right soirées and coffee mornings, just to test the waters, and then he should be ready to make a more public splash in society.'

'At least now you look the part, Robert.'

'I feel like an idiot.'

'That's how you know it's fashionable, dear. You should have seen some of the things my Finlay wore, in his days as a fop. People would complain of eye strain for days after he unveiled a new outfit.'

'We need to talk about Finlay,' said Robert. 'Have you seen him recently? Is he going to make problems over my being the Campbell instead of him? He does have a better claim to the title.'

'Trust me, dear, Finlay doesn't want to be the Campbell. He never did. Finlay wouldn't know what to do with responsibility if you nailed it to his forehead. He's always been the most important thing in his life. I had hoped Evangeline might have changed that, but . . . He came to see me recently. Said he wanted to see the children, which was a first. I'm surprised he could remember their names without prompting.'

'How did it go?'

'Badly. I should have known better. He's never been any good with children. Or anyone else, really. But I have to say he seemed even more out of it than usual. I'd be worried about him, if I could bring myself to give a damn. I really must contact Evie, see how she's doing. Finlay has never really appreciated her. But that can wait. How do you feel now, Robert?'

'Very grateful that you're letting me impose on you. Baxter and I will move out as soon as I can find somewhere . . .'

'Oh, there's no rush. Besides, you'd probably just move into some squalid little bachelor apartment, and we can't have that. If you're to be a part of society, you must have a respectable address. Somewhere men and women of stature can come visiting without feeling they're going slumming. The right address always says a great deal about a man. To

416

begin with, I think we'll get you settled in a suite at one of the better hotels.'

'Addie, I don't have that kind of money! The Clan has no assets, and while the Navy gave me a nice little bonus on leaving, it hardly amounted to a golden handshake. What I've got won't last long, and it certainly won't stretch to a suite.'

'If you're going to be the Campbell, you have to live like the head of a Clan,' Adrienne said firmly, 'or no one is going to take you seriously. Don't you worry about money. Once word gets around that you're back, people will be falling over themselves to pay your bills, in return for future favours. Even the banks will extend you open lines of credit in the hope of handling your business. Everyone knows that a hell of a lot of money went missing when the Campbells crashed, money that the Wolfes never got their hands on.'

'But I haven't got it.'

'They don't know that! If anyone asks you about it, just smile and look enigmatic. Let me worry about such things, dear. You just concentrate on looking the part. How are we doing for clothes, Baxter? Is he ready to go out in public yet?'

'There will have to be further fittings for the more formal evening wear, ma'am, but I think we're ready to risk a few carefully controlled appearances. Did you have anyone in mind, ma'am?'

'Well, to start with,' said Adrienne, 'I thought Constance Wolfe.'

'Are you crazy?' said Robert. 'The Wolfes destroyed my Family! Murdered my uncles, almost killed you, and hunted us down in the street and butchered us like animals!'

'That was then, this is now,' said Adrienne firmly. 'A lot's happened since those days. Jacob Wolfe was head of the Clan at the time. He's dead now. Valentine is on the run, Daniel is missing and Stephanie is so far out of favour with her own people that she can't even see it from where she is. Constance, Jacob's young widow, is currently the Wolfe, and head of the Family. And she has revolutionary ideas about how the Families should behave in the new order. She distrusts Blue Block, supports Parliament and is very keen to mend fences with old enemies. Go and see her, Robert. Turn on the Campbell charm, make it clear you don't hold her responsible for the excesses of her predecessors and you might just find in her a kindred spirit. She'd make a very strong friend and supporter. And it would demonstrate to all the other Families that you don't feel bound by old feuds and vendettas. You're going to have enough enemies as it is, Robert. Make friends where you can.'

'Not back twenty-four hours, and here I am dressed up like a clothes horse and contemplating making deals with a Wolfe,' said Robert disgustedly. 'Some welcome home. But, if I have to . . .'

'You have to,' said Adrienne.

Robert looked to Baxter, who nodded solemnly. 'It will make an excellent beginning, sir. Not to worry; I shall of course be accompanying you.'

'Wonderful,' said Robert. 'Now I've got a nanny as well as a butler.' He glared at Adrienne. 'Anything else you think I ought to know?'

'There is one other thing,' Adrienne said reluctantly. 'Concerning Finlay. You may have to do something about him.'

'You just said he didn't want to be the Campbell.'

'He doesn't. But he's been acting even more erratically than usual, just recently; threatening people. He's made a lot of enemies in his time, many of them major players in society. They might just ask you to deal with Finlay, as a price for their support.'

'Deal with Finlay? As in kill him? What the hell could I do? The man's a legendary fighter and assassin. He's not going to listen to anything I might say, and even if he did accept me as head of the Clan, I doubt very much that he'd accept my authority over him. And I am certainly not stupid enough to try to deal with him myself. Owen Deathstalker might be able to handle him, or Kid Death, but I wouldn't last five minutes against him.'

'There are ways,' said Adrienne, not looking at him. 'In the end, all that matters is the good of the Clan. One man can't be allowed to undermine everything we're hoping to achieve.'

'For God's sake, Adrienne; he's your husband, the father of your children. Don't you have any feelings for him?'

'I don't know him any more. Sometimes I wonder if I ever did.'

Robert Campbell sat upright on an antique chair with spindly legs and an unforgiving seat, holding a full cup of tea in one hand and a large chocolate pastry on a plate in the other, and wondered how the hell he was supposed to get either one of them anywhere near his mouth without losing the other. Also, his new coat was uncomfortably tight across the shoulders, his cravat was half strangling him and his trousers were pinching him in places he didn't even know he had. All in all, this was shaping up to be one hell of a first social call.

His hostess, Constance Wolfe, had the top floor in Tower Wolfe all to herself, and had fitted it out to her personal taste. There were thick rugs on the floor, the very latest fashions in furniture, and stuffed fluffy animals lying everywhere there was a space. Robert felt he could have coped with all that. It was the frankly pornographic murals on the walls that kept throwing him. He'd never seen anything like some of them, and him a Navy man. He also had a terrible suspicion that Constance had posed for at least three of them. In which case, she was not only very beautiful, but incredibly limber as well. She looked very smart in black, still in mourning for her husband, and every inch the head of her Clan. Robert stared determinedly down at his tea and pastry, and tried to beam telepathic appeals for help to Baxter, before remembering that Constance had banished him from the room, along with all her servants, so that he and she could speak privately.

He hoped she wasn't going to jump on him. He'd always been rather shy about such things.

There'd been a lot of guards too, but Constance had dismissed them as a sign of good faith. The two of them were alone together. Robert had been surprised at the sheer number of armed men Constance had around her. He hadn't realized society was that dangerous these days. He supposed he ought to get a few guards himself, if only for show. Constance leaned forward in her chair facing him, and he jumped slightly in spite of himself. Tea slopped out of his cup and into the saucer.

'You don't have to eat the pastry if you don't want it,' said

Constance, smiling. 'Or drink the tea. One of the first things you have to learn at social gatherings is the art of saying no gracefully. Otherwise they'll load you down with food till your arms ache. People do so love to show off their chefs.'

Robert smiled gratefully, looked round for a nearby table or empty surface, realized there wasn't one and finally settled for putting cup and plate down on the floor beside his chair. He straightened up, tried surreptitiously to ease his coat and trousers without much success, and smiled slightly desperately at Constance.

'I like your room. It's very . . . comfortable.'

'One of the few joys of living alone is that you don't have to compromise on your personal ideas of comfort,' said Constance. 'Jacob would have had a fit if I'd done this to his living room while he was still alive. But after he died, I got rid of most of his things as quickly as was decent. Otherwise, everything I saw would have made me think of him. Every object had a story, a memory, a reminder of what I'd lost. So I replaced it all with new things, because I had to make a new life without him. All I kept were a few portraits of him. They're in my bedroom, next to my bed, so his face can be the last thing I see at night. That way, sometimes I get to dream of him. He was the only man I ever loved, you see, and we had such a short time together before he was taken from me so very suddenly. You understand; you lost someone too, didn't you?'

'Yes,' said Robert. 'I understand.'

'His ghost came back to me once,' said Constance, her voice calm and even. 'At Court. But it was just a Ghost Warrior. Just his body, not my Jacob. Poor Daniel went off looking for the Ghost Warrior, convinced his father was still in there somewhere. Daniel always was desperate for his father's approval. Jacob did love his children, in his own way, even Valentine, but he never found it easy expressing things like that. And they were all disappointments to him. I was going to give him new children, but he didn't want to share me with anyone else, so we never got round to it before he was taken from me, so now I never will. Just another loss to grieve.'

'He must have loved you very deeply,' said Robert, struggling for the right thing to say in the face of her calm words.

'I hope so, but I was never really sure. Never really sure whether he loved me as much as I loved him. I was a trophy wife, you see, young and beautiful, something to show off at Court and at parties. It was an arranged marriage, but I grew to love him. He was always kind to me, but . . . he never found it easy to talk about his feelings, even to me. So I was never sure.'

'You must find it very difficult, being a woman alone, and heading such a large Clan,' said Robert, just to be saying something.

'You have no idea,' said Constance dryly. 'I only got the position by default. I keep it by playing my many enemies off against each other and intriguing morning, noon and night. As a result, every word I say, and even the smallest of actions, are analysed endlessly by all concerned, to see if they contain crumbs of valuable information. Sometimes I say things entirely at random, just to get them worrying. There are always people around me now. Moments of privacy like this are rare. Everyone wants to see me, everyone wants something. You'll find that out for yourself, now you're the Campbell.'

'Then why not just walk away from it all?' said Robert. 'You're not trapped, like me. You're only a Wolfe by marriage, not blood. You could give it all up, and no one could stop you.'

'But the Clan is all I have left of Jacob. The one remaining connection to the happy times I shared with him. I owe him a duty not to step down till I can place the Clan in safe hands. That's why I'm marrying Owen Deathstalker.'

'I had heard. Congratulations.'

'Thank you.'

'What's he like, really? I've only ever seen him on the holo. Some say he's a hero, some—'

'Say he's a monster, I know. But he seemed very ordinary to me. Quite likeable. Even charming, in a clumsy sort of way. But he's strong, thoughtful. He'll make a good constitutional monarch, and as his Queen our two Families will merge, and I will be able to give up control to him. Can you think of any hands more secure than those of the legendary Owen Deathstalker?'

'Not really, no. But how do you feel about him?'

'He seemed kind. I'll settle for that. I've had one great love in my life. I don't think I could stand to lose another.'

'Why did you agree to see me?' said Robert. 'You said yourself that you're greatly in demand these days, and I'm not anyone important, yet. And our Families are mortal enemies. So why me?'

'We have a lot in common. We both became head of our Clan much sooner than we ever expected, through the death of a loved one, taking on the responsibility through duty and need. We've both known terrible pain and loss, but it didn't break us. I need someone like you, someone I can talk to, who'll understand. And I need allies I can trust; someone in the Families who isn't afraid of Blue Block.'

'Good reasons,' said Robert. 'As for Blue Block, I don't really know much about them. I was only with them for a short time before my Family took me away and placed me in the Fleet, where they thought I'd be more use to them. I was never introduced into any of their mysteries or secrets. I never realized they were so widespread, so powerful.'

'Very few did,' said Constance. 'Until it was too late. Blue Block was supposed to be the Families' secret defence against Lionstone, just another hidden weapon of last resort. But now the tail is wagging the dog, and no one knows what to do about it. Blue Block makes suggestions with the strength of orders, and we all jump to obey. But we have no idea what Blue Block really is, what they really want. I've seen too much evil in the Families, Robert. Too many of us became inbred and corrupt, misusing our power and abusing our privileges. I was one of the few in the Families who actually approved of the rebellion. I saw in the new order a chance to remake the Families as they should be; the best of the best, leading and guarding, not ruling by fear and oppression. But now Blue Block is putting all that at risk. The Clans are so desperate to regain power, they'll do anything Blue Block says to get it. And maybe only later realize that they've made a deal with the Devil. Someone has to stop Blue Block, and I can't do it alone. I need associates, people of good heart and true, to whom duty is more than just a word. What do you say, Robert Campbell? Have I found a friend in you?'

'I think perhaps you have, Constance Wolfe. God knows I've no love for Blue Block, or the excesses of the Clans. But what can we do to change anything?'

'We can set an example. Show Blue Block we're not afraid of them. If we stand up to be counted, others will join us.'

'I don't know about that,' said Robert. 'In the military, the first man to stand up is usually the first to get his head shot off. But I think you're right in that others might join us, if they knew there were others who thought as they did. What about your Family, before you married Jacob Wolfe? Where do they stand? Would they support us?'

'My Family and I . . . don't talk any more,' said Constance evenly. 'I was the eldest daughter of Clan Devereaux, supposed to attract a suitable young man of lesser stature into the Family to improve the bloodline. Instead, I married a Wolfe, joined his Clan, and my bloodline was lost to the Family for ever. My father declared that I was dead in his eyes. I haven't spoken with any of my Family since.'

'Now that's a shame,' said Robert. 'You should try, Constance. They might feel differently about you now, in your current circumstances.'

'I have my pride.'

'Sometimes pride just gets in the way. The ones we love or admire are always taken from us far too soon, before we get to say all the things we meant to say to them. I lost my parents early, so as I grew older I venerated the head of my Clan, Crawford Campbell. He was a god to me. A great fighting man, and a cunning intriguer. I would have walked through fire for him, if he would only notice me. I always felt guilty that I wasn't there with him in Tower Campbell on the day the Wolfes came, the day he died. I can't help feeling I might have made a difference. That if I'd been there, fighting at his side, the end result might have been otherwise. I'm probably wrong. Odds are, we would all have died anyway. But sometimes . . .'

'I know,' said Constance, 'I understand.'

She leaned forward and put a comforting hand on top of his. And as she touched him, a moment of electricity sparked between them. Their eyes met, wide and startled, and their hearts were suddenly beating faster in their breasts. They looked deep into each other's eyes and saw heaven there, waiting for them. Then Constance jerked her hand away, and everything was back to normal again. For a moment they just sat in silence, looking at anything but each other, while their breathing and heartbeats returned to normal. Robert risked a glance at Constance, and saw the remains of a hot red flush in her face. He wondered if he was blushing too. His cheeks felt uncomfortably hot.

'So, how are preparations going for your wedding to the Deathstalker?' he said finally, a little more heavily than he'd intended.

'Very well, thank you for asking,' said Constance, her voice quite composed. 'It's due to take place six months from now. Barring any . . . complications.'

'Of course,' said Robert. 'You never know when complications are going to arise. You don't love him, do you?'

'No,' said Constance, 'I don't love him.'

'Good,' said Robert. Their eyes met again, and this time they smiled at each other.

Finlay was still in his quarters under the Arenas when he heard an urgent knocking at his door. He frowned. For someone who was supposed to be in hiding, he was getting a hell of a lot of visitors. He strapped on his sword belt and holster, and went carefully over to the door. He really should have invested in a spyhole or a hidden camera. He listened for a moment, couldn't hear anything and finally opened the door just a crack. A familiar voice said his name, and then he was pushed back as the weight of the body leaning against the door forced it open. His hand started towards his gun, and then he grabbed hold of Evangeline as she fell towards him, only just in time to stop her hitting the floor. She was wrapped in a long crimson sheet, part of it bulked into a large unwieldy parcel under one arm. Her face was slack with shock and exhaustion, and spattered with recently dried blood.

Finlay tried to question her, but all she could do was murmur his name, over and over again. She was breathing hard, and her eyes weren't tracking properly, and she clung to him with desperate strength. Finlay gave up trying to get any sense out of her, and got her over to the bed, but she would only sit on the edge, not lie down. Her eyes were red and puffy from crying, and all she wanted to do was hold him. He hugged her in return, trying to reassure her with his presence and calm tone.

'What is it, love? What's happened? You're safe here, you're all right now. What have you got under your arm?'

She still wouldn't or couldn't answer him. He slowly eased out of her grasp, murmuring soothingly all the while, and began unwrapping the bedsheet that enveloped her. And it was only then that he discovered she was naked underneath, apart from her panties, and splashed with a great deal of sticky blood. He checked her quickly for cuts and wounds, and was only partly reassured to find that none of the blood was hers. He eased the bundle out from under her arm, and unwrapped that. Something small and hard fell out on to the floor. It was the hilt of the monofilament knife she'd asked him to get for her. He removed the sheet completely, and discovered two glass cases containing two severed but still living heads. He was so startled he almost dropped them, but managed to fumble them safely to the floor. Their mouths were moving, but he couldn't hear anything. He turned back to Evangeline, and she giggled almost hysterically at the look on his face. She finally controlled herself with an effort, and spoke to him almost in a whisper.

'The man is Professor Wax. I don't know him. The woman is Penny DeCarlo, my oldest friend. My father was holding them prisoner. I rescued them.'

'Your father? You've been to see Gregor Shreck? On your own? What happened? Where did all this blood come from?'

'We talked. And afterwards . . . things got rough.'

'Why didn't you tell me you were going?'

'I couldn't! Gregor had been threatening me, saying he'd kill Penny if I didn't go back to him. He insisted that I go alone. So I went there, to Tower Shreck, into the belly of the beast. And I found he'd . . . done that, to Penny. So I made Gregor give them both up, and I took them away.'

'How the hell did you get him to part with them?'

'I had my monofilament knife, the one you gave me. Such a practical present.' She almost laughed again at the expression on Finlay's face. 'You're not the only one who knows how to fight. I used Gregor as a human shield to get out of the Tower, and then made a run for my gravity sled. A few guards tried to stop me leaving, so I killed them. It was easy. Gregor's people stopped chasing me after a while, so I came here. I didn't know where else to go.'

'Of course you were right to come here, Evie. You'll be safe here. But what happened to your clothes?'

Evangeline gripped his arm fiercely. 'Don't ask me that, Finlay. Don't ever ask me that.'

'All right, I won't. Calm down. Damn, you did a very brave thing, Evie, but you really should have told me. I would have understood. Did he hurt you? Are you injured anywhere? Should I get you a doctor? If Gregor's hurt you, I'll kill the bastard!'

'No,' said Evangeline quickly. 'I'm not hurt. I don't need a doctor, I'm all right. Don't fuss, Finlay. Just . . . let me get my breath back. Now I've freed Penny, Gregor doesn't have any hold over me any more. Everything's going to be all right now.'

'Brave girl,' said Finlay, taking her in his arms again, and kissing her gently on the top of her head. 'My brave girl.'

And then the holoscreen on the wall chimed once, announcing an incoming call. Finlay started to get up to answer it, and Evangeline grabbed his arm with both hands.

'Don't answer it!'

'It's all right, Evie; only a few trusted people know I'm here. I have to answer it, in case it's an emergency.'

He freed himself from her grip, smiled reassuringly at her, got up from the bed and accepted the call. The screen cleared to show the huge flushed face of Gregor Shreck, half covered by a blood-soaked bandage. For a moment he just stared out of the screen, taking in Finlay and Evangeline together. His mouth was trembling and twitching, and his single eye was very bright.

'What do you want, Shreck?' said Finlay. 'And how did you find me here?'

'My people followed Evie all the way home. She thought

she'd lost them. I knew I'd find you both together.' Gregor's voice was strained and high-pitched, but full of venom. 'Told you all about her little adventure at Tower Shreck, has she? But what hasn't she been telling you, eh, Campbell? What about the things she never told you, the secrets she's kept from you all this time? Shall I tell you all about your darling little cloned copy, hmm?'

'I know she's a clone,' said Finlay coldly. 'And I know you murdered the original. We have no secrets, Evangeline and I.'

'Oh, but you do, you do, dear boy. I guarantee it. I'll bet she never told you how much I loved her, or exactly how I loved her. Oh, I loved her dearly and well and very often. I loved every inch of her body. In fact, I took her to my bed and loved her morning, noon and night, as hard as I could. And she loved it.'

'No!' said Evangeline. 'No!'

'You bastard!' screamed Finlay, his face bright red with rage. 'You bastard!'

'I bedded her, Campbell, long before you ever did. She was Daddy's girl, and did whatever Daddy told her to do. And we did all kinds of things. Things she's probably never done for you. She'll always be mine, Campbell, because she was mine first. That's what I had her made for. I'm going to take her back from you, and there's nothing you can do to stop me.'

'I'll kill you!' said Finlay, fighting for breath against the pain in his chest. 'I'll kill you! Kill you!'

Gregor laughed at him, and Finlay drew his gun and shot out the viewscreen. Gregor's face shattered, and the screen fell in pieces to the floor. Smoke rose from the machine's workings. After that it was very quiet, apart from Evangeline who was sobbing on the bed. Finlay stood there, the gun still in his hand, trying to think what to do next, but Gregor's hateful words filled his head to the exclusion of everything else. He never doubted the truth of them. It was the kind of thing Gregor Shreck would do. He finally put away the gun, and turned slowly to look at Evangeline. She stopped her tears by an effort of will, and looked back at him.

'Why didn't you tell me?' said Finlay.

'Because I knew you'd react like this. Because I knew you'd be angry and hurt. Because I thought if you knew . . . you might leave me. That you wouldn't feel the same about me any more.'

'You never . . . cared for Gregor?'

'Of course not! I was his property! I had no choice. I either did what he said, or he'd kill me, and make another clone who would. I did what I had to, to survive.'

'I'm going to kill him,' said Finlay. 'There aren't enough guards in this world to keep me from him. You stay here, and lock the door after me. Don't open it till I come back. And maybe I'll bring you back Gregor's head wrapped in a bedsheet.'

'No, Finlay! He'll be expecting you to go straight there! That's why he contacted you, told you what he did. It has to be a trap!'

'Of course it's a trap. But that won't stop me.'

'You can't just kill him, Finlay. It isn't like the old days, during the rebellion, when you had the protection of the underground. The war is over; they'd call it murder, and no one would speak for you. They'd hang you as a common killer.'

'Let them try,' said Finlay. 'Evie, how could you keep something like this from me? We swore we'd have no secrets between us. How could you not tell me something as important as this? Didn't you trust me?'

'Oh, you're a fine one to talk about keeping secrets, Finlay Campbell! Are you ever going to tell Julian the truth? That the man he admires so much is the same Masked Gladiator who killed his brother Auric?'

'That's different!' said Finlay. Then he stopped, as he heard a strained noise behind him. He looked round, and there, standing in the open doorway, was Julian Skye. Finlay looked at his face, and didn't need to ask how much Julian had heard. The young esper's face was bone-white, but his dark eyes were fixed steadily on Finlay's.

'Julian . . .'

'You should have told me, Finlay. When we first met, you should have told me. How could you do such a thing?'

'I killed a lot of people in the Arena,' said Finlay, 'while I

428

was the second Masked Gladiator. Auric was just one of them. I never knew he was your brother till after we'd become friends. And I never told you then, because I knew how much it would hurt you.'

'And the Masked Gladiator I killed, during the rebellion?'

'That was Georg McCrackin, the first man to wear the mask. He was my teacher. I inherited the role from him.'

'So I killed an innocent man.'

'He stood with the Empress! He would never have surrendered. He would have killed you.'

'An innocent man. You bloody bastard! Did you think it was funny? Did you have a good laugh, at the brother of the man you murdered trotting at your heels like a puppy?'

'No, Julian! It was never like that!'

'I have to think about this. I'm going away for a while. I don't want you to call me. I'll contact you, when I've decided what I'm going to do. When I've decided whether or not I'm going to kill you.'

He turned and left, and Finlay wanted to run after him, but didn't. There was nothing he could say now that wouldn't only make things worse. He stood silent, in the middle of his room, in the ruins of his world. In the space of a few minutes, he'd lost his friend and perhaps his love, the only things that really mattered to him. He wanted to go out and kill Gregor, and seek solace in slaughter, but he couldn't. Not now, with so many matters left unresolved. He went back to the bed, sat down beside Evangeline and took her in his arms and comforted her as best he could.

And let the bloody, red rage simmer in his heart.

In the best suite that the best hotel in the Parade of the Endless had to offer, BB Chojiro took a short rest between official engagements, reclining peacefully on the huge bed while Cardinal Brendan brought her up to date on the latest news. BB enjoyed a little luxury now and again, and saw no point in denying herself just to save her Clan a few pennies. Besides, the people she had to deal with expected to see and meet her in the same kind of surroundings they enjoyed. It was necessary they perceive her as at least their equal, or they wouldn't strike deals with her. She realized that Brendan had stopped talking, and turned her head lazily on the pillow to look at him.

'Yes? Is there a problem?'

'No. I was just wondering . . . how did you get to be the official spokesperson for Blue Block? I'd never even heard of you, before the rebellion.'

BB Chojiro smiled. 'I am spokesperson because Blue Block wants it that way. Which is really all you need to know. But, vanity, vanity, thy name is woman, so it pleases me to inform you that I am the end result of extensive planning and programming, designed for just this task. I am the voice of Blue Block. My thoughts are those that Blue Block gave me.'

'But then . . . how much of you is left?' said Brendan. 'I mean, the real you, the original BB Chojiro?'

'Ah,' said BB. 'You'd be surprised. Let's just say, more than you'd think. But it doesn't matter. Their interests are mine, and vice versa.'

'But why—'

'Did they choose me, out of all the subjects at their command? They've never told me. Genetics, presumably. They had my parents killed when I was very young, and took me away from my Clan, so that I would have no ties or loyalties to anyone but them. I never even met the brothers and sisters of my Clan till I was of adult age. I never knew a Family, or what it could be, so I can't honestly say I lost anything. Blue Block is my father and mother, and all my brothers and sisters too. They made me what I am today.'

'And who are they?' said Brendan. 'I've only ever been on the edges. The mysteries are closed to me. Who is this *they* that run everything?'

'Ah,' said BB, smiling up at the ceiling, 'wouldn't you like to know?'

Cardinal Brendan sighed quietly. He should have known better than to expect a straight answer from BB Chojiro. 'So, where are we going next?' he asked, moving on to the safer ground of the day's business. 'We've been through everyone on my list, but you had me leave the rest of the evening free.'

'So I did,' said BB. 'I'm not exactly sure what's going to happen now. Several trains of event have been set in motion. The only certainty is that this evening, several important members of Blue Block will be journeying here, to discuss forming an alliance with Jack Random.'

'What? You have got to be kidding! The professional rebel himself? Democracy's darling? He hates the aristocracy, and has growing suspicions about Blue Block. What could he possibly have in common with us?'

'Simple. He's a Chojiro.'

Brendan just stared at her for a moment. 'Jack Random is a *Chojiro*?'

'You didn't really think his name was Random, did you? His mother was a part of my Clan. His father was no one important. What matters is that Jack has blood connections to a major Family, and that he feels more isolated than at any other time in his life. And however far we stray, Family is still Family. He used to have his cause to cling to, but now that's gone. He used to be a leader, but now he's just another politician. His dreams betrayed him by coming true. If we could persuade him to join with us, the legendary professional rebel and hero, the man who made the deal with Blue Block . . .'

'It's risky,' said Brendan. 'Too risky. He may be politically isolated at the moment, but he's still a man of power and influence. And on top of all that, he's one of the Maze people. Whatever they are.'

'They are the future,' said BB. 'They are the key to future influence and power. Whoever controls them, or can remove them from the playing field, will control the fate of humanity. However, the Maze people may be powerful, but they all have their weaknesses. Jack Random will succumb to the comforts of Family, of belonging. Ruby Journey needs action, and a direction if not a cause; she's incapable of running her own life, and needs to feel needed. Owen Deathstalker and Hazel d'Ark . . . are a problem. Together they are greater than the sum of their parts, so it is in our best interests to separate them, turn them against each other. Set his idealism against her practicality, and they might well destroy each other.'

'Whatever happens, we have to prevent the forthcoming marriage between Owen and Constance Wolfe,' said

Brendan. 'Owen as Emperor, even just a constitutional Emperor, is unthinkable.'

'Not necessarily,' said BB, stretching languidly. 'If we can't destroy him, we can always manipulate him. More importantly, we have to remove Finlay Campbell from the board. It's vital that Robert be installed unopposed as the Campbell.'

'I've set things in motion,' said Brendan. 'All we have to do is wait. But I don't see that Robert's going to be any improvement as the Campbell. The word is he has no love for aristocrats in general, and Blue Block in particular.'

'But he was Blue Block, for a time, and once you are ours, you are ours for ever. He left before the real programming could begin, but the standard mental commands were implanted in his subconscious. When the time comes, he'll do the right thing. He won't be able to help himself.'

The viewscreen on the wall chimed politely, and Brendan went to answer it. Julian Skye's gaunt face appeared on the screen, and BB quickly lay down again, to ensure Julian couldn't see her. He looked tired, and his eyes were suspiciously puffy as he glared out of the screen at Brendan.

'I want to speak to BB. Now.'

'I'm sorry, Julian. I told you; she doesn't want to talk to you. Not until you've proved your love and your loyalty to her.'

'I can deliver Finlay Campbell. If that's what she wants.'

'That's good news, Julian. I'm sure BB will be very glad to hear that. How soon—'

'Very soon. But I'll only deliver him to BB. In person.'

'I'm sure that can be arranged. Contact me again, when you're ready to make the delivery, and I'll give you a time and place. BB will be there, waiting for you.'

'Tell her . . . tell her I love her.'

'Of course I will. You're doing the right thing, Julian. Take care with Finlay, he's—'

But Julian had already broken contact. Brendan stared at the blank screen, and then turned to BB as she got up off the bed and came over to join him.

'Well,' said Brendan. 'That was unexpected. I hadn't foreseen complete and utter capitulation for days yet.'

'He loves me,' said BB. 'My dear, sweet, vulnerable Julian. He always said he'd do anything for me.'

'Even betray his friends?'

'Of course. What are friends for?'

'But can we trust him to keep his word? You betrayed him to the torturers. You stand for everything he hates.'

'None of that matters. He belongs to me. I made him love me, using all of Blue Block's most subtle techniques. It should have been his more malleable older brother, Auric. He would have been far more useful to us. But he insisted on fighting that stupid duel in the Arena, and was lost. Julian was second choice, but to be fair, he's come much further on his own than I ever thought he would. Another official hero of the rebellion could be of great use to us . . . If he can deliver Finlay Campbell, dead or alive, I will personally take Julian to Blue Block and oversee his programming myself.'

'Do you really think he'd kill his closest friend? His saviour? Even for you?'

'Probably not. More likely he'll bring me Finlay alive but helpless, and make all kinds of conditions before his conscience will allow him to hand Finlay over. It doesn't matter. One way or another, we'll get what we want.'

'Poor Julian,' said Brendan, smiling. 'Already out of his depth and sinking fast. Almost makes you feel sorry for him, doesn't it?'

BB looked at him coolly. 'Are you asking if I have any feelings for him? Of course I do. I'm only human, after all.'

'Really?' said Brendan. 'I thought you were Blue Block.'

Evangeline sat stiffly on the edge of the bed in Finlay's quarters, still wrapped in her bedsheet. Finlay was sitting in a chair opposite her, scowling darkly. They'd been trying to talk, but not getting anywhere. Talking had never been what Finlay did best. The back-up viewscreen chimed suddenly, and Finlay had to think hard for a moment to remember where it was. He'd never had to use it before. He finally found the small screen in the headboard of the bed, and accepted the call. Secretly, he was glad of the interruption. Julian Skye's face appeared on the small screen, and Finlay gave a small sound of relief.

'Julian! I was worried. How are you? Are you all right? Listen—'

'We need to talk, Finlay.'

'Of course we do! Look, I can't leave Evie just now. Why don't you—'

'We have to talk now, Finlay. Come over to my town house. I can't leave; I can't risk being seen. You have to come here. It's important. My old esper contacts have turned up a connection between Gregor Shreck and the Chojiros. They're working with Blue Block on some kind of scheme to undermine or maybe even destroy Parliament. I tried to contact Jack Random, but no one knows where he is. You're the only other person I can trust with this.'

'Yeah; right. Shit, some days everything happens at once. All right, stay where you are. I'll be with you as soon as I can.'

'Sure, Finlay. See you.'

The screen went dead. Finlay turned away to see Evangeline looking at him in disbelief. 'You're not seriously thinking of going out and leaving me, are you?'

'I have to,' said Finlay. 'I need to talk to him, to explain . . . you saw the state of him when he left. And he looks terrible. I'm worried he might do something stupid. I won't be long.'

'What about me? Don't I matter? I don't want to be left alone, Finlay!'

'I'll be back as soon as I can.'

'Finlay!'

'Evie, I have to do this. The Chojiro stuff might be nothing, just an excuse to reach out to me, but I can't afford to assume that. If he's right, I've got to contact a whole bunch of people . . . Evie, you know I wouldn't leave you unless I had to.'

'You're always leaving me, Finlay. Rushing off to kill someone, to be the hero one more time. It's always about what you need. What about what I need?'

'You're safe here. No one can get to you, not past Arena security. I have to go. This is important.'

'And I'm not?'

'I didn't say that!'

'If it's so important, I'm coming with you.'

'Evie, you can't. You're in no condition to go anywhere. And I think Julian and I need to be alone for this. You get some rest. I'll be back soon, I promise.'

'Finlay, if you leave me now, I won't be here when you get back. I mean it.'

He left anyway, as both of them had known he would. Finlay Campbell never could turn down a call to action.

Back in his old home once again, Julian Skye turned away from the deactivated viewscreen. He felt cold and empty and very tired. He couldn't believe that so much had happened in so short a time. Only a few days ago, his life had made sense. It had been ordered, secure, even routine. Now everything he'd ever cared for was gone. Everything but BB Chojiro. But there wasn't time to feel sad, or sorry. There were things he had to do, preparations that had to be made, before Finlay arrived.

Julian moved over to the low wooden table by the fire, and picked up the small silver casket waiting there. Its lid held the Family crest. His father had used it as a snuff box. Julian had used it for other purposes, back in his rebel days. He opened the casket and took out a single black capsule, almost as big as his fingernail. He balanced it in his hand for a moment, considering its surprising weight, and then went looking for a glass of wine. Something that size was going to be hard to swallow, and he'd always had trouble with pills. But he managed it eventually, with the aid of a glass and a half of wine, and a certain amount of strain. It felt decidedly uncomfortable going down, but he was beyond caring about things like that. It was necessary, so he did it.

A single black capsule. Just a little something to hold him together while he talked with BB Chojiro. He hoped he wouldn't need it, but there was always the chance he would.

He went and sat down in the parlour, and waited for Finlay to arrive. It took just under an hour, and when the doorbell rang, Julian was still sitting there. He went to answer the door himself. He'd given the servants the rest of the evening off. He didn't want any witnesses. He opened the front door to Finlay, and the two of them nodded awkwardly to each other. Julian led the way back to his parlour. They sat down on facing chairs before the banked fire, and looked at each other.

'I never meant you to find out,' said Finlay. 'I knew it would hurt you.'

'You killed my brother Auric.'

'Yes, I did. I killed a lot of people fighting in the Arenas.'

'He fought well. You could have just wounded him. The crowd would have turned up their thumbs for him.'

'He fought too well. He'd had armour implanted under his skin, servo-mechanisms in his muscles. I really thought he was going to kill me. I stopped him with a sword-thrust to the only part of him that wasn't armoured; his eye.'

'You were the Masked Gladiator. Undefeated Champion of the Arena. You could have found a way to defeat him without killing him, if you'd wanted to.'

'Maybe, I don't know. There isn't time to think about things like that in the Arena. It's kill or be killed. Your brother knew that.'

'Auric. His name was Auric.'

'What do you want me to say, Julian? That I'm sorry? All right; I'm sorry I killed your brother Auric. But you and I killed a lot of people in the rebellion; especially in the street fighting at the end. Some of them just guards or soldiers, doing their job, their duty as they saw it. They were all someone's brother. I'm sorry for the pain I've caused you, Julian. But there's nothing I can do about it.'

'I know,' said Julian. 'I'm sorry, too. But sometimes, sorry isn't enough.'

He reached out with his esp, and shut down Finlay's mind. The Campbell toppled forward from his chair, and lay still on the carpet. Julian stood up and looked down at his friend's body, and did his best to feel nothing at all. The door to his parlour opened, and three operatives from Blue Block came in, from where they'd been waiting in the next room. The leader looked down at Finlay's still form.

'Is he dead?'

'No,' said Julian, 'just sleeping. He won't wake up till my esp wakes him, and by then we'll be with BB Chojiro. Pick him up and carry him out. And treat him courteously. He was a great man, once.'

The three operatives from Blue Block dropped Finlay's unconscious body on to the floor at BB Chojiro's feet. He lay still, barely breathing, his sword belt and holster gone, one arm falling limply away from his body as though outstretched in supplication to BB. She studied his body for a moment, then looked up to smile at Julian Skye, who stood a little to one side. He didn't smile back, but nodded to her.

'Hello, BB. It's been a while, hasn't it? I like your suite; very airy. I brought you a present. A little something.'

'Hello, Julian. It's good to see you again. You always were very generous to me. I hope you had no trouble getting to see me.'

'I could have lived without the strip-search and the probing fingers, but I can understand your need for security. You have a lot of enemies these days, BB.'

'Successful people always do. You're looking very pale, Julian, almost haggard. Have you been looking after yourself properly?'

'I've not been well. The rebellion took a lot out of me. It'll pass.'

'Good. I've seen all your holo shows. Very dramatic. I understand you're quite the heart-throb these days.'

'Oh, sure. I even have an official fan club. I can get you an autographed photo, if you like. I always knew I had it in me to be a star.'

'So,' said BB. 'Is there anyone . . . special in your life, at present?'

'No,' said Julian. 'You know there isn't. There's only ever been you, BB. You ruined me for anyone else. That's why I'm here, why I brought you Finlay. To show the depths of my feelings for you.'

'Dear Julian. There's never been anyone but you in my life either. I never wanted anyone else. We belong together.'

'Get rid of the shadows,' said Julian, indicating the three Blue Block operatives hovering silently in the background. 'We don't need an audience.'

BB gestured at them, and the three faceless men nodded

and left, closing the door quietly behind them. BB and Julian stood looking at each other, over Finlay's unconscious body. They gazed into each other's eyes, and there was a yearning look in both of their faces that might or might not have been real.

'You're so beautiful,' said Julian. 'You're all I ever wanted. I would have laid down my life for you.'

'Why are you here, Julian?' said BB, her voice very small and very quiet. 'After all the terrible things I did to you?'

'I don't know. I'm still not sure whether I ought to kiss you or kill you. You hurt me, BB. I trusted you, and you ripped the heart right out of me.'

'I know. I had no choice. I've belonged to Blue Block since I was a small child. They were my life, my everything. I could no more reject their programming than I could choose to stop breathing. I loved you, but they made me give you up. I cried for days.'

'Did you, BB? Did you really? I cried in the interrogation cells, but no one came to wipe away my tears. I haven't cried since. I don't think I have it in me any more.'

'Why are you here, Julian? What do you want from me?'

'I had to come. And you know what I want. I want things to be the way they used to be. When we were in love, and so happy, and we thought we'd spend the rest of our lives together.'

'I want that too, Julian. Whoever and whatever I've been, there's always been someone in me who loved you. We can be together again, now you've proved your love. I never doubted you, but Blue Block insisted. I never stopped loving you, Julian. No one ever touched my heart like you did. Blue Block won't stand between us this time. They want us to be together. They've planned a great future for us. We can marry, and you'll become part of Clan Chojiro. We'll forget the past, and the pain, and nothing will ever part us. I'll be yours for ever, and you'll be mine. It's not so bad, being in Blue Block. We can be happy together. All it will take is one last proof of your feelings. All you have to do, for Blue Block, for me, is kill our enemy, Finlay Campbell.'

Julian looked at her, and then looked down at the unconscious body on the floor between them. 'I always thought it might come to that – choose between my love for you, and my love for my friend. That's why you wanted him here. You never cared about him; this was always just about me. And I wondered what I was going to do when we finally got to this point. I never stopped loving you, BB. You were my first love and my first woman, and nothing can change that. But I've been through a lot since we last met. I see things more clearly now. And I know you'd say whatever it took to get me to do what you want. Truth and lies are all the same to you, because the only thing in your life that really matters to you is Blue Block. They own you, body and soul. It's not your fault, not really. But you don't love me. You never did. I don't think you have it in you.'

'You're wrong, Julian, you're so wrong. There's more to me than just my programming.' There were tears glistening in her eyes now. 'Blue Block shaped my mind, but my heart is still my own. We can be happy together. We can.'

'No. If you really loved me, you wouldn't ask me to kill my friend.'

'Then don't,' said BB. 'Let him live. You're more important to me than the death of an enemy.'

She held out her arms to him, and he stumbled forward into them. They clung together, like two drowning people caught in the midst of rapids that threatened to tear them apart. Julian hugged her to him, his head resting on top of hers. He breathed in the subtle scent of her hair; she was so soft and wonderful in his arms. And then BB drew the long thin dagger hidden in her sleeve, and thrust it expertly between his ribs. He cried out in shock and pain, his arms closing round her like a vice. BB relaxed in his dying embrace, and smiled into his face, so close to hers.

'Sorry, my darling. But you were always too dangerous to be allowed to run free. If you had only bound yourself to me, forsaking all others, and allowed me to rein you to Blue Block, we could have been happy together. But I always suspected you were too honourable a man for that. Poor Julian; didn't you know there's no honour left in the world you helped to make?'

Julian smiled at her, and his teeth were red with blood. He was breathing harshly now, and a mist of fine red droplets sprayed her face with his every breath, speckling BB's face with horrid freckles. She didn't flinch. Julian still held her tightly, but she knew the strength would go out of his arms soon. Julian lowered his face to hers. He wanted to be sure she heard what he had to say.

'I knew . . . there was no honour in you, BB. *Wake up, Finlay.*'

He reached out to Finlay with his esp, and the body on the floor was suddenly wide awake again. Finlay surged to his feet, reaching for a sword at his side that wasn't there any more. He glared about him, saw Julian holding BB, and then saw the knife in his side.

'Julian; what . . .'

'You're in Tower Chojiro,' Julian said painfully. 'Get out of here, Finlay. I'm holding the doors shut with my esp, to keep the guards out. You'll have to use the window.'

He flexed his mind, and the steelglass window exploded outwards, leaving a wide opening through which a wind blew, cold as death. Finlay started towards Julian.

'I'm not leaving you here! You're hurt!'

'I'm dying, Finlay! I forgive you everything. You were always my friend. Now get the hell out of here. I've got a bomb in my belly.'

BB gasped, and tried to pull free of him, but his arms held her like bars of iron. Finlay saw the truth in the dying man's face, and threw himself out of the shattered window. BB kicked and struggled, screaming for help. Julian held her to him, their bodies pressed together. He was laughing and crying as he sent the esp signal to the black capsule he'd swallowed earlier.

When the bomb went off, it killed them both instantly, and blew out the whole top floor of Tower Chojiro.

Finlay Campbell didn't know he was on the top floor of Tower Chojiro, thirty storeys up, until after he'd jumped through the great hole in the window. He fell the first few storeys in a state of shock, and then the top floor exploded, snapping him out of it. All the windows blew out at once, and thick black smoke billowed from where they had been. Sharp-edged steelglass shrapnel flew past him, cutting him here and there, as he reached down and struggled to pull back the heel of his right boot. Inside was the coil of superstrong climbing wire he'd used in his old assassin days, during the rebellion. He'd always believed in being prepared. Guards might take your sword and gun, but they rarely took your boots till after you were dead. Julian knew about the boot heel. Finlay had told him enough stories about it. Julian . . . Julian was dead. Finlay squeezed his eyes shut for a moment, and then pushed the thought aside. He'd mourn later, when he had time. Assuming there was a later.

He threw the grapnel on the end of the wire at the side of the Tower, and it snagged on an ornamental outcropping. He wrapped the other end of the line around both his fists, and braced himself. The line snapped taut, straining his arms and biting deep enough into his hands to draw blood. Finlay gritted his teeth, and used the remaining momentum to swing him into the side of the Tower. A moment later he was clinging to the wall like an old friend, flexing his aching hands one at a time, and trying to get his breath back. He couldn't break his way in, all the windows were steelglass, so he'd have to climb the rest of the way down. He looked down cautiously, and counted twenty-one storeys. He shook his head slowly. He was getting too old for this shit.

It took him over an hour to reach the ground, descending carefully foot by foot, avoiding the notice of the Tower guards. Luckily the explosion had taken out the Tower's exterior sensors, and the guards were all inside, trying to put out the fire on what was left of the top floor. Finlay dropped the last few feet, hitting the ground hard. The solid support felt good under his feet. He looked back up the way he'd come. The top of Tower Chojiro was lost in smoke and flames now – Julian's funeral pyre. Finlay still wasn't sure exactly what had happened, but he could guess. He'd always known BB Chojiro would be the death of Julian.

Finlay sighed, and decided the time had come to kill Gregor Shreck. He might as well; everything he cared about had been taken from him. He'd lost his closest friend. He'd lost all hope of contact with Adrienne and the children. And he'd lost Evangeline, too, by walking out on her when she needed him the most. No; he was alone now, and free to do what he should have done a long time ago. The law wouldn't understand. Nor would his former friends and comrades in the rebellion. They'd call him a killer, a renegade, and band together to hunt him down. He knew that. But none of that mattered. All that was left now was to punish Gregor Shreck for all the pain and horror he was responsible for. Finlay nodded once, and then strode away from the burning Tower.

Gregor should have known: the most dangerous man of all is the man with nothing left to lose.

He'd never given up his weapons when he was made to retire as a rebel assassin. He'd always thought he might need them again some day. Just in case the new order didn't work out. He stashed them in a secure lock-up in a part of the city where no one asked questions, and kept their existence a secret. Even Evangeline didn't know about them. She would never have approved. A taxi took Finlay to them in under half an hour. He stopped the driver well short of the destination, and tipped him enough not to remember who his fare had been. Finlay walked the rest of the way with a curiously light heart. For the first time in years, he had no complications in his life. His way was clear and open.

He stopped before the plain steel door and carefully checked that all his hidden tell-tales were still secure. None of them had been triggered – his secret was still safe. He opened the locking system with his thumbprint and voice code, and nodded, satisfied, to see all his old friends just where he'd left them. Blades, axes, energy guns, projectile weapons, grenades, and all the other useful little items he'd acquired during his time as an assassin. There was enough firepower here to take out a small army, and that was just what he intended to do.

He put on his full body armour first. He didn't usually bother with that, but he was determined not to die until he'd reached Gregor Shreck. Next came a force-shield bracelet around his left wrist, and a sword belt went round his waist. The weight of the sword on his hip was reassuring, like coming home. On his other hip, he placed a holster carrying a fully charged disrupter. He slipped a projectile pistol into the back of his belt. He had something special in mind for that. Finally, two bandoliers of assorted grenades, shrapnel and concussion and incendiary devices, crossed his chest and back. Finlay stamped back and forth about the lock-up for a while, getting used to the new weight. He was carrying a lot more than he usually cared to, but the odds were he was going to need all of it. His plan was very simple: he was going to walk in the front door of Tower Shreck, and kill everyone he saw until he got to Gregor Shreck.

And that was what he did. As a plan, it worked surprisingly well. The security in Tower Shreck, as in most of the pastel towers, was mainly concerned with warding off attacks from the air, from gravity sleds, or on the ground, by massive armed forces. They weren't prepared for a single, cold-eyed, cold-hearted killer who no longer cared whether he lived or died. Finlay walked up to the guards by the main door, shot the first one in the face and cut the throat of the other. A shaped charge from his bandolier blew the main door in. He tossed a shrapnel grenade into the lobby, waited till it had gone off and the screaming began, and then stalked into the smoke-filled chamber and cut down the few people the grenade hadn't finished off. Finlay dropped an incendiary to start a distracting fire, and made his way up the stairs to the next floor. He wasn't dumb enough to use the elevator.

Guards came running down the stairs, and he killed them all till blood ran off his armour, and dripped steadily from his sword. The guards weren't organized yet; they didn't know what was going on. Finlay made his way steadily up the stairwell, stopping at each floor to toss around grenades and incendiaries. Those who didn't die in the blasts were soon preoccupied with trying to escape the fires and smoke. Sprinkler systems were doing their best, but had never been designed to cope with anything like this. There were always more guards, and Finlay killed them all, except for those with sense enough to turn and run when they saw death coming.

Finlay's sword-arm began to ache, and the blood that dripped from his armour was sometimes his own now, but he didn't care. He was doing what he was born to do, and doing it well. His force shield deflected energy weapons, and in the narrow stairwell the guards could only come at him a few at a time, and that wasn't enough to stop him, not nearly enough. He stepped over the bodies and kept going.

He'd set fires on half the floors of the Tower by now. Thick black smoke was drifting up the stairwell after him. He could hear screaming and panicking and the screeching of alarm sirens, and it was all music to his ears. Let Tower Shreck burn. He wasn't planning on going back down again.

Finally, Gregor ran out of guards. Their impressive-looking armour wasn't much use in close-quarter fighting. It slowed them down too much, and Finlay knew all the weak spots and hidden defects. And with the Tower burning all around them, most of Gregor's guards decided they weren't being paid enough to deal with this madman, and took to their heels. Finlay carried on up the staircase, breathing hard now, and sometimes coughing from the smoke, but not slowing down in the least. He came to the top floor of the Tower, and made his way down the deserted corridor, kicking open doors till he came to the reinforced door that led into Gregor's private chambers. Finlay blew the door in with a small charge, and strode through the smoke into Gregor's blood-red room. Only to find the Shreck wasn't alone.

Gregor was sitting on his huge rose-petal bed, clutching the sheets defensively around him. Half his oversized face was hidden behind a blood-soaked bandage, and Finlay smiled briefly to see it. Evangeline had done well. But standing beside the bed, gun in hand, was a tall, slender figure, dressed all in black to show off his pale skin and delicate features. Valentine Wolfe. Finlay laughed softly, a disturbing, not altogether sane sound. Gregor flinched. Valentine didn't.

'Well, well,' said Finlay. 'It's all my birthdays come at once. The two men I hate most together in one room. There is a God, and he is good.'

'You and I have never had much to do with Him,' said Valentine easily. 'We've always served a much darker master. But your timing is impeccable, as always. I came here to make an alliance with Gregor, on certain delicate issues that needn't concern you, and you choose this very evening to pursue your somewhat delayed vengeance. Well, I'm afraid I can't allow you to interfere, Finlay, so I'm afraid you're going to have to die.'

Finlay laughed, and it was an ugly sound. Gregor whimpered in his bed. Valentine moved forward to stand between him and Finlay. He put away his gun and drew his sword.

'I've heard many tales of your swordsmanship, Campbell. Let's see how good you really are. Man to man, blade to blade; let's finish what we started in Tower Campbell, so long ago. What do you say?'

'I don't have time for this,' said Finlay, and shot Valentine Wolfe with his disrupter. The energy beam punched through Valentine's chest and exploded out of his back, throwing the Wolfe to the floor. Finlay sniffed once, and turned to Gregor, who snarled soundlessly at him. Finlay strode forward, putting away his sword and gun, and grabbed Gregor by the shirt-front with both hands. He hauled the huge, distended body out of bed, and threw Gregor on the floor. Flames from Valentine's burning clothes had set light to some of the surrounding furnishings, and the flames were spreading. The heat and flickering light and shadows added a suitably hellish touch to the proceedings. Finlay looked down at Gregor.

'You hurt Evangeline. You're a murderer and a traitor and a symbol of everything that's corrupt in the Families and in the Empire. The world will smell better when you're gone. Don't waste my time with threats or warnings. Your guards aren't coming, and I don't care what happens after I'm through with you. All that matters is that you suffer as you made my Evie suffer. I'm going to make you hurt so bad that when you finally die and get to Hell, the fires of the Pit will seem like a release.'

He reached around his back and pulled the projectile weapon out from under his belt. He'd saved it especially for this moment. It was a simple handgun, with eight bullets. He took aim at Gregor's left knee, and pulled the trigger. The kneecap shattered immediately under the bullet's impact, and Gregor screamed shrilly. He'd never known there could be such pain. He clutched at his bloody leg with both fat hands, as though they could force the kneecap back together. Finlay aimed carefully, and shot out the other kneecap with his second bullet. Gregor screamed again, flailing his arms, as though appealing for help that wasn't there. Finlay raised the gun, and shot out Gregor's left elbow. Blood and splintered bone flew on the air, and the forearm swung back and forth at an unnatural angle. Finlay fired again, taking out the right elbow, and the right forearm was almost torn away by the impact.

Gregor was screaming steadily now, barely stopping to suck in new breath between each scream. His eyes bulged, and his mouth stretched impossibly wide. Finlay took his time aiming, and shot Gregor in his grossly distended stomach, just above the navel. This time the impact had a soft, muffled sound. Gregor howled like an animal. Finlay shot him in the groin, and blood spurted high up into the air. Gregor screamed and howled his sanity away, and still couldn't hide from the awful, horrible pain.

Finlay stood and listened to the Shreck scream for a while, smiling his death's-head grin. Half the chamber was on fire now. He looked around for Valentine, but there was no sign of the body anywhere. The Wolfe must have crawled away to die. He wouldn't get far, with half his chest shot away. Finlay turned back to Gregor, still screaming like a soul newly damned to Hell.

'This is for you, Evie,' Finlay murmured, and put a bullet through each of Gregor's eyes, blowing the back of his head away.

Finlay Campbell lowered the empty gun, and looked down on the dead body of his enemy. It comforted him. The flames were all around him now, and no doubt sweeping through all the floors below. There were no windows in Gregor's private quarters, no way out. He could hear explosions everywhere. The Tower wouldn't last much longer. Finlay looked calmly around him.

And wondered what he would do next.

CHAPTER SIX

Cry Havoc

It was all going to hell in a handcart. The Empire, dangerously weakened in its transitional state between the new and
old orders, found itself under attack from all sides at once.
All the old enemies came howling out of the dark, falling like
wolves on the undefended colonies out on the Rim. A
massive fleet of Shub starships, manned by unliving crews,
burst out of the Forbidden Sector, brushing aside the single
quarantining starcruiser, and laid waste every inhabited
planet in its path. Many had the new alien-derived stardrive,
making them effectively unstoppable by anything save the
few remaining E-class ships in the Imperial Fleet.

The great golden ships of the Hadenmen appeared out of
nowhere, striking viciously at unsuspecting planets all along
the Rim. The augmented men had finally begun their second
great Crusade of the Genetic Church, determined to remake
humanity in their own biomechanical image. It soon became
clear that they were emerging from hidden bases deep
beneath the surfaces of uninhabited worlds. The Hadenmen
had established secret Nests all across the Empire, mindful
not to place all their eggs in one fragile basket again. The
Deathstalker's destruction of Brahmin II had proved them
right, and spurred on by the elimination of what should have
been their second homeworld, all the Hadenmen Nests opened at once, and the huge, gleaming ships of feared legend
ranged the long night again, vast and awful, bringing death
and destruction and an end worse than death.

The insect ships were back too. Gliding silently out of the
dark like huge sticky balls of compacted webbing, driven by
unknown forces they passed unaffected through planetary
defences and discharged crawling armies of killer insects of

all shapes and sizes. Whole cities were eaten alive, and nothing was left behind save bare bones from which every last trace of meat had been gnawed. They made no threats, issued no demands, could not be talked to or warned off. They just descended from the skies, a silent horror, on everything that lived, until either they were entirely destroyed or their victims were. Soon there were whole planets out on the Rim covered with scuttling, seething insects, crawling blindly through the ruins of what had once been human cities.

The Empire wasted remarkably little time springing to its own defence. There were those of the old order more than ready to shake a finger and say *I told you so*, but they were told to shut up and join the fight, or get the hell out of the way. Parliament organized Golgotha into one great communications and tactical centre, alerted all planets and colonies in the path of danger and rushed ships, personnel and weapons to defend those not yet fallen or attacked. Luckily, though the rogue AIs of Shub, the Hadenmen and the insects shared a common enemy in humanity, they showed no interest in any form of alliance. They went their own way, chose their own targets and did not cooperate, even when it was clearly in their best interests to do so. But they didn't attack each other either, sticking strictly to their own territories, for the moment.

Planets and colonies fell, one by one, all along the Rim, and the three attacking forces moved steadily inwards, heading for the greater concentrations of humanity and the vulnerable heart of the Empire – Golgotha. Some colonists tried, against all Parliament's wishes and advice, to strike deals with those attacking them. It did no good: Shub agreed to whatever it had to to gain the advantage, and then invaded anyway, showing no mercy to any. The Hadenmen declared their Crusade to be a logical necessity, for the betterment and perfection of humanity, and would not be turned aside. And the insect ships sailed silently overhead, unhearing or uncaring.

General Beckett's devastated Imperial Fleet did what it could, but its capabilities were limited from the first. Only the few surviving E-class ships with the new stardrive were capable of matching the speed and firepower of the huge golden ships and the new Shub attack ships, and they couldn't be everywhere at once. Worlds under attack cried out for help all the time. Beckett sent what was left of his Fleet darting all over the Empire, pulling in every last ship with a crew and working guns, even those patrolling the Darkvoid, and rushed them from one trouble spot to another, but all too often they got there too late to do any real good. Beckett tried splitting up the Fleet, dispatching his most powerful starcruisers to defend those planets in the most immediate danger. But Imperial starcruisers caught on their own were quickly outnumbered and outgunned, and had no choice but to run for their lives, usually heavily damaged. Unnerved by the loss of too many irreplaceable ships, Parliament ordered Beckett to regroup his Fleet and pull them back, to protect the more densely populated inner worlds of the Empire. Everyone else was left to fend for themselves. Whole populations struggled to evacuate their worlds, cramming themselves into the cargo holds of any ship with a working stardrive. Many never reached their destinations. Shub and the Hadenmen and the insect ships showed no mercy. Other populations stood their ground and fought, ready to die rather than give up the worlds they had tamed and cultivated and made their own, through generations of hard work and sacrifice. Not every world fell to the Enemies of Humanity.

The invasion had actually begun to slow when Shub launched its new wave. Vast armadas of new ships made their appearance, without the new stardrive but built from the harvested metal trees of Unseeli, and from these ships issued great armies of Ghost Warriors and Furies, and the deadly biomechanical aliens they had looted from the secret Vaults on Grendel. The huge forces surged inwards, ignoring the incoming fire of opposing armies, trampling over their own fallen to get at the enemy before them. Unstoppable, implacable, they existed only to kill – dead men with computer implants; steel machines in the shape of men. Aliens bioengineered by some forgotten race to be the perfect killing machines. Horror troops. Terror weapons. Just like the insects, they overran humanity's armies, leaving only blood and bone behind. But still humanity resisted, forgetting old animosities and diversions in the face of a common enemy that threatened them all. There were victories as well as losses, but never enough.

The Empire was being invaded on three fronts by its most deadly enemies, and the fighting was spread across worlds already sickened and weakened by the long, bitter fighting of the rebellion. Some just didn't have it in them to fight any more; it was too much to ask of them. There were shortages of everything needed to fight a war, ships and weapons that ought to have stopped the invaders having been used up when humanity fought itself. Shub and the Hadenmen and the insects had chosen their moment well. But humanity fought on, refusing to be beaten. And thanked God that at least the alien Recreated hadn't made an appearance yet. Because there was no one left to watch the Darkvoid.

The people called out for their heroes, the great warriors of the rebellion, but it seemed that most were dead, or nowhere to be found. And the four greatest, the four survivors of the Madness Maze, had been sent off on distant, vital missions, from which they might never return.

The army of the rogue AIs of Shub came to the planet Loki, world of eternal storms, and were invited in by human traitors. Ghost Warriors, human corpses given a new kind of life by tech implants and computer minds, strode unfeeling through the howling winds, side by side with the human turncoats. Outer settlements fell quickly, and the central city of Vidar, overseer of the extensive mining operations, sent out a desperate call for help. There were no ships available, but it was a very valuable planet, so Parliament did the next best thing and sent them two living legends – Jack Random and Ruby Journey.

The *Defiance* dropped out of hyperspace over Loki, hung around just long enough to drop a heavily armoured pinnace and then it was gone again, needed urgently elsewhere. The pinnace, wrapped in four times the usual amount of protective armour, dropped like a stone into the violently swirling atmosphere of Loki. Inside, the two living legends and their reluctant accompanying marine crew clung desperately to every handhold they could find as the roaring winds shook the pinnace like a dog shakes a rat, their crash-webbing swinging them crazily back and forth. The shrieking of the winds outside grew steadily louder as the pinnace plummeted down through the atmosphere, sounding more and more like a whole bunch of seriously pissed-off banshees. There were warning lights flashing all over the place, and everything not actually nailed down flew about the cramped cabin like so much shrapnel. The crew of half a dozen hastily assembled, last-minute volunteer marines hunched their heads down into their shoulders, and did their best to hang on to their last meal. Random tried to look stoic and experienced, while Ruby swung happily back and forth in her webbing, whooping loudly with glee at every new drop and lurch.

'Now this is what I call a ride!' she yelled over the din of the storm and the pinnace's straining engines. 'You'd have to pay good money for a ride like this back in Golgotha's theme parks!'

'Can't you do anything to settle this ship down?' Random yelled to the pilot at the front of the cabin. The floor dropped out from under his feet again, and he clung grimly to a nearby stanchion with both hands. 'I have been in crashing elevators that were less uncomfortable than this!'

'Spoilsport!' said Ruby loudly. 'You're getting old, Random!'

'Shut the hell up and let me concentrate!' the pilot shouted back, entirely unmoved. 'The gyros are useless in weather systems like this; the conditions are changing too suddenly for the computers to cope. The best we can do for now is drop like a brick and hope things improve as we get nearer the surface. Though I wouldn't put money on it. If you don't like the way I fly, there are parachutes under your seats. Of course, the storm lightning will fry you the minute you open the outer hatch, but that's your problem. Thank you for flying with us, and for God's sake try and get some of it in the sick bags.'

'Let the man do his job,' said the massive marine sergeant to Random's left. He was a thirty-year man with a trim muscular form and an impressive number of combat drops to his credit. The kind of man they used to send after Jack

Random, back when he was still the professional rebel. Half the sergeant's face was covered with a spider's-web tattoo, and golden skulls and crossbones hung from both ears. His name tab said *Miller*. 'He's a good pilot. And he's made this drop twice before, which is twice more than anyone else has. He knows what he's doing.'

'I'm glad someone does,' said Ruby from the webbing on Random's right. 'I mean, all right, it's a fun ride down, but normally people who express an interest in visiting Loki of their own free will are immediately grabbed and locked up in a rubber room under industrial-strength sedatives, before they hurt themselves. Loki is the only planet in the Empire with worse weather than Mistworld. They only got colonists to come here by bribing them with massive land grants and more credit than they could spend in a lifetime. If the Empire needed an enema, this world is where they'd stick—'

'We had to come,' said Random. 'We're needed.'

'I was quite happy back on Golgotha,' said Ruby, 'living in a civilized city where the weather does what it's told, chasing down possible Shub connections. But no, Jack bloody Random has to go chasing off to be a hero again, and I get dragged along with him.'

'You know we had to come,' said Random. He looked back at the sergeant. 'You're sure Young Jack Random is down there somewhere?'

'Oh, yes. We've got holovid footage if you want to see it.' Miller's mouth twitched as though he'd just tasted something sour. 'The cameraman got fried before he could broadcast much, but we're pretty sure it's him. I thought you people said he died on Golgotha?'

'He did,' said Random. 'I saw him die. Show us the footage.'

The sergeant made the connection through the pinnace's computers, and the holovid footage played back through Random's and Ruby's comm implants, channelled directly through their optic nerves. The interior of the pinnace cabin vanished, to be replaced by a jerky, uncertain scene of a village in flames. Gusting winds fanned the fires, the low squat buildings burning like bales, and black smoke thick with drifting smuts and cinders billowed through the still streets. There were bodies everywhere, men, women, children, lying in great pools of blood. Not all the bodies were intact.

Ghost Warriors strode stiffly through the inferno, untouched by the intense heat. Dead men walking, their grey flesh rotting on their bones. And at their head, smiling and laughing, a sword dripping blood in one hand, was Young Jack Random. Tall, muscular, handsome, clad in silver armour chased with gold, every inch the hero of legend. A severed human head hung by its blood-slick hair from his other hand. He stopped, suddenly aware of the camera, turned and struck a pose, standing half silhouetted against the crimson flames of a burning house. He smiled widely, showing perfect white teeth. His armour was running with blood, none of it his. He held up the severed head so it faced the camera, its eyes still rolling. Young Jack Random laughed, and gestured with his sword. Two Ghost Warriors moved towards the camera. The scene swung wildly as the cameraman turned to run, but he didn't get far. The footage cut off abruptly, and the pinnace cabin returned. Random and Ruby looked at each other.

'Well?' said Miller. 'Is that him?'

'Oh, yes,' said Ruby. 'That's Young Jack Random, doing what he does best.'

'So what's the story?' demanded the sergeant. 'Officially, the man died a hero, leading the street fighting in the Parade of the Endless. Unofficially, there were all kinds of rumours, because there always are. Some say he was killed by his own side, for betraying the cause. Others say you people killed him, because he wouldn't go along with the deal you struck with Blue Block over the Families. Some say he never died, that he just walked away in disgust from all the killing, but that he'd return again in the hour of the Empire's greatest need. Lot of people liked that one. Word is, when he first appeared on Loki, people flocked to him as a saviour. Until news came back with the few survivors that he was leading an army of Ghost Warriors, and wasn't interested in taking prisoners. So, talk to me. If I'm going to have to face that man dirtside, I have a right to know.'

'Of course you have,' said Random. 'But he's not a man,

he's a machine. A Fury. You can understand why we thought we had to keep that quiet.'

'Jesus,' said Miller. 'But . . . he was a hero. He helped lead the rebellion.'

'Shub was taking the long view,' said Ruby. 'If we won, they wanted one of their own in a position of power and influence. We only found out his true nature by accident. An esper colleague of ours destroyed his body completely. Flattened him out like metal roadkill.'

'So how come he's back here making trouble?'

'It would appear Shub has built another one,' said Random. 'Another me. I suppose I should be flattered. It's psychological warfare, just a little something extra to undermine human morale. Or perhaps a lure to bring me here, for some purpose of their own. When we find the Fury, I'll be sure to put those points to him and see what he has to say for himself. Before I destroy him again.'

'If we can,' said Ruby. 'Furies can take a hell of a lot of punishment. Julian Skye was a powerful esper. There's no guarantee we'll find anyone of his calibre down there.'

'Julian Skye killed the original?' said the sergeant, his face lighting up. 'Damn; I watch his show all the time! He was a real hero!'

'Yes,' said Random. 'One of the few of us who really was. I wish he was here now.'

'Probably too busy doing close-ups,' said Ruby. 'While we get to do the dirty work, as always. What's the matter, Sergeant? Aren't two living legends enough for you?'

'No offence,' said the sergeant, quickly. 'Everyone knows your record. And I'm sure having the real Jack Random to lead them will do wonders for civilian morale.'

The pinnace lurched wildly from side to side as it hit another patch of extreme turbulence. The crash-webbing swung violently back and forth, slamming its human contents against each other. The cabin lights flickered and threatened to go out, but somehow hung on. Thunder rolled almost continuously, lightning crawling the length of the outer hull, and the winds howled like the storm given voice. From up front, the pilot's continuous cursing grew ever more vicious as his hands darted over the controls. The sergeant popped his straps' clasps and swung down out of his webbing, bracing himself against the sudden roll and sway of the drop with two separate handholds.

'I'd better go and see if I can help the pilot. Back in a minute!'

He staggered off down the narrow central aisle, all but throwing himself from stanchion to stanchion till he could drop into the co-pilot's seat and strap himself in next to the pilot. Their lips moved, but Random couldn't hear anything. They'd switched to a private channel on their comm implants, which implied it had to be really bad news. Random looked away, and studied the other marines in their crash-webbing opposite him. They paid him no attention, each lost in their own private rituals of comfort.

One was working a neon rosary, eyes closed, lips moving in silent prayer. Another was trying to tell an endless joke to the man beside him, who was pretending to be asleep. The others were passing a metal flask of something bracing back and forth. They didn't offer any to Random or Ruby. He gestured for her to lean closer, so he could speak practically in her ear. Normally a murmur would have been lost in the din, no matter how close their heads were, but Random and Ruby could always hear each other, no matter what the conditions. Just another gift from the Maze.

'I had been wondering why they chose to send us here, when we were doing so well uncovering Shub connections,' said Random. 'But if that really is Young Jack Random down there, at the head of a Ghost Warrior army, then we could be the only hope Loki has.'

'Maybe,' said Ruby. 'But why us, rather than Owen and Hazel? They're the licensed troubleshooters these days. I can't help wondering if maybe our investigations were bringing us too close to something, or someone, that didn't want to be known about.'

'No,' said Random. 'I would have insisted on this assignment, and they knew it. I need to do this. I wasn't there when my metal duplicate was destroyed. I saw it happen, on the holo footage they confiscated from Toby Shreck, but it wasn't the same. I never got my chance to face him, to test myself against him. I need to see him fall before me, Ruby. I need to tear him apart with my bare hands, for all the terrible things he's done while wearing my face.'

'And not just because, for a while, he seemed a better leader of men than you, and a much more plausible hero?'

'Of course not,' said Random. 'How could you think such a thing of me?'

They smiled dryly at each other, and then the side of the pinnace opposite them exploded. A whole section of the heavily armoured hull disappeared, blown away by a direct hit from a disrupter cannon. All the marines in their crash-webbing were sucked right out of the gaping hole, their security hooks ripped out of the steel floor in a moment. They were gone before they even had time to scream. New alarm sirens sounded, and red warning lights flashed as the cabin atmosphere boiled out of the hull breach, and the temperature plummeted.

The pinnace spun round and round as it fell, spiralling towards the planet's surface as the pilot opened up the engines, struggling to outrun and outmanoeuvre the enemy's tracking systems. The storm howled even louder now, and buffeting winds forced freezing rain into the cabin through the hole. Random and Ruby struggled for air as the cabin pressure dropped, and breathing masks fell down from above them. They tried to reach for the masks, but their crash-webbing was being sucked towards the hull breach, and it was all they could do to hang on to their security straps. Random fought for air, and prayed the webbing's security hooks would hold. There was nothing he or Ruby could do till the ship fell deep enough into the planet's atmosphere to equalize the pressure.

He looked over at Ruby, and saw her struggling to release the belt straps that held her in her webbing. He called out to her, but she wouldn't listen. The straps finally let go, and she lurched out of her webbing on to the slippery steel floor, clinging to a nearby stanchion with fingers like claws. She let go with one hand and grabbed a steel gun locker on the wall. It was almost as wide as it was tall, and had to weigh the best part of a ton. Ruby ripped it off the wall, and with an effort that tore an agonized, silent scream from her, threw the locker in the direction of the hull breach. The hole grabbed the locker in mid-air and sucked it into place, neatly covering the huge gash.

The cabin air pressure quickly re-established itself, and Random fought his way out of his crash-webbing and rushed over to hold the locker in place. Ruby was quickly at his side, blood dripping from her nose, with a hand welder she'd found in a tool box. It took only a few moments to seal the locker securely, and then they both collapsed on to the floor, and sat with their backs propped against the bulkhead. They were both breathing hard, but from effort now rather than asphyxiation.

'Nice throw,' Random said finally.

'Thanks,' said Ruby. 'Nice catch.'

'You stay put and take it easy for a moment. I'll go and have a word with the pilot.'

Ruby nodded wearily, and gingerly massaged her aching shoulder as Random forced himself to his feet and stumbled down the aisle to the front of the pinnace. Neither the pilot nor the sergeant looked round as Random joined them.

'That had to be disrupter cannon,' said Random, with a hand on the back of each of their chairs to steady himself. 'Is there somebody up here with us?'

'I don't think so,' said the sergeant. 'Sensors would have detected another ship, even in all this crap. Must be land-based.'

'Then Shub must have supplied it,' said Random. 'There was nothing in the files to indicate the human traitors had access to that kind of weaponry.'

'Well they do now,' said the pilot. 'And we're a sitting duck up here. It's only the weather and the turbulence that's keeping them from locking on for another shot.'

'Do we have any energy shields?' said Random, leaning over the sergeant's shoulder to try to make sense of the control panels. There seemed to be a hell of a lot of warning lights flashing.

'No. Engines need all their power to fight the storms. And our armour was never intended to cope with energy weapons. Pilot, can you get us down any faster?'

The pilot opened his mouth to say something cutting, and then the steelglass window in front of him exploded into shrapnel as the pinnace took another direct hit. A hundred steelglass shards slammed into and through the pilot in a second, killing him instantly. He jerked back in his chair and then slumped forward over the blood-spattered controls. Air rushed out through the broken window. Random pulled the nearest steel locker off the wall and threw it at the gaping hole. The locker plugged up the gap fairly neatly, with a little seepage round the edges, and the air pressure stabilized again.

The engines whined as the pinnace dropped like a stone. Random hit the pilot's strap releases and hauled the dead body out of his seat. He fastened himself into the command chair and studied the controls. The altitude indicator showed they were a lot nearer the surface than he'd thought, but it was still a hell of a long way down. With no hand at the helm, sky and cloud and snatches of surface swept back and forth before the unblocked part of the steelglass window. Random cleaned the controls of blood with his sleeve as best he could, being very careful not to activate anything till he was sure what it did. He looked across at the sergeant in the co-pilot's seat, but even as he started to ask for help, he realized that Miller was slumped forward, unmoving. Random reached out and pulled the sergeant back in his chair. Miller's head rolled back, and he stared sightlessly up at the cabin ceiling, a large steelglass fragment protruding from one bloody eye socket.

'Dead as a doornail,' said Ruby, moving into view beside Random. 'Our luck is running true to form.'

'Haul his ass out of that chair and take his place,' said Random. 'I'm going to need your help to land this thing.'

Ruby unfastened the straps, pulled Miller's body out of the chair and dumped it on the desk. She took over the co-pilot's seat, studied the blood-smeared controls dubiously, and then looked over at Random. 'You have flown one of these things before, haven't you, Jack?'

'Do you want the bad news or the really bad news?'

'Oh, shit.'

'That just about sums it up. Not only is this a totally new model to me, but those two disrupter hits did a lot of damage to our steering mechanisms. And if I'm interpreting these controls correctly, we have associational damage too. Engine power is dropping, one of the main air tanks is ruptured and the landing computers are shot to shit. Apart from that, putting this unfamiliar craft down in unknown territory in a never-ending storm should be a piece of cake. Any questions?'

'Oh, great,' said Ruby. 'Just great. Where did the sergeant say those parachutes were?'

'Forget it. There's enough lightning out there to turn you into a cinder before you could even pull the ripcord. The ionization on the hull's attracting it.'

'Escape pods? Gravity sleds?'

'In a ship this size? Hey, wait a minute . . . *Oh, shit.*'

Ruby looked at him sharply. 'I really didn't like the way you said that. What is it now?'

'Half the controls just shut down. Apparently the shrapnel from the window has riddled most of the main computers. Enough of them have fallen off-line that the main systems went with them. We are now running entirely on back-up systems. And if I try and cut in the manual controls, this heap of shit will drop like a rock. It's only the few remaining automatic systems that are keeping the engines going.'

'Oh, *shit.*'

'Exactly. We are now plummeting towards the surface of an unknown planet in a crippled ship we can't control, with all the glide factor of half a brick with a nail in it. I think *oh, shit* covers the situation quite accurately. Feel free to chime in if you have any bright ideas that don't include divine intervention.'

'So what are we going to do? Come on, Random; you're the expert strategist, think of a way out of this mess.'

'Strategies require options, and we don't seem to have any. We're just going to have to trust what's left of the on-board computers to manage a landing, or at least crash us as gently as possible.'

'We can't be that helpless! We're Maze people, dammit! Superhumans!'

'Unfortunately, we're still only mortal, and none of our abilities are any use in this situation. But we're tough. We can take a lot of punishment. We should be able to survive a crash that would kill anyone else. Hell, when I attacked the pastel towers back on Golgotha, they shot my gravity sled out of the sky and then set fire to me, and I still walked away from it.'

Ruby stared at the useless controls before her. 'There has to be something we can do, something to improve our chances.'

'There is,' Random said suddenly. 'Give me a hand.'

He hit his strap releases and surged up out of his chair, his face alight with inspiration. He staggered up the slanted central aisle of the shaking ship, and started pulling loose all the remaining chairs and lockers. Ruby hurried after him, new hope in her heart.

'What is it? What have you thought of, Jack?'

'A cocoon. We're going to build a barricade around ourselves, layers of steel and padding, and hope it absorbs most of the impact on landing. Give me a hand here. We've only got a few minutes left before we hit.'

Ruby joined him, tearing attachments loose with her superhuman strength. Everything that wasn't an actual part of the deck or the hull was torn away and ended up as one of the many layers of barricade at the front of the cabin. Finally they ran out of junk and time, and retreated into the heart of the cocoon. They'd left just enough room for the two of them to force their way in, and they sat together in each other's arms, wedged together so tightly they could barely breathe. The alarm sirens had blended into a single hysterical tone now, and the red emergency lighting had washed everything the colour of blood. The storm still raged around them, slapping the falling craft this way and that.

'I never thought I'd die like this,' said Ruby Journey. 'Just sitting helplessly, waiting for the end. I'm a fighter, a warrior. I deserved a warrior's death. A chance to die fighting, on my feet, and take some of my enemies with me. Not like this.'

'We're not dead yet,' said Jack Random. 'I've been close to death more times than I can remember, and I'm still here. Never give up hope, Ruby. It's all that keeps us going.'

'I've always loved you, Jack. Always will. I might not be very good at showing it, but . . .'

'It's all right, I know. Love you too, Ruby. If we get out of this alive, you want to take another stab at living together?'

'Hell, no. I don't love you that much.'

They laughed softly together.

'At least they've stopped shooting,' said Random. 'Either the storm's thrown us out of range, or they must think we're all dead.'

'Let us be thankful for small mercies,' said Ruby. 'You know, that attack was no accident. Someone down there knew we were coming.'

'Yes. We'll have to ask a few pointed questions about that later. Even if it's only through a spirit board.'

'I won't die,' said Ruby. 'I'm not ready to die yet. There's still so much I meant to do.'

'I suppose everyone feels like that. I'm . . . more or less content. I've achieved more than I ever expected to. And I got to meet you, eventually. I'll settle for that.'

'You always were willing to settle for too little, Jack.'

They laughed again, and then the breath was slammed from their bodies as the landing computers cut in and hauled back on the engines, fighting to turn the last of the descent into a landing. The pinnace's speed fell drastically, the engines shrieking and complaining all the way. The hull groaned and flexed, and lights flickered on and off. The whole ship shuddered violently, the scream of the straining engines louder than the storms outside. Random and Ruby held each other tightly, their heads buried in each other's shoulders. And then the pinnace struck a towering black mountain a glancing blow in passing, and the whole right side of the craft bulged inwards. The improvised barricade shook viciously, but held together. The pinnace struck one obstacle after another on its way down, its heavily armoured hull absorbing most of the blows, but Random and Ruby took a lot of the impact too. They cried out at the pain, but were helpless to do anything about it. Fires broke out somewhere in the back of the pinnace, and smoke drifted down the cabin, thick and black and choking. And then the ship finally hit the ground.

The impact seemed to go on for ever. The pinnace skidded across an unyielding, unforgiving surface in a sea of sparks and flames, slowing only gradually, until finally the nose slammed into a dark outcropping and the pinnace came to a final halt, at the end of its journey at last. The engines cut off automatically, and for long moments there was only the roaring of the gale-force winds as they blew out the flames and rocked the open wreck of the pinnace back and forth.

Jack Random came slowly back to consciousness. His initial awareness was of being rocked pleasantly to and fro like an infant in its cradle. It felt wonderfully comfortable, and all he wanted was to lie there and enjoy it, but part of him knew he couldn't do that. Reluctantly he opened his eyes, and was greeted with the hellish red glow of the emergency lighting. At least the damn alarm sirens had shut up at last. His thoughts were slow and sluggish. He didn't know how long he'd been unconscious, but he could hear fires burning at the back of the craft. Not a good sign. He could taste blood in his mouth. He tried to move his arms, and immediately sharp pains erupted in his sides. Several careful movements later, he was satisfied he'd broken most of his ribs, and there was enough blood seeping into his mouth with his breathing that he had to keep spitting it out. Definitely not a good sign. He gritted his teeth against the pain, and tried to stand up. He barely moved an inch. The crash had compacted the barricades around him and Ruby so tightly that there was no room to move. Ruby's eyes were still closed, and she was breathing harshly through her mouth.

'Ruby! Wake up, dammit! I can't do this on my own!'

'Stop shouting,' Ruby mumbled without opening her eyes. 'I've got a headache.'

She lifted her head slowly, and Random winced as her face came into the light. There was a deep and nasty wound on her forehead. Blood was streaming down the side of her face. But when she opened her eyes they were clear and rational.

'Congratulations,' said Random. 'We survived the landing. Unfortunately, the ship is on fire, and I've no way of knowing what condition the engines are in, but I suspect the worst. We have to get out of here, fast.'

'So what's stopping us?' said Ruby.

'We're stuck in our cocoon, and I can't seem to find any leverage I can use to free us. Any suggestions?'

462

'Our feet are still on the deck. If we can't push back, push up.'

They braced themselves against each other, refusing to cry out at the pain of their various injuries for fear of upsetting the other, and forced themselves to their feet. After that, it was a simple but painful task to free themselves from the cocoon that had saved their lives. Leaning heavily on each other, they headed for the single airlock. Neither of them were particularly steady on their feet. Jack's vision wasn't as clear as he would have liked, and his head ached abominably. He just hoped he didn't have concussion. Ruby was favouring one leg, and one of her eyeballs was red with leaking blood inside. Really, not a good sign. Jack decided he'd think about all that later. First get out of the damned pinnace. He hit the airlock controls, and nothing happened. He hit them again, as hard as he could in his weakened state, but the airlock inner door remained stubbornly shut.

'What's taking so long?' said Ruby petulantly. 'I want to lie down. Get some sleep.'

'In a while,' said Random. 'Right now, try talking to this door. It won't listen to me.'

'Airlock's linked to the main controls. And they were wrecked in the landing.'

'Can we repair them?'

'Maybe,' said Ruby, frowning as she tried to concentrate. 'If you're good at jigsaws. Anyway, don't be in such a hurry to leave. From what I remember of the files, surface conditions are atrocious. It's cold, there's high background radiation, and the wind never stops blowing. Let's just sit here and wait to be rescued. I'm tired.'

'I'm afraid we can't do that, Ruby. There's a fire in the hold and it's coming this way. And the engines—'

'Could blow any time. Yeah, I remember. Damn. You're just full of good news, aren't you? All right; there should be manual controls for the door, top and bottom. Toss you for which of us has to bend over.'

In the end, Jack nearly passed out from the pain when he tried to bend down, so Ruby had to do it, cursing and complaining all the way. They cracked the inner airlock door open inch by inch, stumbled into the lock and hit the explosive bolts that blew the outer door open. Outside, it was cold and dark and the gusting wind was ferociously loud. Random put his head out cautiously, and winced as the bitter wind hit his exposed face. It felt like razors. He pulled his head quickly back in.

'Nasty.'

'Told you,' said Ruby. 'The locals wear protective armour when they have to go out, which is as rarely as they can get away with.'

'We don't have the time to improvise any armour. We need to put some distance and protection between us and this ship, in case she blows. I'm pretty sure I saw a cliff face within walking distance, and what might have been caves.'

'You'd better be right about this, Random. OK, you lead, I'll follow.'

They lurched out into the freezing dark, and the howling wind hit them hard, sending them staggering sideways for a moment before they could get their footing. The cold cut into them like a knife, and there was something abrasive in the wind that seared their exposed skin raw. They huddled together, and staggered away from their crashed ship towards the great dark cliff.

Their progress was maddeningly slow. Neither could move very quickly or freely because of their injuries. Strength and determination could only do so much in the face of broken bones and crippling pain. They stumbled on, supporting each other. It wasn't fully dark yet, only just twilight, but there was only a small moon, dropping a sickly blue light over the nightmare landscape. They were in a valley, surrounded on all sides by huge eerie shapes that rose up unexpectedly out of the gloom. There was no sign of anything living. The wind howled like something dying, rising and falling away but never still. The cliff face didn't seem to be getting any closer.

'What are our chances of rescue?' said Ruby, after a while.

'Bad,' said Random. 'The storm and the attack threw us way off course. The last location I had put us about two miles from the main city, Vidar. No other settlements in walking distance. And after a crash like ours, they might not bother with any rescue. No one moves on the surface here unless they absolutely have to. They wouldn't come this far just to identify a few bodies. Even if two of them were rather famous.'

'So,' said Ruby, 'first we get to the cliff face. Then we climb the cliff face till we find a cave. Then we sit and heal. And then we get to walk two miles through this shit to the nearest civilization. Wonderful. Assuming we get through all this alive, I am going to find whoever's idea it was to send us here, rip out his spleen and make him eat it, one bite at a time.'

'You must be feeling better if you can talk that much. Let's speed up the pace.'

'You're a bastard, Jack. Have I told you that recently?'

'Shut up and keep walking.'

The roar of the wind became deafening, slapping tears from their eyes and plucking at their clothes with strong, insistent hands. The dust in the air grated against their exposed skin like sandpaper, but the cold was so bad now they barely felt it. Dark, towering figures loomed about them, rocky outcrops eroded by the winds into disturbing apparitions. The cliff face grew slowly larger as they drew nearer.

'Why the hell did I agree to come here?' said Ruby.

'You volunteered, said you were bored. Wanted a little excitement.'

'This is most certainly not what I had in mind.'

'Ah, you never did want to go anywhere fun.'

They clung to each other as the wind whipped sharply about them, pushing them this way and that like some playground bully. They screwed up their eyes against it till they could barely see, and it filled their noses and mouths with dust that irritated their throats. The ground beneath their feet rose and fell sharply for no obvious reason, hard and unyielding, so that each step sent painful vibrations shuddering through their exhausted bodies.

Random tried to get some impression of his surroundings. The shapes they passed were some kind of black basaltic rock, but their strange enigmatic shapes had a subtly troubling quality. There was something almost organic about them, something strangely familiar, like the shapes we see in dreams, full of significance. Random shook his head, trying to drive out the unsettling thoughts. It was just his imagination, that the rocks looked like creatures who had just sat down to sleep and might awaken at any moment, and turn and pursue him with the slow malevolent patience of all creatures in nightmares. He looked back at the pinnace. It was almost lost in the growing twilight, but he could see well enough to be astonished that he and Ruby had survived the crash-landing at all. The ship had cracked open in several places, the thick-armour plating split and buckled like paper. More than enough to kill any human passengers. Anyone merely human.

At least the engines hadn't blown up yet.

Random turned his head away, and concentrated on the cliff face before him. It was definitely closer. Which was good, because he felt like shit. Every step jolted his broken ribs, and he was pretty sure he had internal injuries too. Either his healing powers were taking a long time kicking in, or his injuries were even more serious than he thought. There was always blood in his mouth now, no matter how often he spat it out. Ruby was leaning on him more and more heavily, and had stopped complaining, which was always a bad sign. They had to find shelter soon, somewhere they could rest and hopefully heal. Even the more than human had their limits.

When they finally stumbled to a sudden halt at the base of the cliff, it seemed like a miracle. Random spotted a cave opening, and pointed it out with a harsh croak that was all that was left of his voice. They hauled themselves up the jagged cliff face with a last burst of strength, buoyed up by a sense of purpose and a possible end to their struggle. The cave opening was a good ten feet in diameter, its interior in impenetrable darkness. Random pulled a penlight from his sleeve, and played the thin yellow beam around the cave's entrance. The interior stretched away before him, further than the light could penetrate. Still leaning on each other, Random and Ruby stumbled into the cave.

It went some way back into the rock, and they followed the tunnel till they reached the sealed end, and then collapsed on the hard floor, their backs against the comforting support of the cave wall. It felt good to be off their feet, good to be sheltered from the storm that still howled outside, as though angry at being cheated of its victims.

The air was still now, and perhaps fractionally warmer. Random and Ruby sat together, shoulder to shoulder, their breathing and their heartbeats slowly returning to normal. Their various pains seemed comfortably far away, for the moment, though neither had the strength to move another inch. Random turned off his penlight. Might need the power yet, and besides, there was really nothing he needed to see right now. He felt deathly tired. Since passing through the Madness Maze, he'd grown accustomed to his occasional wounds healing quickly, but it had been a long time since he'd been busted up this badly. He wondered after all if there was a limit to how much damage his body could repair. If so, this was a hell of a time to find out. He could hear Ruby beside him, breathing jerkily through her mouth. She didn't sound good.

'Ruby? You still with me?'

'Unfortunately, yes.' Her voice was strained and harsh. 'I feel like shit. How about you?'

'I'm getting there.' Random gritted his teeth against a sudden surge of pain from his broken ribs, and then had to cough, which hurt even more. A thick wad of blood and something else came into his mouth, and he spat it out. 'Damn. I have a horrible feeling there was a bit of lung in that.'

'You're just trying to cheer me up. I have been on some low-rent planets in my time, but this place takes first, second and third prize. I always knew I'd end up in Hell, but I never thought I'd get there while I was still alive. Maybe I didn't. Maybe we both died in the crash . . .'

'No,' said Random. 'If this was Hell, all my friends would be here. Sit. Rest. Get your strength back. When morning comes, we've got a two-mile hike ahead of us.'

'Oh, shut up. I'm not going anywhere. Any chance we could contact anyone through our comm implants?'

'Afraid not. Comm traffic on Loki is very limited. The constant storms give this world a supersaturated electrical and magnetic field. Plays hell with all kinds of communications.

We've no way of letting anyone know we're alive. Can't even send up a flare. We're on our own.'

'Somehow I just knew you were going to say that. So, how are we supposed to find our way to Vidar in weather like this?'

'I can feel where it is,' said Random. 'So many people, I can feel their presence. Reach out with your mind. See if you can feel them too.'

'Damn,' said Ruby, after a moment. 'You're right. It's like having a compass in my head. I didn't know we could do this.'

'Unlike you, I haven't been taking my abilities for granted,' said Random. 'I spent my spare time testing what I could do, trying to expand my limits.'

'I'll bet you were teacher's pet at school. It's a pity you didn't work out how to speed up our healing abilities. They're taking a long time to kick in.'

'Be patient, they've got a lot of work to do. We'll heal; in time.'

'Hope you're right, Random. I've never felt this bad in my life. Even hurts to breathe. If I didn't know better, I'd swear I was dying . . .'

Her voice trailed away. Random could hardly hear her breathing. 'Ruby? Ruby? Can you hear me?'

'Don't shout! My head hurts enough without you yelling in my ear. Let me sleep. Maybe when I wake up, everything'll be fixed again.'

'No! I don't think we can trust our bodies to do this much work on their own. We have to do it ourselves, go inside, concentrate, and control the healing process. Otherwise, we might just drift off and never wake up.'

'You're just full of words of comfort, aren't you? All right; I hurt too much to argue. How do you want to do this?'

'I think we have to look inwards. Try and find your healing power, the same way you found the compass in your head. And once you've found it, work it for all it's worth.'

Ruby nodded, and closed her eyes. Random closed his, and focused his thoughts inwards, searching for something he'd know when he found it. He pushed the pains of his broken body from his thoughts, refusing to let them distract him. He shut down all his senses, sinking deeper and deeper into his own mind. He couldn't die here; he refused to die here, when there was still so much work to be done. And he was damned if he'd die such a useless, pointless, stupid death. The legend of his long life deserved a better ending. His anger burned fiercely through him, and something stirred in his back brain, the undermind, that secret part of him he couldn't see, where his power lived. And a new fire ignited there, bursting out through all the rest of him, burning away all pains and weaknesses in its purifying flames. He was remade and reborn, and Random howled aloud in sheer exhilaration at being so alive.

His eyes flew open as he crashed back into his usual state of consciousness, already forgetting that hidden part of himself he'd so briefly touched. He raised his hands in front of him and flexed them, and they were fine. He surged to his feet, grinning like a fool at how well and fit he felt. All his injuries had healed, all his pains were gone, and he didn't even have a scar left to show for it. He realized Ruby was standing beside him, stamping her foot on the ground to test her leg, see that it wasn't broken any more. She looked at him and laughed incredulously, and then they hugged each other fiercely like they'd never stop.

'Damn,' said Ruby, when they finally did release each other. 'I feel good! I feel like I could take on a whole damned army!'

'No pain anywhere?' said Random. 'No weaknesses?'

'Hell, no! You?'

'I feel like I was twenty again. I feel like I could go one on one with a Grendel and dismantle it with my bare hands.' He broke off and looked at Ruby thoughtfully. 'And just a few moments ago we were both knocking on death's door. I'm amazed we even survived the crash, let alone managed to drag ourselves here. Just the shock of so many major injuries should have killed us outright.'

Ruby shrugged. 'We only speeded up what would have happened anyway. This isn't the first time something should have killed us, and we survived. It's part of being who and what we are.'

'But we just did in a few seconds what a regeneration machine would have taken weeks to do. And I have no idea how.'

'Random, will you for once in your life look on the bright side? We are no longer dying, we are back in shape again and the pinnace didn't explode after all. Count your damned blessings. As soon as we get back to civilization, I am going to light candles in as many different churches as I can find. Any religion, I'm not fussy. Now let's get some sleep, so we can set off for Vidar at first light.'

'Yes,' said Random. 'Sleep does sound good. But this is something we need to talk about in the future, Ruby. We don't know nearly enough about our powers. About what we might be able to do if we put our minds to it.'

'We're doing all right,' said Ruby. 'The Madness Maze didn't exactly come with an instruction manual. So we learn by doing.'

'There's still the question of how we do what we do. Where does the energy come from, that powers our abilities? What did we just tap into to heal ourselves, to bring ourselves back from the brink of death? I'm already forgetting most of it, but what I can remember scares the hell out of me. It felt like tapping into God . . .'

'I think you're getting delusions of grandeur,' said Ruby sternly. 'Some questions just don't have answers. At least, not in this world. Now shut up, lie down and get some sleep. We've got a long walk ahead of us in the morning.'

She turned away from him, lay down on the cave floor and closed her eyes in a determined way that indicated that as far as she was concerned, the conversation was over. Random looked down at her for a while, and then lay down beside her. He knew questions didn't go away just because you didn't want to talk about them, but there was no point in pushing the matter now. Still, when this mission was over, he felt it was well past time that all the surviving Maze alumni got together and tried to work out a few answers to the nature of their unique condition. Random had no real objection to becoming more than human; he just wanted some idea of where that road might be taking them all. He closed his eyes and let sleep overtake him, and the storm roared helplessly outside the cave till morning.

In the morning, Jack and Ruby stood together at the mouth of the cave, looking out into the new light. The wind actually seemed to have dropped off a little, but the storm was still going strong. Loki's sun was mostly hidden away behind the boiling clouds, but its pale light was augmented by the lightning that flared constantly overhead, illuminating the land below with a stark bluish light. Sometimes the dust carried in the winds grew thick enough to hide anything not close at hand, but that haze was constantly shifting too, forming and re-forming as the winds changed direction over and over. Random and Ruby watched in silence, getting their first real look at the landscape they'd crossed the night before.

The valley was full of eerie, grotesque shapes of black stone, standing in no apparent pattern, like so many silent watchful sentinels. Beyond them, the pinnace still lay where it had crashed, up against a dark outcrop. It looked like a broken toy, too delicate for rough handling. Long broken skid marks traced its progress down the valley to its final fate. At the far end of the valley, Random could just make out an open plain, dotted with more of the dark forbidding shapes. There was no sign of life anywhere; no vegetation, no insects, no open water. Only the wind-carved landscape, harsh and bleak and utterly alien.

'I suppose life never really got started here,' said Ruby. 'Just as well, really. The last thing we need is more complications, on our little hike to Vidar.'

'That is a terribly self-centred view, Ruby,' said Random.

'So? What's your point?'

'Oh, nothing. I don't know why I take part in these conversations any more. All right, lead the way. And keep your eyes open. Young Jack Random and his bloody Ghost Warriors aren't supposed to be anywhere near here, but you never know.'

'Good point,' said Ruby. 'Let them all come. I could use a little action.'

Random sighed, and followed her out of the cave. Climbing down the cliff face proved a lot easier than going up, and soon they were striding through the valley towards the open plain. The storm winds were still blowing hard, but Random and Ruby just lowered their heads and ploughed through it. Now that they had their strength back, it didn't bother them nearly as much. Even the abrasive dust that got everywhere was only a minor irritant. Vidar's location burned in their minds like a beacon, and they headed for it in the straightest line they could manage. Time faded gradually into the background. With no significant landmarks, it was hard to tell how far they'd come, or how much further they had to go. There was just the storm and the winds and the hard, unyielding ground and the city, still somewhere up ahead. On they went, with nothing to say to each other for the moment.

The world moved slowly past them, always looking much the same. Sometimes Random thought he saw something moving, right out on the edge of his vision; something dark and slow and impossibly large. But by the time he'd stopped and turned to look directly at it, it was gone, lost in the storm. He couldn't be sure he'd really seen anything. Even the standing stones looked as though they might move, if you came on them suddenly. It was just his eyes playing tricks, providing the illusion of movement in a landscape where there was none. He strode on, looking fixedly ahead. And if he thought he sometimes heard strange cries or howlings, far off in the distance, then it was probably just the storm. After all, what kind of life could possibly exist in conditions like this? Even humanity wouldn't be here, if it weren't for the cobalt mines.

He was pretty sure Ruby hadn't seen anything. If she had, she would undoubtedly have taken a shot at it.

They passed the dark stone structures slowly, no one shape like any other, reminding Random of ancient statues of forgotten gods. They varied from simple monoliths the size of a man to great mountains with wind-cut crevices deep enough to drop a starship in. Random would have liked to think about something else, but there was nothing else. Maybe the stones were the evidence of past volcanic activity, driven up through cracks in the ground as molten rock, only to solidify once they hit the cold air. It was as good an explanation as any.

Oh, God, thought Random tiredly. *I am really, really bored.*

And then they reached the top of a long rise and looked down, and there was Vidar, the main city of Loki, spread out on the plain before them. It was a great sprawl of squat black buildings, with dark towers thrusting up here and there; a shadowy fortress with red and yellow furnace eyes, like a mining operation in Hell. A tall metal wall surrounded the city, polished by the abrasive dust to a dark purple sheen, with two massive metal gates at the front. The faint shimmer of a massive energy screen covered the whole city from the walls up. It had to be said that Vidar didn't look the least bit welcoming, but Random and Ruby were used to turning up at places where they weren't wanted. And as long as it promised shelter from the storms, a clean bed and a hot bath to soak in, Random was quite prepared to get down on his knees and kiss the ground inside its gates. Without looking at each other, Random and Ruby made their way down the long grey slope to the dark city below.

A local guard patrol intercepted them as they approached the main gates. There were six of them, moving slowly and clumsily in full body armour, with improvised masks and hoods protecting their faces. They plodded determinedly towards Random and Ruby, stopping a respectful distance away to form a semicircle before them. Each man had an energy gun in a thickly gloved hand, carefully aimed. Random and Ruby came to a stop too, just to be polite. One of the guards stepped forward.

'Who the hell are you?' he yelled, his voice only just carrying over the winds. 'Our sensors confirm you aren't Furies or Ghost Warriors, but nothing human is stupid enough to travel the surface without armour!'

'We are Jack Random and Ruby Journey,' said Random, as courteously as he could while shouting. 'I believe you're expecting us. Sorry we're a bit late.'

'But . . . we saw your ship go down yesterday, over two miles away!'

'We survived the crash, but our crew didn't. So we waited out the night in a cave, and then walked here.'

'You *walked*? Jesus Christ; maybe you are as good as the stories say. Follow me; I'll lead you in. But I'm afraid the weapons stay trained on you till we can positively verify your identity. Shub's been trying all kinds of tricks to get into the city. We don't take chances any more.'

'Understood. Now do you think we could get moving? I've had enough of this storm and dust to last a lifetime.'

'Welcome to Loki,' said the guard leader, and turned and headed for the main gates. Random and Ruby moved after him, the other guards turning slowly to keep them covered. The main gates turned out to be two huge slabs of steel, polished by the winds to a mirror-like finish. Twenty feet high, to match the walls, and eight feet wide, they looked like they could keep out anything up to and including a Grendel in heat. They opened slowly in response to a signal from the guard leader, who led Random and Ruby in. The rest of the guards moved quickly in to surround them, and the gates slammed together, holding out the storm.

It was suddenly very quiet. The roar of the winds was gone, cut off as though someone up above had thrown a switch. Random slowly straightened his aching back, and rubbed the grit from his eyes. Beside him, Ruby was hacking and coughing, trying to clear the dust from her mouth and throat. They were in a huge airlock, big enough to handle fifty men at a time, if they didn't mind crowding. The air was comfortably warm and blessedly clear. Random took several deep breaths before turning to the guard leader, who had taken off his metal and leather face mask, and was now wearily stacking pieces of his armour in the wall compartments. He was young, barely into his twenties, with a long serious face under a thick shock of long yellow hair. There were already deep lines of responsibility and hard life around his mouth and eyes. He grinned suddenly at Random; an engaging, almost shy smile.

'According to the sensors and our computer records, you two are exactly who and what you say you are. And man, are we glad to see you!' He gestured to the other guards, who immediately holstered their weapons and set about removing their own masks and armour. They all looked young and sober and more than capable of handling themselves in a fight. Random guessed the weaker and less responsible elements didn't last long in a place like Loki. The guard leader stuck out his hand, and Random shook it automatically. The leader turned to Ruby, but she just gave him a hard look, so he put his hand away and turned back to Random.

'I'm Peter Savage, guard leader. I wanted to take out a search party to look for you, but the city Council were positive no one could have survived such a crash. I could have told them; I knew it would take a lot more than a crashing ship to finish off the legendary professional rebel!'

There was a loud murmur of agreement from the other guards, and Random looked round to find them regarding him with wide eyes and smiles, and respectful nods. Some of them were so overawed they could barely meet his eyes. Savage was practically glowing with hero-worship. Random indicated Ruby, who'd finally stopped hacking and spitting on the airlock floor.

'I take it you know my companion?'

'Oh, yes,' said Savage, his smile disappearing. 'We know all about Ruby Journey. We watch the holo shows. Please don't let her kill anyone important. Or set fire to anything.'

'Your reputation precedes you,' Random said dryly to Ruby. 'We're really going to have to do something about your public image.'

'I like it just the way it is,' said Ruby.

'Anyway,' said Peter Savage brightly, 'we're delighted to have you here, Sir Random. Maybe you can turn this bloody war around.'

'Our briefing was pretty basic,' said Random. 'Fill in the blanks for us.'

Savage hesitated. 'I'm supposed to take you directly to the city Council, so they can instruct you on the current situation.'

'You can start the process as we go. Tell me about Vidar. How well protected is the city?'

'Walls and doors of solid steel over a foot thick,' said Savage, leading them out of the airlock's inner door. 'The force screen above the walls keeps out the weather. We need the walls and gates because we can't lower the screen, even for a second, or the storms would devastate the city. It's not just the winds; the dust gets into everything. Tech is constantly breaking down, even with the walls and the screen.'

'Don't the storms ever stop?' said Ruby.

'No, ma'am. But there are lulls, sometimes. This way.'

Beyond the airlock lay a simple pattern of narrow streets between the low, squat functional-looking buildings. There was little in the way of colour or ornament or decoration. Vidar was a mining city, with little time for frills and fancies. People rushed by as Savage led his charges on, but they paid little or no attention to the newcomers. They all had business of their own, and no time to waste. They all wore swords and energy guns, even in the supposed safety of the fortress city. Random found that significant.

'The rebel forces have made an alliance with Shub,' said Savage. He made the last word sound like an obscenity. 'They have an army of Ghost Warriors, a few Furies and a whole bunch of high-tech weaponry that falls apart more often than it works. That's Loki for you. Even Shub can't find an answer to the dust. As a result, most of our fighting tends to be hand to hand. Men of flesh and blood against living corpses and men of metal. Not exactly a level playing field, but that's Shub for you. Certainly the rebels don't seem to be objecting. Their leaders no longer care about anything but winning. The disrupter cannon that shot you down was as much a surprise to us as it was to you. They must be really scared of your involvement to risk revealing that powerful a weapon. Think of it as a backhanded compliment.'

'Oh, we do,' Random assured Savage, perfectly straight-faced. 'And we plan to return the compliment, as soon as possible.'

Savage grinned. 'I have to say, I'm really looking forward to working with you, Sir Random. You always were my hero. I've seen all your holo shows. It will be an honour and a privilege to fight beside you.'

The young guard all but brimmed over with sincerity, of a kind Random hadn't seen since his glory days as the great and legendary professional rebel, when he was the only hope against Lionstone's evil Empire. A lot had changed since then. If anything, such hero-worship made Random feel old. He wasn't sure he was the man Savage remembered any more. He felt slightly embarrassed, and Ruby's clear amusement didn't help at all. He moved quickly to change the subject.

'Where is everybody? I expected to see a lot more people in a city this size.'

'With half the outer settlements overrun by the rebel forces, most of the mining equipment on Loki is being operated from Vidar these days, which means we're all working overtime to keep the systems going. Vidar was never meant to carry this heavy a load, but it's not like we have a choice. The mines are Loki's lifeblood. And . . . a lot of people here aren't going to be too sure about you, Sir Random. There's a man out there with your face leading the Shub forces, leaving blood and death and atrocities in his wake. Practically everyone in this city has lost someone to Young Jack Random. Your name has become a curse. That's why you have an armed guard. In case there's . . . trouble.'

'Let them start something,' said Ruby calmly. 'Let anyone start something.'

'Anyway,' said Savage hurriedly, 'the rebels, backed up by Shub's forces, have been systematically wiping out all the outer settlements, knocking out the mining equipment and killing everything that lives before moving on to their next target. They have us surrounded on all sides, and they're moving gradually inwards, heading towards Vidar. Because whoever controls this city controls the world's only starport, as well as all the mining. If we fall, the whole colony falls with us. We don't have much of an army; just security guards and a whole bunch of volunteers. Mostly refugees from settlements that have fallen. We can't even arm all of them. We've never needed an army before; we were always too busy fighting the weather to fight each other.'

'How has your army done in the field?' said Random. 'I take it there have been direct clashes, army to army?'

'Some,' said Savage. 'We go out, when there are lulls in the weather. People die, but nothing gets settled. We have the numbers and the training, but they have Shub. It's all been very inconclusive.'

'Why hasn't Golgotha sent you reinforcements?' said Random, frowning.

'We asked,' said Savage. 'They sent you two. Apparently we're not very high on the priorities list. Everyone's screaming for reinforcements right now, and we're just another mining planet with a relatively small population. We were lucky to get you.'

'Just the two of us, against an army of Ghost Warriors,' said Ruby. 'My kind of odds.'

'The trouble is, she's not joking,' said Random. 'Ignore her. I do, whenever possible. How much further to the Council chambers?'

'We're almost there, Sir Random.'

'Anything else I ought to know?'

Savage hesitated, and lowered his voice. 'Watch yourself. The city Council has always done what it considers best for the Council.'

They walked the next few blocks in silence, each alone with their thoughts. Finally Savage stopped before an ugly, squat building apparently no different from any of the others, and led them through a series of surprisingly stringent security measures. Random was impressed. He still refused to give up his sword and gun when asked, though, and so did Ruby. No one was stupid enough to press the point, though Ruby looked hopeful. Savage knocked diffidently on a door flanked by two armed guards, and a voice from within invited them to enter. Savage opened the door, and then stood back to allow Random and Ruby to go first. Random strode in like he owned the place. He'd learned a long time ago never to appear polite or intimidated by local politicians – they just took advantage. Ruby was right there, striding at his side, but in her case it was just natural arrogance.

They found themselves in a reasonably large room, very well appointed, almost excessively comfortable. It had been decorated by someone with an extensive budget and absolutely no taste. Ruby felt right at home. Random had no interest in his surroundings. He took one look at the five men sitting rather pompously behind the long ironwood table at the far end of the room, and came to a sudden stop. Ruby immediately stopped with him, one hand dropping automatically to her gun. Random glared at the man sitting in the middle of the group, and when he spoke his voice was as cold as death itself.

'André de Lisle! What the hell are you doing here, you son of a bitch? Last I heard, you were rotting in a prison cell!'

'It's good to see you too, Random,' said de Lisle calmly. 'It's been a while since Cold Rock, hasn't it?'

A low growl of anger burst from Random's lips, and suddenly he was surging forward across the gap that separated them. The guards that had followed him in went for their weapons, but Ruby had already turned to face them, gun in hand. They stood very still. De Lisle barely had time to shrink back in his chair before Random had crossed the room, leaped on to the table and reached down to grab a handful of his shirt-front. Random hauled de Lisle up out of his chair and held the big muscular man dangling before him, his legs kicking helplessly in mid-air. The other councillors made shocked noises, but didn't interfere. They weren't stupid. Ruby made the guards drop their weapons and line up against a wall, while Random effortlessly held de Lisle aloft, glaring coldly into the man's reddening face.

'So,' said Ruby dryly, from over her shoulder, 'I take it you two know each other.'

'Oh, yes,' said Random, his voice cold and level and very dangerous. 'This piece of pond scum used to run the mining interests on a planet called Cold Rock. Treated his people like shit. Paid them the lowest wages in that sector, and dealt with any protests through whippings, brandings and the occasional mass execution. He grew rich off their sweat and blood and poverty, and lived the good life while children starved. When I brought my rebellion to Cold Rock, he funded the army that opposed me. Not surprising. He ruled Cold Rock in all but name. After I was betrayed and captured, and my rebellion collapsed, he saw to it that my cell contained a holovid, so I could watch him execute everyone who'd sided with me, and a further one in ten, chosen at random, to punish his people for having dared oppose him. Men, women and children died, under his orders. Sometimes he went along and watched, and laughed.

'His was one of the first arrest orders I signed, after we overthrew Lionstone and her people. I made sure he got the same cell he gave me, for old times' sake. With a holovid, so he could see his people being tried and executed. I wanted him hanged, too, but he had a real good lawyer, and a lot of connections. His kind always do. Even so, I was able to make sure he got life imprisonment, in solitary. No parole, no luxuries, no time off for good behaviour. But now here he is, back in charge of a planet again. And I want to know why.'

'Please put the councillor down, Sir Random,' said Savage diffidently. 'There are an awful lot of armed guards on their way here, and I really don't want to have to order them to take you down.'

'That's right,' Ruby said easily. 'You really don't want to do that. It wouldn't be wise.'

Savage considered the point. 'Then may I at least point out that Councillor de Lisle can't actually answer any questions while being strangled.'

Random nodded reluctantly, and dropped de Lisle on to the table top. Savage let out an audible sigh of relief. De Lisle lay on his back, massaging his bruised throat and gasping down air. Random jumped down from the table and turned to face the other councillors.

'I don't know you, but I might just kill you all anyway, for sitting with de Lisle. So sit tight, and be quiet. Or I'll have Ruby reason with you.'

'Yeah,' said Ruby. 'I can be very reasonable, when I put my mind to it.'

De Lisle resumed his seat behind the table. None of the other councillors moved to help him. His face was very pale as he tried to pull the tatters of his dignity around him. Random fixed him with a deadly eye.

'Now,' said Random, almost calmly. 'Talk to me, de Lisle. Tell me everything. Explain how you came to be here, in a position of power again. Bearing in mind that if your answer isn't extremely convincing, I am going to hang you from the city walls. In pieces.'

No one in the room thought he was joking. De Lisle cleared his throat painfully.

'I was pardoned,' he said flatly. 'The Empire needed someone with mining experience to run this hellhole, and candidates were, understandably, somewhat thin on the ground. I was offered the post, on condition I never leave this planet. I accepted. I should have known better; this planet is just one big prison.'

'My heart bleeds for you,' said Random. 'I can't believe they gave a scumbag like you a pardon.'

'In return for a lifetime's service here,' said de Lisle. 'What's the matter, Sir Random? Doesn't the great rebel hero believe in redemption through atonement?'

'Not in your case. But much as I hate to admit it, I'm going to need your local expertise. So, you're going to be my second in command, arranging the things I need to save this world, as and when I need them. I'll take Peter Savage here as my liaison. If only because having to meet with you on a regular basis would turn my stomach. And don't mess with me, de Lisle. I won't be betrayed again.' De Lisle nodded jerkily. Random looked around at the other councillors. 'Someone fill me in on the political situation here. Exactly who are the rebels, what are they rebelling against, and what in God's good name led them to ally themselves with Shub?'

'My name is Bentley,' said a councillor, after they'd all spent some time looking at each other and waiting for someone else to start. Bentley was a tall, slender man with a shaved head and eyes of so pale a blue they were almost colourless. 'I'm in charge of security. I have no interest in politics, I just do my job. Our situation here is really quite simple. The rebel leaders are the ex-Planetary Controller Matthew Tallon, and the ex-Mayor of this city, Terrence Jacks. They led the rebellion that overthrew the old order here, under Lionstone. Your comrades in the great rebellion, Sir Random. After throwing out or executing Lionstone's people, they put themselves in charge.

'However, they had no real experience in running a planetary economy, and were soon out of their depth, though they wouldn't admit it. They gave the people of Loki the vote, and after a series of blunders and mismanagements that nearly bankrupted the economy, the people voted them out of office. Tallon and Jacks took this very badly, and blamed the whole thing on hidden elements of the old order. They retreated to the outer settlements, and gathered a new rebel force around them, mostly people who were disappointed that the new order hadn't immediately made them all wealthy and powerful. It wasn't much of a force, and they weren't much of a problem. Until the Shub forces arrived to back them up. Apparently, in the last days of their power, Tallon and Jacks had secretly formed an alliance with the Enemies of Humanity. And now Young Jack Random leads the rebel forces. Tallon and Jacks stay pretty much in the background these days.'

'So,' said Random. 'I've been sent here to fight for the established order, against old rebel comrades.'

'Got it in one,' said de Lisle, though he had sense enough not to smile when he said it. 'Funny how things work out, isn't it? It would seem you and I have no choice but to be allies, unless you want Shub to win.'

'Don't push it,' said Random. 'At least now I know why Parliament wanted me here. They think coverage of me fighting rebel forces will tie me more strongly to them. Distance me from any forces that might oppose Parliament's authority. Well, we'll see about that. Right now, Ruby and I need some rest. It was a long walk here. No doubt your quarters are the most comfortable, de Lisle, so we'll take them. You'll have to make your own arrangements. Any problems, talk to Savage, and he will officially ignore them on my behalf. Savage, we're leaving.'

'Yes, Sir Random. Please follow me, and I'll take you to the councillor's quarters.'

Random nodded to the councillors, Ruby nodded to the guards she was covering with her gun, and they stalked out of the room after Savage. And for a long time in the Council chamber, no one said anything.

Some time later, when everyone but the night shift was safely asleep, Savage, Random and Ruby moved quietly through the narrow streets, hidden inside concealing cloaks. Savage had already arranged it so that the guards on duty at the main computer centre were friends of his, and they looked pointedly in the other direction as Savage led Random and Ruby in through the front door, using his new security rating to override the alarm systems. Once inside, Savage searched out the right terminal, seated himself before it and set about calling up all kinds of files he wasn't supposed to know about. If having Random staring over his shoulder made him nervous, he did his best to hide it. Ruby watched the door, gun in hand, just in case.

Random was surprised at how easy it had been. When he'd first explained to Savage that he wanted information only the main city computers were likely to have, he'd expected all kinds of problems. Instead, Savage had arranged everything with only a few quick calls to some old friends. Apparently that was how things were done in Vidar these days. It was that kind of administration, and as above, so below. Knowing de Lisle, Random understood completely.

'Run the names and backgrounds of all the city councillors,' said Random. 'What brought them here, and who put them in authority?'

'Officially, the voters did,' said Savage, working his way past security blocks with the ease of long practice. 'But since we're all very new to democracy here, the winners tend to be those with the most money to spend during elections. As to their backgrounds . . . they're all pardoned war criminals. How about that! All five of them were part of the old order, in positions of authority under Lionstone. They were arrested and tried for crimes against humanity, convicted and imprisoned, but later offered pardons, if they'd come here and run things.'

'And that includes Bentley, the security chief?'

'Yeah. He was the first. Took up his position under Tallon and Jacks. Far as I know, he's always done a good job.'

'Who authorized these pardons?' said Random, frowning. 'And whose idea was it to send them here?'

'That information isn't here, Sir Random. Or if it is, it's buried so deep I can't get at it. But only someone fairly high up in Parliament would have had the authority to set something like this in motion, and keep it quiet. I can tell you none of the colonists here knew about this. A lot of us took part in the original rebellion, and there's no way we would have stood for war criminals of the old order being put in authority over us. Hell, maybe Tallon and Jacks had some justification after all.'

'There's no justification for making an ally of Shub,' said

Random. 'Let's see what else we can find on the councillors. Crack open their bank accounts – I want to see what they're being paid to run this planet.'

Savage had to use a lot of passwords he wasn't supposed to know, but he finally got the answers he was looking for. Even the best systems will fall to an experienced hacker, and as Savage rather sheepishly pointed out, there wasn't a lot to do in Vidar when you were young and restless. Which was why Loki had the highest percentage of cyberats per population of any planet in the Empire. Random's smile fell away as he saw the figures Savage had dug up for him. The councillors were taking a percentage of Loki's gross output. Not just a part of the profits; they were creaming money right off the top. They were also pocketing a large percentage of all tax monies, and every other public purse they could get their hands on. In effect, they were systematically looting the whole planetary economy, and depositing the money in banks on Golgotha. If this continued, the Loki economy would inevitably collapse, though no doubt the councillors would have arranged their escape long before that became obvious.

Savage went from shocked to furious to cold rage in a few seconds. 'If the colonists knew about this, they'd drag the councillors out of their beds and lynch them on the spot. But there's no way these people could have set this up themselves, Sir Random. Someone much higher up has to be covering for them, someone on Golgotha. But why would they want to ruin Loki?'

'Because they could,' said Ruby. 'That's all the reason these people need.'

'Damn,' said Random. 'Maybe I am fighting on the wrong side. If Tallon and Jacks knew about this . . . Look, is there any way we can contact the rebel forces? Secretly? If we could persuade them to settle their grievances through the system, with my support . . .'

'You don't understand,' said Savage, shutting down his terminal and turning to face Random. 'You haven't seen what they've been doing. The rebels fight alongside the Ghost Warriors, sharing in everything they do. They've been wiping out the outer settlements; whole towns and villages, murdered down to the last man, woman and child. Afterwards, the rebels help the Ghost Warriors collect the least damaged adult bodies, so they can be made over into Ghost Warriors. The other bodies . . . they do things with. It's not just Shub that practises atrocities. Let me call up some vid footage we have from their last attack. They let the cameraman live long enough to film it all, so we could see what the rebels have been doing.'

He activated a viewscreen, and Random and Ruby watched Shub and the rebel forces destroy a town with fire and steel and horror. Savage watched their faces more than he watched the screen. He'd already seen the vid footage, and knew he'd never be able to forget what he'd seen.

Ghost Warriors went stalking through the streets, killing everything that moved that wasn't them. Corpses, with grey and blue skin, metal eyes and grinning teeth revealed by cracked and rotting lips. Some so badly damaged that bones showed through tears and exposed meat, or loops of tattered intestine hung from slashed-open bellies. Computer implants moved servo-mechanisms in dead limbs, and men and women who had fallen nobly in the battle against evil were raised ignobly to fight in the name of Shub. Terror weapons, horror troops, they could not be hurt, argued with or stopped. Wounds or damage only slowed them down. As long as the armoured computer implant remained intact, whatever remained of the body would keep going, obeying its merciless orders.

They stalked their human prey with inhuman patience, killing those who stood and fought, chasing down those who fled. They killed with gun and sword or anything that came to hand. Buildings blazed around them, the leaping flames fanned by the endless winds. People ran back and forth, screaming. The living went blade to blade with the dead, to defend their homes or perhaps only to buy time for their loved ones to escape, but they all died, in the end. The Ghost Warriors would not stop till all that lived lay still before them, as dead as they were. That was how they had been programmed. They dragged the last few women and children from their hiding places and put on a show for the camera, tearing their victims apart with inhuman strength. Some ganged up on their victims, rending their limbs away, leaving the head and torso to scream and bleed to death on the already scarlet ground. Shub had always understood the value of a good show. Afterwards, the Ghost Warriors built strange constructions from human pieces, dozens of feet high, with human bones as supports, and eyeless children's faces as ornaments.

The scene faded away, and the viewscreen shut itself down. Random let out a breath he hadn't realized he'd been holding. He'd seen his share of death and slaughter and atrocity down the years, but this relentless, mechanical murder chilled his soul. He looked across at Savage.

'I saw people in there. Humans, not Ghost Warriors. They were killing too, and looting. Rebels?'

'That's right,' said Savage. 'They work with the machines. Partners, allies. They're a part of everything that happens. Like so many other places, there was nothing special or important about that village. Place called Trawl. Population maybe five hundred. I had family there; they're all dead now. Trawl didn't even have any strategic value, but the rebels destroyed it anyway. Just because it was there. And they killed everyone to send us a message – that there was nothing they wouldn't do, and that there was nothing we could do to stop them. I lost all that remained of my family in Trawl. There's nobody else; I am the last of my line, and my name dies with me.'

'Yeah,' said Ruby. 'There's a lot of that about, these days. I can't believe humans would fight alongside Ghost Warriors of their own free will.'

Savage shrugged. 'They're desperate. And a lot of them have old scores to settle. And maybe . . . they've developed a taste for killing, I don't know. Sometimes I think the whole Empire's gone crazy. The old order was bad, but what we've got now is worse.'

'It's just a transition,' said Random. 'There were always bound to be difficulties, in replacing one system with another. Things will get better, in time.'

'I'm sure that's a comfort to all those who die during your transition,' said Savage. 'Or to those who have to watch them die. What happened, Sir Random? I always believed in you. Watched your battle against Lionstone on black-market vids.

Prayed that some day, somehow, you'd succeed. Now I don't know what to believe any more.'

'Have faith,' said Random. 'Not in me, but in the people. They'll put the Empire back together again, and make it stronger than it was. All this will pass.'

'If you start talking about birth pains again, I may puke,' said Ruby.

'Nothing of worth is ever achieved without pain and sacrifice,' said Random, concentrating on Savage. 'We owe it to those who have died to keep on fighting, to keep struggling, for what they and we believe in.'

'I want to believe,' said Savage. 'I want all this death and suffering to have been for something. But what have we achieved, if people like de Lisle can come back into power again?'

'Trust me,' said Random. 'I'll take care of him, once I get back to Golgotha.'

'Can you stop the rebels?' said Savage. 'Can you stop the Ghost Warriors?'

'Of course we can,' said Ruby. 'We're the good guys. Right, Random?'

'Well, I am,' said Random. 'I'm not too sure about you.' He looked straight at Savage. 'We'll do everything we can to save this world from its enemies. I swear it, upon my blood and my honour. Now, I need you to work out a map for me, showing how much territory the rebels control, and what direction they're moving in. I want some idea of what they're going to hit next.'

Savage nodded and got to work at his terminal again. Random gestured unobtrusively to Ruby, and they moved off a way so they could talk quietly in private.

'Originally, I thought we'd been sent here to distract us from our investigations into Shub's connection on Golgotha,' said Random. 'But this is clearly more important. Shub has to be stopped here, and stopped hard, or they'll move from planet to planet, repeating these tactics.'

'But what can we do, against an army of Ghost Warriors?' said Ruby. 'For all our powers, there's only two of us. We can't be everywhere at once. You made a real nice speech to that boy, but I don't see how we're going to back it up. Even trained soldiers have a hard time against Ghost Warriors, and this city's army is strictly amateur hour. If our armies go one on one, Shub will chew them up and spit them out.'

'I do have some experience plotting strategies against superior odds,' said Random. 'I did win my fair share of campaigns, you know.'

'You lost just as many.'

'That was then, this is now. If Savage's map shows what I think it's going to, I have an idea that may win us this war in one blow.'

'A desperate last gamble, against overpowering odds, with everything depending on us. That sort of thing?'

'Yes,' said Random, 'that sort of thing.'

'Ah,' said Ruby, shaking her head. 'Business as usual. Look, just once, why not do the sensible thing – call in half a dozen starcruisers and have them blast the rebel positions from orbit?'

'One; there aren't half a dozen starcruisers available. Two; their sensors wouldn't work accurately through the Loki storms. Three; if we escalate matters, so will Shub. We have to beat them with what we have here, so they'll think twice about trying this anywhere else.'

'I hate it when you go all logical on me,' said Ruby. 'All right, here we go again. Time to snatch victory from the jaws of defeat, once more and with feeling. I guess if we can survive that bloody crash, we can survive anything.'

Savage called politely for their attention, and they all crowded round his monitor to study the map Savage and the computers had put together.

'So far, the rebel forces have been concentrating on hit-and-run attacks,' said Savage. 'They strike during lulls in the weather, destroy the target and then disappear before we can retaliate. Travel has to be on foot, for us and them. Aircraft won't work on Loki; the storms are too much for them. In a sense, that's been our salvation. It limits the damage Shub's been able to do.'

'What about force shields?' said Ruby. 'A good screen could handle any weather this world threw at it.'

'Loki's electromagnetic fields are very unusual. It takes a hell of a lot of power to maintain a shield here. You wouldn't believe how much it takes to maintain Vidar's screen. Nothing short of a starcruiser could generate enough power to maintain a travelling shield on Loki for any length of time.'

'This was all covered in the briefings before we left, Ruby,' said Random. 'I do wish you'd learn to pay attention.'

'Random, even I can see what's happening on this map. The rebels have been quietly surrounding Vidar, cutting the city off from outside help. This is their next target, has to be. Vidar itself.'

'Right,' said Random. 'They're finally ready for the killing stroke.'

'Then we have to do something,' said Savage, turning in his chair to glare at Random and Ruby. 'You've got to do something! You're the great heroes!'

'Easy, boy,' said Ruby. 'We can't just rush out and attack the rebel forces on our own. Even I'm not that crazy.'

'So what do we do? Sit and wait for them to come to us?'

'Almost,' said Random. 'Rather, we make them come to us, in a setting we choose. We can't risk letting them lay siege to Vidar. This city wasn't built to stand off attacks by Ghost Warriors and Shub technology. We need to face them in the field. According to the briefing we were given, your computers can predict lulls in the weather, moments of calm in the storms. Is that right?'

'Well, yes. We're managing about eighty per cent accuracy. But lulls never last for long.'

'This one won't have to. We find our calm spot, occupy it to our best advantage, and then wait for the rebel forces to come to us. And then we kick their ass. The rebels may have Ghost Warriors, but you've got us. And we've never lost a battle yet.'

'Come bloody close sometimes,' muttered Ruby.

'Shut up, Ruby. We can do this, Peter. It'll take every armed man you've got and will mean leaving Vidar practically defenceless, but it's a necessary risk. Our powers will make the difference. One last battle, to end it all.'

'Hold everything,' said Ruby. 'This all depends on the rebels and Shub sending their whole force against us, to fight on ground they must know we've chosen and prepared. Why should they? They're doing fine as they are.'

'They'll come to us because we'll have something they want. Something they want very badly.'

'Like what?' said Ruby.

'Us,' said Random. 'You and me. We hold within us the secrets and powers of the Madness Maze. Shub will risk everything for a chance at us, and you can bet rebel spies in the city will have got the word out by now.'

'Oh, great,' said Ruby. 'Just wonderful. We're going to be the bait in a trap, in a weather lull that may or may not last till the battle's over, with a whole army of Ghost Warriors expressly intent on getting to us at all costs. Have I missed anything?'

'Actually, no,' said Random. 'I think that sums it up rather well. How about it, Savage; what do your computers have to say about imminent lulls in the weather?'

'I'm there,' said Savage, bent over his terminal. 'And it looks like our luck's in, for once. There's a major lull due in the next few days. It should last for several hours, and it'll cover half a square mile around a valley not too far from Vidar. This particular lull turns up on a regular cycle, so it's fairly dependable. Just what the doctor ordered.'

'About time something went our way,' said Ruby. 'I say we go for it, Jack. You're right; this is too good an opportunity to miss.'

'Then let's go and talk to the people who think they're in charge here,' said Random. 'We've got an army to put together, and not a lot of time to do it in.'

In a steel and stone bunker, deep beneath the surface of Loki, dug by Shub technology, the rebel forces planned their next objectives. Or at least, the human element did. Young Jack Random and his Ghost Warriors took their orders from the rogue AIs back on Shub, and mostly they chose not to share their tactics with the human rebels, who were told what they needed to know and nothing else. The leaders of the human rebels, ex-Planetary Controller Matthew Tallon and ex-Mayor of Vidar Terrence Jacks, sat facing each other across a simple metal table, in a cramped room with bare walls and a low ceiling, that served many functions, as necessary. Tallon and Jacks got the room to themselves, for the moment, because they were the leaders. They picked bitterly at the main meal of the day; protein cubes and distilled water, produced by Shub machines. All the elements necessary to sustain life, but that was it. Young Jack Random saw to it that his human allies had everything necessary for survival, but nothing else.

'God, I hate this stuff,' said Jacks, pushing the small chunks of protein about his plate. 'It tastes of nothing, takes ages to chew and it doesn't even come in any interesting colours.'

'I know,' said Tallon. 'I'd kill for a thick steak and a decent wine to wash it down with.'

'We've killed for less than that,' said Jacks, and their eyes met across the table.

'There's been looting again, hasn't there?' said Tallon. 'Even though I forbade it.'

'You can't blame the men. I mean, the dead in the towns don't need their food any more, do they?'

'But there's never enough to go round. Only a taste, for a lucky few. Enough to remind a man how foul this stuff really is. So the men fight each other over the spoils, when they should be conserving their strength for the struggle to come. We can't afford to lose any more people, dammit! I know our life is hard, but we chose it. We chose to be rebels, rather than bow down to tyranny.'

'And a hell of a lot it's got us,' said Jacks. 'Allied with the Enemies of Humanity against our own kind, our own people. We should never have dealt with Shub in the first place.'

'We had no choice! The Empire wouldn't protect us, and the power base they inflicted on us was hopelessly corrupt. Our only chance for a decent life lay with calling in Shub's help.'

'You call this a decent life? Hiding in a hole in the ground, only coming out to kill our own people?'

'Things will get better, you'll see. This is just a time of transition.'

'What have we come to, Matt?' said Jacks. 'Living like rats in their holes, standing by as the Ghost Warriors kill women and children. Some of our men have even started joining in, taking out their anger and frustrations on the defenceless.

Are we any closer to winning this bloody war, because I can't see it. All I can see is our becoming as inhuman as our allies.'

'We do what's necessary.' Tallon held Jacks's gaze unwaveringly. 'We swore an oath during the rebellion against Lionstone, remember? Swore it on our blood and our honour: *Whatever it Takes*. We swore there was nothing we wouldn't do, nothing we'd shrink from, to gain our freedom. That hasn't changed. We're still fighting the same enemy.'

'Are we? Jack Random and Ruby Journey have come here, to fight us! Two of the greatest heroes of the rebellion, the people who inspired us to fight, have come here specifically to fight *us*. How the hell did we end up on opposite sides from *them*? We can't fight them!'

'Yes we can. There's just the two of them. What difference can they make against an army of Ghost Warriors?'

'Are you kidding? They have powers no one understands! They overthrew Golgotha, toppled Lionstone from the Iron Throne and remade the Empire. They're legends!'

'They're monsters. The Madness Maze turned them into something other than human.'

'Isn't that what we've done?' said Jacks, and Tallon had no reply.

'My, my,' said Young Jack Random from the doorway. 'Do I detect despondency? You don't want to worry about Random and Journey. They may be legends, or monsters, but then so am I.'

The two humans looked round sharply, glaring at the machine standing at ease in the doorway. Young Jack Random was a Fury, a robot in human form, hidden inside cloned human skin. He was tall and handsome, clad in silver armour, every inch a hero. A killing machine with a hero's face, without mercy or compassion or honour: leader of the Shub forces on Loki. He smiled charmingly at Tallon and Jacks.

'Sorry to interrupt your meal, gentlemen, but I thought you should know there's been a change of plan, and we'll be moving out soon. Better get your people together and properly motivated. No more sneak attacks; we're going one on one with the colonists. Our army versus theirs, winner takes all.'

'What brought this on all of a sudden?' said Tallon, rising to his feet. 'I've always dictated policy. We've nothing to gain from such open tactics, and everything to lose. What's changed?'

'Jack Random and Ruby Journey will be leading the city forces. And Shub wants them, dead or alive. We could learn so much from studying them.'

Jacks stood up too. 'You want them so badly you're willing to risk all our lives, and our cause, just for a chance at getting your hands on them?'

'Got it in one,' said Young Jack Random.

'No,' said Tallon. 'I can't accept this. My people are still exhausted from their last raid. You can't ask them to go out again.'

'I'm not asking,' said Young Jack Random, smiling. 'Anyone who doesn't march with us, dies here.'

'You need us!' said Jacks.

'Now where did you ever get that idea?' said the Fury. 'You are useful, nothing more. Pray you don't outlast that usefulness.'

'We can't fight Random and Journey!' said Tallon. 'Not them. They're monsters. They can do things no one should be able to do.'

'Not to worry,' said Young Jack Random, still smiling. 'We always thought there was a chance some of the Maze survivors might turn up here. It was a calculated gamble. So we brought along a special little something, just for them. Something that will make them merely human again. And then you'll have no trouble taking them, will you, gentlemen?'

'No,' said Tallon. 'We won't. They perverted and corrupted our cause. They made a deal with the Families, instead of wiping them out, as we were promised. They told us we were free, but nothing's really changed. The same bastards are still running things, same as they always did. To hell with Jack Random, and that psycho bitch Journey.'

'We were betrayed,' said Jacks. 'After everything we'd done for Loki, after all our blood and suffering and the good men we lost, in the end it was all for nothing.'

The two humans looked at each other, seeing again old hurts from the past. Their words had the familiarity of much repetition. Only by continually rehearsing their old wrongs and grievances could they keep their rage fresh, and excuse the terrible things they had seen and done in their alliance with Shub. They needed to believe they were still the heroes of their rebellion.

'When I took over as Planetary Controller, after the rebellion, I thought the war was over,' said Tallon. 'I thought we'd won. I thought I could finally start making changes, real changes; put things right and do what needed to be done. I was going to put the mines in the hands of the miners, see that everyone got a fair share of the profits. I had such great ideas; all the things I'd planned and dreamed of . . . But it was all a sham. My position meant nothing, my ideas were ignored. The people who actually ran things, who controlled the money and the bureaucracy, found more and more ways to obstruct and sideline me. Whatever I tried to create always cost too much, or wasn't practical, or got bogged down in endless committees. The same old order of wealth and privilege continued; the mining business was still riddled with corruption and kickbacks, and safety measures were ignored in the demand for greater and greater profits. I was in charge, officially, but I couldn't enforce my orders. I was helpless, little more than a figurehead, there to fool the people into thinking something had changed.'

'So all that was left to us was to rebel again,' said Jacks. 'And this time, make sure we had enough power on our side that we couldn't be denied. And so we turned to Shub, and they sent you, Young Jack Random, or whatever the hell you really are. You and all your killing machines.'

'And haven't we done an excellent job?' said the Fury. 'Our forces haven't lost a single campaign.'

'Campaign? You call slaughtering defenceless villagers a campaign?' Tallon glared at Young Jack Random, so angry he could barely speak. 'It has to stop! I won't stand for this any more. Stop the massacres now, while we still have some popular support left!'

'We only do what is necessary,' Young Jack Random said calmly. 'We must destroy the morale of the enemy, so that when we finally come to Vidar, they will surrender rather than face extermination. Thus, a lengthy siege and much loss of life on both sides is avoided. You did agree to these tactics, before we began.'

'Yes,' said Jacks, 'we agreed. But we never thought it would go on this long, never knew there'd be so much blood on our hands.'

'Better a few hundred die in a few villages, than thousands in the city,' said Tallon. 'That's how you sold it to us. But Vidar still shows no sign of surrendering, and now they have the real Jack Random, and Ruby Journey. They have monsters on their side.'

'Not to worry,' said Young Jack Random. 'You have me.' And he smiled on them both, and turned and left.

Tallon and Jacks sank back into their seats again, not looking at each other. Tallon's hands were clenched into fists on the table top. Jacks looked sick.

'Monsters,' said Tallon quietly. 'Wherever I look, I see monsters.'

'What have we done, Matt?' said Jacks. 'We've unleashed something we have no hope of controlling.'

'We have to go on,' said Tallon. 'We're in too deep now. We have to go to Vidar and win this, or all the blood and all the deaths will have been for nothing.'

'But . . . say we win. Say we take control of Vidar, and then Loki. You think Shub is just going to pull its forces out, and leave us to get on with running things? What's to stop them just slaughtering us all, and making Loki into another Shub planet?'

'We're allies,' said Tallon.

'Are we? We're sure as hell not equal partners. We have no way of enforcing our side of things. Whatever Shub decides, we'll have no choice but to go along. We're damned, Matt, whatever happens.'

'Then we're damned!' said Tallon. 'And I don't care. Just as long as our enemies fall first. Just let me live long enough to see them all die, and I'll be happy. When all else fails, there is always revenge.'

Jack Random and Ruby Journey strode unhurriedly through the crowded corridors of the city Council building, and people hurried to get out of their way. There was bad news

495

in the air. Everyone could smell it, but no one knew what it was yet, or where it might fall. They kept their heads down, and hoped not to be noticed. Random and Ruby began to walk a little faster. They could sense something was wrong, and the closer they got to the Council chamber, the more wrong it felt.

It was barely morning when Random and Ruby received a call from the city Council, demanding their attendance at once. Normally Random would have told them what they could do with their demand, but something in the barely restrained panic filling the comm clerk's voice had convinced him this was something he and Ruby should see for themselves.

The chamber door was guarded by four armed men, but they moved quickly aside as Random and Ruby approached. One even opened the door for them. Inside, de Lisle and his people were standing together, staring unhappily at two large wooden crates on the floor before them. The crates looked perfectly ordinary, not at all threatening, but the councillors were looking at them as though they expected a Grendel to leap out at any moment. It was a measure of how upset they were that they looked at Random and Ruby with open relief. De Lisle patted at his sweating forehead with a handkerchief, and gestured at the crates with a hand that wasn't as steady as it might have been.

'These were waiting for us here in the chamber when we arrived for work this morning, along with a polite little note, saying A Present from Shub. Nothing else. We have no idea how they got here. Given our current level of security, this should be impossible. I can only assume there are traitors among my people, rebel sympathizers. We haven't dared open the crates. They make threatening noises if they're touched. They make equally threatening noises if we try and leave. We've been trapped in here with them for almost an hour.'

'Typical Shub terror tactics,' said Ruby, studying the crates interestedly. 'Have you tried scanning the contents?'

'Yes. The interiors appear to be lined with something our scanners can't penetrate.'

'Could be a bomb,' said Ruby, crouching down before the

nearest crate and studying the lid with a professional eye. 'No lock, no clasps, no obvious electronic countermeasures. Maybe it's a warning of some kind. If Shub just wanted us dead, these things would have gone off the moment Jack and I entered the room. I say we open the crates, and see what happens.'

'Sounds like a good plan to me,' said Random. 'Ruby and I would probably survive a bomb anyway. But just in case, Councillors, I suggest you retire to the far end of the room.'

The councillors did so hastily, not bothering to take their dignity with them. Random crouched down beside Ruby.

'I don't think we'll encounter any booby traps,' he said thoughtfully. 'Shub wants us to see what's in these crates. Otherwise, they wouldn't have bothered with two. One would have been enough for a bomb, or any other terror weapon.'

'Could contain some kind of Fury,' said Ruby, frowning. 'The crates are big enough for a smallish one. But why bother with a killing machine, when a bomb would be just as effective?'

'Maybe it's something aimed specifically at us,' said Random. 'Some new kind of Shub tech designed with us in mind.'

'Maybe,' said Ruby. She looked at Random, and grinned. 'Want to toss over which one of us gets to open the first crate?'

'I'll open the first,' said Random. 'You always cheat.'

He took a firm hold of the lid on the nearest crate and yanked it off. A puff of refrigerated air rose up, and Random and Ruby backed away quickly, but there was no other response from the crate. They moved cautiously forward, and looked inside. A dead face with pure white skin flecked with frost looked up at them. The open eyes were frosted too. Random and Ruby looked at each other, and then looked back in the crate. A human body had been wrapped around the interior walls of the crate like a snake. He'd been cut open from throat to groin, and his chest and abdomen were strangely flat. Ruby raised an eyebrow.

'Whatever I was expecting, this isn't it. Anyone you know?'

'I don't think so. Why would Shub send us a dead man? And a carefully preserved one, at that?'

'And why arrange him like that? OK, it was probably the only way to get him in the crate, but why not just use a bigger crate?' She reached in and grabbed a handful of the dead man's hair. She tried to pull him out, but the body barely budged, stuck with cold and frost to the interior walls. The frozen tissues gave out loud cracking sounds as they were forcibly stretched. The long abdominal cut opened slowly like a mouth, and it was only then that Random and Ruby realized the body had been completely gutted. Everything inside the chest and abdomen had been removed.

'The cut's so precise it might have been made with a scalpel,' Random said thoughtfully, and Ruby released her handful of hair. The head fell back against the crate wall with a loud thud. Ruby examined her hand. It was already covered with frost. She sniffed, untouched by the cold, and looked back at the hollow man.

'They really emptied him out, Jack. They didn't just take his guts; the bones are gone too. No ribcage, no sternum, even the collarbones are gone. But why send us an eviscerated dead man? Is this supposed to frighten us?'

'Maybe it's a warning of what they mean to do to us all,' said Random warily. 'Kill us, empty us out and make us into Ghost Warriors. Let's look in the other crate. Perhaps the answer's in there.'

Ruby opened the second crate, waving aside the cold air that steamed up from inside, impatient to see what it contained. The she wrinkled her nose, and looked at Random. 'You have got to see this, Jack. This is really disgusting.'

Random leaned over the second crate. A set of human organs had been arranged neatly on the floor of the crate, pale pink and grey and covered with shining frost. Carefully laid human bones kept them separate. The heart had been wrapped in a pretty pink ribbon, tied in a bow.

'The last time I saw anything like this I was still a clonelegger,' said Ruby, staring fascinatedly at the human remains. 'What the hell is the point of this?'

'There's another envelope,' said Random. 'Under the heart.' He reached in and carefully slid the paper out from under the solid organ. He studied the envelope carefully. The thick paper was permeated with frost crystals.

'Interesting. It's addressed to us. Shub knows we're here.'

'Open the damned thing,' said Ruby impatiently.

Inside the envelope was a single sheet of paper with a set of printed instructions on it. Random unfolded it carefully, not wanting the brittle paper to crack apart in his hands. He studied the message in silence for some moments. Ruby pushed up beside him.

'Well? What is it? What does it say?'

'It appears to be a set of instructions, on how to put together a human in kit form. According to this, if you put the bones and organs back in the right order, close him up and thaw him out, the human should start functioning again.'

'Now that is just sick,' said Ruby. 'That is too sick, even for me.'

'Strange, too,' said Random. 'I never knew Shub to show a sense of humour before. This is too . . . human.'

Ruby shook her head. 'I'm still no wiser as to why they sent us this. It doesn't make any sense. Did they think this would frighten us?'

Random shrugged. 'Let's see what the councillors have to say.'

He beckoned them over, and they returned to the crates, somewhat emboldened now that they hadn't exploded after all. Then they looked inside the crates. One just made it to the door before being sick. Two others retreated to the far end of the room again, and refused to come back. Bentley and de Lisle stood their ground, though they were visibly upset.

'I know this man,' Bentley said finally. 'He volunteered to go alone and unarmed to try to negotiate a settlement with the rebel leaders. He used to be a friend and colleague of Terrence Jacks, the ex-Mayor. He thought their friendship would guarantee his safety. He should have known better, after everything they've done. I tried to warn him, but he believed some kind of deal was still possible, with good will on both sides.'

'The rebels did this?' said Ruby. 'What the hell for?'

'To send us a message,' said de Lisle. 'That they're not interested in negotiating. You can see now the nature of the foe we're dealing with. Don't be fooled into thinking of them as your old comrades. Shub is bad enough, but the rebels here are animals. This is just another of their attempts to undermine our morale. We have to keep this quiet; it mustn't go beyond this room. Do you agree, Sir Random?'

'Yeah. The people don't need to know about this. We'll just say the crates contained severed heads from the outer settlements. That's nasty enough to motivate them, without sickening them too much. Dispose of all this secretly. Better incinerate it.'

'I just had a thought,' said Ruby, smiling wickedly. 'What if we followed the instructions, and put the human together? Do you think he'd work? I mean, Shub knows a lot of things. He just might get up and start functioning again.'

The councillor at the door lost what was left of his breakfast. The other councillors looked at her with open revulsion. Random shook his head.

'I don't think that's a road we should go down. Whatever we ended up with, you can be sure it wouldn't be human. Burn it, de Lisle. Burn it all. And then scatter the ashes, just in case.'

Things were relatively quiet after that. The rebels headed for Vidar in one great force, human and Shub, destroying and razing all settlements in their path. The storm winds kept blowing, but everyone knew the lull was coming, and with it the final battle for Loki. Random and Ruby spent all their time struggling to turn Vidar's volunteer force into something like an army. There was no shortage of volunteers, but most didn't know one end of a sword from the other, and had never fired a gun in anger in their life. They were mostly tough enough, and brave; the weak didn't last long on a hard mining world like Loki. But turning even the most willing volunteer into a trained soldier takes time, and everyone knew that time was running out. When the lull came they would have to fight, whatever state they were in.

So it was something of a surprise to everyone when Random excused himself from the training exercise on the second afternoon, left Ruby in charge and disappeared on a mission of his own. Wrapped in a long cloak, with the hood pulled well down to conceal his features, Jack Random made his way through narrow, dirty streets into the really scummy part of Vidar. Every city has a part of town where the mostly respectable can come in secret, in search of the pleasures that may not have a name but certainly have a price. A few local hard men thought to intercept Random on his way, and relieve him of the weight of any valuables he might be burdened with, but a glimpse of energy gun was usually all it took to make them back down. Random had to kill one man, but he didn't seem to be the sort that anyone would miss.

Random finally reached his destination in the late afternoon; a broken-down drinking establishment that had probably looked sleazy and disreputable from the moment it opened. For a while Random stood in the shadows on the other side of the street, making sure he hadn't been followed. He didn't think anyone could sneak up on him any more, with all his powers, but old habits die hard. Nobody looked up when he finally walked into the gloomy bar. It was the kind of place where everyone was careful to mind their own business.

There were no windows, and the lights were kept low to encourage confidentiality. There was an atmosphere of illegal smoke, cheap perfume and general paranoia. Customers sat at rickety tables in twos and threes, talking business in lowered voices, pushing anonymous packages back and forth, or just sitting staring into drinks they didn't touch while they waited for their contacts to show up. There was no sawdust on the floor. Probably someone had stolen it. Random had spent a lot of time in the past meeting people in places like this, searching for the kind of answers that could only be found in such company. He spotted his contact, sitting well back in the shadows, and moved over to join him.

'There had better be a damned good reason for bringing me here,' said Random, as he polished the seat of his chair with a handkerchief before sitting down. 'I've been in some dives in my time, and this is definitely one of them. I'm almost afraid to touch anything in case I catch something. God alone knows what the booze is like here.'

'Actually, it's pretty good,' said Peter Savage. 'For the price. And we're meeting here to talk because it's one of the few places where de Lisle's informers wouldn't dare follow me. I've been digging into those computer files you helped me turn up.'

'All right; what have you found?'

'It's worse than we thought. De Lisle and his cronies were sent here deliberately to wreck Loki's economy. Once they'd done their job and left, their bosses on Golgotha would have moved in and bought everything up at rock-bottom prices. Including the colonists. To pay off their debts, they'd have had to take lifetime indentures: slaves, in all but name. By the time anyone found out about it, it would have been too late to do anything.'

'Can they do that?' said Random. 'I had Parliament pass a whole bunch of laws, just to prevent things like that.'

'The law isn't much good when presented with a *fait accompli*. Someone would have had to sue, and there wouldn't have been anyone left on Loki able to afford the lawyers. Everything was going smoothly. No one suspected anything. They would have got away with it, if the rebels hadn't made their alliance with Shub, and thrown everything into chaos.'

'Tallon must have found out about this. That's what made him desperate enough to call in Shub's forces.'

'Looks that way. Tallon and Jacks were big men in the original rebellion. Hardline idealists, heroes. It must have broken their hearts to discover it had all been for nothing.'

'They didn't have to go to Shub,' said Random. 'They could have got word to Parliament. They could have come to me. I would have done something, if I'd known.'

'You've been busy,' said Savage. 'How many people wanted to talk to you every day, and how many were turned away because there just weren't enough hours in the day to see them all? You had to pick and choose, and rely on your subordinates to weed out the head cases and the time-wasters. And you can bet good money that de Lisle's bosses would have made sure that word never got to you, one way or another.'

Random sat quietly for a while. Savage sipped his wine and watched Random brood. Even sitting calm and silent, the old professional rebel still looked sharp and dangerous. If anyone could save Loki, it might be him. The murmur of

502

hushed conversation went around the bar, rising and falling like a distant tide. Random sighed, and shook his head.

'I won the rebellion. Threw down the Iron Bitch. Weakened if not destroyed the Families. And nothing's changed. I thought when the war was over, I'd finally be allowed to retire; get some peace, some rest. Put down my burden and have a life of my own, at last. I should have known better. No matter how many wars you fight, another always comes along. I thought I could remake myself, put away the warrior's sword and become a politician, a man of peace. But I don't believe in politics; never have. I believe in right and wrong, not deals and compromises.'

'And yet you agreed to the deal with Blue Block,' Savage said carefully. 'Millions would have died or been ruined if you hadn't.'

'Yes, I saved lives, but only by compromising everything I ever believed in. I should have stood firm. Said no, and to hell with the consequences. People would have died, maybe whole worlds, but in the end we would have been rid of the Families and people like de Lisle for ever. A fair price, perhaps, I don't know. All I know is that tomorrow I have to lead an army out to fight rebels who just might have right on their side, to protect the interests of scum like de Lisle. Where's the right in that? Where's the honour? I used to be an honourable man. I was famous for it. I wonder when I lost it.'

'The rebels might have been justified in the beginning,' said Savage. 'But they lost all claim to the moral high ground when they called in Shub, the Enemies of Humanity. What good to save the world, if you lose your soul in the process? They have no excuses. Everyone knows how deals with the Devil work out. I've never forgotten the first footage I saw of Young Jack Random and his Ghost Warriors in action. Rows and rows of men, women and children crucified on metal crosses. Left to die slowly as the abrasive storm winds slowly flayed them alive. I know where I stand, Sir Random, and so does everyone else in Vidar. Even these scumbags sitting around us, making a last few desperate deals, will be with us tomorrow, sword and gun in hand, to fight the war of man against machine. Even them.'

'I'll give you good odds de Lisle and his cronies won't be there.'

'It's not their world, not really. No one expected us to survive when we first came here, let alone turn Loki into a viable colony as well as a mining world, but we did it. We were so hard, the storms of Loki just broke against us. If a whole planet couldn't defeat us, a few tin soldiers and walking corpses aren't going to do it. Even if they are led by Young Jack Random.'

'Don't you worry about him,' said Random. 'He was never more than a flashy imitation of the real thing. I'll deal with him. And then I'll come back and deal with de Lisle. I give you my word.'

'Jack Random's word is good enough for me,' said Peter Savage.

Random smiled for the first time, reached across and took Savage's glass and tried some of the wine. He shuddered, and put the glass down firmly. 'God, you must be tougher than you look if you can drink that stuff voluntarily.' But the smile didn't last long, and his face fell back into brooding lines, so that he looked much older than his apparent youth. 'I've been here before, you know, on worlds like this. Cold Rock, Mistworld . . . but what Loki reminds me of most is Virimonde. What used to be Owen Deathstalker's world.'

'The world Shub destroyed, under Valentine Wolfe,' said Savage, nodding. 'I've seen the holo documentaries. We all have. But that's not going to happen here. We have an army.'

'Yeah. I'm just glad Owen isn't here. It would break his heart to see another world faced with such destruction.'

Savage leaned forward, his eyes shining. 'What's he really like? The Deathstalker? Has he really done all the things they say he has?'

'Most of them, yes. You'd be surprised. If there's a single real hero to come out of the rebellion, it's him, not me. He's never compromised, never once wavered from what he believed in. The best kind of warrior; the man who never wanted to be one, but fought anyway because he believed in the rightness of his cause. I'd given up; the Empire had broken me. But he brought me back . . . What is he like, really? A good man in bad times. The only really honourable man I ever met.'

'Would he come to help us? If we asked him?'

'Probably. But I have no idea where he is right now. Once, I would have known just by thinking about it, we were that close. But we've become distanced since then, grown apart. I gave up who I was to become somebody else, someone I thought I was supposed to be. You don't know what I'm rambling on about, do you, Savage, but you're too polite to interrupt. It doesn't matter: tomorrow we go out to meet the army from Hell, and all problems will be decided then.'

'I can't wait,' said Savage, raising his wine glass in a toast to Random. 'It will be an honour and a privilege to fight beside the legendary professional rebel!'

Random looked at him sadly, and said nothing.

The human army, the army of last resort, Loki's only hope, gathered noisily in the great square before the main gates in the city's huge outer wall. Everyone had a sword, and some had a gun too. Men and women wielded their weapons with grim enthusiasm, and struck bold poses for the hovering holo cameras which would be accompanying them into battle. The war would be broadcast live, shown in real time to those unfortunate enough to be staying behind. Those who were too young, or too old, the sick and the lame and those necessary for the city's security. Like de Lisle and his people, who had chosen not to make an appearance. There were no flyers, no ground vehicles; the storm might be heading for a lull, but the winds in the upper atmosphere would still be strong enough to toss gravity craft around like toys, and the dust floating in the air would be more than enough to short out the motors of any ground craft. Vidar's army would go to victory or damnation on its own two feet.

Jack Random and Ruby Journey stood with their backs to the great airlock, and watched the excited confusion with knowing, experienced eyes. They knew enthusiasm wasn't enough to win battles. When the Vidar army finally clashed with Shub and the rebels, some would inevitably break and run, simply because not everyone has a killer in them. It's not something any man can know until he's tested. But most would stand and fight and die bravely, if need be. They knew they were fighting for something bigger than themselves.

Peter Savage was darting back and forth, trying to be everywhere at once, browbeating and cajoling different groups into some kind of order, anxious for his people to look good in front of his hero, Jack Random. The crowd good-naturedly let Savage get on with it. Bottles of booze were being freely handed back and forth, and Random decided he'd better get his army moving soon. A little booze was good for motivating people, but a drunken army was a losing army. Still, it was a six-hour hike to the chosen spot, and that would sweat most of the booze out of them. So he let them drink a little, before they had to leave. For all their enthusiasm and commitment, this was a crowd of strangers, brought together by need and duty and desperation. They had to win this battle, or lose everything. They couldn't retreat if things went bad, and hope for a second chance. If they fell back, the Ghost Warriors would pursue them tirelessly, to the walls of Vidar and beyond. The rebels were desperate too. If they could break this army, the war would be over, and they knew it. They had to win, while they still thought they had some control over Young Jack Random and his Shub forces.

Savage came over to Random, who nodded approvingly. 'Doing a good job, Savage. They're actually starting to look like an army.'

'Good,' said Savage. 'Because I've just received some news, and it's all bad. The Empire has become concerned enough about the situation here to send two starcruisers, but they're only D-class, so they won't get here for at least a week. Their orders are to negotiate with whoever has control of the mining equipment: the colonists, de Lisle and his people . . . or the rebels.'

'Can they do that?' said Ruby. 'Strike a deal with Shub allies?'

'Sure they can,' said Random. 'Politicians are nothing if not practical people. They need the cobalt this planet produces, and they'll deal with whoever they have to, to get it. Hard times make for hard choices, or at least that's how they'll sell it to the public. If the rebels were to win, and give the appearance of distancing themselves from Shub, Parliament would do business with them. They'd have no choice. It doesn't matter; it's just one more reason why we have to win this battle. Pass the word, Savage. It's time we were moving out. The lull will hit our chosen location in just over six hours, and we don't want to be late. We're going to need every second of that lull.'

Savage bobbed his head and hurried off into the crowd, shouting orders. Men and women gathered in their companies, and formed ranks as they'd been trained. Random turned to Ruby.

'Off we go to save the day, one more time. You know, Ruby, I've missed this. Things are so much simpler on a battlefield.'

'This is where we belong, Jack. Right in the middle of things, in blood up to our armpits. Peace was just a dream. You can't fight destiny.'

'Maybe,' said Random, 'maybe.'

And so the great gates opened, and the last army of Vidar filed through the huge airlock and streamed out into the raging storm, disregarding the violent weather in anticipation of the fighting still to come. They lowered their heads, hunched themselves inside their protective armour, and with two living legends to lead them, the last hope of Vidar and Loki went singing off to battle.

They made good time across the dark jagged landscape, and five hours later they passed through a narrow valley to reach the open plain where the lull was supposed to hit. They set up a temporary camp of reinforced tents, and waited impatiently for the storm to pass, as the computers had promised. When the lull finally came, it was like a kind of magic. The wind's voice fell away like the end of an oratorio, and suddenly there was utter silence. The air was still, like the eye of a hurricane. The constant pressure in the air was gone, and the dust settled slowly to the ground. It was like the end of the world, the last pause before Judgement Day. The people emerged from their tents and looked around them, seeing their world with new eyes. Most had never known anything but the endless storms.

People laughed and joked and cheered, and slapped each other on the shoulder, as though the lull was a sure sign of victory. Savage had them stripping off most of their heavy protective armour, so they'd have more freedom of movement once the fighting began. And when that was over, everyone stood in place, looking expectantly out across the open plain. The world was very still, as though holding its breath, waiting for everything to begin. And then the floating holo cameras out on the plain sent back the first pictures of the rebel and Shub forces. They were on their way. Random and Ruby and Savage crowded round a small monitor screen and nodded, satisfied. The enemy had taken the bait, and committed all their forces.

The Vidar army readied itself quickly, and surged out across the plain. The enemy came to meet them. There was no time or need for subtle tactics. The two opposite forces crashed together, no quarter asked or given, and blood spilled on the dusty ground. Human fighters threw themselves against walking corpses, and the thought of surrender was alien to both of them.

Within an hour, most of the living on both sides were dead.

The battle was a mess, groups of fighters surging this way and that, each concerned only with their personal part of the war. Swords rose and fell, hacking at living and unliving flesh. Axes chopped through human meat and jarred on bone. And from everywhere in the strange, quiet twilight came the sudden flaring and roar of discharging energy weapons. Men and women fell and did not rise again. Ghost Warriors fell too, blown apart by energy beams or surrounded and cut to pieces by howling warriors. The maddened mob surged back and forth on the blood-soaked ground, driven by rage and hatred that could be soothed only by victory or death. And among them moved the unfeeling warriors of the living dead, driven by cold, dispassionate minds that killed and killed and felt nothing at all. The bodies piled up on every side, and still the battle raged on.

Peter Savage fell, unnoticed.

He'd stuck close to Random and Ruby, guarding their backs, awed and amazed by the cold ferocity of their fighting.

He saw men and Ghost Warriors fall under their blades, swept almost casually aside by superior strength and speed, and his heart swelled to be fighting in such company. He thought they were invulnerable, protected by fate and destiny, and because he fought at their side, he must be too. He never even saw the blade that came thrusting out of nowhere, to slam into his ribcage and out again. The power of the blow, driven by servo-mechanism-assisted dead muscles, threw him to the bloody ground, and ignorant feet stamped around him.

At first, Savage thought he'd just had the wind knocked out of him, and tried to get straight back up again. But his legs wouldn't obey him, and when he put his hand to his side, it came away dripping blood. The pain hit him then, and he cried out in spite of himself. He was no quitter: he kept trying to get to his feet, even as his lifeblood drained away. His place was at Random's side, but his body wouldn't listen. The strength quickly went out of him and he died there, unseen and unremarked, not knowing that just to walk in the company of legends was not enough to make him a legend too. Peter Savage was a brave man, a hero to his city, but he was never more than human.

Jack Random and Ruby Journey, on the other hand, fought savagely and tirelessly, dealing out terrible wounds and sudden death with every blow, and what small injuries they took healed almost immediately. They were fighting at the peak of their powers, and no one could stand against them. They never saw Peter Savage fall, or even missed him, until much later. They were too busy doing what they did best; surviving against impossible odds and killing everything within reach. The dead piled up around them, the quivering, blood-streaked skin of the fallen rebel lying next to the grey decaying flesh of fallen Ghost Warriors. But Random and Ruby were so taken up with their own inhuman achievements that they never even noticed that gradually, foot by foot, they were being separated from the main body of the conflict.

It took little more than an hour for the human forces on both sides to pretty much wipe each other out. They never even noticed that the Shub forces had moved away, leaving them to fight their own war. The human survivors on each side, driven by mutual hatred, saw only each other. They circled each other warily, blood-soaked and bone-weary, sensing that the end was near, and unwilling to throw their lives away needlessly. With barely a few hundred human souls left in all, both sides scented victory. They fought doggedly, carefully, so wrapped up in their own needs they never became aware that the real battle for the future of Loki was being fought somewhere else.

There was a long narrow valley between the open plain and the city of Vidar, a straight pass between two huge mountains of black rock. It hadn't looked like much when the city army marched through it, but Random had recognized its strategic importance. It was the only way to reach Vidar that didn't involve a days-long detour. If the Ghost Warriors were to reach Vidar while the lull still held, they had to pass through the valley. So when Random and Ruby finally realized how far they'd been herded from the rest of their army, they wasted no time in cutting their way out of the surrounding Ghost Warriors, and ran like hell for the valley. Since there was no way they could get back to the Vidar army, all that remained was for them to defend the one strategic location that actually meant something. They soon outdistanced their pursuers, and took up a position guarding the entrance to the narrow valley.

It was over a mile long, but barely twenty feet wide, narrowing to ten at the entrance. Which meant that two people could hold off the army, for a time. Especially if the two people were living legends. It all depended on the odds.

Random and Ruby stood together at the entrance to the valley, leaning wearily on each other while they got their breath back. They'd had to cover a long distance at a dead run, and even more than human legs and lungs had their limits. And the fighting itself had been long and hard, with Random and Ruby having to operate at the very limits of their strength and speed to stay alive in the crush of mostly unliving assailants. A flashing sword or a random energy beam didn't care how important you were. After a while, their breathing slowed and their hearts no longer hammered quite so frantically in their breasts, and they were able to stand alone. They looked out at the army of walking corpses watching impassively from the open plain, and swore more or less in unison. There were almost a thousand Ghost Warriors, with swords and guns and a complete readiness to be destroyed if that was what it took to bring the enemy down. They were, after all, just machines, operated by computer minds far, far away.

'Can't say I like the odds,' said Jack Random. 'A thousand to two is just a little worrying.'

'We've faced worse,' said Ruby Journey.

Random looked at her. 'If we have, I must have missed it. A thousand Ghost Warriors would cause even Owen Deathstalker to have doubts. However, they have to come at us from the front, so that means only a handful can reach us at a time. If we pace ourselves, we might just outlast the bastards.'

'Unless they figure out some way to sneak up on us from behind. Or come down the sides of the valley.'

Random looked back into the valley, frowning thoughtfully. 'Unlikely. It would take them days to march round to the other end of the valley, and one way or another, we won't be here that long. And the sides of those mountains are pretty near vertical. Even experienced climbers would get nosebleeds just looking at them. No, Ruby; they have to come straight at us. Head to head.'

'Best way,' Ruby said briskly. 'So all we have to do is hold the Ghost Warriors off until our side wins, and comes to relieve us, right?'

'No,' said Random slowly. 'From what I saw of the fighting, I don't think we can count on anyone joining us. We have to assume that we're all that stands between Vidar and Shub. If we can hold them off till the lull is over and the storms return, then we'll have won. The city will be safe.'

'What about us?' said Ruby.

'We made it to the city through the storms before. We can do it again.'

'And the battle?'

'God knows,' said Random. 'Last I saw, the city army had the rebel forces on the ropes, but the real threat was always the Shub forces. And I don't think we made much of a dent in them. And there's something else that worries me, too.'

'There's always something that worries you,' Ruby said resignedly. 'What is it this time?'

'I haven't seen any sign of Young Jack Random yet. He wasn't anywhere in the battle – I would have known. So where is he, and what is he up to?'

'Damn. You're right, that is worrying.'

'If you don't like that one, you'll love this. Why aren't the Ghost Warriors attacking?'

'All right; I'll bite. Why?'

'Because they're waiting for someone. Most probably Young Jack Random. With reinforcements he didn't commit to the first battle.'

There was a sound out on the plain, and they both turned to look. The sound quickly developed into the rhythmic hammer of marching feet. And a second army of dead men came marching out of the distance, easily a thousand strong, with the shining silver armour-clad figure of Young Jack Random smiling at their head. They joined up with the first force of silently waiting Ghost Warriors, and then stood motionless in ranks, staring unblinking at the narrow opening to the valley, and the two flesh and blood legends who held it.

They ignored the two human forces still fighting it out some distance away. Shub knew where the real threat lay.

'Don't you ever get tired of being right all the time?' said Ruby, almost angrily. 'These are not good odds, Jack. We really might be in trouble here. They really do want us badly, don't they?'

'If there's a choice between being taken dead or alive, I think we'd be wise to go for dead,' said Random. 'Vivisection is probably not much fun at all if you're still aware when they do it.'

'I'm glad I've got you to look on the cheerful side,' said Ruby. 'I suppose running like hell is out of the question?'

'Unfortunately, yes. The Ghost Warriors would pursue us right to the gates of Vidar, and the city wouldn't last an hour against them. We have to hold our ground, to buy time. Time for Vidar's army to defeat the rebels; for the lull in the weather to pass and the storms to return. Or, if all else fails, for us to whittle down the number of Ghost Warriors to the point where the city might stand a chance. Either way, it's all down to us.'

'Of course,' said Ruby Journey. 'It always is, isn't it?'

'We've got eight, maybe nine hours till the lull is over,' said Random calmly. 'We might last till then. After that, things should get really interesting. Forget what I said earlier. They might just decide to come after us anyway, even through the storms. After all, they're dead. They don't feel the wind, or the cold, or the cutting dust. And Shub really does want us very badly. I wonder if that's why they sent Young Jack Random here, to be bait in a trap for us . . . It doesn't matter. We had to come, we were needed. No, Ruby; I think we have to accept that we're here for the duration. Until one side or the other has nothing left to gain.'

'Hold everything,' said Ruby. 'I think the curtain just went up.'

The whole army of Ghost Warriors came surging across the plain towards them, while Young Jack Random stood to one side and cheered them on with a cheerful human voice. The dead men were silent, the only sound on the plain the rumbling thunder of their feet on the hard, unrelenting ground. Random and Ruby hefted their swords and stood at the valley entrance, waiting.

'If we do fall here . . .' said Random.

'Yes?' said Ruby.

'At least it will be a good death. A warrior's death.'

'Yeah. We were dying by inches back on Golgotha. We were never meant for civilization, Jack. You can't cage wild birds.'

'But if by some miracle we do come out of this alive . . .'

'Yes?'

'I'm going to do things differently. No more politics, no more compromises. I'm going to follow my heart and my conscience, and God help anyone who gets in my way.'

'Sounds good to me,' said Ruby.

And then the first of the Ghost Warriors were upon them. They crowded into the narrow entrance to the valley, packed together, struggling to reach their human prey. Random and Ruby stood together and wielded their blades with more than human strength and speed, cutting the Ghost Warriors apart;

literally dismantling the animated corpses until they could no longer function, and fell helpless to the ground. They were quickly hauled out of the way so that more Ghost Warriors could take their place, and the struggle continued. Only five or six could enter the valley at a time, and Random and Ruby had no difficulty in handling that many. At first. Their swords rose and fell, chopping and hacking, and the Ghost Warriors could not stand against them. But there were always more to take the place of those who fell, and the dead never grew tired.

Random and Ruby fought on, but after the first hour they had begun to slow, and their strength was not what it was. Their backs and their sword arms ached unmercifully, and it was growing harder to get their breath. There was never any break, and they dared not retreat so much as a step. Enemy swords were starting to get past their defences, and their wounds were taking longer to heal. The first blood began to spatter on to the valley floor. It had been a long, hard day, even for two living legends. Their breath came raggedly now, burning in their lungs. Sweat ran down their faces, stinging in their eyes and tasting of salt on their lips. The ground grew slippery underfoot with their own blood. And still the Ghost Warriors came, wearing them down slowly but surely, and Random had to admit to himself what he had always known. That while two warriors could hold off an army for a time, they couldn't do it for ever.

So he did the only thing that was left to him. He reached out to Ruby with his mind, and their thoughts met and merged. In a moment that was no time at all, they reached deep within themselves and power blazed up from the back brain, the undermind, up through their altered minds and out into the real world, where it became a wall of searing, consuming fire that surged away from Random and Ruby, burning up everything in its path. Ghost Warriors blackened and shrivelled up like leaves in the impossibly hot flames that blazed so brightly, as though a part of the sun had come down and touched the earth. Dead flesh was consumed, given peace at last, and Shub tech melted down into pools of smoking liquid metal. Over a hundred Ghost warriors were consumed in the first few seconds, and still the wall of heat roared on, devouring everything in its path.

By the time the power behind the fire collapsed, and the flames snapped out, more than half the Shub army had been reduced to blackened husks, scattered across the plain in dark, shrivelled heaps. The survivors stood ranged before Young Jack Random, who was no longer smiling. Back at the valley entrance, Random and Ruby had fallen to their knees, heads hanging down as they leaned on each other for support. They'd put the last of their strength into maintaining that attack, and they had nothing left. The flames they called up had not injured them in the least, but now the heat radiating back from the scorched valley walls was almost overpowering, raising an uncomfortable sweat on their smarting, exposed skin.

'Now that was a good one,' said Ruby, her voice a toneless croak. 'Think we could do it again?'

'Not a chance in hell,' said Random. 'But let's hope Young Jack Random doesn't know that. God, I feel bad.'

'Same here. And we didn't even get most of them. I have a horrible suspicion we may have peaked too early.'

'We had no choice. They would have overwhelmed us.'

'The survivors still might.' Ruby raised her head painfully slowly, and looked out over the plain. 'Shit. We got maybe half of them. And that smug metal bastard's still out there. Wonder what he's waiting for?'

'Probably to see how weakened we are. On your feet, Ruby. Maybe we can still bluff them.'

But they couldn't get up without leaning heavily on each other, and even after they'd forced themselves up on to their trembling legs, their swords still hung limply from their hands. They did their best to hold their heads up.

'I don't know if you've noticed,' said Ruby, 'but our wounds aren't healing any more.'

'I noticed. I think that wall of flame took everything we had. Until we get a chance to rest and recover, we're tapped out. We're just human again. Nothing left but our guns and our steel and our good right arms.'

'Good,' said Ruby. 'I always thought that was a more honest way to fight.'

'There is still one option,' said Random.

'Is there, by God,' said Ruby. 'I'd love to hear it.'

'You get the hell out of here. Run. Make your way back to Vidar, while I hold them here as long as I can. Maybe buy you enough time to get some kind of defence organized in the city.'

'A nice thought,' said Ruby, 'but no.'

'If you stay, we'll both die. Where's the sense in that? At best they'll overwhelm us, cut us down or tear us apart. At worst, we'll have to shoot each other to prevent Shub taking us alive. At least my way, one of us gets to live. Be logical, Ruby.'

'I am. There are no defences left to organize at Vidar. And you should know I never ran from a good fight in my life.'

'If they come again, we're going to die,' said Random. 'We don't stand a chance. I've been in enough tough spots in my time to know a lost cause when I see one. Even the hardest rock can be worn away, if you just keep hitting it.'

'Everyone has to die somewhere,' said Ruby, 'and I never thought I'd die in bed. Never wanted to. This is as good a way to go as any.'

'I always wanted to die in bed,' said Random, smiling. 'Preferably with a belly full of good brandy and my arm around a beautiful woman. But if I have to go down fighting, I can't think of anyone else I'd rather be with.'

'Oh, Jack; you say the nicest things.'

They kissed once, unhurriedly, and then turned to look out at the enemy forces on the plain one last time. And saw Young Jack Random striding towards them, quite alone, his hands empty of weapons. The rest of the Ghost Warrior army stood still and silent, watching. Random and Ruby looked at each other.

'What the hell does he think he's doing?' said Random. 'Surely he doesn't expect us to surrender?'

'Maybe he wants to surrender,' said Ruby, hopefully.

The steel machine in its human covering strode unhurriedly across the plain, smiling his interminable smile, and finally came to a halt a respectful distance away from the two humans guarding the valley entrance. He was still within disrupter range, but Random was pretty sure his Shub double was fast enough to dodge an energy beam if he had to. Young Jack Random was a Fury, and no longer had any reason to hide behind merely human limitations.

'Well, well,' said Young Jack Random pleasantly. 'Here we all are again. Funny how we keep bumping into each other, isn't it? It must be fate. How are you both feeling?'

'Strong enough to kick your metal ass,' growled Ruby.

'What do you want?' said Random.

'To fulfil my mission here,' said Young Jack Random, standing tall and heroic in his silver armour. 'To wipe out every living human on this planet, and make it over into a Shub base.'

'I take it your rebel allies don't know that,' said Random.

'Oh, I think they probably do, deep down, but they don't want to admit it. The human talent for self-deception never ceases to amaze me. Still, they and their pitiful army are irrelevant now. While they're keeping your forces occupied, I will take my army to Vidar and destroy it.'

'You have to get past us first,' said Ruby. 'And you've already seen what we can do when we put our minds to it.'

'Yes, and very impressive it was,' said Young Jack Random. 'But not totally unexpected. Our files on you are really quite extensive. We've studied every use of your remarkable powers, on every occasion. And being the great brains that we are, we came up with an answer. You see, you're really talking to the rogue AIs of Shub. We're running all our forces on this miserable planet through this focus. That's why you couldn't kill us on Golgotha. Only a body died there, and we have so many bodies. This one is very special. We built something very powerful into it, and then sent it here, knowing your human egos would demand you come to face it.'

'Wait a minute,' said Ruby. 'You mean you staged all this, killed all these people, just to get to us?'

'Now isn't that just typical of human egos?' said Young Jack Random. 'No, my dear, you're not that important. Loki is a vital staging point in our expansion into human space. But we also set things up to bring you here, too. You Maze people fascinate us. And we are determined to have you in our laboratories, so we can learn to do what you do. To that

517

end, a very special device was installed in me. Its function: to suppress your more than human powers and abilities. The most powerful esp-blocker ever built.' His smile widened. 'And yes, it's been operating all the time I've been standing here. You are now quite helpless. I advise you to surrender. If not, I will be obliged to hurt you.'

Random and Ruby looked at each other, and began to laugh. Young Jack Random looked from one to the other.

'I really don't see what use hysteria is in this situation . . .'

'You idiot,' said Random. 'Whatever we may be, we're not espers. We established that long ago.'

And he reached inside himself and pulled up the last few sparks of his power. With impossible speed he surged forward, crossing in an instant the space between himself and the machine with his face. He raised his sword and brought it savagely down towards the Fury's head. Flames flared around the steel blade. Young Jack Random raised a hand, as though to block the blow. The blazing sword sheared through the flesh and metal hand, buried itself in Young Jack Random's metal skull, and then continued on down in a shower of sparks, cutting through the steel and flesh body till it erupted out of his groin. The two halves of the Fury fell slowly away from each other, and lay sparking and spitting on the bare ground. Random stood over them, just a little out of breath.

'That . . . isn't possible,' said a cold metallic voice from one side of the sundered head.

'It is if I believe it is,' said Random. 'Now shut the hell up and die.'

He stamped on the left half of the metal head, and crushed it flat under his boot. Ruby came over and stamped on the other side of the head, and then they both used their disrupters on the two halves of the body, blowing them apart. And out on the bare plain, every one of the surviving Ghost Warriors suddenly collapsed and lay still, as though all their strings had been cut.

'Of course,' said Ruby, 'he said he was Shub's focus for all their forces here. With communications being so difficult on Loki, they needed a booster to maintain their control, and that was him. With him gone, they're just so much metal junk. You know what, Jack, I think we just won this war.'

'Of course,' said Random. 'I told you everything would be all right. You should listen to me more.'

Ruby laughed and hugged him. 'We're heroes! We're immortal! We're going to live for ever!'

They hugged each other for a long time, and then let go and just stood companionably together, enjoying being alive.

'I'm taking our survival as a sign,' said Random. 'No more pussyfooting. From now on I do what needs to be done, and God help the guilty.'

'Sounds good to me,' said Ruby. 'Did you have anything particular in mind?'

'Well, first we go find the two human armies, or what's left of them, break up the battle, and persuade the surviving rebel forces that their war is over. Without Young Jack Random and his Ghost Warriors they don't stand a chance, and they know it.'

'And then?'

'And then we go back to Vidar. And clean house.'

Back at the city, the populace went mad with joy over the two legendary heroes who'd saved their city and their planet in their hour of greatest need. So when Jack Random asked them to do something for him, they didn't hesitate. Soon the whole surviving population of Vidar was gathered in the great square before the main gates, watching breathlessly as Vidar's surviving guards fashioned a series of nooses and hung them from the inner wall. To one side knelt Matthew Tallon, once Planetary Controller, and Terrence Jacks, once Mayor of Vidar, and the few dozen rebels who'd survived the last battle. They all had their hands tied behind them. They looked for mercy in the faces of the crowd, but saw none. On Random and Ruby's other side knelt de Lisle and Bentley and all their people, down to the lowest bureaucrat, also securely tied. Jack Random looked down on them all with harsh, unforgiving eyes. Ruby Journey stood beside him, her face cold and expressionless. They knew about Peter Savage now.

'You can't do this!' howled de Lisle. 'I was pardoned! We

519

all were! Parliament put us in charge here! You can't go against the authority of Parliament!'

'Watch me,' said Random. 'You and your people plotted to leech this colony dry and then move on, never once thinking of all the colonists whose lives would be ruined. I call that treason.'

'We have backers!' said de Lisle. 'Powerful backers! I could tell you their names—'

'They'll be in the computers somewhere, we'll find them. There's only one thing I want to know. That man, killed and gutted and placed in two crates. That was your idea, wasn't it?'

'It was Bentley's idea,' de Lisle said quickly. 'We needed something to motivate you, alienate you from the rebels.'

'Who was the man?' said Ruby.

De Lisle shrugged, and looked at Bentley, who said nothing. Ruby kicked the security chief in the ribs.

'Nobody,' said Bentley. 'Just someone we used. He wasn't important.'

'Everyone's important,' said Random. 'That's what separates us from Shub.' De Lisle started to splutter some apology or excuse, but Random just looked at him, and he fell silent.

'They deserve to die,' said Tallon. 'But we only ever had the best interests of Loki at heart. We rebelled because we had legitimate grievances. You of all people should be able to understand that.'

'I understand,' said Random. 'But you allied yourself with Shub, the Enemies of Humanity. The end doesn't always justify the means.'

'Jack,' said Ruby quietly. 'I'm really not sure this is a good idea. Hang a few to make a point, sure, but this . . . De Lisle's right. Parliament is never going to approve this.'

'Then to hell with Parliament,' said Jack Random. He gestured to the guards, survivors of the army he'd led. They looked at him with worshipful eyes. Random gestured at the ropes. 'Hang them. Hang them all!'

The guards dragged the prisoners over to the inner wall. Most went quietly. De Lisle screamed and kicked and sobbed right until they put the noose around his neck and cut off his breath for ever. Tallon looked back at Random and Ruby with prophet's eyes, and raised his voice so the crowd would be sure to hear.

'They're monsters! You can't trust them! They'll turn on you in the end, because you're only human, and they're not. They're monsters! Monsters!'

The noose put an end to his words. The politicians and the rebels hung side by side on the inner wall of Vidar, and the population of the city cheered and cheered and cheered.

Ruby looked at Random.

'Hang them all,' said Random. 'They're all politicians, all dirty. Hang them all.'

It was raining, hard. The rain had started falling on the world known as Lachrymae Christi some several million years earlier, and showed no signs of letting up. Fuelled by the massive ocean that covered three quarters of the planet, the rain fell from eternally cloudy skies on to the endlessly thirsty jungle below, that covered the world's only continent from shore to shore. It fell on the wise and the wicked, the plain and the glorious, the lucky and the unlucky, and the rain it raineth every day. Lachrymae Christi had never known summer or winter, sunshine or snow, and never once had its grey skies been blessed with a rainbow.

The rain fell on the planet's unfortunate colonists, too, in their scattered dwellings. Though colonists isn't perhaps the correct word to describe them. They didn't come to the world of eternal rains through choice. They were rounded up by gloved and helmeted men and herded into the holds of cargo ships, persuaded on their way by long electric prods and drawn guns. They travelled in hardship and despair, and were finally dumped on their new home, to make what kind of life they could for themselves. No one objected; no one cared. They were the lowest of the low, despised by the old order and the new order alike. Supply ships left the bare necessities, now and again, but that was the extent of the Empire's compassion. No one gave a damn whether the unwilling colonists lived or died, as long as they stayed where they were put. They were banned from starflight, banned from civilization, from a humanity that had turned its backs on them. But against all the odds, the colonists survived, and prospered in their fashion. If only to spite those who had abandoned them there.

Lachrymae Christi was a leper colony.

The *Sunstrider II* dropped out of hyperspace and fell into high orbit over the world of eternal tears. Owen Deathstalker sat uncomfortably before the main viewscreen on his yacht's bridge, and studied the silent planet's image, hidden and enigmatic beneath its perpetual swirling shroud of clouds. He didn't know much about Lachrymae Christi. Not many did. It wasn't something respectable people talked about, as though just using the dreaded word might somehow attract the disease's attention. A secret world, to hide a secret shame. For centuries the Empire had boasted that its scientists had defeated disease, and that with the regeneration machines and the cloning tanks, nothing should stop a man of decent means from living a long and healthy life. It was a different matter for the poor, of course, but for them, that was true of everything.

And then, some seventy years before, leprosy returned; an almost forgotten horror from humanity's distant past, and the scientists could do nothing. It spread rapidly from world to world, infecting rich and poor alike with its rotten touch, and soon it was everywhere. No one knew what caused or spread it, and there was no hope or comfort available for its victims. Only isolation, the shunning of friends and neighbours. Rather than have the victims hanging around, as a reminder of science's failure and civilization's lack of compassion, it was decided that once diagnosed, all lepers would be given a one-way ticket to the Rim, and a world no one wanted, where they could be with their own kind, and humanity could comfortably forget them.

Only some people couldn't, wouldn't forget.

Hazel d'Ark slouched on to the bridge, and dropped heavily into the chair next to Owen's. She scowled at the image on the viewscreen, and sniffed loudly. 'You know, we get sent to all the best places. I can't believe you agreed to this mission, Owen. I swear that if I leave here with less than my usual number of fingers, I am personally going to drop-kick you out of the nearest airlock.'

'There's really nothing to worry about,' said Owen, trying hard to sound reassuring. 'All the latest medical information says you can't catch leprosy by casual contact. I checked.'

'They don't know that! They don't know anything for sure. They still haven't even worked out where the hell it came from.'

'What exactly is this leprosy?' said Midnight Blue, from behind them. The tall dark warrior woman was leaning in the doorway, drinking a vitamin extract straight from the bottle. 'We don't have anything like it where I come from.'

'Same here,' said Bonnie Bedlam, pushing past Midnight to claim the only remaining chair on the bridge. Her various piercings clattered loudly as she sat down. 'Are there really people down there with bits falling off them?'

'Only in the worst cases,' said Owen. 'It's a neurological disease. Victims lose all sense of feeling. Even small wounds refuse to heal and become infected. Flesh rots and decays. It's a slow and very nasty way to die. There are some drugs that help, but not much.'

'Is it too late to turn this ship around?' said Bonnie.

'I thought you believed in disfigurement as a fashion statement?' said Midnight.

'There are limits,' said Bonnie. 'Though I never thought I'd hear myself say that.' She leaned in closer to Owen, and he did his best not to flinch away. Bonnie disturbed him. 'You know, Owen, this disease sounds too bad to be true. More like it was manufactured. Could it be some bioweapon that got loose from a lab?'

'You're not the first person to suggest that,' said Hazel. 'Truth is, no one knows. It doesn't appear to be related to any other current disease. It could well have been some damn fool's idea of a last-ditch terror weapon. And it would explain how it just appeared out of nowhere.'

'Of course, that could be nothing more than general paranoia,' said Owen. 'There was a lot of that about during Lionstone's reign.'

'Yeah,' said Hazel. 'Mostly because they really were out to get you.'

'True. Thank God things have changed since then.'

Every alarm on the bridge went off at once, with flashing

523

lights and sirens screaming loud enough to wake the dead. Owen stared in disbelief at the control panels before him.

'I don't believe it!'

'What? What?' said Hazel.

'A Hadenman ship just dropped out of hyperspace right next to us! How the hell did they know we were going to be here?'

'Tell you what,' said Hazel, stabbing desperately at the controls, 'You ask them, and I'll concentrate on getting us the hell out of here.'

'I thought Owen was supposed to be their Redeemer,' said Bonnie.

'Yeah, well,' said Owen, busily activating every defensive shield the *Sunstrider II* had, 'after what we got up to on Brahmin II, I think we can safely consider that particular title obsolete.' He hit the intercom switch. 'Moon! Get your silicon ass up here!'

'I'm already here,' said the grating tones of the augmented man. Tobias Moon strode over to stand beside Owen, studying the image of the vast golden ship on the viewscreen with his glowing golden eyes. 'My people have found us again.'

'Wonderful,' said Owen. 'Some days things wouldn't go right if you paid them. Shields are up, weapon computer systems are all on-line. Hazel?'

'I've put us into a dive, heading for cloud cover. Maybe we can lose them.'

'Unlikely,' Moon said calmly. 'Hadenman sensors are state-of-the-art, far in advance of anything the Empire has. Also, that golden ship has enough firepower to vaporize a small moon. Or a large one, if they were patient. I suggest you concentrate on speed. Although my people built this ship for you, they used the improved stardrive from the original *Sunstrider*. That is still far superior to anything the Hadenmen have.'

'Thank the good Lord for small mercies,' said Hazel. 'Hang on to your breakfast, people. We are going straight down.'

The *Sunstrider II* punched through the swirling atmosphere, the huge golden ship of the Hadenmen right behind her like a whale pursuing a minnow. Both ships plunged down through Lachrymae Christi's atmosphere at dangerously high speeds, ignoring the violent weather systems that heaved and crackled around them. The golden ship opened fire, and the *Sunstrider II*'s shields flared brightly, absorbing as much of the terrible destructive energies as they could.

Inside the yacht, all the alarm sirens were howling at once. The lights on the bridge went out, replaced after a heartstopping pause by the dull red glow of emergency lighting. Owen's gaze darted across the control panels, looking for good news and finding none. More and more systems were shutting down, as the main computers re-routed more and more power to sustain the failing defensive shields. The ship rocked back and forth as it absorbed further punishment, and Owen yelled for everyone to strap themselves into their crash-webbing. Hazel managed to get off a few shots at the pursuing Hadenman ship, but they made no impression on the huge ship's fields. Owen kept one eye on their speed and elevation, and didn't know which worried him the most. If he couldn't throw off the Hadenman pursuit soon, the *Sunstrider II* would be hard-pressed to cut back her speed enough to be sure of a safe landing.

'Can someone please kill those damned alarms!' he said harshly. 'I can't hear myself think in here!'

Hazel hit a section of the control panels with her fist, and a sudden blessed silence fell across the bridge. 'Better?'

'Much,' said Owen. 'Maybe I should just fire you out through the airlock and have you hit the Hadenman ship.'

'Can we do anything to help?' said Bonnie.

'Prayer is probably a good idea about now,' said Hazel. 'Any good deities where you come from?'

'What's our exact situation?' said Midnight.

'Bad, and getting worse,' said Owen. 'We are outgunned, and pursued by a much larger ship with power to burn and one hell of a grudge against us. And if we don't figure out how to slow down real soon now, some unfortunate part of the planet below is going to end up with a crater you could drop a small sun into. Does the phrase "deep shit" ring any bells? Oz, any suggestions?'

'You could always offer to surrender,' said the AI calmly

in his ear. 'Of course, they'd probably kill you slowly, and turn you into Hadenmen . . . but it is an option you haven't considered.'

'Thanks a whole bunch,' said Owen.

'Can't we fight back?' said Bonnie.

'We don't have anything powerful enough to hurt them,' said Hazel. 'And anyway, our targeting systems just went offline. We need the extra power for the shields. Which are currently taking one hell of a battering and are on the brink of collapse.'

'There must be something we can do!' said Midnight.

'I am open to suggestions!' said Owen. 'Moon, those are your people. Can't you . . . talk to them, or something?'

'The augmented men undoubtedly consider me a traitor,' said Moon, his thick buzzing voice calm and unmoved. 'Of us all, they want me dead the most. Our situation would appear to be hopeless. I estimate our shields will collapse in the next thirty seconds.'

There was an explosion at the rear of the yacht, and the whole ship shuddered. The alarms came back on again for a few seconds before Hazel shut them up again, running her hands frantically across the controls.

'Hull breach, Owen! We're losing pressure, and we'll have to drop a hell of a lot further into the planet's atmosphere before the pressures equal out. We have a small fire, but the automatic systems seem to be handling it. Rear shields are down, mid shields . . . are holding. For the moment. Twenty per cent systems failures, all across the board. We can't afford to take any more hits like that.'

'Do we have escape pods?' said Bonnie. 'Grav sleds? Any way off this wreck?'

'I don't believe this,' said Owen. 'I've already had one ship shot out from under me, and been forced to crashland in a jungle. Why is this happening to me again? Moon, think of something!'

There was another explosion in the rear. The ship's engines were shrieking horribly. Warning lights blinked all over the control panels, and then everything shut down. Owen looked at the dead panels before him, and didn't have a clue what to do.

'Oh, shit,' said Hazel. 'Main computers just went down. Shields are down. All weapon systems off-line. Life support is failing. The engines are running out of control. This isn't a ship any more, it's a missile. Owen, with all the computers down, we have no way of landing this baby.'

Everyone looked at each other. Owen thought hard. He had to stay calm, think it through. 'We're all Maze survivors,' he said hesitantly. 'Maybe if we just bailed out, and hope we hit a deep enough part of the ocean . . .'

'No,' said Hazel, 'not at this speed. The impact alone would kill us outright. We're tough, but we're not that tough.'

'Oz?' said Owen. 'There must be something we haven't tried.'

'Sorry, Owen, nothing I can do. Doesn't this remind you of our arrival on Shandrakor? I'm almost nostalgic.'

'That's it!' said Owen, turning quickly to Moon. 'When the Imperial starcruisers shot the hell out of the first *Sunstrider*, and we were heading for a crash in Shandrakor's jungles, you integrated yourself directly into the ship's computers, and guided us down! Can you do the same again?'

'Wait a minute!' said Hazel. 'The last time he tried that we still bloody crashed, and we were lucky to walk away alive!'

'At least we walked away!' said Owen. 'Do you have a better idea?'

'It's moments like this that make me wish I'd stayed a pirate,' said Hazel. 'Moon, get on with it.'

'I have already established a connection with the surviving computer systems,' said Moon, just a little distantly. 'A plan has occurred to me. It is somewhat extreme, but offers a seventy-three per cent chance of success. All other alternatives present distinctly lower chances of survival.'

'Oh, hell, go for it,' said Owen. 'But if you smash up my ship again, I'll melt you down to repair it.'

'Oh ye of little faith,' said Moon calmly, and he shut down the engines. It was suddenly very quiet on the bridge. The few remaining controls went dead, and even the emergency lighting went out.

'Moon,' said Hazel, in a dangerously calm tone of voice. 'What have you done?'

'I've shut everything down,' said the augmented man, his golden eyes glowing bright in the dark. 'I am hoping to convince the Hadenman ship that we are dead in the water. Being an extremely logical people, they should assume that only a total madman would shut down all systems at this point, and that therefore the ship must be fatally damaged. They should then call off their pursuit, and remove themselves from the gravity well while they still can. Once I've estimated that enough time has passed for them to be safely out of range, I will restart the systems and attempt a landing. Of course, with the sensors down I have no way of knowing whether they'll have left or not. And we will be very close to the surface of the planet by the time I restart the engines. Still, it's these little moments of drama that make life worth living, isn't it?'

There was a long pause in the utter darkness of the bridge. 'I'm going to shoot him,' said Hazel finally. 'Moon, say something so I know where to aim. You're completely bloody insane!'

'Quite,' said Moon. 'Which is why the Hadenmen will be fooled. They are incapable of such leaps of the imagination. Fortunately, I am no longer limited to merely logical thinking. I spent my formative years on human planets, and have many human attributes.'

'Oh, great,' said Owen. 'A Hadenman who's acquired a taste for Russian roulette. I feel sick. How much longer do we have to free-fall before you can restart the engines?'

'Ah,' said Moon, 'now that is the tricky bit.'

'What did he say?' said Bonnie. 'What did he just say? And why have I got this terrible feeling in the pit of my stomach that I'm really not going to like his answer?'

'Well,' said Moon, 'to be absolutely sure the golden ship is out of range, I will have to leave it to the last possible moment, taking into account factors of speed and altitude, and then hope there are enough functional systems left in the ship to restart and control the engines. There will not, unfortunately, be any room for error.'

'Right,' said Midnight. 'That is it. Time we were leaving, Bonnie. A good warrior always knows when to cut her losses and head for the horizon. Hazel, nice to have known you, but I think this would be a really good time for you to return Bonnie and I to our own dimensions. Not that I don't have any faith in your demented friend, but I really don't think I want to be here to see how this all turns out.'

'Yeah,' said Bonnie, 'what she said.'

'Tough,' said Hazel. 'I'm not entirely sure how I do what I do, but I'm pretty sure that if I were to send you back right now, you'd both still be travelling at your present speed. Which means you'd probably reappear at the exact spot I took you from, only travelling at something well past the speed of sound. When you eventually hit something solid, they'd have to scrape up your remains with a palette knife. Of course, if you really want to risk it . . .'

'Oh, hell,' said Bonnie, 'we wouldn't think of deserting our friends in their hour of need. Would we, Midnight?'

'Of course not,' said Midnight, 'perish the thought. I think I feel sick.'

'Moon,' said Owen. 'I'm really very sure the golden ship is gone by now. Start the bloody engines.'

'Actually,' said Moon, 'I have been attempting to restart the engines for the past twenty-two seconds, to no avail. I can only assume the damage to the computer systems was more extreme than I conjectured.'

Hazel made a noise in the dark. 'Think of something, Owen!'

'Mostly I'm thinking about strangling Moon,' said Owen.

'I have come up with another plan,' said Moon. 'Your stardrive is derived from alien technology, and therefore has its own separate systems. These appear to be intact. I believe I can maintain a connection long enough to use the alien drive to jump-start the standard engines.'

'Hold everything,' said Bonnie. 'You want to activate a hyperdrive, this far into a planet's gravity well? You could collapse the whole star system! Bad as things are, I have no desire to see what the inside of a black hole looks like!'

'Trust me,' said Moon. 'I'm almost sure I know what I'm doing.'

There was a moment that seemed to last for ever. Space turned inside out, stretching and almost tearing, and colours slowed to a crawl. There was a brilliant light coming from somewhere, but they weren't seeing it with their eyes. A choir of angels was singing a single sustained chord, in a harmony almost too perfect to be borne. And then everything snapped back to normal, and the light was just the bridge's normal lighting and the song was the roar of the ship's engines as Moon fought to slow the *Sunstrider II*'s plummeting descent. Owen looked dazedly about him, and slowly realized that some of the control panels were back on-line again.

'We have sensors!' said Owen. 'No sign of the Hadenman ship, but the surface of the planet is coming up awfully fast! Brace yourselves, people! This is going to hurt!'

The *Sunstrider II* came howling down out of the roiling clouds, slicing through the pouring rain so quickly that the water evaporated before it could even touch the hull. And then the jungle reached up and seized the ship, and the battered yacht tore a ragged path through the heavy towering trees, slowing gradually all the time, until finally it slammed to a halt in a cloud of steam and ripped-up vegetation. The engines shut down, and all was quiet for a while, save for the gentle continuous hiss of rain falling on the superheated hull.

Inside, the yacht's passengers sat slumped in their crash-webbing, letting their heartbeats and breathing slow gradually back to normal before they tried anything complicated, like getting up. Apart from Moon, who appeared entirely unmoved by the whole experience. He'd already thrown aside his webbing and was leaning over the control panels, studying the sensor readings. Owen sighed heavily.

'Well, there goes another bloody yacht. Let's all pray very fervently that the damage is repairable, or we're going to be spending an extended holiday in this charming little paradise. There isn't another supply ship due here for months. Leper colonies aren't high on anybody's list of priorities just now.'

'Then why are we here?' said Hazel.

'Maybe we did something really bad in an earlier life,' said Owen. 'Moon, any life-form readings out there?'

'Just the jungle,' said Moon. 'Plant life, of various kinds. No animals, or insects. And no humans in sensor range. We are alone.'

'Finally, some news from Moon that I can live with,' said Hazel. 'How far are we from Saint Bea's mission?'

'Main computers are still down,' said Moon. 'I am currently unable to access that information.'

'Oz?' said Owen.

'If the ship followed the trajectory I plotted, we're not too far from where we should be,' murmured the AI. 'The mission should be located some ten miles north-north-east of here. Though that is, of course, an estimate. Things got a little hairy there, at the end. Allowing for error, we could be talking a twenty-mile hike. Still, what's a few miles trekking through impenetrable jungle? The exercise will do you good. Shouldn't take you more than a day. Or two. Three, tops.'

Owen shook his head tiredly. 'This is Shandrakor all over again, I just know it.'

'Not necessarily,' said Moon. 'At least this time there are no hungry killer aliens out there. There is no animal life on the entire planet, apart from the colonists. Though the files do contain some rather disturbing accounts of encounters with large and mobile vegetation displaying a distinctly antagonistic attitude.'

'Killer plants,' said Bonnie. 'Wonderful. Look, will somebody please fill me in on what the hell we're doing here? I was quite happily halfway through a four-day bender when I got your message. You made it sound quite sane at the time.'

'The state you were in, you would have volunteered for a mission to Shub,' said Midnight. 'How can you abuse your body in such a fashion?'

'Practice, darling, practice.' Bonnie dropped the black warrior woman a wink, and she looked away, exasperated. Bonnie laughed. 'Come on, somebody fill in the blanks for me. Do I at least get to kill somebody? Preferably lots of somebodies?'

'We're here on a mercy mission,' Owen said patiently. 'Mother Superior Beatrice Christiana, better known as the Saint of Technos III, resigned from running the reformed Church to come and run a mission here, for the leper colonists. Being who she is, she soon turned the mission into a social and communications centre for the whole planet, and combined the various scattered settlements into one people at last. They were actually on the verge of becoming a viable, self-sustaining colony, when the Hadenmen attacked. Which is presumably what that bloody golden ship was doing here. Anyway, there's a force of Hadenmen down here, concentrating their attacks on Saint Bea's mission. We are here to protect the mission and its people.'

'Why us?' said Bonnie. 'Why isn't the regular army here, earning its pay?'

'Because the regular army doesn't give a toss about a colony of lepers. Everyone Saint Bea approached was busy elsewhere. Finally she approached me personally, and,' said Owen, smiling ruefully, 'I find it kind of hard to say no to a saint.'

'Next time ask me,' said Bonnie. 'I'll coach you. There are no saints where I come from, Deathstalker. We ate them.'

'Right,' said Midnight. 'One of the first things we did after overthrowing the Empire was to dissolve the established Church, and replace it with the Mystical Order of Steel. We are warriors, and we follow the warrior way.'

'Sometimes I wonder if our worlds have anything in common apart from the Maze,' said Owen.

'Well, there's always you,' said Midnight, smiling a little too warmly for Owen's liking. 'Wherever there's one of me, there's always one of you. We were fated to be together.'

'Right,' said Bonnie, idly tugging at a gold ring piercing something Owen preferred not to look at. 'Right . . .'

'Now that is interesting,' said Moon, still bent over the control panels. Everyone looked round quickly.

'I really hate it when he says that,' said Hazel. 'It nearly always means something quite appallingly nasty is going on.'

'No, this really is interesting,' said Moon. 'I don't know what it means, but it definitely is interesting.'

Owen moved over to join him, and the others watched his frown slowly deepen as he studied the sensor displays. 'This makes no sense at all,' he said finally. 'It's like something is slowly . . . enveloping the *Sunstrider*. Some kind of organic material.'

'Hold everything,' said Bonnie. 'Are you saying there's something on this benighted world big enough to *swallow* a starship?'

'Not as such,' said Moon. 'Nothing here but plant life, remember?'

'We're going to have to go out and take a look,' said Hazel. 'See what else can go wrong on this bloody mission.'

'Better watch your language when we meet Saint Bea,' said Owen, smiling. 'She'll make you do penance.'

'I already am,' Hazel growled. 'Ever since I met you.'

For a while, the airlock's outer door refused point-blank to open. All the systems were functioning, but the door wouldn't budge. They tried cranking it open with the manual release, but all that happened was that Hazel broke two fingernails straining to shift it. She lost her temper completely, and shot out the locking system with her disrupter. Owen and Moon dragged the door halfway open, and the party took it in turns to squeeze through and drop down to the surface below, gun and sword in hand.

Outside, the jungle was a riot of colour, all of it in shades of red. The black trees had scarlet leaves, the shrubbery and foliage were a blushing crimson, and the thick curling vines were a disturbingly organic shade of pink. The local vegetation never saw any sun, due to the constant driving rain and the ever-present cloud cover, so chlorophyll never really got started. Red was the order of the day in Lachrymae Christi's jungle, and a hell of a lot of it was determinedly draping itself over the *Sunstrider II*.

Owen and his companions cut and hacked their way clear of the airlock, were drenched immediately by the pouring rain, and finally turned and looked back at their ship. A crawling network of shocking-pink vines had already covered much of the outer hull from stem to stern, and more vines were crawling into position over the first, inching doggedly forward like lengths of animated intestine. Thick leaves like scarlet palms slapped against the hull from all sides, adding still more layers, as though the jungle was trying to bury all traces of the intruding ship that had so violently disturbed its peace.

By the time Owen had taken all this in, the airlock opening had already disappeared behind a mat of blood-red lianas. He struggled back through the clinging foliage, trying to cut through the vines with his sword, but the blade clung stickily to the vines, and he had to jerk hard to pull it free. He raised his disrupter and took aim. The energy beam punched a hole through the vines, and went on to do untold further damage inside the airlock. The blackened vines almost caught alight, but the rain quickly put a stop to that. Owen watched numbly as the vines slowly but deliberately repaired and covered over the hole he'd made.

'Ah,' said Moon. 'Now that is unfortunate.'

Owen lost it completely. A shriek of pure rage and frustration burst out of him as he stamped around in a circle, hacking with his sword at any vegetation that got in his way. 'That is it! That is bloody *it*! Not only have I lost my second yacht in a crashlanding; not only have we now been cut off from all our supplies and extra weapons; not only is it at least twenty miles hard going between here and the mission, but it is pouring down and I don't have my cloak with me! I am soaked! I hate being wet like this! Hate it, hate it, hate it!'

He kicked viciously at a patch of vines, got his foot tangled and fell over. No one was stupid enough to laugh. He surged to his feet again, his face crimson as the surrounding vegetation, breathing hard. Moon looked at Hazel.

'Has Owen changed while I was gone? He never used to do that.'

'No,' said Hazel. 'He didn't. Everyone stay put here while I go and have a quiet word with him.'

'My Owen never did anything like that,' said Midnight. 'He was far too dignified.'

'My Owen did all kinds of things,' said Bonnie, playing reflectively with one of her piercings.

'I'll just bet he did,' said Midnight.

Hazel left Moon trying to make sense of the undercurrents in those last few comments, and moved cautiously forward. Owen was leaning with his head against the coal-black bark of a tree trunk. His desperate breathing had slowed somewhat, but he still had his disrupter in his hand. There was something defeated but still dangerous about him. Hazel hadn't found Owen's outburst funny at all. In all the time she'd known him, he'd never once lost his temper like that. Given what he was capable of, if he got angry enough, Hazel found his sudden loss of control worrying. She stopped a respectful distance away from Owen, and cleared her throat politely. He didn't look round.

'Go away, Hazel.'

'What's the matter, Owen?' Hazel said quietly. 'It wasn't that bad a landing, all things considered. I mean; we're alive.'

'It wasn't the landing,' said Owen, staring off into the scarlet jungle. Rain ran down his face, and dripped from his nose and chin. 'It's . . . everything. I am just so damn tired of everything going wrong. I try so hard, and nothing ever comes out the way I plan it. This was supposed to be a simple mission, a quick in and out with no complications. Show up, flash the powers, kick some Hadenman butt, and move on to more important matters. Now look at us. Stranded in the middle of nowhere on a hellplanet colonized by lepers, while all hell is breaking loose in the Empire. I shouldn't be here. I should be out there, fighting the aliens or the Hadenmen or whatever the hell Shub's throwing at us this week. I have a duty, an obligation, to use my abilities to help humanity. But no, I'm stuck here in the back of beyond, when I'm needed elsewhere.'

'You're needed here too,' said Hazel. 'The mission is under attack. Saint Bea wouldn't have asked for us unless things were really desperate here.'

'They're lepers,' Owen said brutally. 'They're dying anyway. The Empire needs us more.'

'Every planet, every people, is just as important as any other,' said Hazel. 'Didn't your time as an outlaw teach you anything? It's not just the big important planets like Golgotha that matter. Everyone matters. I know what this is all about. It's hurt pride. You thought you could just drop in here, act the hero for Saint Bea and then move on to something more high-profile. Instead, you screwed up. You, the Deathstalker, the living legend; and now you're cut off from where the real action is. You think you're the only one that can save the Empire from its enemies. Well, you're wrong. The Empire is perfectly capable of defending itself without you. Even the mighty Deathstalker can't be everywhere at once. Humanity survived perfectly well before we marvellous Maze people came along, and they'll manage just as well when we're gone. The Maze may have made us more than human, but it didn't make us gods. Now cut the crap and shape up, or I'll slap you a good one.'

Owen finally turned his head and looked at her, and something in his cold eyes made Hazel wonder if she'd actually gone too far. But she held her ground, meeting his gaze unflinchingly, and after a moment Owen relaxed just a little, and tried a smile.

'You wouldn't really hit me, would you?'

'Damn right I would.'

'OK. I surrender. No more tantrums. Let's go and see what kind of a fix Saint Bea's got herself into.'

Hazel hesitated. 'Are you . . . all right now, Owen?'

'No. But I am back in control. I'm just tired. Just once, I'd like to take a trip on a ship that doesn't crash, or get attacked, or land me up to my ass in trouble. You said it yourself; I'm supposed to be the great hero, the saviour of humanity, and I can't even make my own life work out properly.'

Hazel had to laugh. 'Owen, that's part of being human. Everyone's life is like that. Now let's get back to the others and work out what we're going to do next, before we all drown in this bloody rain. Doesn't it ever let up?'

'Not for the last few million years. Maybe we could fashion umbrellas out of the local plants.'

'I don't think they'd like that,' said Hazel, looking around her at the surrounding crimson and purple vegetation, all of which seemed to be constantly if slowly on the move. 'This stuff gives me the creeps. Plants should know their place.'

They returned to the others to find Bonnie and Midnight ostentatiously not talking to each other, staring rigidly off in different directions. Moon had given up trying to make sense of the situation, and was pretending interest in a quivering purple shrub the size of a small house. Owen gave his crashed ship a last look. It was already so deeply buried under the strange vegetation that it might never have been there.

'All right,' he said loudly. 'Cut the chatter. It's at least ten miles to Saint Bea's mission, so the sooner we get started, the sooner we can get there and get out of this rain. Oz, give me directions to the mission.'

'Of course, Owen. Just head out of this clearing in the direction of those three trees leaning together, and I'll guide you from there. I feel I should brief you about some of the more impressive local vegetation. It can be rather dangerous.'

'You mean it's poisonous?'

'More like homicidal. Animal life never really got started here, so the plants prey on each other for space, light, water, rooting and so forth. Some of them even consume each other, and down the millennia they've developed some very nasty tactics, and lots of ways of expressing their displeasure when thwarted. I suggest you all stick very close together, and be prepared to defend yourselves at any moment.'

Owen passed this on, and the others received it with varying degrees of disgust.

'As if this planet wasn't unpleasant enough,' said Bonnie. 'Bad enough my piercings will probably rust up in all this rain, but now we have to hack our way through miles of killer plants. I can feel one of my heads coming on. I want to go home.'

'Look on it as a challenge,' said Midnight. 'A warrior never quails from adversity.'

'You look on it as a challenge,' said Bonnie, 'and I'll stand back and watch you doing it.'

'Cool it,' said Hazel. 'Save your spleen for the killer plants. I mean, come on; how dangerous can a few mobile shrubs be?'

'I have a horrible feeling we're going to find out,' said Owen. 'Moon, you take the lead. Feel free to shoot or cut up anything at all you don't like the look of. And let's try to set a good pace, people. I hate to think what this place is like when it gets dark. And in case you were wondering, yes, all our torches are back in the ship.'

'Somehow, I'm not surprised,' said Hazel. 'God, I hate rain.'

They followed Oz's murmured directions into the rain-soaked crimson forest, leaving the buried ship behind them. They all had to fight the urge to keep looking back at the mound under which it lay. The *Sunstrider II* was their last link with civilized, technological Empire. From now on they were on their own.

There was little shelter to be found anywhere; rain dripped

unceasingly from every surface. Soon they were all soaked to the skin, and rain squelched inside their boots with every step. Their hair was plastered to their faces, and they had to keep blinking their eyes to clear them. The ground under their feet was mostly mud, flattened and compacted like stone in places, but it could change without warning into inches-deep gunk in which the party slipped and skidded, when they weren't tripping over exposed roots or various kinds of creeping vine or ivy.

It was a constant struggle to push their pace to more than a slow walk, and the unrelenting rain beat down on their exposed heads like a feeble but persistent bully. After a while, Owen took off his jacket and draped it over his head in an improvised hood. It meant he was now cold as well as wet, but it was worth it for the simple relief it offered. The others soon did the same, except for Moon, who didn't seem at all bothered by the rain, and couldn't understand why everyone got so surly when he said so. He tried pointing out new plant species of interest, but that went down even less well, so he gave up and walked happily on in silence.

The jungle stretched off in every direction, for as far as the eye could see, into the driving rain. Dark-boled trees with jagged black bark soared hundreds of feet up into the sky, their vast bowing branches weighed down with curling, serrated leaves the colour of blood. Owen reached up to touch one of the leaves, and then swore mildly as the jagged edge opened his fingertip like a razor. He gripped the leaf more firmly, and was surprised to find it thick and pulpy, and unpleasantly warm to the touch, almost uncomfortably so. He sucked thoughtfully at his lacerated finger, ignoring Hazel's snide remarks with the ease of long practice.

The jungle was every shade of red imaginable, giving the foliage a disturbingly fleshy look, as though it was accustomed to gorging itself on endless supplies of blood, and as if plasma rather than sap ran through the leaves' distended veins. Owen considered the possibility of vampire plants, but couldn't see what they would have to prey on, apart from each other. He was becoming convinced that on some level the jungle was definitely aware, if not actually sentient, and knew that intruders were passing through it. Leaves rustled as the party approached, and fell silent after they were gone. Vines circled slowly on tree trunks like dreaming snakes, and tall stalks would turn to face the party as they passed, quivering agitatedly till they had been left safely behind. Owen also couldn't help noticing that at least half the vegetation seemed to be slowly but determinedly stalking the other half.

The first attack caught them all by surprise. Long flailing tendrils with inch-long thorns lashed out at them from every side at once, striking with unexpected strength and speed. The barbs drew blood, and the blood-red tendrils sought to wrap themselves round their prey with springy tenacity. But they parted easily under the keen edge of a steel blade, and the oozing remnants sprang away again. More tendrils struck down from above, but the party stood their ground, hacking and cutting about them till the tattered sections were forced to retreat. Owen drew his disrupter and blasted one of the areas where the tendrils had seemed to spring from. The others followed suit, and soon there were half a dozen small fires burning around them. There was a certain amount of quivering and rustling in the surrounding foliage, but what was left of the tendrils showed no signs of contemplating any further aggression.

Owen put his gun away, and looked at the others. 'Anyone badly hurt?'

'Just scratches,' said Hazel. 'Damn, those things were fast.'

'Should we do something about the fires?' said Moon. 'They could spread . . .'

'Let them,' said Midnight, wiping away blood from a cut on her face that had come dangerously close to an eye. 'Treacherous bloody things. Let them all burn.'

'The rain should take care of the fires,' said Owen. 'And the foliage looks too drenched to catch alight. But let's try to remember, there could be colonists' settlements not that far away, so if you have to use your guns, aim carefully.'

'Yes, leader,' said Bonnie. 'I'm sure that would never have occurred to us. How ever did we manage till you came along?'

Owen ignored that, and gestured for Moon to lead off again.

The slow march continued, slogging through deepening mud until their legs ached from the strain. Moon continued to treat it all like a casual nature ramble, stopping every now and again to pull up some unfamiliar piece of plant life, compare it against his data banks and announce happily that since it wasn't officially identified, he had the right to name it. Unfortunately, this tended to involve very laboured puns in Latin, which no one but Moon understood or appreciated, so after a few pointed death threats from certain members of the party, he kept his enthusiasm to himself, silently studying everything that didn't shrink away fast enough.

Given the overall denseness of the jungle, and the way all the plant life fought for every square inch of light and rain, Owen had expected to spend most of his journey hacking a path through the vegetation with his sword, but after the incident with the barbed tendrils, the jungle seemed to be going out of its way to open up a path slowly ahead of them. Owen thought some more about how aware the jungle might be. He raised the subject with Oz, who responded with a running commentary on what was known of Lachrymae Christi's plant life. Most of this was monumentally boring, and Owen tuned it out until something odd caught his attention.

'Hold it, Oz; back up. No insects at all here? Are you sure?'

'Quite sure. Like animal life, they just never caught on here. The plant life is so aggressive on all levels that any other kinds of life never found an ecological niche to prosper in.'

'But if there are no insects, and as far as I can see no flowers . . . how do the plants propagate? How does fertilization occur?'

'Well it certainly doesn't involve the birds and the bees. Take a look over to your right, about four o'clock.'

Owen looked, and saw two large masses of foliage moving together, rocking back and forth. 'Wait a minute; are they doing what I think they're doing?'

'I'm afraid so. Animal life may not have developed here, but certain animal practices apparently did. You should think yourselves lucky you didn't arrive in the rutting season. Do you want to know how the trees do it?'

'No!'

'Suit yourself. You've led a really sheltered life in some ways, Owen.'

The AI went back to talking about how the rain drained away through cracks in the ground, and ended up in vast subterranean lakes that fed the jungle's great root system, and Owen went back to not listening.

They trudged on for another hour or so, getting even wetter and more miserable, before the jungle moved against them again. They'd fallen into a plodding routine, following the path that lay itself open before them, until Oz suddenly pointed out that the path was slowly but surely turning them off course. Owen yelled for everyone to stop, and they all snapped out of their half-daze and looked quickly about them, guns at the ready. Owen calmed them down and explained the situation, and took the lead so he could follow Oz's directions more exactly. But when he tried to turn aside from the path the red foliage clumped stubbornly together before him, forming a thick ragged wall. Owen drew his sword and cut at the wall with all his strength, but just as before, his blade clung stickily to the foliage, limiting the amount of damage he could do. He pulled his sword free, stepped back and opened fire with his disrupter. The energy beam blasted a narrow tunnel through the plant wall, lined with blackened and burning edges. But as soon as Owen moved forward, the scorched sides just closed together again like a slow-moving mantrap.

'Stubborn, isn't it?' said Hazel. 'I get the feeling that's going to happen whichever way we try to go. The jungle really doesn't want us deviating from the path it's chosen.'

'Maybe it's hiding something,' said Midnight. 'Some vulnerable part of itself.'

'Little baby jungle things?' said Bonnie. 'Could we be trespassing on a nursery?'

'How long would it take us to go round whatever it is?' said Moon, looking at Owen.

Owen consulted with Oz, and then shook his head. 'Depends on how large an area the jungle is protecting. Let's try curling around it. If it looks like it's taking us too long, we'll see what some high explosives will do. You do have some, don't you, Hazel?'

'Never without them,' said Hazel cheerfully.

Owen led the way cautiously round the blocked-off area, following the path that formed itself before him. He kept his gun in his hand. It seemed to him there was something sinister in the jungle's slow, deliberate intentions. He looked carefully about him for possible traps or ambush points. He tried to visualize what kind of drowsy, sluggish thoughts a plant might think, and wasn't surprised when he couldn't.

He led the way for a good half-hour before realizing that something was wrong. Except for the foliage that drew slowly apart in front of him to form the path, nothing in the jungle was moving. Not a vine nor a branch nor a leaf. He stared about him into the endless twilight, straining his eyes against the tangle of the jungle and the never-ending rain, but all was still and silent. The only sound was the heavy squelching of his party's boots diving in and out of the mud, and the steady patter of the rain. Owen hefted his disrupter. His instincts were screaming that he was walking into a trap, but he couldn't see anything dangerous or even threatening. If anything, the path ahead seemed wider than usual. But he was haunted by the sense that something was about to happen. Hazel moved up beside him.

'You feel it too, don't you?' she said quietly.

He nodded. 'The jungle's been watching us, leading us here. It's planning something.'

'Intelligent plants,' said Hazel. 'Spooky. Would it help if I apologized for all the salads I've eaten?'

Owen smiled briefly. 'I doubt it. You see anything?'

'Not a damned thing. Nothing above or around us, for as far as I can see. What do we do?'

'Keep moving, and be ready to react whenever whatever it is hits us. We've fought Hadenmen and Grendels. I doubt there's anything a bunch of plants can throw at us that we can't handle.'

'Getting cocky again, Deathstalker.'

While they were busy talking, the ground dropped out from under their feet. Owen's stomach lurched as he plunged down into the mud and just kept going. He scrabbled about him for something to cling on to, but the vegetation nearest to them had drawn back out of reach. There was only the mud, thick and confining, sucking him down. The others were yelling all around him, and from what he could see, were just as badly off as he was. The mud began moving, circling round in a churning, determined way, like a slow-motion whirlpool. It was already up to Owen's waist, and he was still sinking. He fought to stay upright, and tried to remember what he'd heard about dealing with quicksand. You were supposed to be able to swim in it, if you kept your nerve, but when Owen tried to move his legs they barely responded at all. The viscous sucking mud smothered his movements easily, thick and clinging and bitterly cold.

The circling speed of the mud was increasing all the time, a great whirlpool now of mud and grasses and loose vegetation a good twenty feet in diameter, churning remorselessly round in an anticlockwise motion, pulling in everything around it like a relentless meat grinder. Owen tried to see how the others were doing, but the mud held him firmly now, creeping up his stomach towards his chest. He held his arms above him, but there was nothing to cling on to. A great sucking sink-hole appeared in the centre of the whirlpool, pulling everyone towards it. Owen could hear the others shouting as the speeding mud carried them around, but they didn't seem to be making any sense. By now he was shouting too, and doubted he sounded any different. His constant struggle to stay upright and keep his face out of the mud was tiring him out, and getting him nowhere. His heart pounded frantically, and panic threatened to overwhelm his thoughts. Drowning in mud was supposed to be a really bad way to go.

He could almost feel the thick soft weight of it forcing its way down his throat as he sucked for air that never came . . .

Owen took a deep breath, and forced himself to be calm. He had to stay calm, work through his options, think of a way out of this, or he was a dead man. He craned his neck round, and saw Hazel fighting the mud with all her strength. It was already over her chest. Moon had stopped struggling, his face calm. Owen couldn't see Bonnie or Midnight. He hoped they hadn't already been swallowed up. The point was, none of them could help him. He was going to have to do it himself. The mud was getting colder all the time, sucking up his body heat. His teeth had begun to chatter. He was being carried inevitably closer to the sink-hole, the churning mud and grasses moving faster and faster. Owen didn't know where the mud ended up after it had been through the sucking hole, but he didn't think he'd enjoy finding out first-hand.

He tried to summon his Maze powers, but so much was happening he couldn't calm his mind enough to call them up. He tried to reach out to the surrounding foliage, looking for something to grab on to, but it was all well beyond his grasp. Think, think. If he couldn't go to the foliage, maybe he could bring it to him . . . He still had his disrupter in his hand, held up out of the mud to protect it. He aimed carefully and shot a nearby tree dead square at the bottom of its wide trunk.

The energy beam punched straight through the trunk, and the tree toppled slowly forwards across the whirlpool. The splintered remains of its lower trunk and heavy roots held it in place. The surging mud brought Owen sweeping round and slammed him hard against the black trunk. The impact knocked the breath out of him, but he clung desperately to the trunk with both hands and it held him in place, even against the steady pull and pressure of the mud. The others also hit the trunk as they came round, and clung to it and to each other. And after that it was only a matter of strength and determination to drag themselves slowly along the tree trunk and pull themselves out of the mud and on to firmer land. They crawled a safe distance away from the sucking mud, and then collapsed on their backs, letting the rain slowly wash the mud off them. They lay there for some time, getting their breath back, until finally Owen forced himself back on to his feet. He beat away some more of the mud from his legs and waist, and glared at the slowing whirlpool.

'That was no accident,' he said flatly. 'We were herded here. The jungle wanted to be rid of us. On some level, it must be aware, capable of cooperating against anything it sees as a threat.'

Hazel sat up slowly. 'So how are we going to get to Saint

Bea's mission, if the whole damned jungle's determined to stop us?'

'We just have to be more determined than it is,' said Owen. He consulted Oz to make sure he'd got the direction right, and then blasted an opening in the foliage with his disrupter. He waited till the crimson vegetation had closed together, and then borrowed Hazel's disrupter and blasted it open again. 'From now on, we take it in turns to keep blasting a trail, using our guns in sequence as they recharge, backing it up with explosives as necessary, until the jungle learns to respect us, and allows us to go where we want to go.'

And in the end, it was as simple as that. The jungle eventually got fed up with being incinerated and blown into small pieces, and went back to opening up a path as the party dictated. The scarlet and purple vegetation shook angrily around them for a while, but made no further moves to threaten them. Owen continued to lead, weapons at the ready, carefully checking the way ahead for booby traps. The rain kept falling. Everyone was soaked to the skin, and they were all shuddering from the cold. Any normal human would have been in serious trouble by now, sliding into shock as their core body temperature slowly decreased, but all five of the party had been through the Maze. And Moon was a Hadenman.

Along the way, as much to distract himself as anything, Owen brought Bonnie and Midnight up to date on the background of Saint Bea, and her mission. When the rebels finally won the war on Technos III, and put an end to the fighting, Mother Superior Beatrice didn't feel she was needed there any more. So she returned to Golgotha, and set about rebuilding the established Church by throwing out all the political and corrupt elements. Turning the quasi-military organization of the Church of Christ the Warrior into the pacifistic Church of Christ the Redeemer wasn't easy, but it helped that the Saint of Technos III had a huge popular following, not least due to Toby Shreck's docu footage of her working as a nurse in the slaughterhouse field hospital of Technos III, and that the majority of the Church wanted change. Most of those who would have objected either died in the rebellion or were on trial for crimes against humanity.

But after achieving this miracle, Mother Beatrice found herself declared a saint on all sides, especially by the media, and this upset her greatly. She didn't see herself as a saint, and detested the media interest that followed her everywhere. As soon as the new Church was up and running, she renounced her leadership and went to Lachrymae Christi to minister to the lepers. They seemed to need her more than anyone else, and it was possibly the only place where the media wouldn't follow her.

Before her involvement, lepers were just dumped where their ship landed, and left to live or die as best they could. Supply ships were infrequent. Saint Bea changed all that. She used her influence and contacts to get food and tech and medicines dropped on a regular basis, and built her mission into a spiritual and communications centre for the whole leper population. And all went well. Till the Hadenmen came, augmented serpents in paradise.

'Damned if I'd call this place paradise,' said Hazel. 'Why did she contact you, Owen, and not me? Or Jack and Ruby?'

'Apparently Jack and Ruby are off somewhere on a mission of their own. And she probably thought I'd be more . . . approachable.'

'More of a soft touch, certainly.'

Owen grinned, and shrugged. 'My life's been tough enough without having God mad at me.'

'I never really thought of you as religious,' said Hazel. 'You've broken enough commandments in your time.'

'I'm what the Empire made me,' said Owen. 'I never wanted to be a warrior. I was perfectly happy as a scholar, tucked away in my cosy ivory tower. But destiny had other plans for me. As for being religious; I was raised to believe in the Families first, the Iron Throne second and God when I had time. But of them all, only my faith in God remains. That was always a personal thing, irrespective of the established Church, then or now. I like to think that Someone out there watches, and cares.' He looked at Hazel. 'How about you?'

'I believe in hard cash and a loaded gun,' Hazel said

briskly, and Bonnie and Midnight nodded more or less in unison. Hazel would have left it at that, but she could see Owen wanted more. 'I live my life by my own rules, and I've always had problems with authority figures. If there is anything after this life, I'll deal with it when I get there. As for Saint Bea; all right, she's done a lot of good in her time, but so have we. She saved lives in her hospital, and we saved whole worlds by killing the right people. In the end, which of us made the most difference? Let history worry about it. I have more immediate concerns.'

'Saint Bea is a real hero,' Owen said firmly. 'She was a volunteer. An aristo who gave up everything to minister to the needy. We were all dragged into the rebellion, kicking and screaming all the way. So when she asked for my help, I couldn't say no. Not to a real hero. And how does God reward me? Crashes my ship and strands me on a leper colony. Thanks a whole bunch, Big Guy.'

Hazel looked back at Bonnie and Midnight. 'Didn't you have anyone like Saint Bea on your worlds?'

'Nah,' said Bonnie. 'The Church fell apart after the rebellion. Nothing's really replaced it. We live for the day, and let eternity take care of itself.'

Midnight sniffed dismissively. 'In my Empire, the Church found a new role after the rebellion. Everyone is a member of the Church of Christ the Warrior now, but it is a mystical order rather than a religion. We have seen what force of arms can do. Everyone is raised to be a warrior, from childhood on. The people will never be weak again. We have no room for saints, for the weak or the meek; for those who don't have the faith to fight for what's right.'

'I can see you and the Mother Superior are going to have a lot to talk about,' said Owen, and Hazel nodded solemnly. 'Where do you stand on all this, Moon?'

'The Hadenmen believe in the Church of the Genetic Crusade, the perfecting of man. Man becomes God, eventually. I don't believe that any more, but I'm no longer sure what I do believe. So much has changed since I went through the Maze. I touched something there, something much greater than myself, but whether that was the Maze, or something the Maze put me in touch with . . . And afterwards, I

547

died; and was brought back to life again. At least, the Hadenmen repaired my damaged body. My thoughts, my memories, my . . . self, should have been lost for ever, but here I am. I have no memories of being dead. Owen, you said I spoke to you, even after I was killed by the Grendel.'

'You did,' Owen said stubbornly. 'I heard your voice, down in the caverns of the Wolfling World. You told me the right code sequence with which to open the Tomb of the Hadenmen. Without that, everything would have been different.'

'Then I too have something to discuss with Mother Superior Beatrice,' said Moon. 'Even if it is only the exact nature of guilt. I shall be interested to hear her replies.'

'Hold everything,' said Bonnie. 'Back up and go previous. I think I must have missed something along the way. Why the hell do the Hadenmen want this bloody planet anyway? I mean, there's no tech here, no mineral deposits, just a whole crop of plants with attitude and colonists who have to count their fingers after they've shaken hands. Why would the Hadenmen waste troops and resources here when there must be other places that need them more? Moon, is this world of any strategic importance to the Hadenmen?'

'Not as far as I am aware,' said Moon. 'The Hadenman presence here is a complete mystery to me. The colonists are hardly the right material for being made over into Hadenmen, and the planet isn't suitable for a Base or a Nest. I can only assume there is something of a unique nature here that they desire, that is as yet unknown to us.'

'Well, if we stumble across any of the invading army, try and leave one of them alive,' said Owen. 'I'll hold him down, and Hazel can ask him questions.'

'I've got a question of my own, for Saint Bea,' said Hazel. 'Namely, what the hell are just the five of us supposed to do against a whole invading army, with no ship, weapons, or back-up.'

'Maybe she's hoping for a miracle,' said Owen.

In the end, it took them a day and a night and most of the next day of slow, hard slogging through the jungle and mud and rain to reach Saint Bea's mission. They drank water from occasional standing pools. It tasted brackish, and gave them all a mild case of the runs, but at least they were able to keep it down. They'd been less lucky trying to discover which parts of the jungle it was safe to eat. Most of it came straight back up again, tasting twice as bad in the process. There was no real shelter from the rain, so they spent the night sitting miserably together around a tree, trying to snatch what sleep they could. By the time they reached the mission, they were tired, cold, hungry and very wet.

There was no warning. They just forced their way through yet another series of closely set trees, and found themselves looking out into a wide clearing, with the mission set squarely in the middle. It was huge. There was about twenty feet of open ground, and then a tall wooden wall marked the outer boundary of the mission. The wall had been constructed of tightly packed black tree trunks, and looked reassuringly solid. The mission itself was more of a small village, with a long, slanting wooden roof covering everything within its walls. A single gate faced them, some twelve feet tall and ten wide, with a wooden watchtower on each side. *Definitely a low-tech world*, thought Owen. *Hate to see what a disrupter cannon would do to that wall. Hate to think what their plumbing's like.*

He stepped out into the clearing, and the watchtower sentries spotted him immediately and sounded the alarm. Owen led his party slowly across the open space. Armed men appeared on a catwalk inside the top of the outer wall. They were cloaked and hooded figures, some with energy weapons, most with bows and arrows. Owen didn't disparage the bows. An arrow could kill you just as dead as anything else if it hit the right spot. He murmured to the others to keep their hands conspicuously away from their weapons. He kept a careful eye on the watchtower sentries. One had what appeared to be a telescope trained on the newcomers. Hopefully, once they'd identified the approaching party as human, and not Hadenman, the armed figures on the wall would calm down a little, but Owen still kept himself ready to dodge a nervous arrow if he had to. Tired as he was, he was pretty sure he could dodge an arrow. Hell, he could probably shoot the bowman's head off before he'd even finished pulling back his bowstring, but he thought he'd better not. Definitely not the best way to make a good first impression with Saint Bea. *Mother Beatrice*, he thought firmly. *She hates being called Saint Bea*. His party made it all the way to the front gate without anyone on either side developing a twitchy finger, and Owen looked up at the left-hand watchtower, blinking through the pouring rain.

'Owen Deathstalker and party, here at the request of Mother Superior Beatrice Christiana. How about letting us in before we all drown out here?'

'Stay where you are,' said a hoarse voice from the watchtower. 'We've sent a runner to the Mother Superior. She'll have to identify you.'

'Don't be a prat all your life, son,' said another voice from the tower. 'That's the Deathstalker, all right. Seen his face on a dozen holo documentaries, before I came here. He's a hero of the rebellion. And that's Hazel d'Ark beside him.'

'That's *Hazel d'Ark*?' said the first voice. 'Oh, bloody hell. Isn't it bad enough being a leper, without having her here too? Please let me shoot her. It'll save a lot of trouble in the long run.'

Owen looked at Hazel. 'Your reputation is spreading.'

'Good,' said Hazel. 'Now tell them to get a move on or I'll kick their gate in and make them eat the hinges.'

'I heard that,' said the second voice. 'Please leave our gate alone. It's the only one we've got. Give us a minute to draw back the bolts, and we'll let you in. The Mother Superior will be here soon, and there'll be hot food and dry clothes for all of you.'

'And a leash for Hazel d'Ark,' said the first voice.

'I heard that!' said Hazel.

There was a pause. 'Do you know who I am?' said the first voice.

'No.'

'Then I think I'll keep it that way.'

The gate creaked open while Hazel was still trying to come up with a suitably devastating reply, and all animosity was forgotten as Owen and his party hurried inside, glad to get out of the rain at last. The gate opened into a wide square or compound, already half full of cloaked and hooded figures, with more arriving all the time. They all had their hoods pulled well forward to hide their faces, making the crowd eerily alike and anonymous, like a convention of somewhat tattered grey ghosts. Owen stood dripping before them, listening to the very pleasant and reassuring sound of the rain drumming on the protecting roof overhead. Every part of him was soaking wet, as though he'd just stepped out of an ocean. He looked slowly around him, trying to judge his reception, and then the crowd raised their voices in a ragged cheer. Owen let the cheering go on for a while. He rather felt he'd earned it. But finally he raised a hand to get their attention, and the cheer cut off as suddenly as it had begun. All the hoods turned to face him, eerily expectant. *Damn*, thought Owen. *They want a speech.*

'It's good to be here at last,' he said, very seriously. 'The good news is that the Empire got Mother Beatrice's call for help. The bad news is, we're all you're getting. The Empire's fighting a war for survival on half a dozen fronts at once, and we're what they can spare. But Hazel and I have been known to turn around even the most dire of situations, so as soon as we've had a word with Mother Beatrice, and brought our-selves up to speed—'

'I'm here,' said a warm but still subtly commanding voice, and the crowd parted silently to allow the Mother Superior to pass through them. They bowed their heads deeply as she approached. Mother Beatrice wore a simple nun's outfit, with a plain wimple, rather than the much more impressive robes to which her rank entitled her. A simple silver crucifix hung around her neck, and a wooden rosary hung from one hip like a drawn gun. Her face was pale and wan, with dark steady eyes and a determined mouth. 'Thank the good Lord you're here at last, Sir Deathstalker. We've been expecting you for some time. Will you introduce your companions?'

'Hazel d'Ark I'm sure you know,' said Owen. 'Everything you've heard is true, unfortunately. The others are Bonnie Bedlam and Midnight Blue, and Tobias Moon. He's a Had-enman, but he's a good guy. Really. Are there going to be any problems over his presence here?'

'No,' said the Mother Superior. 'All souls are welcome here. Anyone who feels otherwise is welcome to come and discuss the matter with me.'

It'd be a brave man who tried, thought Owen. 'There was mention of hot food and dry clothes . . .'

'Of course,' said Mother Beatrice. 'Please follow me.'

She led them through the crowd, who bowed again as Owen and his party passed, though nowhere near as deeply as they'd bowed to Saint Bea. The compound led on to a series of low buildings with narrow alleys running between them. In the centre was a ramshackle wooden building the size of a barn, built like everything else from the local black trees. The rooms inside turned out to be surprisingly civilized, with all the usual amenities, if few luxuries. Owen and Moon stripped off their soaking-wet clothes in one room, while the women were escorted to another. Thick, hot towels were provided, and Owen rubbed himself down briskly, standing as close to the open fire as he could get. Warmth moved slowly through him, and he stretched luxuriously, as self-centred as a cat. He hadn't known there could be such pleasure in just being dry and warm.

Moon went about his toilet with quiet thoroughness, with no obvious signs of enjoyment. The door opened just enough for an arm to throw in two sets of simple but functional clothing, all in grey, followed by the ubiquitous hooded cloaks, and then the arm withdrew and the door closed again. Owen sorted out a set for himself. The clothes seemed sturdy enough, but showed signs of much hard use and washing. *More than one leper had these before me*, Owen thought uncomfortably, and tried not to wonder how many might have died wearing them. He shrugged mentally, and put them on. It wasn't as if he had a choice.

He glanced over at Moon, who was still towelling himself. Metal implants showed clearly all over his pale skin, but that wasn't what drew Owen's attention. 'Uh, Moon . . .'

'Yes, Owen?'

'I understood that all Hadenmen were . . . desexed.'

'Yes,' said Moon. 'All of the sexual parts are cut away when a human becomes a Hadenman.'

'But you appear to have a full set of . . . well, everything.'

'Yes,' said Moon. 'They grew back. Other changes are taking place in my body, all the time. I believe it to be a part of the changes the Maze is working in me. Certain tech

552

implants have disappeared, absorbed into my body. I don't seem to need them any more. I have detected no lowering in my general efficiency. But I am becoming . . . more human.'

And I've been worrying about the Maze making me less human, thought Owen.

Owen and Moon made their way to the common room, where the three women were already warming themselves before a roaring log fire. They too were wearing the basic grey clothes provided, complete with cloak and hood, though Hazel had lifted up the back of her skirt so she could warm her bare bottom before the fire. She grinned unconcernedly at Owen.

'I see you got the basic outfit too. Apparently grey is in this year.'

'I hate it,' said Bonnie. 'It covers far too much of me. What's the point of having tattoos and piercings if you can't show them off to everyone?'

'I think it's a vast improvement,' said Midnight. 'You've done things to your body I wouldn't do to a dead dog.'

'Prude!' snapped Bonnie.

'Pervert!'

'So?'

Owen gave Hazel a hard look. 'All the alternates you could have called up, and you had to choose these two . . .'

'Don't you take that tone of voice with me, Owen Death-stalker. After all, you married one of them.'

Luckily the door opened at that moment, and Mother Beatrice came in. Everyone immediately shut up, and managed some kind of polite smile. Mother Beatrice laughed.

'Nothing like a nun entering a room to stop a conversation. Don't worry; when you're Mother Confessor to a colony of lepers, there isn't much left that can shock you. I'm afraid those rather boring grey outfits are all the clothes we have to offer you. It's all the Empire provides. Officially, so that if anyone here did get off-planet, they could be recognized immediately. More likely, it's because they're cheap. Still, the cloaks and hoods provide a useful purpose in hiding the ravages of the disease in its later stages. Most of the colonists remain largely unmarked, but they choose to wear the cloak and hood too, as a sign of solidarity. There are those who flaunt their deformities, but that's mostly just a plea for attention. Don't let them bother you.' She looked at Moon for a long moment, and then turned to Owen. 'You should have told me you were bringing a Hadenman with you. I have no objection to his presence, but my people have suffered much at the hands of the augmented men. I don't know how people are going to react to him. I can't guarantee his safety.'

'That's all right,' said Hazel. 'We'll guarantee his safety, by kicking the ass of anyone who even looks at him funny.'

'This is Tobias Moon,' said Owen. 'He turned against his own people, to side with humanity.'

'You mean he's a traitor.'

'No, I mean he's a friend. We've been through a lot together. We all vouch for him. That should be enough.'

'It's more than enough,' said Mother Beatrice. She put out a hand to Moon, and he shook it gravely. 'I'm sorry if I seemed a little cold, Sir Moon. I've never met a Hadenman socially before.'

'That's all right,' said Moon generously. 'I've never met a saint before.'

Mother Beatrice laughed briefly, and shook her head. 'You still haven't. No one's ever met a saint who was alive. It's more of a posthumous award, bestowed by people who never even met the real person.' She looked at Hazel. 'Speaking of reputations, I've heard a lot about you, Hazel d'Ark.'

'You don't want to believe everything you see in the holos,' said Hazel uncomfortably.

'Oh, I don't,' Mother Beatrice assured her. 'You should hear some of the things they've said about me. Last I heard, they were claiming I was feeding this entire colony on five protein cubes and five pints of distilled water. I wish! I'm no saint; just a nun, going where I'm needed. Now, perhaps you'd be good enough to introduce your two friends, whom I confess are unfamiliar to me.'

'Oh, sure,' said Hazel. 'The tall steroids' case with a butcher's axe on her hip is Midnight Blue. The S and M freak is Bonnie Bedlam. They're . . . cousins of mine. Good fighters. Now perhaps you'd be good enough to brief us on the current situation. I was given to understand that things were pretty desperate here, but we travelled through miles of jungle to get here, and never saw a single Hadenman.'

'They come and they go,' said Mother Beatrice. 'We don't know why. They started off attacking the outer settlements, but soon found they were losing more people to the jungle than in the fighting, and focused their attention here. We're the main communications centre, the only starport, and the main distribution centre. Whoever controls the mission controls the fate of the colony. The jungle and the weather make air attacks and ground travel impractical, so they have to come on foot. And though there are always more of them in every attack, so far we've held them off successfully. High-tech weaponry doesn't last long here; the rain gets into everything. So most of the fighting has been hand to hand, steel on steel, which gives us the advantage.'

'Even so,' said Owen, 'how has a simple wooden fort like this stood off a Hadenman army?'

'With increasing difficulty. The jungle is our protector. The Hadenmen have to get through it to get to us, and while the plant life here has always been somewhat aggressive, it really hates the augmented men. By the time they get to us, they're already exhausted and thinned out by what the jungle's put them through. And we do have a number of true warriors here. Some were marines, before their condition was diagnosed. They've made good teachers. And we also have two Sisters of Glory.'

'Bloody hell,' said Hazel, deeply impressed. 'The warrior nuns? I'd back two Sisters of Glory against an army of Hadenmen, no problem. I'd even give odds. How did they come to be here?'

'How do you think?' said Mother Beatrice, and Hazel had the grace to look a little embarrassed.

Owen saw Moon's puzzled frown. 'They're something new, appeared while you were still dead. The Sisters of Glory are nuns who used to be part of the old Church's Brotherhood of Steel, a semi-mystical order within an order, trained to the peak of perfection in all martial arts. The old Church used them as internal police, debt collectors, and for scaring the crap out of the ungodly. After Mother Beatrice reformed the Church, most of the Brotherhood were up on charges for atrocities, mass murder and being massively politically incorrect. So the Mother Superior revamped the few survivors as the Sisters of Glory, and gave them a new mission in life – to fight to put an end to fighting. Protect the weak and the needy. Die fighting, that others might live. The last warriors in a pacifistic Church, the order tends to attract . . . extreme types.'

'Very diplomatically put,' said Mother Beatrice. 'Actually, they're mostly a bunch of homicidal headbangers with strong self-destructive tendencies, and I just wanted a place I could put them all, so I could keep an eye on them. To my surprise, they've turned out to be very good at what they do. They've established themselves as the Church's strong right arm, defenders of the faith and feared and respected fighters. Still a little too keen to martyr themselves for the cause, but I suppose that goes with the territory. Anyway, you'll meet them later.'

'Oh, good,' said Owen. 'Two more homicidal women in my life. Just what I needed.'

'What was that?' said Mother Beatrice. 'Don't mumble, Sir Deathstalker, it's a very annoying habit. Now then; we seem to be in a quiet phase at the moment, so why don't you all take a walk through our little community? It'll be good for their morale, and will give you some idea of the kind of people you'll be fighting alongside. Don't be nervous of them. Bits of them won't fall off if you speak too loudly, and you can't catch it just by shaking hands. They're just people. I should split up into ones or twos; you'll be less intimidating that way. It's not every day we get living legends walking among us. Be back here in an hour, and there'll be a hot meal ready. Now be off with you; I have my rounds to make in the infirmary.'

And she gently but firmly shooed them all out of the common room, and shut the door behind them. Owen shook his head slowly.

'So that's Saint Bea. Seems to have a good head on her shoulders. I was expecting one of the nuns who taught me as a child. All loud voices and stiff necks and a devil with the steel ruler.'

'They probably went on to become Sisters of Glory,' said Hazel.

'Wouldn't surprise me at all. Now pay attention, people; forget what she said, no one is to go off on their own. We don't know enough about the situation here. I don't think Saint Bea would necessarily lie to us, but there could be all kinds of undercurrents here she knows nothing about. So, Hazel and Moon, you come with me; Bonnie and Midnight, stick close together and watch your backs. We'll meet here in an hour.'

'He just loves being in charge,' said Hazel to Bonnie and Midnight, and they nodded knowingly.

'Let's get out of here before he starts making one of his speeches,' said Midnight, and she and Bonnie went off to meet some lepers.

Owen looked haughtily at Hazel. 'I have no idea what you were talking about.'

Hazel grinned at Moon. 'The trouble is, he probably doesn't. Lead the way, Sir Deathstalker, O saviour of humanity.'

Owen sniffed loudly, and set off. Hazel followed, grinning, and a rather mystified Moon brought up the rear.

Bonnie Bedlam freaked the lepers out. She loved sweeping back her clothes to flash people, and show off her many piercings and body modifications. Even after everything they'd been through, the lepers had never seen anyone like Bonnie. Soon a small but fascinated crowd had formed around her. After a while Bonnie and some of the braver lepers began comparing mutilations and trying to get one up and gross each other out. There were shrieks and mock-shocked gasps, and soon Bonnie and the lepers were chatting away as though they'd known each other for years. The idea that someone would voluntarily cut and pierce and modify their own flesh fascinated the colonists, having been victimized by so many for a similar condition over which they had no control. That Bonnie took pride in her being different from the norm just blew them away. It wasn't long before Bonnie had fervent disciples sitting at her feet, working out how to start some piercings of their own. *All flesh is beautiful,* said Bonnie firmly. *Anything can be made sexy*. A spirited argument arose as to whether it was better to pierce dead flesh or that which still had some feeling. Bonnie strongly recommended the latter, to get the full experience.

Midnight Blue stood quietly behind Bonnie, trying hard to be shocked but not quite making it in the face of the lepers' obvious enthusiasm. It had never occurred to them that their disfigurements didn't have to be ugly. The lepers revealed more and more of themselves as they grew more comfortable in Bonnie's presence. Midnight was quietly horrified at what the disease had done to some of its victims, but fought to keep it out of her face. Missing fingers and toes were common, and many had eaten-away noses and ears. It was always the extremities that went first. Many had sores and open wounds that would not heal, sometimes bandaged, sometimes not. There were drugs that helped slow the symptoms, but there'd been no deliveries for some time. The Empire needed all its cargo ships for the war. So the lepers were left to die by inches, because even a saint's pleas had to take second place to the military.

Abandoned yet again, the lepers refused to give in to their condition. They watched themselves and watched each other, and tried to live as normal a life as possible as they fought to establish a self-sufficient colony. Children were being born for the first time, most of them free of the disease, as yet. For the first time, there was hope. For the future, if not for themselves.

When things got too bad, there was the mission infirmary. Not so much a hospital, more a resting place before the end. A place where people could be cared for when they were no longer capable of caring for themselves. Mother Superior Beatrice ran the infirmary. The lepers couldn't say enough about her. She gave them hope and faith, and a reason to live when it would have been so easy just to lie down and die. The lepers worshipped her, much to her discomfort. Among themselves, they had declared her the patron saint of lepers.

Eventually Bonnie moved on, word of her appearance moving ahead of her, so that there were always people waiting to meet her. She made them laugh, and tried to give them pride in themselves again. Many of the lepers were pathetically grateful that anyone had come to fight beside them. They'd been told they were the lowest of the low for so long that many had come to believe it. Bonnie blew that notion away on a cloud of raucous laughter. Midnight began adding the occasional dry comment, just to provide a balance, and found a ready audience for her sharp wit. It had been a long time since the lepers had had anything to laugh at. Bonnie and Midnight passed through the small village of low buildings smiling and chatting and making themselves known, until finally they had to beg for a little time for themselves. The lepers withdrew to a respectful distance, while Bonnie and Midnight pulled up their hoods and lowered their voices so they could talk privately.

'Oh, Jesus,' said Midnight softly, 'the poor bastards. How can you keep smiling like that? They're dying and they know it and they haven't given up. I think of the kind of guts that takes and I feel like nothing in comparison.'

'They're so brave,' said Bonnie. 'And I smile and laugh to make them laugh, because the last thing they need is some outsider weeping buckets over them.'

'They break my heart. It's so unfair. These people had lives, futures, dreams . . . They had friends and families and loved ones. And now they have nothing but the disease that's killing them. And they still believe in God. If I was in their place I'd curse Her name every day. They put me to shame.'

'If you so much as sniffle, I'll slap you a good one,' said Bonnie fiercely. 'We have to be strong, for them.'

'Strength through piercing,' said Midnight. 'A novel approach to psychotherapy.'

'Whatever works. Their bodies have ruled their lives for so long, it's only fair that they get back some control over their flesh.'

'They're strong people,' said the warrior woman. 'They'll make good fighters, when the Hadenmen come again.'

'Of course they will. But can we defend this place indefinitely?'

Midnight shrugged. 'Depends on how many Hadenmen we have to fight off. Which in turn depends on how badly the Hadenmen want this planet. The mission's walls are sturdy, the attackers have to come to us across an open clearing, and apparently we don't have to worry about large-scale weaponry. And there's the Sisters of Glory, that Hazel was so impressed by. The situation could be a lot worse. Anyway, the question's redundant. We'll hold out because we have to. There's nowhere to run, nowhere to hide, no starship to get us off-planet.'

'And no reinforcements,' said Bonnie. 'There's just us. So we'll have to be enough.'

'We don't stand a chance, do we?' said Midnight Blue.

'Not a hope in hell,' said Bonnie Bedlam.

At first, Owen and Hazel had to walk either side of Moon, with their hands hovering over their weapons, because once the lepers recognized a Hadenman, they either ran from him or tried to attack him. The atmosphere got very bad very quick until Owen identified himself, and just like that the mood changed. People came running from all over the village to meet the legendary Deathstalker, and once he'd vouched for the Hadenman, things calmed down a lot. Everyone wanted to meet the great hero of the rebellion, and he warmed in the glow of the appreciation, and was soon at his most charming and gracious. Hazel smiled determinedly in his shadow, and did her best to be polite. Some people wanted Owen's autograph, and everyone wanted to shake his hand. Owen kept his smile steady as he clasped hands that weren't always complete, and had a kind word for everyone. No one wanted to get close enough to Hazel to shake her hand, and no one cared about Moon any more. Soon the crowd around them had got so dense, there was no room to move, so Owen led the way to the compound before the main gate and the crowd sat facing him in neat rows, filling the great open space.

Owen had never felt at ease in front of large audiences, but the hero-worship was unnerving him even more, so he overcame his natural tendency for speech-making and opted for a question-and-answer session. After a little prompting, people began introducing themselves and asking questions, most of them so familiar to Owen that he could have answered them in his sleep. Soon the lepers became just another audience to him, a little better behaved than most, as he began telling them about his time in the rebellion, or at least the parts that were suitable for public consumption. He won points for being quietly witty and self-effacing, and Hazel began chiming in now and again with what she considered telling points. The lepers treated them both with great respect, and Owen and Hazel couldn't help but warm to them. It had never occurred to them that the lepers might be fans of theirs, just like everyone else.

Eventually Owen ran out of things to say, and introduced Moon. The audience listened quietly as he talked of his adventures with Owen and Hazel, and how he had learned humanity from them. So much so that in the end he turned on his own people to side with Owen and Hazel. A voice from the audience asked if he considered himself a traitor to his people, and Moon thought for a moment before finally saying no; that his people were traitors to humanity. He actually got a soft patter of applause for that.

Time went quickly by, and Owen was actually surprised when Oz murmured in his ear that his hour was nearly up. Owen wasn't sure what he'd expected from a colony of lepers; perhaps shambling deathlike figures clanging a bell and shouting *Unclean! Unclean!* These quiet, warm and friendly people were a revelation to him. Previously, he'd seen his commitment to fight for them as a duty. Now he saw it as an honour. They'd been through so much, it didn't seem fair to him that they should have to face the Hadenmen as well.

He announced at last that he had to leave, and a roar of protest went up. He explained that Mother Beatrice had a meal prepared for them, and the mention of the saint's name was all it took to clear the compound. Owen looked at Hazel.

'So, what do you think?'

'They'll fight,' said Hazel. 'But then I never doubted they would. Only hardline fighters would live and prosper in the face of all they have going against them, even before the Hadenmen. But God knows how long we can hold this place against an army. Moon?'

The augmented man frowned. 'I confess I find it hard to understand what the Hadenmen are doing here anyway. The colonists don't have anything worth the taking. There must be something else here, something we're missing. Something the Hadenmen want so badly, they're prepared to commit troops and resources here that must surely be needed elsewhere.'

'Keep thinking,' said Owen. 'If we knew what it was they wanted, maybe we could just give it to them, or destroy it. Then maybe they'd go away and annoy someone else.'

'I wouldn't bet on that,' said Hazel. 'Once the Hadenmen find out we're here, it might well motivate them to raze the whole mission to the ground, just to get us. We did, after all, wipe out what was to be their new homeworld on Brahmin II. And the Hadenmen have never been the most forgiving of people.'

'True,' said Moon.

'Oh, shut up,' said Owen. 'I've got enough problems to think about.'

'I think a new one may be heading our way,' said Hazel quietly. 'Take a look at what just showed up.'

They all looked, with varying degrees of disbelief, as a tall, skeleton-thin creature lurched towards them. Well over six and a half feet tall, the newcomer wore a long black dress of tatters, belted round an impossibly thin waist to support a sword on one bony hip and a gun on the other. She wore tall lace-up boots, long green evening gloves with holes in and a tall, battered witch's hat with long purple streamers flying from the top. Her face was covered with white pancake make-up, pointed up by two bright red cheeks, and metallic green lipstick and eyeshadow. She moved with an uneven, determined gait, her legs barely bending, as though the knees didn't work properly. She looked a lot like a marionette who'd cut her own strings, done something very nasty to the puppeteer, and then gone out into the world to do as much damage as possible before someone finally stopped her.

Owen let his hand drift casually down to the gun at his side. The black-clad witch lurched to a halt before him, waited a moment to make sure all her parts had caught up with her, and then glowered at Owen in what she clearly thought was a friendly fashion.

'Welcome to Hell, Deathstalker. I'm Sister Marion. Bea's second in command. I run the place while she's busy being saintly. I was going to be a saint too, when I was younger, but it turned out I didn't have the right attitude. So they made me a Sister of Glory, and sent me out to kick righteous ass on the kind of missions the Church doesn't like to talk about in public. Then I caught leprosy, and they sent me here. Bastards. Still, a nun serves God wherever she's sent, and God knows this bunch needs all the help it can get. You can say hello now.'

'Hello, Sister Marion,' said Owen, doing his best to appear entirely unperturbed. 'That's a very striking outfit you're wearing.'

The nun stretched her green mouth in a disturbing smile that showed far too many teeth. 'I dress like this to mess with people's heads. And the make-up and gloves help hide the skin lesions. People here will tell you I'm an eccentric. Or a loony tune. Don't listen to them. We all have our own ways of dealing with our condition. Mine is just a little more dramatic than most. Now get your asses in gear and follow me. Bea's got dinner waiting and there are things we need to discuss.'

She turned round sharply, swayed for a moment like a flagpole in a high wind, and then marched stiff-leggedly off without looking to see if anyone was following. Lepers scattered to get out of her way as she strode on, as implacable as a force of nature and twice as dangerous.

'So that's a Sister of Glory,' said Moon.

'Yeah,' said Hazel. 'I don't know what the Hadenmen'll make of her, but she scares the crap out of me. Did you notice she didn't blink once the whole time she was talking to us? That nun is in serious need of psychotherapy. And possibly a hole in her head to let the devils out.'

'You don't get invited to be a Sister of Glory because of your even temperament,' said Owen. 'Personally, I think she's the most encouraging thing I've seen since I got here. At least someone here knows how to fight. Just pull her pin, throw her at the enemy and stand well back.'

'I just hope we can defuse her afterwards,' said Hazel. 'That is a very dangerous person.'

'You should know,' said Owen.

They set off after Sister Marion, and followed her back to

the main building, maintaining a respectful distance at all times. They picked up Bonnie and Midnight along the way. Bonnie admired Sister Marion's dress sense. Midnight managed a frosty greeting. A small crowd of colonists tried to follow them into the main building, not wanting to miss anything. The Sister explained that it was a private meeting. One colonist made the mistake of objecting too loudly and just a little too rudely, and Sister Marion head-butted him in the face. The other colonists discovered they had pressing business elsewhere and managed a dignified retreat that didn't quite involve running. Sister Marion led her guests inside, leaving the unconscious colonist to lie in the street until he remembered his manners. Or at least his name.

To no one's surprise, the meal turned out to be mostly vegetables, spiced up with flavoured protein cubes and bottles of a vicious-looking blue wine distilled from local produce. Owen didn't recognize anything on his plate, which, given his previous experiments at finding something edible in the jungle, reassured him somewhat. He made polite noises to Mother Beatrice and crunched his way determinedly through one unpleasant surprise after another. He couldn't even work out what flavour the protein cubes were supposed to be. He washed everything down with lots of wine, which turned out to be fierce but surprisingly palatable. Everyone drank a lot of it, except Moon. Mother Beatrice in particular put the stuff away as though it was water, knocking it back with the ease of long practice. No one said anything, after a few guarded glares from Sister Marion. Presumably being a saint was hard on the nerves. Owen watched Sister Marion stab at her food with knife and fork as though it might try to escape at any moment, and cleaned his plate with a sense of accomplishment, hoping against hope for a decent dessert. Unless the wine was the dessert. Unfortunately, he must have overdone the polite, appreciative noises, because Mother Beatrice immediately served him a second helping. Owen smiled bravely down at his heaped plate, chewed his way slowly through something very like scarlet seaweed, and listened to Mother Beatrice talk about the planet's history so he wouldn't have to think about what he was eating.

The mission had originally been nothing more than a very basic hospital and a graveyard, in a clearing cut from the jungle with energy weapons and flame-throwers. The clearance had to be renewed daily, or the jungle crept back. There was a landing pad just big enough for one ship to land and take off. The hospital was never intended to be anything more than a place for lepers to die in relative comfort. A lot of the colonists died, at first. The shock of the disease, the diagnosis and being dumped on Lachrymae Christi was simply too much for many people, and they just lay down and died.

The lepers had to bury their own dead. No one but them ever put a foot down on the leper planet. The graveyard quickly became overcrowded, so the colonists let the jungle take it back. The plants consumed the bodies overnight, so no one had to watch. There were still headstones, with names and dates. For the comfort of the living, not the dead. These days, there were rows and rows of markers, with no room to walk between them. It didn't matter.

Everyone knew Lachrymae Christi was where lepers went to die.

Mother Beatrice changed all that. Weary of the compromises and politics that were already creeping into her new Church, she made it her business to discover people who had a taste and a talent for such work, and happily handed it over to them, so that she could get back to what she considered real work for a nun. And so she went to Lachrymae Christi, to give hope to the hopeless where no one else would.

It never occurred to her that she was doing something very brave, or noble, or even self-sacrificing, risking her life in a place no one cared about, for people humanity had discarded. She went because she thought she was needed, because she thought she could do some good.

Because she was Saint Bea.

The lepers took heart from her quiet determination not to be beaten by circumstances, or to give in to despair. She gave them back their pride in themselves, and encouraged them to make as much of their lives as they could, while they still could. And she never once pushed her religion on them. She held regular services, for those who wished to attend, but that was all. A lot of people came anyway, just because it was her. To those who asked why God had allowed such a horrible thing to happen to them, she said *God has a plan for all of us.* And to those who said they didn't believe in God, she just smiled and said, *That's all right. He believes in you.*

The lepers worked hard because she worked harder, and believed in themselves because she believed in them. Working under her guidance and inspiration, they became a colony in truth at last, establishing small settlements further and further out into the jungle. It was a basic kind of life, but better by far than they'd had any right to expect. Everything was going so well. Until the Hadenmen came to Lachrymae Christi.

The lepers had wanted to rename the mission Saint Beatrice's Mission, but she wouldn't hear of it. She said it was her work that was important, not her, and that the mission and the colony would still be there, long after she was gone. The colonists respected her wishes, and only called it Saint Beatrice's Mission when she wasn't around.

Owen got some of this from Mother Beatrice, and some from Sister Marion's acid interventions, and some he knew already from talking with the colonists. It fitted with what he'd previously heard of the Saint of Technos III. He studied her unobtrusively while he was eating, looking for some kind of halo, or a sense of self-righteousness, but Mother Beatrice came across as reassuringly normal and level-headed. But there was still something about her, something . . . focused. Owen wondered idly if that was how people saw him, sometimes. He realized that Sister Marion was snapping at Mother Beatrice, and paid attention. The Sister didn't take any nonsense from anyone, not even Saint Bea.

'If you don't ease up on your workload, you'll end up in one of your own infirmary beds,' said Sister Marion angrily. She hadn't taken her witch's hat off for dinner, and the long plumes bobbed emphatically as she glared at Mother Beatrice. 'You work harder than anyone else, and you don't get nearly enough sleep. You're no good to anyone dead on your feet from exhaustion. And you needn't think I'm going to take over as head nurse. I can cope with the bandages and the bedpans, but I'm no good at talking to them, or holding hands and mopping brows, and all that nonsense. That's your department.'

'Hush, Marion,' said Mother Beatrice affectionately. 'After my time on Technos III, this is a picnic. Besides, I've never needed much sleep.'

Sister Marion glowered at her, unconvinced. This was an argument they'd clearly had many times before, and would again.

'We need to know more about the Hadenman attacks,' said Owen, pushing away his plate. It was still more than half full, so Hazel immediately transferred its contents to her own plate. Owen wasn't surprised. Hazel would eat anything, if she was hungry enough. He concentrated on Beatrice. 'How long is it between each attack? Normally?'

'Sometimes days, sometimes hours,' said Mother Beatrice. She sounded suddenly tired. 'The Hadenmen first came just over a month ago. There was no warning, no ultimatums. We were completely unprepared. The first we knew of it was when some of the outer settlements stopped answering our calls. Then the first refugees arrived, bringing tales of death and destruction. The few who'd tried to surrender were cut down without mercy. We lost a lot of people, until I gave the order for the outer settlements to be abandoned. Then the Hadenmen came here. We've strengthened our fortifications, and everyone here has learned to use a weapon. The Sisters of Glory have proved excellent teachers. And then there's Colonel William Hand, and Otto. You'll meet them later.'

'Much later, if you've got any sense,' said Sister Marion.

'They're good fighters,' said Mother Beatrice reprovingly.

'They're complete bloody psychopaths!'

'Takes one to know one, dear. And these days, their . . . attitude is something of an advantage.' Mother Beatrice frowned down at her hands, clasped together on the table before her. 'Every time the Hadenmen come, we lose more people. Every victory carries a high price. My people are brave enough, and they fight well, but lepers have their limitations as warriors. Even the smallest wound can turn deadly very quickly. It's the rain, and the ever-present mois- ture. Everything rots. Everything.'

'How long has it been since the last attack?' said Moon, in his buzzing, inhuman voice.

'Three days,' said Sister Marion, pruning her green finger-nails with her dinner knife. 'They could come any time.' She looked up and fixed Moon with her bright cold eyes. 'Ready for a little action, Hadenman?'

'Call me Moon. And yes, I will fight. To protect my friends. Isn't that why anyone fights?'

There was a moment of silence that might have become uncomfortable, but it was interrupted by a polite knock at the door. Sister Marion went to answer it, and then came back to murmur in Mother Beatrice's ear. She rose to her feet.

'You'll have to excuse us. We're needed at the infirmary. Make yourselves at home. We'll talk more later.'

The room seemed very quiet after the Sister of Glory and the saint had left. Everyone looked at each other, except Hazel, who was mopping up the last traces of anything edible from her plate. Everyone else looked at her with varying shades of disgust and amusement. She glanced up and saw them watching.

'What?'

'I'm impressed,' said Owen. 'Really. I couldn't manage two helpings of that stuff if you put a gun to my head.'

'I'm hungry! And you'd better learn to get used to it; we could be here a long time.'

'Parliament will send a ship, as soon as they learn we're stranded here,' said Owen. 'We're too valuable to the war effort to be abandoned.'

Hazel shrugged. 'On the other hand, we've made a lot of enemies in our time. Enemies who might be quite happy to see us sidelined. Face it, Owen; we're not getting off this planet any time soon.'

Owen shook his head angrily. 'One thing at a time. Let's deal with the Hadenmen first. Moon, any ideas on how we can carry the fight to the enemy? Anything we can do to turn the odds more in our favour?'

Moon frowned. 'We have no way of knowing where the Hadenman forces are, or how large they are. We don't know what they want, or how big a force they're prepared to field to get it. I will think on the matter further. Now, if you will excuse me, I need some time alone.'

He got to his feet. The others looked quickly at each other. 'I don't think that's such a good idea, Moon,' said Owen. 'Lots of people here have no reason to love the Hadenmen.'

'I'll be fine, Owen. I don't need a nursemaid.' He headed for the door, not looking back. 'Don't wait up for me.'

'Watch your back!' said Owen, and then the door closed, and the Hadenman was gone.

Bonnie and Midnight got to their feet. 'Getting late,' said Bonnie. 'Time for one last stroll before bed. These lepers are fascinating.'

'And I want to check out the fortifications, look for weak spots,' said Midnight. 'See you in the morning.'

They left too. Owen looked at Hazel. 'Was it something I said?'

'For once, no. I think everyone just needs some time to themselves, Owen. For all Saint Bea's upbeat attitude, this is still at heart a grim and depressing place. People came here to die, and just when they thought they'd made a life for themselves against all the odds, along came the Hadenmen to put the boot in. I've got a bad feeling about this place, Owen. We've cheated death many times, one way or another, but I've never seen anywhere as steeped in death as this. This is the place where death always wins. Maybe we've finally come to the one place no one escapes from. I'm going to go and get some sleep, on a real bed with warm dry blankets, and try not to dream. You should get some sleep too. We're going to need all our strength when the Hadenmen return.' She got to her feet, and looked round the empty room. 'We should never have come here, Owen. Something bad is going to happen.'

She left the room without a backward glance, not bothering to shut the door behind her. Owen leaned back in his chair and stretched tiredly. Not for the first time in his eventful life, a lot had happened in a short time, but he wasn't ready to sleep yet. Not while he was still trying to work out what the hell to do for the best. From what he'd seen of the mission so far, it was going to be hell to defend. Wooden walls, wooden buildings, wooden roof. The constant rain would help to suppress fires, but if the Hadenmen had access to the right accelerants, they could set fires no rain would be able to put out. Maybe that was what they'd gone to get.

The lepers seemed willing enough to fight, but they were still basically only invalid civilians with limited training. One on one, they wouldn't stand a chance. The augmented men were designed and constructed to be efficient, merciless killers. They had internal armour, steel mesh under their skin, servo-motors in their muscles, inhuman speed and built-in disrupters. It was a wonder and a miracle that the mission hadn't fallen already. But then, a man always fought hardest when defending his home. And when he knew there was nowhere else to go.

Owen got to his feet. Hazel was right; the place stank of death. He walked slowly over to the door, still too restless to sleep. An impulse made him pull his cloak around him, and bring his hood well forward so its shadow hid his face. Perhaps if he walked among the lepers as one of them, they would speak freely in front of him, and he could learn more of the truth of the situation. He needed the truth. He couldn't make plans in the dark.

He made his way slowly through the narrow streets and alleys of the mission. Despite the dark and the late hour, there were people everywhere. It seemed Owen wasn't the only one who couldn't sleep. He moved unhurriedly along, going nowhere in particular, being as careful as everyone else not to bump into anyone. The never-ending rain drummed loudly on the wooden roof overhead. Indoors, you learned to tune out the sound, but now it was like an endless drum roll, foreshadowing the action to come. Owen found himself looking out over the compound, the only large open space inside the mission. Torches blazed at regular intervals, casting pools of gold and amber light, surrounded by shifting shadows. People stood or sat in small groups; eating, drinking, preparing weapons or just talking quietly. No one noticed one more cloaked and hooded figure as Owen moved into the compound to join the crowd.

He found Sister Marion and another Sister of Glory holding an impromptu class on the best ways to set booby traps and pitfalls for use in case the Hadenmen ever got past the outer wall. The two Sisters passed a bottle of the local wine back and forth as they lectured the attentive group before them, and leaned on each other heavily when they thought no one was watching. Sister Kathleen looked more in keeping with what Owen thought of as a nun, in sweeping black robes and traditional starched wimple, but she too wore a sword on one hip and a disrupter on the other. She was of average height, a strapping woman with a man's large bony hands. She all but crackled with nervous energy, stalking back and forth like a trapped animal, her hand stabbing out to point at her audience when she wanted to emphasize something. She had the word LOVE tattooed on both sets of knuckles. She had a long, horsy face, a wide mouth full of protruding teeth and a voice like an angel. Owen could have listened to her for hours. Sister Marion stood beside her like a ghastly scarecrow, interjecting the odd word or comment whenever she felt the need.

'Caltrops,' said Sister Kathleen cheerfully, holding up two nails twisted together. 'However you drop them, they always land point up. And even a Hadenman won't get far with three inches of steel rammed through the sole of his foot. Don't forget to dip the points in fresh dung before you drop them; that'll make the wounds fester. Every little helps. Now, you've all seen the deadfalls we've arranged. Memorize where the triggers are so you won't set one off accidentally. Same with the spiked pits and the half-dozen landmines we've improvised. And don't forget; never hit a Hadenman when he's down; put the boot in, it's safer. And if you're down, go for his hamstrings and cripple the bastard. A Hadenman may have the edge in strength and speed, but no one's ever matched a human for sheer dirty fighting.'

'Don't forget the nooses,' said Sister Marion.

'I was getting to the nooses!'

'A dangling noose inside the doorway of a darkened room can take out even the most experienced warrior.'

'I was going to tell them that!'

'Of course you were, dear. You carry on. Don't mind me.'

'Thank you.'

'And if the noose doesn't kill them immediately, yank on their ankles till their necks break.'

'Marion! Do you want to give this lecture?'

'Of course not, dear. You do it so well.'

This had the sound of a conversation that could go on for some time, so Owen left them to it. He moved on through the compound, seeing what there was to see, listening to scraps of conversation that mostly revolved around everyday things. It was as though the colonists wanted to savour their few happy memories while they still could, before everything was lost in the fighting. No one seemed particularly optimistic about the final outcome.

Owen found Colonel William Hand and Otto sitting together on a bench outside their hut, polishing their swords and quietly singing an old marine marching song. The colonel still wore his old uniform, ragged and tattered but still scrupulously clean. His chest bore an impressive display of medal ribbons, carefully maintained. He didn't bother with the usual cloak and hood. He had leprosy, and didn't care who knew it. His grey skin was dotted with dark patches of dead matter, and half his nose was eaten away. He might have been handsome once – it was hard to tell. He looked to be in his late fifties, a large and muscular man now running to fat. His long dark hair was greasy and stringy, held back out of his face with a plain leather headband.

His companion Otto was a hunchbacked dwarf, barely four feet tall. His over-large head was touched with decay here and there, and most of his hair had fallen out. He too wore a marine uniform, but it was filthy dirty and he looked like he hadn't bathed in weeks. For a hunchbacked dwarf with leprosy, he seemed cheerful enough.

The colonel looked up at Owen, and fixed him with a cold, flat gaze. 'You must be new, boy, or you wouldn't be hanging around us. Even lepers have their pariahs. Got time to sit and talk for a while?'

'Of course,' said Owen. He sat down on the bench next to the colonel. 'May I ask what makes you a pariah here?'

The colonel snorted. 'Well, I don't think the sun shines out of Saint Bea's ass. I don't have any time for her peace and love nonsense. I'm a killer, boy. Made a career out of it. Bloody good at it, too. Joined the marines as soon as I was able, and never looked back. Never wanted anything else.'

'You seem to have had an impressive career, Colonel,' said Owen, indicating the medal ribbons.

'Bet your ass, boy. I've fought in every campaign of note for the past thirty years. Killed men and aliens on a hundred worlds, first to advance and last to retreat, and loved every minute of it. I was never happier than when I was wading in blood, cutting down the enemy, doing what I was born to do. No regrets, no bad dreams, no stirrings of conscience in the wee small hours. Mother Bea never could understand that, and for a saint she's remarkably unforgiving to anyone who won't toe the party line. She wants me to make confession, say I'm sorry and make my peace with God. Well, I'm not sorry, and I won't say I was, and when I finally get to stand before God, I'll look him right in the eye and say *You made me a killer. I just did what you made me to do. Now, where's the next enemy?*'

He laughed shortly, rooting around in the ruined half of his nose with a fingertip. 'I was one of the best, but they still sent me here the moment I was diagnosed. I'm not bitter, not really. I would have done the same thing. But it came hard at the time, to give up my career for this shithole. I was in line for General, dammit. Ironic, really. All the battles I fought, all the odds I beat, and in the end it wasn't a sword or an energy blast that got me; just a stupid mindless disease, killing me by inches. Not at all how I expected to die.'

'You never expected to die,' said Otto. 'You thought you were so special you'd live for ever.'

'Maybe,' said the colonel. He looked at Owen. 'Don't suppose you brought any cigars with you? No, of course not. Just as well; filthy habit anyway. But it's one of the few things I do miss . . . I missed the rebellion, you know. Biggest bloody war in the history of the Empire, and I never got to fight in it. Had to just sit and watch it on the holo. Shame. I would have liked to test myself against the Deathstalker and his crew. They would have been worthy adversaries. Still, Empress or Parliament, it makes no difference in the end. Neither one is going to let us off this planet.'

'No one cares about us,' said Otto. 'They're ashamed of us. We have no place in their bright, new, shining Empire.' He sniffed wetly, and rubbed at his nose with the back of his hand. 'I was gengineered like this, in case you were wondering, by my parents. They ran a travelling circus, and since hunchbacked dwarves don't tend to occur naturally any more, they made one of their own. I was one of the stars of the show. Audiences loved to come and pity me from a safe distance. But no one ever asked me what I wanted, what my dreams were. So the minute I hit sixteen I went straight to the nearest recruiting office, and signed on. I was supposed to be a mascot, but I quickly demonstrated such a natural aptitude for killing people that I got upgraded to full service inside a year. Never looked back.'

'We fought side by side in a hundred battles,' said the colonel. 'Nasty little man. Very good with a gutting knife. And when I came here, he came with me. He didn't have leprosy, then. A good friend, but dumb as shit.'

'True,' said Otto. 'How true.'

'Thank God for the Hadenmen. They gave us purpose again. At least now I have a real enemy to vent my spleen on. And a chance to die a warrior's death, instead of rotting away, day after day. And best of all, after months of open disapproval for my past wicked ways, Saint Bea had to come to me to help train her people how to fight. Must have stuck in her craw something fierce, but she did it. Came and asked us, right in front of everybody.'

'Looked like she was chewing a wasp while she said it, mind,' said Otto.

'What do you think of our chances against the Hadenmen?' said Owen.

Colonel Hand grinned nastily. 'Don't you worry, boy. I've fought all kinds before, and I'm still here to talk about it. Hadenmen will die just as readily as anyone else, if you stick your knife in the right place and twist it. Besides, if a shitty disease and a rotten planet like this couldn't beat us, a bunch of walking appliances with attitude isn't going to do it.'

Owen nodded, made his goodbyes, got up and moved on. He thought he'd enjoyed about as much of the colonel and Otto's company as he could stand. But for all the old soldier's venom, Owen couldn't help thinking that maybe he had a point. Lepers were the dark, unspoken secret of the Empire; the forbidden subject that was never openly discussed. No cure, no hope, so just dump the poor bastards out of sight where the rest of us don't have to look at them. Owen had known about Lachrymae Christi, vaguely, but it had never occurred to him to do anything about it. Leprosy was something that happened to other people. But now, having had his face rubbed in it, he vowed to do something about it. Assuming he and they survived.

He rounded a corner and saw Moon, sitting alone, crying his eyes out. His shoulders were shaking with the force of his sobs, and tears ran jerkily down his face from his glowing golden eyes. There was no one near him, no obvious cause for his sorrow. In fact, those few lepers near him seemed to be trying their best to ignore him. Owen hurried over to the crying augmented man, and then stood awkwardly over him, not sure what to do.

'Moon? Tobias? What is it? Has someone said something, done something . . . Dammit, if anyone's been having a go at you, I'll rip his lights out!'

The Hadenman stopped crying abruptly, and looked up. 'Oh, hello, Owen,' he said, quite calmly. 'There's nothing wrong, no one has upset me. I was just trying out the emotion, to see what it felt like. Please, sit and talk with me.'

Owen frowned, shrugged, and sat down next to his friend. Moon wiped at his face with a cloth, quite unselfconsciously. Owen looked at him. 'So . . . nothing's wrong? You're all right?'

'I don't know. I confess I've become very confused, of late. This is my second life, Owen, and many things are still new to me. Memories of my first life are always returning, but jumbled, distorted, often strangely removed, like the actions of someone else seen dimly on a holoscreen. I can remember doing things, but not why I did them, or how I felt while doing them. I spent most of my first life living among humans, developing human traits, but most of that is lost to me now. I am like a child, having to learn everything anew. I have emotions, I . . . feel things, but they are strange, puzzling things, because I have no frame of reference to put them in. I'm like a blind man seeing colours for the first time. So I laugh and cry, savouring their unfamiliar flavours, trying to discover what separates them, how they relate to the world I live in. I see the lepers here, living and fighting and dying so bravely, and I think tears are appropriate, but it is hard to be sure. It's very hard to be human, Owen. I don't know how you manage it so effortlessly.'

'You'll get the hang of it,' said Owen. 'You just need to practice. That's how everyone learns. And yes, tears are appropriate here. If I had any left, I'd shed them. But I've seen so many people die, fought in so many desperate last-ditch battles, it's hard for me to find room for such emotions. I have to be strong, unmoved, because everyone else needs me to be strong for them. I'd love to have the luxury of being weak again, Moon. To have someone else be strong, be the hero, so I could lean on them. It's hard work being a living legend.'

'Yes,' said Moon, 'I remember you being a hero. You risked your life to open the Tomb of the Hadenmen, after I failed. After I deserted you, leaving you and the others to fight the Empire while I went off on my own, convinced that it was my destiny to reawaken my people. I was wrong. I won't let you down again, Owen. I'll never desert you again.'

'Of course you won't,' said Owen. 'I never thought otherwise.'

'There are more new things in me, apart from my emotions,' said Moon. 'I recently attempted to run a diagnostic on my tech implants, the internal mechanisms that make me an augmented man. To my surprise, I found most of them to be missing. It seems my body has absorbed them. But I am as strong and fast as I ever was, my senses as clear, my thoughts as sharp. It's as though I don't need the tech to be more than human any more.'

'It's the Maze,' said Owen, nodding. 'When you passed through with the rest of us, it put its mark on you too. We've all been through . . . changes.'

'I am neither man nor Hadenman any more,' said Moon, frowning. 'I'm becoming something else, something different. My eyes still glow and my voice still buzzes, but perhaps only because I expect them to. You're further down the road than me, Owen. What am I becoming?'

'I don't know,' said Owen. 'Perhaps something we have no name or even a concept for. Yet.'

'I feel something when I consider this, Owen. I think . . . I'm scared.'

'We all are. The unknown is always scary. But no doubt the caterpillar fears becoming a butterfly, even as its instincts compel it to construct its own cocoon. What does the tadpole think when it grows legs, and something it can't understand forces it out of the water and into the air? We have no control over what's happening to us, so . . . enjoy the ride. And remember, you're among friends.'

'I have observed the lepers. If they can face their changes with such courage, so can I.' He looked sideways at Owen. 'Everyone who went through the Madness Maze developed powers. Different powers. I think something new is developing in me. I can . . . sense things; things not apparent to anyone else. It's not telepathy. More like empathy, perhaps. Either way, believe me when I say we're not alone here. There's something else, out in the jungle. Something hidden, and very powerful.'

'The Hadenman army?'

'No. I'd know my own people. This is alive, but it's like nothing else I've ever encountered. It thinks slow thoughts, but it's growing angry. And it knows where we are.'

'Does it have a name? An identity?'

'Oh, yes,' said Tobias Moon. 'It's the Red Brain.'

Hazel d'Ark had joined up with her two alternate selves, and was having fun trading gossip over their respective Owens, when a single leper woman approached them, limping tiredly into their path. The three women stopped abruptly, rather than run her over, and the leper woman dropped to her knees before Hazel.

'Forgive my impertinence, blessed one, but you are Hazel d'Ark, the liberator of Golgotha?'

'Well, yes,' said Hazel. 'Though I didn't exactly do it alone. Was there something you wanted?'

The leper pushed back her cowl, revealing a face half eaten away by rot. Patches of bare skull showed through the sparse remaining hair, and her teeth showed clearly where her left cheek should have been. Up close, the smell was appalling, though Hazel and the others tried hard not to show it. The leper woman produced one grey hand from under her cloak. It was skeletal, and only had two fingers on it. The leper woman held it out in supplication to Hazel.

'You have been touched by God, lady. You have worked miracles. I have seen it, on the holo. So work one more miracle, for me, I beg you. Heal me.'

Hazel fell back a step, shocked. 'I . . . I can't. I don't know how.'

'You have healed your own terrible wounds. You are blessed by God. Only lay your hand on me, and I too shall be healed, I know it.'

Hazel looked to Bonnie and Midnight for help, but they were stunned too. Hazel looked back at the leper woman before her, and didn't have one damned clue what to say. So in the end she reached out a hand, her flesh crawling, and laid it firmly on the leper's bowed head. They both waited a few moments, but nothing happened. After a while, the leper woman sighed, and got to her feet again.

'Thank you for trying, lady. My faith was not strong enough. I won't trouble you again.'

And she pulled her hood back over her ruined head, and limped slowly away. Hazel looked after her, and then back at her hand. She rubbed it hard against her side, and then stopped, almost guiltily. She realized there were other lepers watching her.

'I would have helped her, if I could.'

No one said anything, and after a while Hazel walked on. Bonnie and Midnight followed her, some distance behind.

The Hadenmen attacked just after first light. The rain was coming down like it had a grudge, but the augmented men didn't even seem to notice. They came streaming into the clearing from all sides, forcing their way through the packed tree line by sheer brute force. Wood splintered and cracked under their servo-motor-driven strength, and soon the clearing was full of Hadenmen. The guards in the watchtowers sounded the first alarm, and lepers went running to the walls to defend the mission. Hundreds of Hadenmen came marching through the rain in silence, attacking without challenge or war cries; they were beyond such things. They strode endlessly out of the jungle, tall and perfect like living gods, graceful beyond hope, with the sun burning in their eyes and energy weapons in their hands.

A fusillade of arrows rained down on them, mostly glancing off their internal armour. When the arrows did pierce flesh, the augmented men merely pulled them out and let them drop to the ground. They felt no pain. They opened fire with their hand disrupters, punching holes in the wooden outer wall, concentrating their fire to create holes large enough to enter through. The wooden wall burned briefly here and there, but the driving rain soon put it out. And then the Hadenmen reached the outer wall, and the first few broke through into the compound beyond, and it was all hand-to-hand fighting after that.

The lepers up on the catwalks kept up a steady rain of arrows on their enemy, and now and again an augmented man crashed to the ground and did not rise again, an arrow in his eye. Other defenders poured boiling oil on the Hadenmen climbing through the holes they'd made in the wall. Those few defenders with energy weapons picked their targets carefully, and cursed the long two minutes it took for their guns to recharge between shots. Inside the wall, defenders rushed to meet the intruders, and held them in place by sheer weight of numbers.

Owen and Hazel fought side by side before the largest hole in the outer wall, and every Hadenman that came within reach of their weapons died. They swung their swords with far more than human strength, and the heavy steel blades sheared clean through internal armour and implanted steel mesh to pierce the more vulnerable organs beyond. Fast as the augmented men were, Owen and Hazel were faster. They stopped the invaders in their tracks, and step by step they pushed the Hadenmen back out into the clearing, kicking aside the bodies of the fallen to get at their inhuman foe.

Bonnie Bedlam and Midnight Blue danced among the augmented men, glorying in blood and slaughter, laughing and singing as they killed. Bonnie threw herself into the thick of the combat, cutting at everything within reach, ignoring the injuries she took herself. The wounds healed so quickly she barely felt the pain, and wouldn't have cared if she had.

Pain and she were old friends. She was death and destruction, and nothing could stand before her. Midnight teleported back and forth across the compound, blinking in and out of existence just long enough to strike down an enemy and be gone again. She seemed to be everywhere at once, and everywhere she was, a Hadenman fell.

The two Sisters of Glory came howling out of nowhere, swinging their swords too fast for the human eye to follow. They cut viciously at the Hadenmen, darting in and out again, slashing at vulnerable joints and unprotected throats. Sister Marion strode woodenly into the thickest part of the fighting, lurching and swaying and somehow never where her enemy thought she would be. She brought her sword round in a long sweeping arc, cutting right through a Hadenman's glowing eyes, and then finished off her blinded prey with a knife to the heavy veins at the top of the thigh. Blood splashed her uncanny witch's outfit, and looked perfectly at home there.

Sister Kathleen swung her sword with both hands, cutting a path through the enemy by sheer determination. She ducked and darted, bobbed and wove, coming at the augmented men from unexpected angles. She slipped between them, elusive as mercury, leaving dead men in her wake.

Colonel William Hand went to meet the Hadenmen with grim purpose and some satisfaction, glad at last to be doing what he was meant to do, and did so well. He roared and chanted old battle cries as his sword rose and fell in simple butchery, and his heart was glad. He'd been dying for so long he'd forgotten how good it felt to be alive. The augmented men tried ganging up on him, but Otto was always there to watch his back, hacking at the long legs of the Hadenmen and bringing them down so his knife could reach their throats and faces. He laughed and sniggered as he killed, revelling in the destruction of such perfection of form.

And everywhere, inside the mission and without, the lepers fought as best they could, with guns and swords and sharpened farm implements, or anything that came to their grey and rotting hands. Anyone who could stand came out to fight, throwing themselves at the enemy with the calm desperation of those who knew they were dying anyway, and have nothing left to lose. And also because they were determined to preserve the few things in their lives that still had value and meaning: the mission, their homes and the saint who had come to give them hope when they thought they had lost it for ever.

They would fight for the mission, but they would die for Saint Bea.

Slowly the Hadenmen were forced back out of the mission and into the clearing beyond, though many died on both sides in the process. Ironically, the greater open space favoured the augmented men, giving them more room to move, to exploit their strength and speed. The defenders stuck close to the outer wall, guarding the open holes, refusing to be tempted further. And still the Hadenmen came streaming out of the surrounding jungle, hundreds and hundreds of them, tall and perfect, and perfectly deadly.

A group of Hadenmen felled one of the trees with their energy weapons, and used it as a great battering ram against the main gate of the mission. As long as the gate held, the lepers were safe from the main force of the augmented men, and both sides knew it. The heavy wooden gates shuddered under every blow, the great steel hinges groaning loudly. The guards in the watchtowers rained down arrow after arrow at the straining Hadenmen, but even when one fell, another was immediately there to take his place. The gate began to bow inwards as the massive weight of the tree slammed into it again and again. After a while the constant back-and-forth motion of the Hadenmen churned the ground beneath them into thick mud, and the weight of the tree sent them slipping and sliding in the treacherous morass. And then Owen and Hazel arrived to save the day.

They came running through the scattered battles, cutting down anyone who got in their way with effortless speed and style. The augmented men dropped the tree trunk and turned to face their new enemy with inhuman speed, servo-motors humming loudly in their limbs, and met Owen and Hazel with sword blows so fast they were blurs in the rain. Owen and Hazel countered them easily, and took the fight to the Hadenmen. They were quickly separated by the press of bodies, and soon they were all slipping and sliding in the mud, often hanging on to the tree trunk for support while they cut and hacked.

Hazel went one on one with a giant Hadenman, revelling in the chance to fight someone at last who operated on levels close to her own. Blows and parries and counters came and went inhumanly fast, and sparks flew from their blades with every contact. The rain drove down around them, running down their intent faces. In the end, Hazel beat the Hadenman's sword aside with her superior strength, and rammed her sword through his chest and out of his back. He fell to his knees, the golden light slowly going out of his eyes. Hazel jerked her sword free in a last flurry of blood, and looked around for fresh prey.

Owen moved swiftly between the Hadenmen, his lighter frame enabling him to move more freely in the muddy conditions. His sword flashed in and out, come and gone in a moment, always that little bit too fast for the augmented men who tried to crowd around him. He seemed to grow stronger and faster the longer he fought, as though something was awakening in him, until he was more than a fighter, more than a warrior. He felt invincible, like some unstoppable force of nature sent to teach the Hadenmen the error of their ways. He stamped and lunged, and then he slipped in the mud, and fell.

He landed awkwardly, jarring his right elbow on something solid, and his sword flew from his momentarily numbed fingers. Immediately there were Hadenmen all around him, stabbing down at him again and again, and only their uncertain footing in the mud gave Owen the few moments he needed to scrabble to his feet. He shot a Hadenman through the chest at point-blank range, and the others fell back. Owen grabbed for the knife he kept in his boot, cursing and blaspheming as he looked frantically about for his lost sword.

And then he looked up, just in time to see the blunt end of the great wooden battering ram coming straight at him. Four of the Hadenmen had broken away from him to pick it up, servo-motors straining loudly, and they surged forward, driving themselves and their burden on through the mud and rain. Owen just had time to see his death coming, and then the huge end of the tree trunk, easily five feet in diameter, hit him squarely and slammed him back against the immovable main gate.

For a moment, it was like a dream. The end of the tree blotted out the light, as though night had fallen especially for him. Then he was hit hard from the front, and from behind a moment later, and it felt like the whole world was pressing down on him. He could feel his whole body, his bones and his organs, actually flattening under the impact, before things began breaking. And then the pain hit him, and it wasn't like a dream at all.

His ribs cracked and gave way under the impact, collapsing inwards to spear his lungs and heart. His organs crushed and flattened. A river of blood spurted out of his mouth and anus. The tree trunk swung back, but Owen stayed where he was, stuck to the main gate by his own blood. Light filled his eyes again. There was more blood, from his nose and ears and eyes. The pain was unbelievable, so bad he couldn't even think through it, and he stood trapped in the agony of that moment like a fly trapped in amber. His punctured lungs trembled in his chest, unable to draw breath in or push it out. His arms and legs were broken, white shards of bone protruding through the bloody flesh, and his face was smashed to a pulp. He slid slowly, helplessly, down the gate, leaving a thick trail of dark blood behind him on the wood, which had actually cracked and splintered under the force of the impact.

Owen lay still in the mud, not breathing, barely thinking, his heart clenching in a few last sporadic pulses in his crushed chest. He never heard Hazel scream with horror and rage, never saw her fall upon the Hadenmen and kill all that remained. He lay in the mud, the rain slowly washing the blood from his ruined face, and thought, *Such a stupid way to die; so many things still left to do.* And then he thought, *No. I won't die. I refuse to die. Not here, not now, when I'm still needed.*

He reached inside himself, deep down into the undermind, the back brain, into that mysterious part of his mind where his power lay, and he pulled it forth by the brute force of his will, whether it wanted to come or not. He hauled it up out of the dark place where he couldn't see, and thrust it into his broken, dying body. Healing energies crackled through him, and he wanted to scream at the new pain as his splintered bones slowly knitted themselves together again; but it wasn't until his lungs healed and reinflated that he could manage even the smallest of whimpers. His heart healed itself in a moment, beating strong and hard. Bones became whole, organs sound, and it all hurt like the pits of Hell. And then the power retreated back into the depths of his mind, leaving Owen lying there in the mud, soaked in his own blood and as weak as a kitten, but brought back from the brink of death itself by his own refusal to be beaten by anything, even the near-destruction of his own body.

Well, he thought finally, *there's another thing I didn't know I could do*.

Hazel dropped to her knees beside him, her eyes wide at the sight of so much blood soaking him. 'Lie still, Owen, I'll get help.' Her voice was unsteady with barely held-back tears. 'Don't die. Don't you dare die on me, Owen! I won't stand for it.'

'Easy, love,' said Owen, his voice little more than a whisper. 'I'm all right. Healed myself. Help me back on my feet.'

Hazel checked his chest first with experienced probing fingers, to reassure herself he was still basically intact, and then hauled him up to his feet. 'Hell's teeth, Owen; when I saw that bloody tree slam into you, I thought I'd lost you for sure. Can anything kill us any more?'

Owen smiled grimly. 'Oh, I think a direct energy shot to the head would probably do it. That, or a stake through the heart. But we're getting tougher all the time. Now help me back inside – I'm no use to anyone till I've got my breath back.'

Hazel got him over to the nearest hole in the wall. The Hadenmen gave them both plenty of room.

Bonnie Bedlam danced among the Hadenmen, sudden death on two legs. Every blow was a killing blow, and she never bothered with a defence. When she was cut or hurt she just laughed aloud, glorying in the rush of healing flesh. She darted in between the battling bodies, never still long enough to be a serious target, or get involved in a direct confrontation. She slipped through the stamping, thrusting mêlée like a ghost, dispensing a cut here and a stab there, flashing her teeth in a death's-head grin. Not for her the honour of one-on-one combat, and if she'd heard of fair play, it was only to laugh at it. She came and went, her sword flashing out of nowhere to pierce an undefended side or a turned back. Bonnie Bedlam was a fighter, not a warrior, and had no time at all for honour. It just got in the way. She cut down the enemy with vicious, heartless attacks, and ignored the cries for help or support from the lepers fighting around her. She wasn't there to be anyone's shield or partner. She defended the mission as she saw best, and saw no point in putting herself at risk by going to the aid of others. Her powers and abilities made her far more vital to the mission's defence than any damn fool colonist who needed his hand held.

Midnight Blue wielded her axe with both hands, lopping off heads and limbs with her inhuman strength. Hadenmen blood struck her again and again like an invigorating shower, and she wore it proudly. She roared the sacred chants of her warrior order, cutting her way through the battle like a forester opening up a new path in a crowded wood. Hadenmen fell almost helplessly before her cold, focused anger, and did not rise again. She took fierce blows and wounds without flinching, ignoring or rising above the pain in her battle fury. Most of her wounds closed almost immediately, and for those that took a little longer, she paid them no heed. She fought at the head of a small group of lepers, and watched their backs as if they were her own. She could have teleported anywhere in the battle, but would not leave while she felt she was needed.

Sometimes one of her people would fall despite everything she could do to protect them, and then her heart would fill with rage till it seemed there was no room for anything else. They all fought so very bravely, but in the end they were no match for Hadenmen. One by one they fell, until Midnight was left alone again. She vanished then, reappearing somewhere else where she was needed, to protect another group of lepers for as long as she could.

Bonnie and Midnight came together in the middle of the fighting, and when they stood their ground, back to back, no one could move them. They blocked the way to the biggest hole in the mission wall, and the Hadenmen came at them in an endless tide, only to fall back dead or dying like waves crashing against an immovable rock. The Hadenmen had energy weapons, but in the constantly moving crush of bodies, even their augmented computer minds found it hard to hit any one target, even when they no longer cared about hitting their own. And so the battle raged, until the sheer press and numbers of Hadenmen gained enough momentum to drive Bonnie and Midnight back, step by step, until they were standing in the hole in the wall itself, and from there they would not be moved. Until the Hadenmen brought forward a large object, wrapped in layers of thick waterproofing. The augmented men fighting Bonnie and Midnight took one look, and fell back immediately, hurrying to get out of the way. Bonnie and Midnight lowered their weapons and looked at each other, and then at the object, as the Hadenmen pulled away the wrapping to reveal a portable disrupter cannon. Bonnie glared at Midnight.

'Get out of here, teleporter. Vanish.'

'I won't leave you here to die.'

'I regenerate, remember?'

'Not from that, you won't.'

'Teleport, damn you! I'd run, if I thought I'd get anywhere.'

'Bonnie . . .'

'Go. I've always known I'll die alone.'

Midnight cried out once, in rage and anguish, and vanished. Air rushed in to fill the space she'd left. She reappeared behind the crew of the disrupter cannon, hewing about her with her axe.

But even as the Hadenmen fell away, dead or dying, one of them had already aimed and fired. The energy beam surged forth, an unstoppable storm of raging power. Energies that could vaporize steel or punch through force shields crossed the space between the cannon and Bonnie in under a second, and when the beam finally shut down, there was a hole in the wall big enough to lead an army through, and no sign anywhere of Bonnie Bedlam.

Midnight Blue howled with loss, at the death of someone

she might have been, at the death of a good comrade-in-arms. And perhaps just a little at the knowledge that no matter how fast or strong she was, she couldn't save everyone, even when it mattered most to her. She cut down the rest of the cannon's crew and held the cannon over her head, her arm muscles bulging. She'd never lifted anything that heavy before, but in that moment she felt like she could hold it aloft for ever. She looked around her, picked the heaviest concentration of Hadenmen, and threw the cannon into their midst with all her strength. The cannon exploded on impact, and a sudden intense light swept through the augmented men, blowing them away, scorched and broken, like leaves in a firestorm. When the dust finally settled, there was a great crater, and broken bodies everywhere. Some of them were lepers. Midnight tried to feel something for them, and couldn't, not just yet. Not while she still had that numb hole in her life where Bonnie used to be. She stumbled back to the wall, to guard the gaping hole. And that was when she heard the sound from inside.

Midnight stepped through and saw what was left of Bonnie Bedlam lying some distance from her. It was mostly bones, scorched and blackened by the terrible energies of the disrupter beam, but somehow still held together by strands of bloody meat. Bits and pieces of organs could be seen pulsing inside the broken ribs and shattered sternum. Terribly, the thing was still alive, and suffering. Midnight stumbled forward and knelt beside the body. The skull grinned at her with broken teeth, but incredibly, there was an intact eye in one of the sockets. As Midnight watched, another eye slowly formed in the second socket. Strands of muscle formed out of nowhere, creeping over the bone like worms, pulling the lower jaw back into place. Further down the body, the organs were repairing themselves. The heart was beating, though its blood just splashed everywhere for the moment. The lungs reinflated, sucking in air. Long red muscles formed striations and linked the arms and legs together. Midnight looked back at the head. Skin covered the wet red flesh, and lips formed slowly over the teeth. The mouth opened, and breath hissed in and out.

'Told you I could take it,' whispered Bonnie Bedlam,

smiling painfully. 'We survived a direct hit from a cannon once before, on Mistworld, remember? Of course, Owen was with us then. We were always stronger together.'

'Jesus, you're a mess,' said Midnight, caught between tears and laughter. 'I'll get you to the infirmary.'

'No time. You guard that hole in the wall while I finish regenerating. And if you see them setting up another disrupter cannon, pick me up and run like hell, because there's no way I could survive another blast like that.'

'You got it,' said Midnight Blue. 'If anyone gets past me, bite their ankles.'

She moved back to the wall, stepped into the great hole and defied the Hadenmen to get past her. She stood there with her axe in her hands, laughing at the augmented men, ready to stand her ground till the battle was over, till death or till Hell froze, whichever came first.

The two Sisters of Glory, Marion and Kathleen, were seemingly everywhere at once, urging their leper charges on, leading from the front, singing hymns and psalms as they killed everything that came against them. The leper colonists fought with the souls of warriors, holding their own against the Hadenmen for as long as they could. For all their strength and speed, their implanted armour and steel mesh, the augmented men couldn't stand against enemies who threw themselves into the fray not caring whether they lived or died. One leper would cling to a Hadenman's sword arm, holding it down while another leper went for the throat. Some deliberately took a sword in the belly, trapping the blade so others could drag the killer down. The Hadenmen were efficient, trained killers, but the lepers were inspired. The battle surged back and forth, towards the mission and away again, with neither side able to hold the advantage for long.

Sister Kathleen saw the bomb first. Caught for a moment in a quiet eddy, she looked around for a new opponent, and saw six Hadenmen carrying a heavy explosive device between them, heading slowly for the main gate of the mission. A bodyguard of six more Hadenmen surrounded the bomb, using their disrupters indiscriminately to clear the way before them. Kathleen recognized the device. She'd worked in mining before she came to the Church. She called out to Marion, naming the new threat, and together they carved a path through the surging crowd towards the bomb.

Sister Marion stalked through the crush, in her tattered black and her Hallowe'en face, emerald lips stretched in a smile that had no mercy in it. Sister Kathleen swung her sword in complex patterns, moving so swiftly and unexpectedly that neither she nor her blade were ever where her opponents expected them to be. The two Sisters reached the bomb's honour guard together, and threw themselves at the unsuspecting Hadenmen. Their guns exhausted, the augmented men stood their ground with naked steel, and would not be moved. The Sisters of Glory fought savagely, but they had been fighting for so very long, and they were after all very sick women, their strength and stamina eaten away by the leprosy. The servo-motors in the arms of the Hadenmen never grew tired. The progress of the bomb had been stopped, not far from the edge of the clearing, but the Sisters couldn't reach it.

They battled on, their faith pushing them forward when any other might have retired, or dropped from sheer exhaustion, but in the end only Kathleen saw what was needed. She said a last prayer to God, and forced her way between two Hadenmen by throwing everything she had into an attack that left her totally defenceless. She burst through, heading for the bomb, and two swords hit her from behind at once, slamming into her back and kidneys. She cried out once, blood spraying from her mouth, but kept going, the headlong momentum of her last desperate charge bringing her to the bomb. She flailed wildly about her with her sword, killing one of the Hadenmen carrying the bomb, and the device crashed to the ground. And then it was the simplest thing in the world for Kathleen to reach forward and activate the five-minute timer.

Sister Marion saw what had happened, and cried out helplessly as Kathleen threw herself over the bomb, clinging to it determinedly so that the Hadenmen couldn't get to it and undo what she'd done. Sister Marion turned and ran for the mission, yelling to the lepers to retreat. Others took up the cry, trusting her decision, and soon all the defenders of Saint Bea's mission had broken away from the battle and were sweeping back across the clearing, heading for the main gate and the larger holes in the outer wall. At first the Hadenmen pursued them, but they quickly realized something was wrong, and stopped, suspecting a trap or a trick of some kind.

Back at the bomb, the Hadenmen cut and hacked at Kathleen, trying to force her to let go, but she clung on with the last of her strength, feeling her life draining out of her, crying out at the horrid pain of her wounds but refusing to release her grip. The Hadenmen had to be careful where they hit her, for fear of damaging the bomb. Kathleen had positioned herself very carefully. Finally she died, though it took the augmented men some time to realize she'd gone. They pried her hands off the bomb, breaking her fingers in the process, and threw the dead nun aside. Only then did they see the timer, and realize what Kathleen had bought with her stubborn, defiant death. The Hadenmen turned to run, and the bomb went off.

The blast killed every Hadenman still in the clearing, flattened some of the trees on the periphery and shook the walls of the mission. The lepers had made it inside, and secured the main gate in time, and although there was some structural damage among the smaller buildings, the colonists and their champions survived. After the last tremors of the explosion had died away, and the walls and the ground had stopped shaking, Sister Marion opened the main gate and looked out. All that remained of the attacking army were a few half-melted metal shapes here and there. The Hadenman force was gone, as though it had never been. There was no trace at all of Sister Kathleen. Sister Marion sighed, and sniffed loudly.

'Teach those metal bastards to play with dangerous toys. God bless you and keep you, Sister Kathleen, and damn all the Hadenmen to Hell.'

After the battle came the clearing up. The holes in the outer wall had to be repaired or barricaded, the injured were taken to the infirmary as fast as it could cope with them, and the dead were piled up in one of the storage huts. There would be time for funerals later, hopefully. Each of the dead had to be identified first, so that friends and loved ones could say a last goodbye. Sometimes the bodies were so damaged or disfigured that identification was difficult. Those unfortunates were laid out in lines in a separate hut, and tearful survivors moved slowly down the narrow aisles between the bodies, looking for something familiar.

Collecting the dead, and either identifying or laying them out, was a disturbing, depressing business, but it had to be done. Most of those who'd gone out to fight were in no shape to do it, physically or mentally, so the duty fell to those who'd stayed within the mission, as a last line of defence to protect those too ill to fight. Colonel William Hand and Otto had ended up guarding the main gate and overseeing tactics, much to their disgust, and now used their military experience to deal with the business of the dead. There were always more, as men and women died waiting to get to the infirmary.

Hand and Otto weren't bothered by the dead. They'd seen enough bodies in their time to know the trick of treating them as objects, rather than as the people they'd been. Tobias Moon worked with them. He hadn't been allowed to go outside and fight, because he might easily have been mistaken for one of the enemy. At least, that's what they'd told him, and he went along with it. So now he carried the dead into the long narrow hut and laid them in their rows, his augmented arms carrying the load long after even the most determined of the lepers had been forced to give up through sheer exhaustion. He was glad for a chance to be doing something to help. The dead bodies didn't bother him at all. He'd been there.

William Hand walked slowly up and down the ranks, giving each body a number, and making notes of things like personal jewellery, to help with the identification. Otto staggered in and out with blankets wrapped around collections of body parts. They'd be matched up later, if possible. For now, he just dumped them all in a pile in one corner, and thanked God there were no rats on Lachrymae Christi. He dropped his last load on to the chest-high pile with an emphatic grunt, turned round and pulled a face.

'Jesus, this place stinks, Colonel. Couldn't they at least have chosen a hut with windows?'

'Splash some disinfectant around,' said Hand, not looking up from his clipboard. 'And if you see anything small and wriggling, hit it with something heavy.'

'Can't,' said Otto. 'Saint Bea's commandeered all the disinfectant for the infirmary. She's even rounded up all the booze in the camp, as back-up. Next time, Colonel, let's not get distracted from the fighting. I'd rather take on a whole army of Hadenmen with my hump on backwards than go through this shit again. Too much like working for a living.' The dwarf looked around him, and was quiet for a long moment. 'We lost a lot of good people out there, Colonel. Fifteen, maybe twenty per cent of us. And a lot more'll be dead by morning.'

'Hadenmen lost a damn sight more.'

'Yeah, but let's face it, that was just a preliminary skirmish. An advance force, sent in to test the defences. That's what I'd have done. The real army is still out there in the jungle somewhere, digesting the lessons it's learned. And they could come at us any time.'

'You know, Otto, it's your cheerful personality that keeps me going. Don't you have any work to do?'

'Nope. No more body parts. I had to use a shovel and a bucket for the last lot, though how you're planning to match up things like ears and teeth and red and purple blobby bits is beyond me. Don't know what we'll do with them if they're not claimed. Except maybe make soap out of them. Or soup, if things get really desperate.'

The colonel looked up from his clipboard. 'Of course, your people were cannibals, weren't they?'

'Only on holy days. And only if we really didn't like someone.'

'Finished,' said Tobias Moon, from the doorway. 'There are no more bodies, though many remain gravely ill. I think you two should rest for a while now. I can continue with your work, I'm not tired at all.'

'Then you're the only one in this mission who isn't,' said the colonel. He looked at his clipboard, then opened his hand

and let it drop to the floor. 'Take ten, Otto. I think we've earned it.'

The two of them sat down on the floor, as far away from the bodies and the smell as they could get, and wearily set their backs against the hut wall. Otto produced a battered gunmetal flask from somewhere about his person, winked at the colonel and they both drank deeply from it. Moon hovered uncertainly in the doorway. Hand beckoned for him to come over.

'Join us, Sir Moon. You've earned a break too, even if you don't need it. Pull up a piece of floor and sit down. Fancy a drop of something bad for you?'

'Thank you,' said Moon. Alcohol did nothing for him, but he took the proffered flask anyway. He understood that that was part of being sociable. He sat down beside the colonel, took a modest drink and then passed the flask back. 'It has an . . . unusual flavour.'

Otto laughed. 'The flavour isn't why you drink it, friend. You've been out in the main compound. What's the latest news?'

Moon hesitated, running the information available through a filter of what most people found interesting. 'The holes in the wall have been dealt with. The few fires did remarkably little damage.'

'The people, Moon,' said Hand impatiently. 'What about your friends, the living legends?'

'The Deathstalker was badly injured, but has recovered. Hazel d'Ark and Midnight Blue are helping Mother Beatrice in the infirmary. Bonnie Bedlam suffered extensive damage, but is healing at an accelerated rate and expects to be fully functional within an hour or two. Those of us who have been through the Madness Maze are very hard to kill.'

'Yeah,' said the colonel, 'we noticed. You're probably even immune to what we've got.' Hand looked at Moon for a long moment. 'What would you have done, if the Hadenmen had broken through our defences and got in here? Would you have fought your own kind?'

'Yes,' said Moon immediately, 'because they are not my people any more. I am neither man nor Hadenman. I owe allegiance to no race now, only to my friends.'

'In the end, that's all any of us have,' said Hand, lifting the flask to his grey lips again. 'Friendship and honour. Nothing else matters.'

'But what if honour requires that you turn against your friends?' said Moon.

'Tricky one,' said Hand. 'That's something everyone has to decide for himself. I guess you have to ask yourself; would they still be your friends, if they knew you'd betrayed your honour?'

'It is very hard to be human,' said Moon, sighing.

'Got that right,' said Otto.

By the time things had started to settle down, it was night. The dark fell early on Lachrymae Christi. Saint Bea and Sister Marion were still working in the infirmary, struggling to save lives with insufficient medicines and instruments. It was starting to look less like a hospital, and more like a slaughterhouse. Hazel d'Ark and Midnight Blue helped as much as they could, taking breaks outside when they could no longer stand the screams or the suffering or the stench of exposed guts. They sat together on the steps outside, breathing in the fresh air, gathering up the courage to go back in again. It was hard to be so powerful and so helpless at the same time. After a while, Bonnie Bedlam came striding out of the shadows to join them. She wore the standard grey clothing, and was perfectly healed, so much so they barely recognized her. All her piercings and tattoos and body modifications were gone, blasted away by the energy beam, and had not been recreated when she healed. She was scowling fiercely as she sat down beside Hazel, just a little unsteadily.

'I hate looking like this, like everyone else. Years of hard work gone in an instant! Even my old leathers were destroyed, that I was wearing under my cloak. I've had them for years. Made them out of the skin of an old enemy. And I'm still weak from the regeneration; never had to do that much work before. If the Hadenmen attacked now, I couldn't beat them off with a paper towel.'

'Nice to see you too,' said Midnight. 'We're fine, thanks.'

'You look a lot more like me, now,' said Hazel.

'Oh, God,' said Bonnie, 'it's not that bad, is it?'

'Any disturbances out in the jungle?' said Midnight.

'Just the plants, eating and humping each other. How's it going in the infirmary?'

'Depends on how you look at it,' said Hazel. 'We're losing more than we're saving, but given the appalling conditions, it's a miracle we're saving so many. She really is a saint, you know. Been working all day, and she's still going when we're out on our feet. I've never seen so much blood in one place. The floor's awash with it, no matter how much disinfectant we sling about. Shock kills a lot of them, either from their wounds or from the surgery. I guess leprosy weakens all the body's defences.'

'It's not fair,' said Midnight. 'They fought so bravely. They won the battle. They deserve better than the little we're able to do for them.'

'Yeah,' said Bonnie. 'It's one thing for us to go out and fight; we're practically unkillable. We can get hurt, but nothing really threatens us.'

'And in the end, Sister Kathleen turned the battle round,' said Midnight, 'not one of us. And gave her life to do it. Didn't even hesitate.'

'Lord, what marvels these mortals be,' said Bonnie.

'We're like the monsters in the old stories,' said Hazel. 'Cut us, shoot us, burn us; we just keep coming back for more. Unless they stick stakes through our hearts, cut off our heads, burn them and scatter the ashes. I don't think even you could come back from that, Bonnie.'

'I'd give it a bloody good try,' said Bonnie.

'The Hadenmen,' said Midnight. 'They're the real monsters. Giving up their humanity for their love of tech. Perfection isn't achieved through the body, but through the spirit. What honour is there in attacking a mission full of sick people?'

'They want something,' said Bonnie. 'And they never let anything get in the way of what they want, least of all morality. They're ruthless, utterly without mercy or compassion, and they never step aside for anyone. I can respect that. Sometimes, in order to achieve anything of value, you have to be prepared to sacrifice something else of value. Friends, honour, morality . . . love. I love my Owen with all my rotten heart, but I'd sacrifice him to save the Empire, and he knows it. Can you say you wouldn't do the same?'

'I lost my Owen,' said Midnight. 'I would sacrifice the Empire and everything in it, to have him in my arms again.'

'But how would he feel about that?' said Hazel.

'Oh, he'd be appalled,' said Midnight. 'But then, Owen always was much more honourable than me.'

'Where's your Owen?' said Bonnie to Hazel.

'Around,' said Hazel. 'He was overseeing the repairs to the wall, but I haven't seen him for ages. Been too busy. I thought he was going to die today, but once again he pulled himself back from the brink. Man's got more lives than a basket full of cats. But . . . just for a moment, while he was lying there in his own blood, I thought, *What would I do without him? What would there be for me to live for, with him gone?*'

'Why don't you tell him that?' said Midnight softly. 'If the Hadenmen come again, you might not get another chance.'

'Later, maybe,' said Hazel. 'We're still needed here.'

'I can help out for a while,' said Bonnie. 'Go and find your Owen.'

Hazel looked down at the ground before her. 'I never wanted commitment, to be bound to any one person. I've spent my whole life fighting to be free, defying any kind of authority, just to be sure that no one ran my life but me. And then I met Owen, and fate bound us together no matter how much we struggled. I . . . admire him greatly. He's brave and kind and honourable, and he loves me. I've always known that. But I've never loved anyone in my whole life. I don't know if I have it in me to love anyone, even a man as fine as Owen. I'm not the loving kind.'

'I thought that, for a long time,' said Midnight. 'I didn't realize the truth till my Owen was dead, and lost to me for ever. Don't make the mistake I did, and wait too long. We heroes tend to live dangerous and often tragically short lives.'

'Go and talk to the man,' said Bonnie. 'I'll cover for you with Saint Bea. Come on, Midnight, you hold them down and I'll do the stitches.'

They got up, squared their shoulders and went back into

the slaughterhouse. Hazel sat alone on the steps, staring silently out into the gloom.

Owen Deathstalker moved through the open compound, anonymous again in his leper's cloak and pulled-down hood, listening to the people talk. They sat in small clumps around open fires, passing their last few bottles of booze back and forth. It was supposed to have gone to the infirmary, for emergency use, but it hadn't taken the lepers long to decide that if their current need wasn't an emergency, they didn't know what was, since they could all be dead tomorrow anyway. They dug up the hidden bottles they'd stashed away for a dry day, and poured the stuff down their necks as fast as they could stand it. The cheer of victory hadn't blinded them to the reality of their situation. They knew they were just waiting for the next act. So they talked and laughed and sang, praised Saint Bea and the Sisters of Glory, and compared notes on the living legends who had come to lead and protect them.

'They say the Deathstalker died, and brought himself back to life,' said a leper with half his face eaten away.

'Nah,' said another man, his face hidden in the shadows of a broad-brimmed hat. 'When you're dead, you're dead, like the blessed Sister Kathleen. When you're gone, you don't come back.'

'That's for the likes of us,' said the third man at the fire, a tall, gangling sort, sitting hugging his bony knees to his chest. 'We're human. He isn't. Not any more.'

'Of course he's human,' said the first man. 'He was born among us, to become more than us, to lead us to victory. Like he led the rebels in the great war against the Empress.'

'That was Jack Random,' said the second man, 'the professional rebel. Though they say he's immortal too, these days. And Ruby Journey and Hazel d'Ark, and that bloody Hadenman Moon. Every bugger except us, seems like.'

'Yeah,' said the third man. 'But they're still human. Old Daft Sally asked Hazel d'Ark to heal her, by laying on of hands. Didn't work.'

'Maybe Sally just didn't have enough faith,' said the first man.

Owen decided he didn't like the way the conversation was going. He stepped forward into the light of the fire. 'May I join you, friends?'

'Sure,' said the first man. 'Take a pew. I'm Harry. The one with the stupid hat is Sigurd, and the boring one is Glum.'

'I'm Giles,' said Owen. 'I'm . . . new. I've met the Death-stalker. He didn't seem all that special to me. Just a man, trying to do what's right.'

'Then you must have had your eyes shut,' said Harry, picking at a scab on the side of his face he still had left. 'He's been touched by God. Has to have been, to do all the things he's done. They say angels fought alongside him in the great rebellion, and were seen flying in the skies above all the great battles.'

'He's no saint,' said Sigurd. 'There's only one saint here, and she's still up to her elbows in guts in the infirmary. And I saw the Deathstalker on the holo, fighting in the streets on Golgotha, and there weren't any bloody angels there. Just Hazel d'Ark, and she sure as hell isn't an angel. Unless it's the fallen kind. Nice tits, though.'

'Angels wouldn't show up on a film,' said Harry patiently. 'They're spiritual creatures.'

'If he was a saint, he'd heal us,' said Glum, still looking down at his knees. 'Save us all, and wipe out the Hadenmen with a wave of his hand. But he didn't, because he can't. No, he's powerful all right, but he's still one of us.'

'There are those who say he's a monster,' Owen said quietly. 'That no one should be able to do the things he can do. That all power corrupts . . .'

'Bull!' said Harry angrily. 'He was born an aristo, to a life of riches and pleasures, but he gave it all up to champion the downtrodden! He gave up wealth and position of his own free will, refusing to live in comfort while the people lived in slavery! He's a hero, a legend.'

'That was Jack Random,' said Sigurd stubbornly.

'Random was a failure on his own, everyone knows that. The Deathstalker fought for us when no one else would. Freed Jack Random from prison, and put new life into him. He could have been Emperor, if he wanted, but he turned it down.' Harry shook his head wonderingly. 'You only see his like once in a thousand years.'

'He gave the Hadenmen a chance at redemption,' said Glum, looking up for the first time. 'Who else would have done that? All right, they betrayed him in the end, but that's Hadenmen for you.'

'They say he killed a Grendel with his bare hands,' said Harry reverently. 'A Grendel, mind you! No man could do that who wasn't touched by God.'

'But doesn't it scare you, some of the things he can do?' said Owen.

'Oh, hell,' said Sigurd. 'What does it matter? Of course he's scary. Heroes always are. They're all pretty spooky, all the Maze people. If they did go bad, who could stop them? They could kill us all, lay waste to whole planets, destroy the damned Empire if the whim took them. They could be monsters. But the point is, they aren't. The Deathstalker came here to save us, when no one else would. He could die here, along with us, and no one would ever know. But he came anyway, because it was the right thing to do. In the end, that's all that matters.'

'Touched by God,' said Glum. 'Driven by destiny. Chosen to be a hero. Poor bastard.'

'Yeah,' said Harry. 'He could have taken the crown. I would have. Instead, he's here with us. In Hell.'

'Oh, I don't know,' said Owen. 'From what I've heard, Parliament's an even more dangerous place than this. At least here you can be sure who your enemies are.' He got to his feet. 'I have to go. Thanks for your company, friends.'

He left them sitting around their fire, and made his way back across the compound, heading nowhere in particular. He'd heard them talk about Owen Deathstalker as a hero and a legend, and as some poor bastard touched by God, and didn't recognize himself in either vision. Already people were beginning to forget the facts, or dress them up to fit their own beliefs. No one understood who he really was, or why he'd done the things he'd done. As a historian, he'd always known such revision and reinvention of his life was inevitable, but it came hard to see himself already disappearing behind the old masks of myth and folk hero. They'd be saying he was born in a manger next, with three wise Lords come to visit him.

His feet took him to the infirmary, where Hazel was. When in doubt, he always went to Hazel. She was perhaps the only person who'd known him from the beginning, who'd been through all the changes with him. Perhaps the only person left who knew the real him. He found her sitting on the steps outside the wooden building, her head hanging tiredly down. He sat down beside her, and she grunted an acknowledgement.

'You should get some sleep,' said Owen gently. 'It's been a long day. You've done enough.'

'You're the one who should be sleeping,' said Hazel. 'Hell, you nearly died today.'

Owen shrugged. 'Business as usual. Saint Bea still working in there?'

'Yeah. Nearly finished, though. Those who were going to die have done so, and the rest have all been attended to. She's just mopping the place out now, getting ready for tomorrow. How many do you think we'll lose tomorrow, Owen?'

'Too many. They fight well, and they're brave enough, but most of them belong in sickbeds. And even if they were fit, they'd be no match for an army of Hadenmen. I don't think anything is, under these conditions. Maybe not even us. The real army will be here tomorrow, and maybe even sometime tonight, and then the walls to this place will come down like matchsticks, and the real butchery will begin. What the hell do they want here? Moon said there's something out there in the jungle; something he could sense but not describe. Called it the Red Brain. Maybe that's what the Hadenmen want.'

'What we need is a miracle,' said Hazel. 'Maybe if we asked Saint Bea very nicely . . .'

'I don't think God's listening to us right now,' Owen said tiredly. 'We're on our own.'

'Nonsense,' said Mother Beatrice briskly, coming out of the infirmary in a brand new nun's outfit, freshly starched and spotlessly clean. 'God is always with us. He just won't fight our battles for us.'

'I don't believe in God any more,' said Hazel. 'Not after

600

everything I've seen. All the evil, all the suffering, all the death.'

'People were responsible for that evil,' said Mother Beatrice, 'not God. And you have lived to see much of that evil come to an end. Be content with that.' She sat down beside Owen on the steps, rubbing at her hands with a damp cloth. There were still specks of dried blood around her fingernails.

'Why did you come here?' said Hazel. 'Didn't you have enough of seeing people die after Technos III?'

'I came here because I was needed,' said Mother Beatrice calmly. 'Why do you and Owen keep throwing yourselves into danger?'

'Same reason, I suppose,' said Owen. 'People need us; no one else can do what we do. I still believe in the old virtues of duty and honour, even though they seem to have gone out of fashion in today's new order of deals and compromises.'

Mother Beatrice smiled. 'And that part of you is the part that hears God's voice. You can't ignore it any more than I can.'

'I fight because I'm good at it,' Hazel said stubbornly. 'My life's revolved around violence and killing for as long as I can remember. Everywhere I've been, it was always kill or be killed. Where's God's voice in that?'

'It isn't what you do that matters,' said Mother Beatrice patiently. 'It's why you do it. It is the cause we fight for that defines us. God gave you the warrior's gift, Hazel, but left it up to you how to use it.'

'I never wanted to be a warrior,' said Owen. 'It was thrust upon me, by circumstances.'

'Maybe, in the beginning,' said Mother Beatrice. 'Nobody sane wants to be a hero. Few tales of real heroes have happy endings. But you became what you are because of who you are, because you couldn't look aside and do nothing while evil flourished. You are the best kind of warrior, Owen; the man who never wanted to be one. I never wanted to be a saint. I still wince inside whenever anyone uses the word. I know I'm not worthy. Hell, I only joined the Church originally to get out of marrying Valentine Wolfe. But I found my faith, or it found me, and I can no more turn aside from those who need help than I could stop breathing. In the end, honour defines us all. Without honour, our lives would have no meaning at all.'

Owen listened, and wanted so desperately to believe, but still couldn't be sure.

The three of them looked up sharply as all hell seemed to be breaking loose in the jungle around the mission. It sounded like there was a war going on out there, and someone was losing badly. Owen and Hazel drew their guns, forced aside their tiredness, and ran for the outer wall. People ran alongside them, rubbing sleep from their eyes and shouting questions no one had answers for. Owen and Hazel sprinted up the wooden steps that led to the catwalk inside the top of the outer wall, and looked out across the clearing at the jungle beyond. The light from the mission didn't penetrate far into the dark, and there was no moon above to light the scene. Hazel called for more light to be brought. Owen listened intently to the commotion raging in the jungle, but couldn't make any sense of it. Were the Hadenmen fighting each other? Soon the catwalk was packed with people, most of them holding up torches or lanterns, and for the first time movements could be seen in the jungle, of dark forces rushing back and forth. And then the first screams came out of the jungle, in the unmistakable buzzing tones of Hadenmen, torn from unwilling, horrified throats, followed by the familiar deadly sound of energy weapons discharging.

Owen strained his eyes against the dark and the rain. The clearing was utterly deserted. Whatever was happening was limited to the jungle. He could hear screams and cries of anger, and the sound of people running, crashing through the heavy foliage. Sudden glows came and went among the trees as energy beams started fires, and the rain put them out. Dark figures could be seen fighting and struggling. They might have been Hadenmen. But there were other shapes too, dark and indistinct, moving too fast to be defined. And wherever they went, the screaming rose anew. Mother Beatrice pushed in beside Owen.

'What is it, Sir Deathstalker? What's happening out there?'

'Damned if I know. But at a guess, I'd say someone or something is kicking Hadenman ass. And making a damn good job of it.'

'Could they be reinforcements? Marines, perhaps?'

'I don't think so,' said Hazel. 'The attackers don't seem to be using guns. And they don't move like anything human. Are there any creatures on this planet that we don't know about, Mother Beatrice?'

'No. Nothing at all.'

'Angels,' said a voice from further down the catwalk. 'Angels have come to save us.'

'I don't think so,' said Owen. 'These seem more like devils. I never heard a Hadenman scream before. What could be so deadly, so terrible, that even the Hadenmen are afraid of them?'

'Well, you could always go out and take a look, but if you do, you're going on your own,' said Hazel firmly. 'I'm not putting one foot outside this wall until there's enough light to see what I'm aiming at.'

'The Hadenmen have disrupters,' said Mother Beatrice. 'It doesn't seem to be doing them any good, does it?'

The tumult in the jungle suddenly broke off, the last few screams choked off abruptly. The crashing and the thrashing stopped, and there was no sign of movement anywhere. The night was completely still, and the mission's defenders stood silently on the catwalk, listening to nothing but the crackling of torches, the endless pattering of rain on the roof and their own breathing. The jungle was dark and calm, holding its secrets within.

'Well,' said Owen finally, 'at a guess, I'd say that whatever it was, it's over now. I think we'd better post double guards for tonight, on three-hour shifts. Everyone else, go and get some sleep. Just because a few Hadenmen apparently got their just desserts, it doesn't necessarily mean we won't be facing a whole army of the bastards out there tomorrow. And we're going to need all our strength to see them off.'

'Shouldn't we send someone out to check for bodies?' said a voice further down the catwalk.

'After you,' said Hazel, and snorted, unimpressed, when there was no response.

'Any bodies can wait till the morning,' said Mother Beatrice. 'Everything can wait till the morning. The Deathstalker's right; post the extra guards, and everyone else get some sleep.'

And since no one ever argued with Saint Bea, the watchers slowly dispersed, going to find what rest they could before morning. The guards left behind turned their guns on the dark jungle, ready to shoot first and ask questions much later, if at all. Owen and Hazel headed for the nearest steps, and ran into Bonnie Bedlam and Midnight Blue coming the other way.

'A good performance,' said Bonnie. 'I felt like applauding.'

'Don't mind her,' said Midnight, 'she's just being herself. What do you think just hit the Hadenmen?'

'I couldn't make out much,' said Owen. 'But what I did see seemed almost . . . familiar.'

'Anyone who kills Hadenmen is fine with me,' said Hazel. 'I mean, come on; what could be worse than an army of augmented men?'

'I have a horrible suspicion we're going to find out, come the morning,' said Midnight. 'At least the Hadenmen were a known quantity. We could make plans against them. Now . . .'

'Right,' said Bonnie. 'The enemy of my enemy isn't always bound to be my friend. Especially if they're the Enemies of Humanity.'

Hazel looked at her sharply. 'Shub? You think there are Shub forces out there?'

'What else could take out a force of Hadenmen so easily? You ask me, that jungle is full of Ghost Warriors and Furies.'

'I want to go home,' said Hazel.

'But what the hell would Shub want here?' said Owen, exasperated. 'There's nothing here!'

'Except the Red Brain,' said Moon, emerging suddenly from the gloom. 'I can feel its presence, more and more strongly all the time.'

'Red . . .' said Bonnie. 'Could it be some part of the jungle? Some plant that has developed intelligence?'

'It's vast,' said Moon. 'Very large and very complex, and utterly alien. I have no idea what it is, but what I can detect of its slow thoughts makes no sense at all. All I can be sure of is that it's very dangerous. And it's slowly becoming aware

604

of our presence. If I were a little more certain of my humanity, I think . . . I'd be scared. It's so big, and we're so very small . . .'

'But what is it?' said Hazel.

'It's the Red Brain,' said Moon. 'And if it's as powerful and as dangerous as I think it is, then Haden or Shub would be right to commit any number of troops here, either to seize it, or destroy it.'

'But then . . . why are they attacking the mission?' said Owen.

'We're just in the way,' said Moon. 'I don't think Haden or Shub is in the mood to share its prize.'

He turned and walked back into the gloom, and was soon gone. Hazel glared after him. 'I think I preferred him when he was just inhuman. He was much less irritating.'

'He's certainly picked a hell of a time to go mystical on us,' said Owen. 'Maybe we should send him to Saint Bea, and see if she can get some sense out of him.'

'The Red Brain . . .' said Bonnie. 'Sounds like one of those evil, criminal masterminds from the old holo serials, when I was just a kid. Maybe we should put out a call to the Grim Grey Avenger to come and save us.'

'Did you have those shows on your world?' said Midnight. 'I was always a big fan of his. He was my hero, when I was little.'

'Yeah!' said Hazel. 'I had all his tapes, and his special decoder ring, the one you had to send away for . . .'

Owen left them chattering happily together, and went off on his own to get some sleep before he fell down. Saving his own life had taken a lot out of him. And he had a strong feeling that when morning came, and he finally saw what was waiting outside the mission, he wasn't going to like it at all.

Dawn came suddenly on Lachrymae Christi, right on schedule. Everyone who could pack themselves on to the catwalks was there waiting, when the sunlight suddenly forced its way past the clouds, throwing back the gloom, and the view outside the mission appeared again. And there, standing still and silent in the rain, in the clearing all the way round the mission, were row upon row of Grendel aliens. Owen looked dumbly down from the wall, his mouth dry, and could all but feel the confidence draining out of the mission's defenders.

Gengineering killing machines from the Vaults of the Sleepers, held in suspended animation for unknown centuries, perhaps even millennia, but now reborn into an unprepared universe. Living horrors with spiked crimson armour that was somehow a part of them, and steel teeth and claws. Deadly, remorseless, invincible killers, they existed only to destroy, programmed by their unknown creators in all the subtle arts of slaughter. Shub looted hundreds of thousands of them from the Vaults of the Sleepers, and no one ever saw any of them again. Until now.

'That's it,' said Hazel grimly. 'It's official. Things just got worse. I'd recommend running, if there was anywhere to run to.'

'Are they really so much more dangerous than the Hadenmen?' said Mother Beatrice.

'We stood a chance against the Hadenmen,' said Owen, almost bitterly. 'I've killed any number of augmented men. I only ever killed one Grendel, and it very nearly killed me. It was stronger than I was, faster. It took my hand. I still have nightmares. And now there are thousands of them out there.'

'Swords won't stop them,' said Hazel. 'A direct hit with a disrupter only slows them down, unless you hit one of its very few vital spots. They were created to be unstoppable. We are in deep shit, people.'

Mother Beatrice turned to Sister Marion, at her side. 'Tell everyone to arm themselves, even the wounded. Get everyone who can stand to defensive positions. Reactivate all the booby traps, and arm the explosives.' Sister Marion nodded grimly, her tall black hat bobbing, and hurried off.

'Explosives?' said Owen.

'A last resort,' said Mother Beatrice. 'We used them for clearing spaces in the jungle, to establish new settlements. They're all linked together in one place, enough to take out the whole compound. A last gesture of defiance, if it's obvious there's no other way.'

'Put someone in charge of the button who doesn't panic easily,' said Hazel. 'We're going to do our best to give these bastards a good run for their money. Right, Owen?'

'Right,' said Owen, flexing the fingers of the hand he'd regrown. 'We've been in impossible situations before, Mother Beatrice, and we're still here. But if you do have a direct line to the good Lord, now would be a really good time to put in a claim for a miracle.'

Mother Beatrice smiled. 'Every legend has its ending, Sir Deathstalker, and every hero falls at last, but if that's all that's left to us, let us at least die well. God expects no less. Now, if you'll excuse me, I must return to the infirmary. I think I'm going to be needed there.'

She left, her back perfectly straight, her head bent in thought, or perhaps prayer, and people made way for her as she passed, and bowed respectfully.

'She'd have made one hell of a warrior,' said Hazel.

'Sure,' said Owen. 'She's always been a fighter, in her own way. The mild-mannered don't tend to last long enough to become living saints.'

'Grendels,' said Hazel bitterly. 'Why did it have to be bloody Grendels? At least we stood a chance against the Hadenmen.'

'It isn't over till the fat lady croaks,' said Owen. 'If nothing else, let's see how many of them we can take with us.'

There were startled yells from other people on the catwalk, and Owen and Hazel turned back to see the Grendels come rushing forward as one, triggered at last by some unknown signal. They surged in from all sides, advancing in utter silence, crossing the wide clearing in a few seconds. They threw themselves against the great wooden wall, hammering on it till the whole length of the wall sounded like a giant drum. A fusillade of disrupter fire stabbed down, punching holes through the crimson silicon armour, but the Grendels didn't fall. Their heavy spiked fists tore chunks out of the thick black wood, and the wall shuddered under the impact. Some Grendels came scrambling up the wall, steel talons and claws digging deep into the wood as they climbed, steel mouths grinning mercilessly. Owen leaned over the edge and shot one of the Grendels through its broad heart-shaped head. It convulsed and fell backwards, arms and legs still grabbing at nothing. It hit the ground hard, and lay still, and the other Grendels swarmed right over it.

Everyone with a gun was on the catwalk now, all the length of the wall, and the roar of so many discharging energy weapons was deafening. The rain burst into clouds of steam, and Grendels fell everywhere. But in the end there just weren't enough guns, and there were far too many Grendels; when the steam cleared, and the defenders lowered their exhausted guns, the Grendels were still surging forward and scrambling up the wall, trampling over the bodies of their own fallen to get at their prey. The disrupters were useless till their energy crystals recharged, and a lot could happen in two minutes. There were few projectile guns; there were no animals on Lachrymae Christi. So the next step was bow and arrow. The archers stepped forward, leaned precariously out over the wall, and let fly. Every arrow struck its target, and glanced harmlessly away. And that just left steel. The mission's defenders lifted swords and axes and farm implements with newly sharpened edges, and waited for the enemy to come to them.

The Grendels scrabbled up and over the outer wall in one great boiling wave, red as blood, savage as Satan, and threw themselves upon the catwalk defenders. Swords flashed and axes chopped, only to rebound helplessly from the living crimson armour. The Grendels tore their way through fragile human flesh, killing everything that came within reach. They ripped away limbs and tore off heads. A Grendel plunged its spiked hand into a leper's belly and tore out a handful of guts. Steel teeth closed on throats and faces. Screaming men fell from the high catwalk, hit the ground hard and never moved again. Some jumped, rather than face the Grendels. Blood spilled everywhere, and the air was full of screams.

Outside, in the rain, Grendels smashed their way through the wall repairs and barricades, and poured through in an unstoppable flood. It only took a few moments before the compound was swarming with the scarlet devils, and the real slaughter began. Men and women ran screaming everywhere, but the Grendels ran faster.

Owen Deathstalker swung his sword double-handed, with all his more than human strength, and sometimes the edge would cut through the crimson armour, and sometimes it wouldn't. The sheer strength of his blows was enough to send the Grendels staggering backwards, but he couldn't hurt them. Hazel d'Ark fought at his side, darting and dodging in the space available on the catwalk, searching for weak spots in the armour, thrusting the point of her sword into exposed joints and twisting it, and all to no avail. Like Owen, her strength was enough to keep the Grendels at bay, but that was all. Owen tried knocking the Grendels off the catwalk with sweeping blows of his arm, but even the long drop to the hard ground below didn't seem to bother them. Step by step, Owen and Hazel were driven back, while their merely human fellow defenders died around them and they could do nothing to save them. The lepers fought well and bravely, but they didn't stand a chance; they never had. Soon the catwalk was littered with the dead and dying, and slick with rivers of blood that dripped from the edges of the catwalk in another endless rain. And still more Grendels came swarming over and through the wall.

'Fall back! Fall back!' yelled Colonel William Hand, down in the compound. 'Fall back to the inner redoubt, and let the booby traps do their work!'

The surviving lepers on the catwalk turned and ran, crowding down the narrow stairways, the Grendels falling on those at the back. Owen and Hazel continued to retreat slowly, trying to buy the lepers near them some time. A Grendel ducked under the arc of Owen's blade, and went for his throat. Owen lashed out instinctively, and his fist smashed through the heart-shaped head, splintering the crimson armour. The Grendel convulsed as Owen seized a handful of its brains and ripped them out of its skull. The creature spun helplessly in place, until its fellows pulled it down and trampled it underfoot.

'Nice touch,' said Hazel, just a little breathlessly.

'Yeah,' said Owen. 'Think I broke my bloody hand.'

'In case you hadn't noticed, we're cut off from the stairs.'

'Then we'll just have to jump.'

'The fall will kill us!'

'We're not that lucky. Jump!'

They beat aside the nearest Grendels, avoided the snapping jaws, ran to the edge of the catwalk and threw themselves out into the air. It was a long way down, and for a few wonderful moments it was almost like flying. And then they hit the ground hard, driving the breath from their lungs, and all they could do was lie on the blood-soaked ground and gasp for breath. Up above them, the catwalk was completely overrun.

Owen forced himself back on to his feet through sheer will-power, and grabbed Hazel by the shoulder, pulling her up. There were people and Grendels running everywhere. A steel smile lunged for Hazel's throat. She grabbed the Grendel with both hands, whipped it up over her head and threw it into the nearest concentration of Grendels. They went down in a pile of thrashing limbs. Owen and Hazel ran for the inner redoubt, the hall-sized communications centre, set up as the only practical place to retreat to, if the outer defences were breached.

Lepers ran with them, dodging or leaping over the hidden traps and pitfalls. Grendels raced after them. They fell into the spike-bottomed pits, flattened the spikes, rose unharmed and leaped right out again. Weight-driven spikes and sword blades flew out of hiding, only to glance harmlessly from the aliens' spiked silicon armour. The improvised landmines erupted all across the compound in sudden spurts of smoke and flames, throwing Grendels into the air, and even damaging a few. But there were always more, always more.

An army of death, created to be invincible.

The defenders streamed into the last redoubt, packing it full. There were steel shutters on the windows, and heavy bolts on the doors. Owen and Hazel took up a position before the great hall, and went head to head with the first Grendels to arrive, trying to occupy the attention of as many aliens as they could, to buy the arriving lepers a few more moments of precious time. Owen stamped and thrust, dodging flashing claws and snapping teeth, moving faster than he ever had before. Hazel guarded his side, warding off Grendels through the sheer ferocity of her attack.

Bonnie Bedlam was there too, with Midnight Blue. Bonnie laughed aloud in sheer exuberance as the Grendels swarmed around her, glorying in a battle that tested her as never before. She swung her sword with all her strength, beating Grendels to the ground and cracking open their armour. She was bleeding constantly from wounds that never had the time to heal properly before they were torn open again, but she repelled the growing weakness in her arms, relishing the never-ending rush of pain and regeneration. She was very happy.

Midnight Blue teleported back and forth in a circle around her comrade-in-arms, blinking in and out of view just long enough to land a telling blow with her axe before vanishing again. She concentrated on the broad heart-shaped heads, slamming her axe deep into the crimson skulls by repeated blows to the same spot. And here and there Grendels fell to the bloody ground and scrabbled there helplessly, often torn apart by their own kind for getting in the way. Midnight chanted her order's battle songs to the rhythm of her blows, but the strength was going out of her arms. Teleporting continuously took a lot out of her, and it was getting harder all the time to concentrate. She could feel herself slowing down, and the Grendels were starting to shake off her blows.

All the Maze people were slowing down, as they burned up the energies that fuelled them. The human body was never meant to operate at such extremes for long.

Colonel William Hand and Otto took their stand at the entrance to the maze of narrow alleys that led between the huts. Many lepers had gone to ground there, barricading themselves inside familiar surroundings. Hand didn't give much for their chances, but he did his best to buy them all the time he could. He fought savagely, calling up old skills as his strength quickly gave out. Otto guarded his side, as always. But the colonel was a long way past his prime, a man in his fifties already weakened by a terrible disease, and after a few desperate minutes the Grendels knocked him down and swarmed right over him. He lay on his back, bleeding heavily from a dozen vicious wounds, trying to find the sword he'd dropped as crimson armoured legs stamped down around him. A Grendel loomed over him, and steel claws slashed down. Hand cried out in spite of himself, and then Otto was there one last time, throwing himself across his colonel. The steel claws sank deep into his back, and ripped away his hunch and half his spine. Otto shuddered once, and died. The Grendel moved on.

Hand tried to move the dead dwarf off him, and couldn't. There was no feeling in his hands, and no strength in his arms. His throat hurt, and he could hear his breath whistling strangely. He forced one hand to his neck, and it came away soaked in blood. One of the Grendels had cut him a good one, and he hadn't even noticed. The colonel let his hand fall back on the hard ground. He'd always thought he'd welcome a warrior's death, rather than let the leprosy eat him away by inches, but now the time was here, he would have traded everything for just a few more days, a few more hours, of life. But God didn't make deals.

He would have liked time to put his affairs in order, write a few letters . . . his thoughts drifted for a moment, before they snapped back into focus. He couldn't die yet, not while he still had one last duty to perform, one last order to carry out. He forced his cold right hand to the remote control Saint Bea had given to him. She'd trusted him to know the right time to use it, and have the guts to hit the switch no matter what.

The colonel smiled grimly, his mouth leaking blood. 'Goodbye, Otto,' he said, or thought he said. He hit the switch.

The explosives planted under the compound floor all went off at once, a massive thunderclap that threw the ground up into the roof, and tore the packed Grendels apart. The whole compound disappeared in a cloud of smoke, the wall blasted outwards by the shaped and positioned charges, while the huts of the village stood untouched. Alien guts and shards of crimson armour pattered back to the cratered ground. No trace remained anywhere of Colonel William Hand, and Otto.

Owen and Hazel fought doggedly on before the communications centre, tired beyond pain or hope, driven now only by a determination not to fall while they were still needed. They were both bleeding freely from a dozen bad wounds, and the strength was going out of their blows. Owen looked around him. Nearly all the lepers were inside now – just a few more left. And then they were inside. A voice yelled for him to get inside too, so they could close and bolt the doors. Owen considered it. Time seemed to slow right down, so that he had all the time in the world to make up his mind. He looked to his left, and saw Bonnie and Midnight fighting back to back, their faces slack with pain and exhaustion, surrounded by Grendels. There was no way they could get to the hall in time. And besides, the hall wasn't much of a sanctuary anyway. The mission's outer wall had been far stronger, and it hadn't even slowed the Grendels down. He looked to his right and saw Hazel, still fighting, dripping with her own blood. No, Owen decided. He wasn't going to turn and run. He sighed regretfully. Time to play his last trump card, and hope it was good enough.

'Shut the door!' he yelled.

He turned back to face the enemy. He reached inside himself, diving deep into his mind, through the undermind to the back brain, and tapped into the power that lived there. He threw back his head and howled the old war cry of his Clan, *Shandrakor! Shandrakor!* and all his rage and frustration and need to defend the lepers of the mission came roaring up through him and burst out into the material world, beating on the air like the wings of a huge and powerful bird. The Grendels sensed that something new had entered the fray, and stopped and looked about them, confused. The ground shook, undulating under their feet, throwing them off balance. A great wind roared across what was left of the compound, scattering the Grendels like leaves in a hurricane. Owen looked about him, smiled once, and let loose his anger on the aliens.

Those nearest to him blew apart in sudden explosions of blood and guts and shattered armour. Owen stalked unsteadily forward, his eyes wide and unblinking, his rage beating on the air in time to his heartbeat, his face grim and relentless. He had given himself up to his power as never before. He could feel it tearing him apart, and didn't give a damn. He turned his head, and Grendels died where he looked. His boots hit the ground, and earthquakes split apart the cratered earth of the compound. The Deathstalker had released his rage, and the Grendels could not stand against it. They blew apart or were blown away, and not one of them could get close enough to touch him. Owen knew the power was killing him. He could feel things tearing apart, breaking down, inside. He knew he should shut the power down while he still could. That mortal man was not meant to burn so very brightly. But he couldn't, not while the innocent still needed him. So he walked slowly on, killing Grendels, dying inside a little more with every step, killing himself as he killed his enemy.

Deathstalker.

But all too quickly there came a time when even need and determination couldn't drive him forward another step. His mortal frame had never been meant to channel so much power for so long, and finally, it had nothing left to give. Owen fell to his knees. He felt very tired. He'd done so much. Maybe he could sleep now, and if he was lucky, he wouldn't dream. He fell forward, and his face slammed into the blood-soaked ground. The winds shut down, the ground stopped shaking, and the rage of the Deathstalker no longer flew upon the air.

Hazel d'Ark saw his last moment of glory, saw him fall. She'd watched in awe as his anger swept aside the Grendels, but now she cried out, and ran to him. She put a hand on his shoulder, but there was no response. Hazel cried out again, in shock and horror and the pain of a heart breaking at last. She would have cried, but she didn't know how. She never had.

She looked up and saw the remaining Grendels re-forming. Owen had killed a lot of them, but there were still a hell of a lot left. More than enough to tear down the communications hall and kill every living thing within it. They moved slowly forward, baring their steel teeth, flexing steel claws, and Hazel looked at them and smiled the coldest smile of her life. They were going to pay for what they had done – all of them.

She'd tried to tell herself that her particular power wasn't needed; that the mission already had enough defenders. That she didn't need to call up alternates of herself, and see them die over and over again. Bonnie and Midnight had made her alternates real to her, as never before. But she needed them now, and so she called on them, not in her own name, but in Owen's. Called them forth to avenge the Deathstalker.

And they came.

Suddenly the compound was full of Hazel d'Arks, screaming in rage and loss. And all the Grendels who hadn't died under Owen's attack suddenly found themselves facing an army of warrior women of varying face and forms, but all of them united in pain and sorrow. There was a moment, as both sides looked at each other and recognized a worthy adversary, and then they surged forward and clashed together, and the dying began. Guns roared and steel flashed, and metal teeth and claws tore human flesh, but for every Hazel that fell, another appeared to take her place. Hazel d'Ark had made herself a doorway, through which an endless stream of alternates could appear, for as long as they were needed, or for as long as Hazel d'Ark could stand it.

She knew the effort was killing her, and didn't give a damn. She would save the lepers, not so much because she cared about them, but because Owen had. She knelt beside him, her strength seeping out of her like blood from an opened vein, and put one gentle hand upon his shoulder. She'd come this far with Owen Deathstalker, and if she had to follow him into the lands of the dead, she could do that too.

Someone was calling her name. Over and over, in a strange buzzing voice. She turned her head slowly, and saw Tobias Moon kneeling beside her.

'We can't win this way!' he said urgently. 'There's too many of them. But seeing you use your power has shown me how to use mine. I know what to do. Trust me! Reach out to me, and we can win this fight a different way!'

'How?' said Hazel.

'The Red Brain,' said Moon. 'It isn't in the jungle. It *is* the jungle.'

And his mind reached out to hers, and made contact. And through her, Moon touched all the other Hazels. Bonnie and Midnight were there too, and Owen. They all joined together, melding and merging, becoming something far more powerful than the sum of their parts. They reached out and gathered up all the living minds in the mission, from the sickest leper to Saint Bea herself. And together they turned outwards, forged into one force, one thought, and touched the Red Brain: the gestalt consciousness of all the plant life on Lachrymae Christi. The jungle, millions of square miles of it, was all one connected body, and its mind was the Red Brain.

This was what the Hadenmen had come in search of, what Shub had sent the Grendels to seize or control or destroy. A whole new form of consciousness, unknown anywhere else in the Empire. A mind the size of a world. The Red Brain's thoughts were slow, moving with the rhythm of day and night and the turning of the seasons, endlessly dying, endlessly living, immeasurably old. Alone for millennia, until the new mind touched it. Friendship was new, and joy, at being alone no longer, but it learned need and necessity too, and stretched out its vast and mighty body to help its new friend.

The jungle around the mission erupted into movement, driven at a speed it had never known before. Trees uprooted themselves and fell across the fallen mission wall. And across these bridges the jungle advanced and fell upon the Grendels. Barbed flails and crawling vines wrapped themselves around the scarlet aliens and tore them apart with slow, implacable strength. Deadly plants with gaping maws and hideous strength erupted out of the broken ground of the compound, called up from deep below by the jungle's voice. Grendels were swallowed up or ripped to pieces, too small to stand against the will of the jungle. The aliens turned and tried to flee the killing ground, but once they left the mission, huge sucking pits appeared under their feet and dragged them down. And only a few minutes after it had begun, the jungle grew still again, because there were no more Grendels left to kill.

The Red Brain and the mass human mind touched again. It hadn't really noticed the human presence on Lachrymae Christi before; they hadn't been there long enough. Far, far in its unimaginable past, there had been a time when it was not alone, but that was so long ago it was more instinct than memory. Recognizing another, it was overjoyed to have companionship again, and it begged the human mind not to abandon it. For all its age, it was really only a child. The human mind reassured it. There were espers among the lepers. Communication would be possible, now that they both knew what they were looking for. And now that the Red Brain had showed its strength, Haden and Shub would never

616

dare come again. The human mind looked around the mission, sorrowing over its many dead, and then fell back into its many bodies. There was much work to be done.

After that, it was mostly a case of clearing up. Much of the mission would have to be rebuilt, but this time the jungle would help. Once again, bodies had to be cleared up and identified, and Saint Bea worked long hours in her infirmary, tending the sick. And if sometimes she laid her hands on a helpless case, and whispered a quiet prayer, who could blame her. Especially when so many of them lived.

Owen Deathstalker woke up in the infirmary, astonished to be alive. Bonnie and Midnight lay in beds on either side of him, and Hazel took it in turns to sit with each of them. The link with the Red Brain, and its immense mental strength, had saved them, pulling them back from the brink one more time. They were all still weak as half-drowned kittens, but strength was coming slowly back to them. Which was just as well; Hazel meant well, but she was bloody useless as a nurse. She just didn't have the temperament. They all complained a lot, and made a nuisance of themselves, and by the evening Sister Marion said they were all well enough, and would they please oblige her by getting the hell out of her infirmary so the rest of the patients could get some peace?

It was still raining, drumming loudly on the wooden roof. Owen and Hazel walked slowly across the uneven ground of the compound. The bodies were all gone, but the place itself was still a mess. They took it in turns to lean on each other, their inner energies at an all-time low. For the time being, they were only human again, and they made the most of it. Everywhere they went, the lepers bowed and saluted and called out their names like prayers or hymns. Owen and Hazel smiled uncomfortably back, noting that for all their fervour, the lepers maintained a careful distance. Living legends were one thing; living gods were quite another.

Tobias Moon came to meet them. His eyes no longer glowed, and only the faintest buzz remained in his voice. He was moving beyond such things as the Maze continued to work its changes in him. There was a new serenity to him, a calmness in himself, as though many things had at last become clear to him.

'I'm not going with you when you leave,' he said calmly. 'I'm staying. The people here will need a lot of help rebuilding their mission and their lives, and I think I could be of use. Until the espers learn how, I will be their contact with the Red Brain.' He shook his head slowly. 'That was the most fascinating experience of my life. It's been alone so long, just like me, the only one of its kind. And the lepers . . . perhaps it took the dying to teach me the meaning and value of life. Anyway, I'm staying. To guard the lepers, and be the voice of the jungle.'

'Never really thought of you as a gardener, Moon,' said Owen dryly, and Moon laughed politely. He was still working on humour.

Owen and Hazel walked on. Bonnie and Midnight were overseeing repairs on the other side of the compound, but they waved a hand in greeting. Owen and Hazel waved back. All was peaceful and serene, like the quiet after the storm has passed.

'Well,' said Owen finally, 'we won another one.'

'Yeah,' said Hazel. 'Came bloody close to losing it, though. If Moon hadn't come through at the last minute, we could have died here. I really thought I'd lost you.'

'A salutary reminder that even we have limits,' said Owen. 'That for all we can do, we're still bound by merely human limitations. In a strange way, I find that comforting. That for all our powers and abilities, we haven't left humanity behind.'

Hazel sniffed loudly. 'I didn't find nearly bloody dying at all comforting. And let's hope the jungle didn't miss any Grendels. I couldn't steal candy from a baby in my current condition. And that was always one of my best tricks.'

'Our strength will return, eventually,' said Owen. 'It always has before.' He stopped and looked about him, lost for a moment in memories. 'So many died here. I wish we could have saved more.'

'William Hand and Otto,' said Hazel. 'Sister Kathleen. They didn't have our powers, but they did just as much to save the mission as we did. They were the real heroes here.'

'Of course,' said Owen. 'They were all heroes here, the

living and the fallen. Now, if you'll excuse me, I've got an appointment in the communications centre. They're trying to get a ship for us, so we can get off-planet. Lachrymae Christi may be safe now, but the rest of the Empire is still in deep trouble.'

'Now that is typical of you, Deathstalker,' said Hazel. 'You've barely got over nearly dying, twice, and already you're talking about charging back into battle again. Aren't we entitled to some time off?'

'Sure,' said Owen. 'When the war's over.'

'The wars are never over,' said Hazel. 'Not for us.'

Owen put his hands on her shoulders, and kissed her. 'You'd be bored in a week, and you know it.'

'Maybe. I really thought I'd lost you, Owen. Don't you ever do that again.'

'Never,' said Owen. 'We're a team. Nothing's ever going to separate us.'

'Promise me we'll always be together. For ever.'

'For ever and ever. Even death can't part us now.'

He kissed her again, and moved off towards the communications centre. Hazel watched him go for a while, and then turned away and looked out over the compound. People were slowly filling in the deep gashes and craters in the ground. The outer wall was being raised again, section by section. The battle was over, and life went on. Hazel felt strangely left out. Maybe Owen was right; that all they knew how to be was warriors.

And then someone called her name, in a familiar voice, but hoarse and filled with pain. She looked round, and there was Owen, leaning against the side of a hut. He looked like hell, deathly tired, face gaunt, his clothes stained and blood-ied. It took a moment for Hazel to realize that it wasn't the grey clothing of the lepers. It was the same clothes Owen had been wearing when he appeared out of nowhere to save her life on Virimonde. He was looking at her with such loss and longing, and he held out a hand to her, as though trying to warn her of something. She started towards him, and a sudden horror filled his face. She took another step, and a silver, shimmering energy field appeared around her, pinning her to the spot. She beat on the energy field with her fists, and it spat static, discharging loudly through the broken earth, but the field didn't weaken at all. And she had no power left to break it. She called out to Owen to help her, but he was gone.

Owen Deathstalker came running out of the communications centre. He'd heard her call his name, even from so far away. He saw her standing trapped in the shimmering energy field, and recognized it immediately. The Blood Runners of the Obeah Systems had used it once before to try and kidnap Hazel, claiming she owed them her body for experiments, to pay off a debt incurred by her captain, back when she was still a clonelegger. Owen had saved her then by breaking the field, but now he didn't have the power.

He ran towards her, pulling the disrupter from his holster. Hazel was still struggling inside the field, but her image was growing fainter as the field disappeared, taking her with it. Bonnie Bedlam and Midnight Blue were making their way across the compound too, heading for the shimmering field.

Strange figures appeared around the silver energy. Tall and willowy, albinos with milk-white hair and blood-red eyes. They wore long robes of swirling colours, their faces ritually scarred in vicious patterns – Blood Runners. They laughed soundlessly at Owen and then disappeared, taking the energy field and Hazel with them.

Owen cried out in horror and stumbled to a halt, looking at the empty place where Hazel had been. He heard the flat sound of air rushing in to fill a space where something had been a moment before, and looked round to see that Bonnie and Midnight had disappeared too. Without Hazel to maintain their presence, they couldn't stay. They no longer had anything to link them to this universe. Owen felt numb, paralysed with shock. Hazel was gone, in the hands of torturers, and he had no way to reach her. He had no idea where they'd taken her; she could be anywhere in the Obeah Systems. And he didn't even have a ship, to get him off the planet. He'd never felt so helpless.

Owen Deathstalker, the conqueror of armies and toppler of Empires, and he couldn't even save the one he loved.

Hang in there, Hazel, I'm coming for you. Somehow, I'll find you, whatever it takes. And if they've hurt you, I'll drown the whole Obeah Systems in blood.

Owen Deathstalker will return
one last time
in
Deathstalker Destiny

Also available in Vista paperback

Deathstalker

SIMON R. GREEN

The first volume in the epic adventure series

Owen Deathstalker, last of his line, is a quiet man, a historian, remote from the stench of corruption and intrigue surrounding the Iron Throne at the heart of the galaxy-spanning, tyrannical Empire.

And then, inexplicably, Deathstalker is outlawed, forced to flee from one end of the Empire to the other. And as he does so, he discovers that resistance is growing, everywhere, to the Iron Bitch on the Iron Throne.

DEATHSTALKER

Outlawing him could be the Iron Bitch's biggest mistake.

ISBN 0 575 60160 4

Deathstalker Rebellion

SIMON R. GREEN

The second volume in the epic adventure series

At the heart of the galaxy-spanning tyrannical Empire lies Golgotha, the planet of the Iron Throne. Once it was impregnable. Now . . . the Iron Bitch may have made a fatal mistake. In outlawing Owen Deathstalker, she has woken a lust for revenge in a quiet man – and unwittingly created a focus for a galaxy full of hatred for her loathsome rule.

At last the espers and the clones, the AIs and the freaks, the innocent and the damned alike, have someone to look to, someone to lead the

DEATHSTALKER REBELLION

And then, the killing begins . . .

ISBN 0 575 60011 X

VISTA

Deathstalker War

SIMON R. GREEN

The third volume in the epic adventure series

Owen Deathstalker, last of his line, was wrongly outlawed by the evil Empress Lionstone XIV . . . but in making an enemy of Deathstalker, the Iron Bitch sowed the bitter seeds of revenge. Now the rebellion Deathstalker has been fomenting has blossomed into war.

Opening skirmishes on Mistworld, Haceldama and Virimonde reveal just a few of the horrors the Iron Bitch is prepared to unleash upon the rebels, but the opposition only fuels their determination to win justice.

This time it's war.

DEATHSTALKER WAR

No quarter, no prisoners, no compromises.

ISBN 0 575 60061 6

VISTA